ENQUIRY CONCERNING
POLITICAL JUSTICE

William Godwin, the famous philosopher and novelist, was born in East Anglia in 1756. The son of a Presbyterian minister, he was himself educated at Hoxton Academy for that calling. However, after five years he left the ministry, having lost his faith in God. He then devoted his time to writing. In 1797 he married Mary Wollstonecraft, and in 1801 he married Mrs Clairmont. He became a firm believer in the doctrine of 'enlightenment' and has been described as a 'kind of Puritanical anarchist'. He published a great deal of journalism and historical writing but is now mainly remembered for his philosophical work, *An Enquiry Concerning Political Justice* (1793), and one of the earliest propaganda novels, *Caleb Williams, or Things as They Are* (1794).

Isaac Kramnick was born in 1938 and educated at Harvard University, where he received a B.A. degree in 1959 and a Ph.D. in 1965, and at Peterhouse. He has taught at Harvard, Brandeis, Yale and Cornell, where he is now Professor of Government. He is married to Miriam Brody Kramnick and lives in Ithaca, New York, in the United States. Among his publications are *Bolingbroke and His Circle* and *Conservatism and Personality: The Ambivalence of Edmund Burke*.

William Godwin

ENQUIRY
CONCERNING
POLITICAL JUSTICE

AND ITS INFLUENCE ON MODERN MORALS
AND HAPPINESS

PENGUIN BOOKS

Penguin Books Ltd, Harmondsworth, Middlesex, England
Penguin Books Inc., 7110 Ambassador Road, Baltimore, Maryland 21207, U.S.A
Penguin Books Australia Ltd, Ringwood, Victoria, Australia
Penguin Books Canada Ltd, 41 Steelcase Road West, Markham, Ontario, Canada
Penguin Books (N.Z.) Ltd,
182–190 Wairau Road, Auckland 10, New Zealand

—

First published 1798
Published in Pelican Books 1976

—

Made and printed in Great Britain
by Richard Clay (The Chaucer Press), Ltd,
Bungay, Suffolk
Set in Linotype Baskerville

Contents

Introduction

EVERY political philosophy has its prophet and sacred text. For liberalism it is Locke and *The Second Treatise on Civil Government*; for democracy it is Rousseau and his *Social Contract*; for conservatism Burke and the *Reflections on the Revolution in France*; for socialism Marx and the *Communist Manifesto*. Anarchism is no exception. Its prophet is William Godwin and its first sacred text, his *Enquiry Concerning Political Justice*. James Joll, historian of anarchism, writing in 1964 describes the

one English writer who, starting from the commonplaces of eighteenth century philosophical belief, elaborated the most complete and worked-out statement of rational anarchist belief ever attempted, a philosophy of anarchism carried through to its logical conclusions, however surprising and absurd these might be. This was William Godwin.[1]

His contemporaries in the last decade of the eighteenth century were even more impressed and dazzled by this man they called 'the Philosopher'. William Hazlitt has described how in 1793 Godwin

blazed as a sun in the firmament of reputation; no one was more talked of, more looked up to, more sought after, and wherever liberty, truth, justice was the theme, his name was not far off; no work in our time gave such a blow to the philosophical mind of the country as the celebrated *Enquiry Concerning Political Justice*. Tom Paine was considered for the time as a Tom Fool to him; Paley an old woman; Edmund Burke a flashy sophist. Truth, moral truth, it was supposed had here taken up its abode; and these were the oracles of thought. 'Throw aside your books of chemistry,' said Words-

1. James Joll, *The Anarchists* (Eyre & Spottiswoode, London, 1964), p. 31.

worth to a young man, a student in the Temple, 'and read Godwin on necessity.[2]

Godwin moved in the midst of the literary and intellectual circle that gloried in the early years of the French Revolution, the years that Wordsworth immortalized as:

> Bliss was it that dawn to be alive.
> But to be young was very heaven! Oh, Times . . .
> when reason seemed the most to assert her rights.

Wordsworth's young friend Coleridge also sang the praises of Godwin in a sonnet, 'To William Godwin, author of *Political Justice*'.

> And hymn thee, Godwin! With ardent lay:
> For that thy voice, in Passion's stormy day
> When wild I roamed the blackheath of distress,
> Bade the bright form of justice meet my way
> And told me that her name was happiness.

The reign of reason, justice and happiness was short-lived and with the advent of the 'Terror' Wordsworth, Coleridge and most of the English intellectual community turned on both the Revolution and Godwin's anarchism. By the turn of the century, Hazlitt had accurately described how Godwin's 'reputation had sunk below the horizon'. Some have argued, on the other hand, that it was more than simply the reaction to the excesses of the French Revolution that turned opinion against Godwin. The Victorian Leslie Stephen suggests it was the abstract absurdity of Godwin's anarchism itself that brought about this reversal.

Godwin's dreams were but gorgeous bubbles, destined to speedily collapse when brought into contact with the hard facts of the actual world . . . He must have been a quiet and amiable dreamer, able to ignore all inconvenient facts, whose opinions were too deeply rooted in abstract speculation to be

2. William Hazlitt, *Spirit of the Age*, Everyman Edition (London, 1964), p. 202

upset by any storms raging in the region of concrete pheno-mena.[3]

But not everyone shared this revulsion at Godwin's anarchism. In 1812, Percy Shelley, then nineteen and recently expelled from Oxford, discovered that Godwin, long since past his prime was, however, still alive. Shelley had fallen in love with the ideas of *Political Justice* and wrote extravagantly to Godwin seeking advice and friend-ship.

It is now a period of more than two years since first I saw your inestimable book on *Political Justice*; it opened to my mind fresh and more extensive views; it materially influ-enced my character, and I rose from its perusal a wiser and better man . . . to you, as the regulator and former of my mind, I must ever look with real respect and veneration.[4]

Shelley and Godwin did indeed become fast friends and their personal lives became closely enmeshed, as we shall note below. Of even greater importance was the influence of Godwin's anarchist ideas on Shelley's poetry.

This edition provides the modern reader the original set of anarchist ideas that so dazzled Shelley and subse-quent generations of libertarians and anarchists.

1. Godwin's Life: From Calvinism to Anarchism

Like so many of the radicals in eighteenth-century Eng-land, Godwin's roots were non-conformist. His grand-father, uncle and father were dissenting ministers. Exclu-ded from Oxford and Cambridge, excluded from munici-pal and governmental jobs, dissenters were in turn freed from the stifling orthodoxy of establishment church, state and school. From their own academies these presbyterians, baptists and unitarians produced men and women at the

3. Leslie Stephen, *History of English Thought in the Eighteenth Century* (Rupert Hart-Davis, London, 1962), I.I, p. 238.
4. Quoted in Ford K. Brown, *The Life of William Godwin* (Dent, London, 1926), p. 258.

forefront of innovation in the religious, political, scientific and industrial life of England from 1750 to 1800. Wedgwood, Priestley, Wilkinson, Watt, Price, were all products of this marginal yet incredibly productive segment of English life.

William Godwin, born in 1756, was schooled from 1775 to 1778 in one of these hotbeds of critical enquiry, the dissenting academy at Hoxton, near London. In 1778, he, like his forbears, took the position of minister to a congregation of dissenters in Ware (Hertfordshire). It would not to be his lifelong calling, however. His Calvinist faith was shaken, first by his readings of the French philosophers, Rousseau, d'Holbach and Helvétius, and then by the doctrines of Joseph Priestley. Unlike Priestley, Godwin would not settle for the more rationalist religion of unitarianism; by 1783 he left the ministry and in 1787 embraced total religious scepticism. After a short and unsuccessful career as a teacher he began what would be a half-century of literary activity.

His dissenting past behind him Godwin the emancipated writer moved to London in 1783 at the age of twenty-seven. Here he remained for the rest of his long life. The output of the 1780s was relatively undistinguished – some religious essays before his fall, some biography, a play, and a large number of reviews and essays written for the weekly literary and political journals that flourished in late Georgian London. He made his way in the intense and close world of Grub Street political journalism and Soho-city intellectualism, a partial success. But true fame came to Godwin with the French Revolution and the excitement it brought to the complacent world of the London literati. The Revolution, which according to Wordsworth seemed to mark the 'blissful dawn' of a new age, turned Godwin to political enquiry and study. He started attending meetings of radical political societies. He was, in fact, present at the famous sermon given on 4 November 1789 by the great dissenting minister and political radical Richard Price at the Old Jewry chapel. It was this sermon that provoked the wrath of Edmund Burke as expressed in his *Reflections on the Revolution in France*. Burke's book, a conservative attack on the French Revolution, was just as much if not even more a bitter condemnation of English radicalism and its efforts to reform Parliament. The radical replies to Burke came quickly and often. Mary Wollstonecraft wrote her *Vindication of the Rights of Man* and then later the pioneer feminist tract, the *Vindication of the Rights of Women*. Tom Paine wrote the immensely popular *Rights of Man* and James Mackintosh offered the more scholarly rebuttal to Burke with his *Vindicae Gallicae*. But, as Hazlitt informs us in the early nineties, it was Godwin who emerged as the English philosopher of freedom, who eclipsed all the others as visionary for the new post Revolutionary political and social order.

Godwin wrote in his diary that he conceived the idea of *Political Justice* in May 1791, just after Paine's *Rights of Man* had appeared. Paine's reply to Burke was moving and intelligent, but Paine was no philosopher and Godwin felt that what was needed was a treatise not on taxation and representation or on the problems of unwritten constitutions, but one which dealt with the grander philosophical issues of truth, reason and education. His diary records that 'there began to form in my mind a work that would philosophically place the principles of politics on an immovable basis, which would overbear and annihilate all oppositions'.[5] He sold the idea to the radical publisher Johnson in July of 1791 and worked on his book for the next sixteen months.

The first edition of Godwin's *Enquiry Concerning the Principles of Political Justice* finally appeared in February 1793. Instantly it made Godwin famous. Nearly everyone seems to have heard of him or his anarchist vision. In his diary Godwin recorded that everywhere he went they knew of his book: 'I was nowhere a stranger ... I was

5. *William Godwin: His Friends and Contemporaries*, edit. L. Kegan Paul (London, 1876), I, p. 67.

everywhere received with curiosity and kindness.' People called themselves 'Godwinians', or 'Godwinites'; they referred to him as the 'philosopher' or the 'Grand Master'.[6]

It is not clear how much of this fame was based on actual purchase and reading of the book. The price of the two-volume edition was an extraordinarily high three guineas (Burke's *Reflections* sold at one tenth that price, and Paine's *Rights of Man* could be had in tract form for sixpence). Pitt is alleged to have argued in Cabinet that there was no need to suppress Godwin's book, as he had Paine's, since such an expensive book could cause little trouble. What is clear, however, is that Godwin's book had a tremendous impact on the young, as we have seen, on youthful radicals like Wordsworth, Southey, Coleridge and Shelley. In 1795 Crabb Robinson, a radical playwright and diarist, wrote:

> It was in the spring of this year that I read a book which gave a turn to my mind, and in effect directed the whole course of my life – a book which often producing a powerful effect on the youth of that generation, has now sunk into unmerited oblivion . . . I entered fully into its spirit, it left all others behind in my admiration, and I was willing even to become a martyr for it.[7]

As fast as the rise to fame, so, then, equally as fast Godwin sank to oblivion. The public mood had changed in but two short years. England and France were at war; news of the Terror reached London. Revolutionaries, visionaries and philosophical anarchists were silenced by Pitt's repression and hunted down by angry Church and King mobs. The young poets Wordsworth, Coleridge and Southey turned against the French 'experiment' and Godwin as well – to remain, for the duration of their careers, social and political conservatives. In the midst of this conservative and chauvinistic reaction Godwin was singled out with particular malice. The absurdities of reform were

6. ibid, I, p. 213.

7. Crabb Robinson, *On Books and Their Writers* (Dent, London, 1938), p. 21.

conjured up by anti-Jacobin pamphlets merely by referring to the schemes envisioned in *Political Justice*. Godwin's name was synonymous with licence, atheism and
sin in traditionalist circles. Crabb Robinson wrote in his
diary of an 'eminent clergyman who was accustomed
when any incident of unnatural depravity or abandoned
profligacy was mentioned, to say 'I should not have supposed any man capable of such an action except Godwin.'[8]

That Godwin should have been the scapegoat for the
loyalist reaction was inevitable. Paine after all had fled
and *Political Justice* had been recognized as the high-
water mark of sympathetic responses to the French Revolution. But, as we shall see below, while perhaps inevitable, the attack on Godwin was by no means just; he had
in *Political Justice* cautioned against revolution and popular tumult and had even spoken out against popular
radical agitators in London. But these details were less
well known. He stood condemned as the pre-eminent
English philosophical disciple of Rousseau and Helevétius,
who were by now accepted as the bloody forerunners of
the terror.

Godwin's decline in public fortune in the later years
of the 1790s was matched by a tragic setback in his personal affairs. He had met Mary Wollstonecraft, the radical feminist, in 1791. But only in 1796 did he begin to
spend much time with her, by which time she was the well-
known authoress of the controversial *Vindication of the
Rights of Woman*. They both had enlightened views on
cohabitation and marriage. In *Political Justice* Godwin
had written that marriage was a stifling monopoly, that
each partner ought to exist separately and independently.
Mary Wollstonecraft, in turn, wrote, 'it is my wish that
Mr Godwin shall visit and dine out as formerly, and I
shall do the same; in short, I still mean to be independent'.[9]

In keeping to these views, the liberated couple main-

8. ibid., p. 25.
9. Ford K. Brown, *The Life of William Godwin*, op. cit., p. 117.

tained separate dwellings and communicated by note and met for meals. They did, however, finally bow to conventional morality, when Mary became pregnant. They were married in March 1797. Their political views on marriage and the relationship of the sexes was further grist for the mill of conservative ridicule and satire. The *Anti-Jacobin Review* lampooned 'the promiscuous intercourse of the sexes, as one of the highest improvements to result from Political Justice'.[10] A child, Mary Godwin, was born to the couple on 30 August 1797. Ten days later Mary Wollstonecraft the mother lay dead. In a tragic irony of fate the feminist succumbed in childbirth – a woman's lot. Godwin was prostrate with grief. His beloved was dead and he at forty-one was left with the care of two children – little Mary, and a four year-old, Wollstonecraft's child by a previous liaison.

Godwin never recovered from the public and private despair of the years 1795–7. He continued to write a great deal both to recoup his fame and to provide the money needed to raise his children. His novel *Caleb Williams* (1794), which rendered the theme of *Political Justice* in fiction, was somewhat successful (it is even available today in paperback editions – history's recognition of permanent impact). He tried another long essay in political philosophy, *The Enquirer*, in 1797, in which he re-stated most of the themes of his earlier work, with minor concessions to his critics. He then turned to writing plays. Nothing worked. He became a virtual unknown, constantly borrowing money, writing hack children's books and dictionaries. He re-married in 1803, but that was equally unsuccessful. It was in such relative obscurity, then, that Godwin was 're-discovered' by the young Shelly in 1812. Godwin was no fool, he cultivated the young heir to £6,000 a year and thus opened the next fascinating chapter in his life.

Shelley began to turn the ideas of Godwin's *Political Justice* – buried for twenty years – into verse. *Queen Mab*

10. *Anti-Jacobin Review*, July 1797, p. 91.

appeared in March 1813. Godwin meanwhile turned to Shelley for cash, and so it would be for many years. Shelley lived off Godwin's ideas and Godwin lived off loans and gifts from the poet. Their lives were destined to become even further entwined, however, for Percy fell in love with sixteen-year-old Mary Godwin. In 1814 Shelley's wife Harriet left him and he and Mary went off to France. Godwin was angry. All the earlier emancipated views on marriage had died with Wollstonecraft in the 1790s; this was his daughter and the impropriety infuriated him. For the next two years Godwin refused to see his daughter and Shelley, though he still communicated with them for loans of money. In December 1816 Harriet Shelley committed suicide and Percy and Mary were married. Only then did Godwin visit his daughter and benefactor son-in-law. Mary Godwin Shelley would, like her husband, also help to immortalize Godwin's ideas. In 1818, when only twenty-one, she wrote *Frankenstein*, in which there are many links to the social and psychological doctrines of her father's *Political Justice*.

Godwin lived on for two more decades, during which time as an old man he repudiated most of the visionary and radical aspects of *Political Justice*. Whereas earlier he had taught Coleridge, now Coleridge led Godwin back to religion via the mysteries of pantheism. In the late 1820s Godwin spoke out against the increasingly powerful movement for suffrage reform. Once again, as we shall discuss in detail below, a close reading of *Political Justice* would not find these positions so startling. He wrote more plays, usually unsuccessful, and dabbled in publishing, also with little success. The only important book produced in these two decades was his study *Of Population* in 1820. In this work he answered Malthus, who in *An Essay on the Principle of Population* had criticized Godwin's utopian vision of men conquering sickness and even death through reason. What would such numbers subsist on, asked Malthus? Godwin's *Of Population* suggested that rational man would sense the folly of unlimited procreation and self-consciously limit population growth in the victory of reason and intellect over passion.

His last years were marked by even more financial troubles, compounded in 1822 by the drowning of his son-in-law Shelley. Mary Shelley, then twenty-five, stayed close to her father in his declining years, as he continued to write and publish. A long philosophical treatise *Thoughts on Man* appeared in 1831, in which he repudiated many of the positions he had taken in 1793. He wrote a play in 1830, another in 1833. Some token of public recognition finally came to Godwin when he was seventy-seven. In 1833, with the Whigs in power for the first time since before the French Revolution, Lord Grey rewarded Godwin with the sinecure office of Yeoman Usher of the Exchequer at £200 a year. His life and career had come to this, he lived to be the beneficiary of government, of that very brute force his anarchism had condemned. Godwin died in 1836 at the age of eighty; in his will he asked to be buried next to his first wife, his beloved Mary Wollstonecraft.

2. *The 'Euthanasia of Government': The Attack on The Liberal Tradition and Political Authority in Political Justice*

Godwin's anarchism is epitomized most simply in his plea in *Political Justice* for 'the dissolution of political government, of that brute engine, which has been the only perennial cause of the vices of mankind'. But the doctrines of this, one of the most sacred texts in the anarchist tradition, are by no means so generally obvious and straightforward. It is useful, therefore, so schematize the development of the argument in *Political Justice*, in the following manner. Two stages of destruction are followed by one of visionary reconstruction. The first negative stages involves an assault on the liberal tradition, carried out primarily by invoking Rousseau. Then follows the attack on law and political authority in the name of the liberal values of private judgement and individuality. There is, to be sure, some tension, incompatibility and even contradiction between these two destructive aspects of the argument, some of which remains and cannot be reasoned away. But much of this tension is resolved in the positive vision of anarchist society. The synthesizing agent is the principle of sincerity. In bare outline, then, these are the stages in Godwin's philosophy of anarchism. One can turn now in greater detail to each stage in the argument.

Godwin begins *Political Justice* with a root-and-branch attack on the Lockean natural rights tradition. His main charge is that it is too egotistical, too concerned with the individual's right to do as he wills. Sacrificed in this world view, according to Godwin, are duty, justice and concern for the common good. Writers like Locke, he contends, in their 'unprofitable disquisitions ... respecting the probable origin of government', and in investigating rights, have failed to ask what form of government was the most conducive to public welfare.[11] Godwin repudiates any notion of contract based on some original promise. He does this by simply repeating the arguments of Hume.[12]

What irritates him even more is the basic liberal notion of rights, for as far as Godwin is concerned rights 'are all of them superseded and rendered null by the superior claims of justice'. Man has no permissive grant to do as he wishes, based on some supposed ethic of self-justification. He is bound by justice to do his duty, to employ his talents, his understanding, his strength and his time in the production of the greatest quantity of general good. One's duty is to see that his every act is 'bound to ... the general weal, that is, for the benefit of the individuals of whom the whole is composed.'[13]

Godwin is perfectly willing to dispense with the most fundamental of liberal rights. Man, he states, has no right even to his life, 'when his duty calls him to resign it'.

11. See below, p. 167.
12. See below, pp. 212, 216–17, 234.
13. See below, pp. 197, 175, 87–8.

17

Neighbours are duty-bound to deprive one another of liberty and even life, he suggests, if to do so is absolutely necessary to the prevention of greater evil. Godwin sees such calculations of duty as by and large easy. It is, after all, blatantly clear that should one's 'brother or father' and Archbishop Fénelon (The French social thinker and critic of Louis XIV's despotism) be trapped together in a burning house the latter should be saved. Not only has Godwin thus repudiated Locke and Hobbes, he also repudiates what will be one of Mill's major liberal contentions. Men have to amend the errors of anyone they may see or know, suggests Godwin. 'It is absurd to suppose that certain points are especially within my province, and therefore [that my neighbour] ... may not afford me, invited or uninvited, his assistance in arriving at a right decision'.[14]

Like Rousseau, his exemplar in much of this criticism, Godwin's thought is very close to that of the eighteenth-century French *philosophes*. He shares the interest of these Enlightenment philosophers in right reason, truth and justice. Indeed, at this point there is every good reason to expect Godwin to continue his Rosseauean assault on liberal government by repudiating its negativism, its failure positively to promote virtue, the good life or at least the general good. All he has written to this point in the argument tends in that direction. If not an enlightened despot, the solution of some *philosophes*, like Helvétius and Voltaire, then at least a democratic sovereign finding duty and right reason via the law of the general will – Rousseau's proposal – seems in order. But Godwin follows neither of the two alternatives taken by the French *philosophes*; he sets out on his own path to anarchism. Is it the duty of governments to watch over the manners of the people, he asks? Ought it to superintend the sentiments of the people and 'encourage such as are favorable to virtue, and to check in the bud such as may lead to disorder and corruption?' 'Surely,' he states ironically,

14. See below, pp. 194-5.

'government can do some positive good.'[15] But no, alas, it cannot, he proclaims. Helvétius and Rousseau are both rejected, and in an abrupt about-face there is the anarchist Godwin one expected.

> Government is, in all cases, an evil; it ought to be introduced as sparingly as possible. Man is a species of being whose excellence depends on his individuality; and who can be neither great nor wise, but in proportion as he is independent.[16]

This turn in the argument introduces Godwin's second destructive stage, his assault on law and political authority in the name of private judgement and individuality. The mood shifts decisively and one finds the traditional liberal preoccupation with individual freedom pushed to extremes – to anarchist extremes. But the anti-liberal Godwin, the critic of rights and the defender of duty and a higher public good, will eventually return. He will eventually proclaim a vision of an ideal society, where not governments but friends and neighbours will lead men to truth and virtue. In this early stage of the argument, however, he is concerned with the defence of private judgement and the need to replace the brute engine, government.

Godwin argues, then, that self-determination and independence are basic to the nature of man. Free man consults his own reason and draws his own conclusions. He then will conscientiously conform to whatever are his own ideas of propriety. The free man is one who exercises his own judgement and 'stands by himself, and rests upon his own understanding'. He seeks truth and right through his own rational faculties. The only principle which legitimately imposes upon him any specific conduct is the conviction of his individual understanding.[17] We are unmistakably in the camp of individualistic liberalism.

15. See below, p. 556.
16. See below, p. 556.
17. See below, p. 198.

It is only necessary for Godwin now to push this liberalism to the finality of anarchism. This he does by criticizing first governmental authority, then law, and finally punishment.

Anything that moves man to action other than his own private judgement, Godwin contends, is by definition force or coercion. Government, which sets up other men as permanent arbiters over the actions of individuals, is the ultimate determinant of most men's destinies. As such, 'government is nothing but regulated force; force is its appropriate claim upon your attention.[18] But Godwin's rejection of government is much more complex than this often-quoted passage. Government is only the third of three possible forms of authority. In the first, the authority of reason, the individual obeys simply himself. Reason, indeed, represents the absence of government. The second form of authority is confidence in and deference to some esteemed figure and his decisions. As Godwin rightly points out, this is the original meaning of the word authority; it represents 'compliance which is the offspring of respect'.[19] Godwin regards only the third form of authority as purely political that is, unnatural. This is governmental authority, to which compliance is based not upon esteem and respect but upon force and power. Self-government, the first form of authority, is obviously the ideal. Of the two forms of external authority, the second, the natural deference to superiority, is clearly preferable to the third, according to Godwin, especially when the individual has reason to believe that another person knows better than he what is proper to do. If this is the case, then one ought to conform to such direction. The door is opened here, we must note now and return to later, for an élitist appreciation of enlightened tutelage, an idea not at all uncongenial to the eighteenth-century *philosophes* enamoured of the vision of enlightened despotism. But, nothing, Godwin writes, can justify the third

18. See below, p. 242.
19. See below, p. 243.

form of authority. It is totally contrary to reason and justice to surrender one's private judgement, that is to obey another man because he is superior in station 'or because of concurrence of circumstances has produced him a share in the legislative and executive government of our country'. But men need not, indeed ought not, to take arms to overthrow this brute engine that Godwin calls government. Such forms of government are doomed anyway, he writes, for all government will ultimately wither away. People obey government only because they are ignorant. When knowledge and virtue increase, men will discover that there is 'no mystery in government which uninitiated mortals must not presume to penetrate'. At some point they no longer will need nor will they tolerate authority of governments, the third form of authority. Formal governments will be abandoned and only the authority of the truly esteemed and wise will operate. But, as knowledge and virtue further increase, men will be themselves wise and defer to the authority of no one but themselves. With the inexorable passage of time, then, and with the progressive dissemination of knowledge and wisdom, all forms of government, formal and informal, will slowly be put to rest.

In other words, government cannot proceed but upon confidence, as confidence on the other hand cannot exist without ignorance. The true supporters of government are the weak and uninformed, and not the wise. In proportion as weakness and ignorance shall diminish, the basis of government will also decay. This, however, is an event which ought not to be contemplated with alarm. A catastrophe of this description would be the true euthenasia of government.[20]

Godwin is no revolutionary, then. Implicit in the argument of *Political Justice* is the assumption that anarchism will in and of itself win the day as ignorance retreats before advancing enlightenment. We shall return later to the importance of waiting out the gradual evolution of

20. See below, pp. 247–8.

the anarchist ideal. But returning to his argument, having disposed of governmental authority, Godwin turns next on law. None of Rousseau's rhapsodic appreciation of law is found here. Godwin's central point is that the diversity of human experience defies generalization, one important form of which is abstract law. No action of any man is the same as another's. Law is either stretched on a Procrustean bed to fit new cases, or else a new general law is made. In either case, Godwin argues, instead of being certain and eliminating ambiguity, law is cloaked in uncertainty. Few can thus know what to expect at the hands of the law. Moreover, it 'fixes the human mind in a stagnant condition', and substitutes permanence for progress.[21] Because of these shortcomings law must be abolished and replaced by what Godwin calls situational wisdom. Reason, he holds, must be applied anew to each incident, and all the many and unique factors of each case must be heard and understood. Only this conduct befits a rational people.

The final step in the destructive phase of Godwin's anarchism is his attack on the doctrine of punishment. It is essential for his anarchism that he question the legitimacy and the utility of punishment, since, as he himself concedes, the most important justification for government is that in order to prevent the hostile actions of one member of society upon another there must be the sanction of criminal punishment. Punishment is unjust, however, Godwin contends, because it assumes free will when in fact necessity and circumstance propel the criminal to his action. In a famous passage Godwin suggests that the assassin can no more prevent the murder he commits than can his dagger.[22] Moreover, he adds, punishment is a useless method of dealing with a wrongdoer. Like all forms of political coercion it is a mere recourse to force that has no intrinsic capacity to convince. 'It is no argument ... it begins with violently alienating the mind from the truth with which we wish it to be impressed.' One ought to rea-

21. See below, p. 688.
22. See below, p. 633.

son with a criminal and convince him of his errors, for, as Godwin firmly believes, no man can reject truth and choose falsehood when the evidence is clearly and fairly presented.[23]

So much, then, for the destructive phase of Godwin's anarchism. Government, law and coercion are pushed aside by self-determined wise men who use their own private judgement and their own reason. These men are independent and autonomous. 'Each man should be wise enough to govern himself, without the intervention of any compulsory restraint.' So keen is Godwin on protecting this individual autonomy that he pushes his anarchic-individualist ideal to the elimination of all forms of co-operation. 'Everything that is usually understood by the term co-operation,' he writes, 'is in some degree an evil'.[24] And that degree is the extent to which co-operation inhibits a man's individuality and prevents his thinking for himself. Meals in common and communal labour are suspect. Men may now have to work crowded together in factories, but technology will soon, he predicts, make the most extensive operations within the reach of one solitary man. Theatrical and musical performances will go, too. Autonomous men may very well cease to 'repeat words and ideas that are not their own', or music composed by others. Though they may find pleasure in one another's company, solitude will be the greatest delight of autonomous men: they 'ought to be able to do without one another'. And so one comes to Godwin's famous views on marriage, which he sees as both unjust and monopolistic. Even more harmful is its unnecessary emphasis on co-operation and its infringement on personal independence.[25]

In these prophetic passages of *Political Justice* one finds the quintessential statement of Godwin's anarchic individualism – the ideal of independent, self-determined,

23. See below, pp. 572, 563.
24. See below, p. 758.
25. See below, pp. 759–62.

non-co-operative man. This is the often parodied Godwin that has amused his detractors, ranging from the staff of the *Anti-Jacobin Review* of his day to the Victorian Leslie Stephen. But Godwin's anarchism, and anarchist thought after him, does not end with this longing for individual privacy and autonomy. It moves on to a second stage, more positive and less liberal – the vision of an ideal order, in which emphasis shifts dramatically to values of community, co-operation and solidarity, all achieved through the coercion of virtuous and duty-seeking neighbours. Paradoxically, the new order will enshrine co-operation, but a co-operation by no means as 'usually understood'.

3. *'Political Simplicity': Utopian Anarchism in* Political Justice

Godwin's vision of anarchist society is constructed around three basic principles: 'political simplicity', 'public inspection' and 'positive sincerity'. One must begin with 'political simplicity', for the two other principles presume its prior existence. The practice of sincerity and the performance of public inspection require the geopolitical reorganization of society. The masses of mankind have been duped, claims Godwin, 'by the mysterious complicated nature of the social system'[26] the social order must therefore be simplified. Simplicity of political arrangement would liberate men and could be achieved through localism and federalism. If nations were broken down into smaller autonomous units, parishes that regulated their own affairs, they would cease their tyranny:

The ideas of a great empire and legislative unity are plainly the barbarous remains of the days of military heroism. In proportion as political power is brought home to the citizens and simplified into something of the nature of parish regulation; the danger of misunderstanding and rivalship will be nearly annihilated. In proportion as the science of

26. See below, p. 552.

government is divested of its present mysterious appearances, social truth will become obvious, and the districts pliant and flexible to the dictates of reason.[27]

A general assembly of these parishes would be a rare and extraordinary event. Normally, representatives of the parishes would assemble but once a year to adjust their few differences. This assembly would pass no laws, take no votes. To do so would be an affront to reason and justice, 'the deciding upon truth by the casting out of numbers'. As part of the generally nostalgic flavour of Godwin's ideal order, this yearly assembly would merely perform the medieval task of hearing complaints and representations from constituents.[28]

Within the parish no political institutions would be necessary. Occasional disputes would be settled by calling a jury, but these juries would have no coercive power. They would only invite and reason. They would persuade, not dictate. Political authority in the parish would be replaced by public persuasion. The entire system is made to work by the power 'of public inspection'. In a simple and small unit the 'observant eye of public judgement' would prompt each individual to seek the common good. Godwin was not the first, nor the last, to suggest that men are less moral under the cover of a large society and more virtuous in the face-to-face contacts of simpler and more local surroundings. Extensive governments require coercion and force; smaller units allow the sway of opinion. 'The inspection of every man over the conduct of his neighbours, when unstained with caprice, would constitute a censorship of the most irresistible nature.' Law and government are replaced, then, in Godwin's anarchist utopia, by the watchful and censuring eye of public opinion. The disapprobation of one's neigbours is enough, he holds, to make everyone shy away from vice.[29]

Public inspection and censorship would work, however,

27. See below, p. 610.
28. See below, p. 551.
29. See below, p. 554.

only if neighbours tell the truth to one another; that is, only if they are sincere. Godwin's preoccupation with sincerity, his quaint insistence that one must not have one's butler lie when one is in but not eager to see company, is more than simply the eccentricity of a bookish crank. It is, in fact, a principle basic to his vision of a new order, for public persuasion can only work if each citizen is his neighbour's 'ingenious censor' and if they proclaim one another's 'virtues, good deeds, meanness and follies'. Only through such just and impartial evaluation can vice presumably be discouraged and virtue encouraged. In the telling of these truths, neighbours should not be restrained by private protections like libel laws. The occasional false charge or mistaken censor, Godwin insists, is a small price to pay for the advantages of unlimited and sincere criticism.[30] It is in light of this important political purpose, then, that one is to understand Godwin's claim that sincerity is 'the most powerful engine of human improvement'. But sincerity does more; it helps bring together the anti-liberal and the liberal aspects of his anarchism. Liberated from governmental coercion, men in Godwin's parishes will freely exercise their private judgements, but they will not leave each other alone. They will not till their gardens in passive liberal enjoyment of private rights. They will recognize their fundamentally non-liberal duty, 'the most indispensable business of man, to study and promote his neighbour's welfare'.[31] Their exercise of private judgement will be in the service of others. It will pursue a higher will, a higher realm of truth. This pursuit will take the form not of legislative enactment of a general will but rather of positive, constructive, and sincere neighbourly advice and criticism. There is, according to Godwin, no plurality of ideals. The nature of man and the nature of his good life are not relative. 'There is but one perfection to man; one thing most honourable ... all else is deviation and error; a disease to

30. See below, pp. 312–13, 593–603.
31. See below, pp. 320–21.

be cured, not to be encouraged.' That single and overriding ideal is 'benevolence', or as he calls it elsewhere, 'disinterested transport'. The goal of man's social existence is 'to make others free, virtuous and wise'. Godwin is convinced that 'there is but one best mode of social existence', which can be deduced from the principles of human nature, for there must be one code of truth on the subject of our reciprocal duties.[32] It is as if Rousseau's legislator and general will are replaced by Adam Smith's neutral observer. Godwin describes it as:

Putting ourselves in the place of an impartial spectator, of an angelic nature, – beholding us from an elevated station, and uninfluenced by our prejudices, conceiving that would be his estimate of the intrinsic circumstances of our neighbour and acting accordingly.[33]

Each individual is obliged to see that his neighbour lives up to the uniform code of truths which teach benevolence and public spirit. To do this, he must, however, break the cold reserve that keeps men at a distance from one another. Men must end the charade in which they talk to one another without disclosing their feelings or opinions. They must sincerely and openly speak to each other about their moral character, 'how they ought to be employed, and how to be improved'.[34]

Sincerity is the key, then, to understanding the relationship of the diverse parts of Godwin's argument, as well as being the essential value in his simple, face-to-face, nonpolitical society. Laws would be unnecessary, for example, in this vision of political simplicity. The inhabitants of a small parish, seeing that laws were irrational, would judge each case not by written axioms but by the circumstances and demands of the particular case, what Godwin calls the 'spontaneous justice' of the parish. But even this would become unnecessary at some point, for eventually

32. See below, pp. 249, 302.

33. See below, pp. 173–4, and Adam Smith, *The Theory of Moral Sentiments*.

34. See below, p. 288.

crime would be totally eliminated. Public disapproval
would turn all knaves honest. Who would commit a crime
when faced by 'the sober condemnation of every spectator'? Even the 'legal' crime and murder of governments
would come to an end in the new order, for they were
indelibly associated with the false notions of extensive
territory and dreams of glory, empire and national greatness.[35]

The new anarchist order would see the decline of crime
for reasons much more basic than simply the public disapproval of knaves. The very motivation to crime would
dry up. For, according to Godwin, its most important
source was economic inequality. If this were changed,
crime would cease. Godwin is dramatically outspoken
in his condemnation of inequality. Few English Jacobins
of the 1790s would outdo his indignation at social injustice; perhaps only his wife, Mary Wollstonecraft, and
Tom Paine could match him on this score. The rich,
Godwin claims, were 'in all countries directly or indirectly
the legislators of the state'. Their laws invariably favoured
their interests over those of the poor and 'reduced oppression into a system'.[36] He points out that while the
rich, for example, could associate for monopoly and gain,
the law of Parliament prevented working men combining
in unions. The effect of this inequality on the poor was
disastrous. To be born poor, Godwin writes in his *Enquirer*, 'may be said under another name to be born a
slave'. Any potential for distinction and intellectual
achievement in the lower orders was dashed by 'the present
ordering of society ... the great slaughter-house of genius
and of mind'.[37]

The great ally of the rich in this oppression and bru-
talization of the poor was, according to Godwin, modern
technology. Godwin here sets the pattern for subsequent

35. See below, pp. 611, 693, 598, 659.
36. See below, p. 92.
37. Godwin, *The Enquirer: Reflections on Education, Manners,
and Literature*, (London, 1797), p. 162; 17.

generations of anarchists in the condemnation of the machine age. Like many of them, however, he also relished the progressive potential of technology. Would not, for example, the drudgery and oppression of communal factory work be ended with the invention of one great machine operated by a solitary individual? But his response in this, his anti-technological, mood was in fact a rather acute anticipation of later notions of alienation, for the end product of the factory system, he argued, in his novel *Fleetwood* was the estrangement of man from himself, his transformation from worker to machine.

A mechanic becomes a sort of machine; his limbs and articulations are converted, as it were, into wood and wires. Tamed, lowered, torpified into this character, he may be said perhaps to be content.[38]

The most grievous political result of this constant and unmerciful exercise of superiority by the rich was, according to Godwin, that it produced crime, which in turn could be used as justification for punishment and, therefore, as a rationale for government. The exploitation by the rich led the poor to seek reprisals. The poor see 'the state of society as a state of war'. In his most popular novel, *Caleb Williams,* Godwin has his pathetic hero, driven to crime, exclaim in his defence:

Oh poverty! Thou art indeed omnipotent! Thou grindest us into desperation; thou confoundest all our boasted and most deep rooted principles; thou fillest us to the very brim with malice and revenge, and render us capable of acts of unknown horror.[39]

The inequality and injustice of this economic system would disappear in the simple anarchist society described in *Political Justice*. The oppression of the factory, taxation of the poor, legislation by the rich, oppression and misery leading to class crime – all these would be replaced simply and magically in the transition to a frugal agrarian econ-

38. Godwin, *Fleetwood* (London, 1805), I, 277.
39. Godwin, *Caleb Williams* (London, 1794), II, 30.

omy. Once again Godwin anticipated generations of future
anarchists. Taxation would be unnecessary in the parish,
he holds, since there would be no foreign wars, no domestic office holders. The usual army of government functionaries, clerks, collectors, etc. would not be needed. But Godwin felt that the right to private property, on the other
hand, was still legitimate, and was in fact, essential for the
exercise of private judgement and independence. Too
great and too unequal an accumulation of property was,
to be sure, unjust, but the small and simple parish society
would restrain this accumulation by 'the good sense of the
community, and the inspection of all exercised upon all'.
Eventually the parish would see an equality of holdings
with no man having for his personal use more than his
necessities required. Man in his parish society would work
only in simple manual industry and agriculture. No one
would accumulate unearned property produced by the
labour of others; 'the mathematician, the poet, and the
philosopher will derive a new stock of cheerfulness and
energy from the recurring labour that makes them feel they
are man'.[40] No one in Godwin's utopia would manufacture
luxuries, however – an unnecessary chore that occupied
many men in modern nations. Whereas the object of
modern society was to multiply labour, Godwin's parish
economy would simplify it, would produce 'a state of the
most rigid simplicity'. In the England of 1790s one in
twenty worked on agriculture, he conjectured (a rather
wildly erroneous guess); but in his utopia all men would
work in the fields at some time. All other jobs would be
eliminated. The job of supplying the community with
the absolute necessities of life would be parcelled out to
all men and thus occupy one-twentieth of every man's
time. Each member of the community would perform
manual labour about half an hour a day; the rest of the
day he would enjoy life, learning and nature in his idyllic
rural paradise.[41] And of course there was the duty of using

40. See below, pp. 625, 710, 694, 744.
41. See below, pp. 744-7.

free time to inspect and give sincere advice to neighbours.

Here, too, Godwin anticipates and sets the pattern for later anarchist ambivalence. While much of the argument for equality expresses itself in images of communal solidarity, it is also expressed in the language of radical and competitive individualism. One dimension of his assault on inequality is couched in the language of bourgeois liberalism. The enemy is aristocratic privilege. In *Political Justice* some of Godwin's most vitriolic prose is directed at the feudal notions of rank and status. In their place he pleads for the liberal principles of careers and rewards open to talent, industry and merit. He speaks directly of equality of opportunity, as he makes the classic liberal argument for a fair race, free of special advantages, and with victory assured the best runner:

Remove from me and my fellows all arbitrary hindrances; let us start fair; render all the advantages and honours of social institution accessible to every man, in proportion to his talents and exertions.[42]

In passages such as these Godwin echoes the progressive bourgeois ideology found in the writings of men like Priestley and articulated in the circles of industrial religious dissenters around Wilkinson and Wedgwood.

This is, it must be repeated, but one side of his message. Godwin, the ambivalent anarchist, also speaks to the past; indeed, much of the imagery of his visionary parish society was familiar to Englishmen of his day. Alongside sentiments championed by the new men of industrial talent there is also in Godwin rural nostalgia and the longing for the simplicity of a frugal economy and a face-to-face society, themes often found in earlier opposition writings under Walpole, both from Tories, like Bolingbroke and Gay, and radicals like Trenchard and Gordon. These themes are also writ large in the Toryism of Goldsmith's 'Deserted Village' and the radicalism of Southey's *Wat*

42. See below, p. 472.

Tyler. Godwin, in his novel *Imogen*, written in 1784, had himself depicted an idyllic community of Druids with no government, and no ranks of distinction. His sincere and simple protagonists, Imogen and Edwin, roundly overcame the villain Roderick. But the vision of *Political Justice* differs from other nostalgic pastorals and from the spate of English imitations of Rousseau in its transcendence of mere social and economic nostalgia and its thoroughgoing political radicalism – in short, in its complete dismissal of the political.

Even here, however, one wonders if perhaps Godwin didn't have a model for his vision. Where else, for example, might he find a vision of a community free of law, free of coercion, free of institutions, free of power, indeed free of politics? Where else might he find a community of spontaneous solidarity and zealous regard for one another's moral well-being? The answer may well be that Godwin, the former dissenting minister, could never quite free himself from the anarchic vision of the primitive Christian community – but that is another story. Suffice it to point out here that Godwin held no illusion that if the government of Britain were dissolved in 1793 his simple parish society would immediately flourish. The citizenry were still unregenerate, and not fit for this dispensation; it would come only in due time. Before one speculates on this eventuality, however, one must make clear how Godwin felt this dispensation would *not* come about. The radical ideal of anarchic political simplicity, he was certain, could never be brought about by radical political agitation or reform.

4. 'Tumult and Violence': The Critique of Radical Politics in Political Justice

In the preface to the first edition of *Political Justice* Godwin credits many of his insights to the recent experiments in America and France. He was persuaded 'of the desirableness of a govenment in the utmost degree simple' by the ideas suggested in the French Revolution.[43] That event, he confesses, more than anything else, prompted his writing the *Enquiry*. Like Price's sermon at Old Jewry, Paine's *Rights of Man*, Mackintosh's *Vindiciae Gallicae*, and Wollstonecraft's *Vindication of the Rights of Woman*, Godwin's *Political Justice* was part of the literary outburst produced among English Jacobins by the French Revolution.[44] But Godwin's response when examined closely has very much the flavour of another written in those years, Burke's *Reflections*. Godwin, the philosophical radical, would have no truck with any political action designed to encourage or hasten the achievement of anarchism. The Revolution in France had, to be sure, awakened Godwin's love for freedom, but it had also irredeemably frightened the calm philosophical sceptic in him. Thus in *Political Justice* Godwin specifically repudiates reform politics, which means in the context of the 1790s that he opposed radical change through political action.

'Tumult and violence', the phrase he habitually used in *Political Justice* to describe the hurly-burly of radical politics, could never bring about an ideal order, he argued. Only when the great majority of society were persuaded would 'the chains fall off of themselves'. Any effort to introduce political change – no matter how excellent theoretically – that did not consider the state of the public mind would be both absurd and injurious. Men ought to speculate on the ideal form of political society, Godwin felt, but they should be on guard against precipitate measures. Ideals could be securely established only when there was a general preference in their favour. Philosophers might well know that one form of government is most desirable, but inferior forms of government must still be tolerated since immediate efforts to remove them would

43. See below, p. 69.
44. The English reformers of this period often called themselves or were called by their opponents, Jacobin, which is the party designation of the radical revolutionaries in France. The English Jacobins were, on the whole, reformers, not revolutionaries.

introduce something far worse, chaos and turbulence. All the wheels, he writes, must move together lest the fragile structure of society break down:

> The interests of the human species requires a gradual, but uninterrupted change. He who should make these principles the regulators of his conduct would not rashly insist upon instant abolition of all existing abuses ... Truth, however unreserved be the mode of its enunciation, will be sufficiently gradual in its progress. It will be fully comprehended only by slow degrees, by its most assiduous votaries; and the degrees will be still more temperate by which it will pervade so considerable a portion of the community as to render them mature for a change of their common institutions ... we shall have many reforms, but no revolutions ... Revolutions are the produce of passion, not of sober and tranquil reason.[45]

The proper task for the friends of humanity was not to introduce new practices in politics, but 'enquiry, communication, and discussion'. Godwin assailed Rousseau on this very point. He felt that Rousseau's recourse to a civic religion in the effort to transform the public mentality enlisted a new authority over a people not yet capable of perceiving the wisdom of the new order. Duping men to receive a system whose reasonableness is not a part of their understanding is, Godwin suggests, 'a questionable method for rendering them sober, judicious, reasonable, and happy'. Burke, too, is criticized on this score for his suggestion that men cherish their prejudices. Lulling men not to use their own understanding is wrong when used to uphold the established order as well as when used to change it.[46]

The major thrust of Godwin's caution, however, is directed against the 'domestic spoilers' who preach immediate disolution of all governments. Godwin contends that if this should occur in 1793, in a period when political truth had not yet permeated the understandings of all, an

45. See below, pp. 251–2.
46. See below, pp. 496–7, 504.

anarchy of barbarism and violence would follow, not the
reasoned anarchy of political simplicity, positive sincerity and public censorship. The resultant insecurity and
disorder would be far worse than the preceding despotism. Particularly vulnerable were not the poor and the
exploited, but men the very likes of Godwin, 'the wisest,
the brightest, the most generous and bold'. In a state of
barbaric and violent anarchy one 'must bid farewell, to the
patient lubrications of the philosopher, and the labour
of the midnight oil'. True anarchy would not result from
headlong and impatient action:

In order to anarchy being rendered a seed of future justice,
reflection and enquiry must have gone before; the regions
of philosophy must have been penetrated, and political truth
have opened her school to mankind.[47]

Godwin is so outspoken in his opposition to any form
of resistance or revolution that he even rejects the argument from Locke so often cited by English radicals.
Nations have no right, Godwin answers, to shake off
governments simply because of an alleged break with a
social contract or usurpation of traditional rights. Since
government is founded on opinion, he argues, even bad
governments must have come to be accepted by whatever
be the current level of popular understanding. If the
people are unenlightened and unprepared for a state of
freedom, then resistance is inappropriate, and if political
knowledge has spread among them, then their resistance
is unnecessary, for subjection of the people even by foreign
forces will be futile and short-lived. The theme is constantly reiterated: 'if the nation be not right for a state
of freedom' no resistance is justified.[48]

Godwin is careful in *Political Justice* to remind his
readers that 'the great cause of humanity' has two enemies,
the Burkean friends of prejudice and antiquity, on the

47. See below, pp. 663–6.
48. See below, pp. 258ff, 294.

one hand, and the 'friends of innovation' on the other. Having warned of two enemies he concentrates, however, on only one, those 'impatient of suspense, inclined violently to interrupt the calm, incessant, rapid and auspicious progress which thought and reflection appear to be making in the world'. He even uses the misgivings of the one enemy to combat the other. Like Burke, Godwin keenly saw the paradoxes inherent in the Jacobin-Revolutionary mentality. Resisting tyranny, the revolutionaries became tyrants themselves, scrutinizing men's thoughts punishing their opinions. 'To dragoon men into adoption of what we think right,' Godwin writes, 'is an intolerable tyranny.'[49]

Much like an orthodox Marxist of a later day, Godwin, in the next stage of his attack on radical reform, cautions against rushing the inevitable developments of progressive change. 'There is a condition of political society best adapted to every different stage of individual improvement.' Everything is in order, and succeeds at its appointed time. History must unfold in its predetermined stages, one cannot impatiently hurry it to its conclusion. The historical passage is long and arduous; 'and if we aspire to the final result, we must submit to the portion of misery and vice, which necessarily fills the span in between,' he writes. One such evil is the unfair distribution of wealth. This, too, cannot be changed by premature violence or even legislative action: it can only come from a 'revolution of opinions'. Men should be careful lest they rip down too hastily the institutions of property and its inequalities which are so woven into the social fabric. If private property were suddenly abolished, or if even the principles of feudal rights and privileges of rank were instantly dissolved, thousands of men, indeed whole classes, would be reduced to immediate wretchedness, Godwin contends, and all manner of calamity, convulsion and upheaval would ensue more dreadful than the evil remedied. It is Godwin the proto-Marxist historicist again who writes,

49. See below, p. 262.

'the inequalities of property perhaps constitute a state, through which it would be necessary for us to pass'.[50]

It is more than simply anachronistic, however, to label Godwin thus. His historical caution on this score is, after all, informed by the fundamental convictions of a property-owning class. Like Proudhon Godwin sees property as crucial to the independence and autonomy of anarchist man.

> Without permitting to every man, to a considerable degree, the exercise of his own discretion, there can be no independence, no improvement, no virtue and no happiness. This is a privilege in the highest degree sacred; for its maintenance no exertions and sacrifices can be too great. Thus deep is the foundation of the doctrine of property. It is, in the last resort, the palladium of all that ought to be dear to us, and must ever be approached but with awe and veneration.[51]

Burke might well agree with Godwin's criticism of the politics of resistance, revolution and redistribution, but Burke would never agree with Godwin's more basic and unique assault on political associations, parties and political life in general. Political parties, associations – any form of co-operative political endeavour – all fall before Godwin's ruthless philosophical bias. Sounding much like a contemporary student of group politics, Godwin insists that in any such collective gathering the intemperate and artful push aside the 'prudent, the sober, the sceptical, and the contemplative'. Truth could never emerge from the superficial convictions of committed partisans; it would only come from rigorous and laborious enquiry. Party, Godwin argues, puts a premium not on thinking for one's self but on identifying one's creed with that of one's associates. There is no encouragement to enquiry when all the diversity of opinion has been reduced to the position of one common mass. Political meetings encourage harangue and declamation, he contends, which lead

50. See below, pp. 667. 716, 698–9, 273, 263.
51. See below, p. 752.

only to passion and not argument. Orators and party leaders work on the passions of their followers, playing on hopes and fears. 'Truth can scarcely be acquired in crowded halls and amidst noisy debates'.[52]

Burke, who had championed party in his *Causes of the Present Discontent* (1770), need not have feared, different as their opinions on party were. In these passages Godwin was not criticizing the Rockingham Party (the particular Whig connection that Burke worked and wrote for) nor the Whigs, old or new. His clearly intended victims were the radicals, those who thought that politics and not philosophy would usher in the new political age.

5. *Philosophy and Action: Godwin and the Politics of Pitt's Repression*

This theoretical repudiation of activism found in the bible of anarchism, Godwin's *Political Justice*, was soon tested in the arena of Jacobin politics. In 1795 and 1796 Godwin's philosophical anarchism and the politics of radical agitation met head-on. The second party to the confrontation was the London Corresponding Society and its leader John Thelwall.

The London Corresponding Society, founded in 1792 by a shoemaker, Thomas Hardy, hardly seems to merit Burke's assessment as 'the mother of all mischief'.[53] Its membership, according to Frances Place, an early official of the Society, was about two thousand; more generous estimates place it around twenty thousand. The social types attracted by the Society were artisans; mainly hatters, bakers, grocers, booksellers, and shoemakers – 'the thinking part of the working people' – as Place characterized them.[54] The division meetings of the Society were devoted to political discussion and communication with other radical societies, often with the two very large ones in Sheffield and Nor-

52. See below, pp. 285–6.
53. Quoted in Thomas Hardy, *Memoirs* (London, 1832) p. 109.
54. British Museum, *Add. Mss.* 35, 143. f/9.

wich. Pamphlets and broadsides were periodically published proclaiming the Society's positions on issues of the day. The ideology of the group was simple and straightforward and was shared by most of the Jacobin groups of the 1790s. It stood for three principles: annual parliaments, universal suffrage and parliamentary reform. Despite a liberal dose of Paine's ahistorical and non-constitutional argument from nature and natural rights, most of the Society's rhetoric was still couched in terms of recapturing ancient lost English rights. Communications and pamphlets were as often signed 'Anglo-Saxon' as 'citizen'. The ancient constitution, freed from its 'Norman Yoke', was authority enough on which to base true English liberty in the three areas of reform. There were in the Society a very few who, according to Place, 'were desirers of confusion, and for all sorts of absurd and violent measures'. Some members, for example, accepted Paine's Republicanism, but even they assumed that it would be achieved after the House of Commons was reformed and the King and Lords set aside peacefully. The L.C.S. (as it was known in its day) was, in short, an asociation of sober shopkeepers, craftsmen and journeymen. Some indication of the extent of its threat to the social order can be gathered from Place's evaluation years later of his association with the Society. It had a profound moral impact on its artisan membership, he wrote. Instead of wasting time in the public house, they were encouraged to read books, to think for and respect themselves. In addition, Place wrote, it encouraged them to educate their children: Lest this general assessment be doubted Place related how in 1822 at an anniversary dinner for Hardy he saw twenty-four men whom he knew at the Society in the middle of the 1790s. 'Of the twenty-four, twenty were then journeymen or shopmen; they were now all in business and all flourishing men.'[55]

How surprising then that in May 1794 Pitt's government should try the leaders of the L.C.S. for treason! The

55. *Add. Mss.* 35, 143. f/93.

great treason trial of that year brought to an end the first
stage of Pitt's repression of the radical Jacobin community.
It had begun over a year earlier with his decision to ban
Paine's *Rights of Man*, and with Paine's subsequent flight
and trial *in absentia*. Anti-Jacobin societies quickly spread
across England and Scotland, as did John Reeve's Church
and King Associations, groups heavily assisted by Pitt's
Government. (The full name of Reeve's group was 'The
Association for the Protection of Property against Republicans and Levellers'.) Moreover, in 1793, the French King
was killed, and England went to war. The blissful dawn
that had so moved Wordsworth had turned to dusk. The
campaign of repression was so widespread that few were
surprised in May of 1794 when Pitt accused the Corresponding Society and other leading radicals of plotting:

To assemble a pretended convention of the people, for the
purpose of assuming the character of a general representation
of the nation, superseding the representative capacity of the
House and arrogating the legislative power of the country at
large.[56]

The Tory newspapers echoed Pitt's charge. 'The whole
system of insurection lay in the monstrous doctrine of the
Rights of Man, and the Corresponding Society composed
of the meanest and most despicable of people.'[57] Godwin
knew most of the accused. Three of them – Jerrald, Thelwall and Horne Tooke – were good friends. One defendant,
Thomas Holcroft, the writer, was Godwin's closest friend.
Nevertheless, Godwin had little love for the Society. It
stood condemned of all he had written about political
associations. Moreover, in *Political Justice* he had even
criticized those who argued for change in the name of
antiquity, having heaped ridicule on 'those governed by
the dicta of their remotest ancestors'. In his book he had
criticized the narrowness of groups like the L.C.S. groups

56. Quoted in Philip A. Brown, *The French Revolution in English History* (Lockwood, London, 1918), p. 112.
57. *New Annual Register*, 1794, pp. 190–191.

that opposed 'a specific tax perhaps' or sought to remedy 'some temporary grievance'.[58] He had, after all, proposed a truly radical restructuring of society, albeit not readily attained. Friendship and the conviction that Pitt's charges were based not on actions but on publications and speeches won out, however, and Godwin anonymously published an attack on the court. Shortly thereafter, the defendants were found innocent by the jury, and at least one of them, Horne Took, credited this to Godwin's *Cursory Strictures on the Charge Delivered by Lord Chief Justice Eyre to the Grand Jury*. Soon, however, the basic differences between Godwin and the L.C.S. would surface, and true to his own creed of outspoken and sincere censorship no amount of friendship would quiet Godwin and prevent the confrontation within the Jacobin family.

The essential ingredient for the evolution of the controversy was the emergence after the trial in 1794 of one of its defendants, John Thelwall, as the leading figure in the L.C.S. He gave to the Society a new and decidedly more radical face. Poet, playwright, pamphleteer and politician, Thelwall cut a fascinating figure in the 1790s. Friend and confidant of Coleridge, author of Rousseauean pastorals, publisher of a weekly radical newspaper and ever-present agitator at public meetings and lecture halls, Thelwall may well deserve a place in history as one of the first great leaders of the English urban working class. His ideas are not our central concern here; in this story they are less important than his actions. Suffice it to say, however, that he was an intellectual disciple of Godwin's. In his *Tribune* articles and in his very popular *Rights of Man* (1796) he, too, was a perfectionist, who wrote on necessity, the fraud of punishment and hypocrisy of patriotism, marriage, and gratitude, and one who recognized the obligations of sincerity and truth over friendship. He refused, however, to follow Godwin into the utopia of 'political simplicity'. Much more concerned with economic and social questions, he wrote primarily of specific re-

58. See below, pp. 252, 260.

forms required to improve the lot of the working man. One English historian has recently described Thelwall as having taken 'Jacobinism to the borders of Socialism'. He also took it 'to the borders of revolutionism', which is much more our concern.[59] Thelwall led the L.C.S. in the post-trial period in its vigorous opposition to Pitt and the legions of Church and King. His tactic was twofold: first, he gave rousing lectures with great rhetorical flourish, lectures which soon became the source of inspiration for scores of militant Jacobins. Much more courageous was his second tactic, the mass meeting; he organized and spoke to meetings at least three of which, in 1795 alone, drew more than 100,000 people to London. Whatever his cause – universal suffrage, annual parliaments, shorter working hours or redistribution of wealth – he brought to it an intensity and activism that pushed the L.C.S. from moderation to agitation and active intervention in the street politics of London. As an activist he was disdainful of philosophical and literary fellow-travellers like Godwin who refused to participate in Jacobin agitation. He wrote in his weekly newspaper, *The Tribune*:

Moderation! Moderation! A compromise between right and wrong! I detest it ... for what is moderation of principle, but a compromise between right and wrong; an attempt to find out some path of expediency, without going to the first principles of justice. Such attempts must always be delusive to the individual and fatal to mankind. If there is anything sacred, it is principle! Let every man investigate seriously and solemnly the truth and propriety of the principles he adopts, but having adopted, let him pursue them into practice: let him tread on the path which they dictate.[60]

The change in direction Thelwall brought to the once sober L.C.S. did not go unchallenged within the organization, and within its own meetings, quietly and beneath the surface there occurred the first skirmish between his

59. E. P. Thompson, *The Making of the English Working Class* (Penguin Books, Harmondsworth, 1968), p. 160.
60. *The Tribune*, ix, Saturday, 19 May 1795.

tactics and Godwin's principles. A serious split developed in the Society over the issue of large mass meetings, a split between Thelwall's activist followers and the disciples of Godwin who saw the group as merely engaged in educational work disseminating political wisdom and truth through publication and discussion. The Godwinians lost, as evidenced by the resignation of twenty-one members, 'who deplored the increase of factious spirit, the preference given to measures the most inconsiderate and violent'.[61] The General Committee of the Society answered with an attack on 'those many weak minded persons who have attempted to propagate an opinion, that all endeavours to promote the cause of liberty in Britain by means of popular associations must necessarily prove fruitless.'[62] Under Thelwall's leadership, Place informs us, many in the Society came to believe that repeated mass meetings and agitation would provoke a crisis that would 'force the House of Commons to consent to radical reform in the state of representation'.[63] Place, a good Godwinian, resigned, however, rather than agree to such coercive tactics.

This disagreement took place solely within the radical family, but the next and more devastating confrontation took place out of doors for all to see. It came to a head in late 1795 and early 1796 with the introduction into Parliament of Pitt's notorious Anti-Sedition Acts. Pitt's response to L.C.S. agitation was not the reform of Parliament but instead the introduction of two laws abrogating freedom of speech, freedom of assembly and freedom of the press. Fearful for its survival, Pitt's Government was lashing back. Food riots had spread through England in the summer and autumn of 1795; inflammatory tracts appeared at the same time with titles like *King Killing, the Reign of the English Robespierre,* or the *Happy Reign of George the Last.* On the way to Parliament, the King was hissed and booed by some two hundred thousand London-

61. *Add. Mss.* 27, 185. f/165–6.
62. *Add. Mss.* 27, 815. f/184.
63. *Add. Mss.* 35, 143. f/15.

ers thronging the streets. His carriage window was broken by a stone, and he is alleged to have gasped, 'My Lord, I, I, I've been shot at.'[64] For many, the nightmare world of Versailles seemed to have arrived at St James's. The Anti-Sedition Acts were Pitt's response to all of this. The Foxite opposition fought the bills unsuccessfully, and upon their passage *habeas corpus* was suspended for eight years. The two acts having been passed, Pitt's repression succeeded. The L.C.S. and the English Jacobins were stilled, only to revive in the short-lived naval mutinies of 1797.

Where did Godwin, the anarchist and philosopher of freedom and truth, stand in all of this? As a careful reading of *Political Justice* might have predicted, he criticized the L.C.S. and most specifically his one-time friend, John Thelwall. His position is found in his pamphlet *Considerations on Lord Grenville's and Mr Pitt's Bills Concerning Treasonable and Seditious Practices and Unlawful Assemblies*, published anonomously by 'a lover of order'. (Did he find it so hard to betray a friend that he violated his own canon of candour?) The pamphlet begins with a general lecture on the principle of philosophical anarchy, as differentiated from false anarchy, offered by one 'untainted with the headlong rage of faction'. Governing men in a 'petty and limited circle', he contends, is easy and can be done not by institutions but by reason alone. All men will 'exercise an inspection over all', and no deeds can be concealed from the general censure or applause. But in nations with millions of men, 'there is no eye penetrating enough to detect every mischief in its commencement'. Governments are needed in such states to keep order and provide security. Shifting to the language of Burke, Godwin describes the fragility and complexity of society and government.

He that deliberately views the machine of human society,

64. Anonymous. *Truth and Treason! Or a Narrative of the Royal Procession* (London, 1795), p. 3.

will even in his speculations approach it with awe. He will recollect with alarm, that in this scene 'fools rush in, where angels fear to tread'. The fabric that we contemplate is sort of a fairy edifice, and though it consists of innumerable parts, and hides its head among the clouds, the hand of a child almost, if suffered with neglect, may shake it into ruins.[65]

There are, to be sure, abuses in societies; there are, for example, large numbers of poor and very few rich. But these abuses, Godwin quickly adds, are woven into the fabric of society and must be painstakingly corrected with careful judgement and deliberation lest one destroy faster than one creates, and rear up only false anarchy and barbarism. Government has as its major responsibility the protection of order and security, 'the blessings we already possess, from the rashness of presumptuous experiment'. The major threat to this security, Godwin insists, is the L.C.S. Like the Jacobin party in France, it is filled with impetuous and ardent zealots. It threatens civil order by 'the immense multitudes it collects' who wreak disorder in the city streets. Its speeches and resolutions lack all temperance. Having done with the L.C.S., Godwin turns next on its leader Thelwall, whose lectures and public addresses violate all reasonable tenets of political life. The public mind ought to be enlightened, Godwin insists, and a uniformity of understanding reached such that no minister or monopolist would ever be powerful enough to withstand it. Could such a transformation occur in Thelwall's crowded, noisy meetings? No, he answers, and he condemns Thelwall:

Oh reform! Genial and benignant power! How often has thy name been polluted by profane and unhallowed lips! How often has thy standard been unfurled by demagogues, and by assassins been drenched and disfigured with human gore![66]

Thelwall, Godwin continues, is a dangerous demagogue. An impatient and headlong reformer, he is in no position

65. *Considerations* ... (London, 1795), p. 4.
66. ibid., pp. 7, 13, 17.

to weigh his words with proper deliberation and purvey the truth while prompted by the demoralizing stimulus of the clamorous applause of large, excited audiences. He appeals to their passions and not reason, and if as 'saving clauses' he urges the practice of universal benevolence and utters warnings against violence, he is like 'Lord George Gordon preaching peace to the rioters in Westminster Hall', or 'Iago adjuring Othello not to dishonour himself by giving harbour to a thought of jealousy'.[67]

While outspoken in his criticism of Thelwall and the L.C.S., Godwin was also critical in his pamphlet of Thelwall's persecutors. Godwin assailed the legislation offered by Pitt and Grenville as fundamental threats to the freedoms of speech and assembly. The L.C.S. agitation was an evil affront to the orderly process of change but the legislative remedy was far more pernicious than that which it sought to cure. It was no less than 'the consecrated engine of tyranny'.[68] But this assault on the treason and sedition acts notwithstanding, what strikes one about the pamphlet is the outspoken condemnation of Thelwall. The defence of a free press and the right of assembly was, after all, by no means an unexpected position for a man to take who had opposed even libel laws in *Political Justice* as unnecessary restrictions on speech and print, or who had just a few months earlier in his pamphlet *Censory Strictures* turned opinion against Chief Justice Eyre's charges to the jury in the State Treason Trial. Thelwall was a defendant at that trial and Godwin's invocation of the legal safeguards of the British Constitution seemed to many to have convinced the jury to acquit. What shocked Thelwall now was that in addition to the anticipated rebuke of Pitt's repressive legislation Godwin saw fit to lash out at him and the L.C.S. But what Thelwall didn't know and indeed what few have known until very recently is that two years earlier Godwin had already spoken out, albeit anony-

67. ibid., p. 21.
68. ibid., p. 30.

mously, against the disruptive radical associations. Only recently have the letters been attributed to him that Godwin wrote in January 1793 to *the Morning Chronicle*. Written at the very time he was finishing *Political Justice*, these earlier letters expressed the same moderate position he would take in 1795 – a plague on both houses! He condemned the repressive excesses of Reeves and the Anti-Jacobins, but he was equally as critical of the radical associations, 'the intemperate advocates of reform', whose methods of appealing to public opinion were characterized as 'such instruments disgraceful to a civilized community'.[69]

Thelwall's surprise at the attack contained in the *Considerations* seems to indicate that he knew nothing of Godwin's authorship of those anonymous notices of 1793 and in his bi-weekly issues of the *Tribune* he lamented that even Godwin, his friend and defender for so long, should have turned on him when all the forces of Pitt's repression sought to shut him up. But Thelwall should have known that candour and sincerity were more important values for Godwin than friendship, and that, true to his own teaching, Godwin was obliged to censor his neighbour, to show his shortcomings, and thus to contribute to the formation of a more virtuous character. Nor would Thelwall be alone in receiving the lash of Godwin's pen in criticism of activist and revolutionary zeal. While *Political Justice* might envision an utterly drastic transformation of social and political life, in practical politics Godwin was a man of moderation with only harsh words for those who lacked patience and philosophic detachment. Some years later Godwin cautioned an impetuous Shelley off to Ireland to help free the Catholics. Such organized political action was foolhardy, Godwin wrote.

Discussion, reading, enquiry, perpetual communication,

69. *Uncollected Writings (1785–1822) By William Godwin* edited by J. H. Marken and B. R. Pollin (Gainesville, Florida, 1968), p. 115.

these are my favourite methods for the improvement of mankind, but associations, organized societies, I firmly condemn. You may as well tell the adder not to sting ... as tell organized societies of men, associated to obtain their rights and to extinguish oppression – prompted by a deep aversion to inequality, luxury, enormous taxes, and the evils of war – to be innocent, to employ no violence, and calmly to await the progress of truth. I never was at a public political dinner that I did not see how the enthusiasm was lighted up, how the fire caught from man to man, how fast the dictates of sober reason were obliterated by the gusts of passion, and how near the assembly was to go forth and fire the city.[70]

What alarmed Godwin most about the L.C.S. was the absence at its meetings of 'persons of eminence, distinction, and importance in the country', who could temper the enthusiasm of those 'not much in the habits of regular thinking'. In addition, Godwin charged that Thelwall, the popular leader, was 'not calmed and consecrated by the mild spirit of philosophy'.[71] As in his attack on reformers in general, the intellectual and elitist disdain shown here was by no means a novel departure in Godwin's public writings. *Political Justice* had been just as outspoken on this score. There, for example, Godwin described the greater part of people as 'mere parrots' who mouthed arguments of which they understood little or nothing about. Burke's depiction of the democratic masses constantly setting their minds on every 'floating fashion and fancy' was no more arrogant than Godwin's castigating a constantly changing public opinion by writing '... what is it they desire? They know not. It would probably be easy to show that what they professed to desire is little better than what they hate'.[72] One obvious answer, then, is given to the question raised earlier. 'Political simplicity' cannot be realized by popular agitation led

70. Quoted in Ford K. Brown, *Life of William Godwin*, pp. 261–2.
71. *Considerations*, pp. 14, 19.
72. See below, p. 260.

by radical reformers. Nor, for that matter, would widespread popular education suffice. Unlike Tom Paine and Mary Wollstonecraft, both of whom advocated a government-run school system, Godwin saw schemes of national education as only further examples of coercive interference with the individual's unfettered exercise of private judgement.[73]

If the age of felicity could not be entered through the schoolhouse, nor through street pressure on a weak parliament, how would it be accomplished? How would the simple and sincere order come about? Enlightened despotism, according to Godwin, was clearly not the answer. Power and force could never be the allies of truth and reason; nor for that matter could monarchs ever be capable of encouraging progress. The same could be said for the clergy and aristocracy. As for the middle class of newly enriched commoners, they too were ruled out as too selfish to be champions of reform. The lawyers who favoured the rich over the poor and discouraged candour were also incapable of this task.[74] The only social group capable of the noble mission of moving society to its blissful future was for Godwin, as for legions of future anarchists, the literary and intellectual elite. At bottom, Godwin harbours the one basic prejudice shared by all the enlightenment philosophers, save Rousseau – the unreflecting faith in the power of reflective man. '*Political Justice*,' he informs the reader in his preface, is 'an appeal to men of study and reflection'. If only a small number of 'liberally educated and reflecting members' would serve as the 'people's guides and instructors', then, Godwin holds, 'the business would be done'. The 'elevated system of the preceptor' would push aside 'the grovelling views of the great mass of mankind'. These few preceptors 'having stored their minds with reading and reflection' would communicate their wisdom to all, and through *them*, not through national schooling, enlightenment would filter down to

73. See below, pp. 612–18.
74. See below, pp. 448–86, 91–2, 108, 728ff., 679, 703.

all mankind.[75] The social and political mission of the intellectual elite is most succinctly described by Godwin in his *Enquirer* of 1797.

Men of genius must rise up ... to analyse the machine of society, to demonstrate how the parts are connected together ... and point out the defects and the remedy. 'It is thus only that important reforms can be produced ... He who is a friend to general happiness, will neglect no chance of producing in his pupil or his child, one of the long-looked for saviours of the human race.[76]

There is no doubt who these men of genius were. They could be found in the literary and philosophical circle that always had Godwin at its centre, the circle of Holcroft and Godwin's wife, Mary Wollstonecraft, and that of Coleridge, Hazlitt and Godwin's son-in-law, Shelley. Writing to a friend, Godwin unabashedly described himself and his correspondent as 'of course among the few enlightened'.[77] His close friend Hazlitt wrote that Godwin 'has the happiness to think an author the greatest character in the world'.[78] His friend Coleridge, however, soon to leave the fold of eighteenth-century rationalism, did not even in 1795 share its and Godwin's high hopes for the intellectual elite. In two sentences he repudiates the intellectualism of Godwin in particular and the *philosophes* in general.

The annals of the French Revolution prove that the knowledge of the few cannot counteract the ignorance of the many ... the light of philosophy, when it is confined to a small minority, points out the possessors as the victims rather than the illuminators of the multitude.[79]

75. See below, pp. 70, 152–3, 114, 289.
76. *Enquirer*, pp. 10–11.
77. C. Kegan-Paul, *William Godwin: His Friends and Contemporaries* (London, 1876), II, p. 195.
78. *Spirit of the Age*, p. 204.
79. S. T. Coleridge, *Essay on His Times* (London, 1850), I, 7–8.

6. Political Justice *and Anarchism Today*

Godwin's *Political Justice* was the first great trumpet blast against the 'brute engine' – government. Since 1793 anarchism has developed into a rich and varied, albeit not terribly successful, ideology. To the left, first of the liberals and democrats, and then even of the socialists and communists, have stood these quintessential nay-sayers. Politics itself is unnecessary. Power, force and coercion – no matter who or what class be the wielder is itself instrinsically evil. Some nineteenth- and twentieth-century anarchists have read Godwin's *Political Justice,* some have not. Be that as it may, the themes of *Political Justice* echo through the tradition. They can be heard in the rather representative words of the great nineteenth-century Russian anarchist Tolstoy:

The modern state is nothing but a conspiracy to exploit, but most of all to demoralize its citizens ... I understand moral and religious laws, not compulsory for everyone but leading forward and promising a more harmonious future; I feel the laws of art, which always bring happiness. But political laws seem to me such prodigious lies ... I regard all governments, not only the Russian government, as intricate institutions, sanctified by tradition and custom, for the purpose of committing by force and with impunity the most revolting crimes. And I think the efforts of all those who wish to improve our social life should be directed towards the liberation of themselves from national governments whose evil, and above all whose futility, is in our time becoming more and more apparent.[80]

The echoes can be heard in the writings of the Frenchman Proudhon, the Russian Kropotkin, and even in the German Marx, who despite his constant warfare with the Bakuninite anarchists in the International still conjures up an anarchist vision for his post-revolutionary society. In nineteenth-century America the echoes of *Political Jus-*

80. Quoted in G. Woodcock, *Anarchism* (Penguin Books, Harmondsworth, 1963), pp. 209–10.

tice are heard in the writings of Henry David Thoreau. *On the Duty of Civil Disobedience* (1849) expresses the conviction that the final arbiter of any action must be the conscience of the individual, not the dictate of government, while in his *Walden* Thoreau repeats the anarchist themes of retreat – retreat from the city, from competition, from materialism.

As a fringe ideology anarchism is very much alive and well in today's world, and here, too, there are echoes of *Political Justice* and its plea for 'simplicity' and 'sincerity'. Much of the socio-political attitudes of 'the counter-culture', the 'Age of Aquarius', the 'Consciousness III', is anarchist in nature. Politics, the making of rules to decide among conflicting interests, has no place in the new culture. The competition and self-interest that have previously generated the need for rules and authority disappear in an 'Age of Aquarius'. Conflict is replaced by spontaneous harmony and joy – unassisted by any state, government or laws. For many simplicity and freedom are achieved in communes. Here in a life of harmony and real community, politics, force and government does not exist. It is replaced as it was in Godwin's parishes by non-coercive/non-authoritarian mutual co-operation or in the language of the great Russian anarchist Kropotkin, by 'mutual aid'. Like Godwin's anarchism, latter-day anarchism is still ambivalent on its commitment to the individual alone and autonomous or the individual submerged in communal solidarity. There is, however, one important aspect of some varieties of modern anarchism that is not found in *Political Justice* – the revival in many areas of the counter-culture of self-conscious and programmatic recourse to violence. The romanticism of the 'dinamitero' and the 'pétroleuse' is the anarchism of Bakunin and Nechaev, not Godwin.

But it is not only among the young today for whom anarchism has its appeal. It thrives in the academy, too, and here also the echo of *Political Justice* can be heard. The doctrine toes no partisan line. It is implicit in the laissez-faire liberal visions (we call them conservative today) of a Chamberlain, a Hayek or a Freedman, with their spontaneous self-regulating market place. And it is found on the left in Robert Paul Wolff's *In Defense of Anarchism* or Herbert Marcuse's plea for

The new radicalism [which] militates against the centralized bureaucratic communist as well as against the semi-democratic liberal organization. There is a strong element of spontaneity, even anarchism, in this rebellion, expression of the new sensibility, sensitivity against domination: the feeling, the awareness, that the joy of freedom and the need to be free must precede liberation.[81]

So, too, the echoes of the plea in *Political Justice* for decentralization and simplicity, regionalism and revitalization of local community and small group democracy – notions that would be so important in Proudhon's anarchism in nineteenth-century France – are heard today in the writings of American anarchists like Paul Goodman, and English anarchists like Colin Ward and Nicolas Walter.

Godwin's own writings exemplified the characteristic intellectualism of the Enlightment. Many modern anarchists would leave Godwin the *philosophe* behind. In fact, much of nineteenth- and twentieth-century anarchism is an outright repudiation of the Enlightenment rationalism that the founder of anarchism so typified. For many more recent anarchists, politics is in fact equated with reason and because of this to be superseded with and by apolitical action. It could well be argued that Thelwall's street politics was, in fact, a more accurate anticipation of the future anarchist style. Still, in *Political Justice* Godwin gives to anarchism qualities that endure despite the philosophical, methodological and cultural gap that may separate him and the doctrine's later proponents. As it was in his presentation, anarchism after him is torn between the

81. H. Marcuse, *An Essay on Liberation* (Penguin Books, Harmondsworth, 1972), p. 91.

liberal values of individuality, independence, autonomy, privacy and self-determination, on the one hand, and the non-liberal values of community, solidarity and the encouragement of virtue through social pressure, on the other. So, too, later anarchists waver, like Godwin, between a progressive, futuristic orientation with assumptions of perfectibility and endless innovation and improvement, and a nostalgic yearning for a simple, agrarian and pre-industrial existence. Finally, Godwin may also have stamped anarchism with its touch of elitism, an abiding conviction that if only all men were as wise or as sensitive as the anarchist then governments would be superfluous, and that until this were the case all government represents pure coercion. The anarchist's role meanwhile is first to tutor and then to emancipate the ignorant 'great mass of mankind', whether slowly and imperceptibly, as by Godwin, through reason and enlightenment or hastily, as by Bakunin, with the dramatic flourish of exquisite acts.

A Note to the Reader

POLITICAL JUSTICE is long and often irritating to the modern reader. Godwin was a philosopher and the conventions of eighteenth-century letters required a general treatise of this sort to range broadly over areas that are now much more compartmentalized. The book has, therefore, lengthy excursions into what now might be considered the domain of psychology, ethics, metaphysics, epistomology, as well as politics. To the eighteenth-century mind these formed the natural background of a disquisition on justice in society. Added to this is Godwin's own stylistic predilection to discuss every and all issues, to enter into every conceivable controversy, to push each subject to its outermost limits. Despite the comprehensive length and the more than occasional excursion into subjects far beyond the central anarchist theme, I have decided not to shorten Godwin's text. To do so might well render it more amenable to modern taste, and less difficult to read. On the other hand Godwin's text deserves to be read in its entirety, and this Penguin edition provides the only complete edition of the text available now in print. In reading this edition, then, you will encounter not only themes of enduring relevance, that are concerned with the equity of social, economic and political power, but also occasional themes like duelling or associationism, which while they were of pressing interest in the eighteenth-century, have declined as the principal stuff of today's intellectual debate.

The text can, of course, be read with great value even if parts are omitted. Godwin himself in a footnote in the chapter 'On Free Will and Necessity' (p. 336) recommends that 'the reader who is indisposed to abstruse speculations will find the other members of the Treatise sufficiently connected without an express reference to this and the three following chapters of the present book.' I see no reason why, then, it would be inappropriate to offer my own personal suggestions on what might be skipped without great loss to the more general reader. The following chapters may be passed over without jeopardy to the more important arguments in the book: 'The Characters of Men Originate in their External Circumstances' (pp. 96–116); 'The Voluntary Actions of Men Originate in their Opinions' (pp. 116–46); 'Of Free Will and Necessity' (pp. 335–50); 'Inferences from the Doctrine of Necessity' (pp. 350–60); 'Of the Mechanism of the Human Mind' (pp. 360–77); 'Of Self-Love and Benevolence' (pp. 377–88); these latter four chapters second Godwin's own advice.

A number of minor changes have been made. The original heavy punctuation is distracting to the modern reader, so that some punctuation marks, particularly obtruding commas used where they would not now be used, have been removed. Spelling has been modernized in the few cases where it differs from today's spelling.

A Note on the Text

GODWIN himself supervised the publication of *Political Justice* in 1793, 1796 and 1798. The text used here is his third and final revision. In the second edition Godwin made a substantial number of changes which he justified in his preface on two grounds. There were firstly, 'many things that now appear to the author upon a review, not to have been meditated with a sufficiently profound reflection, and to have been too hastily obtruded upon the reader'. In addition, he suggested, an author should 'keep his mind awake to correction and improvement'. In the third edition he made few substantive changes. All that seemed necessary was 'to remove a few of the crude and juvenile remarks'. The changes from the first to the second edition, then, deserve some comment.

Despite the number of changes he made, Godwin insisted in the preface of the second edition that he had not tampered with 'the spirit and great outlines of the work'. On the whole his own assessment stands up. The most important thrust of his revisions was to render the text more unified and coherent. The first edition had been hastily delivered in parts to the printer. By 1796 Godwin had leisure to reorganize the work as a whole. While the political positions are by no means toned down – the assault on monarchy, aristocracy, law and government in general – there does, however, seem to be some retreat from the strident rationalism of the first edition. In the second edition Godwin gave more importance to the role of feeling and sentiment. This is indicated in small but by no means trivial changes. The discussion on p. 170, for example, about the moral choice between rescuing from a fire the distinguished Fénelon or his valet who might be 'my brother, my father', was posed in the first edition as a choice between Fénelon and his chambermaid, who might be 'my wife or mother'. Other changes indicate a general softening on the issue of marriage. It is still criticized, but in the second edition more specifically in terms of the then current aristocratic practice of arranged marriages. In general there is good evidence that Godwin's greater receptivity to the realm of feeling in the second and third editions reflects his several happy and tender years with Mary Wollstonecraft. In some of these changes in *Political Justice* Godwin anticipates the more important changes of doctrine that would appear in his later works and other philosophical writings, which in their greater stress on the role of feeling place him as an important link to the romantic movement of the nineteenth century. But it ought still to be noted that the changes in *Political Justice* are minimal – the anarchist political doctrine remains unchanged from one edition to another. As such, then, there seems every justification to reproduce here in its entirety Godwin's third edition, which, according to the author, is how he wished his book read by posterity, free of 'crude and juvenile remarks'. We have taken but one liberty in reproducing this 1798 edition. In its original format it appeared in two volumes, 463 and 554 pages respectively. Books 1–4 were contained in the first, Books 5–8 in the second volume. This edition renders the two volumes as one and has in turn run the page numbers consecutively. Godwin's footnotes are indicated by asterisks, etc., whilst the editors notes are shown by superior numbers and placed at the end of the book.

Facsimile of the title page of Vol. I of the third edition of *Enquiry Concerning Political Justice*, reproduced by kind permission of The Board of Trinity College, Dublin.

ENQUIRY

CONCERNING

POLITICAL JUSTICE,

AND

ITS INFLUENCE

ON

MORALS AND HAPPINESS.

BY

WILLIAM GODWIN.

THE THIRD EDITION CORRECTED.

IN TWO VOLUMES.

VOL. I.

LONDON:

PRINTED FOR G. G. AND J. ROBINSON,
PATERNOSTER-ROW.
1798.

CONTENTS

Contents

BOOK III
PRINCIPLES OF GOVERNMENT

BOOK IV
OF THE OPERATION OF OPINION IN SOCIETIES AND INDIVIDUALS

BOOK V
OF LEGISLATIVE AND EXECUTIVE POWER

Contents

BOOK VI

OF OPINION CONSIDERED AS A SUBJECT OF POLITICAL INSTITUTION

Contents

BOOK VII
OF CRIMES AND PUNISHMENT

BOOK VIII
OF PROPERTY

Contents

PREFACE

FEW works of literature are held to be of more general use than those which treat in a methodical and elementary way of the principles of science. But the human mind in every enlightened age is progressive; and the best elementary treatises, after a certain time, are reduced in value by the operation of subsequent discoveries. Hence it has always been desired by the intelligent that new works of this kind should from time to time be brought forward, including the improvements which had not yet been realized when former complications upon the subject were produced.

It would be strange if something of this kind were not requisite in the science of politics, after the concussion that the minds of men have suffered upon this subject, and the materials that have been furnished, by the recent experiments of America and France. A sense of the value of such a work, if properly executed, was the motive which gave birth to these volumes.[1]

Authors who have formed the design of supplying the defects of their predecessors will be found, if they were in any degree equal to the task, not merely to have collected the scattered information that had been produced upon the subject, but to have enlarged the science by the effect of their own meditations. In the following work principles will occasionally occur which it will not be just to reject without examination, upon the ground of their apparent novelty. It was impossible perseveringly to reflect upon so comprehensive a science, and a science which may be said to be yet in its infancy, without being led into ways of thinking that were in some degree uncommon.

Another argument in favour of the utility of such a

work was frequently in the author's mind, and therefore ought to be mentioned. He conceived politics to be the proper vehicle of a liberal morality. That description of ethics will be found perhaps to be worthy of slight estimation which confines itself to petty detail and the offices of private life, instead of designing the combined and simultaneous improvement of communities and nations. But, if individual correction ought not to be the grand purpose of ethics, neither ought it by any means to be overlooked. It appeared sufficiently practicable to make of such a treatise, exclusively of its direct political use, an advantageous vehicle for this subordinate purpose. The author was accordingly desirous of producing a work from the perusal of which no man should rise without being strengthened in habits of sincerity, fortitude and justice.

Having stated the considerations in which the work originated, it is proper to mention a few circumstances of the outline of its history. It was projected in the month of May 1791: the composition was begun in the following September, and has therefore occupied a space of sixteen months. This period was for the most part devoted to the purpose with unusual ardour. It were to be wished it had been longer; but the state of the public mind and of the general interests of the species operated as a strong argument in favour of an early publication.

The printing of the following treatise, as well as the composition, was influenced by the same principle, a desire to reconcile a certain degree of dispatch with the necessary deliberation. The printing was for that reason commenced long before the composition was finished. Some disadvantages have arisen from this circumstance. The ideas of the author became more perspicuous and digested as his enquiries advanced. The longer he considered the subject, the more clearly he seemed to understand it. This circumstance has led him into some inaccuracies of language and reasoning, particularly in the earlier part of the work, respecting the properties and

utility of government. He did not enter upon the subject
without being aware that government by its very nature
counteracts the improvement of individual intellect; but,
as the views he entertains in this particular are out of the
common road, it is scarcely to be wondered at that he
understood the proposition more completely as he proceeded, and saw more distinctly into the nature of the
remedy. This defect, together with some others, might,
under a different mode of preparation, have been avoided.
The judicious reader will make a suitable allowance.
The author judges upon a review that the errors are not
such as essentially to affect the object of the work, and
that more has been gained than lost by the conduct he
has pursued.*

In addition to what is here stated it may not be
useless to describe the progress by which the author's
mind was led to its present sentiments. They are not the
suggestions of any sudden effervescence of fancy. Political
enquiry had long held a considerable place in the writer's
attention. It is now twelve years since he became satisfied
that monarchy was a species of government essentially
corrupt. He owed this conviction to the political writings
of Swift and to a perusal of the Latin historians. Nearly
at the same time he derived much additional stimulus
from several French productions on the nature of man,
which fell into his hands in the following order, the
Système de la Nature, the works of Rousseau, and those
of Helvetius. Long before he projected the present work,
his mind had been familiarized to several of the speculations suggested in it respecting justice, gratitude, the
rights of man, promises, oaths and the omnipotence of
opinion. Of the desirableness of a government in the utmost degree simple he was not persuaded but in consequence of ideas suggested by the French revolution. To

---

*The defects here alluded to have been attempted to be rectified
in the second edition. It is impossible perhaps so to improve a crude
and unequal performance, as to remove every vestige of its original
blemish.

the same event he owes the determination of mind which gave birth to the present work.

The period in which it makes its appearance is singular. The people of England have assiduously been excited to declare their loyalty, and to mark every man as obnoxious who is not ready to sign the Shibboleth of the constitution. Money is raised by voluntary subscription to defray the expense of prosecuting men who shall dare to promulgate heretical opinions, and thus to oppress them at once with the authority of government, and the resentment of individuals. This was an accident unforeseen when the work was undertaken; and it will scarcely be supposed that such an accident could produce any alteration in the writer's designs. Every man, if we may believe the voice of rumour, is to be prosecuted who shall appeal to the people by the publication of any unconstitutional paper or pamphlet; and it is added that men are to be punished for any unguarded words that may be dropped in the warmth of conversation and debate.* It is now to be tried whether, in addition to these alarming encroachments upon our liberty, a book is to fall under the arm of the civil power which, beside the advantage of having for one of its express objects the dissuading from tumult and violence, is by its very nature an appeal to men of study and reflection. It is to be tried whether an attempt shall be made to suppress the activity of mind, and put an end to the disquisitions of science. Respecting the event in a personal view the author has formed his resolution. Whatever conduct his countrymen may pursue, they will not be able to shake his tranquillity. The duty he conceives himself most bound to discharge is the assisting the progress of truth; and, if he suffer in any respect for such a proceeding, there is certainly no vicissitude that can befall

---

* The first conviction of this kind, which the author was far from imagining to be so near, was of a journeyman tallow-chandler, 8 January 1793, who, being shown the regalia at the Tower, was proved to have vented a coarse expression against royalty to the person that exhibited them.

him that can ever bring along with it a more satisfactory consolation.

But, exclusively of this precarious and unimportant consideration, it is the fortune of the present work to appear before a public that is panic struck, and impressed with the most dreadful apprehensions respecting such doctrines as are here delivered. All the prejudices of the human mind are in arms against it. This circumstance may appear to be more essential than the other. But it is the property of truth to be fearless, and to prove victorious over every adversary. It requires no great degree of fortitude to look with indifference upon the false fire of the moment, and to foresee the calm period of reason which will succeed.

LONDON

7 JANUARY 1793

PREFACE
TO THE SECOND EDITION

THE reception of the following work has been such as to exceed what the author dared to promise himself. Its principles and reasonings have obtained the attention of the public to a considerable extent. This circumstance he has construed as imposing upon him the duty of a severe and assiduous revisal. Every author figures to himself, while writing, a numerous and liberal attention to his lucubrations: if he did not believe that he had something to offer that was worthy of public notice, it is impossible that he should write with any degree of animation. But the most ardent imagination can scarcely be expected to come in competition with sense. In the present instance there are many things that now appear to the author upon a review not to have been meditated with a sufficiently profound reflection, and to have been too hastily obtruded upon the reader. These things have been pruned away with a liberal hand. The wish nearest to his heart is that there should be nothing in the book unworthy of the cause it was intended to serve. But, though he professes to have done much, much yet remains to be done. After repeated revisals the jealous eye of a man habituated to the detection of errors still discovers things that might be better. Some are obscure; some are doubtful. As to the last, the author did not conceive himself at liberty to retract any thing without a conviction, or something near a conviction, that he was wrong. He deemed it by no means justifiable to suppress any opinion because it was inconsistent with the prejudice or persuasion of others. A circumstance by which it was originally intended that this book should be characterized was a perfect explicitness and unreserve; and even if this intention should at last be an improper one, it was apparently too late to reverse it. It would have been an act incompatible with every pretension to integrity to have rescinded sentiments originally advanced as true, so long as they stood forward to the author's mind accompanied with their original evidence.

It will perhaps be asked by some persons in perusing the present edition, how it has happened that the author has varied in so many points from the propositions advanced in the former? and this variation may even be treated as a topic of censure. To this he has only to answer, in the first place, that the spirit and great outlines of the work, he believes, remain untouched, and that it is reasoned in various particulars with more accuracy from the premises and fundamental positions than it was before. Secondly, he presumes to ascribe the variations to an industrious and conscientious endeavour to keep his mind awake to correction and improvement. He has in several instances detected error; and, so far is he from feeling mortified at the discovery that he hopes yet, by such activity and impartiality as he shall be able to exert, to arrive at many truths of which he has scarcely at present perhaps the slightest presentiment.

Some apology is due to the purchasers of the former edition respecting the variations that appear in this. It was extremely the wish of the author that the variations should be printed separately for their use. But how was this possible? They grew under his hands; and at last, out of eight books of which the work consists, the four first and the last may, without impropriety, be said to be re-written. An obvious alternative unavoidably offers itself. If the work be of that useless sort with which the press is daily encumbered, these purchasers will not be very solicitous about the variations of such a performance. If on the contrary it be a production of any value, they will probably sympathize with the author. He feels himself particularly indebted to them for having enabled him to bring the work to its present state of correction; and it is to be hoped that they will not regret the having been instrumental to that purpose.

The parts of the work in which the most material variations of deduction or statement appear will be found under the following titles, The Characters of Men Originate in their External Circumstances, The Voluntary Actions of Men Originate in their Opinions, Of Personal Virtue and Duty, Of Rights, Of Promises, Of Obedience, Of Forms of Government,* Illustrations of Sincerity, Of Self-love and Benevolence, Of Good and Evil, Principles of Property, and Of the Supposed Advantages of Luxury. Important explanations are also subjoined on the topics of marriage and longevity, Book VIII, Appendices to Chap. VIII, and IX. To these the author would wish particularly to call the attention of his former readers. Inferior variations are scattered everywhere, and are impossible to be enumerated.

The *Enquiry concerning Political Justice* has been treated by some persons as of a seditious and inflammatory nature. This is probably an aspersion. If the political

---

* The principles delivered on this subject in the last chapter of Book III are more fully developed in the three first chapters of Book IV.

principles in favour of which it is written have no solid foundation, they have little chance to obtain more than a temporary fashion; and the present work is ill calculated to answer a temporary purpose. If on the contrary they be founded in immutable truth, it is highly probable, to say the least, that they will one day gain a decisive ascendancy. In that case, the tendency of such a disquisition will be to smooth the gradation, and to prepare the enlightened to sympathize with the just claims of the oppressed and the humble. No man can more fervently deprecate scenes of commotion and tumult than the author of this book; no man would more anxiously avoid the lending his assistance in the most distant manner to animosity and bloodshed; but he persuades himself that, whatever may be the events with which the present crisis of human history shall be distinguished, the effect of his writings, as far as they are in any degree remembered, will be found favourable to the increase and preservation of general kindness and benevolence.

29 OCTOBER 1795

ADVERTISEMENT

THE author has not failed to make use of the opportunity afforded him by the third edition to revise the work throughout. The alterations however that he has made, though numerous, are not of a fundamental nature. Their object has been merely to remove a few of the crude and juvenile remarks which, upon consideration, he thought himself able to detect in the book as it originally stood.

JULY 1797

SUMMARY OF PRINCIPLES

ESTABLISHED AND REASONED UPON IN THE FOLLOWING WORK

The reader who would form a just estimate of the reasonings of these volumes cannot perhaps proceed more judiciously than by examining for himself the truth of these principles, and the support they afford to the various inferences interspersed through the work

I

THE true object of moral and political disquisition is pleasure or happiness.

The primary, or earliest, class of human pleasures is the pleasures of the external senses.

In addition to these, man is susceptible of certain secondary pleasures, as the pleasures of intellectual feeling, the pleasures of sympathy, and the pleasures of self-approbation.

The secondary pleasures are probably more exquisite than the primary:

Or, at least,

The most desirable state of man is that in which he has access to all these sources of pleasure, and is in possession of a happiness the most varied and uninterrupted.

This state is a state of high civilization.

II

The most desirable condition of the human species is a state of society.

The injustice and violence of men in a state of society produced the demand for government.

Government, as it was forced upon mankind by their

75

vices, so has it commonly been the creature of their ignorance and mistake.

Government was intended to suppress injustice, but it offers new occasions and temptations for the commission of it.

By concentrating the force of the community, it gives occasion to wild projects of calamity, to oppression, despotism, war and conquest.

By perpetuating and aggravating the inequality of property, it fosters many injurious passions, and excites men to the practice of robbery and fraud.

Government was intended to suppress injustice, but its effect has been to embody and perpetuate it.

III

The immediate object of government is security.

The means employed by government is restriction, an abridgement of individual independence.

The pleasures of self-approbation, together with the right cultivation of all our pleasures, require individual independence.

Without independence men cannot become either wise, or useful, or happy.

Consequently, the most desirable state of mankind is that which maintains general security, with the smallest incroachment upon individual independence.

IV

The true standard of the conduct of one man towards another is justice.

Justice is a principle which proposes to itself the production of the greatest sum of pleasure or happiness.

Justice requires that I should put myself in the place of an impartial spectator of human concerns, and divest myself of retrospect to my own predilections.

Justice is a rule of the utmost universality, and prescribes a specific mode of proceeding, in all affairs by which the happiness of a human being may be affected.

V

Duty is that mode of action which constitutes the best application of the capacity of the individual to the general advantage.

Right is the claim of the individual to his share of the benefit arising from his neighbours' discharge of their several duties.

The claim of the individual is either to the exertion or the forbearance of his neighbours.

The exertions of men in society should ordinarily be trusted to their discretion; their forbearance, in certain cases, is a point of more pressing necessity, and is the direct province of political superintendence, or government.

VI

The voluntary actions of men are under the direction of their feelings.

Reason is not an independent principle, and has no tendency to excite us to action; in a practical view, it is merely a comparison and balancing of different feelings.

Reason, though it cannot excite us to action, is calculated to regulate our conduct, according to the comparative worth it ascribes to different excitements.

It is to the improvement of reason therefore that we are to look for the improvement of our social condition.

VII

Reason depends for its clearness and strength upon the cultivation of knowledge.

The extent of our progress in the cultivation of knowledge is unlimited.

Hence it follows,

1. That human inventions, and the modes of social existence, are susceptible of perpetual improvement.

2. That institutions calculated to give perpetuity to any

particular mode of thinking, or condition of existence, are pernicious.

VIII

The pleasures of intellectual feeling, and the pleasures of self-approbation, together with the right cultivation of all our pleasures, are connected with soundness of understanding.

Soundness of understanding is inconsistent with prejudice: consequently, as few falsehoods as possible, either speculative or practical, should be fostered among mankind.

Soundness of understanding is connected with freedom of enquiry: consequently, opinion should, as far as public security will admit, be exempted from restraint.

Soundness of understanding is connected with simplicity of manners, and leisure for intellectual cultivation: consequently, a distribution of property extremely unequal is adverse to the most desirable state of man.

BOOK I

OF THE POWERS OF MAN CONSIDERED IN HIS SOCIAL CAPACITY

CHAPTER I

INTRODUCTION

Subject of enquiry – of the first book. – Received ideas of political institution. – Propriety of these ideas questioned. – Plan of the first book.

THE object proposed in the following work is an investigation concerning that form of public or political society, that system of intercourse and reciprocal action, extending beyond the bounds of a single family, which shall be found most to conduce to the general benefit. How may the peculiar and independent operation of each individual in the social state most effectually be preserved? How may the security each man ought to possess, as to his life, and the employment of his faculties according to the dictates of his own understanding, be most certainly defended from invasion? How may the individuals of the human species be made to contribute most substantially to the general improvement and happiness? The enquiry here undertaken has for its object to facilitate the solution of these interesting questions.

In entering upon this investigation nothing can be more useful than to examine into the extent of the influence that is to be ascribed to political institutions; in other words, into the powers of man, as they have modified, or may hereafter modify his social state of existence.

Upon this subject there has been considerable difference of opinion.

The most usually received hypothesis is that which considers the effects of government or social institutions, whether acting by express regulations or otherwise, as rather of a negative than positive nature. No doubt the purposes for which government was established are in their strictest sense negative; to maintain us in the possession of certain advantages against the occasional hostility either of domestic or foreign invaders. But does the influence of government stop at the point for the sake of which mankind were first prevailed on to adopt it?

Those who believe that it does or can stop at this point necessarily regard it as a matter of subordinate disquisition, or at most only co-ordinate with several others. They survey man in his individual character, in his domestic connections, and in the pursuits and attachments which his feelings may incline him to adopt. These of course fill the principal part of the picture. These are supposed, by the speculators of whom we now speak, to be in ordinary cases independent of all political systems and establishments. It is only in peculiar emergencies and matters that depart from the accustomed routine of affairs that they conceive a private individual to have any occasion to remember, or to be in the least affected by the government of his country. If he commit or is supposed to commit any offence against the general welfare, if he find himself called upon to repress the offence of another, or if any danger from foreign hostility threaten the community in which he resides, in these cases and these only is he obliged to recollect that he has a country. These considerations impose upon him the further duty of consulting, even when no immediate danger is nigh, how political liberty may best be maintained, and maladministration prevented.

Many of the best patriots and most popular writers on the subject of government appear to have proceeded upon the principles here delineated. They have treated morality and personal happiness as one science, and politics as a different one. But, while they have considered the virtues and pleasures of mankind as essentially independent of civil policy, they have justly remarked that the security with which the one can be exercised and the other enjoyed will be decided by the wisdom of our public institutions and the equity with which they are administered; and have earnestly pressed it upon the attention of mankind not to forget, in the rectitude or happiness of the present moment, those precautions and that 'generous plan of power'* which may tend to render it impregnable to the stratagems of corruption or the insolence of tyranny.†

But, while we confess ourselves indebted to the labours of these writers, and perhaps still more to the intrepid language and behaviour of these patriots, we are incited to enquire whether the topic which engaged their attention be not of higher and more extensive importance than they suspected. Perhaps government is not merely in some cases the defender, and in other the treacherous foe of the domestic virtues. Perhaps it insinuates itself into our personal dispositions, and insensibly communicates its own spirit to our private transactions. Were not the inhabitants of ancient Greece and Rome indebted in some degree to their political liberties for their excellence in art, and the illustrious theatre they occupy in the moral history of mankind? Are not the governments of modern Europe accountable for the slowness and inconstancy of its literary efforts, and the unworthy selfishness that characterizes its inhabitants? Is it not owing to the governments of the East that that part of the world can scarcely be said to have made any progress in intellect or science?

*Addison: *Cato*, Act iv.

†These remarks will for the most part apply to the English writers upon politics, from Sydney[2] and Locke[3] to the author of the *Rights of Man*.[4] The more comprehensive view has been strikingly delineated by Rousseau,[5] and Helvétius[6].

When scepticism or a spirit of investigation has led us to start these questions, we shall be apt not to stop at them. A wide field of speculation opens itself before us. If government thus insinuate itself in its effects into our most secret retirements, who shall define the extent of its operation? If it be the author of thus much, who shall specify the points from which its influence is excluded? May it not happen that the grand moral evils that exist in the world, the calamities by which we are so grievously oppressed, are to be traced to political institution as their source, and that their removal is only to be expected from its correction? May it not be found that the attempt to alter the morals of mankind singly and in detail is an injudicious and futile undertaking; and that the change of their political institutions must keep pace with their advancement in knowledge, if we expect to secure to them a real and permanent improvement? To prove the affirmative of these questions shall be the business of this first book.

The method to be pursued for that purpose shall be, first, to take a concise survey of the evils existing in political society;* secondly, to show that these evils are to be ascribed to public institutions;† and thirdly, that they are not the inseparable condition of our existence, but admit of removal and remedy.‡

*Chap. II, III.
†Chap. IV.
‡Chap. V, VI, VII, VIII.

CHAPTER II

HISTORY OF POLITICAL SOCIETY

*War. – Frequency of war – among the ancients
– among the moderns – the French – the English
– Causes of war. – Penal laws. – Despotism. –
Deduction from the whole.*

THE extent of the influence of political systems will be forcibly illustrated by a concise recollection of the records of political society.

It is an old observation that the history of mankind is little else than a record of crimes. Society comes recommended to us by its tendency to supply our wants and promote our well being. If we consider the human species, as they were found previously to the existence of political society, it is difficult not to be impressed with emotions of melancholy. But, though the chief purpose of society is to defend us from want and inconvenience, it effects this purpose in a very imperfect degree. We are still liable to casualties, disease, infirmity and death. Famine destroys its thousands, and pestilence its ten thousands. Anguish visits us under every variety of form, and day after day is spent in languor and dissatisfaction. Exquisite pleasure is a guest of very rare approach, and not less short continuance.

But, though the evils that arise to us from the structure of the material universe are neither trivial nor few, yet the history of political society sufficiently shows that man is of all other beings the most formidable enemy to man. Among the various schemes that he has formed to destroy and plague his kind, war is the most terrible. Satiated with petty mischief and retail of insulated crimes, he rises in this instance to a project that lays nations waste, and thins the population of the world. Man directs the murderous engine against the life of his brother; he invents with indefatigable care refinements in destruction; he proceeds in the midst of gaiety and pomp to the execution of his horrid purpose; whole ranks of sensitive beings, endowed with the most admirable faculties, are mowed down in an instant; they perish by inches in the midst of agony and neglect, lacerated with every variety of method that can give torture to the frame.

This is indeed a tremendous scene! Are we permitted to console ourselves under the spectacle of its evils by the rareness with which it occurs, and the forcible reasons that compel men to have recourse to this last appeal of human society? Let us consider it under each of these heads.

War has hitherto been found the inseparable ally of political institution. The earliest records of time are the annals of conquerors and heroes, a Bacchus, a Sesostris, a Semiramis and a Cyrus. These princes led millions of men under their standard, and ravaged innumerable provinces. A small number only of their forces ever returned to their native homes, the rest having perished by diseases, hardship and misery. The evils they inflicted, and the mortality introduced in the countries against which their expeditions were directed, were certainly not less severe than those which their countrymen suffered.

No sooner does history become more precise than we are presented with the four great monarchies, that is, with four successful projects, by means of bloodshed, violence and murder, of enslaving mankind. The expeditions of Cambyses against Egypt, of Darius against the Scythians, and of Xerxes against the Greeks, seem almost to set credibility at defiance by the fatal consequences with which they were attended. The conquests of Alexander cost innumerable lives, and the immortality of Caesar is computed to have been purchased by the death of one million two hundred thousand men.

Indeed the Romans, by the long duration of their wars, and their inflexible adherence to their purpose, are to be ranked among the foremost destroyers of the human species. Their wars in Italy continued for more than four hundred years, and their contest for supremacy with the Carthaginians two hundred. The Mithridatic war began with a massacre of one hundred and fifty thousand Romans, and in three single actions five hundred thousand men were lost by the Eastern monarch. Sylla, his ferocious conqueror, next turned his arms against his country, and the struggle between him and Marius was attended with proscriptions, butcheries and murders that knew no restraint from humanity or shame. The Romans, at length, suffered the evils they had been so prompt to inflict upon others; and the world was vexed for three hundred years by the irruptions of Goths, Vandals, Ostrogoths, Huns and innumerable hordes of barbarians.

I forbear to detail the victorious progress of Mahomet and the pious expeditions of Charlemagne. I will not enumerate the crusades against the infidels, the exploits of Tamerlane, Gengiskan and Aurungzebe, or the extensive murders of the Spaniards in the new world. Let us examine Europe, the most civilized and favoured quarter of the world, or even those countries of Europe which are thought the most enlightened.

France was wasted by successive battles during a whole century, for the question of the Salic law, and the claim of the Plantagenets. Scarcely was this contest terminated, before the religious wars broke out, some idea of which we may form from the siege of Rochelle, where, of fifteen thousand persons shut up, eleven thousand perished of hunger and misery; and from the massacre of Saint Bartholomew, in which the numbers assassinated were forty thousand. This quarrel was appeased by Henry the fourth, and succeeded by the thirty years war in Germany for superiority with the house of Austria, and afterwards by the military transactions of Louis the fourteenth.

In England the war of Cressy and Agincourt only gave place to the civil war of York and Lancaster, and again after an interval to the war of Charles the first and his parliament. No sooner was the constitution settled by the revolution than we were engaged in a wide field of continental hostilities by king William, the duke of Marlborough, Maria Theresa and the king of Prussia.

And what are in most cases the pretences upon which war is undertaken? What rational man could possibly have given himself the least disturbance for the sake of choosing whether Henry the sixth or Edward the fourth should have the style of king of England? What Englishman could reasonably have drawn his sword for the purpose of rendering his country an inferior dependency of France, as it must necessarily have been if the ambition of the Plantagenets had succeeded? What can be more deplorable than to see us first engage eight years in war rather than suffer the haughty Maria Theresa to live with a diminished sovereignty or in a private station; and then eight years more to support the free-booter who had taken advantage of her helpless condition?

The usual causes of war are excellently described by Swift. 'Sometimes the quarrel between two princes is to decide which of them shall dispossess a third of his dominions, where neither of them pretends to any right. Sometimes one prince quarrels with another, for fear the other should quarrel with him. Sometimes a war is entered upon because the enemy is too strong; and sometimes because he is too weak. Sometimes our neighbours want the things which we have, or have the things which we want; and we both fight, till they take ours, or give us theirs. It is a very justifiable cause of war to invade a country after the people have been wasted by famine, destroyed by pestilence, or embroiled by factions among themselves. It is justifiable to enter into a war against our nearest ally, when one of his towns lies convenient for us, or a territory of land that would render our dominions round and compact. If a prince sends forces into a nation where the people are poor and ignorant, he may lawfully put the half of them to death, and make slaves of the rest, in order to civilize and reduce them from their barbarous way of living. It is a very kingly, honourable and frequent practice, when one prince desires the assistance of another to secure him against an invasion, that the assistant, when he has driven out the invader, should seize on the dominions himself, and kill, imprison or banish the prince he came to relieve.'*

If we turn from the foreign transactions of states with each other to the principles of their domestic policy, we shall not find much greater reason to be satisfied. A numerous class of mankind are held down in a state of abject penury, and are continually prompted by disappointment and distress to commit violence upon their more fortunate neighbours. The only mode which is employed to repress this violence, and to maintain the order and peace of society, is punishment. Whips, axes and gibbets, dungeons, chains and racks are the most approved and established methods of persuading men to obedience, and impressing upon their minds the lessons of reason. There are few subjects upon which human ingenuity has been more fully displayed than in inventing instruments of torture. The lash of the whip a thousand times repeated and flagrant on the back of the defenceless victim, the bastinado on the soles of the feet, the dislocation of limbs, the fracture of bones, the faggot and the stake, the cross, impaling, and the mode of drifting pirates on the Volga, make but a small part of the catalogue. When Damiens, the maniac, was arraigned for his abortive attempt on the life of Louis XV of France, a council of anatomists was summoned to deliberate how a human being might be destroyed with the longest protracted and most diversified agony. Hundreds of victims are annually sacrificed at the shrine of positive law and political institution.

Add to this the species of government which prevails over nine tenths of the globe, which is despotism: a government, as Locke justly observes, altogether 'vile and

* *Gulliver's Travels*, Part IV, Ch. V.

miserable', and 'more to be deprecated than anarchy itself'.*

Certainly every man who takes a dispassionate survey of this picture will feel himself inclined to pause respecting the necessity of the havoc which is thus made of his species, and to question whether the established methods for protecting mankind against the caprices of each other are the best that can be devised. He will be at a loss which of the two to pronounce most worthy of regret, the misery that is inflicted, or the depravity by which it is produced. If this be the unalterable allotment of our nature, the eminence of our rational faculties must be considered as rather an abortion than a substantial benefit; and we shall not fail to lament that, while in some respects we are elevated above the brutes, we are in so many important ones destined for ever to remain their inferiors.

---

* Locke on Government, Book I, Ch. i, § 1; and Book II, Ch. vii, § 91.

Most of the above arguments may be found much more at large in Burke's *Vindication of Natural Society*; a treatise in which the evils of the existing political institutions are displayed with incomparable force of reasoning and lustre of eloquence, while the intention of the author was to show that these evils were to be considered as trivial.

CHAPTER III

SPIRIT OF POLITICAL INSTITUTIONS

*Robbery and fraud, two great vices in society –
originate, 1. in extreme poverty – 2. in the ostentation of the rich – 3. in their tyranny –
rendered permanent – 1. by legislation – 2. by
the administration of law – 3. by the manner in
which property is distributed.*

ADDITIONAL perspicuity will be communicated to our
view of the evils of political society if we reflect with
further and closer attention upon what may be called its
interior and domestic history.

Two of the greatest abuses relative to the interior
policy of nations, which at this time prevail in the world,
consist in the irregular transfer of property, either first by
violence, or secondly by fraud. If among the inhabitants
of any country there existed no desire in one individual
to possess himself of the substance of another, or no desire
so vehement and restless as to prompt him to acquire it
by means inconsistent with order and justice, undoubtedly in that country guilt could scarcely be known but by
report. If every man could with perfect facility obtain the
necessaries of life, and, obtaining them, feel no uneasy
craving after its superfluities, temptation would lose its
power. Private interest would visibly accord with public
good; and civil society become what poetry has feigned
of the golden age. Let us enquire into the principles to
which these abuses are indebted for their existence.

First then it is to be observed that, in the most refined
states of Europe, the inequality of property has risen to
an alarming height. Vast numbers of their inhabitants are
deprived of almost every accommodation that can render
life tolerable or secure. Their utmost industry scarcely
suffices for their support. The women and children lean
with an insupportable weight upon the efforts of the man,
so that a large family has in the lower orders of life be-

come a proverbial expression for an uncommon degree of poverty and wretchedness. If sickness or some of those casualties which are perpetually incident to an active and laborious life be added to these burthens, the distress is yet greater.

It seems to be agreed that in England there is less wretchedness and distress than in most of the kingdoms of the continent. In England the poors' rates amount to the sum of two millions sterling per annum. It has been calculated that one person in seven of the inhabitants of this country derives at some period of his life assistance from this fund. If to this we add the persons who, from pride, a spirit of independence, or the want of a legal settlement, though in equal distress receive no such assistance, the proportion will be considerably increased.

I lay no stress upon the accuracy of this calculation; the general fact is sufficient to give us an idea of the greatness of the abuse. The consequences that result are placed beyond the reach of contradiction. A perpetual struggle with the evils of poverty, if frequently ineffectual, must necessarily render many of the sufferers desperate. A painful feeling of their oppressed situation will itself deprive them of the power of surmounting it. The superiority of the rich, being thus unmercifully exercised, must inevitably expose them to reprisals; and the poor man will be induced to regard the state of society as a state of war, an unjust combination, not for protecting every man in his rights and securing to him the means of existence, but for engrossing all its advantages to a few favoured individuals, and reserving for the portion of the rest want, dependence and misery.

A second source of those destructive passions by which the peace of society is interrupted is to be found in the luxury, the pageantry and magnificence with which enormous wealth is usually accompanied. Human beings are capable of encountering with cheerfulness considerable hardships when those hardships are impartially shared with the rest of the society, and they are not in-sulted with the spectacle of indolence and ease in others, no way deserving of greater advantages than themselves. But it is a bitter aggravation of their own calamity to have the privileges of others forced on their observation, and, while they are perpetually and vainly endeavouring to secure for themselves and their families the poorest conveniences, to find others revelling in the fruits of their labours. This aggravation is assiduously administered to them under most of the political establishments at present in existence. There is a numerous class of individuals who, though rich, have neither brilliant talents nor sublime virtues; and, however highly they may prize their education, their affability, their superior polish and the elegance of their manners, have a secret consciousness that they possess nothing by which they can so securely assert their pre-eminence and keep their inferiors at a distance as the splendour of their equipage, the magnificence of their retinue and the sumptuousness of their entertainments. The poor man is struck with this exhibition; he feels his own miseries; he knows how unwearied are his efforts to obtain a slender pittance of this prodigal waste; and he mistakes opulence for felicity. He cannot persuade himself that an embroidered garment may frequently cover an aching heart.

A third disadvantage that is apt to connect poverty with discontent consists in the insolence and usurpation of the rich. If the poor man would in other respects compose himself in philosophic indifference, and, conscious that he possesses every thing that is truly honourable to man as fully as his rich neighbour, would look upon the rest as beneath his envy, his neighbour will not permit him to do so. He seems as if he could never be satisfied with his possessions unless he can make the spectacle of them grating to others; and that honest self-esteem, by which his inferior might otherwise attain to tranquillity, is rendered the instrument of galling him with oppression and injustice. In many countries justice is avowedly made a subject of solicitation, and the man of the highest rank and most splendid connections almost infallibly carries his cause against the unprotected and friendless. In countries where this shameless practice is not established, justice is frequently a matter of expensive purchase, and the man with the longest purse is proverbially victorious. A consciousness of these facts must be expected to render the rich little cautious of offence in his dealings with the poor, and to inspire him with a temper overbearing, dictatorial and tyrannical. Nor does this indirect oppression satisfy his despotism. The rich are in all such countries directly or indirectly the legislators of the state; and of consequence are perpetually reducing oppression into a system, and depriving the poor of that little commonage of nature which might otherwise still have remained to them.

The opinions of individuals, and of consequence their desires, for desire is nothing but opinion maturing for action, will always be in a great degree regulated by the opinions of the community. But the manners prevailing in many countries are accurately calculated to impress a conviction that integrity, virtue, understanding and industry are nothing, and that opulence is everything. Does a man whose exterior denotes indigence expect to be well received in society, and especially by those who would be understood to dictate to the rest? Does he find or imagine himself in want of their assistance and favour? He is presently taught that no merit can atone for a mean appearance. The lesson that is read to him is, 'Go home; enrich yourself by whatever means; obtain those superfluities which are alone regarded as estimable; and you may then be secure of an amicable reception.' Accordingly poverty in such countries is viewed as the greatest of demerits. It is escaped from with an eagerness that has no leisure for the scruples of honesty. It is concealed as the most indelible disgrace. While one man chooses the path of undistinguishing accumulation, another plunges into expenses which are to impose him upon the world as more opulent than he is. He hastens to the reality of that penury the appearance of which he dreads; and, together with his property, sacrifices the integrity, veracity and character which might have consoled him in his adversity.

Such are the causes that, in different degrees under the different governments of the world, prompt mankind openly or secretly to encroach upon the property of each other. Let us consider how far they admit either of remedy or aggravation from political institution. Whatever tends to decrease the injuries attendant upon poverty decreases at the same time the inordinate desire and the enormous accumulation of wealth. Wealth is not pursued for its own sake, and seldom for the sensual gratifications it can purchase, but for the same reasons that ordinarily prompt men to the acquisition of learning, eloquence and skill, for the love of distinction and the fear of contempt. How few would prize the possession of riches if they were condemned to enjoy their equipage, their palaces and their entertainments in solitude, with no eye to wonder at their magnificence, and no sordid observer ready to convert that wonder into an adulation of the owner? If admiration were not generally deemed the exclusive property of the rich, and contempt the constant lacquey of poverty, the love of gain would cease to be an universal passion. Let us consider in what respects political institution is rendered subservient to this passion.

First then, legislation is in almost every country grossly the favourer of the rich against the poor. Such is the character of the game-laws, by which the industrious rustic is forbidden to destroy the animal that preys upon the hopes of his future subsistence, or to supply himself with the food that unsought thrusts itself in his path. Such was the spirit of the late revenue-laws of France, which in several of their provisions fell exclusively upon the humble and industrious, and exempted from their operation those who were best able to support it. Thus in England the land-tax at this moment produces half a million less than it did a century ago, while the taxes on consumption have experienced an addition of thirteen millions per annum during the same period. This is an attempt, whether effectual or no, to throw the burthen from the rich upon the poor, and as such is an example of the spirit of legislation. Upon the same principle robbery and other offences, which the wealthier part of the community have no temptation to commit, are treated as capital crimes, and attended with the most rigorous, often the most inhuman punishments. The rich are encouraged to associate for the execution of the most partial and oppressive positive laws; monopolies and patents are lavishly dispensed to such as are able to purchase them; while the most vigilant policy is employed to prevent combinations of the poor to fix the price of labour, and they are deprived of the benefit of that prudence and judgement which would select the scene of their industry.

Secondly, the administration of law is not less iniquitous than the spirit in which it is framed. Under the late government of France the office of judge was a matter of purchase, partly by an open price advanced to the crown, and partly by a secret douceur paid to the minister. He who knew best how to manage his market in the retail trade of justice could afford to purchase the good will of its functions at the highest price. To the client justice was avowedly made an object of personal solicitation; and a powerful friend, a handsome woman, or a proper present were articles of much greater value than a good cause. In England the criminal law is administered with greater impartiality so far as regards the trial itself; but the number of capital offences, and of consequence the frequency of pardons, open a wide door to favour and abuse. In causes relating to property the practice of law is arrived at such a pitch as to render its nominal impartiality utterly nugatory. The length of our chancery suits, the multiplied appeals from court to court, the enormous fees of counsel, attorneys, secretaries, clerks, the drawing of briefs, bills, replications and rejoinders, and what has sometimes been called the 'glorious uncertainy' of the law, render it frequently more advisable to resign a property than to contest it, and particularly exclude the impoverished claimant from the faintest hope of redress.

Thirdly, the inequality of conditions usually maintained by political institution is calculated greatly to enhance the imagined excellence of wealth. In the ancient monarchies of the east, and in Turkey at the present day, an eminent station could scarcely fail to excite implicit deference. The timid inhabitant trembled before his superior; and would have thought it little less than blasphemy to touch the veil drawn by the proud satrap over his inglorious origin. The same principles were extensively prevalent under the feudal system. The vassal, who was regarded as a sort of live stock upon the estate, and knew no appeal from the arbitrary fiat of his lord, would scarcely venture to suspect that he was of the same species. This however constituted an unnatural and violent situation. There is a propensity in man to look further than the outside; and to come with a writ of enquiry into the title of the upstart and the successful. By the operation of these causes the insolence of wealth has been in some degree moderated. Meantime it cannot be pretended that even among ourselves the inequality is not strained so as to give birth to very unfortunate consequences. If, in the enormous degree in which it prevails in some parts of the world, it wholly debilitate and emasculate the human race, we shall feel some reason to believe that, even in the milder state in which we are accustomed to behold it, it is still pregnant with the most mischievous effects.

CHAPTER IV*

THE CHARACTERS OF MEN ORIGINATE IN THEIR EXTERNAL CIRCUMSTANCES

Theory of the human mind. – Subject of the present chapter – of the next. – Erroneous opinions refuted. – I. Innate principles. – This hypothesis, 1. superflous – 2. unsatisfactory – 3. absurd. – II. Instincts. – Examination of this doctrine – of the arguments by which it has been enforced: from the early actions of infants – from the desire of self-preservation – from self-love – from pity. – III. Effects of antenatal impressions and original structure. – Variableness of the characters of men. – Ease with which impressions may be counteracted. – Form of the infant undetermined. – Habits of men and other animals compared. – Inference. – Importance of these speculations. – IV. Reasonings of the present chapter applied. – Three sorts of education – 1. accident – 2. precept – 3. political institution.

THUS far we have argued from historical facts, and from them have collected a very strong presumptive evidence that political institutions have a more powerful and extensive influence than it has been generally the practice to ascribe to them.

But we can never arrive at precise conceptions relative

*In the plan of this work it was originally conceived that it was advisable not to press matters of close and laborious speculation in the outset. It appeared as if moral and political philosophy might assume something more than had been usual of a popular form, without deducting from the justness and depth of its investigation. Upon revisal however, it was found that the inferences of the First Book had been materially injured by an overscrupulousness in that point. The fruit of the discovery was this and the following chapter, as they now stand. It is recommended, to the reader who finds himself deterred by their apparent difficulty, to pass on to the remaining divisions of the enquiry.

to this part of the subject without entering into an analysis of the human mind,* and endeavouring to ascertain the nature of the causes by which its operations are directed. Under this branch of the subject I shall attempt to prove two things: first, that the actions and dispositions of mankind are the offspring of circumstances and events, and not of any original determination that they bring into the world; and, secondly, that the great stream of our voluntary actions essentially depends, not upon the direct and immediate impulses of sense, but upon the decisions of the understanding. If these propositions can be sufficiently established, it will follow that the happiness men are able to attain is proportioned to the justness of the opinions they take as guides in the pursuit; and it will only remain, for the purpose of applying these premises to the point under consideration, that we should demonstrate the opinions of men to be,

*Some persons have of late suggested doubts concerning the propriety of the use of the word mind. An accurate philosophy has led modern enquirers to question the existence of two classes of substances in the universe, to reject the metaphysical denominations of spirit and soul, and even to doubt whether human beings have any satisfactory acquaintance with the properties of matter. The same accuracy, it has been said, ought to teach us to discard the term mind. But this objection seems to be premature. We are indeed wholly uncertain whether the causes of our sensations, heat, colour, hardness and extension (the two former of these properties have been questioned in a very forcible manner by Locke, *Hum. Understanding*, the two latter by Berkeley and Hume) be in any respect similar to the ideas they produce. We know nothing of the substance or substratum of matter, or of that which is the recipient of thought and perception. We do not even know that the idea annexed to the word substance is correct, or has any counterpart in the reality of existence. But, if there be any one thing that we know more certainly than another, it is the existence of our own thoughts, ideas, perceptions or sensations (by whatever term we may choose to express them), and that they are ordinarily linked together so as to produce the complex notion of unity or personal identity. Now it is this series of thoughts thus linked together, without considering whether they reside in any or what substratum, that is most aptly expressed by the term mind; and in this sense the term is intended to be used throughout the following work.

for the most part, under the absolute control of political institution.

First, the actions and dispositions of men are not the offspring of any original bias that they bring into the world in favour of one sentiment or character rather than another, but flow entirely from the operation of circum·stances and events acting upon a faculty of receiving sensible impressions. There are three modes in which the human mind has been conceived to be modified, independently of the circumstances which occur to us, and the sensations excited: first, innate principles; secondly, instincts; thirdly, the original differences of our structure, together with the impressions we receive in the womb. Let us examine each of these in their order.

First, innate principles of judgement. Those by whom this doctrine has been maintained have supposed that there were certain branches of knowledge, and those perhaps of all others the most important, concerning which we felt an irresistible persuasion, at the same time that we were wholly unable to trace them through any channels of external evidence and methodical deduction. They conceived therefore that they were orignally written in our hearts; or perhaps, more properly speaking, that there was a general propensity in the human mind suggesting them to our reflections, and fastening them upon our conviction. Accordingly, they established the universal consent of mankind as one of the most infallible criterions of fundamental truth. It appeared upon their system that we were furnished with a sort of sixth sense, the existence of which was not proved to us, like that of our other senses, by direct and proper evidence, but from the consideration of certain phenomena in the history of the human mind, which cannot be otherwise accounted for than by the assumption of this hypothesis.

There is an essential deficiency in every speculation of this sort. It turns entirely upon an appeal to our ignorance. Its language is as follows: 'You cannot account for certain events from the known laws of the subjects to which they belong; therefore they are not deducible from those laws; therefore you must admit a new principle into the system for the express purpose of accounting for them.' But there cannot be a sounder maxim of reasoning than that which points out to us the error of admitting into our hypotheses unnecessary principles, or referring the phenomena that occur to remote and extraordinary sources, when they may with equal facility be referred to sources which obviously exist, and the results of which we daily observe. This maxim alone is sufficient to persuade us to reject the doctrine of innate principles. If we consider the infinitely various causes by which the human mind is perceptibly modified, and the different principles, argument, imitation, inclination, early prejudice and imaginary interest, by which opinion is generated, we shall readily perceive that nothing can be more difficult than to assign any opinion, existing among the human species, and at the same time incapable of being generated by any of these causes and principles.

A careful enquirer will be strongly inclined to suspect the soundness of opinions which rest for their support on so ambiguous a foundation as that of innate impression. We cannot reasonably question the existence of facts; that is, we cannot deny the existence of our sensations, or the series in which they occur. We cannot deny the axioms of mathematics; for they exhibit nothing more than a consistent use of words, and affirm of some idea that it is itself and not something else. We can entertain little doubt of the validity of mathematical demonstrations, which appear to be irresistible conclusions deduced from identical propositions. We ascribe a certain value, sometimes greater and sometimes less, to considerations drawn from analogy. But what degree of weight shall we attribute to affirmations which pretend to rest upon none of these grounds? The most preposterous propositions, incapable of any rational defence, have in different ages and countries appealed to this inexplicable authority, and passed for infallible and innate. The enquirer that has no other object than truth, that refuses to be misled, and is determined to proceed only upon just and sufficient evidence will find little reason to be satisfied with dogmas which rest upon no other foundation than a pretended necessity impelling the human mind to yield its assent.

But there is a still more irresistible argument proving to us the absurdity of the supposition of innate principles. Every principle is a proposition: either it affirms, or it denies. Every proposition consists in the connection of at least two distinct ideas, which are affirmed to agree or disagree with each other. It is impossible that the proposition can be innate, unless the ideas to which it relates be also innate. A connection where there is nothing to be connected, a proposition where there is neither subject nor conclusion, is the most incoherent of all suppositions. But nothing can be more incontrovertible than that we do not bring pre-established ideas into the world with us.

Let the innate principle be that 'virtue is a rule to which we are obliged to conform'. Here are three principal and leading ideas, not to mention subordinate ones, which it is necessary to form, before we can so much as understand the proposition. What is virtue? Previously to our forming an idea corresponding to this general term, it seems necessary that we should have observed the several features by which virtue is distinguished, and the several subordinate articles of right conduct, that taken together constitute that mass of practical judgements to which we give the denomination of virtue. These are so far from being innate that the most impartial and laborious enquirers are not yet agreed respecting them. The next idea included in the above proposition is that of a rule or standard, a generical measure with which individuals are to be compared, and their conformity or disagreement with which is to determine their value. Lastly, there is the idea of obligation, its nature and source, the obliger and the sanction, the penalty and the reward.

Who is there in the present state of scientifical improvement that will believe that this vast chain of perceptions and notions is something that we bring into the world with us, a mystical magazine, shut up in the human embryo, whose treasures are to be gradually unfolded as circumstances shall require? Who does not perceive that they are regularly generated in the mind by a series of impressions, and digested and arranged by association and reflection?

But, if we are not endowed with innate principles of judgement, it has nevertheless been supposed by some persons that we might have instincts to action, leading us to the performance of certain useful and necessary functions, independently of any previous reasoning as to the advantage of these functions. These instincts, like the innate principles of judgement we have already examined, are conceived to be original, a separate endowment annexed to our being, and not any thing that irresistibly flows from the mere faculty of perception and thought, as acted upon by the circumstances, either of our animal frame, or of the external objects, by which we are affected. They are liable therefore to the same objection as that already urged against innate principles. The system by which they are attempted to be established is a mere appeal to our ignorance, assuming that we are fully acquainted with all the possible operations of known powers, and imposing upon us an unknown power as indispensable to the accounting for certain phenomena. If we were wholly unable to solve these phenomena, it would yet behove us to be extremely cautious in affirming that known principles and causes are inadequate to their solution. If we are able upon strict and mature investigation to trace the greater part of them to their source, this necessarily adds force to the caution here recommended.

An unknown cause is exceptionable, in the first place, inasmuch as to multiply causes is contrary to the experienced operation of scientifical improvement. It is exceptionable, secondly, because its tendency is to break that train of antecedents and consequents of which the history of the universe is composed. It introduces an action apparently extraneous, instead of imputing the nature of what follows to the properties of that which preceded. It bars the progress of enquiry by introducing that which is occult, mysterious and incapable of further investigation. It allows nothing to the future advancement of human knowledge; but represents the limits of what is already known, as the limits of human understanding.

Let us review a few of the most common examples adduced in favour of human instincts, and examine how far they authorize the conclusion that is attempted to be drawn from them: and first, some of those actions which appear to rise in the most instantaneous and irresistible manner.

A certain irritation of the palm of the hand will produce that contraction of the fingers which accompanies the action of grasping. This contraction will at first take place unaccompanied with design, the object will be grasped without any intention to retain it, and let go again without thought or observation. After a certain number of repetitions, the nature of the action will be perceived; it will be performed with a consciousness of its tendency; and even the hand stretched out upon the approach of any object that is desired. Present to the child, thus far instructed, a lighted candle. The sight of it will produce a pleasurable state of the organs of perception. He will probably stretch out his hand to the flame, and will have no apprehension of the pain of burning till he has felt the sensation.

At the age of maturity, the eyelids instantaneously close when any substance from which danger is apprehended is advanced towards them; and this action is so constant as to be with great difficulty prevented by a grown person, though he should explicitly desire it. In infants there is no such propensity; and an object may be approached to their organs, however near and however suddenly, without producing this effect. Frowns will be totally indifferent to a child, who has never found them associated with the effects of anger. Fear itself is a species of foresight, and in no case exists till introduced by experience.

It has been said that the desire of self-preservation is innate. I demand what is meant by this desire? Must we not understand by it a preference of existence to nonexistence? Do we prefer anything but because it is apprehended to be good? It follows that we cannot prefer existence, previously to our experience of the motives for preference it possesses. Indeed the ideas of life and death are exceedingly complicated, and very tardy in their formation. A child desires pleasure and loathes pain long before he can have any imagination respecting the ceasing to exist.

Again, it has been said that self-love is innate. But there cannot be an error more easy of detection. By the love of self we understand the approbation of pleasure, and dislike of pain: but this is only the faculty of perception under another name. Who ever denied that man was a percipient being? Who ever dreamed that there was a particular instinct necessary to render him percipient?

Pity has sometimes been supposed an instance of innate principle; particularly as it seems to arise with greater facility in young persons, and persons of little refinement, than in others. But it was reasonable to expect that threats and anger, circumstances that have been associated with our own sufferings, should excite painful feelings in us in the case of others, independently of any laboured analysis. The cries of distress, the appearance of agony or corporal infliction, irresistibly revive the memory of the pains accompanied by those symptoms in ourselves. Longer experience and observation enable us to separate the calamities of others and our own safety, the existence of pain in one subject and of pleasure or benefit in others, or in the same at a future period, more accurately than we could be expected to do previously to that experience.

If then it appear that the human mind is unattended either with innate principles or instincts, there are only two remaining circumstances that can be imagined to anticipate the effects of institution, and fix the human character independently of every species of education: these are, the qualities that may be produced in the human mind previously to the era of our birth, and the differences that may result from the different structure of the greater or subtler elements of the animal frame.

To objections derived from these sources the answer will be in both cases similar.

First, ideas are to the mind nearly what atoms are to the body. The whole mass is in a perpetual flux; nothing is stable and permanent; after the lapse of a given period not a single particle probably remains the same. Who knows not that in the course of a human life the character of the individual frequently undergoes two or three revolutions of its fundamental stamina? The turbulent man will frequently become contemplative, the generous be changed into selfish, and the frank and good-humoured into peevish and morose. How often does it happen that, if we meet our best loved friend after an absence of twenty years, we look in vain in the man before us for the qualities that formerly excited our sympathy, and, instead of the exquisite delight we promised ourselves, reap nothing but disappointment? If it is thus in habits apparently the most rooted, who will be disposed to lay any extraordinary stress upon the impressions which an infant may have received in the womb of his mother?

He that considers human life with an attentive eye will not fail to remark that there is scarcely such a thing in character and principles as an irremediable error. Persons of narrow and limited views may upon many occasions incline to sit down in despair; but those who are inspired with a genuine energy will derive new incentives from miscarriage. Has any unfortunate and undesirable impression been made upon the youthful mind? Nothing will be more easy than for a judicious superintendent, provided its nature is understood, and it is undertaken sufficiently early, to remedy and obliterate it. Has a child passed a certain period of existence in ill-judged indulgence and habits of command and caprice? The skilful parent, when the child returns to its paternal roof, knows that this evil is not invincible, and sets himself with an undoubting spirit to the removal of the depravity. It often happens that the very impression which, if not counteracted, shall decide upon the pursuits and fortune of an entire life might perhaps under other circumstances be reduced to complete inefficiency in half an hour.

It is in corporeal structure as in intellectual impressions. The first impressions of our infancy are so much upon the surface that their effects scarcely survive the period of the impression itself. The mature man seldom retains the faintest recollection of the incidents of the two first years of his life. Is it to be supposed that that which has left no trace upon the memory can be in an eminent degree powerful in its associated effects? Just so in the structure of the animal frame. What is born into the world is an unfinished sketch, without character or decisive feature impressed upon it. In the sequel there is a correspondence between the physiognomy and the intellectual and moral qualities of the mind. But is it not reasonable to suppose that this is produced by the continual tendency of the mind to modify its material engine in a particular way? There is for the most part no essential difference between the child of the lord and of the porter. Provided he do not come into the world infected with any ruinous distemper, the child of the lord, if changed in the cradle, would scarcely find any greater difficulty than the other in learning the trade of his softer father, and becoming a carrier of burthens. The muscles of those limbs which are most frequently called into play are always observed to acquire peculiar flexibility or strength. It is not improbable, if it should be found that the capacity of the skull of a wise man is greater than that of a fool, that this enlargement should be produced by the incessantly repeated action of the intellectual faculties, especially if we recollect of how flexible materials the skulls of infants are composed, and at how early an age persons of eminent intellectual merit acquire some portion of their future characteristics.

In the meantime it would be ridiculous to question the real differences that exist between children at the period of their birth. Hercules and his brother, the robust infant whom scarcely any neglect can destroy, and the infant that is with difficulty reared, are undoubtedly from the moment of parturition very different beings. If each of them could receive an education precisely equal and eminently wise, the child labouring under original disadvantage would be benefited, but the child to whom circumstances had been most favourable in the outset would always retain his priority. These considerations however do not appear materially to affect the doctrine of the present chapter; and that for the following reasons.

First, education never can be equal. The inequality of external circumstances in two beings whose situations most nearly resemble is so great as to baffle all power of calculation. In the present state of mankind this is eminently the case. There is no fact more palpable than that children of all sizes and forms indifferently become wise. It is not the man of great stature or vigorous make that outstrips his fellow in understanding. It is not the man who possesses all the external senses in the highest perfection. It is not the man whose health is most vigorous and invariable. Those moral causes that awaken the mind, that inspire sensibility, imagination and perseverance, are distributed without distinction to the tall or the dwarfish, the graceful or the deformed, the lynx-eyed or the blind. But, if the more obvious distinctions of animal structure appear to have little share in deciding upon their associated varieties of intellect, it is surely in the highest degree unjustifiable to attribute these varieties to such subtle and imperceptible differences as, being out of our power to assign, are yet gratuitously assumed to account for the most stupendous effects. This mysterious solution is the refuge of indolence or the instrument of imposture, but incompatible with a sober and persevering spirit of investigation.

Secondly, it is sufficient to recollect the nature of moral causes to be satisfied that their efficiency is nearly unlimited. The essential differences that are to be found between individual and individual originate in the opinions they form, and the circumstances by which they are controlled. It is impossible to believe that the same moral train would not make nearly the same man. Let us suppose a being to have heard all the arguments and been subject to all the excitements that were ever addressed to any celebrated character. The same arguments, with all their strength and all their weakness, unaccompanied with the smallest addition or variation, and retailed in exactly the same proportions from month to month and year to year, must surely have produced the same opinions. The same excitements, without reservation, whether direct or accidental, must have fixed the same propensities. Whatever science or pursuit was selected by this celebrated character must be loved by the person respecting whom we are supposing this identity of impressions. In fine, it is impression that makes the man, and, compared with the empire of impression, the mere differences of animal structure are inexpressibly unimportant and powerless.

These truths will be brought to our minds with much additional evidence if we compare in this respect the case of brutes with that of men. Among the inferior animals, breed is a circumstance of considerable importance, and a judicious mixture and preservation in this point is found to be attended with the most unequivocal results. But nothing of that kind appears to take place in our own species. A generous blood, a gallant and fearless spirit is by no means propagated from father to son. When a particular appellation is granted, as is usually practised in the existing governments of Europe, to designate the descendants of a magnanimous ancestry, we do not find, even with all the arts of modern education, to assist, that such descendants are the legitimate representatives of departed heroism. Whence comes this difference? Probably from the more irresistible operation of moral causes. It is not impossible that among savages those differences would be conspicuous which with us are annihilated. It is not unlikely that if men, like brutes, were withheld from the more considerable means of intellectual improvement, if they derived nothing from the discoveries and sagacity of their ancestors, if each individual had to begin absolutely *de novo* in the discipline and arrangement of his ideas, blood or whatever other circumstances distinguish one man from another at the period of his nativity would produce as memorable effects in man as they now do in those classes of animals that are deprived of our advantages. Even in the case of brutes, education and care on the part of the man seem to be nearly indispensable, if we would not have the foal of the finest racer degenerate to the level of the cart-horse. In plants the peculiarities of soil decide in a great degree upon the future properties of each. But who would think of forming the character of a human being by the operations of heat and cold, dryness and moisture upon the animal frame? With us moral considerations swallow up the effects of every other accident. Present a pursuit to the mind, convey to it the apprehension of calamity or advantage, excite it by motives of aversion or motives of affection, and the slow and silent influence of material causes perishes like dews at the rising of the sun.

The result of these considerations is that at the moment of birth man has really a certain character, and each man a character different from his fellows. The accidents which pass during the months of percipiency in the womb of the mother produce a real effect. Various external accidents, unlimited as to the period of their commencement, modify in different ways the elements of the animal frame. Everything in the universe is linked and united together.

No event, however minute and imperceptible, is barren of a train of consequences, however comparatively evanescent those consequences may in some instances be found. If there have been philosophers that have asserted otherwise, and taught that all minds from the period of birth were precisely alike, they have reflected discredit by such an incautious statement upon the truth they proposed to defend.

But, though the original differences of man and man be arithmetically speaking something, speaking in the way of a general and comprehensive estimate they may be said to be almost nothing. If the early impressions of our childhood may by a skilful observer be as it were obliterated almost as soon as made, how much less can the confused and unpronounced impressions of the womb be expected to resist the multiplicity of ideas that successively contribute to wear out their traces? If the temper of the man appear in many instances to be totally changed, how can it be supposed that there is anything permanent and inflexible in the propensities of a new-born infant? and, if not in the character of the disposition, how much less in that of the understanding?

Speak the language of truth and reason to your child, and be under no apprehension for the result. Show him that what you recommend is valuable and desirable, and fear not but he will desire it. Convince his understanding, and you enlist all his powers animal and intellectual in your service. How long has the genius of education been disheartened and unnerved by the pretence that man is born all that it is possible for him to become? How long has the jargon imposed upon the world which would persuade us that in instructing a man you do not add to, but unfold his stores? The miscarriages of education do not proceed from the boundedness of its powers, but from the mistakes with which it is accompanied. We often inspire disgust, where we mean to infuse desire. We are wrapped up in ourselves, and do not observe, as we ought, step by step the sensations that pass in the mind of our hearer. We mistake compulsion for persuasion, and delude ourselves into the belief that despotism is the road to the heart.

Education will proceed with a firm step and with genuine lustre when those who conduct it shall know what a vast field it embraces; when they shall be aware that the effect, the question whether the pupil shall be a man of perseverance and enterprise or a stupid and inanimate dolt, depends upon the powers of those under whose direction he is placed and the skill with which those powers shall be applied. Industry will be exerted with tenfold alacrity when it shall be generally confessed that there are no obstacles to our improvement which do not yield to the powers of industry. Multitudes will never exert the energy necessary to extraordinary success, till they shall dismiss the prejudices that fetter them, get rid of the chilling system of occult and inexplicable causes, and consider the human mind as an intelligent agent, guided by motives and prospects presented to the understanding, and not by causes of which we have no proper cognisance and can form no calculation.

Apply these considerations to the subject of politics, and they will authorize us to infer that the excellencies and defects of the human character are not derived from causes beyond the reach of ingenuity to modify and correct. If we entertain false views and be involved in pernicious mistakes, this disadvantage is not the offspring of an irresistible destiny. We have been ignorant, we have been hasty, or we have been misled. Remove the causes of this ignorance or this miscalculation, and the effects will cease. Show me in the clearest and most unambiguous manner that a certain mode of proceeding is most reasonable in itself or most conducive to my interest, and I shall infallibly pursue that mode, as long as the views you suggested to me continue present to my mind. The conduct of human beings in every situation is governed by the judgements they make and the sensations that are communicated to them.

It has appeared that the characters of men are determined in all their most essential circumstances by education. By education in this place I would be understood to convey the most comprehensive sense that can possibly be annexed to that word, including every incident that produces an idea in the mind, and can give birth to a train of reflections. It may be of use for a clearer understanding of the subject we here examine to consider education under three heads: the education of accident, or those impressions we receive independently of any design on the part of the preceptor; education commonly so called, or the impressions which he intentionally communicates; and political education, or the modification our ideas receive from the form of government under which we live. In the course of this successive review we shall be enabled in some degree to ascertain the respective influence which is to be attributed to each.

It is not unusual to hear persons dwell with emphasis on the wide difference of the results in two young persons who have been educated together; and this has been produced as a decisive argument in favour of the essential differences we are supposed to bring into the world with us. But this could scarcely have happened but from extreme inattention in the persons who have so argued. Innumerable ideas, or changes in the state of the percipient being, probably occur in every moment of time. How many of these enter into the plan of the preceptor? Two children walk out together. One busies himself in plucking flowers or running after butterflies, the other walks in the hand of their conductor. Two men view a picture. They never see it from the same point of view, and therefore strictly speaking never see the same picture. If they sit down to hear a lecture or any piece of instruction, they never sit down with the same degree of attention, seriousness or good humour. The previous state of mind is different, and therefore the impression received cannot be the same. It has been found in the history of several eminent men, and probably would have been found much oftener had their juvenile adventures been more accurately recorded, that the most trivial circumstance has sometimes furnished the original occasion of awakening the ardour of their minds and determining the bent of their studies.

It may however reasonably be suspected whether the education of design be not, intrinsically considered, more powerful than the education of accident. If at any time it appear impotent, this is probably owing to mistake in the project. The instructor continually fails in wisdom of contrivance, or conciliation of manner, or both. It may often happen, either from the pedantry of his habits, or the impatience of his temper, that his recommendation shall operate rather as an antidote than an attraction. Preceptors are apt to pique themselves upon disclosing part and concealing part of the truth, upon a sort of common place, cant exhortation to be addressed to youth, which it would be an insult to offer to the understandings of men. But children are not inclined to consider him entirely as their friend whom they detect in an attempt to impose upon them. Were it otherwise, were we sufficiently frank and sufficiently skilful, did we apply ourselves to excite the sympathy of the young and to gain their confidence, it is not to be believed but that the systematical measures of the preceptor would have a decisive advantage over the desultory influence of accidental impression. Children are a sort of raw material put into our hands, a ductile and yielding substance, which, if we do not ultimately mould in conformity to our wishes, it is because we throw away the power committed to us, by the folly with which we are accustomed to exert it. But there is another error not less decisive. The object we choose is an improper one. Our labour is expended, not in teaching truth, but in teaching falsehood. When that is the case, education is necessarily and happily maimed of half its powers. The success of an attempt to mislead can never be complete. We continually communicate in spite of ourselves the materials of just reasoning; reason is the genuine exercise, and truth the native element of an intellectual nature; it is no wonder therefore that, with a crude and abortive plan to govern his efforts, the preceptor is perpetually baffled, and the pupil, who has been thus stored with systematic delusions, and partial, obscure, and disfigured truths, should come out anything rather than that which his instructor intended him.

It remains to be considered what share political institution and forms of government occupy in the education of every human being. Their degree of influence depends upon two essential circumstances.

First, it is nearly impossible to oppose the education of the preceptor, and the education we derive from the forms of government under which we live, to each other; and therefore, however powerful the former of these may be, absolutely considered, it can never enter the lists with the latter upon equal terms. Should anyone talk to us of rescuing a young person from the sinister influence of a corrupt government by the power of education, it will be fair to ask who is the preceptor by whom this talk is to be effected? Is he born in the ordinary mode of generation, or does he descend among us from the skies? Has his character been in no degree modified by that very influence he undertakes to counteract? It is beyond all controversy that men who live in a state of equality, or that approaches equality, will be frank, ingenuous and intrepid in their carriage; while those who inhabit where a great disparity of ranks has prevailed will be distinguished by coldness, irresoluteness, timidity and caution. Will the preceptor in question be altogether superior to these qualities? Which of us is there who utters his thoughts in the fearless and explicit manner that true wisdom would prescribe? Who, that is sufficiently critical and severe, does not detect himself every hour in some act of falsehood or equivocation that example and early habits have planted too deeply to be eradicated? But the question is not what extraordinary persons can be found who may shine illustrious exceptions to the prevailing degeneracy of their neighbours. As long as parents and teachers in general shall fall under the established rule, it is clear that politics and modes of government will educate and infect us all. They poison our minds before we can resist, or so much as suspect their malignity. Like the barbarous directors of the Eastern seraglios, they deprive us of our virility, and fit us for their despicable employment from the cradle. So false is the opinion that has too generally prevailed that politics is an affair with which ordinary men have little concern.

Secondly, supposing the preceptor had all the qualifications that can reasonably be imputed, let us recollect for a moment what are the influences with which he would have to struggle. Political institution, by the consequences with which it is pregnant, strongly suggests to everyone who enters within its sphere what is the path he should avoid, as well as what he should pursue. Under a government fundamentally erroneous, he will see intrepid virtue proscribed, and a servile and corrupt spirit uniformly encouraged. But morality itself is nothing but a calculation of consequences. What strange confusion will the spectacle of that knavery which is universally practised through all the existing classes of society produce in the mind? The preceptor cannot go out of the world, or prevent the intercourse of his pupil with human beings of a character different from his own. Attempts of this kind are generally unhappy, stamped with the impression of artifice, intolerance and usurpation. From earliest infancy therefore there will be two principles contending for empire, the peculiar and elevated system of the preceptor, and the grovelling views of the great mass of mankind. These will generate confusion, uncertainty and irresolution. At no period of life will the effect correspond to what it would have been if the community were virtuous and wise. But its effect, obscure and imperceptible for a time, may be expected to burst into explosion at the period of puberty. When the pupil first becomes master of his own actions, and chooses his avocations and his associates, he will necessarily be acquainted with many things of which before he had very slender notions. At this time the follies of the world wear their most alluring face. He can scarcely avoid imagining that he has hitherto laboured under some species of delusion. Delusion, when detected, causes him upon whom it was practised to be indignant and restive. The only chance which remains is that, after a time, he should be recalled and awakened: and against this chance there are the progressive enticements of society; sensuality, ambition, sordid interest, false ridicule and the incessant decay of that unblemished purity which attended him in his outset. The best that can be expected is that he should return at last to sobriety and truth, with a mind debilitated and relaxed by repeated errors, and a moral constitution in which the seeds of degeneracy have been deeply and extensively sown.

CHAPTER V

THE VOLUNTARY ACTIONS OF MEN ORIGINATE IN THEIR OPINIONS

IF by the reasons already given, we have removed the supposition of any original bias in the mind that is inaccessible to human skill, and shown that the defects to which we are now subject are not irrevocably entailed upon us, there is another question of no less importance to be decided, before the ground can appear to be sufficiently cleared for political melioration. There is a doctrine the advocates of which have not been less numerous than those for innate principles and instincts, teaching 'that the conduct of human beings in many important particulars is not determined upon any grounds of reasoning and comparison, but by immediate and irresistible impression, in defiance of the conclusions and conviction of the understanding. Man is a compound being,' say the favourers of this hypothesis, 'made up of powers of reasoning and powers of sensation. These two principles are in perpetual hostility; and, as reason will in some cases subdue all the allurements of sense, so there are others in which the headlong impulses of sense will for ever defeat the tardy decisions of judgement. He that should attempt to regulate man entirely by his understanding, and supersede the irregular influences of material excitement; or that should imagine it practicable by any process and in any length of time to reduce the human species under the influence of general truth*; would show himself profoundly ignorant of some of the first laws of our nature.'

This doctrine, which in many cases has passed so current as to be thought scarcely a topic for examination, is highly worthy of a minute analysis. If true, it no less than the doctrine of innate principles opposes a bar to the efforts of philanthropy, and the improvement of social institutions. Certain it is that our prospects of melioration depend upon the progress of enquiry and the general advancement of knowledge. If therefore there be points, and those important ones, in which, so to express myself,

---

* Objections have been started to the use of the word truth in this absolute construction, as if it implied in the mind of the writer the notion of something having an independent and separate existence, whereas nothing can be more certain than that truth, that is, affirmative and negative propositions, has strictly no existence but in the mind of him who utters or hears it. But these objections seem to have been taken up too hastily. It cannot be denied that there are some propositions which are believed for a time and afterwards refuted; and others, such as most of the theorems of mathematics, and many of those of natural philosophy, respecting which there is no probability that they ever will be refuted. Every subject of enquiry is susceptible of affirmation and negation; and those propositions concerning it which describe the real relations of things may in a certain sense, whether we be or be not aware that they do so, be said to be true. Taken in this sense, truth is immutable. He that speaks of its immutability does nothing more than predict with greater or less probability, and say, 'This is what I believe, and what all reasonable beings, till they shall fall short of me in their degree of information, will continue to believe.'

knowledge and the thinking principle in man cannot be brought into contact, if, however great be the improvement of his reason, he will not the less certainly in many cases act in a way irrational and absurd, this consideration must greatly overcloud the prospect of the moral reformer.

There is another consequence that will flow from the vulgarly received doctrine upon this subject. If man be, by the very constitution of his nature, the subject of opinion, and if truth and reason when properly displayed give us a complete hold upon his choice, then the search of the political enquirer will be much simplified. Then we have only to discover what form of civil society is most conformable to reason, and we may rest assured that, as soon as men shall be persuaded from conviction to adopt that form, they will have acquired to themselves an invaluable benefit. But, if reason be frequently inadequate to its task, if there be an opposite principle in man resting upon its own ground, and maintaining a separate jurisdiction, the most rational principles of society may be rendered abortive, it may be necessary to call in mere sensible causes to encounter causes of the same nature, folly may be the fittest instrument to effect the purposes of wisdom, and vice to disseminate and establish the public benefit. In that case the salutary prejudices and useful delusions[7] (as they have been called) of aristocracy, the glittering diadem, the magnificent canopy, the ribands, stars and titles of an illustrious rank, may at last be found the fittest instruments for guiding and alluring to his proper ends the savage, man.*

Such is the nature of the question to be examined, and such its connection with the enquiry concerning the influence of political institutions.

The more accurately to conceive the topic before us, it is necessary to observe that it relates to the voluntary actions of man.

The distinction between voluntary and involuntary

* Book V, Chap. XV.

action, if properly stated, is exceedingly simple. That action is involuntary which takes place in us either without foresight on our part, or contrary to the full bent of our inclinations. Thus, if a child or a person of mature age burst into tears in a manner unexpected or unforeseen by himself, or if he burst into tears though his pride or any other principle make him exert every effort to restrain them, this action is involuntary. Voluntary action is where the event is foreseen previously to its occurrence, and the hope or fear of that event forms the excitement, or, as it is most frequently termed, the motive,* inducing us, if hope be the passion, to endeavour to forward, and, if fear, to endeavour to prevent it. It is this motion, in this manner generated, to which we annex the idea of voluntariness. Let it be observed that the word action is here used in the sense of natural philosophers, as descriptive of a charge taking place in any part of the universe, without entering into the question whether that change be necessary or free.

Now let us consider what are the inferences that immediately result from the above simple and unquestionable explanation of voluntary action.

'Voluntary action is accompanied with foresight; the hope or fear of a certain event is its motive.' But foresight is not an affair of simple and immediate impulse: it implies a series of observations so extensive as to enable us from like antecedents to infer like consequents. Voluntary action is occasioned by the idea of consequences to result. Wine is set before me, and I fill my glass. I do this either because I foresee that the flavour will be agreeable to my palate, or that its effect will be to produce gaiety and exhilaration, or that my drinking it will prove the

---

*The term motive is applicable in all cases where the regular operations of inanimate matter are superseded by the interference of intelligence. Whatever sensation or perception in the mind is capable of influencing this interference is called motive. Motive therefore is applicable to the case of all actions originating in sensation or perception, whether voluntary or involuntary.

kindness and good humour I feel towards the company with which I am engaged. If in any case my action in filling dwindle into mechanical or semi-mechanical, done with little or no adverting of the mind to its performance, it so far becomes an involuntary action. But, if every voluntary action be performed for the sake of its consequences, then in every voluntary action there is comparison and judgement. Every such action proceeds upon the apprehended truth of some proposition. The mind decides 'this is good' or 'desirable'; and immediately upon that decision, if accompanied with a persuasion that we are competent to accomplish this good or desirable thing, the limbs proceed to their office. The mind decides 'this is better than something else'; either wine and cordials are before me, and I choose the wine rather than the cordials; or the wine only is presented or thought of, and I decide that to take the wine is better than to abstain from it. Thus it appears that in every voluntary action there is preference or choice, which indeed are synonymous terms.

This full elucidation of the nature of voluntary action enables us to proceed a step further. Hence it appears that the voluntary actions of men in all cases originate in their opinions. The actions of men, it will readily be admitted, originate in the state of their minds immediately previous to those actions. Actions therefore which are preceded by a judgement 'this is good', or 'this is desirable', originate in the state of judgement or opinion upon that subject. It may happen that the opinion may be exceedingly fugitive; it may have been preceded by aversion and followed by remorse; but it was unquestionably the opinion of the mind at the instant in which the action commenced.

It is by no means uninstructive to remark how those persons who seem most to have discarded the use of their reason have frequently fallen by accident, as it were, upon important truths. There has been a sect of Christians who taught that the only point which was to determine

the future everlasting happiness or misery of mankind
was their faith. Being pressed with the shocking immorality of their doctrine, and the cruel and tyrannical
character it imputed to the author of the universe, some
of the most ingenious of them have explained themselves
thus.

'Man is made up of two parts, his internal sentiments
and his external conduct. Between these two there is a
close and indissoluble connection; as are his sentiments,
so is his conduct. Faith, that faith which alone entitles to
salvation, is indeed a man's opinion, but not every
opinion he may happen openly to profess, not every
opinion which floats idly in his brain, and is only recollected when he is gravely questioned upon the subject.
Faith is the opinion that is always present to the mind,
that lives in the memory, or at least infallibly suggests
itself when any article of conduct is considered with which
it is materially connected. Faith is that strong, permanent
and lively persuasion of the understanding with which
no delusive temptations will ever be able successfully to
contend. Faith modifies the conduct, gives a new direction
to the dispositions, and renders the whole character pure
and heavenly. But heavenly dispositions only can fit a
man for the enjoyment of heaven. Heaven in reality is
not so properly a place as a state of the mind; and, if a
wicked man could be introduced into the society of
'saints made perfect', he would be miserable. God therefore, when he requires faith alone as a qualification for
heaven, is so far from being arbitrary that he merely executes the laws of reason, and does the only thing it was
possible for him to do.'

In this system there are enormous absurdities, but the
view it exhibits of the source of voluntary action, sufficiently corresponds with the analysis we have given of the
subject.

The author of the *Characteristics* has illustrated this
branch of the nature of man in a very masterly manner.
He observes: 'There are few who think always consist-

ently, or according to one certain hypothesis upon any subject so abstruse and intricate as the cause of all things, and the œconomy or government of the universe. For it is evident in the case of the most devout people, even by their own confession, that there are times when their faith hardly can support them in the belief of a supreme wisdom; and that they are often tempted to judge disadvantageously of a providence and just administration in the whole.

'That alone therefore is to be called a man's opinion, which is of any other the most habitual to him, and occurs upon most occasions. So that it is hard to pronounce certainly of any man, that he is an atheist, because, unless his whole thoughts are at all seasons and on all occasions steadily bent against all supposition or imagination of design in things, he is no perfect atheist. In the same manner, if a man's thoughts are not at all times steady and resolute against all imagination of chance, fortune, or ill design in things, he is no perfect theist. But, if any one believes more of chance and confusion than of design, he is to be esteemed more an atheist than a theist [this is surely not a very accurate or liberal view of the atheistical system], from that which most predominates, or has the ascendant. And, in case he believes more of the prevalency of an ill designing principle than of a good one, he is rather a demonist, and may be justly so called, from the side to which the balance or his judgement most inclines.'*

From this view of the subject we shall easily be led to perceive how little the fact of the variableness and inconstancy of human conduct is incompatible with the principle here delivered, that the voluntary actions of men in all cases originate in their opinions. The persuasion that exists in the mind of the drunkard in committing his first act of intoxication, that in so doing he complies with the most cogent and irresistible reasons capable of being assigned upon the subject, may be ex-

* *Characteristics*; Treatise IV, B, I, Part i, § 2.

ceedingly temporary; but it is the clear and unequivocal persuasion of his mind at the moment that he determines upon the action. The thoughts of the murderer will frequently be in a state of the most tempestuous fluctuation; he may make and unmake his diabolical purpose fifty times in an hour; his mind may be torn a thousand ways by terror and fury, malignity and remorse. But, whenever his resolution is formed, it is formed upon the suggestions of the rational faculty; and, when he ultimately works up his mind to the perpetration, he is then most strongly impressed with the superior recommendations of the conduct he pursues. One of the fallacies by which we are most frequently induced to a conduct which our habitual judgement disapproves is that our attention becomes so engrossed by a particular view of the subject as wholly to forget, for the moment, those considerations which at other times were accustomed to determine our opinion. In such cases it frequently happens that the neglected consideration recurs the instant the hurry of action has subsided, and we stand astonished at our own infatuation and folly.

This reasoning, however clear and irresistible it may appear, is yet exposed to one very striking objection. 'According to the ideas here delivered, men always proceed in their voluntary actions upon judgements extant to their understanding. Such judgements must be attended with consciousness; and, were this hypothesis a sound one, nothing could be more easy than for a man in all cases to assign the precise reason that induced him to any particular action. The human mind would then be a very simple machine, always aware of the grounds upon which it proceeded, and self-deception would be impossible. But this statement is completely in opposition to experience and history. Ask a man the reason why he puts on his clothes, why he eats his dinner, or performs any other ordinary action of his life. He immediately hesitates, endeavours to recollect himself, and often assigns a reason the most remote from what the true philosophy of motive would have led us to expect. Nothing is more clear than that of the moving cause of this action was not expressly present to his apprehension at the time he performed it. Self-deception is so far from impossible that it is one of the most ordinary phenomena with which we are acquainted. Nothing is more usual than for a man to impute his actions to honourable motives, when it is nearly demonstrable that they flowed from some corrupt and contemptible source. On the other hand many persons suppose themselves to be worse than an impartial spectator will find any good reason to believe them. A penetrating observer will frequently be able to convince his neighbour that upon such an occasion he was actuated by motives very different from what he imagined. Philosophers to this hour dispute whether human beings in their most virtuous exertions are under the power of disinterested benevolence, or merely of an enlightened self-interest. Here then we are presented, in one or other of these sets of philosophers, with a striking instance of men's acting from motives diametrically opposite to those which they suppose to be the guides of their conduct. Self-examination is to a proverb one of the most arduous of those tasks which true virtue imposes. Are not these facts in express contradiction to the doctrine that the voluntary actions of men in all cases originate in the judgements of the understanding?'

Undoubtedly the facts which have been here enumerated appear to be strictly true. To determine how far they affect the doctrine of the present chapter, it is necessary to return to our analysis of the phenomena of the human mind. Hitherto we have considered the actions of human beings only under two classes, voluntary and involuntary. In strictness however there is a third class, which belongs to neither, yet partakes of the nature of both.

We have already defined voluntary action to be that of which certain consequences, foreseen, and considered either as objects of desire or aversion, are the motive.

Foresight and volition are inseparable. But what is foreseen must, by the very terms, be present to the understanding. Every action therefore, so far as it is perfectly voluntary, flows solely from the decision of the judgement. But the actions above cited, such as relate to our garments and our food, are only imperfectly voluntary.*

In respect of volition there appear to be two stages in the history of the human mind. Foresight is the result of experience; therefore foresight, and by parity of reasoning volition, cannot enter into the earliest actions of a human being. As soon however as the infant perceives the connection between certain attitudes and gestures and the circumstance of receiving such, for example, he is brought to desire those preliminaries for the sake of that result. Here, so far as relates to volition and the judgement of the understanding, the action is as simple as can well be imagined. Yet, even in this instance, the motive may be said to be complex. Habit, or custom, has its share. This habit is founded in actions originally involuntary and mechanical, and modifies after various methods such of our actions as are voluntary.

But there are habits of a second sort. In proportion as our experience enlarges, the subjects of voluntary action become more numerous. In this state of the human being, he soon comes to perceive a considerable similarity between situation and situation. In consequence he feels inclined to abridge the process of deliberation, and to act today conformably to the determination of yesterday. Thus the understanding fixes for itself resting places, is no longer a novice, and is not at the trouble continually to go back and revise the original reasons which determined it to a course of action. Thus the man acquires habits from which it is very difficult to wean him, and which he obeys without being able to assign either to him-

* This distribution is in substance the same as that of Hartley[9]; but is here introduced without any attention to adopt the peculiarities of his phraseology. *Observations on Man*, Chap. I, § iii, Prop. 21.

self or others any explicit reason for his proceeding. This is the history of prepossession and prejudice.

Let us consider how much there is of voluntary, and how much of involuntary in this species of action. Let the instance be of a man going to church today. He has been accustomed, suppose, to a certain routine of this kind from his childhood. Most undoubtedly then, in performing this function today, his motive does not singly consist of inducements present to his understanding. His feelings are not of the same nature as those of a man who should be persuaded by a train of reasoning to perform that function for the first time in his life. His case is partly similar to that of a scholar who has gone through a course of geometry, and who now believes the truth of the propositions upon the testimony of his memory, though the proofs are by no means present to his understanding. Thus the person in question is partly induced to go to church by reasons which once appeared sufficient to his understanding, and the effects of which remain, though the reasons are now forgotten, or at least are not continually recollected. He goes partly for the sake of decorum, character, and to secure the good will of his neighbours. A part of his inducement also perhaps is that his parents accustomed him to go to church at first, from the mere force of authority, and that the omission of a habit to which we have been formed is apt to fit awkwardly and uneasily upon the human mind. Thus it happens that a man who should scrupulously examine his own conduct in going to church would find great difficulty in satisfying his mind as to the precise motive, or proportion contributed by different motives, which maintained his adherence to that practice.

It is probable however that, when he goes to church, he determines that this action is right, proper or expedient, referring for the reasons which prove this rectitude or expediency to the complex impression which remains in his mind, from the inducements that at different times inclined him to that practice. It is still more reasonable to believe that, when he sets out, there is an express volition, foresight or apprehended motive inducing him to that particular action, and that he proceeds in such a direction because he knows it leads to the church. Now, so much of this action as proceeds from actually existing foresight and apprehended motive, it is proper to call perfectly voluntary. So much as proceeds upon a motive, out of sight, and the operation of which depends upon habit, is imperfectly voluntary.

This sort of habit however must be admitted to retain something of the nature of voluntariness for two reasons. First, it proceeds upon judgement, or apprehended motives, though the reasons of that judgement be out of sight and forgotten; at the time the individual performed the first action of the kind, his proceeding was perfectly voluntary. Secondly, the custom of language authorizes us in denominating every action as in some degree voluntary which a volition, foresight or apprehended motive in contrary direction might have prevented from taking place.

Perhaps no action of a man arrived at years of maturity is, in the sense above defined, perfectly voluntary; as there is no demonstration in the higher branches of the mathematics which contains the whole of its proof within itself, and does not depend upon former propositions, the proofs of which are not present to the mind of the learner. The subtlety of the human mind in this respect is incredible. Many single actions, if carefully analysed and traced to their remotest source, would be found to be the complex result of different motives, to the amount perhaps of some hundreds.

In the meantime it is obvious to remark that the perfection of the human character consists in approaching as nearly as possible to the perfectly voluntary state. We ought to be upon all occasions prepared to render a reason of our actions. We should remove ourselves to the furthest distance from the state of mere inanimate machines, acted upon by causes of which they have no understanding. We should be cautious of thinking it a sufficient reason for an action that we are accustomed to perform it, and that we once thought it right. The human understanding has so powerful a tendency to improvement that it is more than probable that, in many instances, the arguments which once appeared to us sufficient would upon re-examination appear inadequate and futile. We should therefore subject them to perpetual revisal. In our speculative opinions and our practical principles we should never consider the book of enquiry as shut. We should accustom ourselves not to forget the reasons that produced our determination, but be ready upon all occasions clearly to announce and fully to enumerate them.

Having thus explained the nature of human actions, involuntary, imperfectly voluntary and voluntary, let us consider how far this explanation affects the doctrine of the present chapter. Now it should seem that the great practical political principle remains as entire as ever. Still volition and foresight, in their strict and accurate construction, are inseparable. All the most important occasions of our lives are capable of being subjected at pleasure to a decision, as nearly as possible, perfectly voluntary. Still it remains true that, when the understanding clearly perceives rectitude, propriety and eligibility to belong to a certain conduct, and so long as it has that perception, that conduct will infallibly be adopted. A perception of truth will inevitably be produced by a clear evidence brought home to the understanding, and the constancy of the perception will be proportioned to the apprehended value of the thing perceived. Reason therefore and conviction still appear to be the proper instrument, and the sufficient instrument for regulating the actions of mankind.

Having sufficiently established the principle that in all cases of volition we act, not from impulse, but opinion, there is a further obstacle to be removed before this reasoning can be usefully applied to the subject of political melioration. It may be objected, by a person who should admit the force of the above arguments, 'that little was gained by this exposition to the cause it was intended to promote. Whether or no the actions of men frequently arise, as some authors have asserted, from immediate impression, it cannot however be denied that the perturbations of sense frequently seduce the judgement, and that the ideas and temporary notions they produce are too strong for any force that can be brought against them. But, what man is now in this respect he will always to a certain degree remain. He will always have senses, and, in spite of all the attempts which can be made to mortify them, their pleasures will always be accompanied with irritation and allurement. Hence it appears that all ideas of vast and extraordinary improvement in man are visionary, that he will always remain in some degree the dupe of illusion, and that reason, and absolute, impartial truth, can never hope to possess him entire.'

The first observation that suggests itself upon this statement is that the points already established tend in some degree to set this new question in a clearer light. From them it may be inferred that the contending forces of reason and sense, in the power they exercise over our conduct, at least pass through the same medium, and assume the same form. It is opinion contending with opinion, and judgement with judgement; and this consideration is not unattended with encouragement. When we discourse of the comparative powers of appetite and reason, we speak of those actions which have the consent of the mind, and partake of the nature of voluntary. The question neither is nor deserves to be respecting cases where no choice is exerted, and no preference shown. Every man is aware that the cases into which volition enters either for a part or the whole are sufficiently numerous to decide upon all that is most important in the events of our life. It follows therefore that, in the contention of sense and reason, it cannot be improbable to hope that the opinion which is intrinsically the best founded shall ultimately prevail.

But let us examine a little minutely these pleasures of sense, the attractions of which are supposed to be so irresistible. In reality they are in no way enabled to maintain their hold upon us but by means of the adscititious ornaments with which they are assiduously connected. Reduce them to their true nakedness, and they would be generally despised. Where almost is the man who would sit down with impatient eagerness to the most splendid feast, the most exquisite viands and highly flavoured wines, 'taste after taste upheld with kindliest change',* if he must sit down alone, and it were not relieved and assisted by the more exalted charms of society, conversation and mutual benevolence? Strip the commerce of the sexes of all its attendant circumstances; and the effect would be similar. Tell a man that all women, so far as sense is concerned, are nearly alike. Bid him therefore take a partner without any attention to the symmetry of her person, her vivacity, the voluptuous softness of her temper, the affectionate kindness of her feelings, her imagination or her wit. You would probably instantly convince him that the commerce itself, which by superficial observers is put for the whole, is the least important branch of the complicated consideration to which it belongs. It is probable that he who should form himself with the greatest care upon a system of solitary sensualism would come at last to a decision not very different from that which Epicurus is said to have adopted in favour of fresh herbs and water from the spring.

'But let it be confessed that the pleasures of sense are unimportant and trivial. It is next to be asked whether, trifling as they are, they may not nevertheless possess a delusive and treacherous power by means of which they may often be enabled to overcome every opposition?'

The better to determine this question, let us suppose a man to be engaged in the progressive voluptuousness of

* Milton: *Paradise Lost*, Book V.

the most sensual scene. Here, if ever, we may expect sensation to be triumphant. Passion is in this case in its full career. He impatiently shuts out every consideration that may disturb his enjoyment; moral views and dissuasives can no longer obtrude themselves into his mind; he resigns himself, without power of resistance, to his predominant idea. Alas, in this situation, nothing is so easy as to extinguish his sensuality! Tell him at this moment that his father is dead, that he has lost or gained a considerable sum of money, or even that his favourite horse is stolen from the meadow, and his whole passion shall be instantly annihilated: So vast is the power which a mere proposition possesses over the mind of man. So conscious are we of the precariousness of the fascination of the senses that upon such occasions we provide against the slightest interruption. If our little finger ached, we might probably immediately bid adieu to the empire of this supposed almighty power. It is said to be an experiment successfully made by sailors and persons in that class of society, to lay a wager with their comrades that the sexual intercourse shall not take place between them and their bedfellow the ensuing night, and to trust to their veracity for a confession of the event. The only means probably by which any man ever succeeds in indulging the pleasures of sense, in contradiction to the habitual persuasion of his judgement, is by contriving to forget everything that can be offered against them. If, notwithstanding all his endeavours, the unwished for idea intrudes, the indulgence instantly becomes impossible. Is it to be supposed that the power of sensual allurement, which must be carefully kept alive, and which the slightest accident overthrows, can be invincible only to the artillery of reason, and that the most irresistible considerations of justice, interest and happiness will never be able habitually to control it?

To consider the subject in another point of view. It seems to be a strange absurdity to hear men assert that the attractions of sensual pleasure are irresistible, in contradition to the multiplied experience of all ages and countries. Are all good stories of our nature false? Did no man ever resist temptation? On the contrary, have not all the considerations which have power over our hopes, our fears, or our weaknesses been, in competition with a firm and manly virtue, employed in vain? But what has been done may be done again. What has been done by individuals cannot be impossible, in a widely different state of society, to be done by the whole species.

The system we are here combating, of the irresistible power of sensual allurements, has been numerously supported, and a variety of arguments has been adduced in its behalf. Among other things it has been remarked 'that, as the human mind has no innate and original principles, so all the information it has is derived from sensation; and everything that passes within it is either direct impression upon our external organs, or the substance of such impressions modified and refined through certain intellectual strainers and alembics. It is therefore reasonable to conclude that the original substance should be most powerful in its properties, and the pleasures of external sense more genuine than any other pleasure. Every sensation is, by its very nature, accompanied with the idea of pleasure or pain in a vigorous or feeble degree. The only thing which can or ought to excite desire is happiness or agreeable sensation. It is impossible that the hand can be stretched out to obtain anything except so far as it is considered as desirable; and to be desirable is the same thing as to have a tendency to communicate pleasure. Thus, after all the complexities of philosophy, we are brought back to this simple and irresistible proposition, that man is an animal purely sensual. Hence it follows that in all his transactions much must depend upon immediate impression, and little is to be attributed to the generalities of ratiocination.'

All the premises in the objection here stated are unquestionably true. Man is just such an animal as the objection describes. Everything within him that has a tendency to voluntary action is an affair of external or internal sense, and has relation to pleasure or pain. But it does not follow from hence that the pleasures of our external organs are more exquisite than any other pleasures. It is by no means unexampled for the result of a combination of materials to be more excellent than the materials themselves. Let us consider the materials by means of which an admirable poem, or, if you will, the author of an admirable poem, is constructed, and we shall immediately acknowledge this to be the case. In reality the pleasures of a savage, or, which is much the same thing, of a brute, are feeble indeed compared with those of the man of civilization and refinement. Our sensual pleasures, commonly so called, would be almost universally despised had we not the art to combine them with the pleasures of intellect and cultivation. No man ever performed an act of exalted benevolence without having sufficient reason to know, at least so long as the sensation was present to his mind, that all the gratifications of appetite were contemptible in the comparison. That which gives the last zest to our enjoyments is the approbation of our own minds, the consciousness that the exertion we have made was such as was called for by impartial justice and reason; and this consciousness will be clear and satisfying in proportion as our decision in that respect is unmixed with error. Our perceptions can never be so luminous and accurate in the belief of falsehood as of truth.

The great advantage possessed by the allurements of sense is 'that the ideas suggested by them are definite and precise, while those which deal in generalities are apt to be faint and obscure. The difference is like that between things absent and present; of the recommendations possessed by the latter we have a more vivid perception, and seem to have a better assurance of the probability of their attainment. These circumstances must necessarily, in the comparison instituted by the mind in all similar cases, to a certain degree incline the balance towards that side. Add to which, that what is present forces itself upon our attention, while that which is absent depends for its recurrence upon the capriciousness of memory.'

But these advantages are seen upon the very face of them to be of a precarious nature. If my ideas of virtue, benevolence and justice, or whatever it is that ought to restrain me from an improper leaning to the pleasures of sense, be now less definite and precise, they may be gradually and unlimitedly improved. If I do not now sufficiently perceive all the recommendations they possess, and their clear superiority over the allurements of sense, there is surely no natural impossibility in my being made to understand a distinct proposition, or in my being fully convinced by an unanswerable argument. As to recollection, that is certainly a faculty of the mind which is capable of improvement; and the point, of which I have been once intimately convinced and have had a lively and profound impression, will not easily be forgotten when the period of action shall arrive.

It has been said 'that a rainy day will frequently convert a man of valour into a coward'. If that should be the case, there is no presumption in affirming that his courage was produced by very slight and inadequate motives. How long would a sensation of this kind be able to hold out against the idea of the benefits to arise from his valour, safety to his family and children, defeat to an unjust and formidable assailant, and freedom and felicity to be secured to his country? In reality, the atmosphere, instead of considerably affecting the mass of mankind, affects in an eminent degree only a small part of that mass. The majority are either above or below it; are either too gross to feel strongly these minute variations, or too busy to attend to them. The case is to a considerable degree the same with the rest of our animal sensations. 'Indigestion,' it has been said, 'perhaps a fit of the tooth ache, renders a man incapable of strong thinking and spirited exertion.' How far would they be able to maintain their ground against an unexpected piece of intelligence of the most delightful nature?

Pain is probably more formidable in its attacks upon us, and more exquisitely felt than any species of bodily pleasure. Yet all history affords us examples where pain has been contemned and defied by the energies of intellectual resolution. Do we not read of Mutius Scaevola who suffered his hand to be destroyed by fire without betraying any symptom of emotion, and archbishop Cranmer who endured the same trial two hundred years ago in our own country? Is it not recorded of Anaxarchus that, while suffering the most excruciating tortures, he exclaimed, 'Beat on, tyrant! Thou mayest destroy the shell of Anaxarchus, but thou canst not touch Anaxarchus himself'? The very savage Indians sing amidst the wanton tortures that are inflicted on them, and tauntingly provoke their tormentors to more ingenious cruelty. When we read such stories, we recognize in them the genuine characteristics of man. Man is not a vegetable to be governed by sensations of heat and cold, dryness and moisture. He is a reasonable creature, capable of perceiving what is eligible and right, of fixing indelibly certain principles upon his mind, and adhering inflexibly to the resolutions he has made.

Let us attend for a moment to the general result of the preceding discussions. The tendency of the whole is to ascertain an important principle in the science of the human mind. If the arguments here adduced to be admitted to be valid, it necessarily follows that whatever can be adequately brought home to the conviction of the understanding may be depended upon as affording a secure hold upon the conduct. We are no longer at liberty to consider man as divided between two independent principles, or to imagine that his inclinations are in any case inaccessible through the medium of his reason. We find the principle within us to be uniform and simple; in consequence of which we are entitled to conclude that it is in every respect the proper subject of education and persuasion, and is susceptible of unlimited improvement. There is no conduct, in itself reasonable, which the refutation of error, and dissipating of uncertainty, will not make appear to be such. There is no conduct which can be shown to be reasonable, the reasons of which may not sooner or later be made impressive, irresistible and matter of habitual recollection. Lastly, there is no conduct, the reasons of which are thus conclusive and thus communicated, which will not infallibly and uniformly be adopted by the man to whom they are communicated.

It may not be improper to attend a little to the light which may be derived from these speculations upon certain maxims, almost universally received, but which, as they convey no distinct ideas, may be productive of mischief, and can scarcely be productive of good.

The first of these is that the passions ought to be purified, but not to be eradicated. Another, conveying nearly the same lesson, but in different words, is that passion is not to be conquered by reason, but by bringing some other passion into contention with it.

The word passion is a term extremely vague in its signification. It is used principally in three senses. It either represents the ardour and vehemence of mind with which any object is purified; or secondly, that temporary persuasion of excellence and desirableness which accompanies any action performed by us contrary to our more customary and usual habits of thinking; or lastly, those external modes or necessities to which the whole human species is alike subject, such as hunger, the passion between the sexes, and others. In which of these senses is the word to be understood in the maxims above stated?

In the first sense, it has sufficiently appeared that none of our sensations, or, which is the same thing, none of our ideas, are unaccompanied with a consciousness of pleasure or pain; consequently all our volitions are attended with complacence or aversion. In this sense without doubt passion cannot be eradicated; but in this sense also passion is so far from being incompatible with reason that it is inseparable from it. Virtue, sincerity, justice and all those principles which are begotten and cherished in

us by a due exercise of reason will never be very strenuously espoused till they are ardently loved; that is, till
their value is clearly perceived and adequately understood. In this sense nothing is necessary but to show us
that a thing is truly good and worthy to be desired, in
order to excite in us a passion for its attainment. If therefore this be the meaning of passion in the above proposition, it is true that passion ought not to be eradicated,
but it is equally true that it cannot be eradicated: it is
true that the only way to conquer one passion is by the
introduction of another; but it is equally true that, if we
employ our rational faculties, we cannot fail of thus
conquering our erroneous propensities. The maxims
therefore are nugatory.

In the second sense, our passions are ambition, avarice,
the love of power, the love of fame, envy, revenge and
innumerable others. Miserable indeed would be our condition if we could only expel one bad passion by another
of the same kind, and there was no way of rooting out
delusion from the mind but by substituting another delusion in its place. But it has been demonstrated at large
that this is not the case. Truth is not less powerful, or
less friendly to ardent exertion, than error, and needs not
fear its encounter. Falsehood is not, as such a principle
would suppose, the only element in which the human
mind can exist, so that, if the space which the mind
occupies be too much rarefied and cleared, its existence
or health will be in some degree injured. On the contrary,
we need not fear any sinister consequences from the
subversion of error, and introducing as much truth into
the mind as we can possibly accumulate. All those notions
by which we are accustomed to ascribe to anything a
value which it does not really possess should be eradicated
without mercy; and truth, a sound and just estimate of
things, which is not less favourable to zeal or activity,
should be earnestly and incessantly cultivated.

In the third sense of the word passion, as it describes
the result of those circumstances which are common to

the whole species, such as hunger and the propensity to the intercourse of the sexes, it seems sufficiently reasonable to say that no attempt ought to be made to eradicate them. But this sentiment was hardly worth the formality of a maxim. So far as these propensities ought to be conquered or restrained, there is no reason why this should not be effected by the due exercise of the understanding. From these illustrations it is sufficiently apparent that the care recommended to us not to extinguish or seek to extinguish our passions is founded in a confused or mistaken view of the subject.

Another maxim not inferior in reputation to those above recited is that of following nature. But the term nature here is still more loose and unintelligibble than the term passion was before. If it be meant that we ought to accommodate ourselves to hunger and the other appetites which are common to our species, this is probably true. But these appetites, some of them in particular, lead to excess, and the mischief with which they are pregnant is to be corrected, not by consulting our appetites, but our reason. If it be meant that we should follow instinct, it has been proved that we have no instincts. The advocates of this maxim are apt to consider whatever now exists among mankind as inherent and perpetual, and to conclude that this is to be maintained, not in proportion as it can be shown to be reasonable, but because it is natural. Thus it has been said that man is naturally a religious animal, and for this reason, and not in proportion to our power of demonstrating the being of a God or the truth of Christianity, religion is to be maintained. Thus again it has been called natural that men should form themselves into immense tribes or nations, and go to war with each other. Thus persons of narrow views and observation regard everything as natural and right that happens, however capriciously or for however short a time, to prevail in the society in which they live. The only things which can be said to compose the nature or constitution of man are our external structure, which itself is capable of being modified with indefinite variety; the appetites and impressions growing out of that structure; and the capacity of combining ideas and inferring conclusions. The appetites common to the species we cannot wholly destroy: the faculty of reason it would be absurd systematically to counteract, since it is only by some sort of reasoning, bad or good, that we can so much as adopt any system. In this sense therefore no doubt we ought to follow nature, that is, to employ our understandings and increase our discernment. But, by conforming ourselves to the principles of our constitution in this respect, we most effectually exclude all following, or implicit assent. If we would fully comport ourselves in a manner correspondent to our properties and powers, we must bring everything to the standard of reason. Nothing must be admitted either as principle or precept that will not support this trial. Nothing must be sustained because it is ancient, because we have been accustomed to regard it as sacred, or because it has been unusual to bring its validity into question. Finally, if by following nature be understood that we must fix our preference upon things that will conduce to human happiness, in this there is some truth. But the truth it contains is extremely darkened by the phraseology in which it is couched. We must consider our external structure so far as relates to the mere question of our preservation. As to the rest, whatever will make a reasonable nature happy will make us happy; and our preference ought to be bestowed upon that species of pleasure which has most independence and most animation.

The corollaries respecting political truth, deducible from the simple proposition, which seems clearly established by the reasonings of the present chapter, that the voluntary actions of men are in all instances conformable to the deductions of their understanding, are of the highest importance. Hence we may infer what are the hopes and prospects of human improvement. The doctrine which may be founded upon these principles may perhaps best be expressed in the five following propositions: Sound reasoning and truth, when adequately communicated, must always be victorious over error: Sound reasoning and truth are capable of being so communicated: Truth is omnipotent: The vices and moral weakness of man are not invincible: Man is perfectible, or in other words susceptible of perpetual improvement.

These propositions will be found in part synonymous with each other. But the time of the enquirer will not be unprofitably spent in copiously clearing up the foundations of moral and political system. It is extremely beneficial that truth should be viewed on all sides, and examined under different aspects. The propositions are even little more than so many different modes of stating the principal topic of this chapter. But, if they will not admit each of a distinct train of arguments in its support, it may not however be useless to bestow upon each a short illustration.

The first of these propositions is so evident that it needs only be stated in order to the being universally admitted. Is there anyone who can imagine that, when sound argument and sophistry are fairly brought into comparison, the victory can be doubtful? Sophistry may assume a plausible appearance, and contrive to a certain extent to bewilder the understanding. But it is one of the prerogatives of truth, to follow it in its mazes and strip it of disguise. Nor does any difficulty from this consideration interfere with the establishment of the present proposition. We suppose truth not merely to be exhibited, but adequately communicated; that is, in other words, distinctly apprehended by the person to whom it is addressed. In this case the victory is too sure to admit of being controverted by the most inveterate scepticism.

The second proposition is that sound reasoning and truth are capable of being adequately communicated by one man to another. This proposition may be understood of such communication, either as it affects the individual, or the species. First of the individual.

In order to its due application in this point of view, opportunity for the communication must necessarily be supposed. The incapacity of human intellect at present requires that this opportunity should be of long duration or repeated recurrence. We do not always know how to communicate all the evidence we are capable of communicating in a single conversation, and much less in a single instant. But, if the communicator be sufficiently master of his subject, and if the truth be altogether on his side, he must ultimately succeed in his undertaking. We suppose him to have sufficient urbanity to conciliate the good will, and sufficient energy to engage the attention, of the party concerned. In that case, there is no prejudice, no blind reverence for established systems, no false fear of the inferences to be drawn, that can resist him. He will encounter these one after the other, and he will encounter them with success. Our prejudices, our undue reverence, and imaginary fears, flow out of some views the mind has been induced to entertain; they are founded in the belief of some propositions. But every one of these propositions is capable of being refuted. The champion we describe proceeds from point to point; if in any his success have been doubtful, that he will retrace and put out of the reach of mistake; and it is evidently impossible that with such qualifications and such perseverance he should not ultimately accomplish his purpose.

Such is the appearance which this proposition assumes when examined in a loose and practical view. In strict consideration it will not admit of debate. Man is a rational being. If there be any man who is incapable of making inferences for himself, or of understanding, when stated in the most explicit terms, the inferences of another, him we consider as an abortive production, and not in strictness belonging to the human species. It is absurd therefore to say that sound reasoning and truth cannot be communicated by one man to another. Whenever in any case he fails, it is that he is not sufficiently laborious, patient and clear. We suppose of course the person who undertakes to communicate the truth really to possess it, and be master of his subject; for it is scarcely worth an observation to say that that which he has not himself he cannot communicate to another.

If truth therefore can be brought home to the conviction of the individual, let us see how it stands with the public or the world. Now in the first place, it is extremely clear that, if no individual can resist the force of truth, it can only be necessary to apply this proposition from individual to individual, and we shall at length comprehend the whole. Thus the affirmation in its literal sense is completely established.

With respect to the chance of success, this will depend, first, upon the precluding all extraordinary convulsions of nature, and after this upon the activity and energy of those to whose hands the sacred cause of truth may be entrusted. It is apparent that, if justice be done to its merits, it includes in it the indestructible germ of ultimate victory. Every new convert that is made to its cause, if he be taught its excellence as well as its reality, is a fresh apostle to extend its illuminations through a wider sphere. In this respect it resembles the motion of a falling body, which increases its rapidity in proportion to the squares of the distances. Add to which that when a convert to truth has been adequately informed it is barely possible that he should ever fail in his adherence; whereas error contains in it the principle of its own mortality. Thus the advocates of falsehood and mistake must continually diminish, and the well informed adherents of truth incessantly multiply.

It has sometimes been affirmed that, whenever a question is ably brought forward for examination, the decision of the human species must ultimately be on the right side. But this proposition is to be understood with allowances. Civil policy, magnificent emoluments and sinister motives may upon many occasions, by distracting the attention, cause the worse reason to pass as if it were the better. It is not absolutely certain that, in the controversy brought forward by Clarke[10] and Whiston[11] against the doctrine of the Trinity, or by Collins[12] and Woolston[13] against the Christian revelation, the innovators had altogether the worst of the argument. Yet fifty years after the agitation of these controversies, their effects could scarcely be traced, and things appeared on all sides as if the controversies had never existed. Perhaps it will be said that, though the effects of truth may be obscured for a time, they will break out in the sequel with double lustre. But this at least depends upon circumstances. No comet must come in the meantime and sweep away the human species: no Attila must have it in his power once again to lead back the flood of barbarism to deluge the civilized world: and the disciples, or at least the books of the original champions must remain, or their discoveries and demonstrations must be nearly lost to the world.

The third of the propositions enumerated is that truth is omnipotent. This proposition, which is convenient for its brevity, must be understood with limitations. It would be absurd to affirm that truth, unaccompanied by the evidence which proves it to be such, or when that evidence is partially and imperfectly stated, has any such property. But it has sufficiently appeared from the arguments already adduced that truth, when adequately communicated, is, so far as relates to the conviction of the understanding, irresistible. There may indeed be propositions which, though true in themselves, may be beyond the sphere of human knowledge, or respecting which human beings have not yet discovered sufficient arguments for their support. In that case, though true in themselves, they are not truths to us. The reasoning by which they are attempted to be established is not sound reasoning. It may perhaps be found that the human mind is not capable of arriving at absolute certainty upon any subject of enquiry; and it must be admitted that human science is attended with all degrees of certainty, from the highest moral evidence to the slightest balance of probability. But human beings are capable of apprehending and weighing all these degrees; and to know the exact quantity of probability which I ought to ascribe to any proposition may be said to be in one sense the possessing certain knowledge. It would further be absurd, if we regard truth in relation to its empire over our conduct, to suppose that it is not limited in its operations by the faculties of our frame. It may be compared to a connoisseur who, however consummate be his talents, can extract from a given instrument only such tones as that instrument will afford. But, within these limits, the deduction which forms the principal substance of this chapter proves to us that whatever is brought home to the conviction of the understanding, so long as it is present to the mind, possesses an undisputed empire over the conduct. Nor will he who is sufficiently conversant with the science of intellect be hasty in assigning the bounds of our capacity. There are some things which the structure of our bodies will render us forever unable to effect; but in many cases the lines which appear to prescribe a term to our efforts will, like the mists that arise from a lake, retire further and further, the more closely we endeavour to approach them.

Fourthly, the vices and moral weakness of man are not invincible. This is the preceding proposition with a very slight variation in the statement. Vice and weakness are founded upon ignorance and error; but truth is more powerful than any champion that can be brought into the field against it; consequently truth has the faculty of expelling weakness and vice, and placing nobler and more beneficent principles in their stead.

Lastly, man is perfectible. This proposition needs some explanation.

By perfectible, it is not meant that he is capable of being brought to perfection. But the word seems sufficiently adapted to express the faculty of being continually made better and receiving perpetual improvement; and in this sense it is here to be understood. The term perfectible, thus explained, not only does not imply the capacity of being brought to perfection, but stands in express opposition to it. If we could arrive at perfection, there would be an end to our improvement. There is however one thing of great importance that it does imply: every perfection or excellence that human beings are competent to conceive, human beings, unless in cases that are palpably and unequivocally excluded by the structure of their frame, are competent to attain.

This is an inference which immediately follows from the omnipotence of truth. Every truth that is capable of being communicated is capable of being brought home to the conviction of the mind. Every principle which can be brought home to the conviction of the mind will infallibly produce a correspondent effect upon the conduct. If there were not something in the nature of man incompatible with absolute perfection, the doctrine of the omnipotence of truth would afford no small probability that he would one day reach it. Why is the perfection of man impossible?

The idea of absolute perfection is scarcely within the grasp of human understanding. If science were more familiarized to speculations of this sort, we should perhaps discover that the notion itself was pregnant with absurdity and contradiction.

It is not necessary in this argument to dwell upon the limited nature of the human faculties. We can neither be present to all places nor to all times. We cannot penetrate into the essences of things, or rather we have no sound and satisfactory knowledge of things external to ourselves, but merely of our own sensations. We cannot discover the causes of things, or ascertain that in the antecedent which connects it with the consequent, and discern nothing but their contiguity.* With what pretence can a being thus shut in on all sides lay claim to absolute perfection?

* Book IV, Chap. VII.

But, not to insist upon these considerations, there is one principle in the human mind which must forever exclude us from arriving at a close of our acquisitions, and confine us to perpetual progress. The human mind, so far as we are acquainted with it, is nothing else but a faculty of perception. All our knowledge, all our ideas, everything we possess as intelligent beings, comes from impression. All the minds that exist set out from absolute ignorance. They received first one impression, and then a second. As the impressions became more numerous, and were stored by the help of memory, and combined by the faculty of association, so the experience increased, and with the experience the knowledge, the wisdom, everything that distinguishes man from what we understand by a 'clod of the valley'. This seems to be a simple and incontrovertible history of intellectual being; and, if it be true, then as our accumulations have been incessant in the time that is gone, so, as long as we continue to perceive, to remember or reflect, they must perpetually increase.

CHAPTER VI

OF THE INFLUENCE OF CLIMATE[14]

Means by which liberty is to be introduced. –
Their efficacy illustrated. – Facts in confirmation
of these reasonings. – Inference.

TWO points further are necessary to be illustrated, in order to render our view of man in his social capacity impartial and complete. There are certain physical causes which have commonly been supposed to oppose an immovable barrier to the political improvement of our species: climate, which is imagined to render the introduction of liberal principles upon this subject in some cases impossible: and luxury, which, in addition to this disqualification, precludes their revival even in countries where they had once most eminently flourished.

An answer to both these objections is included in what has been offered upon the subject of the voluntary actions of man. If truth, when properly displayed, be omnipotent, then neither climate nor luxury are invincible obstacles. But so much stress has been laid upon these topics, and they have been so eloquently enforced by poets and men like poets, that it seems necessary to bestow upon them a distinct examination.

'It is impossible,' say some, 'to establish a system of political liberty in certain warm and effeminate climates.' To enable us to judge of the reasonableness of this affirmation, let us consider what process would be necessary in order to introduce political liberty into any country.

The answer to this question is to be found in the answer to that other, whether freedom have any real and solid advantages over slavery? If it have, then our mode of proceeding respecting it ought to be exactly parallel to that we should employ in recommending any other benefit. If I would persuade a man to accept a great estate, supposing that possession to be a real advantage; if I would induce him to select for his companion a beautiful and accomplished woman, or for his friend a wise, a brave and disinterested man; if I would persuade him to prefer ease to pain, and gratification to torture, what more is necessary than that I should inform his understanding, and make him see these things in their true and genuine colours? Should I find it necessary to enquire first of what climate he was a native, and whether that were favourable to the possession of a great estate, a fine woman, or a generous friend?

The advantages of liberty over slavery are not less real, though unfortunately they have been made less palpable in their application to the welfare of communities at large, than the advantages to accrue in the cases above enumerated. Every man has a confused sense of the real state of the question; but he has been taught to believe that men would tear each other to pieces if they had not priests to direct their consciences, lords to consult for their tranquillity, and kings to pilot them in safety through the dangers of the political ocean. But whether they be misled by these or other prejudices, whatever be the fancied terror that induces them quietly to submit to have their hands bound behind them, and the scourge vibrated over their heads, all these are questions of reason. Truth may be presented to them in such irresistible evidence, perhaps by such just degrees familiarized to their apprehension, as ultimately to conquer the most obstinate prepossessions. Let the press find its way into Persia or Indostan, let the political truths discovered by the best of the European sages be transfused into their language, and it is impossible that a few solitary converts should not be made. It is the property of truth to spread; and, exclusively of any powerful counteraction, its advocates in each succeeding year will be somewhat more numerous than in that which went before. The causes which suspend its progress arise, not from climate, but from the watchful and intolerant jealousy of despotic sovereigns. – What is here stated is in fact little more than a branch of the principle which has been so generally recognized, 'that government is founded in opinion'.*

Let us suppose then that the majority of a nation, by however slow a progress, is convinced of the desirableness, or, which amounts to the same, the practicability of freedom. The supposition would be parallel if we were to imagine ten thousand men of sound intellect, shut up in a madhouse, and superintended by a set of three or four keepers. Hitherto they have been persuaded, for what absurdity has been too great for human intellect to entertain? that they were destitute of reason, and that the superintendence under which they were placed was necessary for their preservation. They have therefore

*Hume's *Essays*, Part I, Essay iv.

submitted to whips and straw and bread and water, and perhaps imagined this tyranny to be a blessing. But a suspicion is at length by some means propagated among them that all they have hitherto endured has been an imposition. The suspicion spreads, they reflect, they reason, the idea is communicated from one to another through the chinks of their cells, and at certain times when the vigilance of their keepers has not precluded them from mutual society. It becomes the clear perception, the settled persuasion of the majority of the persons confined.

What will be the consequence of this opinion? Will the influence of climate prevent them from embracing the obvious means of their happiness? Is there any human understanding that will not perceive a truth like this, when forcibly and repeatedly presented? Is there a mind that will conceive no impatience of so horrible a tyranny? In reality the chains fall off of themselves when the magic of opinion is dissolved. When a great majority of any society are persuaded to secure any benefit to themselves, there is no need of tumult or violence to effect it. The effort would be to resist reason, not to obey it. The prisoners are collected in their common hall, and the keepers inform them that it is time to return to their cells. They have no longer the power to obey. They look at the impotence of their late masters, and smile at their presumption. They quietly leave the mansion where they were hitherto immured, and partake of the blessings of light and air like other men.

It may perhaps be useful to consider how far these reasonings upon the subject of liberty are confirmed to us by general experience as to the comparative inefficacy of climate, and the superior influence of circumstances, political and social. The following instances are for the most part abridged from the judicious collections of Hume upon the subject.*

1. If the theory here asserted be true, we may expect to

* *Essays*, Part I, Essay xxi.

find the inhabitants of neighbouring provinces in different states widely discriminated by the influence of government, and little assimilated by resemblance of climate. Thus the Gascons are the gayest people in France; but the moment we pass the Pyrenees, we find the serious and saturine character of the Spaniard. Thus the Athenians were lively, penetrating and ingenious; but the Thebans unpolished, phlegmatic and dull. 2. It would be reasonable to expect that different races of men, intermixed with each other, but differently governed, would afford a strong and visible contrast. Thus the Turks are brave, open and sincere; but the modern Greeks mean, cowardly and deceitful. 3. Wandering tribes closely connected among themselves, and having little sympathy with the people with whom they reside, may be expected to have great similarity of manners. Their situation renders them conspicuous, the faults of individuals reflect dishonour upon the whole, and their manners will be particularly sober and reputable, unless they should happen to labour under so peculiar an odium as to render all endeavour after reputation fruitless. Thus the Armenians in the East are as universally distinguished among the nations with whom they reside as the Jews in Europe; but the Armenians are noted for probity, and the Jews for extortion. 4. What resemblance is there between the ancient and the modern Greeks, between the old Romans and the present inhabitants of Italy, between the Gauls and the French? Diodorus Siculus describes the Gauls as particularly given to taciturnity, and Aristotle affirms that they are the only warlike nation who are negligent of women.

If on the contrary climate were principally concerned in forming the characters of nations, we might expect to find that heat and cold producing an extraordinary effect upon men, as they do upon plants and inferior animals. But the reverse of this appears to be the fact. Is it supposed that the neighbourhood of the fun renders men gay, fantastic and ingenious? While the French, the

Greeks and the Persians have been remarkable for their gaiety, the Spaniards, the Turks and the Chinese are not less distinguished by the seriousness of their deportment. It was the opinion of the ancients that the northern nations were incapable of civilization and improvement; but the moderns have found that the English are not inferior in literary eminence to any nation in the world. Is it asserted that the northern nations are more hardy and courageous, and that conquest has usually travelled from that to the opposite quarter? It would have been truer to say that conquest is usually made by poverty upon plenty. The Turks, who from the deserts of Tartary invaded the fertile provinces of the Roman empire, met the Saracens half way, who were advancing with similar views from the no less dreary deserts of Arabia. In their extreme perhaps heat and cold may determine the characters of nations, of the negroes for example on one side, and the Laplanders on the other. Not but that, in this very instance, much may be ascribed to the wretchedness of a sterile climate on the one hand, and to the indolence consequent upon a spontaneous fertility on the other. As to what is more than this, the remedy has not yet been discovered. Physical causes have already appeared to be powerful till moral ones can be brought into operation.

Has it been alleged that carnivorous nations are endowed with the greatest courage? The Swedes, whose nutriment is meagre and sparing, have ranked with the most distinguished modern nations in the operations of war.

It is usually said that northern nations are most addicted to wine, and southern to women. Admitting this observation in its full force, it would only prove that climate may operate upon the grosser particles of our frame, not that it influences those finer organs upon which the operations of intellect depend. But the truth of the first of these remarks may well be doubted. The Greeks appear to have been sufficiently addicted to the pleasures of the bottle. Among the Persians no character was more coveted than that of a hard drinker. It is easy to obtain anything of the negroes, even their wives and children, in exchange for liquor.

As to women the circumstances may be accounted for from moral causes. The heat of the climate obliges both sexes to go half naked. The animal arrives sooner at maturity in hot countries. And both these circumstances produce vigilance and jealousy, causes which inevitably tend to inflame the passions.

The result of these reasonings is of the utmost importance to him who speculates upon principles of government. There have been writers on this subject who, admitting and even occasionally declaiming with enthusiasm upon the advantages of liberty and the equal claims of mankind to every social benefit, have yet concluded 'that the corruptions of despotism, and the usurpations of aristocracy, were congenial to certain ages and divisions of the world, and under proper limitations entitled to our approbation'. But this hypothesis will be found unable to endure the test of serious reflection. There is no state of mankind that renders them incapable of the exercise of reason. There is no period in which it is necessary to hold the human species in a condition of pupillage. If there were, it would seem but reasonable that their superintendents and guardians, as in the case of infants of another sort, should provide for the means of their subsistence without calling upon them for the exertions of their own understanding. Wherever men are competent to look the first duties of humanity in the face, and to provide for their defence against the invasions of hunger and the inclemencies of the sky, it can scarcely be thought that they are not equally capable of every other exertion that may be essential to their security and welfare.

The real enemies of liberty in any country are not the people, but those higher orders who find their imaginary profit in a contrary system. Infuse just views of society into a certain number of the liberally educated and reflecting members; give to the people guides and instructors; and the business is done. This however is not to be accomplished but in a gradual manner, as will more fully appear in the sequel. The error lies, not in tolerating the worst forms of government for a time, but in supporting a change impracticable, and not incessantly looking forward to its accomplishment.

CHAPTER VII

OF THE INFLUENCE OF LUXURY

The object stated. – Source of this objection. – refuted from mutability – from mortality – from sympathy. – The probability of perseverance considered.

THE second objection to the principles already established is derived from the influence of luxury, and affirms 'that nations, like individuals, are subject to the phenomena of youth and old age, and that, when a people by effeminacy and depravation of manners have sunk into decrepitude, it is not within the compass of human ability to restore them to vigour and innocence'.

This idea has been partly founded upon the romantic notions of pastoral life and the golden age. Innocence is not virtue. Virtue demands the active employment of an ardent mind in the promotion of the general good. No man can be eminently virtuous who is not accustomed to an extensive range of reflection. He must see all the benefits to arise from a disinterested proceeding, and must understand the proper method of producing those benefits. Ignorance, the slothful habits and limited views of uncultivated life, have not in them more of true virtue, though they may be more harmless, than luxury, vanity and extravagance. Individuals of exquisite feeling, whose disgust has been excited by the hardened selfishness or the unblushing corruption which have prevailed in their own times, have recurred in imagination to the forests of Norway or the bleak and uncomfortable Highlands of Scotland in search of a purer race of mankind. This imagination has been the offspring of disappointment, not the dictate of reason and philosophy.

It may be true that ignorance is nearer than prejudice to the reception of wisdom, and that the absence of virtue is a condition more auspicious than the presence of its opposite. In this case it would have been juster to compare a nation sunk in luxury to an individual with confirmed habits of wrong, than to an individual whom a debilitated constitution was bringing fast to the grave. But neither would that comparison have been fair and equitable.

The condition of nations is more fluctuating, and will be found less obstinate in its resistance to a consistent endeavour for their improvement, than that of individuals. In nations some of their members will be less confirmed in error than others. A certain number will be only in a very small degree indisposed to listen to the voice of truth. This number, from the very nature of just sentiments, must in the ordinary course of things perpetually increase. Every new convert will be the means of converting others. In proportion as the body of disciples is augmented, the modes of attack upon the prejudices of others will be varied, and suited to the variety of men's tempers and prepossessions.

Add to this that generations of men are perpetually going off the stage, while other generations succeed. The next generation will not have so many prejudices to subdue. Suppose a despotic nation by some revolution in its affairs to become possessed of the advantages of freedom. The children of the present race will be bred in more firm and independent habits of thinking; the suppleness, the timidity, and the vicious dexterity of their fathers will give place to an erect mien and a clear and decisive judgement. The partial and imperfect change of character which was introduced at first will in the succeeding age become more unalloyed and complete.

Lastly, the power of reasonable and just ideas in changing the character of nations is in one respect infinitely greater than any power which can be brought to bear upon a solitary individual. The case is not of that customary sort, where the force of theory alone is tried in curing any person of his errors; but is as if he should be placed in an entirely new situation. His habits are broken through, and his motives of action changed. Instead of being perpetually recalled to vicious practices by the recurrence of his former connections, the whole society receives an impulse from the same cause that acts upon the individual. New ideas are suggested, and the languor and imbecility which might be incident to each are counteracted by the spectacle of general enthusiasm and concert.

But it has been further alleged 'that, even should a luxurious nation be induced, by intolerable grievances, and notorious usurpation, to embrace just principles of human society, they would be unable to perpetuate them, and would soon be led back by their evil habits to their former vices and corruption': that is, they would be capable of the heroic energy that should expel the usurper, but not of the moderate resolution that should prevent his return. They would rouse themselves so far from their lethargy as to assume a new character and enter into different views; but, after having for some time acted upon their convictions, they would suddenly become incapable of understanding the truth of their principles and feeling their influence.

Men always act upon their apprehensions of preferableness. There are few errors of which they are guilty which may not be resolved into a narrow and inadequate view of the alternative presented for their choice. Present pleasure may appear more certain and eligible than distant good. But they never choose evil as apprehended to be evil. Wherever a clear and unanswerable notion of any subject is presented to their view, a correspondent action or course of actions inevitably follows. Having thus gained one step in the acquisition of truth, it cannot easily be conceived as lost. A body of men, having detected the injurious consequences of an evil under which they have long laboured, and having shaken it off, will scarcely voluntarily restore the mischief they have annihilated. No recollection of past error can reasonably be supposed to have strength enough to lead back, into absurdity and uncompensated subjection, men who have once been thoroughly awakened to the perception of truth.

CHAPTER VIII

HUMAN INVENTIONS SUSCEPTIBLE OF PERPETUAL IMPROVEMENT

Perfectibility of man – instanced, first, in language – Its beginning. – Abstraction. – Complexity of Language. – Second instance: aphabetical writing. – Hieroglyphics at first universal. – Progressive deviations. – Application.

BEFORE we proceed to the direct subject of the present enquiry, it may not be improper to resume the subject of human improvableness, and consider it in a somewhat greater detail. An opinion has been extensively entertained 'that the differences of the human species in different ages and countries, particularly so far as relates to moral principles of conduct, are extremely insignificant and trifling; that we are deceived in this respect by distance and confounded by glare; but that in reality the virtues and vices of men, collectively taken, always have remained, and of consequence,' it is said, 'always will remain, nearly at the same point'.

The erroneousness of this opinion will perhaps be more completely exposed by a summary recollection of the actual history of our species than by the closest deductions of abstract reason. We will in this place simply remind the reader of the great changes which man has undergone as an intellectual being, entitling us to infer the probability of improvements not less essential, to be realized in future. The conclusion to be deduced from this delineation, that his moral improvements will in some degree keep pace with his intellectual, and his actions correspond with his opinions, must depend for its force upon the train of reasoning which has already been brought forward under that head.*

Let us carry back our minds to man in his original state, a being capable of impressions and knowledge to an unbounded extent, but not having as yet received the one or cultivated the other; let us contrast this being with all that science and genius have effected; and from hence we may form some idea what it is of which human nature is capable. It is to be remembered that this being did not, as now, derive assistance from the communications of his fellows, nor had his feeble and crude conceptions amended by the experience of successive centuries; but that in the state we are figuring all men were equally ignorant. The field of improvement was before them, but for every step in advance they were to be indebted to their untutored efforts. Nor is it of consequence whether such was actually the progress of mind, or whether, as others teach, the progress was abridged, and man was immediately advanced half way to the end of his career by the interposition of the author of his nature. In any case it is an allowable, and will be found no unimproving speculation, to consider mind as it is in itself, and to enquire what would have been its history if, immediately upon its production, it had been left to be acted upon by those ordinary laws of the universe with whose operation we are acquainted.

One of the acquisitions most evidently requisite as a preliminary to our present improvements is that of lan-

* Chap. V.

guage. But it is impossible to conceive an acquisition that must have been in its origin more different from what at present it is found, or that less promised that copiousness and refinement it has since exhibited.

Its beginning was probably from those involuntary cries which infants, for example, are found to utter in the earliest stages of their existence, and which, previously to the idea of exciting pity or procuring assistance, spontaneously arise from the operation of pain upon our animal frame. These cries, when actually uttered, become a subject of perception to him by whom they are uttered; and, being observed to be constantly associated with certain antecedent impressions and to excite the idea of those impressions in the hearer, may afterwards be repeated from reflection and the desire of relief. Eager desire to communicate any information to another will also prompt us to utter some simple sound for the purpose of exciting attention: this sound will probably frequently recur to organs unpractised to variety, and will at length stand as it were by convention for the information intended to be conveyed. But the distance is extreme from these simple modes of communication, which we possess in common with some of the inferior animals, to all the analysis and abstraction which languages require.

Abstraction indeed, though, as it is commonly understood, it be one of the sublimest operations of mind, is in some sort coeval with and inseparable from the existence of mind.* The next step to simple perception is that of

---

*The question whether or not the human mind is capable of forming abstract ideas has been the subject of much profound and serious disquisition. It is certain that we have a general standard of some sort, in consequence of which, if an animal is presented to our view, we can in most cases decide that it is, or is not a horse, a man, &c.; nor is it to be imagined that we should be unable to form such judgements, even if we were denied the use of speech.

It is a curious fact, and on that account worthy to be mentioned in this place, that the human mind is perhaps incapable of entertaining any but general ideas. Take, for example, a wine glass. If,

comparison, or the coupling together of two ideas and the perception of their resemblances and differences. Without comparison there can be no preference, and without preference no voluntary action: though it must be acknowledged that this comparison is an operation

---

after this glass is withdrawn, I present to you another from the same set, you will probably be unable to determine whether it is another or the same. It is with a like inattention that people in general view a flock of sheep. The shepherd only distinguishes the features of every one of his sheep from the features of every other. But it is impossible so to individualize our remarks as to cause our idea to be truly particular, and not special. Thus there are memorable instances of one man so nearly resembling another as to be able to pass himself upon the wife and all the relatives of this man as if he were the same.

The opposition which has been so ingeniously maintained against the doctrine of abstract ideas seems chiefly to have arisen from a habit of using the term idea, not, as Locke has done, for every conception that can exist in the mind, but as constantly descriptive of an image, or picture. The following view of the subject will perhaps serve in some degree to remove any ambiguity that might continue to rest upon it.

Ideas, considering that term as comprehending all perceptions, both primary, or of the senses, and secondary, or of the memory, may be divided into four classes: 1. perfect. The existence of these we have disproved. 2. imperfect, such as those which are produced in us by a near and careful inspection of any visible object. 3. imperfect, such as those produced by a slight and distant view. 4. imperfect, so as to have no resemblance to an image of any external object. The perception produced in us in slight and current discourse by the words river, field, are of this nature; and have no more resemblance to the image of any visible object than the perception ordinarily produced in us by the words conquest, government, virtue.

The subject of this last class of ideas is very ingeniously treated by Burke, in his *Enquiry into the Sublime*, Part V. He has however committed one material error in the discussion, by representing these as instances of the employment of 'words without ideas'. If we recollect that brutes have similar abstractions, and a general conception, of the female of their own species, of man, of food, of the smart of a whip, &c. we shall probably admit that such perceptions (and in all events they are perceptions, or, according to the established language upon the subject, ideas) are not necessarily connected with the employment of words.

which may be performed by the mind without adverting to its nature, and that neither the brute nor the savage has a consciousness of the several steps of the intellectual progress. Comparison immediately leads to imperfect abstraction. The sensation of today is classed, if similar, with the sensation of yesterday, and an inference is made respecting the conduct to be adopted. Without this degree of abstraction, the faint dawnings of language already described could never have existed. Abstraction, which was necessary to the first existence of language, is again assisted in its operations by language. That generalization, which is implied in the very notion of a thinking being, being thus embodied and rendered a matter of sensible impression, makes the mind acquainted with its own powers, and creates a restless desire after further progress.

But, though it be by no means impossible to trace the causes that concurred to the production of language, and to prove them adequate to their effect, it does not the less appear that this is an acquisition of slow growth and inestimable value. The very steps, were we to pursue them, would appear like an endless labyrinth. The distance is immeasurable between the three or four vague and inarticulate sounds uttered by animals, and the copiousness of lexicography or the regularity of grammar. The general and special names by which things are at first complicated and afterwards divided, the names by which properties are separated from their substances, and powers from both, the comprehensive distribution of parts of speech, verbs, adjectives and particles, the inflections of words by which the change of their terminations changes their meaning through a variety of shadings, their concords and their governments, all of them present us with such a boundless catalogue of science that he who on the one hand did not know that the task had been actually performed, or who on the other was not intimately acquainted with the progressive nature of mind, would pronounce the accomplishment of them impossible.

A second invention, well calculated to impress us with a sense of the progressive nature of man, is that of alphabetical writing. Hieroglyphical or picture-writing appears at some time to have been universal, and the difficulty of conceiving the gradation from this to alphabetical is so great as to have induced Hartley, one of the most acute philosophical writers, to have recourse to miraculous interposition as the only adequate solution. In reality no problem can be imagined more operose than that of decomposing the sounds of words into four and twenty simple elements or letters, and again finding these elements in all other words. When we have examined the subject a little more closely, and perceived the steps by which this labour was accomplished, perhaps the immensity of the labour will rather gain upon us, as he that shall have counted a million of units will have a vaster idea upon the subject than he that only considers them in the gross.

In China hieroglyphical writing has never been superseded by alphabetical, and this from the very nature of their language, which is considerably monosyllabic, the same sound being made to signify a great variety of objects, by means of certain shadings of tone too delicate for an alphabet to represent. They have however two kinds of writing, one for the learned, and another for the vulgar. The learned adhere closely to their hieroglyphical writing, representing every word by its corresponding picture; but the vulgar are frequent in their deviations from it.

Hieroglyphical writing and speech may indeed be considered in the first instance as two languages running parallel to each other, but with no necessary connection. The picture and the word, each of them, represent the idea, one as immediately as the other. But, though independent, they will become accidentally associated; the picture at first imperfectly, and afterwards more constantly suggesting the idea of its correspondent sound. It is in this manner that the mercantile classes of China began to corrupt, as it is styled, their hieroglyphical writing. They had a word suppose of two syllables to write. The character appropriate to that word they were not acquainted with, or it failed to suggest itself to their memory. Each of the syllables however was a distinct word in the language, and the characters belonging to them perfectly familiar. The expedient that suggested itself was to write these two characters with a mark signifying their union, though in reality the characters had hitherto been appropriated to ideas of a different sort, wholly unconnected with that now intended to be conveyed. Thus a sort of rebus or charade was produced. In other cases the word, though monosyllabic, was capable of being divided into two sounds, and the same process was employed. This is a first step towards alphabetical analysis. Some word, such as the interjection *O!* or the particle *A*, is already a sound perfectly simple, and thus furnishes a first stone to the edifice. But, though these ideas may perhaps present us with a faint view of the manner in which an alphabet was produced, yet the actual production of a complete alphabet is perhaps of all human discoveries that which required the most persevering reflection, the luckiest concurrence of circumstances, and the most patient and gradual progress.

Let us however suppose man to have gained the two first elements of knowledge, speaking and writing; let us trace him through all his subsequent improvements, through whatever constitutes the inequality between Newton and the ploughman, and indeed much more than this, since the most ignorant ploughman in civilized society is infinitely different from what he would have been when stripped of all the benefits he has derived from literature and the arts. Let us survey the earth covered with the labours of man, houses, enclosures, harvests, manufactures, instruments, machines, together with all the wonders of painting, poetry, eloquence and philosophy.

Such was man in his original state, and such is man as

we at present behold him. Is it possible for us to contemplate what he has already done without being impressed with a strong presentiment of the improvements he has yet to accomplish? There is no science that is not capable of additions; there is no art that may not be carried to a still higher perfection. If this be true of all other sciences, why not of morals? If this be true of all other arts, why not of social institution? The very conception of this as possible is in the highest degree encouraging. If we can still further demonstrate it to be a part of the natural and regular progress of mind, our confidence and our hopes will then be complete. This is the temper with which we ought to engage in the study of political truth. Let us look back, that we may profit by the experience of mankind; but let us not look back as if the wisdom of our ancestors was such as to leave no room for future improvement.

BOOK II

PRINCIPLES OF SOCIETY

CHAPTER I

INTRODUCTION

*Nature of the enquiry. – Connection of politics
and morals. – Mistakes to which the enquiry has
been exposed. – Distinction between society and
government.*

IN the preceding book we have cleared the foundations
for the remaining branches of enquiry, and shown what
are the prospects it is reasonable to entertain as to future
political improvement. The effects which are produced by
positive institutions have there been delineated, as well as
the extent of the powers of man, considered in his social
capacity. It is time that we proceed to those disquisitions
which are more immediately the object of the present
work.

Political enquiry may be distributed under two heads:
first, what are the regulations which will conduce to the
well being of man in society; and, secondly, what is the
authority which is competent to prescribe regulations.

The regulations to which the conduct of men living in
society ought to be conformed may be considered in two
ways: first, those moral laws which are enjoined upon us
by the dictates of enlightened reason; and, secondly, those
principles a deviation from which the interest of the community may be supposed to render it proper to repress by
sanctions and punishment.

Morality is that system of conduct which is determined

by a consideration of the greatest general good: he is entitled to the highest moral approbation whose conduct is, in the greatest number of instances, or in the most momentous instances, governed by views of benevolence, and made subservient to public utility. In like manner the only regulations which any political authority can be justly entitled to enforce are such as are best adapted to public utility. Consequently, just political regulations are nothing more than a certain select part of moral law. The supreme power in a state ought not, in the strictest sense, to require anything of its members that an understanding sufficiently enlightened would not prescribe without such interference.*

These considerations seem to lead to the detection of a mistake which has been very generally committed by political writers of our own country. They have for the most part confined their researches to the question of What is a just political authority or the most eligible form of government, consigning to others the delineation of right principles of conduct and equitable regulations. But there appears to be something preposterous in this mode of proceeding. A well constituted government is only the means for enforcing suitable regulations. One form of government is preferable to another in exact proportion to the security it affords that nothing shall be done in the name of the community which is not conducive to the welfare of the whole. The question therefore, What it is which is thus conducive, is upon every account entitled to the first place in our disquisitions.

One of the ill consequences which have resulted from this distorted view of the science of politics is a notion very generally entertained, that a community, or society of men, has a right to lay down whatever rules it may think proper for its own observance. This will presently be proved to be an erroneous position.† It may be prudent in an individual to submit in some cases to the usurpation

* Chap. V of the following Book.
† Chap. V of this Book.

of a majority; it may be unavoidable in a community to proceed upon the imperfect and erroneous views they shall chance to entertain: but this is a misfortune entailed upon us by the nature of government, and not a matter of right.*

A second ill consequence that has arisen from this proceeding is that, politics having been thus violently separated from morality, government itself has no longer been compared with its true criterion. Instead of enquiring what species of government was most conducive to the public welfare, an unprofitable disquisition has been instituted respecting the probable origin of government; and its different forms have been estimated, not by the consequences with which they were pregnant, but the source from which they sprung. Hence men have been prompted to look back to the folly of their ancestors, rather than forward to the benefits derivable from the improvements of human knowledge. Hence, in investigating their rights, they have recurred less to the great principles of morality than to the records and charters of a barbarous age. As if men were not entitled to all the benefits of the social state till they could prove their inheriting them from some bequest of their distant progenitors. As if men were not as justifiable and meritorious in planting liberty in a soil in which it had never existed as in restoring it where it could be proved only to have suffered a temporary suspension.

The reasons here assigned strongly tend to evince the necessity of establishing the genuine principles of society, before we enter upon the direct consideration of government. It may be proper in this place to state the fundamental distinction which exists between these topics of enquiry. Man associated at first for the sake of mutual assistance. They did not foresee that any restraint would be necessary to regulate the conduct of individual members of the society towards each other, or towards the whole. The necessity of restraint grew out of the errors

* Chap. V.

and perverseness of a few. An acute writer has expressed this idea with peculiar felicity. 'Society and government,' says he, 'are different in themselves, and have different origins. Society is produced by our wants, and government by our wickedness. Society is in every state a blessing; government even in its best state but a necessary evil.'*

CHAPTER II

OF JUSTICE

Extent and meaning of justice. – Subject of justice: mankind. – Its distribution by the capacity of its subject – by his usefulness. – Self-love considered. – Family affection. – Gratitude. – Objections: from ignorance – from utility. – An exception stated. – Remark. – Degrees of justice. – Application. – Idea of political justice.

FROM what has been said it appears that the subject of our present enquiry is strictly speaking a department of the science of morals. Morality is the source from which its fundamental axioms must be drawn, and they will be made somewhat clearer in the present instance if we assume the term justice as a general appellation for all moral duty.

That this appellation is sufficiently expressive of the subject will appear, if we examine mercy, gratitude, temperance, or any of those duties which, in looser speaking, are contradistinguished from justice. Why should I pardon this criminal, remunerate this favour, or abstain from this indulgence? If it partake of the nature of morality, it must be either right or wrong, just or unjust. It must tend to the benefit of the individual, either without trenching upon, or with actual advantage to the mass of individuals.

* *Common Sense*, page 1.

Either way it benefits the whole, because individuals are parts of the whole. Therefore to do it is just, and to forbear it is unjust. – By justice I understand that impartial treatment of every man in matters that relate to his happiness, which is measured solely by a consideration of the properties of the receiver, and the capacity of him that bestows. Its principle therefore is, according to a well known phrase, to be 'no respecter of persons'.

Considerable light will probably be thrown upon our investigation if, quitting for the present the political view, we examine justice merely as it exists among individuals. Justice is a rule of conduct originating in the connection of one percipient being with another. A comprehensive maxim which has been laid down upon the subject is 'that we should love our neighbour as ourselves'. But this maxim, though possessing considerable merit as a popular principle, is not modelled with the strictness of philosophical accuracy.

In a loose and general view I and my neighbour are both of us men; and of consequence entitled to equal attention. But, in reality, it is probable that one of us is a being of more worth and importance than the other. A man is of more worth than a beast; because, being possessed of higher faculties, he is capable of a more refined and genuine happiness. In the same manner the illustrious archbishop of Cambray was of more worth than his valet, and there are few of us that would hesitate to pronounce, if his palace were in flames, and the life of only one of them could be preserved, which of the two ought to be preferred.

But there is another ground of preference, beside the private consideration of one of them being further removed from the state of a mere animal. We are not connected with one or two percipient beings, but with a society, a nation, and in some sense with the whole family of mankind. Of consequence that life ought to be preferred which will be most conducive to the general good. In saving the life of Fénelon,[15] suppose at the moment he conceived the project of his immortal Telemachus, I should have been promoting the benefit of thousands who have been cured by the perusal of that work of some error, vice and consequent unhappiness. Nay, my benefit would extend further than this; for every individual, thus cured, has become a better member of society, and has contributed in his turn to the happiness, information and improvement of others.

Suppose I had been myself the valet; I ought to have chosen to die, rather than Fénelon should have died. The life of Fénelon was really preferable to that of the valet. But understanding is the faculty that perceives the truth of this and similar propositions; and justice is the principle that regulates my conduct accordingly. It would have been just in the valet to have preferred the archbishop to himself. To have done otherwise would have been a breach of justice.*

Suppose the valet had been my brother, my father or my benefactor. This would not alter the truth of the proposition. The life of Fénelon would still be more valuable than that of the valet; and justice, pure, unadulterated justice, would still have preferred that which was most valuable. Justice would have taught me to save the life of Fénelon at the expense of the other. What magic is there in the pronoun 'my', that should justify us in overturning the decisions of impartial truth? My brother or my father may be a fool or a profligate, malicious, lying or dishonest. If they be, of what consequence is it that they are mine?

'But to my father I am indebted for existence; he supported me in the helplessness of infancy.' When he first subjected himself to the necessity of these cares, he was probably influenced by no particular motives of benevolence to his future offspring. Every voluntary benefit however entitles the bestower to some kindness and retribu-

---

*The question how far impartial justice is a motive capable of operating upon the mind will be found examined at length, Book IV, Chap. X.

tion. Why? Because a voluntary benefit is an evidence of benevolent intention, that is, in a certain degree, of virtue. It is the disposition of the mind, not the external action separately taken, that entitles to respect. But the merit of this disposition is equal, whether the benefit were conferred upon me or upon another. I and another man cannot both be right in preferring our respective benefactors, for my benefactor cannot be at the same time both better and worse than his neighbour. My benefactor ought to be esteemed, not because he bestowed a benefit upon me, but because he bestowed it upon a human being. His desert will be in exact proportion to the degree in which that human being was worthy of the distinction conferred.

Thus every view of the subject brings us back to the consideration of my neighbour's moral worth, and his importance to the general weal, as the only standard to determine the treatment to which he is entitled. Gratitude therefore, if by gratitude we understand a sentiment of preference which I entertain towards another, upon the ground of my having been the subject of his benefits, is no part either of justice or virtue.*

It may be objected 'that my relation, my companion, or my benefactor, will of course in many instances obtain an uncommon portion of my regard: for, not being universally capable of discriminating the comparative worth of different men, I shall inevitably judge most favourably of him of whose virtues I have received the most unquestionable proofs; and thus shall be compelled to prefer the man of moral worth whom I know, to another who may possess, unknown to me, an essential superiority.'

This compulsion however is founded only in the imperfection of human nature. It may serve as an apology for my error, but can never change error into truth. It will always remain contrary to the strict and universal deci-

*This argument is stated with great clearness in an *Essay on the Nature of True Virtue*, by Jonathan Edwards, author of a celebrated work on the Freedom of the Will.

sions of justice. The difficulty of conceiving this, is owing merely to our confounding the disposition from which an action is chosen, with the action itself. The disposition that would prefer virtue to vice, and a greater degree of virtue to a less, is undoubtedly a subject of approbation; the erroneous exercise of this disposition, by which a wrong object is selected, if unavoidable, is to be deplored, but can by no colouring and under no denomination be converted into right.*

It may in the second place be objected 'that a mutual commerce of benefits tends to increase the mass of benevolent action, and that to increase the mass of benevolent action is to contribute to the general good'. Indeed! Is the general good promoted by falsehood, by treating a man of one degree of worth as if he had ten times that worth? or as if he were in any degree different from what he really is? Would not the most beneficial consequences result from a different plan; from my constantly and carefully enquiring into the deserts of all those with whom I am connected, and from their being sure, after a certain allowance for the fallibility of human judgement, of being treated by me exactly as they deserved? Who can describe the benefits that would result from such a plan of conduct, if universally adopted?

It would perhaps tend to make the truth in this respect more accurately understood to consider that, whereas the received morality teaches me to be grateful, whether in affection or in act, for benefits conferred on myself, the reasonings here delivered, without removing the tie upon me from personal benefits (except where benefit is conferred from an unworthy motive), multiply the obligation, and enjoin me to be also grateful for benefits conferred upon others. My obligation towards my benefactor, supposing his benefit to be justly conferred, is in no sort dissolved; nor can anything authorize me to supersede it but the requisition of a superior duty. That which ties me to my benefactor, upon these principles, is the moral

*Chap. IV.

worth he has displayed; and it will frequently happen that I shall be obliged to yield him the preference, because, while other competitors may be of greater worth, the evidence I have of the worth of my benefactor is more complete.

There seems to be more truth in the argument, derived chiefly from the prevailing modes of social existence, in favour of my providing, in ordinary cases, for my wife and children, my brothers and relations, before I provide for strangers, than in those which have just been examined. As long as the providing for individuals is conducted with its present irregularity and caprice, it seems as if there must be a certain distribution of the class needing superintendence and supply, among the class affording it; that each man may have his claim and resource. But this argument is to be admitted with great caution. It belongs only to ordinary cases; and cases of a higher order, or a more urgent necessity, will perpetually occur in competition with which these will be altogether impotent. We must be severely scrupulous in measuring the quantity of supply; and, with respect to money in particular, should remember how little is yet understood of the true mode of employing it for the public benefit.

Nothing can be less exposed to reasonable exception than these principles. If there be such a thing as virtue, it must be placed in a conformity to truth, and not to error. It cannot be virtuous that I should esteem a man, that is, consider him as possessed of estimable qualities, when in reality he is destitute of them. It surely cannot conduce to the benefit of mankind that each man should have a different standard of moral judgement, and preference, and that the standard of all should vary from that of reality. Those who teach this impose the deepest disgrace upon virtue. They assert in other words that, when men cease to be deceived, when the film is removed from their eyes, and they see things as they are, they will cease to be either good or happy. Upon the system opposite to theirs, the soundest criterion of virtue is to put ourselves in the place of an impartial spectator, of an angelic nature, suppose, beholding us from an elevated station, and uninfluenced by our prejudices, conceiving what would be his estimate of the intrinsic circumstances of our neighbour, and acting accordingly.

Having considered the persons with whom justice is conversant, let us next enquire into the degree in which we are obliged to consult the good of others. And here, upon the very same reasons, it will follow that it is just I should do all the good in my power. Does a person in distress apply to me for relief? It is my duty to grant it, and I commit a breach of duty in refusing. If this principle be not of universal application, it is because, in conferring a benefit upon an individual, I may in some instances inflict an injury of superior magnitude upon myself or society. Now the same justice that binds me to any individual of my fellow men binds me to the whole. If, while I confer a benefit upon one man, it appear, in striking an equitable balance, that I am injuring the whole, my action ceases to be right, and becomes absolutely wrong. But how much am I bound to do for the general weal, that is, for the benefit of the individuals of whom the whole is composed? Everything in my power. To the neglect of the means of my own existence? No; for I am myself a part of the whole. Beside, it will rarely happen that the project of doing for others everything in my power will not demand for its execution the preservation of my own existence; or in other words, it will rarely happen that I cannot do more good in twenty years than in one. If the extraordinary case should occur in which I can promote the general good by my death more than by my life, justice requires that I should be content to die. In other cases, it will usually be incumbent on me to maintain my body and mind in the utmost vigour, and in the best condition for service.*

Suppose, for example, that it is right for one man to possess a greater portion of property than another,

* Appendix, No. I, p. 177.

whether as the fruit of his industry, or the inheritance of his ancestors. Justice obliges him to regard this property as a trust, and calls upon him maturely to consider in what manner it may be employed for the increase of liberty, knowledge and virtue. He has no right to dispose of a shilling of it at the suggestion of his caprice. So far from being entitled to well earned applause, for having employed some scanty pittance in the service of philanthropy, he is in the eye of justice a delinquent if he withhold any portion from that service. Could that portion have been better or more worthily employed? That it could is implied in the very terms of the proposition. Then it was just it should have been so employed. – In the same manner as my property, I hold my person as a trust in behalf of mankind. I am bound to employ my talents, my understanding, my strength and my time, for the production of the greatest quantity of general good. Such are the declarations of justice, so great is the extent of my duty.

But justice is reciprocal. If it be just that I should confer a benefit, it is that another man should receive it, and, if I withhold from him that to which he is entitled, he may justly complain. My neighbour is in want of ten pounds that I can spare. There is no law of political institution to reach this case, and transfer the property from me to him. But in a passive sense, unless it can be shown that the money can be more beneficently employed, his right is as complete (though actively he have not the same right, or rather duty, to possess himself of it) as if he had my bond in his possession, or had supplied me with goods to the amount.*

To this it has sometimes been answered 'that there is more than one person who stands in need of the money I have to spare, and of consequence I must be at liberty to bestow it as I please'. By no means. If only one person offer himself to my knowledge or search, to me there is but one. Those others that I cannot find belong to other

*Chap. V.

rich men to assist (every man is in reality rich who has more than his just occasions demand), and not to me. If more than one person offer, I am obliged to balance their claims, and conduct myself accordingly. It is scarcely possible that two men should have an exactly equal claim, or that I should be equally certain respecting the claim of the one as of the other.

It is therefore impossible for me to confer upon any man a favour; I can only do him right. Whatever deviates from the law of justice, though it should be in the too much done in favour of some individual or some part of the general whole, is so much subtracted from the general flock, so much of absolute injustice.

The reasonings here alleged are sufficient clearly to establish the competence of justice as a principle of deduction in all cases of moral enquiry. They are themselves rather of the nature of illustration and example, and, if error be imputable to them in particulars, this will not invalidate the general conclusion, the propriety of applying moral justice as a criterion in the investigation of political truth.

Society is nothing more than an aggregation of individuals. Its claims and duties must be the aggregate of their claims and duties, the one no more precarious and arbitrary than the other. What has the society a right to require from me? The question is already answered: everything that it is my duty to do. Anything more? Certainly not. Can it change eternal truth, or subvert the nature of men and their actions? Can it make my duty consist in committing intemperance, in maltreating or assassinating my neighbour? – Again, what is it that the society is bound to do for its members? Everything that is requisite for their welfare. But the nature of their welfare is defined by the nature of mind. That will most contribute to it which expands the understanding, supplies incitements to virtue, fills us with a generous consciousness of our independence, and carefully removes whatever can impede our exertions.

Should it be affirmed 'that it is not in the power of
political system to secure to us these advantages', the conclusion will not be less incontrovertible. It is bound to
contribute everything it is able to these purposes. Suppose its influence in the utmost degree limited; there must
be one method approaching nearer than any other to the
desired object, and that method ought to be universally
adopted. There is one thing that political institutions
can assuredly do, they can avoid positively counteracting
the true interests of their subjects. But all capricious rules
and arbitrary distinctions do positively counteract them.
There is scarcely any modification of society but has in it
some degree of moral tendency. So far as it produces
neither mischief nor benefit, it is good for nothing. So far
as it tends to the improvement of the community, it ought
to be universally adopted.

Appendix I page 174

OF SUICIDE

*Motives of suicide: 1. Escape from pain. –
Benevolence. – Martyrdom considered.*

THIS reasoning will throw some light upon the long disputed case of suicide. 'Have I a right to destroy myself
in order to escape from pain or distress?' Circumstances
that should justify such an action can rarely occur. There
are few situations that can exclude the possibility of
future life, vigour and usefulness. It will frequently happen that the man who once saw nothing before him but
despair, shall afterwards enjoy a long period of happiness
and honour. In the meantime the power of terminating
our own lives is one of the faculties with which we are
endowed; and therefore, like every other faculty, is a subject of moral discipline. In common with every branch
of morality, it is a topic of calculation, as to the balance

of good and evil to result from its employment in any indivdual instance. We should however be scrupulously upon our guard against the deceptions that melancholy and impatience are so well calculated to impose. We should consider that, though the pain to be suffered by ourselves is by no means to be overlooked, we are but one, and the persons nearly or remotely interested in our possible usefulness innumerable. Each man is but the part of a great system, and all that he has is so much wealth to be put to the account of the general stock.

There is another case of suicide of more difficult estimation. What shall we think of the reasoning of Lycurgus,[17] who, when he determined upon a voluntary death, remarked 'that all the faculties a rational being possessed were capable of being benevolently employed, and that, after having spent his life in the service of his country, a man ought, if possible, to render his death a source of additional benefit'? This was the motive of the suicide of Codrus, Leonidas and Decius. If the same motive prevailed in the much admired suicide of Cato, and he were instigated by reasons purely benevolent, it is impossible not to applaud his intention, even if he were mistaken in the application. The difficulty is to decide whether in any instance the recourse to a voluntary death can overbalance the usefulness to be displayed, in twenty years of additional life.

Additional importance will be reflected upon this disquisition if we remember that martyrs ($\mu\alpha\rho\tau\upsilon\rho\epsilon\varsigma$) are suicides by the very signification of the term. They die for a testimony ($\mu\alpha\rho\tau\upsilon\rho\iota\upsilon$). But that would be impossible if their death were not to a certain degree a voluntary action. We must assume that it was possible for them to avoid this fate, before we can draw any conclusion from it in favour of the cause they espoused. They were determined to die, rather than reflect dishonour on that cause.

Of Duelling

Appendix II

OF DUELLING

Motives of duelling – 1. Revenge. – 2. Reputation. – Objection answered. – Illustration.

IT may be proper in this place to bestow a moment's consideration upon the trite but very important case of duelling. A short reflection will suffice to set it in its true light.

This despicable practice was originally invented by barbarians for the gratification of revenge. It was probably at that time thought a very happy project for reconciling the odiousness of malignity with the gallantry of courage.

But in this light it is now generally given up. Men of the best understanding who lend it their sanction are unwillingly induced to do so, and engage in single combat merely that their reputation may sustain no slander.

In examining this subject we must proceed upon one of two suppositions. Either the lives of both the persons to be hazarded are worthless, or they are not. In the latter case, the question answers itself, and cannot stand in need of discussion. Useful lives are not to be hazarded, from a view to the partial and contemptible obloquy that may be annexed to the refusal of such a duel, that is, to an act of virtue.

When the duellist tells me that he and the person that has offended him are of no possible worth to the community, I may reasonably conclude that he talks the language of spleen. But, if I take him at his word, is it to be admitted, though he cannot benefit the community, that he should injure it? What would be the consequence if we allowed ourselves to assail everyone that we thought worthless in the world? In reality, when he talks this language, he deserts the ground of vindicating his injured honour, and shows that his conduct is that of a vindictive and brutalized savage.

'But the refusing a duel is an ambiguous action. Cowards may pretend principle to shelter themselves from a danger they dare not meet.'

This is partly true and partly false. There are few actions indeed that are not ambiguous, or that with the same general outline may not proceed from different motives. But the manner of doing them will sufficiently show the principle from which they spring.

He that would break through a received custom because he believes it to be wrong must no doubt arm himself with fortitude. The point in which we principally fail is in not accurately understanding our own intentions, and taking care beforehand to purify ourselves from every alloy of weakness and error. He who comes forward with no other idea but that of rectitude, and who expresses, with the simplicity and firmness which conviction never fails to inspire, the views with which he is penetrated, is in no danger of being mistaken for a coward. If he hesitate, it is because he has not an idea perfectly clear of the sentiment he intends to convey. If he be in any degree embarrassed, it is because he has not a feeling sufficiently generous and intrepid of the demerit of the action in which he is urged to engage.

If courage have any intelligible nature, one of its principal fruits must be the daring to speak truth at all times, to all persons, and in every possible situation in which a well informed sense of duty may prescribe it. What is it but the want of courage that should prevent me from saying, 'Sir, I will not accept your challenge. Have I injured you? I will readily and without compulsion repair my injustice to the uttermost mite. Have you misconstrued me? State to me the particulars, and doubt not that what is true I will make appear to be true. I should be a notorious criminal were I to attempt your life, or assist you in an attempt upon mine. What compensation will the opinion of the world make for the recollection of so vile and brutal a proceeding? There is no true applause but where the heart of him that receives it beats in unison. There is no censure terrible while the heart repels it with conscious integrity. I am not the coward to do a deed that my soul detests because I cannot endure the scoffs of the mistaken. Loss of reputation is a serious evil. But I will act so that no man shall suspect me of irresolution and pusillanimity.' He that should firmly hold this language, and act accordingly, would soon be acquitted of every dishonourable imputation.

CHAPTER III

OF THE EQUALITY OF MANKIND

Physical equality. – Objection. – Answers. – Moral equality. – How limited. – Province of political justice.

THE principles of justice, as explained in the preceding chapter, proceed upon the assumption of the equality of mankind. This equality is either physical or moral. Physical equality may be considered either as it relates to the strength of the body or the faculties of the mind.

This part of the subject has been exposed to cavil and objection. It has been said 'that the reverse of this equality is the result of our experience. Among the individuals of our species, we actually find that there are not two alike. One man is strong, and another weak. One man is wise, and another foolish. All that exists in the world of the inequality of conditions is to be traced to this as their source. The strong man possesses power to subdue, and the weak stands in need of an ally to protect. The consequence is inevitable: the equality of conditions is a chimerical assumption, neither possible to be reduced into practice, nor desirable if it could be so reduced.'

Upon this statement two observations are to be made. First, this inequality was in its origin infinitely less than it is at present. In the uncultivated state of man, diseases, effeminacy and luxury were little known; and, of consequence, the strength of everyone much more nearly approached to the strength of his neighbour. In the uncultivated state of man, the understandings of all were limited, their wants, their ideas and their views nearly upon a level. It was to be expected that, in their first departure from this state, great irregularities would introduce themselves; and it is the object of subsequent wisdom and improvement to mitigate these irregularities.

Secondly, notwithstanding the encroachments that have been made upon the equality of mankind, a great and substantial equality remains. There is no such disparity among the human race as to enable one man to hold several other men in subjection, except so far as they are willing to be subject. All government is founded in opinion. Men at present live under any particular form because they conceive it their interest to do so. One part indeed of a community or empire may be held in subjection by force; but this cannot be the personal force of their despot; it must be the force of another part of the community, who are of opinion that it is their interest to support his authority. Destroy this opinion, and the fabric which is built upon it falls to the ground. It follows therefore that all men are essentially independent. – So much for the physical equality.

The moral equality is still less open to reasonable exception. By moral equality I understand the propriety of applying one unalterable rule of justice to every case that may arise. This cannot be questioned, but upon arguments that would subvert the very nature of virtue. 'Equality,' it has been affirmed, 'will always be an unintelligible fiction, so long as the capacities of men shall be unequal, and their pretended claims have neither guarantee nor sanction by which they can be enforced.'* But surely justice is sufficiently intelligible in its own nature,

---

* 'On a dit – que nous avons tous les mêmes droits. J'ignore ce que c'est rue les mêmes droits, où il y a inégalité de talens ou de force, et nulle garantie, nulle sanction.' Raynal, *Révolution d'Amérique*, p. 34.

abstractedly from the consideration whether it be or be not reduced into practice. Justice has relation to beings endowed with perception, and capable of pleasure and pain. Now it immediately results from the nature of such beings, independently of any arbitrary constitution, that pleasure is agreeable and pain odious, pleasure to be desired and pain to be disapproved. It is therefore just and reasonable that such beings should contribute, so far as it lies in their power, to the pleasure and benefit of each other. Among pleasures, some are more exquisite, more unalloyed and less precarious than others. It is just that these should be preferred.

From these simple principles we may deduce the moral equality of mankind. We are partakers of a common nature, and the same causes that contribute to the benefit of one will contribute to the benefit of another. Our senses and faculties are of the same denomination. Our pleasures and pains will therefore be alike. We are all of us endowed with reason, able to compare, to judge and to infer. The improvement therefore which is to be desired for one is to be desired for another. We shall be provident for ourselves, and useful to each other in proportion as we rise above the sphere of prejudice. The same independence, the same freedom from any such restraint, as should prevent us from giving the reins to our own understanding, or from uttering, upon all occasions, whatever we think to be true, will conduce to the improvement of of all. There are certain opportunities and a certain situation most advantageous to every human being, and it is just that these should be communicated to all, as nearly as the general economy will permit.

There is indeed one species of moral inequality, parallel to the physical inequality that has been already described. The treatment to which men are entitled is to be measured by their merits and their virtues. That country would not be the seat of wisdom and reason where the benefactor of his species was regarded with no greater degree of complacence than their enemy. But in reality this distinction, so far from being adverse to equality in any tenable sense, is friendly to it, and is accordingly known by the appellation of equity, a term derived from the same origin. Though in some sense an exception, it tends to the same purpose to which the principle itself is indebted for its value. It is calculated to infuse into every bosom an emulation of excellence. The thing really to be desired is the removing as much as possible arbitrary distinctions, and leaving to talents and virtue the field of exertion unimpaired. We should endeavour to afford to all the same opportunities and the same encouragement, and to render justice the common interest and choice.

It should be observed that the object of this chapter is barely to present a general outline of the principle of equality. The practical inferences that flow from it must remain to be detailed under subsequent heads of enquiry.

CHAPTER IV

OF PERSONAL VIRTUE AND DUTY

Of virtuous action. – Of a virtuous agent. – Capacity – in inanimate substances – in man. – Inference. – Of benevolent error. – Nature of vice. – Illustrations – Mutability of the principle of belief. – Complexity in the operation of motives. – Deduction. – Of duty. – It is never our duty to do wrong.

THERE are two subjects of the utmost importance to a just delineation of the principles of society, which are, on that account, entitled to a separate examination: the duties incumbent on men living in society, and the rights accruing to them. These are merely different modes of expressing the principle of justice, as it shall happen to be considered in its relation to the agent or the patient. Duty is the treatment I am bound to bestow upon others; right is the treatment I am entitled to expect from them. This will more fully appear in the sequel.

First, of personal virtue and duty.

Virtue, like every other term of general science, may be understood either absolutely, or as the qualification and attribute of a particular being: in other words, it is one thing to enquire whether an action is virtuous, and another to enquire whether a man is virtuous. The former of these questions is considerably simple; the latter is more complex, and will require an examination of several circumstances before it can be satisfactorily determined.

In the first sense I would define virtue to be any action or actions of an intelligent being proceeding from kind and benevolent intention and having a tendency to contribute to general happiness. Thus defined, it distributes itself under two heads; and, in whatever instance either the tendency or the intention is wanting, the virtue is incomplete. An action, however pure may be the intention of the agent, the tendency of which is mischievous, or which shall merely be nugatory and useless in its character, is not a virtuous action. Were it otherwise, we should be obliged to concede the appellation of virtue to the most nefarious deeds of bigots, persecutors and religious assassins, and to the weakest observances of a deluded superstition. Still less does an action the consequences of which shall be supposed to be in the highest degree beneficial, but which proceeds from a mean, corrupt and degrading motive, deserve the appellation of virtue. A virtuous action is that of which both the motive and the tendency concur to excite our approbation.

Let us proceed from the consideration of the action to that of the agent. Before we can decide upon the degree in which any man is entitled to be denominated virtuous, we must compare his performance with his means. It is not enough that his conduct is attended with an overbalance of good intention and beneficial results. If it appear that he has scarcely produced the tenth part of that benefit, either in magnitude or extent, which he was capable of producing, it is only in a very limited sense that he can be considered as a virtuous man.

What is it therefore, we are led to enquire, that constitutes the capacity of any man? Capacity is an idea produced in the mind by a contemplation of the assemblage of properties in any substance, and the uses to which a substance so circumstanced may be applied. Thus a given portion of metal may be formed, at the pleasure of the manufacturer, into various implements, a knife, a razor, a sword, a dozen of coat-buttons, etc. This is one stage of capacity. A second is when it has already received the form of a knife, and, being dismissed by the manufacturer, falls into the hands of the person who intends it for his private use. By this person it may be devoted to purposes, beneficial, pernicious or idle. – To apply these considerations to the nature of a human being.

We are not here enquiring respecting the capacity of man absolutely speaking, but of an individual; the performer of a given action, or the person who has engaged in a certain series of conduct. In the same manner therefore as the knife may be applied to various purposes at the pleasure of its possessor, so an individual endowed with certain qualifications may engage in various pursuits, according to the views that are presented to him, and the motives that actuate his mind.

Human capacity however is a subject attended with greater ambiguity than the capacity of inanimate substances. Capacity assumes something as fixed, and enquires into the temporary application of these permanent qualities. But it is easier to define, with tolerable precision, the permanent qualities of an individual knife, for example, than of an individual man. Everything in man may be said to be in a state of flux; he is a Proteus whom we know not how to detain. That of which I am capable, for instance, as to my conduct today falls extremely short of that of which I am capable as to my conduct in the two or three next ensuing years. For what I shall do today I am dependent upon my ignorance in some things, my want of practice in others, and the erroneous habits I may in any respect have contracted. But many of these disadvantages may be superseded when the question is respecting what I shall produce in the two or three next years of my life. Nor is this all. Even my capacity of today is in a great degree determinable by the motives that shall excite me. When a man is placed in circumstances of a very strong and impressive nature, he is frequently found to possess or instantaneously to acquire capacities which neither he nor his neighbours previously suspected. We are obliged however in the decisions of morality to submit to these uncertainties. It is only after having formed the most accurate notions we are able respecting the capacity of a man, and comparing this capacity with his performance, that we can decide, with any degree of satisfaction, whether he is entitled to the appellation of virtuous.

There is another difficulty which adheres to this question. Is it the motive alone that we are entitled to take into consideration, when we decide upon the merits of the individual, or are we obliged, as in the case of virtue absolutely taken, to consider both the motives and the tendency of his conduct? The former of these has been frequently asserted. But the assertion is attended with serious difficulties.

First, vice as it is commonly understood is, so far as regards the motive, purely negative. To virtue it is necessary that it proceed from kind and benevolent intention; but malevolence, or a disposition to draw a direct gratification from the sufferings of others, is not necessary to vice. It is sufficient that the agent regards with neglect those benevolent considerations which are allied to general good. This mode of applying the terms of morality seems to arise from the circumstance that, in estimating the merits of others, we reasonably regard the actual benefit or mischief that is produced as the principal point; and consider the disposition that produces it merely as it tends to ensure to us a continuation of benefit or injury.

Secondly, actions in the highest degree injurious to the

public have often proceeded from motives uncommonly conscientious. The most determined political assassins, Clement, Ravaillac, Damiens and Gerard, seem to have been deeply penetrated with anxiety for the eternal welfare of mankind. For these objects they sacrificed their ease, and cheerfully exposed themselves to tortures and death. Benevolence probably had its part in lighting the fires of Smithfield, and pointing the daggers of Saint Bartholomew. The authors of the Gunpowder Treason were, in general, men remarkable for the sanctity of their lives, and the austerity of their manners.

The nature whether of religious imposture, or of persevering enterprise in general, seems scarcely to have been sufficiently developed by the professors of moral enquiry. Nothing is more difficult than for a man to recommend with enthusiasm that which he does not think intrinsically admirable. Nothing is more difficult than for a man to engage in an arduous undertaking that he does not persuade himself will in some way be extensively useful. When archbishop Becket set himself against the whole power of Henry the second, and bore every species of contumely with an unalterable spirit, we may easily discover the haughtiness of the priest, the insatiable ambition that delighted to set its foot upon the neck of kings, and the immeasurable vanity that snuffed with transport the incense of an adoring multitude; but we may see with equal evidence that he regarded himself as the champion of the cause of God, and expected the crown of martyrdom in a future state.

Precipitate and superficial judges conclude that he who imposes upon others is in most cases aware of the delusion himself. But this seldom happens. Self-deception is of all things the most easy. Whoever ardently wishes to find a proposition true may be expected insensibly to veer towards the opinion that suits his inclination. It cannot be wondered at, by him who considers the subtlety of the human mind,* that belief should scarcely ever rest upon

* Book I, Chap. V, p. 127.

the mere basis of evidence, and that arguments are always viewed through a delusive medium, magnifying them into Alps, or diminishing them to nothing.

In the same manner as the grounds of our opinions are complicated, so are the motives to our actions. It is probable that no wrong action is perpetrated from motives entirely pure. It is probable that conscientious assassins and persecutors have some mixture of ambition or the love of fame and some feelings of animosity and ill will. But the deception they put upon themselves may nevertheless be complete. They stand acquitted at the bar of their own examination; and their injurious conduct, if considered under the head of motive only, is probably as pure as much of that conduct which falls with the best title under the denomination of virtue.

For, thirdly, those actions of men which tend to increase the general happiness and are founded in the purest motives have some alloy in the causes from which they proceed. It has been seen that the motives of each single action, in a man already arrived at maturity, are innumerable*: into this mixture it is scarcely to be supposed that something improper, mean and inconsistent with that impartial estimate of things which is the true foundation of virtue will not insinuate itself. It seems reasonable to believe that such actions as are known most admirably to have contributed to the benefit of mankind have sprung from views of all others the least adulterated. But it cannot be doubted that many actions, considerably useful, and to a great degree well intended, have had as much alloy in their motive as other actions which, springing from a benevolent disposition, have been extensively detrimental.

From all these considerations it appears that, if we were to adjust the standard of virtue from intention alone, we should reverse all the received ideas respecting it, giving the palm to some of the greatest pests of mankind, at the expense of others who have been no contemptible bene-

* Book I, Chap. V, p. 127.

factors. Intention no doubt is of the essence of virtue. But it will not do alone. In deciding the merits of others, we are bound, for the most part, to proceed in the same manner as in deciding the merits of inanimate substances. The turning point is their utility. Intention is of no further value than as it leads to utility: it is the means, and not the end. We shall overturn therefore every principle of just reasoning if we bestow our applause upon the most mischievous of mankind, merely because the mischief they produce arises from mistake; or if we regard them in any other light than we would an engine of destruction and misery that is constructed of very costly materials.

The reasonings of the early part of this chapter upon the subject of virtue may equally be applied to elucidate the term duty. Duty is that mode of action on the part of the individual which constitutes the best possible application of his capacity to the general benefit. The only distinction to be made between what was there adduced upon the subject of personal virtue, and the observations which most aptly apply to the consideration of duty, consists in this: that, though a man should in some instances neglect the best application of his capacity, he may yet be entitled to the appellation of virtuous; but duty is uniform, and requires of us that best application in every situation that presents itself.

This way of considering the subject furnishes us with the solution of a question which has been supposed to be attended with considerable difficulty. Is it my duty to comply with the dictates of my erroneous conscience? Was it the duty of Everard Digby[18] to blow up king James and his parliament with gunpowder? Certainly not. Duty is the application of capacity to the real, not imaginary, benefit of mankind. It was his duty to entertain a sincere and ardent desire for the improvement and happiness of others. With this duty he probably complied. But it was not his duty to apply that desire to a purpose dreadful and pregnant with inexhaustible mischief. With the prejudices he entertained, perhaps it was impossible for him to do otherwise. But it would be absurd to say that it was his duty to labour under prejudice. Perhaps it will be found that no man can in any instance act otherwise than he does.* But this, if true, will not annihilate the meaning of the term duty. It has already been seen that the idea of capacity and the best application of capacity is equally intelligible of inanimate substances. Duty is a species under this generical term, and implies merely the best application of capacity in an intelligent being, whether that application originate in a self-moving power, or in the irresistible impulse of motives and considerations presented to the understanding. To talk of the duty of doing wrong can answer no other purpose than to take away all precision and meaning from language.

CHAPTER V

OF RIGHTS

Active rights exploded. – Province of morality unlimited. – Objection. – Consequences of the doctrine of active rights. – Admonition considered. – Rights of kings – of communities. – Passive rights irrefragable. – Of discretion.

THE rights of man have, like many other political and moral questions, furnished a topic of eager and pertinacious dispute more by a confused and inaccurate statement of the subject of enquiry than by any considerable difficulty attached to the subject itself.

The real or supposed rights of man are of two kinds, active and passive; the right in certain cases to do as we list; and the right we possess to the forbearance or assistance of other men.

The first of these a just philosophy will probably induce us universally to explode.

*Book IV, Chap. VII.

There is no sphere in which a human being can be supposed to act where one mode of proceeding will not, in every given instance, be more reasonable than any other mode. That mode the being is bound by every principle of justice to pursue.

Morality is nothing else but that system which teaches us to contribute upon all occasions, to the extent of our power, to the well-being and happiness of every intellectual and sensitive existence. But there is no action of our lives which does not in some way affect that happiness. Our property, our time, and our faculties may all of them be made to contribute to this end. The periods which cannot be spent in the active production of happiness may be spent in preparation. There is not one of our avocations or amusements that does not, by its effects, render us more or less fit to contribute our quota to the general utility. If then every one of our actions fall within the province of morals, it follows that we have no rights in relation to the selecting them. No one will maintain that we have a right to trespass upon the dictates of morality.

It has been observed by natural philosophers that a single grain of land more or less in the structure of the earth would have produced an infinite variation in its history. If this be true in inanimate nature, it is much more so in morals. The encounter of two persons of opposite sexes, so as to lead to the relation of marriage, in many cases obviously depends upon the most trivial circumstances, anyone of which, being changed, the relation would not have taken place. Let the instance be the father and mother of Shakespeare. If they had not been connected, Shakespeare would never have been born. If any accident had happened to the wife during her pregnancy, if she had on any day set her foot half an inch too far and fallen down a flight of stairs, if she had turned down one street instead of another, through which, it may be, some hideous object was passing, Shakespeare might never have come alive into the world. The determination of mind, in consequence of which the child contracts some of his earliest propensities, which call out his curiosity, industry and ambition, or on the other hand leave him unobserving, indolent and phlegmatic, is produced by circumstances so minute and subtle as in few instances to have been made the subject of history. The events which afterwards produce his choice of a profession or pursuit are not less precarious. Every one of these incidents, when it occurred, grew out of a series of incidents that had previously taken place. Everything is connected in the universe. If any man asserted that, if Alexander had not bathed in the river Cydnus, Shakespeare would never have written, it would be impossible to prove that his assertion was untrue.

To the inference we are deducing from this statement of facts, it may be objected 'that it is true that all events in the universe are connected, and that the most memorable revolutions may depend for their existence upon trivial causes; but it is impossible for us to discern the remote bearings and subtle influences of our own actions; and by what we cannot discern it can never be required of us to regulate our conduct.' This is no doubt true, but its force in the nature of an objection will be taken away if we consider first that, though our ignorance will justify us in neglecting that which, had we been better informed, we should have seen to be most beneficial, it can scarcely be considered as conferring on us an absolute right to incur that neglect. Secondly, even under the limited powers of our discernment, it will seldom happen to a man eminently conscientious and benevolent, to see no appearance of superiority, near or remote, direct or indirect, in favour of one side of any alternative proposed to his choice, rather than the other. We are bound to regulate ourselves by the best judgement we can exert. Thirdly, if anything remain to the active rights of man after this deduction, and if he be at liberty to regulate his conduct in any instance, independently of the dictates of morality, it will be, first, an imperfect, not an absolute right, the offspring of ignorance and imbecility; and, secondly, it will relate only to such insignificant matters, if such there be, as, after the best exercise of human judgement, cannot be discerned to have the remotest relation to the happiness of mankind.

Few things have contributed more to undermine the energy and virtue of the human species than the supposition that we have a right, as it has been phrased, to do what we will with our own. It is thus that the miser, who accumulates to no end that which diffused would have conduced to the welfare of thousands, that the luxurious man, who wallows in indulgence and sees numerous families around him pining in beggary, never fail to tell us of their rights, and to silence animadversion and quiet the censure of their own minds, by observing 'that they came fairly into possession of their wealth, that they owe no debts, and that of consequence no man has authority to enquire into their private manner of disposing of that which appertains to them'. We have in reality nothing that is strictly speaking our own. We have nothing that has not a destination prescribed to it by the immutable voice of reason and justice; and respecting which, if we supersede that destination, we do not entail upon ourselves a certain portion of guilt.

As we have a duty obliging us to a certain conduct respecting our faculties and our possessions, so our neighbour has a duty respecting his admonitions and advice. He is guilty of an omission in this point if he fail to employ every means in his power for the amendment of our errors, and to have recourse for that purpose, as he may see occasion, to the most unreserved animadversion upon our propensities and conduct. It is absurd to suppose that certain points are especially within my province, and therefore he may not afford me, invited or uninvited, his assistance in arriving at a right decision. He is bound to form the best judgement he is able respecting every circumstance that falls under his observation; what he thinks, he is bound to declare to others; and, if to others, certainly not less to the party immediately concerned. The worst consequences, through every rank and department of life, have arisen from men's supposing their personal affairs in any case to be so sacred that everyone, except themselves, was bound to be blind and dumb in relation to them.

The ground of this error has been a propensity, to which we are frequently subject, of concluding from the excess to the thing itself. Undoubtedly our neighbour is to be directed in his animadversions, not by a spirit of levity and impertinence, but by a calculation of the eventual utility Undoubtedly there is one person who must, in almost all instances, be the real actor, and other persons may not, but with caution and sober reflection occupy his time with their suggestions as to the conduct he ought to pursue. There is scarcely any tyranny more gross than that of the man who should perpetually intrude upon us his crude and half-witted advices, or who, not observing when, in point of strength and clearness, he had done justice to his own conception, should imagine it to be his duty to repeat and press it upon us without end. Advice perhaps requires above all things that it should be administered with simplicity, disinterestedness, kindness and moderation. – To return.

It has been affirmed by the zealous advocates of liberty 'that princes and magistrates have no rights'; and no position can be more incontrovertible. There is no situation of their lives that has not its correspondent duties. There is no power entrusted to them that they are not bound to exercise exclusively for the public good. It is strange that persons adopting this principle did not go a step further, and perceive that the same restrictions were applicable to subjects and citizens.

It is scarcely necessary to add that, if individuals have no rights, neither has society, which possesses nothing but what individuals have brought into a common stock. The absurdity of the common opinion, as applied to this subject, is still more glaring, if possible, than in the view in which we have already considered it. According to the usual sentiment, every club assembling for any civil purpose, every congregation of religionists assembling for the worship of God, has a right to establish any provisions or ceremonies, no matter how ridiculous or detestable, provided they do not interfere with the freedom of others. Reason lies prostrate at their feet; they have a right to trample upon and insult her as they please. It is in the same spirit we have been told that every nation has a right to choose its form of government. An acute and original author was probably misled by the vulgar phraseology on this subject when he asserted that 'at a time when neither the people of France nor the national assembly were troubling themselves about the affairs of England or the English parliament, Mr Burke's conduct was unpardonable in commencing an unprovoked attack upon them.'*

It is, no doubt, the inevitable result of human imperfection that men and societies of men should model their conduct by the best judgement they are able to form, whether that judgement be sound or erroneous. But, as it has been before shown that it cannot be their duty to do anything detrimental to the general happiness,† so it appears with equal evidence that they cannot have a right to do so. There cannot be a more absurd proposition than that which affirms the right of doing wrong. A mistake of this sort has been attended with the most pernicious consequences in public and political affairs. It cannot be too strongly inculcated that societies and communities of men are in no case empowered to establish absurdity and injustice; that the voice of the people is not, as has sometimes been ridiculously asserted, 'the voice of truth and of God'; and that universal consent cannot convert wrong into right. The most insignificant individual ought to hold himself free to animadvert upon the decisions of the most august assembly; and other men are

---

* *Rights of Man*, p. 1.
† Chap. IV, pp. 190–91.

196

bound in justice to listen to him, in proportion to the soundness of his reasons, and the strength of his remarks, and not for any accessory advantages he may derive from rank or exterior importance. The most crowded forum, or the most venerable senate, cannot make one proposition to be a rule of justice that was not substantially so previously to their decision. They can only interpret and announce that law which derives its real validity from a higher and less mutable authority. If we submit to their decisions in cases where we are not convinced of their rectitude, this submission is an affair of prudence only; a reasonable man will lament the emergence while he yields to the necessity. If a congregation of men agree universally to cut off their right hand, to shut their ears upon free enquiry, or to affirm two and two upon a particular occasion to be sixteen, in all these cases they are wrong, and ought unequivocally to be censured for usurping an authority that does not belong to them. They ought to be told, 'Gentlemen, you are not, as in the intoxication of power you have been led to imagine, omnipotent; there is an authority greater than yours, to which you are bound assiduously to conform yourselves.' No man, if he were alone in the world, would have a right to make himself impotent or miserable.

So much for the active rights of man, which, if there be any cogency in the preceding arguments, are all of them superseded and rendered null by the superior claims of justice. His passive rights, when freed from the ambiguity that has arisen from the improper mixture and confounding of these two heads, will probably be found liable to little controversy.

In the first place he is said to have a right to life and personal liberty. This proposition, if admitted, must be admitted with great limitation. He has no right to his life when his duty calls him to resign it. Other men are bound (it would be improper in strictness of speech, upon the ground of the preceding explanations, to say they have a right) to deprive him of life or liberty, if that should appear in any case to be indispensably necessary to prevent a greater evil. The passive rights of man will be best understood from the following elucidation.

Every man has a certain sphere of discretion which he has a right to expect shall not be infringed by his neighbours. This right flows from the very nature of man. First, all men are fallible: no man can be justified in setting up his judgement as a standard for others. We have no infallible judge of controversies; each man in his own apprehension is right in his decisions; and we can find no satisfactory mode of adjusting their jarring pretensions. If everyone be desirous of imposing his sense upon others, it will at last come to be a controversy, not of reason, but of force. Secondly, even if we had an infallible criterion, nothing would be gained, unless it were by all men recognized as such. If I were secured against the possibility of mistake, mischief and not good would accrue, from imposing my infallible truths upon my neighbour, and requiring his submission independently of any conviction I could produce in his understanding. Man is a being who can never be an object of just approbation, any further than he is independent. He must consult his own reason, draw his own conclusions and conscientiously conform himself to his ideas of propriety. Without this, he will be neither active, nor considerate, nor resolute, nor generous.

For these two reasons it is necessary that every man should stand by himself, and rest upon his own understanding. For that purpose each must have his sphere of discretion. No man must encroach upon my province, nor I upon his. He may advise me, moderately and without pertinaciousness, but he must not expect to dictate to me. He may censure me freely and without reserve; but he should remember that I am to act by my deliberation and not his. He may exercise a republican boldness in judging, but he must not be peremptory and imperious in prescribing. Force may never be resorted to but, in the most extraordinary and imperious emergency. I ought to exercise my talents for the benefit of others; but that exercise must be the fruit of my own conviction; no man must attempt to press me into the service. I ought to appropriate such part of the fruits of the earth as by any accident comes into my possession, and is not necessary to my benefit, to the use of others; but they must obtain it from me by argument and expostulation, not by violence. It is in this principle that what is commonly called the right of property is founded. Whatever then comes into my possession, without violence to any other man, or to the institutions of society, is my property. This property, it appears by the principles already laid down, I have no right to dispose of at my caprice; every shilling of it is appropriated by the laws of morality; but no man can be justified, in ordinary cases at least, in forcibly extorting it from me. When the laws of morality shall be clearly understood, their excellence universally apprehended, and themselves seen to be coincident with each man's private advantage, the idea of property in this sense will remain, but no man will have the least desire, for purposes of ostentation or luxury, to possess more than his neighbours.

A second branch of the passive rights of man consists in the right each man possesses to the assistance of his neighbour. This will be fully elucidated hereafter.*

*Vol. II, Book VIII.

CHAPTER VI

OF THE RIGHT OF PRIVATE JUDGEMENT

The most essential Right

Foundation of virtue. — Human actions regulated: 1. by the nature of things. — 2. by positive institution. — Tendency of the latter: 1. to excite virtue. — Its equivocal character in this respect. — 2. to inform the judgement. — Its inaptitude for that purpose. — Province of conscience considered. — Tendency of an interference with that province. — Unsuitableness of punishment — either to impress new sentiments — or to strengthen old ones. — Recapitulation.

IT has appeared that the most essential of those rights which constitute the peculiar sphere appropriate to each individual, and the right upon which every other depends as its basis, is the right of private judgement. It will therefore be of use to say something distinctly on this head.

To a rational being there can be but one rule of conduct, justice, and one mode of ascertaining that rule, the exercise of his understanding.

If in any instance I am made the mechanical instrument of absolute violence, in that instance I fall under a pure state of external slavery. If on the other hand, not being under the influence of absolute compulsion, I am wholly prompted by something that is frequently called by that name, and act from the hope of reward or the fear of punishment, the subjection I suffer is doubtless less aggravated, but the effect upon my moral habits may be in a still higher degree injurious.

In the meantime, with respect to the conduct I should observe upon such occasions, a distinction is to be made. Justice, as it was defined in a preceding chapter, is coincident with utility. I am myself a part of the great whole, and my happiness is a part of that complex view of things by which justice is regulated. The hope of reward therefore, and the fear of punishment, however wrong in themselves, and inimical to the improvement of the mind, are motives which, so long as they are resorted to in society, must and ought to have some influence with my mind.

There are two descriptions of tendency that may belong to any action, the tendency which it possesses by the necessary and unalterable laws of existence, and the tendency which results from the arbitrary interference of some intelligent being. The nature of happiness and misery, pleasure and pain, is independent of positive institution. It is immutably true that whatever tends to procure a balance of the former is to be desired, and whatever tends to procure a balance of the latter is to be rejected. In like manner there are certain features and principles inseparable from such a being as man; there are causes which, in their operation upon him, are in their own nature generative of pleasure, and some of a pleasure more excellent than others. Every action has a result which may be said to be peculiarly its own, and which will always follow upon it, unless so far as it may happen to be superseded by the operation of other and extrinsical causes.

The tendency of positive institution is of two sorts, to furnish an additional motive to the practice of virtue or right; and to inform the understanding as to what actions are right and what actions are wrong. Much cannot be said in commendation of either of these tendencies.

First, positive institution may furnish an additional motive to the practice of virtue. I have an opportunity of essentially contributing to the advantage of twenty individuals; they will be benefited, and no other persons will sustain a material injury. I ought to embrace this opportunity. Here let us suppose positive institution to interfere, and to annex some great personal reward to the discharge of my duty. This immediately changes the nature of the action. Before, I preferred it for its intrinsic excellence. Now, so far as the positive institution operates,

I prefer it because some person has arbitrarily annexed to it a great weight of self-interest. But virtue, considered as the quality of an intelligent being, depends upon the disposition with which the action is accompanied. Under a positive institution then, this very action, which is intrinsically virtuous, may, so far as relates to the agent, become vicious. The vicious man would before have neglected the advantage of these twenty individuals, because he would not bring a certain inconvenience or trouble upon himself. The same man, with the same disposition, will now promote their advantage, because his own welfare is concerned in it. Twenty, other things equal, is twenty times better than one. He that is not governed by the moral arithmetic of the case, or who acts from a disposition directly at war with that arithmetic, is unjust.* In other words, moral improvement will be forwarded in proportion as we are exposed to no other influence than that of the tendency which belongs to an action by the necessary and unalterable laws of existence. This is probably the meaning of the otherwise vague and obscure principle, 'that we should do good, regardless of the consequences', and by that other, 'that we may not do evil, from the prospect of good to result from it'. The case would have been rendered still more glaring if, instead of the welfare of twenty, we had supposed the welfare of millions to have been concerned. In reality, whether the disparity be great or small, the inference must be the same.

Secondly, positive institution may inform the understanding as to what actions are right and what actions are wrong. Here it may be of advantage to us to reflect upon the terms understanding and information. Understanding, particularly as it is concerned with moral subjects, is the percipient of truth. This is its proper sphere. Information, so far as it is genuine, is a portion detached from the great body of truth. You inform me 'that Euclid asserts the three angles of a plane triangle to be equal

* Book IV, Chap. X.

202

to two right angles'. Still I am unacquainted with the truth of this proposition. 'But Euclid has demonstrated it. His demonstration has existed for two thousand years, and, during that term, has proved satisfactory to every man by whom it has been understood.' I am nevertheless uninformed. The knowledge of truth lies in the perceived agreement or disagreement of the terms of a proposition. So long as I am unacquainted with the middle term by means of which they may be compared, so long as they are incommensurate to my understanding, you may have furnished me with a principle from which I may reason truly to further consequences; but, as to the principle itself, I may strictly be said to know nothing.

Every proposition has an intrinsic evidence of its own. Every consequence has premises from which it flows; and upon them, and not upon anything else, its validity depends. If you could work a miracle to prove 'that the three angles of a triangle were equal to two right angles', I should still know that the proposition had been either true or false previously to the exhibition of the miracle; and that there was no necessary connection between any one of its terms and the miracle exhibited. The miracle would take off my attention from the true question to a question altogether different, that of authority. By the authority adduced I might be prevailed on to yield an irregular assent to the proposition; but I could not properly be said to perceive its truth.

But this is not all. If it were, it might perhaps be regarded as a refinement foreign to the concerns of human life. Positive institutions do not content themselves with requiring my assent to certain propositions, in consideration of the testimony by which they are enforced. This would amount to no more than advice flowing from a respectable quarter, which, after all, I might reject if it did not accord with the mature judgement of my own understanding. But in the very nature of these institutions there is included a sanction, a motive either of punishment or reward, to induce me to obedience.

It is commonly said 'that positive institutions ought to leave me free in matters of conscience, but may properly interfere with my conduct in civil concerns'. But this distinction seems to have been very lightly taken up. What sort of moralist must he be whose conscience is silent as to what passes in his intercourse with other men? Such a distinction proceeds upon the supposition 'that it is of great consequence whether I bow to the east or the west; whether I call the object of my worship Jehovah or Allah; whether I pay a priest in a surplice or a black coat. These are points in which an honest man ought to be rigid and inflexible. But as to those other, whether he shall be a tyrant, a slave or a free citizen; whether he shall bind himself with multiplied oaths impossible to be performed, or be a rigid observer of truth; whether he shall swear allegiance to a king *de jure* or a king *de facto*, to the best or the worst of all possible governments; respecting these points he may safely commit his conscience to the keeping of the civil magistrate.' In reality, by as many instances as I act contrary to the unbiassed dictate of my own judgement, by so much I abdicate the most valuable part of the character of man.

I am satisfied at present that a certain conduct, suppose it be a rigid attention to the confidence of private conversation, is incumbent on me. You tell me 'there are certain cases of such peculiar emergency as to supersede this rule'. Perhaps I think there are not. If I admit your proposition, a wide field of enquiry is opened respecting what cases do or do not deserve to be considered as exceptions. It is little likely that we should agree respecting all these cases. How then does the law treat me for my conscientious discharge of what I conceive to be my duty? Because I will not turn informer (which, it may be, I think an infamous character) against my most valued friend, the law accuses me of misprision of treason, felony or murder, and perhaps hangs me. I believe a certain individual to be a confirmed villain and a most dangerous member of society, and feel it to be my duty to warn others, perhaps the public, against the effect of his vices. Because I publish what I know to be true, the law convicts me of libel, *scandalum magnatum*, and crimes of I know not what complicated denomination.

If the evil stopped here, it would be well. If I only suffered a certain calamity, suppose death, I could endure it. Death has hitherto been the common lot of men, and I expect, at some time or other, to submit to it. Human society must, sooner or later, be deprived of its individual members, whether they be valuable, or whether they be inconsiderable. But the punishment acts, not only retrospectively upon me, but prospectively upon my contemporaries and countrymen. My neighbour entertains the same opinion respecting the conduct he ought to hold as I did. The executioner of public justice however interposes with a powerful argument, to convince him that he has mistaken the path of abstract rectitude.

What sort of converts will be produced by this unfeeling logic? 'I have deeply reflected,' suppose, 'upon the nature of virtue, and am convinced that a certain proceeding is incumbent on me. But the hangman, supported by an act of parliament, assures me I am mistaken.' If I yield my opinion to his *dictum*, my action becomes modified, and my character also. An influence like this is inconsistent with all generous magnanimity of spirit, all ardent impartiality in the discovery of truth, and all inflexible perseverance in its assertion. Countries exposed to the perpetual interference of decrees, instead of arguments, exhibit within their boundaries the mere phantoms of men. We can never judge from an observation of their inhabitants what men would be if they knew of no appeal from the tribunal of conscience, and if, whatever they thought, they dared to speak, and dared to act.

At present there will perhaps occur to the majority of readers but few instances of laws which may be supposed to interfere with the conscientious discharge of duty. A considerable number will occur in the course of the present enquiry. More would readily offer themselves to a patient research. Men are so successfully reduced to a common standard by the operation of positive law that, in most countries, they are capable of little more than, like parrots, repeating what others have said. This uniformity is capable of being produced in two ways, by energy of mind and indefatigableness of enquiry, enabling a considerable number to penetrate with equal success into the recesses of truth; and by pusillanimity of temper, and a frigid indifference to right and wrong, produced by the penalties which are suspended over such as shall disinterestedly enquire, and communicate and act upon the result of their enquiries. It is easy to perceive which of these is the cause of the uniformity that prevails in the present instance.

One thing more in enforcement of this important consideration. 'I have done something,' suppose, 'which, though wrong in itself, I believe to be right; or I have done something which I usually admit to be wrong; but my conviction upon the subject is not so clear and forcible as to prevent my yielding to a powerful temptation.' There can be no doubt that the proper way of conveying to my understanding a truth of which I am ignorant, or of impressing upon me a firmer persuasion of a truth with which I am acquainted, is by an appeal to my reason. Even an angry expostulation with me upon my conduct will but excite similar passions in me, and cloud, instead of illuminate, my understanding. There is certainly a way of expressing truth with such benevolence as to command attention, and such evidence as to enforce conviction in all cases whatever.

Punishment inevitably excites in the sufferer, and ought to excite, a sense of injustice. Let its purpose be to convince me of the truth of a position which I at present believe to be false. It is not, abstractedly considered, of the nature of an argument, and therefore it cannot begin with producing conviction. Punishment is a comparatively specious name; but is in reality nothing more than force put upon one being by another who happens to be stronger. But strength apparently does not constitute justice. The case of punishment, in the view in which we now consider it, is the case of you and me differing in opinion, and your telling me that you must be right, since you have a more brawny arm, or have applied your mind more to the acquiring skill in your weapons than I have.

But let us suppose 'that I am convinced of my error, but that my conviction is superficial and fluctuating, and the object you propose is to render it durable and profound'. Ought it to be thus durable and profound? There are no doubt arguments and reasons calculated to render it so. Is the subject in reality problematical, and do you wish by the weight of your blows to make up for the deficiency of your logic? This can never be defended. An appeal to force must appear to both parties, in proportion to the soundness of their understanding, to be a confession of imbecility. He that has recourse to it would have no occasion for this expedient if he were sufficiently acquainted with the powers of that truth it is his office to communicate. If there be any man who, in suffering punishment, is not conscious of injury, he must have had his mind previously debased by slavery, and his sense of moral right and wrong blunted by a series of oppressions. If there be any truth more unquestionable than the rest, it is that every man is bound to the exertion of his faculties in the discovery of right, and to the carrying into effect all the right with which he is acquainted. It may be granted that an infallible standard, if it could be discovered, would be considerably beneficial. But this infallible standard itself would be of little use in human affairs, unless it had the property of reasoning as well as deciding, of enlightening the mind as well as constraining the body. If a man be in some cases obliged to prefer his own judgement, he is in all cases obliged to consult that judgement, before he can determine whether the matter in question be of the sort provided for or no. So that from this reasoning it ultimately appears that the conviction of a man's individual understanding is the only legitimate principle imposing on him the duty of adopting any species of conduct.

Such are the genuine principles of human society. Such would be the unconstrained condition of its members in a state where every individual within the society and every neighbour without was capable of listening with sobriety to the dictates of reason. We shall not fail to be impressed with considerable regret if, when we descend to the present mixed characters of mankind, we find ourselves obliged in any degree to depart from so simple and grand a principle. The universal exercise of private judgement is a doctrine so unspeakably beautiful that the true politician will certainly feel infinite reluctance in admitting the idea of interfering with it. A principal object in the subsequent stages of enquiry will be to discuss the emergency of the cases that may be thought to demand this interference.

BOOK III

PRINCIPLES OF GOVERNMENT

CHAPTER I

SYSTEMS OF POLITICAL WRITERS

The question stated. – First hypothesis: government founded in superior strength. – Second hypothesis: government jure divino. *– Third hypothesis: the social contract. – The first hypothesis examined. – The second. – Criterion of divine right:* 1. *patriarchal descent –* 2. *justice*

HAVING in the preceding book attempted a general delineation of the principles of rational society, it is proper that we, in the next place, proceed to the topic of government.

It has hitherto been the persuasion of communities of men in all ages and countries that there are occasions, in which it becomes necessary, to supersede private judgement for the sake of public good, and to control the acts of the individual, by an act to be performed in the name of the whole.

Previously to our deciding upon this question, it will be of advantage to enquire into the nature of government, and the manner in which this control may be exercised with the smallest degree of violence and usurpation in regard to the individual. This point, being determined, will assist us finally to ascertain both the quantity of evil which government in its best form involves, and the urgency of the case which has been supposed to demand its interference.

There can be little ground to question the necessity, and consequently the justice, of force to be, in some cases, interposed between individual and individual. Violence is so prompt a mode of deciding differences of opinion and contentions of passion that there will infallibly be some persons who will resort to this mode. How is their violence to be repressed, or prevented from being accompanied occasionally with the most tragical effects? Violence must necessarily be preceded by an opinion of the mind dictating that violence; and, as he who first has resort to force instead of argument is unquestionably erroneous, the best and most desirable mode of correcting him is by convincing him of his error. But the urgency of the case when, for example, a dagger is pointed to my own breast or that of another may be such as not to afford time for expostulation. Hence the propriety and duty of defence.

Is not defence equally necessary, on the part of a community, against a foreign enemy, or the contumacy of its own members? This is perhaps the most forcible view in which the argument in favour of the institution of government has yet been placed. But, waiving this question for the present, the enquiry now proposed is, if action on the part of the community should in any instance be found requisite, in what manner is it proper or just that the force, acting in behalf of the community, should be organized?

There are three hypotheses that have been principally maintained upon this subject. First, the system of force, according to which it is affirmed 'that, inasmuch as it is necessary that the great mass of mankind should be held under the subjection of compulsory restraint, there can be no other criterion of that restraint than the power of the individuals who lay claim to its exercise, the foundation of which power exists, in the unequal degrees in which corporal strength, and intellectual sagacity, are distributed among mankind'.

There is a second class of reasoners, who deduce the

origin of all government from divine right, and affirm 'that, as men derived their existence from an infinite creator at first, so are they still subject to his providential care, and of consequence owe allegiance to their civil governors, as to a power which he has thought fit to set over them'.

The third system is that which has been most usually maintained by the friends of equality and justice; the system according to which the individuals of any society are supposed to have entered into a contract with their governors or with each other, and which founds the authority of government in the consent of the governed.

The two first of these hypotheses may easily be dismissed. That of force appears to proceed upon the total negation of abstract and immutable justice, affirming every government to be right that is possessed of power sufficient to enforce its decrees. It puts a violent termination upon all political science; and is calculated for nothing further than to persuade men to sit down quietly under their present disadvantages, whatever they may be, and not exert themselves to discover a remedy for the evils they suffer. The second hypothesis is of an equivocal nature. It either coincides with the first, and affirms all existing power to be alike of divine derivation; or it must remain totally useless, till a criterion can be found to distinguish those governments which are approved by God from those which cannot lay claim to that sanction. The criterion of patriarchal descent will be of no avail till the true claimant and rightful heir can be discovered. If we make utility and justice the test of God's approbation, this hypothesis will be liable to little objection; but then on the other hand little will be gained by it, since those who have not introduced divine right into the argument will yet readily grant that a government which can be shown to be agreeable to utility and justice is a rightful government.

The third hypothesis demands a more careful examination. If any error have insinuated itself into the support of truth, it becomes of particular consequence to detect it. Nothing can be of more importance than to separate prejudice and mistake on the one hand from reason and demonstration on the other. Wherever they have been confounded, the cause of truth must necessarily be the sufferer. The cause, so far from being injured by a dissolution of the unnatural alliance, may be expected to derive from that dissolution a superior degree of prosperity and lustre.

CHAPTER II

OF THE SOCIAL CONTRACT

Queries proposed. – Who are the contracting parties? – What is the form of engagement? – Over how long a period does the contract extend? – To how great a variety of propositions? – Can it extend to laws hereafter to be made? – Addresses of adhesion considered. – Power of a majority.

UPON the first statement of the system of a social contract various difficulties present themselves. Who are the parties to this contract? For whom did they consent, for themselves only or for others? For how long a time is this contract to be considered as binding? If the consent of every individual be necessary, in what manner is that consent to be given? Is it to be tacit, or declared in express terms?

Little will be gained for the cause of equality and justice if our ancestors, at the first institution of government, had a right indeed of choosing the system of regulations under which they thought proper to live, but at the same time could barter away the understandings and independence of all that came after them, to the latest posterity. But, if the contract must be renewed in each successive generation, what periods must be fixed on for that purpose? And if I be obliged to submit to the established government till my turn comes to assent to it, upon what principle is that obligation founded? Surely not upon the contract into which my father entered before I was born?

Secondly, what is the nature of the consent in consequence of which I am to be reckoned a party to the frame of any political constitution? It is usually said 'that acquiescence is sufficient; and that this acquiescence is to be inferred from my living quietly under the protection of the laws'. But if this be true, an end is as effectually put to all political science, all discrimination of better and worse, as by any system invented by the most slavish sycophant. Upon this hypothesis every government that is quietly submitted to is a lawful government, whether it be the usurpation of Cromwell, or the tyranny of Caligula. Acquiescence is frequently nothing more than a choice on the part of the individual of what he deems the least evil. In many cases it is not so much as this, since the peasant and the artisan, who form the bulk of a nation, however dissatisfied with the government of their country, seldom have it in their power to transport themselves to another. It is also to be observed upon the system of acquiescence, that it is in little agreement with the established opinions and practices of mankind. Thus what has been called the law of nations lays least stress upon the allegiance of a foreigner settling among us, though his acquiescence is certainly most complete; while natives removing into an uninhabited region are claimed by the mother country, and removing into a neighbouring territory are punished by municipal law, if they take arms against the country in which they were born. But surely acquiescence can scarcely be construed into consent while the individuals concerned, are wholly unapprised of the authority intended to be rested upon it.*

Locke, the great champion of the doctrine of an ori-

* Hume's *Essays*, Part II, Essay xii.

ginal contract, has been aware of this difficulty, and therefore observes that 'a tacit consent indeed obliges a man to obey the laws of any government, as long as he has any possessions, or enjoyment of any part of the dominions of that government; but nothing can make a man a member of the commonwealth, but his actually entering into it by positive engagement and express promise and compact.'* A singular distinction! implying upon the face of it that an acquiescence such as has just been described is sufficient to render a man amenable to the penal regulations of society; but that his own consent is necessary to entitle him to the privileges of a citizen.

A third objection to the social contract will suggest itself as soon as we attempt to ascertain the extent of the obligation, even supposing it to have been entered into in the most solemn manner by every member of the community. Allowing that I am called upon, at the period of my coming of age for example, to declare my assent or dissent to any system of opinions or any code of practical institutes; for how long a period does this declaration bind me? Am I precluded from better information for the whole course of my life? And, if not for my whole life, why for a year, a week or even an hour? If my deliberate judgement, or my real sentiment, be of no avail in the case, in what sense can it be affirmed that all lawful government is founded in consent?

But the question of time is not the only difficulty. If you demand my assent to any proposition, it is necessary that the proposition should be stated simply and clearly. So numerous are the varieties of human understanding, in all cases where its independence and integrity are sufficiently preserved, that there is little chance of any two men coming to a precise agreement about ten successive propositions that are in their own nature open to debate. What then can be more absurd than to present to me the laws of England in fifty volumes folio, and call upon me to give an honest and uninfluenced vote upon their contents?

* *Treatise of Government*, Book II, Chap. viii, § 119, 122.

But the social contract, considered as the foundation of civil government, requires of me more than this. I am not only obliged to consent to all the laws that are actually upon record, but to all the laws that shall hereafter be made. It was under this view of the subject that Rousseau, in tracing the consequences of the social contract, was led to assert that 'the great body of the people in whom the sovereign authority resides can neither delegate nor resign it. The essence of that authority,' he adds, 'is the general will; and will cannot be represented. It must either be the same or another; there is no alternative. The deputies of the people cannot be its representatives; they are merely its attorneys. The laws which the community does not ratify in person, are no laws, are nullities.'*

The difficulty here stated has been endeavoured to be provided against by some late advocates for liberty, in the way of addresses of adhesion; addresses originating in the various districts and departments of a nation, and without which no regulation of constitutional importance is to be deemed valid. But this is a very superficial remedy. The addressers of course have seldom any other alternative than that above alluded to, of indiscriminate admission or rejection. There is an infinite difference between the first deliberation and the subsequent exercise of a negative. The former is a real power, the latter is seldom more than the shadow of a power. Not to add that addresses are a most precarious and equivocal mode of collecting the sense of a nation. They are usually voted in a tumultuous and summary manner; they are carried along by the tide of party; and the signatures annexed to

---

* 'La souveraineté ne peut être représentée, par le même raison qu'elle ne peut être aliénée; elle consiste essentiellement dans la volonté générale, et la volonté ne se représente point: elle est la même, ou elle est autre; il n'y a point de milieu. Les députés du peuple ne sont donc point ses représentans, ils ne sont que ses commissaires; ils ne peuvent rien conclure définitivement. Toute loi que le peuple en personne n'a pas ratifiée, est nulle; ce n'est point une loi.' *Du Contrat Social*, Liv. III, Chap. XV.

them are obtained by indirect and accidental methods, while multitudes of bystanders, unless upon some extraordinary occasion, remain ignorant of or indifferent to the transaction.

Lastly, if government be founded in the consent of the people, it can have no power over any individual by whom that consent is refused. If a tacit consent be not sufficient, still less can I be deemed to have consented to a measure upon which I put an express negative. This immediately follows from the observations of Rousseau. If the people, or the individuals of whom the people is constituted, cannot delegate their authority to a representative, neither can any individual delegate his authority to a majority, in an assembly of which he is himself a member. That must surely be a singular species of consent the external indications of which are often to be found in an unremitting opposition in the first instance, and compulsory subjection in the second.

CHAPTER III

OF PROMISES

Promises not the foundation of morality – are, absolutely considered, an evil – are of unfrequent necessity. – Imperfect promises unavoidable. – Perfect promises in some cases necessary. –Obligation of promises – of the same nature as the obligation not to invade another man's property – admits of gradations. – Recapitulation. – Application.

THE whole principle of an original contract rests upon the obligation under which we are conceived to be placed to observe our promises. The reasoning upon which it is founded is 'that we have promised obedience to government, and therefore are bound to obey'. The doctrine of a social contract would never have been thought worth the formality of an argument had it not been presumed to be one of our first and paramount obligations to perform our engagements. It may be proper therefore to enquire into the nature of this obligation.

And here the first observation that offers itself, upon the principle of the doctrines already delivered,* is that promises and compacts are in no sense the foundation of morality.

The foundation of morality is justice. The principle of virtue is an irresistible deduction from the wants of one man, and the ability of another to relieve them. It is not because I have promised that I am bound to do that for my neighbour which will be beneficial to him and not injurious to me. This is an obligation which arises out of no compact, direct or understood; and would still remain, though it were impossible that I should experience a return, either from him or any other human being. It is not on account of any promise or previous engagement that I am bound to tell my neighbour the truth. Undoubtedly one of the reasons why I should do so is because the obvious use of the faculty of speech is to inform, and not to mislead. But it is an absurd account of this motive, to say that my having recourse to the faculty of speech amounts to a tacit engagement that I will use it for its genuine purposes. The true ground of confidence between man and man is the knowledge we have of the motives by which the human mind is influenced; our perception that the motives to deceive can but rarely occur, while the motives to veracity will govern the stream of human actions.

This position will be made still more incontrovertible if we bestow a moment's attention upon the question, Why should we observe our promises? The only rational answer that can be made is because it tends to the welfare of intelligent beings. But this answer is equally cogent if applied to any other branch of morality. It is therefore

* Book II, Ch. II, &c.

absurd to rest the foundation of morality thus circuitously upon promises, when it may with equal propriety be rested upon that from which promises themselves derive their obligation.*

Again; when I enter into an engagement, I engage for that which is in its own nature conducive to human happiness, or which is not so. Can my engagement always render that which before was injurious agreeable to, and that which was beneficial the opposite of duty? Previously to my entering into a promise, there is something which I ought to promise, and something which I ought not. Previously to my entering into a promise, all modes of action were not indifferent. Nay, the very opposite of this is true. Every conceivable mode of action has its appropriate tendency, and shade of tendency, to benefit, or to mischief, and consequently its appropriate claim to be performed or avoided. Thus clearly does it appear that promises and compacts are not the foundation of morality.

Secondly, I observe that promises are, absolutely considered, an evil, and stand in opposition to the genuine and wholesome exercise of an intellectual nature.

Justice has already appeared to be the sum of moral and political duty. But the measure of justice is the useful or injurious characters of the men with whom I am concerned; the criterion of justice is the influence my conduct will have upon the stock of general good. Hence it inevitably follows that the motives by which duty requires me to govern my actions must be such as are of general application.

What is it then to which the obligation of a promise applies? What I have promised is what I ought to have performed, if no promise had intervened, or it is not. It is conducive, or not conducive, to the generating of human happiness. If it be the former, then promise comes in merely as an additional inducement, in favour of that which, in the eye of morality, was already of indispensable

* Hume's *Essays*, Part II, Essay xii.

obligation. It teaches me to do something from a precarious and temporary motive which ought to be done for its intrinsic recommendations. If therefore right motives and a pure intention are constituent parts of virtue, promises are clearly at variance with virtue.

But promises will not always come in reinforcement of that which was duty before the promise was made. When it is otherwise, there is obviously a contention between what would have been obligatory, if no promise had intervened, and what the promise which has been given has a tendency to render obligatory.

Nor can it with much cogency be alleged in this argument that promises may at least assume an empire over things indifferent. There is nothing which is truly indifferent. All things in the universe are connected together.* It is true that many of these links in human affairs are too subtle to be traced by our grosser optics. But we should observe as many of them as we are able. He that is easily satisfied as to the morality of his conduct will suppose that questions of duty are of rare occurrence, and perhaps lament that there is so little within his sphere to perform. But he that is anxiously alive to the inspirations of virtue will scarcely find an hour in which he cannot, by act or preparation, contribute to the general weal. If then every shilling of our property, and every faculty of our mind, have received their destination from the principles of unalterable justice, promises have scarcely an atom of ground upon which they can properly and legitimately be called to decide.

There is another consideration of great weight in this case. Our faculties and our possessions are the means by which we are enabled to benefit others. Our time is the theatre in which only these means can unfold themselves. There is nothing the right disposal of which is more sacred. In order to the employing our faculties and our possessions in the way most conducive to the general good, we are bound to acquire all the information which our

* Book II, Chap. V, p. 192.

opportunities enable us to acquire. Now one of the principal means of information is time. We must therefore devote to that object all the time our situation will allow. But we abridge, and that in the most essential point, the time of gaining information, if we bind ourselves today to the conduct we will observe two months hence. He who thus anticipates upon the stores of knowledge is certainly not less improvident than he who lives by anticipating the stores of fortune.

An active and conscientious man will continually add to his materials of judgement. Nor is it enough to say that every man ought to regard his judgement as immature, and look forward with impatience to the moment which shall detect his present oversights. Beside this, it will always happen that, however mature the faculties of any individual may deserve to be considered, he will be perpetually acquiring new information as to that respecting which his conduct is to be decided at some future period. Let the case be of an indentured servant. Why should I, unless there be something in the circumstances obliging me to submit to this disadvantage, engage to allow him to reside for a term of years under my roof, and to employ towards him a uniform mode of treatment, whatever his character may prove in the sequel? Why should he engage to live with and serve me however tyrannical, cruel or absurd may be my carriage towards him? We shall both of us hereafter know more of each other, and of the benefits or inconveniences attendant on our connection. Why preclude ourselves from the use of this knowledge? Such a situation will inevitably generate a perpetual struggle between the independent dictates of reason, and the conduct which the particular compact into which we have entered may be supposed to prescribe.

It follows from what has been here adduced that promises, in the same sense as has already been observed of government, are an evil, though, it may be, in some cases a necessary evil. – To remove the obscurity which might otherwise accompany this mode of expression, it is perhaps proper to advert to the sense in which the word evil is here used.

Evil may be either general or individual: an event may either be productive of evil in its direct and immediate operation, or in a just balance and comprehensive estimate of all the effects with which it is pregnant. In whichsoever of these senses the word is understood, the evil is not imaginary, but real.

Evil is a term which differs from pain only as it has a more comprehensive meaning. It may be defined to signify whatever is painful itself, or is connected with pain, as an antecedent is connected with its consequent. Thus explained, it appears that a thing not immediately painful may be evil, but in a somewhat improper and imperfect sense. It bears the name of evil not upon its own account. Nothing is evil in the fullest sense but pain.

To this it may be added that pain is always an evil. Pleasure and pain, happiness and misery, constitute the whole ultimate subject of moral enquiry. There is nothing desirable but the obtaining of the one and the avoiding of the other. All the researches of human imagination cannot add a single article to this summary of good. Hence it follows that, wherever pain exists, there is evil. Were it otherwise, there would be no such thing as evil. If pain in one individual be not an evil, then it would not be an evil for pain to be felt by every individual that exists, and forever. The universe is no more than a collection of individuals.

To illustrate this by an obvious example. The amputation of a leg is an evil of considerable magnitude. The pain attendant on the operation is exquisite. The cure is slow and tormenting. When cured, the man who has suffered the amputation is precluded for ever from a variety both of agreeable amusements and useful occupations. Suppose him to suffer this operation from pure wantonness, and we shall then see its calamity in the most striking light. Suppose, on the other hand, the operation to be the only alternative for stopping a mortification, and it becomes relatively good. But it does not, upon this account, cease to be an absolute evil. The painful sensation, at least to a considerable degree, remains; and the abridgement of his pleasures and utility for the rest of his life is in no respect altered.

The case of promises is considerably similar to this. So far as they have any effect, they depose us, as to the particular to which they relate, from the use of our own understanding; they call off our attention from the direct tendencies of our conduct, and fix it upon a merely local and precarious consideration. There may be cases in which they are necessary and ought to be employed: but we should never suffer ourselves by their temporary utility to be induced to forget their intrinsic nature, and the demerits which adhere to them independently of any peculiar concurrence of circumstances.

Thirdly, it may be added to the preceding observations that promises are by no means of so frequent necessity as has been often imagined.

It may be asked, 'How, without the intervention of promises, can the affairs of the world be carried on?' To this it will be a sufficient answer in the majority of instances to say that they will be best carried on by rational and intelligent beings acting as if they were rational and intelligent. Why should it be supposed that affairs would not for the most part go on sufficiently well, though my neighbour could no further depend upon my assistance than it appeared reasonable to grant it? This will, upon many occasions, be a sufficient dependence, if I be honest; nor will he, if he be honest, desire anything further.

But it will be alleged, 'Human pursuits are often of a continued tenour, made up of a series of actions, each of which is adopted, not for its own sake, but for the sake of some conclusion in which it terminates. Many of these depend for their success upon co-operation and concert. It is therefore necessary that I should have some clear and specific reason to depend upon the fidelity of my coadjutor, that so I may not be in danger, when I have for a length of time persisted in my exertions, of being frustrated by some change that his sentiments have undergone in the interval.' To this it may be replied that such a pledge of fidelity is less frequently necessary than is ordinarily imagined. Were it to be superseded in a variety of cases, men would be taught to have more regard to their own exertions, and less to the assistance of others, which caprice may refuse, or justice oblige them to withhold. They would acquire such merit as should oblige every honest man, if needful, to hasten to their succour; and engage in such pursuits as, not depending upon the momentary caprice of individuals, rested for their success upon the less precarious nature of general circumstances.

Having specified the various limitations that exist as to the utility of promises, it remains for us to discuss their form and obligation in the cases where they may be conceived to be necessary.

Promises are of two kinds, perfect and imperfect. A perfect promise is where the declaration of intention is made by me, for the express purpose of serving as a ground of expectation to my neighbour respecting my future conduct. An imperfect promise is where it actually thus serves as a ground of expectation, though that was not my purpose when I made the declaration. Imperfect promises are of two classes: I may have reason, or I may have no reason, to know, when I make the declaration, that it will be acted upon by my neighbour, though not assuming the specific form of an engagement.

As to imperfect promises it may be observed that they are wholly unavoidable. No man can always refrain from declaring his intention as to his future conduct. Nay, it should seem that, in many cases, if a man enquire of me the state of my mind in this respect, duty obliges me to inform him of this as I would of any other fact. Were it otherwise, a perpetual coldness and reserve would pervade all human intercourse. But the improvement of mankind rests upon nothing so essentially as upon the habitual practice of candour, frankness and sincerity.

Perfect promises will also in various instances occur. I have occasion for an interview with a particular person tomorrow. I inform him of my intention of being upon a certain spot at a given hour of the day. It is convenient to him to go to the same place at the same time, for the purpose of meeting me. In this case, it is impossible to prevent the mutual declaration of intention from serving as a sort of pledge of the performance. Qualifying expressions will make little alteration: the ordinay circumstances which qualify engagements will in most cases be understood, whether they are stated or no. Appointments of this sort, so far from deserving to be uniformly avoided, ought in many cases to be sought, that there may be as little waste of time or exertion on either side as the nature of the situation will admit.

To proceed from the manner in which engagements are made to the obligation that results from them. This obligation is of different degrees according to the nature of the case; but it is impossible to deny that it may be of the most serious import. We have already seen that each man is entitled to his sphere of discretion, which another may not, unless under the most imperious circumstances, infringe.* But I infringe it as substantially by leading him into a certain species of conduct through the means of delusive expectations, as by any system of usurpation it is possible to employ. A person promises me, I will suppose, five hundred pounds for a certain commodity, a book it may be, which I am to manufacture. I am obliged to spend several months in the production. Surely, after this, he can rarely be justified in disappointing me, and saying I have found a better object upon which to employ my money. The case is nearly similar to that of the labourer who, after having performed his day's work, should be refused his wages. Take the case the other way, and suppose that, I having contracted to produce the commodity, the other party to the contract has advanced me three out of the five hundred pounds. Suppose further,

* Book II, Chap. V.

that I am unable to replace this sum. Surely I am not at liberty to dispense myself from the performance of my engagement.

The case here is of the same nature as of any other species of property. Property is sacred: there is but one way in which duty requires the possessor to dispose of it, but I may not forcibly interfere, and dispose of it in the best way in his stead. This is the ordinary law of property, as derived from the principles of universal morality.* But there are cases that supersede this law. The principle that attributes to every man the disposal of his property, as well as that distributes to every man his sphere of discretion, derives its force in both instances from the consideration that a greater sum of happiness will result from its observance than its infringement. Wherever therefore the contrary to this is clearly the case, there the force of the principle is suspended. What shall prevent me from taking by force from my neighbour's store, if the alternative be that I must otherwise perish with hunger? What shall prevent me from supplying the distress of my neighbour from property that, strictly speaking, is not my own, if the emergence be terrible, and will not admit of delay? Nothing; unless it be the punishment that is reserved for such conduct in some instances; since it is no more fitting that I should bring upon myself calamity and death than that I should suffer them to fall upon another.

The vesting of property in any individual admits of different degrees of fullness, and, in proportion to that fullness, will be the mischief resulting from its violation. If then it appear that, even when the vesting amounts to the fullness of regular possession, there are cases in which it ought to be violated, the different degrees that fall short of this will admit of still greater modification. It is in vain that the whole multitude of moralists assures us that the sum I owe to another man is as little to be infringed upon as the wealth of which he is in possession.

* Book VIII.

Everyone feels the fallacy of this maxim. The sum I owe to another may in many cases be paid, at my pleasure, either today or tomorrow, either this week or next. The means of payment, particularly with a man of slender resources, must necessarily be fluctuating, and he must employ his discretion as to the proportion between his necessary and his gratuitous disbursements. When he ultimately fails of payment, the mischief he produces is real, but is not so great, at least in ordinary cases, as that which attends upon robbery. In fine, it is a law resulting from the necessity of nature that he who has any species of property in trust, for however short a time, must have have a discretion, sometimes less and sometimes greater, as to the disposal of it.

To return once more to the main principle in this gradation. The property, most completely sanctioned by all the general rules that can be devised, is yet not inviolable. The imperious principle of self-preservation may authorize me to violate it. A great and eminent balance of good to the public may authorize its violation; and upon this ground we see proprietors occasionally compelled to part with their possessions, under every mode of government in the world. As a general maxim it may be admitted that force is a legitimate means of prevention, where the alternative is complete, and the employment of force will not produce a greater evil, or subvert the general tranquillity. But, if direct force be in certain cases justifiable, indirect force, or the employment of the means placed in my hands without an anxious enquiry respecting the subordinate regulations of property, where the benefit to be produced is clear, is still more justifiable. Upon this ground, it may be my duty to relieve, upon some occasions, the wretchedness of my neighbour, without having first balanced the debtor and creditor side of my accounts, or when I know that balance to be against me. Upon this ground, every promise is considered as given under a reserve for unforeseen and imperious circumstances, whether that reserve be specifically stated or no. Upon the same ground an appointment for an interview is considered as subject to a similar reserve; though the time of my neighbour which I dissipate upon that supposition, is as real a property as his wealth, is a part of that sphere over which every man is entitled to the exercise of his separate discretion. It is impossible that human society can subsist without frequent encroachments of one man upon his neighbour: we sufficiently discharge our duty if we habitually recollect that each man has his province, and endeavour to regulate our conduct accordingly.

These principles are calculated to set in a clearer light than they have often been exhibited the cases that authorize the violation of promises. Compact is not the foundation of morality; on the contrary, it is an expedient to which we are sometimes obliged to have resort, but the introduction of which must always be regarded by an enlightened observer with jealousy. It ought never to be called forth but in cases of the clearest necessity. It is not the principle upon which our common happiness reposes; it is only one of the means for securing that happiness. The adherence to promises therefore, as well as their employment in the first instance, must be decided by the general criterion, and maintained only so far as, upon a comprehensive view, it shall be found productive of a balance of happiness.

There is further an important distinction to be made between a promise given without an intention to perform it, and a promise which information, afterwards acquired, persuades me to violate. The first can scarcely in any instance take place without fixing a stain upon the promiser, and exhibiting him, to say the least, as a man greatly deficient in delicacy of moral discrimination. The case of the second is incomparably different. Every engagement into which I have entered an adherence to which I shall afterwards find to be a material obstacle to my utility (suppose an engagement not to write anything in derogation of the thirty-nine articles) ought to be violated: nor can there be any limitation upon this maxim, except where the violation will greatly encroach upon the province and jurisdiction of my neighbour.

Let us apply these remarks upon the nature of promises to the doctrine of a social contract. It is not through the medium of any supposed promise or engagement that we are induced to believe that the conduct of our neighbour will not be ridiculously inconsistent or wantonly malicious. If he protest in the most solemn way against being concluded by any such promise, at the same time that he conducts himself in a rational and sober manner, he will not find us less disposed to confide in him. We depend as readily upon a foreigner that he will not break the laws, and expose himself to their penalties (for this has been supposed to be one of the principal branches of the social contract), as we do upon our countryman. If we do not depend equally upon the Arabs who inhabit the plains of Asia, it is not because we impute to them a deficiency in their social contract, but because we are ignorant of their principles of conduct, or know that those principles do not afford us a sufficient security as to the particulars of our intercourse with them. Tell a man what will be the solid and substantial effects of his proceeding, how it will affect his neighbours, and what influence it will have upon his own happiness, and you speak to the unalienable feelings of the human mind. But tell him that, putting these things for the present out of our consideration, it is sufficient that he has promised a certain conduct, or that, if he have not expressly promised it, he has promised it by implication, or that, if he have not promised it, his ancestors a few generations back promised it for him; and you speak of a motive that scarcely finds a sympathetic chord in one human breast, and that few will so much as understand.

Few things can be more absurd than to talk of our having promised obedience to the laws. If the laws depend upon promises for their execution, why are they accompanied with sanctions? Why is it considered as the great arcanum of legislation to make laws that are easy of execution, and that need no assistance from the execrable intervention of oaths and informers? Again, why should I promise that I will do everything that a certain power, called the government, shall imagine it convenient, or decide that it is fitting, for me to do? Is there in this either morality, or justice, or common sense? Does brute force alone communicate to its possessor a sufficient claim upon my veneration? For, be it observed, the wisdom or duty of obedience proceeds upon exactly the same principle, whether it be to a tyrant, or to the most regularly elected house of representatives. There is but one power to which I can yield a heart-felt obedience, the decision of my own understanding, the dictate of my own conscience. The decrees of any other power, especially if I have a firm and independent mind, I shall obey with reluctance and aversion. My obedience is purely an affair of composition: I choose to do that which, in itself considered, my judgement disapproves, rather than incur the greater evil which the power from whom the mandate issues annexes to my disobedience.*

There is another principle concerned in this subject, and that is sincerity: I may not evade the laws of the society by any dishonourable subterfuge or contemptible duplicity. But the obligation of sincerity, like all the other great principles of morality, is not founded in promises, but in the indefeasible benefit annexed to its observance. Add to which, the sincerity I am bound to practise towards the magistrate, particularly in a case where his requisition shall be unjust, is not different in its principle, and is certainly of no higher obligation, than the sincerity I am bound to practise towards a private individual.

Let us however suppose that the assertion of an implied contract in every community is true, or let us take the case where an actual engagement has been entered into by the members of the society. This appears from what has been already delivered to be of that class of

*Chap. VI.

promises which are of slightest obligation. In the notion of a social contract little is made over, little expectation is excited, and therefore little mischief is included in its breach. What we most expect and require in a member of the same community is the qualities of a man, and the conduct that ought to be observed indifferently by a native or a stranger. Where a promise or an oath is imposed upon me superfluously, as is always the case with promises of allegiance; or where I am compelled to make it by the operation of a penalty; the treatment I suffer is atrociously unjust, and of consequence the breach of such a promise is peculiarly susceptible of apology. A promise of allegiance is a declaration that I approve the actual constitution of things, and, so far as it is binding, an engagement that I will continue to support that constitution. But I shall support for as long a time, and in as great a degree, as I approve of it, without needing the intervention of a promise. It will be my duty not to undertake its destruction by precipitate and unpromising means, for a much more cogent reason than can be deduced from any promise I have made. An engagement for anything further than this is both immoral and absurd: it is an engagement to a non-entity, a constitution; a promise that I will abstain from doing that which I believe to be beneficial to my fellow citizens.

CHAPTER IV

OF POLITICAL AUTHORITY

*Common deliberation the true foundation of
government – proved from the equal claims of
mankind – from the nature of our faculties –
from the object of government – from the
effects of common deliberation. – Delegation
vindicated. – Difference between the doctrine
here maintained and that of a social contract. –
Remark.*

HAVING rejected the hypotheses that have most generally
been advanced as to the rational basis of a political authority, let us enquire whether we may not arrive at the
same object by a simple investigation of the obvious
reason of the case, without refinement of system or fiction
of process.

Government then being first supposed necessary for
the welfare of mankind, the most important principle
that can be imagined relative to its structure seems to be
this; that, as government is a transaction in the name and
for the benefit of the whole, every member of the community ought to have some share in the selection of its
measures. The arguments in support of this proposition
are various.

First, it has already appeared that there is no satisfactory criterion marking out any man, or set of men, to
preside over the rest.

Secondly, all men are partakers of the common faculty,
reason; and may be supposed to have some communication with the common instructor, truth. It would be
wrong in an affair of such momentous concern that any
chance for additional wisdom should be rejected; nor
can we tell, in many cases, till after the experiment, how
eminent any individual may be found in the business of
guiding and deliberating for his fellows.

Thirdly, government is a contrivance instituted for the

security of individuals; and it seems both reasonable that each man should have a share in providing for his own security; and probable that partiality and cabal will by this means be most effectually excluded.

Lastly, to give each man a voice in the public concerns comes nearest to that fundamental purpose of which we should never lose sight, the uncontrolled exercise of private judgement. Each man will thus be inspired with a consciousness of his own importance, and the slavish feelings that shrink up the soul in the presence of an imagined superior will be unknown.

Admitting then the propriety of each man having a share in directing the affairs of the whole in the first instance, it seems necessary that he should concur in electing a house of representatives, if he be the member of a large state; or, even in a small one, that he should assist in the appointment of officers and administrators*; which implies, first, a delegation of authority to these officers, and, secondly, a tacit consent, or rather an admission of the necessity, that the questions to be debated should abide the decision of a majority.

But to this system of delegation the same objections may be urged that were cited from Rousseau under the head of a social contract. It may be alleged that 'if it be the business of every man to exercise his own judgement, he can in no instance surrender this function into the hands of another'.

To this objection it may be answered, first, that the parallel is by no means complete between an individual's exercise of his judgement in a case that is truly his own, and his exercise of his judgement in an article where the province of a government is already admitted. If there be something contrary to the simplest ideas of justice in such a delegation, this is an evil inseparable from political government. The true and only adequate apology of gov-

---

* We shall be led, in a subsequent branch of this enquiry, to investigate how far either of these measures is inseparable from the maintenance of social order. Book V, Chap. XXIV.

ernment is necessity; the office of common deliberation is solely to supply the most eligible means of meeting that necessity.

Secondly, the delegation we are here considering is not, as the word in its most obvious sense may seem to imply, the act of one man committing to another a function which, strictly speaking, it became him to exercise for himself. Delegation, in every instance in which it can be reconciled with justice, proposes for its object the general good. The individuals to whom the delegation is made are either more likely, from talents or leisure, to perform the function in the most eligible manner, or there is at least some public interest requiring that it should be performed by one or a few persons, rather than by every individual for himself. This is the case whether in that first and simplest of all political delegations, the prerogative of a majority, or in the election of a house of representatives, or in the appointment of public officers. Now all contest as to the person who shall exercise a certain function and the propriety of resigning it is frivolous the moment it is decided how and by whom it can most advantageously be exercised. It is of no consequence that I am the parent of a child when it has once been ascertained that the child will live with greater benefit under the superintendence of a stranger.

Lastly, it is a mistake to imagine that the propriety of restraining me, when my conduct is injurious, rises out of any delegation of mine. The justice of employing force upon certain emergencies was at least equally cogent before the existence of society.* Force ought never to be resorted to but in cases of absolute necessity; and, when such cases occur, it is the duty of every man to defend himself from violation. There is therefore no delegation necessary on the part of the offender; but the community, in the censure it exercises over him, puts itself in the place of the injured party.

From what is here stated, we may be enabled to form the

* Chap. I, pp. 209–10.

clearest and most unexceptionable idea of the nature of government. Every man, as was formerly observed,* has a sphere of discretion; that sphere is limited by the co-ordinate sphere of his neighbour. The maintenance of this limitation, the office of taking care that no man exceeds his sphere, is the first business of government. Its powers, in this respect, are a combination of the powers of individuals to control the excesses of each other. Hence is derived to the individuals of the community a second and indirect province, of providing, by themselves or their representatives, that this control is not exercised in a despotical manner, or carried to an undue excess.

It may perhaps be imagined by some persons that the doctrine here delivered, of the justice of proceeding in common concerns by a common deliberation, is nearly coincident with that which affirms a lawful government to derive its authority from a social contract. Let us consider what is the true difference between them: and this seems principally to lie in the following particular.

The principle of a social contract is an engagement to which a man is bound by honour, fidelity or consistency to adhere. According to the principle here laid down, he is bound to nothing. He joins in the common deliberation because he foresees that some authority will be exercised, and because this is the best chance that offers itself for approximating the exercise of that authority, to the dictates of his own understanding. But, when the deliberation is over, he finds himself as much disengaged as ever. If he conform to the mandate of authority, it is either because he individually approves it, or from a principle of prudence, because he foresees that a greater mass of evil will result from his disobedience than of good. He obeys the freest and best constituted authority, upon the same principle that would lead him, in most instances, to yield obedience to a despotism; only with this difference, that, if the act of authority be erroneous, he finds it less probable that it will be corrected in the first instance

* Book II, Chap. V.

than in the second, since it proceeds from the erroneous judgement of a whole people. – But all this will appear with additional evidence when we come to treat of the subject of obedience.

Too much stress has undoubtedly been laid upon the idea, as of a grand and magnificent spectacle, of a nation deciding for itself upon some great public principle, and of the highest magistracy yielding its claims when the general voice has pronounced. The value of the whole must at last depend upon the quality of their decision. Truth cannot be made more true by the number of its votaries. Nor is the spectacle much less interesting of a solitary individual, bearing his undaunted testimony in favour of justice, though opposed by misguided millions. Within certain limits however the beauty of the exhibition may be acknowledged. That a nation should exercise undiminished its function of common deliberation is a step gained, and a step that inevitably leads to an improvement of the character of individuals. That men should agree in the assertion of truth is no unpleasing evidence of their virtue. Lastly, that an individual, however great may be his imaginary elevation, should be obliged to yield his personal pretensions to the sense of the community at least bears the appearance of a practical confirmation of the great principle that all private considerations must yield to the general good.

CHAPTER V

OF LEGISLATION

Society can declare and interpret, but cannot enact. – Its authority only executive.

HAVING thus far investigated the nature of political functions, it seems necessary that some explanation should be given upon the subject of legislation. 'Who is it that has authority make laws? What are the characteristics of that man or body of men in whom the tremendous faculty is vested of prescribing to the rest of the community what they are to perform, and what to avoid?'

The answer to these questions is exceedingly simple: Legislation, as it has been usually understood, is not an affair of human competence. Immutable reason is the true legislator, and her decrees it behoves us to investigate. The functions of society extend, not to the making, but the interpreting of law; it cannot decree, it can only declare that which the nature of things has already decreed, and the propriety of which irresistibly flows from the circumstances of the case.

Montesquieu says that 'in a free state, every man will be his own legislator'.* This is not true, in matters the most purely individual, unless in the limited sense already explained. It is the office of conscience to determine, 'not like an Asiatic cadi, according to the ebbs and flows of his own passions, but like a British judge, who makes no new law, but faithfully declares that law which he finds already written'.† The same distinction is to be made upon the subject of political authority. All government is, strictly speaking, executive. It has appeared to be necessary, with respect to men as we at present find them, that force should sometimes be employed in repressing injustice; and for the same reasons that this force should, as far as possible, be vested in the community. To the public support of justice therefore the authority of the community extends. But no sooner does it wander in the smallest degree from the line of justice than its proper authority is at an end; it may be submitted to by its subjects from necessity; from necessity it may be exercised, as an individual complies with his ill-informed conscience in default of an enlightened one; but it ought never to

---

* 'Dans un état libre, tout homme qui est censé avoir une âme libre, doit être gouverné par lui–même.' *Esprit des lois*; Liv. XI, Ch. vi.

† Sterne's Sermons – 'Of a Good Conscience'.

be confounded with the lessons of real duty, or the decisions of impartial truth.

CHAPTER VI

OF OBEDIENCE

Rational obedience not founded in contract. – Kinds of obedience. – Compulsory obedience often less injurious than confidence. – Kinds of authority. – Limitations of confidence. – Reverence to superiors considered. – Government founded in ignorance.

THE two great questions upon which the theory of government depends are: Upon what foundation can political authority with the greatest propriety rest? and, What are the considerations which bind us to political obedience? Having entered at length into the first of these questions, it is time that we should proceed to the examination of the second.

One of the most popular theories, relative to the foundation of political authority, we have seen to be that of an original contract, affirming that the criterion of political justice is to be found in the conventions and rules which have been adjusted by the community at large. In pursuance of this original position, the same theorists have necessarily gone on and affirmed that the true source of obligation to political obedience was to be found in the same principle, and that, in obeying a government regularly constituted, we did nothing more than perform our engagements.

The reasonings in support of this hypothesis are obvious. 'Suppose a number of persons living in any neighbourhood should perceive that great common benefit would accrue from building a bridge, sinking a canal, or making a highway. The simplest mode for them to adopt is to consult together, and raise the money necessary for effecting this desirable purpose, by each man assessing himself according to his ability, and contributing his quota to a common fund. Now it is plain that, in this case, each pays his assessment (supposing the payment to be voluntary) in consideration of the previous agreement; his contribution would be of no avail, however desirable was the object to be effected, had he not reason to depend upon the rest of the neighbourhood, that they would pay theirs. But government,' say the advocates of an original contract, 'when regularly constituted, is precisely such a provision as the one here stated for building a bridge, or making a road: it is a consultation and settlement among the different members of a community as to the regulations most conducive to the benefit of the whole. It is upon this principle that taxes are paid, and that the force of the community is drawn out in such proportions as are necessary to repress the external or internal disturbers of its tranquillity. The ground therefore upon which each man contributes his share of effort or property is that he may perform his contract, and discharge that for which he has engaged as a member of the community.'

The refutation of this hypothesis has been anticipated in the preceding chapters. – Government can with no propriety be compared to the construction of a bridge or a canal, a matter of mere convenience and refinement. It is supposed to be of the most irresistible necessity; it is indisputably an affair of hardship and restraint. It constitutes other men the arbitrators of my actions, and the ultimate disposers of my destiny. – Almost every member of every community that has existed on the face of the earth might reasonably say, 'I know of no such contract as you describe; I never entered into any such engagement; I never promised to obey; it must therefore be an iniquitous imposition to call upon me to do something under pretence of a promise I never made.' – The reason a man lives under any particular government is partly necessity; he cannot easily avoid living under some government, and it is often scarcely in his power to abandon the country in which he was born: it is also partly a choice of evils; no man can be said, in this case, to enjoy that freedom which is essential to the forming a contract, unless it could be shown that he had a power of instituting, somewhere, a government adapted to his own conceptions. – Government in reality, as has abundantly appeared, is a question of force, and not of consent. It is desirable that a government should be made as agreeable as possible to the ideas and inclinations of its subjects; and that they should be consulted, as extensively as may be, respecting its construction and regulations. But, at last, the best constituted government that can be formed, particularly for a large community, will contain many provisions that, far from having obtained the consent of all its members, encounter even in their outset a strenuous, though ineffectual, opposition. – From the whole of these reasonings it appears that, in those measures which have the concurrence of my judgement, I may reasonably be expected to co-operate with willingness and zeal; but, for the rest, my only justifiable ground of obedience is that I will not disturb the repose of the community, or that I do not perceive the question to be of sufficint magnitude to authorize me in incurring the penalty.

To understand the subject of obedience with sufficient accuracy, it is necessary that we should attend to the various shades of meaning of which the word is susceptible.

Every voluntary action is an act of obedience; in performing it, we comply with some view, and are guided by some incitement or motive.

The purest kind of obedience is where an action flows from the independent conviction of our private judgement, where we are directed, not by the precarious and mutable interference of another, but by a recollection of the intrinsic and indefeasible tendency of the action to be performed.* In this case the object of obedience is the dic-

* Book II, Chap. VI.

tate of the understanding: the action may, or may not, be such as my neighbours or the community will approve, but this approbation does not constitute its direct motive.

The kind of obedience which stands next to this in its degree of voluntariness arises in the following manner. Every man is capable of comparing himself with his fellow. Every man will find that there are some points in which he is the equal or perhaps the superior of other men, but that there are certainly some points in which other men are superior to him. The superiority in question in the present instance is superiority of intellect or information. It may happen that the point in which another man surpasses me is a point of some importance to my welfare or convenience. I want, for example, to build a house, or to sink a well. It may happen that I have not leisure or means to acquire the science necessary for this purpose. Upon that supposition I am not to be blamed if I employ a builder for the first, or a mechanic for the second; nor shall I be liable to blame if I work in person under his direction. This sort of obedience is distinguished by the appellation of confidence; and to justify, in a moral view, the reposing of confidence, the only thing necessary is that it should be fitter and more beneficial, all things considered, that the function to be performed should be performed by me.

The third and last kind of obedience necessary to be adverted to upon the present occasion is where I do that which is not prescribed to me by my private judgement, merely on account of the mischievous consequences that I foresee will be annexed to my omission by the arbitrary interference of some voluntary being.

The most important observation that arises upon the statement of this scale of obedience is that obedience in the second degree ought to be guarded with as much jealousy, and kept by the person yielding obedience within as narrow limits, as possible. The last sort of obedience will frequently be necessary. Voluntary beings constitute a large portion of the universe; we shall often have occasion to foresee their arbitrary determinations and conduct, nor can knowledge, as such, in any instance fail to be a desirable acquisition; our conduct therefore must and ought to be modified by their interferences. Morality, as has already been frequently observed, consists entirely in an estimate of consequences; he is the truly virtuous man who produces the greatest portion of benefit his situation will admit. The most exalted morality indeed, that in which the heart reposes with the most unmingled satisfaction, relates to the inherent and indefeasible tendencies of actions. But we shall be by no means excusable if we overlook, in our system of conduct, the arbitrary awards of other men. Nothing can be more certain than that an action, suppose of inferior moment or utility, which for its own sake might be right to be performed, it may become my duty to neglect if I know that by performing it I shall incur the penalty of death.

The mischiefs attendant on the frequent recurrence of this species of obedience, and the grounds upon which its interference is to be guarded against, as extensively as circumstances will admit, have already been stated.* Yet obedience flowing from the consideration of a penalty is less a source of degradation and depravity than a habit of obedience founded in confidence. The man who yields it may reserve, in its most essential sense, his independence. He may be informed in judgement, and resolved in purpose, as to every moral and social obligation. He may suffer his understanding neither to be seduced nor confounded; he may observe, in its fullest extent, the mistake and prepossession of his neighbour, to which he thus finds it necessary to accommodate himself. It seems possible that he who thus pities the folly, while he complies with the necessity, may still, even under this discipline, grow in discrimination and sagacity.

The greatest mischief that can arise in the progress of obedience is, where it shall lead us, in any degree, to depart from the independence of our understanding, a

* Book II, Chap. VI.

departure which general and unlimited confidence necessarily includes. In this view, the best advice that could be
given to a person in a state of subjection is, 'Comply,
where the necessity of the case demands it; but criticize
while you comply. Obey the unjust mandates of your
governors; for this prudence and a consideration of the
common safety may require; but treat them with no false
lenity, regard them with no indulgence. Obey; this may
be right; but beware of reverence. Reverence nothing but
wisdom and skill: government may be vested in the fittest
persons; then they are entitled to reverence, because they
are wise, and not because they are governors: and it may
be vested in the worst. Obedience will occasionally be right
in both cases: you may run south, to avoid a wild beast
advancing in that direction, though you want to go north.
But be upon your guard against confounding things so
totally unconnected with each other as a purely political
obedience and respect. Government is nothing but regulated force; force is its appropriate claim upon your
attention. It is the business of individuals to persuade; the
tendency of concentrated strength is only to give consistency and permanence to an influence more compendious
than persuasion.'

All this will be made somewhat clearer if we reflect on
the proper correlative of obedience, authority: and here
let us recur to the three sorts of obedience above specified.

The first kind of authority, then, is the authority of
reason, what is really such, or is only conceived to be such.
The terms, both authority and obedience, are less frequently employed in this sense than in either of the
following.

The second species of authority is that which depends
for its validity upon the confidence of him with whom it
prevails, and is where, not having myself acquired such
information as to enable me to form a judicious opinion,
I yield a greater or less degree of deference to the known
sentiment and decision of another. This seems to be the

strictest and most precise meaning of the word authority; as obedience, in its most refined sense, denotes that compliance which is the offspring of respect.

Authority in the last of the three senses alluded to is where a man, in issuing his precept, does not deliver that which may be neglected with impunity; but his requisition is attended with a sanction, and the violation of it will be followed with a penalty. This is the species of authority which properly connects itself with the idea of government. It is a violation of political justice to confound the authority which depends upon force, with the authority which arises from reverence and esteem; the modification of my conduct which might be due in the case of a wild beast, with the modification which is due to superior wisdom. These two kinds of authority may happen to vest in the same person; but they are altogether distinct and independent of each other.

The consequence which has flowed from confounding them has been a greater debasement of the human character than could easily have followed upon direct and unqualified slavery. The principle of confidence, and the limitations with which it ought to be attended, are capable of an easy and convincing explication. I am bound, to the fullest extent that is consistent with my opportunities and situation, to exercise my understanding. Man is the ornament of the universe only in proportion as he consults his judgement. Whatever I submit to from the irresistible impulse of necessity is not mine, and debases me only as it tends gradually to shackle the intrepidity of my character. With respect to some men therefore it may be innoxious. But, where I make the voluntary surrender of my understanding, and commit my conscience to another man's keeping, the consequence is clear. I then become the most mischievous and pernicious of animals. I annihilate my individuality as a man, and dispose of my force as an animal to him among my neighbours who shall happen to excel in imposture and artifice, and to be least under restraint from the scruples of integrity and justice. I put an end, as to my own share, to that happy collision of understandings upon which the hopes of human improvement depend. I can have no genuine fortitude, for fortitude is the offspring of conviction. I can have no conscious integrity, for I do not understand my own principles, and have never brought them to the test of examination. I am the ready tool of injustice, cruelty and profligacy; and, if at any time I am not employed in their purposes, it is the result of accident, not of my own precaution and honesty.

The understanding must first be consulted, and then, no doubt, confidence will come in for its share of jurisdiction. The considerations which will have influence in the mind of an impartial enquirer to enforce, or to give an air of doubtfulness to, his opinions, are numerous. Among these, he will not refuse attention to the state of opinion in the present or any preceding generation of men. In the meantime it will rarely happen that the authority of other men's judgement in cases of general enquiry will be of great weight. Either men of equal talents and integrity have embraced both sides; or their prejudice, and deficiency as to the materials of judging, have been such as extremely to weaken their testimony. Add to this, that the only ground of opinion, strictly so called, is the intrinsic evidence of the opinion itself; upon that our judgement must be formed; and the decision of others can have no effect but that of increasing or diminishing our doubt of the rectitude of our own perceptions. The direct province of confidence is to supply, in the best way the case will admit, the defect of our knowledge; but it can never, strictly speaking, furnish knowledge itself. Its proper use belongs rather to the circumstance of actions immediately to be determined on, than to matters of speculation and principle. Thus, I ought not perhaps to refuse weight to the advice of some men, even when the reasons by which they enforce their advice are conceived by me to be problematical: and thus, I am bound, as before stated, to trust another, in the moment of emergency, in the art he has studied, rather than myself by whom that study was never undertaken. Except when the nature of my situation calls upon me to act, I shall do more wisely in refraining from any decision, in questions where I am not assisted to decide by information that is properly my own.

One of the lessons most assiduously inculcated upon mankind in all ages and countries is that of reverence to our superiors. If by this maxim be intended our superiors in wisdom, it may be admitted, but with some qualification. But, if it imply our superiors in station only, nothing can be more contrary to reason and justice. Is it not enough that they have usurped certain advantages over us to which they can show no equitable claim; and must we also humble our courage, and renounce our independence, in their presence? Why reverence a man because he happens to be born to certain privileges; or because a concurrence of circumstances (for wisdom, as we have already seen, gives a claim to respect utterly distinct from power) has procured him a share in the legislative or executive government of our country? Let him content himself with the obedience which is the result of force; for to that only is he entitled.

Reverence to our superiors in wisdom is to be admitted, but with considerable limitations. I am bound, as has already appeared, to repose certain functions, such as that of building my house, or educating my child, in the hands of him by whom those functions will most properly be discharged. It may be right that I should act under the person to whom I have thus given my suffrage, in cases where I have reason to be persuaded of his skill, and cannot be expected to acquire the necessary skill myself. But in those cases of general justice which are equally within the province of every human understanding, I am a deserter from the requisitions of duty if I do not assiduously exert my faculties, or if I be found to act contrary to the conclusions they would dictate, from deference to the opinions of another. – The reverence we are here considering is a reverence prompting us to some kind of obedience; there is another kind, terminating in esteem only, that, so far from deserving to be confined within these strict limitations, we are bound to extend to every man who is the possessor of estimable qualities.

The reverence which is due from a child to his parent, or rather to his senior in age and experience, falls under the same rules as have already been delivered. Wherever I have good reason to believe that another person knows better than myself what is proper to be done, there I ought to conform to his direction. But the advantage which he possesses must be obvious, otherwise I shall not be justified in my proceeding. If I take into the account every chance for advantage, I shall never act upon the result of my own reflections. The mind of one man is essentially distinct from the mind of another. If each do not preserve his individuality, the judgement of all will be feeble, and the progress of our common understanding inexpressibly retarded. Hence it follows that the deference of a child becomes vicious whenever he has reason to doubt that the parent possesses essential information of which he is deprived. Nothing can be more necessary for the general benefit than that we should divest ourselves, as soon as the proper period arrives, of the shackles of infancy; that human life should not be one eternal childhood; but that men should judge for themselves, unfettered by the prejudices of education, or the institutions of their country.

To a government, therefore, that talked to us of deference to political authority, and honour to be rendered to our superiors, our answer should be: 'It is yours to shackle the body, and restrain our external actions; that is a restraint we understand. Announce your penalties; and we will make our election of submission or suffering. But do not seek to enslave our minds. Exhibit your force in its plainest form, for that is your province; but seek not to inveigle and mislead us. Obedience and external submission is all you are entitled to claim; you can have no right to extort our deference, and command us not to see, and disapprove of, your errors. In the meantime it should be observed that it is by no means a necessary consequence that we should disapprove of all the measures of government; but there must be disapprobation wherever there is a question of strict political obedience.

A corollary which flows from these principles is deserving of our attention. Confidence is in all cases the offspring of ignorance. It must therefore continually decline, in relation, as was above stated, to 'those cases of general justice which are equally within the province of every human understanding',* in proportion as wisdom and virtue shall increase. But the questions that belong to the department of government are questions of general justice. The conduct of an enlightened and virtuous man can only be conformable to the regulations of government so far as those regulations are accidentally coincident with his private judgement, or as he acts with prudent and judicious submission to the necessity of the case. He will not act from confidence; for he has himself examined, as it was his duty to do, the merits of the action: and he has not failed to detect the imposture that would persuade us there is a mystery in government which uninitiated mortals must not presume to penetrate. Now it is sufficiently known that the empire of government is built in opinion;† nor is it enough for this purpose that we refuse to contribute to overturn it by violence, the opinion must go to the extent of prompting us to actual support. No government can subsist in a nation the individuals of which shall merely abstain from tumultuous resistance, while in their genuine sentiments they censure and despise its institution. In other words, government cannot proceed but upon confidence, as confidence on the other hand cannot exist without ignorance. The true supporters of government are the weak and uninformed, and not the wise. In proportion as weakness and ignorance shall

* p. 245.
† Book 1, Chap. VI, p. 148; Book II, Chap. III, pp. 181–2.

diminish, the basis of government will also decay. This however is an event which ought not to be contemplated with alarm. A catastrophe of this description would be the true euthanasia of government. If the annihilation of blind confidence and implicit opinion can at any time be effected, there will necessarily succeed in their place an unforced concurrence of all in promoting the general welfare. But, whatever may be the event in this respect, and the future history of political societies,* we shall do well to remember this characteristic of government, and apply it as the universal touchstone of the institution itself. As in the commencement of the present Book we found government indebted for its existence to the errors and perverseness of a few, so it now appears that it can no otherwise be perpetuated than by the infantine and uninstructed confidence of the many. It may be to a certain degree doubtful whether the human species will ever be emancipated from their present subjection and pupillage, but let it not be forgotten that this is their condition. The recollection will be salutary to individuals, and may ultimately be productive of benefit to all.

CHAPTER VII

OF FORMS OF GOVERNMENT

Uniformity of the nature of man. – Different degrees in which he possesses information. – Imperfect schemes of society estimated. – Mode in which improvements are to be realized.– Inference.

THERE is one other topic relative to general principles of government, which it seems fitting and useful to examine in this place. 'Is there a scheme of political institution which, as coming nearest to perfection, ought to be

* Book V, Chap. XXII, XXIV.

prescribed to all nations; or, on the other hand, are different forms of government best adapted to the condition of different nations, each worthy to be commended in its peculiar place, but none proper to be transplanted to another soil?'

The latter part of this alternative is the creed which has ordinarily prevailed; but it is attended with obvious objections.

If one form of government makes one nation happy, why should it not equally contribute to the felicity of another?

The points in which human beings resemble are infinitely more considerable than those in which they differ. We have the same senses; and the impressions on those senses which afflict me may ordinarily be expected to be sources of anguish to you. It is true that men differ in their habits and tastes. But these are accidental varieties. There is but one perfection to man; one thing most honourable; one thing that, to a well organized and healthful mind, will produce the most exquisite pleasure. All else is deviation and error; a disease, to be cured, not to be encouraged. Sensual pleasure on the one hand, or intellectual on the other, is, absolutely speaking, the highest and most desirable. We are not to make too much account of the perversions of taste. Men long inured to slavery, for example, undoubtedly have a less exquisite sense of its hatefulness; perhaps instances may be found where it is borne without a murmur. But this is by no means a proof that it is the fit and genuine state of the beings who suffer it. To such men we ought to say, 'You are satisfied with an oblivion of all that is eminent in man; but we will awake you. You are contented with ignorance; but we will enlighten you. You are not brutes: you are not stones. You sleep away existence in a miserable neglect of your most valuable privileges: but you are capable of exquisite delights; you are formed to glow with benevolence, to expatiate in the fields of knowledge, to thrill with disinterested transport, to enlarge your thoughts, so as to take in the wonders of the material universe, and the principles that bound and ascertain the general happiness.'

If then it appears that the means which are beneficial to one man ought, in the most important instances, to be deemed most desirable for others, the same principle which applies to all other sources of moral influence will also apply to government. Every political system must have a certain influence upon the moral state of the nation among whom it exists. Some are more favourable, or less inimical, to the general interest than others. That form of society which is most conducive to improvement, to the exalted and permanent pleasure of man, the sound politician would wish to see universally realized.

Such is the true theory of this subject, taken in its most absolute form; but there are circumstances that qualify the universality of these principles.

The best gift that can be communicated to man is valuable only so far as it is esteemed. It is in vain that you heap upon me benefits that I neither understand nor desire. The faculty of understanding is an essential part of every human being, and cannot with impunity be over-looked, in any attempt to alter or meliorate his condition. Government, in particular, is founded in opinion; nor can any attempt to govern men otherwise than in con-formity to their own conceptions be expected to prove salutary. A project therefore to introduce abruptly any species of political institution, merely from a view to its absolute excellence, and without taking into account the state of the public mind, must be absurd and injurious. The best mode of political society will, no doubt, be con-sidered by the enlightened friend of his species, as the ultimate object of his speculations and efforts. But he will be on his guard against precipitate measures. The only mode for its secure and auspicious establishment is through the medium of a general preference in its favour.

The consequence which flows from this view of the sub-ject is, in a certain degree, favourable to the ideas which were stated in the beginning of the chapter, as constituting the more general and prevailing opinion.

'Different forms of government, are best adapted to the condition of different nations.' Yet there is one form, in itself considered, better than any other form. Every other mode of society, except that which conduces to the best and most pleasurable state of the human species, is at most only an object of toleration. It must of necessity be ill in various respects; it must entail mischiefs; it must foster unsocial and immoral prejudices. Yet upon the whole, it may be, like some excrescences and defects in the human frame, it cannot immediately be removed without introducing something worse. In the machine of human society all the wheels must move together. He that should violently attempt to raise any one part into a condition more exalted than the rest, or force it to start away from its fellows, would be the enemy, and not the benefactor, of his contemporaries.

It follows however, from the principles already detailed, that the interests of the human species require a gradual, but uninterrupted change. He who should make these principles the regulators of his conduct would not rashly insist upon the instant abolition of all existing abuses. But he would not nourish them with false praise. He would show no indulgence to their enormities. He would tell all the truth he could discover, in relation to the genuine interests of mankind. Truth, delivered in a spirit of universal kindness, with no narrow resentments or angry invective, can scarcely be dangerous, or fail, so far as relates to its own operation, to communicate a similar spirit to the hearer. Truth, however unreserved be the mode of its enunciation, will be sufficiently gradual in its progress. It will be fully comprehended only by slow degrees by its most assiduous votaries; and the degrees will be still more temperate by which it will pervade so considerable a portion of the community as to render them mature for a change of their common institutions.

Again: if conviction of the understanding be the compass which is to direct our proceedings in the general affairs, we shall have many reforms, but no revolutions.* As it is only in a gradual manner that the public can be instructed, a violent explosion in the community is by no means the most likely to happen as the result of instruction. Revolutions are the produce of passion, not of sober and tranquil reason. There must be an obstinate resistance to improvement on the one side, to engender a furious determination of realizing a system at a stroke on the other. The reformers must have suffered from incessant counteraction, till, inflamed by the treachery and art of their opponents, they are wrought up to the desperate state of imagining that all must be secured in the first favourable crisis, as the only alternative for its being ever secured. It would seem therefore that the demand of the effectual ally of the public happiness, upon those who enjoy the privileges of the state, would be, 'Do not give us too soon; do not give us too much; but act under the incessant influence of a disposition to give us something.'

Government, under whatever point of view we examine this topic, is unfortunately pregnant with motives to censure and complaint. Incessant change, everlasting innovation, seem to be dictated by the true interests of mankind. But government is the perpetual enemy of change. What was admirably observed of a particular system of government† is in a great degree true of all: They 'lay their hand on the spring there is in society, and put a stop to its motion'. Their tendency is to perpetuate abuse. Whatever was once thought right and useful they undertake to entail to the latest posterity. They reverse the genuine propensities of man, and, instead of suffering us to proceed, teach us to look backward for perfection. They prompt us to seek the public welfare, not in alteration and improvement, but in a timid reverence for the decisions of our ancestors, as if it were the nature of the human mind always to degenerate, and never to advance.

---

* Book IV, Chap. II.
† The Spartan: Logan's *Philosophy of History*, p. 69.

Man is in a state of perpetual mutation. He must grow either better or worse, either correct his habits or confirm them. The government under which we are placed must either increase our passions and prejudices by fanning the flame, or, by gradually discouraging, tend to extirpate them. In reality, it is impossible to conceive a government that shall have the latter tendency. By its very nature positive institution has a tendency to suspend the elasticity and progress of mind. Every scheme for embodying imperfection must be injurious. That which is today a considerable melioration will at some future period, if preserved unaltered, appear a defect and disease in the body politic. It is earnestly to be desired that each man should be wise enough to govern himself, without the intervention of any compulsory restraint; and, since government, even in its best state, is an evil, the object principally to be aimed at is that we should have as little of it as the general peace of human society will permit.

BOOK IV

OF THE OPERATION OF OPINION IN SOCIETIES AND INDIVIDUALS

CHAPTER I

OF RESISTANCE

Subject of the fourth book. – First branch of the subject. – Question of resistance stated. – Resistance of a nation. – Ambiguity of the term nation. – Case of a military subjection considered. – Resistance of a majority – of a minority. – Further ambiguity of the term nation. – Nature of liberty. – Remark. – Resistance of the individual.

HAVING now made some progress in the enquiry originally instituted, it may be proper to look back, and consider the point at which we are arrived. We have examined, in the first place, the powers of man as they relate to the subject of which we treat; secondly, we have delineated the principles of society, as founded in justice and general interest, independently of, and antecedent to, every species of political government; and, lastly, have endeavoured to ascertain the fundamental conditions which must belong to the most rational system of government. We might now proceed to investigate the different objects of government, and deduce the inferences respecting them which are pointed out to us by the preceding reasonings. But there are various miscellaneous considerations which, though they have not fallen under the former heads, are of considerable importance to our disquisition, and may usefully occupy the remainder of the present volume. They are of different classes, and in a certain degree detached from each other; but may perhaps without impropriety be ranged under two branches: the mode in which the speculative opinions of individuals are to be rendered effectual for the melioration of society; and the mode in which opinion is found to operate in modifying the conduct of individuals.

The strong hold of government has appeared hitherto to have consisted in seduction. However imperfect might be the political constitution under which they lived, mankind have ordinarily been persuaded to regard it with a sort of reverential and implicit respect. The privileges of Englishmen, and the liberties of Germany, the splendour of the most Christian, and the solemn gravity of the Catholic king, have each afforded a subject of exultation to the individuals who shared, or thought they shared, in the advantages these terms were conceived to describe. Each man was accustomed to deem it a mark of the peculiar kindness of providence that he was born in the country, whatever it was, to which he happened to belong. The time may come which shall subvert these prejudices. The time may come when men shall exercise the piercing search of truth upon the mysteries of government, and view without prepossession the defects and abuses of the constitution of their country. Out of this new order of things a new series of duties will arise. When a spirit of impartiality shall prevail, and loyalty shall decay, it will become us to enquire into the conduct which such a state of thinking shall make necessary. We shall then be called upon to maintain a true medium between blindness to injustice and calamity on the one hand, and an acrimonious spirit of violence and resentment on the other. It will be the duty of such as shall see these subjects in the pure light of truth to exert themselves for the effectual demolition of monopolies and usurpation; but effectual demolition is not the offspring of crude projects and precipitate measures. He who dedicates himself to these may be suspected to be under the domination of passion, rather than benevolence. The true friend of equality will do nothing unthinkingly, will cherish no wild schemes of uproar and confusion, and will endeavour to discover the mode in which his faculties may be laid out to the greatest and most permanent advantage.

The whole of this question is intimately connected with the enquiry which has necessarily occupied a share in the disquisitions of all writers on the subject of government, concerning the propriety and measures of resistance. 'Are the worst government and best equally entitled to the toleration and forbearance of their subjects? Is there no case of political oppression that will authorize the persons who suffer it to take up arms against their oppressors? Or, if there be, what is the quantity of oppression at the measure of which insurrections begin to be justifiable? Abuses will always exist, for man will always be imperfect; what is the nature of the abuse which it would be pusillanimous to oppose by words only, and which true courage would instruct us was to be endured no longer?'

No question can be conceived more important than this. In the examination of it philosophy almost forgets its nature; it ceases to be speculation, and becomes an actor. Upon the decision, according as it shall be decided in the minds of a bold and resolute party, the existence of thousands may be suspended. The speculative enquirer, if he live in a state where abuse is notorious and grievances frequent, knows not, while he weighs the case in the balance of reason, how far that which he attempts to describe is already realized in the apprehension of numbers of his countrymen. Let us enter upon the question with the seriousness which so critical an enquiry demands.

Resistance may have its source in the emergencies either of the public or the individual. 'A nation,' it has commonly been said, 'has a right to shake off any authority that is usurped over it.' This is a proposition that has generally passed without question, and certainly no proposition can appear more plausible. But, if we examine it minutely, we shall find that it is attended with equivocal circumstances. What do we mean by a nation? Is the whole people concerned in this resistance, or only a part? If the whole be prepared to resist, the whole is persuaded of the injustice of the usurpation. What sort of usurpation is that which can be exercised by one or a few persons over a whole nation universally disapproving of it? Government is founded in opinion.* Bad government deceives us first, before it fastens itself upon us like an incubus, oppressing all our efforts. A nation in general must have learned to respect a king and a house of lords, before a king and a house of lords can exercise any authority over them. If a man or a set of men, unsanctioned by any previous prejudice in their favour, pretend to exercise sovereignty in a country, they will become objects of derision rather than of serious resistance. Destroy the existing prejudice in favour of any of our present institutions, and they will fall into similar disuse and contempt.

It has sometimes been supposed 'that an army, foreign or domestic, may be sufficient to hold a people in subjection, completely against their inclination'. A domestic army at least will in some degree partake of the opinions and sentiments of the people at large. The more precautions are employed to prevent the infection, the doctrine will probably spread with so much the more certainty and rapidity. Show me that you are afraid of my entertaining certain opinions or hearing certain principles, and you will infallibly, sooner or later, awaken my curiosity. A domestic army will always be found a very doubtful instrument of tyranny in a period of crisis. – A foreign army after a time will become domesticated. If the question be of importing a foreign army for the specific purpose of supporting tottering abuse, great alarm will inevitably be excited. These men, it may be, are

* Book I, Chap. VI, p. 148; Book II, Chap. III, pp. 181–2.

adapted for continuing the reign of tyranny; but who will pay them? A weak, superstitious or ignorant people may be held in the chains of foreign power; but the school of moral and political independence sends forth pupils of a very different character. In the encounter with their penetration and discernment, tyranny will feel itself powerless and transitory. In a word, either the people are unenlightened and unprepared for a state of freedom, and then the struggle and the consequences of the struggle will be truly perilous; or the progress of political knowledge among them is decisive, and then everyone will see how futile and short-lived will be the attempt to hold them in subjection, by means of garrisons and a foreign force. The party attached to liberty is, upon that supposition, the numerous one; they are the persons of true energy, and who have an object worthy of their zeal. Their oppressors, few in number, and degraded to the rank of lifeless machines, wander with no certain destination or prospect over the vast surface, and are objects of pity rather than serious alarm. Every hour diminishes their number and their resources; while, on the other hand, every moment's delay gives new strength to the cause, and fortitude to the champions, of liberty. Men would not be inclined pertinaciously to object to a short delay, if they recollected the advantages and the certainty of success with which it is pregnant. – Meanwhile these reasonings turn upon the probability that the purposes of liberty will be full as effectually answered without the introduction of force: there can be little doubt of the justifiableness of a whole nation having recourse to arms, if a case can be made out in which it shall be impossible for them to prevent the introduction of slavery in any other way.

The same reasonings, with little variation, will apply to the case of an unquestionable majority of a nation, as to that of the whole. The majority of a nation is irresistible; it as little needs to have recourse to violence; there is as little reason to expect that any usurper will be so mad as to contend with it. If ever it appear to be otherwise, it is because, in one of two ways, we deceive ourselves with the term majority. First, nothing is more obvious than the danger incident to a man of a sanguine temper of overestimating the strength of his party. He associates perhaps only with persons of his own way of thinking, and a very small number appears to him as if it were the whole world. Ask persons of different tempers and habits of life how many republicans there are at this hour in England or Scotland, and you will immediately be struck with the very opposite answers you will receive. There are many errors of a sanguine temper that appear, at first sight, innocent or even useful: but surely every man of integrity and conscience will hesitate, before he suffers the possibility that an error of this sort should encourage him to plunge a nation in violence, and open a sea of blood. He must have a heart of strange composition who, for the precarious inferences he draws in moral or political calculation, would volunteer a mandate of death, or be the first to unsheath the sword of summary execution.

A second deception that lurks under the word majority lies, not in the question of number, but of quality and degree of illumination. A majority, we say perhaps, is dissatisfied with the present state of things, and wishes for such a specific alteration. Alas, it is to be feared that the greater part of this majority are often mere parrots who have been taught a lesson of the subject of which they understand little or nothing. What is it they dislike? A specific tax perhaps, or some temporary grievance. Do they dislike the vice and meanness that grow out of tyranny, and pant for the liberal and ingenuous virtue that would be fostered in their own minds in a different condition? No. They are very angry, and fancy themselves very judicious. What is it they desire? They know not. It would probably be easy to show that what they profess to desire is little better than what they hate. What they hate is not the general depravation of the human character; and what they desire is not its improvement. It is an insult upon human understanding, when we speak of persons in this state of infantine ignorance, to say that the majority of the nation is on the side of political renovation. Few greater misfortunes can befall any country than for such persons to be instigated to subvert existing institutions, and violently to take the work of political reformation into their own hands.

There is an obvious remedy to each of the deceptions here enumerated: Time: Is it doubtful whether the reformers be a real majority of the inhabitants of any country? Is it doubtful whether the majority truly understand the object of their professed wishes, and therefore whether they be ripe for its reception, and competent to its assertion? Wait but a little while, and the doubt will probably be solved in the manner that the warmest friend of human happiness and improvement would desire. If the system of independence and equality be the truth, it may be expected hourly to gain converts. The more it is discussed, the more will it be understood, and its value cherished and felt. If the state of the majority be doubtful, a very few years, perhaps a shorter time, will tend to place it beyond the reach of controversy. The great cause of humanity, which is now pleading in the face of the universe, has but two enemies; those friends of antiquity, and those friends of innovation, who, impatient of suspense, are inclined violently to interrupt the calm, the incessant, the rapid and auspicious progress which thought and reflection appear to be making in the world. Happy would it be for mankind if those persons who interest themselves most zealously in these great questions would confine their exertions to the diffusing, in every possible mode, a spirit of enquiry, and the embracing every opportunity of increasing the stock, and generalizing the communication, of political knowledge!

A third situation, which may be conceived to exist in a country where political reform has been made a topic of considerable attention, is that where neither the whole, nor the majority, of the nation is desirous of the reform in question, but where the innovators are an unquestionable minority. In this case nothing can be more indefensible than a project for introducing by violence that state of society which our judgements may happen to approve. In the first place, no persons are ripe for the participation of a benefit the advantage of which they do not understand. No people are competent to enjoy a state of freedom who are not already imbued with a love of freedom. The most dreadful tragedies will infallibly result from an attempt to goad mankind prematurely into a position, however abstractedly excellent, for which they are in no degree prepared. Secondly, to endeavour to impose our sentiments by force is the most detestable species of persecution. Others are as much entitled to deem themselves in the right as we are. The most sacred of all privileges is that by which each man has a certain sphere, relative to the government of his own actions, and the exercise of his discretion, not liable to be trenched upon by the intemperate zeal or dictatorial temper of his neighbour.* To dragoon men into the adoption of what we think right is an intolerable tyranny. It leads to unlimited disorder and injustice. Every man thinks himself in the right; and, if such a proceeding were universally introduced, the destiny of mankind would be no longer a question of argument, but of strength, presumption or intrigue.

There is a further ambiguity in the term nation, as employed in the proposition above stated, 'that a nation has a right forcibly to shake off any authority that is usurped over it'. A nation is an arbitrary term. Which is most properly termed a nation, the Russian empire, or the canton of Berne? Or is everything a nation upon which accident shall bestow that appellation? It seems most accurate to say that any number of persons who are able to establish and maintain a system of mutual regulation for themselves conformable to their own opinions, without imposing a system of regulation upon a considerable number of others inconsistent with the opinion of

* Book II, Chap. V, VI.

these others, have a right, or, more properly speaking, a duty obliging them to adopt that measure. That any man, or body of men, should impose their sense upon persons of a different opinion is, absolutely speaking, wrong, and in all cases deeply to be regretted: but this evil it is perhaps in some degree necessary to incur, for the sake of a preponderating good. All government includes in it this evil, as one of its fundamental characteristics.

There is one circumstance of much importance to be attended to in this disquisition. Superficial thinkers lay great stress upon the external situation of men, and little upon their internal sentiments. Persevering enquiry will probably lead to a mode of thinking the reverse of this. To be free is a circumstance of little value, if we could suppose men in a state of external freedom, without the magnanimity, energy and firmness that constitute almost all that is valuable in a state of freedom. On the other hand, if a man have these qualities, there is little left for him to desire. He cannot be degraded; he cannot readily become either useless or unhappy. He smiles at the impotence of despotism; he fills up his existence with serene enjoyment and industrious benevolence. Civil liberty is chiefly desirable as a means to procure and perpetuate this temper of mind. They therefore begin at the wrong end, who make haste to overturn and confound the usurped powers of the world. Make men wise, and by that very operation you make them free. Civil liberty follows as a consequence of this; no usurped power can stand against the artillery of opinion. Everything then is in order, and succeeds at its appointed time. How unfortunate is it that men are so eager to strike and have so little constancy to reason!

It is probable that this question of resistance would never have admitted of so long a controversy, if the advocates of the system of liberty promulgated in the last century had not, unobserved to themselves, introduced a confusion into the question. Resistance may be employed, either to repel the injuries committed against the nation generally, or such as, in their immediate application, relate to the individual. To the first of these the preceding reasonings principally apply. The injuries to a nation depend for their nature, for the most part, upon their permanency, and therefore admit of the utmost sobriety and deliberation as to the mode in which they are to be remedied. Individuals may be injured or destroyed by a specific act of tyranny, but nations cannot; the principal mischief to the nation lies in the presage contained in the single act, of the injustice that is to continue to be exercised. Resistance, by the very meaning of the term, as it is used in political enquiry, signifies a species of conduct that is to be adopted in relation to an established authority: but an old grievance seems obviously to lead, as its counterpart, to a gradual and temperate remedy.

The consideration which, by being confounded with this, has served to mislead certain enquirers is that of what is commonly known by the name of self-defence, or, more properly, the duty obliging each individual to repel, as far as lies in his power, any violent attack made either upon himself or another. This, by the terms of the question, is a circumstance that does not admit of delay; the benefit of the remedy entirely depends upon the time of the application. The principle in this case is of easy development. Force is an expedient the use of which is much to be deplored. It is contrary to the nature of intellect, which cannot be improved but by conviction and persuasion. It corrupts the man that employs it, and the man upon whom it is employed. But it seems that there are certain cases so urgent as to oblige us to have recourse to this injurious expedient: in other words, there are cases where the mischief to accrue from not violently counteracting the perverseness of the individual is greater than the mischief which the violence necessarily draws along with it. Hence it appears that the ground justifying resistance, in every case where it can be justified, is that of the good likely to result from such interference being greater than the good to result from omitting it.

There are probably cases where, as in a murder for example about to be committed on a useful and valuable member of society, the chance of preventing it by any other means than instantaneous resistance is so small as by no means to vindicate us in incurring the danger of so mischievous a catastrophe. But will this justify us, in the case of an individual oppressed by the authority of a community? Let us suppose that there is a country in which some of its best citizens are selected as objects of vengeance by an alarmed and jealous tyranny. It cannot reasonably be doubted that every man, a condemned felon or murderer, is to be commended for quietly withdrawing himself from the execution of the law; much more such persons as have now been described. But ought those well affected citizens that are still at large to rise in behalf of their brethren under persecution? Every man that is disposed to enter into such a project, and who is anxious about the moral rectitude of his conduct, must rest its justification upon one of the two grounds above stated: either the immediate purpose of his rising is the melioration of public institutions, or it is to be estimated with reference to the meritoriousness of the individuals in question. The first of these has been sufficiently discussed; we will suppose therefore that he confines himself to the last. Here, as has been already observed, the whole, as a moral question, will turn upon the comparative benefit or mischief to result from the resistance to be employed. The disparity is great indeed between the resistance ordinarily suggested by the term self-defence, and the resistance which must expect to encounter in its progress the civil power of the country. In the first, the question is of a moment; if you succeed in the instant of your exertion, you may expect the applause, rather than the prosecution, of executive authority. But, in the latter, the end will scarcely be accomplished but by the overthrow of the government itself. Let the lives of the individuals in supposition be as valuable as you please, the value will necessarily be swallowed up in the greater questions that occur in the sequel. Those questions therefore are the proper topics of attention; and we shall be to blame if we suffer ourselves to be led unawares into a conduct the direct tendency of which is the production of one sort of event, while all we intended was the production of another. The value of individuals ought not to be forgotten; there are men whose safety should be cherished by us with anxious attention; but it is difficult to imagine a case in which, for their sake, the lives of thousands, and the fate of millions, should be committed to risk.

CHAPTER II

OF REVOLUTIONS

Duty of a citizen as to the constitution of his country. – No scheme of government perfect or final. – Revolutionary measures, during their operation, inimical to independence – and intellectual enquiry. – Period of their operation. – Revolutions accompanied with blood – crude and premature in their effects – uncertain in point of success. – Conviction of the understanding an adequate means of demolishing political abuse. – The progress of conviction not tardy and feeble – not precarious. – Revolutions in some cases to be looked for.

THE question of resistance is closely connected with that of revolutions. It may be proper therefore, before we dismiss this part of the subject, to enter into some disquisition respecting the nature and effects of that species of event which is commonly known by this appellation, and the sentiments which a good citizen should entertain concerning it.

And here one of the first observations that offers itself

is that it is not unworthy of a good member of society to be the adversary of the constitution of his country.

In contradiction to this proposition it has been said, 'that we live under the protection of this constitution; and protection, being a benefit conferred, obliges us to a reciprocation of support in return'.

To this it may be answered, first, that the benefit of this protection is somewhat equivocal. That civilization is a benefit may perhaps be conceded; but civilization, though in some degree preserved by the political constitution of every country in Europe, can scarcely be considered as the characteristic of a bad constitution, or as inseparably involved with the imperfections of any. A good member of society will, probably, be anxious to favour the cause of civilization; but his attachment to that cause may well excite his wishes to see it freed from the slough of corrupt and partial institutions.

Secondly, gratitude, in the sense in which it is here spoken of, has already been proved not to be a virtue, but a vice. Every man and collection of men ought to be treated by us in a manner founded upon their intrinsic qualities and capacities, and not according to a rule, which has existence only in relation to ourselves.*

Add to this, thirdly, that no motive can be more equivocal than the gratitude here recommended. Gratitude to the constitution, an abstract idea, an imaginary existence, is altogether unintelligible. Affection to my countrymen will be much better proved by exertions to procure them a substantial benefit than by my supporting a system which I believe to be fraught with injurious consequences.

A demand of the nature which is here controverted is similar to the demand upon me to be a Christian because I am an Englishman, or a Mahometan because I am a native of Turkey. Instead of being an expression of respect, it argues contempt of all religion and government, and everything sacred among men. If government be an institution conducive to the public welfare, it

* Book II, Chap. II, p. 170.

deserves my attention and investigation. I am bound, in proportion as I desire the happiness of others, to consider it with all the accuracy my circumstances will allow, and employ my talents, and every honest influence I am able to exert, to render it such as justice and reason may require.

This general view of the duties of a citizen in relation to the government under which he lives being premised, we may now proceed with advantage to the particular points which are calculated to influence our judgement as to the conduct we ought to hold with respect to revolutions.

There is one extensive view upon the subject of revolutions which will be of great consequence in determining the sentiments and conduct we ought to maintain respecting them. The wise man is satisfied with nothing. It is scarcely possible there should be any institution in which impartial disquisition will not find defects. The wise man is not satisfied with his own attainments, or even with his principles and opinions. He is continually detecting errors in them; he suspects more; there is no end to his revisals and enquiries. Government is in its nature an expedient, a recourse to something ill to prevent an impending mischief; it affords therefore no ground of complete satisfaction. Finite things must be perpetually capable of increase and advancement; it would argue therefore extreme folly to rest in any given state of improvement, and imagine we had attained our summit. The true politician confines neither his expectations nor desires within any specific limits; he has undertaken a labour without end. He does not say, 'Let me attain thus much, and I will be contented; I will demand no more; I will no longer counteract the established order of things; I will set those who support them at rest from further importunity.' On the contrary, the whole period of his existence is devoted to the promotion of innovation and reform.

The direct inference from these sentiments seems to be

unfavourable to revolutions. The politician who aims at a limited object, and has shut up his views within that object, may be forgiven if he manifest some impatience for its attainment. But this passion cannot be felt in an equal degree by him who aims at improvement, not upon a definite, but an indefinite scale. This man knows that, when he has carried any particular point, his task is far from complete. He knows that, when government has been advanced one degree higher in excellence, abuses will still be numerous. Many will be oppressed; many will be exposed to unjust condemnation; discontent will have its empire and its votaries; and the reign of inequality will be extensive. He can mark therefore the progress of melioration with calmness; though it will have all the wishes of his heart, and all the exertions of his understanding. That progress, which may be carried on through a longer time, and a greater variety of articles, than his foresight can delineate, he may be expected to desire should take place in a mild and gradual, though incessant advance, not by violent leaps, not by concussions which may expose millions to risk, and sweep generations of men from the stage of existence.

And here let us briefly consider what is the nature of revolution. Revolution is engendered by an indignation against tyranny, yet is itself ever more pregnant with tyranny. The tyranny which excites its indignation can scarcely be without its partisans; and, the greater is the indignation excited, and the more sudden and vast the fall of the oppressors, the deeper will be the resentment which fills the minds of the losing party. What more unavoidable than that men should entertain some discontent at being violently stripped of their wealth and their privileges? What more venial than that they should feel some attachment to the sentiments in which they were educated, and which, it may be, but a little before, were the sentiments of almost every individual in the community? Are they obliged to change their creed, precisely at the time at which I see reason to alter mine? They have but remained at the point at which we both stood a few years ago. Yet this is the crime which a revolution watches with the greatest jealousy, and punishes with the utmost severity. The crime which is thus marked with the deepest reprobation is not the result of relaxation of principle, of profligate living, or of bitter and inexorable hatred. It is a fault not the least likely to occur in a man of untainted honour, of an upright disposition, and dignified and generous sentiments.

Revolution is instigated by a horror against tyranny, yet its own tyranny is not without peculiar aggravations. There is no period more at war with the existence of liberty. The unrestrained communication of opinions has always been subjected to mischievous counteraction, but upon such occasions it is trebly fettered. At other times men are not so much alarmed for its effects. But in a moment of revolution, when everything is in crisis, the influence even of a word is dreaded, and the consequent slavery is complete. Where was there a revolution in which a strong vindication of what it was intended to abolish was permitted, or indeed almost any species of writing or argument, that was not, for the most part, in harmony with the opinions which happened to prevail? An attempt to scrutinize men's thoughts, and punish their opinions, is of all kinds of despotism the most odious; yet this attempt is peculiarly characteristic of a period of revolution.

The advocates of revolution usually remark 'that there is no way to rid ourselves of our oppressors, and prevent new ones from starting up in their room, but by inflicting on them some severe and memorable retribution'. Upon this statement it is particularly to be observed that there will be oppressors as long as there are individuals inclined, either from perverseness, or rooted and obstinate prejudice, to take party with the oppressor. We have therefore to terrify not only the man of crooked ambition but all those who would support him, either from a corrupt motive, or a well-intended error. Thus, we propose to make men free; and the method we adopt is to influence them, more rigorously than ever, by the fear of punishment. We say that government has usurped too much, and we organize a government tenfold more encroaching in its principles and terrible in its proceedings. Is slavery the best project that can be devised for making men free? Is a display of terror the readiest mode for rendering them fearless, independent and enterprising?

During a period of revolution, enquiry, and all those patient speculations to which mankind are indebted for their greatest improvements, are suspended. Such speculations demand a period of security and permanence; they can scarcely be pursued when men cannot foresee what shall happen tomorrow, and the most astonishing vicissitudes are affairs of perpetual recurrence. Such speculations demand leisure, and a tranquil and dispassionate temper; they can scarcely be pursued when all the passions of man are afloat, and we are hourly under the strongest impressions of fear and hope, apprehension and desire, dejection and triumph. Add to this, what has been already stated,* respecting the tendency of revolution, to restrain the declaration of our thoughts, and put fetters upon the licence of investigation.

Another circumstance proper to be mentioned is the inevitable duration of the revolutionary spirit. This may be illustrated from the change of government in England in 1688. If we look at the revolution strictly so called, we are apt to congratulate ourselves that the advantages it procured, to whatever they may amount, were purchased by a cheap and bloodless victory. But, if we would make a solid estimate, we must recollect it as the procuring cause of two general wars, of nine years under king William, and twelve under queen Anne; and two intestine rebellions (events worthy of execration, if we call to mind the gallant spirit and generous fidelity of the Jacobites,[19] and their miserable end) in 1715 and 1745. Yet this was, upon the whole, a mild and auspicious revolu-

* p. 270.

tion. Revolutions are a struggle between two parties, each persuaded of the justice of its cause, a struggle not decided by compromise or patient expostulation, but by force only. Such a decision can scarcely be expected to put an end to the mutual animosity and variance.

Perhaps no important revolution was ever bloodless. It may be useful in this place to recollect in what the mischief of shedding blood consists. The abuses which at present exist in political society are so enormous, the oppressions which are exercised so intolerable, the ignorance and vice they entail so dreadful, that possibly a dispassionate enquirer might decide that, if their annihilation could be purchased by an instant sweeping of every human being now arrived at years of maturity from the face of the earth, the purchase would not be too dear. It is not because human life is of so considerable value that we ought to recoil from the shedding of blood. Alas! the men that now exist are for the most part poor and scanty in their portion of enjoyment, and their dignity is no more than a name. Death is in itself among the slightest of human evils. An earthquake, which should swallow up a hundred thousand individuals at once, would chiefly be to be regretted for the anguish it entailed upon survivors; in a fair estimate of those it destroyed, it would often be comparatively a trivial event. The laws of nature which produce it are a fit subject of investigation; but their effects, contrasted with many other events, are scarcely a topic of regret. The case is altogether different when man falls by the hand of his neighbour. Here a thousand ill passions are generated. The perpetrators, and the witnesses of murders, become obdurate, unrelenting and inhuman. Those who sustain the loss of relations or friends by a catastrophe of this sort are filled with indignation and revenge. Distrust is propagated from man to man, and the dearest ties of human society are dissolved. It is impossible to devise a temper more inauspicious to the cultivation of justice and the diffusion of benevolence.

To the remark that revolutions can scarcely be unaccompanied with the shedding of blood, it may be added that they are necessarily crude and premature. Politics is a science. The general features of the nature of man are capable of being understood, and a mode may be delineated which, in itself considered, is best adapted to the condition of man in society. If this mode ought not, everywhere, and instantly, to be fought to be reduced into practice, the modifications that are to be given it in conformity to the variation of circumstances, and the degrees in which it is to be realized, are also a topic of scientifical disquisition. Now it is clearly the nature of science to be progressive in its advances. How various were the stages of astronomy before it received the degree of perfection which was given it by Newton? How imperfect were the lispings of intellectual science before it attained the precision of the present century? Political knowledge is, no doubt, in its infancy; and, as it is an affair of life and action, will, in proportion as it gathers vigour, manifest a more uniform and less precarious influence upon the concerns of human society. It is the history of all science to be known first to a few, before it descends through the various descriptions and classes of the community. Thus, for twenty years, and *Principia* of Newton had scarcely any readers, and his system continued unknown; the next twenty perhaps sufficed to make the outlines of that system familiar to almost every person in the slightest degree tinctured with science.

The only method according to which social improvements can be carried on, with sufficient prospect of an auspicious event, is when the improvement of our institutions advances in a just proportion to the illumination of the public understanding. There is a condition of political society best adapted to every different stage of individual improvement. The more nearly this condition is successively realized, the more advantageously will the general interest be consulted. There is a sort of provision in the nature of the human mind for this species of progress. Imperfect institutions, as has already been shown,* cannot long support themselves when they are generally disapproved of, and their effects truly understood. There is a period at which they may be expected to decline and expire, almost without an effort. Reform, under this meaning of the term, can scarcely be considered as of the nature of action. Men feel their situation; and the restraints that shackled them before vanish like a deception. When such a crisis has arrived, not a sword will need to be drawn, not a finger to be lifted up in purposes of violence. The adversaries will be too few and too feeble to be able to entertain a serious thought of resistance against the universal sense of mankind.

Under this view of the subject then it appears that revolutions, instead of being truly beneficial to mankind, answer no other purpose than that of marring the salutary and uninterrupted progress which might be expected to attend upon political truth and social improvement. They disturb the harmony of intellectual nature. They propose to give us something for which we are not prepared, and which we cannot effectually use. They suspend the wholesome advancement of science, and confound the process of nature and reason.

We have hitherto argued upon the supposition that the attempt which shall be made to effect a revolution shall be crowned with success. But this supposition must by no means be suffered to pass without notice. Every attempt of this sort, even if menaced only, and not carried into act, tends to excite a resistance which otherwise would never be consolidated. The enemies of innovation become alarmed by the intemperance of its friends. The storm gradually thickens, and each party arms itself in silence with the weapons of violence and stratagem. Let us observe the consequence of this. So long as the contest is merely between truth and sophistry, we may look with tolerable assurance to the progress and result. But, when

* Book I, Chap. VI.

we lay aside arguments, and have recourse to the sword, the case is altered. Amidst the barbarous rage of war, and the clamorous din of civil contention, who shall tell whether the event will be prosperous or adverse? The consequence may be the riveting on us anew the chains of despotism, and ensuring, through a considerable period, the triumph of oppression, even if it should fail to carry us back to a state of torpor, and obliterate the memory of all our improvements.

If such are the genuine features of revolution, it will be fortunate if it can be made appear that revolution is wholly unnecessary, and the conviction of the understanding a means fully adequate to the demolishing political abuse. But this point has already been established in a former part of our enquiry.* It is common to affirm 'that men may sufficiently know the error of their conduct, and yet be in no degree inclined to forsake it'. This assertion however is no otherwise rendered plausible than by the vague manner in which we are accustomed to understand the term knowledge. The voluntary actions of men originate in their opinions.* Whatever we believe to have the strongest inducements in its behalf, that we infallibly choose and pursue. It is impossible that we should choose anything as evil. It is impossible that a man should perpetrate a crime in the moment that he sees it in all its enormity. In every example of this sort, there is a struggle between knowledge on one side, and error or habit on the other. While the knowledge continues in all its vigour, the ill action cannot be perpetrated. In proportion as the knowledge escapes from the mind, and is no longer recollected, the error or habit may prevail. But it is reasonable to suppose that the permanence, as well as vigour, of our perceptions is capable of being increased to an indefinite extent. Knowledge in this sense, understanding by it a clear and undoubting apprehension, such as no delusion can resist, is a thing totally different from what is ordinarily called by that name, from a sentiment seldom

* Book I, Chap. V.

recollected, and, when it is recollected, scarcely felt or understood.*

The beauty of the conception here delineated, of the political improvement of mankind, must be palpable to every observer. Still it may be urged 'that, even granting this, truth may be too tardy in its operation. Ages will elapse,' we shall be told, 'before speculative views of the evils of privilege and monopoly shall have spread so wide, and been felt so deeply, as to banish these evils without commotion or struggle. It is easy for a reasoner to sit down in his closet, and amuse himself with the beauty of the conception, but in the meantime mankind are suffering, injustice is hourly perpetrated, and generations of men may languish, in the midst of fair promises and hopes, and leave the stage without participating in the benefit. Cheat us not then,' it will be said, 'with remote and uncertain prospects; but let us embrace a method which shall secure us speedy deliverance from evils too hateful to be endured.'

In answer to this representation, it is to be observed, first, that every attempt suddenly to rescue a whole community from an usurpation the evils of which few understand has already been shown to be attended, always with calamity, frequently with miscarriage.

Secondly, it is a mistake to suppose that, because we have no popular commotions and violence, the generation in which we live will have no benefit from the improvement of our political principles. Every change of sentiment, from moral delusion to truth, every addition we make to the clearness of our apprehension on this subject, and the recollectedness and independence of our mind, is itself abstracted from the absolute change of our institutions, an unquestionable acquisition. Freedom of institution is desirable chiefly because it is connected with independence of mind; if we gain the end, we may reasonably consent to be less solicitous about the means.†

* Book I, Chap. V.
† Chap. 1, p. 263.

In reality however, wherever the political opinions of a community, or any considerable portion of a community, are changed, the institutions are affected also. They relax their hold upon the mind; they are viewed with a different spirit; they gradually, and almost without notice, sink into oblivion. The advantage gained in every stage of the progress without commotion is nearly the precise advantage it is most for the interest of the public to secure.

In the meantime it is impossible not to remark a striking futility in the objection we are endeavouring to answer. The objectors complain 'that the system which trusts to reason alone is calculated to deprive the present generation of the practical benefit of political improvements'. Yet we have just shown that it secures to them great practical benefit; while, on the other hand, nothing is more common than to hear the advocates of force themselves confess that a grand revolution includes in it the sacrifice of one generation. Its conductors encounter the calamities attendant on fundamental innovation, that their posterity may reap the fruits in tranquillity.

Thirdly, it is a mistake to suppose that the system of trusting to reason alone is calculated to place fundamental reform at an immeasurable distance. It is the nature of all science and improvement to be slow, and in a manner imperceptible, in its first advances. Its commencement is as it were by accident. Few advert to it; few have any perception of its existence. It attains its growth in obscurity; and its result, though long in the preparation, is to a considerable degree sudden and unexpected. Thus it is perhaps that we ought to regard the introduction of printing as having given its full security to the emancipation of mankind. But this progressive consequence was long unsuspected; and it was reserved for the penetrating mind of Wolfey to predict almost three centuries ago, speaking in the name of the Romish clergy, 'We must destroy the press; or the press will destroy us.' At present, it requires no extraordinary sagacity to perceive that the most enormous abuses of political institution are hastening to their end. There is no enemy to this auspicious crisis more to be feared than the well meaning, but intemperate, champion of the general good.

There is a passage in a work of Helvétius written to be published after his death, which happened in 1771, so much in the tone of the dissatisfied and despairing advocates of public liberty at present, as to deserve to be cited in this place. 'In the history of every people,' says he, 'there are moments in which, uncertain of the side they shall choose, and balanced between political good and evil, they feel a desire to be instructed; in which the soil, so to express myself, is in some manner prepared, and may easily be penetrated by the dew of truth. At such a moment, the publication of a valuable book may give birth to the most auspicious reforms: but, when that moment is no more, the nation, become insensible to the best motives, is, by the nature of its government, irrecoverably plunged in ignorance and stupidity. The soil of intellect is then hard and impenetrable; the rains may fall, may spread their moisture upon the surface, but the prospect of fertility is gone. Such is the condition of France. Her people are become the contempt of Europe. No salutary crisis shall ever restore them to liberty.'*

It is scarcely necessary to add that the French revolution was at this time preparing by an incessant chain of

---

* 'Dans chaque nation il est des momens où les citoyens, incertains du parti qu'ils doivent prendre, et suspendus entre un bon et un mauvais gouvernement, éprouvent la soif de l'instruction, où les esprits, si je l'ose dire, préparés et ameublis peuvent être facilement pénétrés de la rosée de la vérité. Qu'en ce moment un bon ouvrage paroisse, il peut opérer d'heureuses réformes: mais cet instant passé, les citoyens, insensibles à la gloire, sont par la forme de leur gouvernement invinciblement entraînés vers l'ignorance et l'abrutissement. Alors les esprits sont la terre endurcie: l'eau de la vérité y tombe, y coule, mais sans la féconder. Tel est l'état de la France. Cette nation avilie est aujourd'hui le mépris de l'Europe. Nulle crise salutaire ne lui rendra la liberté.' *De l'Homme*, Préface.

events; and that the train may particularly be considered as taking its date from the circumstance, the destruction of the parliaments by Louis XV, which inspired Helvétius with so melancholy a presage.

An additional support to the objection we are here attempting to remove may be derived from the idea, not only 'that truth is slow in its progress', but 'that it is not always progressive, but subject, like other human things, to the vicissitudes of flux and reflux'. This opinion has hitherto been of great influence in public affairs, and it has been considered as 'the part of a wise statesman to embrace the opportunity, when the people are inclined to any measure in which he wishes to engage them, and not to wait till their fervour has subsided, and the moment of willing co-operation is past'.

Undoubtedly there is the appearance of flux and reflux in human affairs. In subordinate articles, there will be a fashion, rendering one truth more popular, and more an object of attention, at one time, than at another. But the mass of truth seems too large a consideration to be susceptible of these vicissitudes. It has proceeded, from the revival of letters to the present hour, with an irresistible advance; and the apparent deviousnesses of literature seem to resolve themselves into a grand collective consistency. Not one step has been made in retrogression. Mathematics, natural philosophy, moral philosophy, philology and politics, have reached, by regular improvements, to their present degree of perfection.

'But, whatever may be said of the history of the human mind since the revival of letters, its history from the earliest records of man displays a picture of a different sort. Here certainly it has not been all progression. Greece and Rome present themselves like two favoured spots in the immense desert of intellect; and their glory in this respect was exceedingly transient. Athens arrived at an excellence so great, in poetry, in eloquence, in the acuteness and vigour of its philosophers, and in skill in the fine arts, as all the ages of the world are not able to parallel.

But this skill was attained, only to be afterwards forgotten; it was succeeded by a night of barbarism; and we are at this moment, in some of these points, exerting ourselves to arrive at the ground which they formerly occupied. The same remarks which apply to individual improvement equally apply to the subject of politics; we have not yet realized the political advantages, to which they were indebted for their greatness.'

There is but one consideration that can be opposed to this statement: the discovery of printing. By this art we seem to be secured against the future perishing of human improvement. Knowledge is communicated to too many individuals to afford its adversaries a chance of suppressing it. The monopoly of science, though, from the love of distinction, which so extensively characterizes the human race, it has been endeavoured to be prolonged, is substantially at an end. By the easy multiplication of copies, and the cheapness of books, everyone has access to them. The extreme inequality of information among different members of the same community, which existed in ancient times is diminished. A class of men is become numerous which was then comparatively unknown, and we see vast multitudes who, though condemned to labour for the perpetual acquisition of the means of subsistence, have yet a superficial knowledge of most of the discoveries and topics which are investigated by the learned. The consequence is that the possessors of knowledge being more, its influence is more certain. Under different circumstances, it was occasionally only that men were wrought upon to extraordinary exertions; but with us the whole is regular and systematical.

There is one general observation which ought to be made before the subject is dismissed. It has perhaps sufficiently appeared, from the preceding discussion, that revolutions are necessarily attended with many circumstances worthy of our disapprobation, and that they are by no means essential to the political improvement of mankind. Yet, after all, it ought not to be forgotten that, though the connection be not essential or requisite, revolutions and violence have too often been coeval with important changes of the social system. What has so often happened in time past is not unlikely occasionally to happen in future. The duty therefore of the true politician is to postpone revolution if he cannot entirely prevent it. It is reasonable to believe that the later it occurs, and the more generally ideas of political good and evil are previously understood, the shorter, and the less deplorable, will be the mischiefs attendant on revolution. 'The friend of human happiness will endeavour to prevent violence; but it would be the mark of a weak and valetudinarian temper to turn away our eyes from human affairs in disgust, and refuse to contribute our labours and attention to the general weal, because perhaps, at last, violence may forcibly intrude itself. It is our duty to make a proper advantage of circumstances as they arise, and not to withdraw ourselves because everything is not conducted according to our ideas of propriety. The men who grow angry with corruption, and impatient at injustice, and through those sentiments favour the abettors of revolution, have an obvious apology to palliate their errors; theirs is the excess of a virtuous feeling. At the same time, however amiable may be the source of their error, the error itself is probably fraught with consequences pernicious to mankind.

CHAPTER III

OF POLITICAL ASSOCIATIONS

Arguments in their favour. – Answer. – Asso-
ciations put a part for the whole – are attended
with party spirit – declamation – cabal – con-
tentious disputes – restlessness – and tumult.
– Utility of social communication. – Exception
in favour of associations. – Another exception. –
Conclusion.

A QUESTION suggests itself under this branch of enquiry, respecting the propriety of associations among the people at large for the purpose of operating a change in their political institutions.

Many arguments have been alleged in favour of such associations. It has been said 'that they are necessary to give effect to public opinion, which, in its insulated state, is incapable of counteracting abuses the most generally disapproved, or of carrying into effect what is most generally desired'. They have been represented 'as indispensable for the purpose of ascertaining public opinion, which must otherwise forever remain in a great degree problematical'. Lastly, they have been pointed out 'as the most useful means for generating a sound public opinion, and diffusing, in the most rapid and effectual manner, political information'.

In answer to these allegations, various things may be observed. That opinion will always have its weight;* that all government is founded in opinion;† and that public institutions will fluctuate with the fluctuations of opinion, without its being necessary for that purpose that opinion should be furnished with an extraordinary organ;‡ are points perhaps sufficiently established in the preceding divisions of this work. These principles amount

---

* Book I, Chap. V.
† Book I, Chap. VI. p. 148; Book II, Chap. III, pp. 144–5.
‡ Book I, Chap. V; Book III, Chap. VII; Book IV, Chap. II.

to a sufficient answer to the two first arguments in favour
of political associations: the third shall receive a more
particular discussion.

One of the most obvious features of political association is its tendency to make a part stand for the whole.
A number of persons, sometimes greater and sometimes
less, combine together. The tendency of their combination, often avowed, but always unavoidable, is to give to
their opinion a weight and operation which the opinion
of unconnected individuals cannot have. A greater number, some from the urgency of their private affairs, some
from a temper averse to scenes of concourse and contention, and others from a conscientious disapprobation of
the measures pursued, withhold themselves from such
combinations. The acrimonious, the intemperate, and the
artful will generally be found among the most forward in
matters of this kind. The prudent, the sober, the sceptical, and the contemplative, those who have no resentments to gratify, and no selfish purposes to promote, will
be overborne and lost in the progress. What justification
can be advanced for a few persons who thus, from mere
impetuosity and incontinence of temper, occupy a post
the very principle of which is the passing them for something greater and more important in the community
than they are? Is the business of reform likely to be well
and judiciously conducted in such hands? Add to this
that associations in favour of one set of political tenets
are likely to engender counter-associations in favour of
another. Thus we should probably be involved in all the
mischiefs of resistance, and all the uproar of revolution.

Political reform cannot be usefully effected but through
the medium of the discovery of political truth. But truth
will never be investigated in a manner sufficiently promising if violence and passion be not removed to a distance.
To whatever property adhering to the human mind, or
accident affecting it, we are to ascribe the phenomenon,
certain it is that truth does not lie upon the surface. It
is laborious enquiry that has, in almost all instances, led

to important discovery. If therefore we are desirous to liberate ourselves and our neighbours from the influence of prejudice, we must suffer nothing but arguments to bear sway in the discussion. The writings and the tenets which offer themselves to public attention should rest upon their own merits. No patronage, no recommendations, no lift of venerable names to bribe our suffrage, no importunity to induce us, to bestow upon them our consideration, and to consider them with favour. These however are small matters. It is much worse than this, when any species of publications is patronized by political associations. The publications are then perused, not to see whether what they contain is true or false, but that the reader may learn from them how he is to think upon the subjects of which they treat. A sect is generated, and upon grounds not less irrational than those of the worst superstition that ever infested mankind.

If we would arrive at truth, each man must be taught to enquire and think for himself. If a hundred men spontaneously engage the whole energy of their faculties upon the solution of a given question, the chance of success will be greater than if only ten men are so employed. By the same reason, the chance will also be increased in proportion as the intellectual operations of these men are individual, and their conclusions are suggested by the reason of the thing, uninfluenced by the force either of compulsion or sympathy. But, in political associations, the object of each man is to identify his creed with that of his neighbour. We learn the Shibboleth of a party. We dare not leave our minds at large in the field of enquiry, lest we should arrive at some tenet disrelished by our party. We have no temptation to enquire. Party has a more powerful tendency than perhaps any other circumstance in human affairs to render the mind quiescent and stationary. Instead of making each man an individual, which the interest of the whole requires, it resolves all understandings into one common mass, and substracts from each the varieties that could alone distinguish him from a brute machine. Having learned the creed of our party, we have no longer any employment for those faculties which might lead us to detect its errors. We have arrived, in our own opinion, at the last page of the volume of truth; and all that remains is by some means to effect the adoption of our sentiments as the standard of right to the whole race of mankind. The indefatigable votary of justice and truth will adhere to a mode of proceeding the opposite of this. He will mix at large among his species; he will converse with men of all orders and parties; he will fear to attach himself in his intercourse to any particular set of men, lest his thoughts should become insensibly warped, and he should make to himself a world of petty dimensions, instead of that liberal and various scene in which nature has permitted him to expatiate. In fine, from these considerations it appears that associations, instead of promoting the growth and diffusion of truth, tend only to check its accumulation, and render its operation, as far as possible, unnatural and mischievous.

There is another circumstance to be mentioned, strongly calculated to confirm this position. A necessary attendant upon political associations is harangue and declamation. A majority of the members of any numerous popular society will look to these harangues as the school in which they are to study, in order to become the reservoirs of practical truth to the rest of mankind. But harangues and declamation lead to passion, and not to knowledge. The memory of the hearer is crowded with pompous nothings, with images and not arguments. He is never permitted to be sober enough to weigh things with an unshaken hand. It would be inconsistent with the art of eloquence to strip the subject of every meretricious ornament. Instead of informing the understanding of the hearer by a flow and regular progression, the orator must beware of detail, must render everything rapid, and from time to time work up the passions of his hearers to a tempest of applause. Truth can scarcely be acquired in crowded halls and amidst noisy debates. Where hope and fear, triumph and resentment, are perpetually afloat, the severer faculties of investigation are compelled to quit the field. Truth dwells with contemplation. We can seldom make much progress in the business of disentangling error and delusion but in sequestered privacy, or in the tranquil interchange of sentiments that takes place between two persons.

In every numerous association of men there will be a portion of rivalship and ambition. Those persons who stand forward in the assembly will be anxious to increase the number of their favourers and adherents. This anxiety will necessarily engender some degree of art. It is unavoidable that, in thinking much of the public, they should not be led, by this propensity, to think much also of themselves. In the propositions they bring forward, in the subjects they discuss, in the side they espouse of these subjects, they will inevitably be biassed by the consideration of what will be most acceptable to their partisans, and popular with their hearers. There is a sort of partiality to particular men that is commendable. We ought to honour usefulness, and adhere to worth. But the partiality which is disingenuously cultivated by weakness on both sides is not commendable. The partiality which grows out of a mutual surrender of the understanding, where the leader first resigns the integrity of his judgement, that he may cherish and take advantage of the defects of his followers, bears an unfavourable aspect upon the common welfare. In this scene truth cannot gain; on the contrary it is forgotten, that error, a more accommodating principle, may be exhibited to advantage, and serve the personal ends of its professors.

Another feature attendant on collections of men meeting together for the transaction of business is contentious dispute and long consultation about matters of the most trivial importance. Every human being possesses, and ought to possess, his particular mode of seeing and judging. The business upon such occasions is to twist and distort the sense of each, so that, though they were all different at first, they may in the end be all alike. Is any proposition, letter, or declaration, to be drawn up in the name of the whole? Perhaps it is confided to one man at first, but it is amended, altered and metamorphosed, according to the fancy of many, till at last, what once perhaps was reasonable comes out the most inexplicable jargon. Commas are to be adjusted, and particles debated. Is this an employment for rational beings? Is this an improvement upon the simple and inartificial scene of things, when each man speaks and writes his mind, in such eloquence as his sentiments dictate, and with unfettered energy; not anxious, while he gives vent to the enthusiasm of his conceptions, lest his words should not be exactly those in which his neighbours would equally have chosen to express themselves?

An appetite perpetually vexing the minds of political associators is that of doing something, that their association may not fall into insignificancy. Affairs must wait upon them, and not they wait upon affairs. They are not content to act when some public emergence seems to require their interference, and point out to them a just mode of proceeding; they must make the emergence to satisfy the restlessness of their disposition. Thus they are ever at hand, to mar the tranquillity of science, and the unshackled and unobserved progress of truth. They terrify the rest of the community from boldness of opinion, and chain them down to their prejudices, by the alarm which is excited by their turbulence of character. – It should always be remembered in these cases that all confederate action is of the nature of government, and that consequently every argument of this work, which is calculated to display the evils of government, and to recommend the restraining it within as narrow limits as possible, is equally hostile to political associations. They have also a disadvantage peculiar to themselves, as they are an obvious usurpation upon the rights of the public, without any pretence of delegation from the community at large.

The last circumstance to be enumerated among the disadvantages of political association is its tendency to disorder and tumult. Nothing is more notorious than the ease with which the conviviality of a crowded feast may degenerate into the depredations of a riot. While the sympathy of opinion catches from man to man, especially among persons whose passions have been little used to the curb of judgement, actions may be determined on which the solitary reflection of all would have rejected. There is nothing more barbarous, blood-thirsty and unfeeling than the triumph of a mob. It should be remembered that the members of such associations are ever employed in cultivating a sentiment peculiarly hostile to political justice, antipathy to individuals; not a benevolent love of equality, but a bitter and personal detestation of their oppressors.

But, though association, in the received sense of that term, must be granted to be an instrument of very dangerous nature, unreserved communication, especially among persons who are already awakened to the pursuit of truth, is of no less unquestionable advantage. There is at present in the world a cold reserve that keeps man at a distance from man. There is an art in the practice of which individuals communicate for ever, without anyone telling his neighbour what estimate he forms of his attainments and character, how they ought to be employed, and how to be improved. There is a sort of domestic tactics, the object of which is to elude curiosity, and keep up the tenour of conversation, without the disclosure either of our feelings or opinions. The friend of justice will have no object more deeply at heart than the annihilation of this duplicity. The man whose heart overflows with kindness for his species will habituate himself to consider, in each successive occasion of social intercourse, how that occasion may be most beneficently improved. Among the topics to which he will be anxious to awaken attention, politics will occupy a principal share.

Books have by their very nature but a limited operation; though, on account of their permanence, their methodical disquisition, and their easiness of access, they are entitled to the foremost place. The number of those who almost wholly abstain from reading is exceedingly great. Books, to those by whom they are read, have a sort of constitutional coldness. We review the arguments of an 'insolent innovator' with sullenness, and are unwilling to expand our minds to take in their force. It is with difficulty that we obtain the courage to strike into untrodden paths, and question tenets that have been generally received. But conversation accustoms us to hear a variety of sentiments, obliges us to exercise patience and attention, and gives freedom and elasticity to our disquisitions. A thinking man, if he will recollect his intellectual history, will find that he has derived inestimable benefit from the stimulus and surprise of colloquial suggestions; and, if he review the history of literature, will perceive that minds of great acuteness and ability have commonly existed in a cluster.

It follows that the promoting the best interests of mankind eminently depends upon the freedom of social communication. Let us figure to ourselves a number of individuals who, having stored their minds with reading and reflection, are accustomed, in candid and unreserved conversation, to compare their ideas, suggest their doubts, examine their mutual difficulties and cultivate a perspicuous and animated manner of delivering their sentiments. Let us suppose that their intercourse is not confined to the society of each other, but that they are desirous extensively to communicate the truths with which they are acquainted. Let us suppose their illustrations to be not more distinguished by impartiality and demonstrative clearness than by the mildness of their temper, and a spirit of comprehensive benevolence. We shall then have an idea of knowledge as perpetually gaining ground, unaccompanied with peril in the means of its diffusion. Their hearers will be instigated to impart their acquisitions to still other hearers, and the circle of instruction will perpetually increase. Reason will spread, and not a brute and unintelligent sympathy.

Discussion perhaps never exists with so much vigour and utility as in the conversation of two persons. It may be carried on with advantage in small and friendly circles. Does the fewness of their numbers imply the rarity of such discussion? Far otherwise: show to mankind, by an adequate example, the advantages of political disquisition, undebauched by political enmity and vehemence, and the beauty of the spectacle will soon render it contagious. Every man will commune with his neighbour. Every man will be eager to tell, and to hear, what the interests of all require them to know. The bolts and fortifications of the temple of truth will be removed. The craggy steep of science, which it was before difficult to ascend, will be levelled. Knowledge will be generally accessible. Wisdom will be the inheritance of man, and none will be excluded from it but by their own heedlessness and prodigality. Truth, and above all political truth, is not hard to acquisition, but from the superciliousness of its professors. It has been slow and tedious of improvement, because the study of it has been relegated to doctors and civilians. It has produced little effect upon the practice of mankind, because it has not been allowed a plain and direct appeal to their understandings. Remove these obstacles, render it the common property, bring it into daily use, and we may reasonably promise ourselves consequences of inestimable value.

But these consequences are the property only of independent and impartial discussion. If once the unambitious and candid disquisitions of enquiring men be swallowed up in the insatiate gulf of noisy assemblies, the opportunity of improvement is annihilated. The happy varieties of sentiment which so eminently contribute to intellectual acuteness are lost. A fallacious uniformity of opinion is produced, which no man espouses from conviction, but which carries all men along with a resistless tide. Truth disclaims the alliance of marshalled numbers.

The same qualifications belong to this subject, as before to the head of revolutions. Though, from what has been said, it may sufficiently appear that association is scarcely in any case to be desired, there are considerations which should lead us sometimes to judge it with moderation and forbearance. There is one mode according to which the benefit of mankind may best be promoted, and which ought always to be employed. But mankind are imperfect beings. While opinion is advancing with silent step, impatience and zeal may be expected somewhat to outrun her progress. Associations, as a measure intrinsically wrong, the wise man will endeavour to check and postpone, as much as he can. But, when the crisis arrives, he will not be induced by the irregularities of the friends of equality to remain neutral, but will endeavour to forward her reign, as far as the nature of the case shall appear to admit. It may even happen that, in the moment of convulsion, and the terror of general anarchy, something in the nature of association may be indispensably connected with the general safety. But, even granting this, it need not be prepared beforehand. Such preparation has a tendency to wear out the expedient. In a crisis really auspicious to public liberty, it is reasonable to believe that there will be men of character and vigour, called out on the spur of the occasion, and by the state of political knowledge in general, who will be adequate to the scenes they have to encounter. The soil in which such men are to be matured is less that of action than of enquiry and instruction.

Again; there are two objects which association may propose to itself, general reform and the remedy of some pressing and momentary evil. These objects may be entitled to a different treatment. The first ought surely to proceed with a leisurely step, and in all possible tranquillity. The second appears to require somewhat more of activity. It is the characteristic of truth to trust much to its own energy, and to resist invasion rather by the force of conviction than of arms. The oppressed individual however seems particularly entitled to our assistance; and this can best be afforded by the concurrence of many. It appears reasonable that, when a man is unjustly attacked by the whole force of the party in power, he should be countenanced and protected by men who are determined to resist such oppressive partiality, and prevent the rights of all from being wounded through the medium of the individual, as far as that can be done consistently with peace and good order. It is probable however that every association will degenerate, and become a mass of abuses that is suffered to perpetuate itself, or to exist longer than is necessary, for the single and momentary purpose for which only it can justly be instituted.

It seems scarcely necessary to add in treating this subject that the individuals who are engaged in the transactions here censured have frequently been excited by the best intentions, and inspired with the most liberal views. It would be in the highest degree unjust if their undertakings should be found of dangerous tendency, to involve the authors in indiscriminate censure for consequences they did not foresee. But, in proportion to the purity of their views and the soundness of their principles, it were to be desired they should seriously reflect on the means they employ. It will be greatly to be lamented if those who, so far as regards their intention, are among the truest friends to the welfare of mankind should, by the injudiciousness of their conduct, rank themselves among its practical enemies.

CHAPTER VI

OF TYRANNICIDE

Diversity of opinions on this subject. – Argument in its vindication. – The destruction of a tyrant not a case of exception. – Consequences of tyrannicide. – Assassination described. – Importance of sincerity.

A QUESTION connected with the mode of effecting political melioration, and which has been eagerly discussed among political reasoners, is that of tyrannicide. The moralists of antiquity contended for the lawfulness of this practice; by the moderns it has been generally condemned.

The arguments in its favour are built upon a very obvious principle. 'Justice ought universally to be administered. Crimes of an inferior description are restrained, or pretended to be restrained, by the ordinary operations of jurisprudence. But criminals by whom the welfare of the whole is attacked, and who overturn the liberties of mankind, are out of the reach of this restraint. If justice be partially administered in subordinate cases, and the rich man be able to oppress the poor with impunity, it must be admitted that a few examples of this sort are insufficient to authorize the last appeal of human beings. But no man will deny that the case of the usurper and the despot is of the most atrocious nature. In this instance, all the provisions of civil policy being superseded, and justice poisoned at the source, every man is left to execute for himself the decrees of immutable equity.'

It may however be doubted whether the destruction of a tyrant be, in any respect, a case of exception from the rules proper to be observed upon ordinary occasions. The tyrant has indeed no particular sanctity annexed to his person, and may be killed with as little scruple as any other man, when the object is that of repelling personal assault. In all other cases, the extirpation of the offender

293

by a self-appointed authority does not appear to be the appropriate mode of counteracting injustice.

For, first, either the nation whose tyrant you would destroy is ripe for the assertion and maintenance of its liberty, or it is not. If it be, the tyrant ought to be deposed with every appearance of publicity. Nothing can be more improper than for an affair, interesting to the general weal, to be conducted as if it were an act of darkness and shame. It is an ill lesson we read to mankind, when a proceeding, built upon the broad basis of general justice, is permitted to shrink from public scrutiny. The pistol and the dagger may as easily be made the auxiliaries of vice, as of virtue. To proscribe all violence, and neglect no means of information and impartiality, is the most effectual security we can have, for an issue conformable to reason and truth.

If, on the other hand, the nation be not ripe for a state of freedom, the man who assumes to himself the right of interposing violence may indeed show the fervour of his conception, and gain a certain notoriety; but he will not fail to be the author of new calamities to his country. The consequences of tyrannicide are well known. If the attempt prove abortive, it renders the tyrant ten times more bloody, ferocious and cruel than before. If it succeed, and the tyranny be restored, it produces the same effect upon his successors. In the climate of despotism some solitary virtues may spring up. But, in the midst of plots and conspiracies, there is neither truth, nor confidence, nor love, nor humanity.

Secondly, the true merits of the question will be still further understood if we reflect on the nature of assassination. The mistake which has been incurred upon this subject is to be imputed principally to the superficial view that has been taken of it. If its advocates had followed the conspirator through all his windings, and observed his perpetual alarm, lest truth should become known, they would probably have been less indiscriminate in their applause. No action can be imagined more directly at war with a principle of ingenuousness and candour. Like all that is most odious in the catalogue of vices, it delights in obscurity. It shrinks from the piercing light of day. It avoids all question, and hesitates and trembles before the questioner. It struggles for a tranquil gaiety, and is only complete where there is the most perfect hypocrisy. It changes the use of speech, and composes every feature the better to deceive.

> Between the acting of a dreadful thing
> And the first motion, all the interim*

is mystery and reserve. Is it possible to believe that a person who has upon him all the indications of guilt is engaged in an action which virtue enjoins? The same duplicity follows him to the last. Imagine to yourself the conspirators kneeling at the feet of Caesar, as they did the moment before they destroyed him! not all the virtue of Brutus can save them from your indignation.

There cannot be a better instance than that of which we are treating, to prove the importance of general sincerity. We see in this example that an action which has been undertaken from the best motives may, by a defect in this particular, tend to overturn the very foundations of justice and happiness. Wherever there is assassination, there is an end to all confidence among men. Protests and asseverations go for nothing. No man presumes to know his neighbour's intention. The boundaries that have hitherto served to divide the honest man from the profligate are gone. The true interests of mankind require, not the removal, but the confirmation of these boundaries. All morality proceeds upon mutual confidence and esteem, will grow and expand as the grounds of that confidence shall be more evident, and must inevitably decay, in proportion as they are undermined.

*Shakespeare: *Julius Caesar*, Act ii.

CHAPTER V

OF THE CULTIVATION OF TRUTH

*Source of the aristocratical system. – The oppo-
site principle stated. – Subject of this chapter –
of the next. – Importance of science as conducing – to our happiness – to our virtue. –
Virtue the best gift of man – proved by its un-
decaying excellence – by its manner of adapting
itself to all siuations – cannot be effectually
propagated but by a cultivated mind. – Misguided virtue considered. – Importance of
science to our political improvement.*

THAT we may adequately understand the power and
operation of opinion in meliorating the institutions of
society, it is requisite that we should consider the value
and energy of truth. There is no topic more fundamental
to the principles of political science, or to the reasonings
of this work. It is from this point that we may most
perspicuously trace the opposite tenets, of the advocates
of privilege and aristocracy on the one hand, and the
friends of equality, and one universal measure of justice,
on the other. The partisans of both, at least the more enlightened and honourable partisans, acknowledge one
common object, the welfare of the whole, of the community and mankind. But the adherents of the old systems of government affirm 'that the imbecility of the
human mind is such as to make it unadviseable that man
should be trusted with himself; that his genuine condition is that of perpetual pupillage; that he is regulated
by passions and partial views, and cannot be governed
by pure reason and truth; that it is the business of a wise
man not to subvert, either in himself or others, delusions
which are useful, and prejudices which are salutary; and
that he is the worst enemy of his species who attempts, in
whatever mode, to introduce a form of society where no
advantage is taken to restrain us from vices by illusion,

from which we cannot be restrained by reason.' Every
man who adheres, in whole, or in part, to the tenets here
enumerated will perhaps, in proportion as he follows
them into their genuine consequences, be a partisan of
aristocracy.

Tenets the opposite of these constitute the great outline of the present work. If there be any truth in the
reasonings hitherto adduced, we are entitled to conclude
that morality, the science of human happiness, the principle which binds the individual to the species, and the
inducements which are calculated to persuade us to model
our conduct in the way most conducive to the advantage
of all, does not rest upon imposture and delusion, but
upon grounds that discovery will never undermine, and
wisdom never refute. We do not need therefore to be led
to that which is fitting and reasonable, by deceitful allurements. We have no cause to fear that the man who shall
see furthest and judge with the most perfect penetration
will be less estimable and useful, or will find fewer charms
in another's happiness and virtue, than if he were under
the dominion of error. If the conduct I am required to
observe be reasonable, there is no plainer or more forcible
mode of persuading me to adopt it than to exhibit it in its
true colours, and show me the benefits that will really
accrue from it. As long as these benefits are present to my
mind I shall have a desire, an ardour for performing the
action which leads to them, to the full as great as the
occasion will justify; and, if the occasion be of real magnitude, my ardour will be more genuine, and better endure
the test of experiment, than it can when combined with
narrow views or visionary credulity. Truth and falsehood
cannot subsist together: he that sees the merits of a case
in all their clearness cannot in that instance be the dupe
either of prejudice or superstition. Nor is there any reason
to believe that sound conviction will be less permanent
in its influence than sophistry and error.*

The value of truth will be still further illustrated if we

* Book I, Chap. V; Book V, Chap. XV.

consider it in detail, and enquire into its effects, either abstractedly, under which form it bears the appellation of science and knowledge; or practically, as it relates to the incidents and commerce of ordinary life, where it is known by the denomination of sincerity.

Abstractedly considered, it conduces to the happiness and virtue of the individual, as well as to the improvement of our social institutions.

In the discovery and knowledge of truth seems to be comprised, for the most part, all that an impartial and reflecting mind is accustomed to admire. No one is ignorant of the pleasures of knowledge. In human life there must be a distribution of time, and a variety of occupations. Now there is perhaps no occupation so much at our command, no pleasure of the means of which we are so likely to be deprived, as that which is intellectual. Sublime and expansive ideas produce delicious emotions. The acquisition of truth, the perception of the regularity with which proposition flows out of proposition, and one step of science leads to another, has never failed to reward the man who engaged in this species of employment. Knowledge contributes two ways to our happiness: first by the new sources of enjoyment which it opens upon us, and next by furnishing us with a clue in the selection of all other pleasures. No well informed man can seriously doubt of the advantages with respect to happiness of a capacious and improved intellect over the limited conceptions of a brute. Virtuous sentiments are another source of personal pleasure, and that of a more exquisite kind than intellectual improvements. But virtue itself depends for its value upon the energies of intellect. If the beings we are capable of benefiting were susceptible of nothing more than brutes are, we should have little pleasure in benefiting them, or in contemplating their happiness. But man has so many enjoyments, is capable of so high a degree of perfection, of exhibiting, socially considered, so admirable a spectacle, and of himself so truly estimating and favouring the spectacle, that, when we are engaged in promoting his benefit, we are indeed engaged in a sublime and ravishing employment. This is the case whether our exertions are directed to the advantage of the species or the individual. We rejoice when we save an ordinary man from destruction more than when we save a brute, because we recollect how much more he can feel, and how much more he can do. The same principle produces a still higher degree of congratulation in proportion as the man we save is more highly accomplished in talents and virtues.

Secondly, truth conduces to our improvement in virtue. Virtue, in its purest and most liberal sense, supposes an extensive survey of causes and their consequences that, having struck a just balance between the benefits and injuries that adhere to human affairs, we may adopt the proceeding which leads to the greatest practicable advantage. Virtue, like every other endowment of man, admits of degrees. He therefore must be confessed to be most virtuous who chooses with the soundest judgement the greatest and most universal overbalance of pleasure. But, in order to choose the greatest and most excellent pleasures, he must be intimately acquainted with the nature of man, its general features and its varieties. In order to forward the object he has chosen, he must have considered the different instruments for impressing mind, and the modes of applying them, and must know the properest moment for bringing them into action. In whatever light we consider virtue, whether we place it in the act or the disposition, its degree must be intimately connected with the degree of knowledge. No man can so much as love virtue sufficiently who has not an acute and lively perception of its beauty, and its tendency to produce the most solid and permanent happiness. What comparison can be made between the virtue of Socrates, and that of a Hottentot or a Siberian? A humorous example how universally this truth has been perceived may be taken from Tertullian,[20] who, as a father of the church, was obliged to maintain the hollowness and insignificance of pagan virtues, and accordingly assures us, 'that the most ignorant peasant under the Christian dispensation possesses more real knowledge than the wisest of the ancient philosophers'.*

We shall be more fully aware of the connection between virtue and knowledge if we consider that the highest employment of virtue is to propagate itself. Virtue alone deserves to be considered as leading to true happiness, the happiness which is most solid and durable. Sensual pleasures are momentary; they fill a very short portion of our time with enjoyment, and leave long intervals of painful vacuity. They charm principally by their novelty; by repetition they first abate of their poignancy, and at last become little less than wearisome. It is perhaps partly to be ascribed to the high estimation in which sensual pleasures are held that old age is so early and regular in its ravages. Our taste for these pleasures necessarily declines; with our taste our activity; and with our activity gradually crumble away the cheerfulness, the energy and the lives, of those whose dependence was placed upon these resources. Even knowledge, and the enlargement of intellect, are poor when unmixed with sentiments of benevolence and sympathy. Emotions are scarcely ever thrilling and electrical without something of social feeling. When the mind expands in works of taste and imagination, it will usually be found that there is something moral in the cause which gives birth to this expansion; and science and abstraction will soon become cold, unless they derive new attractions from ideas of society. In proportion therefore to the virtue of the individual will be the permanence of his cheerfulness, and the exquisiteness of his emotions. Add to which, benevolence is a resource which is never exhausted; but on the contrary, the more habitual are our patriotism and philanthropy, the more will they become invigorating and ardent.

It is also impossible that any situation can occur in

* *Apologia,* Cap. xlvi. See this subject further pursued in the Appendix.

which virtue cannot find room to expatiate. In society there is continual opportunity for its active employment. I cannot have intercourse with a human being who may not be the better for that intercourse. If he be already just and virtuous, these qualities are improved by communication. If he be imperfect and erroneous, there must always be some prejudice I may contribute to destroy, some motive to delineate, some error to remove. If I be prejudiced and imperfect myself, it cannot however happen that my prejudices and imperfections shall be exactly coincident with his. I may therefore inform him of the truths that I know, and, even by the collision of prejudices, truth is elicited. It is impossible that I should strenuously apply myself to his improvement with sincere motives of benevolence, without some good being the result. Nor am I more at a loss in solitude. In solitude I may accumulate the materials of social benefit. No situation can be so desperate as to preclude these efforts. Voltaire,[21] when shut up in the Bastille, and for aught he knew for life, deprived of the means either of writing or reading, arranged and in part executed the project of his Henriade.*

All these reasonings are calculated to persuade us that the most precious boon we can bestow upon others is virtue, and that the highest employment of virtue is to propagate itself. But, as virtue is inseparably connected with knowledge in my own mind, so by knowledge only can it be imparted to others. How can the virtue we have just been contemplating be produced but by infusing comprehensive views, and communicating energetic truths? Now that man alone is qualified to infuse these views, and communicate these truths, who is himself pervaded with them.

Let us suppose for a moment virtuous dispositions existing without knowledge or outrunning knowledge, the last of which is certainly possible; and we shall pre-

---

*Vie de Voltaire, par M***. A Geneve, 1786. Chap. iv. This is probably the best history of this great man which has yet appeared.

sently find how little such virtue is worthy to be propagated. The most generous views will, in such cases, frequently lead to the most nefarious actions. A Cranmer[22] will be incited to the burning of heretics, and a Digby contrive the Gunpowder Treason. But, to leave these extreme instances: in all cases where mistaken virtue leads to cruel and tyrannical actions, the mind will be rendered discontented and morose by the actions it perpetrates. Truth, immortal and ever present truth, is so powerful, that, in spite of all his prejudices, the upright man will suspect himself when he resolves upon an action that is at war with the plainest principles of morality. He will become melancholy, dissatisfied and anxious. His firmness will degenerate into obstinacy, and his justice into inexorable severity. The further he pursues his system, the more erroneous will he become. The further he pursues it, the less will he be satisfied with it. As truth is an endless source of tranquillity and delight, error will be a prolific fountain of new mistakes and discontent.

As to the third point, which is most essential to the enquiry in which we are engaged, the tendency of truth to the improvement of our political institutions, there can be little room for scepticism or controversy. If politics be a science, investigation must be the means of unfolding it. If men resemble each other in more numerous and essential particulars than those in which they differ, if the best purposes that can be accomplished respecting them be to make them free, virtuous and wise, there must be one best method of advancing these common purposes, one best mode of social existence deducible from the principles of their nature. If truth be one, there must be one code of truths on the subject of our reciprocal duties. Nor is investigation only the best mode of ascertaining the principles of political justice and happiness; it is also the best mode of introducing and establishing them. Discussion is the path that leads to discovery and demonstration. Motives ferment in the minds of great bodies of men, till their modes of society experience a variation, not less memorable than the variation of their sentiments. The more familiar the mind becomes with the ideas of which these motives consist, and the propositions that express them, the more irresistibly is it propelled to a general system of proceeding in correspondence with them.

Appendix, page 300

OF THE CONNECTION BETWEEN UNDERSTANDING AND VIRTUE

Can eminent virtue exist unconnected with talents? – Nature of virtue. – It is the offspring of understanding. – It generates understanding. – Illustration from other pursuits – love – ambition – applied.
Can eminent talents exist unconnected with virtue? – Argument in the affirmative from analogy – in the negative from the universality of moral speculation – from the nature of vice as founded in mistake. – The argument balanced. – Importance of a sense of justice. – Its connection with talents. – Illiberality with which men of talents are usually treated.

A PROPOSITION which, however evident in itself, seems never to have been considered with the attention it deserves is that which affirms the connection between understanding and virtue. Can an honest ploughman be as virtuous as Cato? Is a man of weak intellects and narrow education as capable of moral excellence as the sublimest genius or the mind most stored with information and science?

To determine these questions it is necessary we should recollect the nature of virtue. Considered as a personal quality, it consists in the disposition of the mind, and may be defined a desire to promote the happiness of intelligent beings in general, the quantity of virtue being as the quantity of desire. Now desire is wholly inseparable from preference, or a perception of the excellence, real or supposed, of any object. I say real or supposed, for an object totally destitute of real and intrinsic excellence may become an object of desire on account of the imaginary excellence that is ascribed to it. Nor is this the only mistake to which human intellect is liable. We may desire an object of absolute excellence, not for its real and genuine recommendations, but for some fictitious attractions we may impute to it. This is always in some degree the case when a beneficial action is performed from an ill motive.

How far is this mistake compatible with real virtue? If I desire the happiness of intelligent beings, without a strong and vivid perception of what it is in which their happiness consists, can this desire be admitted for virtuous? Nothing seems more inconsistent with our ideas of virtue. A virtuous preference is the preference of an object for the sake of certain qualities which really belong to it. To attribute virtue to any other species of preference would be nearly the same as to suppose that an accidental effect of my conduct, which was out of my view at the time of adopting it, might entitle me to the appellation of virtuous.

Hence it appears, first, that virtue consists in a desire of the happiness of the species: and, secondly, that that desire only can be eminently virtuous which flows from a distinct perception of the value, and consequently of the nature, of the thing desired. But how extensive must be the capacity that comprehends the full value and the real ingredients of true happiness? It must begin with a collective idea of the human species. It must discriminate, among the different causes that produce a pleasurable state of mind, that which produces the most exquisite and durable pleasure. Eminent virtue requires that I should have a grand view of the tendency of knowledge to produce happiness, and of just political institution to favour the progress of knowledge. It demands that I should perceive in what manner social intercourse may be made conducive to virtue and felicity, and imagine the unspeakable advantages that may arise from a coincidence and succession of generous efforts. These things are necessary, not merely for the purpose of enabling me to employ my virtuous disposition in the best manner, but also of giving to that disposition a just animation and vigour. God, according to the ideas usually conceived of that being, is more benevolent than man because he has a constant and clear perception of the nature of that end which his providence pursues.

A further proof that a powerful understanding is inseparable from eminent virtue will suggest itself, if we recollect that earnest desire, in matters that fall within the compass of human exertion, never fails in some degree to generate capacity.

This proposition has been beautifully illustrated by the poets, when they have represented the passion of love as immediately leading, in the breast of the lover, to the attainment of many arduous accomplishments. It unlocks his tongue, and enables him to plead the cause of his passion with insinuating eloquence. It renders his conversation pleasing, and his manners graceful. Does he desire to express his feelings in the language of verse? It dictates to him the most natural and pathetic strains, and supplies him with a just and interesting language, which the man of more reflection and science has often sought for in vain.

No picture can be more truly founded in a knowledge of human nature than this. The history of all eminent talents is of a similar kind. Did Themistocles desire to eclipse the trophies of the battle of Marathon? The uneasiness of this desire would not let him sleep, and all his thoughts were occupied with the invention of means to accomplish the purpose he had chosen. It is a well known maxim in the forming of juvenile minds that the instruction which is communicated by mere constraint makes a slow and feeble impression; but that, when once you have inspired the mind with a love for its object, the scene and the progress are entirely altered. The uneasiness of mind which earnest desire produces doubles our intellectual activity; and as surely carries us forward with increased velocity towards our goal as the expectation of a reward of ten thousand pounds would prompt a man to walk from London to York with firmer resolution and in a shorter time.

Let the object be for a person uninstructed in the rudiments of drawing to make a copy of some celebrated statue. At first, we will suppose, his attempt shall be mean and unsuccessful. If his desire be feeble, he will be deterred by the miscarriage of this essay. If his desire be ardent and invincible, he will return to the attack. He will derive instruction from his failure. He will examine where and why he miscarried. He will study his model with a more curious eye. He will correct his mistakes, derive encouragement from a partial success, and new incentives from miscarriage itself.

The case is similar in virtue as in science. If I have conceived an earnest desire of being the benefactor of my species, I shall, no doubt, find out a channel in which for my desire to operate, and shall be quick-sighted in discovering the defects, or comparative littleness, of the plan I may have chosen. But the choice of an excellent plan for the accomplishment of an important purpose, and the exertion of a mind perpetually watchful to remove its defects, imply considerable understanding. The further I am engaged in the pursuit of this plan, the more will my capacity increase. If my mind flag and be discouraged in the pursuit, it will not be merely want of understanding, but want of desire. My desire and my virtue will be less than those of the man who goes on with unremitted constancy in the same career.

Thus far we have only been considering how impossible it is that eminent virtue should exist in a weak understanding; and it is surprising that such a proposition should ever have been contested. It is a curious question to examine how far the converse of this proposition is true, and in what degree eminent talents are compatible with the absence of virtue.

From the arguments already adduced, it appears that virtuous desire is wholly inseparable from a strong and vivid perception of the nature and value of the object of virtue. Hence it seems most natural to conclude that, though understanding, or strong percipient power, is the indispensable prerequisite of virtue, yet it is necessary that this power should be exercised upon this object, in order to its producing the desired effect. Thus it is in art. Without genius no man ever was a poet; but it is necessary that general capacity should have been directed to this particular channel, for poetical excellence to be the result.

There is however some difference between the two cases. Poetry is the business of a few, virtue and vice are the affair of all men. To every intellect that exists, one or other of these qualities must properly belong. It must be granted that, where every other circumstance is equal, that man will be most virtuous whose understanding has been most actively employed in the study of virtue. But morality has been, in a certain degree, an object of attention to all men. No person ever failed, more or less, to apply the standard of just and unjust to his own actions and those of others; and this has, of course, been generally done with most ingenuity by men of the greatest capacity.

It must further be remembered that a vicious conduct is always the result of narrow views. A man of powerful capacity, and extensive observation, is least likely to commit the mistake, either of seeing himself as the only object of importance in the universe, or of conceiving that his own advantage may best be promoted by trampling on that of others. Liberal accomplishments are surely, in some degree, connected with liberal principles. He who takes into his view a whole nation as the subjects of his operation, or the instruments of his greatness, may be expected to entertain some kindness for the whole. He whose mind is habitually elevated to magnificent conceptions is not likely to sink, without strong reluctance, into those sordid pursuits which engross so large a portion of mankind.

But, though these general maxims must be admitted for true, and would incline us to hope for a constant union between eminent talents and great virtues, there are other considerations which present a strong drawback upon so agreeable an expectation. It is sufficiently evident that morality, in some degree, enters into the reflections of all mankind. But it is equally evident that it may enter for more or for less; and that there will be men of the highest talents who have their attention diverted to other objects, and by whom it will be meditated upon with less earnestness, than it may sometimes be by other men, who are, in a general view, their inferiors. The human mind is in some cases so tenacious of its errors, and so ingenious in the invention of a sophistry by which they may be vindicated, as to frustrate expectations of virtue, in other respects, the best founded.

From the whole of the subject it seems to appear that men of talents, even when they are erroneous, are not destitute of virtue, and that there is a fullness of guilt of which they are incapable. There is no ingredient that so essentially contributes to a virtuous character as a sense of justice. Philanthropy, as contradistinguished to justice, is rather an unreflecting feeling than a rational principle. It leads to an absurd indulgence, which is frequently more injurious than beneficial, even to the individual it proposes to favour. It leads to a blind partiality, inflicting calamity, without remorse, upon many perhaps, in order to promote the imagined interest of a few. But justice measures by one unalterable standard the claims of all, weighs their opposite pretensions, and seeks to diffuse happiness, because happiness is the fit and proper condition of a conscious being. Wherever therefore a strong sense of justice exists, it is common and reasonable to say that in that mind exists considerable virtue, though the individual, from an unfortunate concurrence of circumstances, may, with all his great qualities, be the instrument of a very small portion of benefit. Can great intellectual power exist without a strong sense of justice?

It has no doubt resulted from a train of speculation similar to this, that poetical readers have commonly remarked Milton's devil[23] to be a being of considerable virtue. It must be admitted that his energies centred too much in personal regards. But why did he rebel against his maker? It was, as he himself informs us, because he saw no sufficient reason for that extreme inequality of rank and power which the creator assumed. It was because prescription and precedent form no adequate ground for implicit faith. After his fall, why did he still cherish the spirit of opposition? From a persuasion that he was hardly and injuriously treated. He was not discouraged by the apparent inequality of the contest: because a sense of reason and justice was stronger in his mind than a sense of brute force; because he had much of the feelings of an Epictetus[24] or a Cato,[25] and little of those of a slave. He bore his torments with fortitude, because he disdained to be subdued by despotic power. He sought revenge, because he could not think with tameness of the unexpostulating authority that assumed to dispose of him. How beneficial and illustrious might the temper from which these qualities flowed have been found, with a small diversity of situation!

Let us descend from these imaginary existences to real history. We shall find that even Caesar and Alexander had their virtues. There is great reason to believe that, however mistaken was their system of conduct, they imagined it reconcilable, and even conducive, to the general interest. If they had desired the general good more earnestly, they would have understood better how to promote it.

Upon the whole it appears that great talents are great energies, and that great energies cannot flow but from a powerful sense of fitness and justice. A man of uncommon genius is a man of high passions and lofty design; and our passions will be found, in the last analysis, to have their surest foundation in a sentiment of justice. If a man be of an aspiring and ambitious temper, it is because at present he finds himself out of his place, and wishes to be in it. Even the lover imagines that his qualities, or his passion, give him a title superior to that of other men. If I accumulate wealth, it is because I think that the most rational plan of life cannot be secured without it; and, if I dedicate my energies to sensual pleasures, it is that I regard other pursuits as irrational and visionary. All our passions would die in the moment they were conceived were it not for this reinforcement. A man of quick resentment, of strong feelings, and who pertinaciously resists everything that he regards as an unjust assumption, may be considered as having in him the seeds of eminence. Nor is it easily to be conceived that such a man should not proceed from a sense of justice, to some degree of benevolence; as Milton's hero felt real compassion and sympathy for his partners in misfortune.

If these reasonings are to be admitted, what judgement shall we form of the decision of Johnson,[26] who, speaking of a certain obscure translator of the odes of Pindar, says that he was 'one of the few poets to whom death needed not to be terrible'?* Let it be remembered that the error is by no means peculiar to Johnson, though there are few instances in which it is carried to a more violent extreme than in the general tenour of the work from which this quotation is taken. It was natural to expect that there would be a combination among the multitude to pull down intellectual eminence. Ambition is common to all men; and those who are unable to rise to distinction are at least willing to reduce others to their own standard. No man can completely understand the character of him with whom he has no sympathy of views; and we may be allowed to revile what we do not understand. But it is

* *Lives of the Poets*: Life of West.

deeply to be regretted that men of talents should so often have entered into this combination. Who does not recollect with pain the vulgar abuse that Swift has thrown upon Dryden, and the mutual jealousies and animosities of Rousseau and Voltaire, men who ought to have cooperated for the salvation of the world?

CHAPTER VI

OF SINCERITY

Its favourable tendencies in respect to – innocence – energy – intellectual improvement – and philanthropy. History – and effects of insincerity. – Sincerity delineated. – Character of its adherents.

IT was further proposed to consider the value of truth in a practical view, as it relates to the incidents and commerce of ordinary life, under which form it is known by the denomination of sincerity.

The powerful recommendations attendant upon sincerity are obvious. It is intimately connected with the general dissemination of innocence, energy, intellectual improvement, and philanthropy.

Did every man impose this law upon himself, did he regard himself as not authorized to conceal any part of his character and conduct, this circumstance alone would prevent millions of actions from being perpetrated in which we are now induced to engage by the prospect of secrecy and impunity. We have only to suppose men obliged to consider, before they determined upon an equivocal action, whether they chose to be their own historians, the future narrators of the scene in which they were acting a part, and the most ordinary imagination will instantly suggest how essential a variation would be introduced into human affairs. It has been justly observed that the popish practice of confession is attended with some salutary effects. How much better would it be if, instead of an institution thus equivocal, and which has been made so dangerous an instrument of ecclesiastical despotism, every man were to make the world his confessional, and the human species the keeper of his conscience?

There is a further benefit that would result to me from the habit of telling every man the truth, regardless of the dictates of worldly prudence and custom. I should acquire a clear, ingenuous and unembarrassed air. According to the established modes of society, whenever I have a circumstance to state which would require some effort of mind and discrimination to enable me to do it justice, and state it with the proper effect, I fly from the talk, and take refuge in silence or equivocation. But the principle which forbad me concealment would keep my mind for ever awake, and for ever warm. I should always be obliged to exert my attention, lest, in pretending to tell the truth, I should tell it in so imperfect and mangled a way as to produce the effect of falsehood. If I spoke to a man of my own faults or those of his neighbour, I should be anxious not to suffer them to come distorted or exaggerated to his mind, or to permit what at first was fact to degenerate into satire. If I spoke to him of the errors he had himself committed, I should carefully avoid those inconsiderate expressions which might convert what was in itself beneficent into offence; and my thoughts would be full of that kindness, and generous concern for his welfare, which such a talk necessarily brings along with it. Sincerity would liberate my mind, and make the eulogiums I had occasion to pronounce, clear, copious and appropriate. Conversation would speedily exchange its present character of listlessness and insignificance, for a Roman boldness and fervour; and, accustomed, at first by the fortuitous operation of circumstances, to tell men of things it was useful for them to know, I should speedily learn to study their advantage, and never rest satisfied with my conduct till I had discovered how to spend the hours I was in their company in the way which was most rational and improving.

The effects of sincerity upon others would be similar to its effects upon him that practised it. How great would be the benefit if every man were sure of meeting in his neighbour the ingenuous censor, who would tell him in person, and publish to the world, his virtues, his good deeds, his meannesses and his follies? We have never a strong feeling of these in our own case, except so far as they are confirmed to us by the suffrage of our neighbours. Knowledge, such as we are able to acquire it, depends in a majority of instances, not upon the single efforts of the individual, but upon the consent of other human understandings sanctioning the judgement of our own. It is the uncertainty of which every man is conscious as to his solitary judgement that produces, for the most part, zeal for proselytism, and impatience of contradiction. It is impossible I should have a true satisfaction in my dispositions and talents, or even any precise perceptions of virtue and vice, unless assisted by the concurrence of my fellows.

An impartial distribution of commendation and blame to the actions of men would be a most powerful incentive to virtue. But this distribution, at present, scarcely in any instance exists. One man is satirized with bitterness, and the misconduct of another is treated with inordinate lenity. In speaking of our neighbours, we are perpetually under the influence of sinister and unacknowledged motives. Everything is disfigured and distorted. The basest hypocrite passes through life with applause; and the purest character is loaded with unmerited aspersions. The benefactors of mankind are frequently the objects of their bitterest hatred and most unrelenting ingratitude. What encouragement then is afforded to virtue? Those who are smitten with the love of distinction will rather seek it in external splendour, and unmeaning luxury, than in moral attainments. While those who are led to benevolent pursuits by the purest motives yet languish under the privation of that honour and esteem which would give new firmness to rectitude, and ardour to benevolence.

A genuine and unalterable sincerity would not fail to reverse the scene.* Every idle or malignant tale now produces its effect, because men are unaccustomed to exercise their judgement upon the probabilities of human action, or to possess the materials of judgement. But then the rash assertions of one individual would be corrected by the maturer information of his neighbour. Exercised in discrimination, we should be little likely to be misled. The truth would be known, the whole truth, and the unvarnished truth. This would be a trial that the most stubborn obliquity would be found unable to withstand. If a just and impartial character were awarded to all human actions, vice would be universally deserted, and virtue everywhere practised. Sincerity therefore, once introduced into the manners of mankind, would necessarily bring every other virtue in its train.

Men are now feeble in their temper because they are not accustomed to hear the truth. They build their confidence in being personally treated with artificial delicacy, and expect us to abstain from repeating what we know to their disadvantage. But is this right? It has already appeared that plain dealing, truth, spoken with kindness, but spoken with sincerity, is the most wholesome of all disciplines. How then can we be justified in thus subverting the nature of things, and the system of the universe, in breeding a set of summer insects upon which the breeze of sincerity may never blow, and the tempest of misfortune never beat?

In the third place, sincerity is, in an eminent degree, calculated to conduce to our intellectual improvement. If from timidity of disposition, or the danger that attends a disclosure, we suppress the reflections that occur to us, we shall neither add to, nor correct them. From the act of telling my thoughts, I derive encouragement to proceed.

* Book VI, Chap. VI.

Nothing can more powerfully conduce to perspicuity than the very attempt to arrange and express them. If they be received cordially by others, they derive from that circumstance a peculiar firmness and consistency. If they be received with opposition and distrust, I am induced to revise them. I detect their errors; or I strengthen my arguments, and add new truths to those which I had previously accumulated. It is not by the solitary anchorite, who neither speaks, nor hears, nor reads the genuine sentiments of man, that the stock of human good is eminently increased. The period of bold and unrestricted communication is the period in which the materials of happiness ferment and germinate. What can excite me to the pursuit of discovery if I know that I am never to communicate my discoveries? It is in the nature of things impossible that the man who has determined never to utter the truths he may be acquainted with should be an intrepid and indefatigable thinker. The link which binds together the inward and the outward man is indissoluble; and he that is not bold in speech will never be ardent and unprejudiced in enquiry.

What is it that, at this day, enables a thousand errors to keep their station in the world; priestcraft, tests, bribery, war, cabal and whatever else excites the disapprobation of the honest and enlightened mind? Cowardice; the timid reserve which makes men shrink from telling what they know; and the insidious policy that annexes persecution and punishment to an unrestrained and spirited discussion of the true interests of society. Men either refrain from the publication of unpalatable opinions because they are unwilling to make a sacrifice of their worldly prospects; or they publish them in a frigid and enigmatical spirit, stripped of their true character, and incapable of their genuine operation. If every man today would tell all the truth he knew, it is impossible to predict how short would be the reign of usurpation and folly.

Lastly, a still additional benefit attendant on the prac-

tice of sincerity is good humour, kindness and benevolence. At present, men meet together with the temper
less of friends than enemies. Every man eyes his neighbour, as if he expected to receive from him a secret
wound. Every member of a polished and civilized community goes armed. He knows many things of his associate, which he conceives himself obliged not to allude
to in his hearing, but rather to put on an air of the pro-
foundest ignorance. In the absence of the person concerned, he scarcely knows how to mention his defects,
however essential the advertisement may be, lest he
should incur the imputation of a calumniator. If he mention them, it is under the seal of secrecy. He speaks of
them with the sentiments of a criminal, conscious that
what he is saying he would be unwilling to utter before
the individual concerned. Perhaps he does not fully advert to this artificial character in himself; but he at least
notes it with infallible observation in his neighbour. In
youth, it may be, he accommodates himself with a pliant
spirit to the manners of the world; and, while he loses no
jot of his gaiety, learns from it no other lessons than those
of selfishness and cheerful indifference. Observant of the
game that goes forward around him, he becomes skilful
in his turn to elude the curiosity of others, and smiles in-
wardly at the false scent he prompts them to follow. Dead
to the emotions of a disinterested sympathy, he can calmly
consider men as the mere neutral instruments of his enjoyments. He can preserve himself in a true equipoise between love and hatred. But this is a temporary character.
The wanton wildness of youth at length subsides, and
he is no longer contented to stand alone in the world.
Anxious for the consolations of sympathy and frankness,
he remarks the defects of mankind with a different spirit.
He is seized with a shuddering at the sensation of their
coldness. He can no longer tolerate their subterfuges and
disguises. He searches in vain for an ingenuous character,
and loses patience at the eternal disappointment. The
defect that he before regarded with indifference he now

considers as the consummation of vice. What wonder that, under these circumstances, moroseness, sourness and misanthropy become the ruling sentiments of so large a portion of mankind?

How would the whole of this be reversed by the practice of sincerity? We could not be indifferent to men whose custom it was to tell us the truth. Hatred would perish from a failure in its principal ingredient, the duplicity and impenetrableness of human actions. No man could acquire a distant and unsympathetic temper. Reserve, deceitfulness, and an artful exhibition of ourselves take from the human form its soul, and leave us the unanimated semblance of what man might have been; of what he would have been, were not every impulse of the mind thus stunted and destroyed. If our emotions were not checked, we should be truly friends with each other. Our character would expand: the luxury of indulging our feelings, and the exercise of uttering them, would raise us to the stature of men. I should not conceive alarm from my neighbour, because I should be conscious that I knew his genuine sentiments. I should not harbour bad passions and unsocial propensities, because the habit of expressing my thoughts would enable me to detect and dismiss them in the outset. Thus every man would be inured to the sentiment of love, and would find in his species objects worthy of his affection. Confidence is upon all accounts the surest foil of mutual kindness.

The value of sincerity will be still further illustrated by a brief consideration of the nature of insincerity. Viewed superficially and at a distance, we are easily reconciled, and are persuaded to have recourse to it upon the most trivial occasions. Did we examine it in detail, and call to mind its genuine history, the result could not fail to be different. Its features are neither like virtue, nor compatible with virtue. The sensations it obliges us to undergo are of the most odious nature. Its direct business is to cut off all commerce between the heart and the tongue. There are organs however of the human frame more difficult to be commanded than the mere syllables and phrases we utter. We must be upon our guard, or our cheeks will be covered with a conscious blush, the awkwardness of our gestures will betray us, and our lips will falter with their unwonted task. Such is the issue of the first attempt, not merely of the liar, but of him who practises concealment, or whose object it is to mislead the person with whom he happens to converse. After a series of essays we become more expert. We are not, as at first, detected by the person from whom we intended to withhold what we knew; but we fear detection. We feel uncertainty and confusion; and it is with difficulty we convince ourselves that we have escaped unsuspected. Is it thus a man ought to feel? At last perhaps we become consummate in hypocrisy, and feel the same confidence and alacrity in duplicity that we before felt in entire frankness. Which, to an ordinary eye, would appear the man of virtue; he who, by the depth of his hypocrisy, contrived to keep his secret wholly unsuspected, or he who was precipitate enough to be thus misled, and to believe that his neighbour made use of words for the purpose of being understood?

But this is not all. It remains for the deceiver, in the next place, to maintain the delusion he has once imposed, and to take care that no unexpected occurrence shall betray him. It is upon this circumstance that the common observation is founded that 'one lie will always need a hundred others to justify and cover it'. We cannot determine to keep anything secret without risking to be involved in artifices, quibbles, equivocations and falsehoods without number. The character of the virtuous man seems to be that of a firm and unalterable resolution, confident in his own integrity. But the character that results from insincerity, begins in hesitation, and ends in disgrace. Let us suppose that the imposition I practised is in danger of detection. Of course it will become my wisdom to calculate this danger, and, if it be too imminent, not to think of attempting any further disguise. But, if the secret be important, and the danger problematical, I shall probably persist. The whole extent of the danger can be known only by degrees. Suppose the person who questions me return to the charge, and affirm that he heard the fact, as it really was, but not as I represent it, from another. What am I now to do? Am I to asperse the character of the honest reporter, and at the same time, it may be, instead of establishing the delusion, only astonish my neighbour with my cool and intrepid effrontery?

What has already been adduced may assist us to determine the species of sincerity which virtue prescribes, and which alone can be of great practical benefit to mankind. Sincerity may be considered as of three degrees. First, a man may conceive that he sufficiently preserves his veracity if he never utter anything that cannot be explained into a consistency with truth. There is a plain distinction between this man and him who makes no scruple of the most palpable and direct falsehood. Or, secondly, it may happen that his delicacy shall not stop here, and he may resolve, not only to utter nothing that is literally untrue, but also nothing which he knows or believes will be understood by the hearer in a sense that is untrue. This he may consider as amounting for the most part to an adequate discharge of his duty; and he may conceive that there is little mischief in the frequently suppressing information which it was in his power to supply. The third and highest degree of sincerity consists in the most perfect frankness, discards every species of concealment or reserve, and, as Cicero expresses it, 'utters nothing that is false, and withholds nothing that is true'.

The two first of these by no means answer the genuine purposes of sincerity. The former labours under one disadvantage more than direct falsehood. It is of little consequence, to the persons with whom I communicate, that I have a subterfuge by which I can, to my own mind, explain my deceit into a consistency with truth; while at the same time the study of such subterfuges is more adverse to courage and energy than a conduct which unblushingly avows the laxity of its principles. The second of the degrees enumerated, which merely proposes to itself the avoiding every active deception, seems to be measured less by the standard of magnanimity than of personal prudence. If, as Rousseau has asserted,* 'the great duty of man be to do no injury to his neighbour', then this negative sincerity may be of considerable value: but, if it be the highest and most indispensable business of man to study and promote his neighbour's welfare, a virtue of this sort will contribute little to so honourable an undertaking. If sincerity be, as we have endeavoured to demonstrate, the most powerful engine of human improvement, a scheme for restraining it within so narrow limits cannot be entitled to considerable applause. Add to this, that it is impossible, in many cases, to suppress information without great mastery in the arts of ambiguity and evasion, and such a perfect command of countenance as shall prevent it from being an index to our real sentiments. Indeed the man who is frequently accustomed to seem ignorant of what he really knows, though he will escape the open disgrace of him who is detected in direct falsehood or ambiguous imposition, will yet be viewed by his neighbours with coldness and distrust, and esteemed an unfathomable and selfish character.

Hence it appears that the only species of sincerity which can in any degree prove satisfactory to the enlightened moralist and politician is that where the frankness is perfect, and every degree of reserve is discarded.

Nor is there any danger that such a character should degenerate into ruggedness and brutality. Sincerity, upon the principles on which it is here recommended, is practised from a consciousness of its utility, and from sentiments of philanthropy. It will communicate frankness to the voice, fervour to the gesture and kindness to the

* *Emile,* liv. ii.

heart. Even in expostulation and censure, friendliness of intention and mildness of proceeding may be eminently conspicuous. There should be no mixture of disdain and superiority. The interest of him who is corrected, not the triumph of the corrector, should be the principle of action. True sincerity will be attended with that equality which is the only sure foundation of love, and that love which gives the best finishing and lustre to a sentiment of equality.

Appendix I

ILLUSTRATIONS OF SINCERITY

Question proposed. – Erroneous maxims upon this head refuted. – General principles and theories estimated. – An injurious distinction exposed. – Limitations of sincerity. – Arguments, affirmative and negative. – Inference. – Conclusion.

THERE is an important enquiry which cannot fail to suggest itself in this place. 'Universal sincerity has been shown to be pregnant with unspeakable advantages. The enlightened friend of the human species cannot fail anxiously to anticipate the time when each man shall speak truth with his neighbour. But what conduct does it behove us to observe in the interval? Are we to practise an unreserved and uniform sincerity, while the world about us acts upon so different a plan? If sincerity should ever become characteristic of the community in which we live, our neighbour will then be prepared to hear the truth, and to make use of the comunication in a way that shall be manly, generous and just. But, at present, we shall be liable to waken the resentment of some, and to subject to a trial beyond its strength the fortitude of others. By a direct and ill-timed truth we may not only incur the forfeiture of our worldly prospects, but of our usefulness, and sometimes of our lives.'

Ascetic and puritanical systems of morality have accustomed their votaries to give a short answer to these difficulties, by directing us 'to do our duty, without regard to consequences, and uninfluenced by a consideration of what may be the conduct of others'. But these maxims will not pass unexamined with the man who considers morality as a subject of reasoning, and places its foundation in a principle of utility. 'To do our duty without regard to consequences,' is, upon this principle, a maxim completely absurd and self-contradictory. Morality is nothing else but a calculation of consequences, and an adoption of that mode of conduct which, upon the most comprehensive view, appears to be attended with a balance of general pleasure and happiness. Nor will the other part of the precept above stated appear, upon examination, to be less erroneous. There are many instances in which the selection of the conduct I should pursue altogether depends upon a foresight of 'what will be the conduct of others'. To what purpose contribute my subscription to an object of public utility, a bridge, for example, or a canal, at a time when I certainly foreknow that the subscription will not be generally countenanced? Shall I go and complete such a portion of masonry upon the spot as, if all my neighbours would do the same, would effect the desired purpose, though I am convinced that no one beside myself will move a finger in the undertaking? There are various regulations respecting our habits of living, expenditure and attire which, if generally adopted, would probably be of the highest benefit, which yet, if acted upon by a single individual, might be productive of nothing but injury. I cannot pretend to launch a ship or repel an army by myself, though either of these might be things, absolutely considered, highly proper to be done.

The duty of sincerity is one of those general principles which reflection and experience have enjoined upon us as conducive to the happiness of mankind. Let us enquire then into the nature and origin of general principles. Engaged, as men are, in perpetual intercourse with their neighbours, and constantly liable to be called upon without the smallest previous notice, in cases where the interest of their fellows is deeply involved, it is not possible for them, upon all occasions, to deduce, through a chain of reasoning, the judgement which should be followed. Hence the necessity of resting-places for the mind, of deductions, already stored in the memory, and prepared for application as circumstances may demand. We find this necessity equally urgent upon us in matters of science and abstraction as in conduct and morals. Theory has also a further use. It serves as a perpetual exercise and aliment to the understanding, and renders us competent and vigorous to judge in every situation that can occur. Nothing can be more idle and shallow than the competition which some men have set up between theory and practice. It is true that we can never predict, from theory alone, the success of any given experiment. It is true that no theory, accurately speaking, can possibly be practical. It is the business of theory to collect the circumstances of a certain set of cases, and arrange them. It would cease to be theory if it did not leave out many circumstances; it collects such as are general, and leaves out such as are particular. In practice however, those circumstances inevitably arise which are necessarily omitted in the general process: they cause the phenomenon, in various ways, to include features which were not in the prediction, and to be diversified in those that were. Yet theory is of the highest use; and those who decry it may even be proved not to understand themselves. They do not mean that men should always act in a particular case, without illustration from any other case, for that would be to deprive us of all understanding. The moment we begin to compare cases, and infer, we begin to theorize; no two things in the universe were ever perfectly alike. The genuine exercise of man therefore is to theorize, for this is, in other words, to sharpen and improve his intellect; but not to become the slave of theory, or at any time to forget that it is, by its very nature, precluded from comprehending the whole of what claims our attention.

To apply this to the case of morals. General principles of morality are so far valuable as they truly delineate the means of utility, pleasure, or happiness. But every action of any human being has its appropriate result; and, the more closely it is examined, the more truly will that result appear. General rules and theories are not infallible. It would be preposterous to suppose that, in order to judge fairly, and conduct myself properly, I ought only to look at a thing from a certain distance, and not consider it minutely. On the contrary, I ought, as far as lies in my power, to examine everything upon its own grounds, and decide concerning it upon its own merits. To rest in general rules is sometimes a necessity which our imperfection imposes upon us, and sometimes the refuge of our indolence; but the true dignity of human reason is, as much as we are able, to go beyond them, to have our faculties in act upon every occasion that occurs, and to conduct ourselves accordingly.

There is an observation necessary to be made, to prevent any erroneous application of these reasonings. In the morality of every action two things are to be considered, the direct, and the remote consequences with which it is attended. There are numerous modes of proceeding which might be productive of immediate pleasure that would have so ill an effect upon the permanent state of one or many individuals as to render them, in every rational estimate, objects, not of choice, but of aversion. This is particularly the case in relation to that view of any action whereby it becomes a medium enabling the spectator to predict the nature of future actions. It is with the conduct of our fellow beings, as with the course of inanimate nature: if events did not succeed each other in a certain order, there could be neither judgement, nor wisdom, nor morality. Confidence, in the order of the seasons, and the progress of vegetation, encourages us to sow our field, in expectation of a future harvest. Confidence, in the characters of our fellow men, that they will for the most part be governed by the reason of the case, that they will neither rob, nor defraud, nor deceive us, is not less essential to the existence of civilized society. Hence arises a species of argument in favour of general rules, not hitherto mentioned. The remote consequences of an action, especially as they relate to the fulfilling, or not fulfilling, the expectation excited, depend chiefly on general circumstances, and not upon particulars; belong to the class, and not to the individual. But this makes no essential alteration in what was before delivered. It will still be incumbent on us, when called into action, to estimate the nature of the particular case, that we may ascertain where the urgency of special circumstances is such as to supersede rules that are generally obligatory.

To return to the particular case of sincerity. Sincerity and plain dealing are obviously, in the majority of human actions, the best policy, if we consider only the interest of the individual, and extend our calculation of that interest only over a very short period. No man will be wild enough to assert, even in this limited sense, that it is seldomer our policy to speak truth than to lie. Sincerity and plain dealing are eminently conducive to the interest of mankind at large, because they afford ground for that confidence and reasonable expectation which are essential both to wisdom and virtue. Yet it may with propriety be asked, 'Whether cases do not exist of peculiar emergency where the general principle of sincerity and speaking the truth ought to be superseded?'

Undoubtedly this is a question to the treatment of which we should advance with some degree of caution and delicacy. Yet it would be a strange instance of inconsistency that should induce us, right or wrong, to recommend a universal frankness, from an apprehension of the abuses which may follow from an opposite doctrine; and thus incur a charge of deception, in the very act of persuading our neighbours that deception is in no instance to be admitted.

Some persons, from an extreme tenderness of countenancing any particle of insincerity, at the same time that they felt the difficulty of recommending the opposite practice in every imaginable case, have thought proper to allege, 'that it is not the propagation of truth, but of falsehood we have to fear; and that the whole against which we are bound to be upon our guard is the telling truth in such a manner as to produce the effects of falsehood'.

This will perhaps be found upon examination to be an injudicious and mischievous distinction. In the first place, it is of great benefit to the cause of morality that things should be called by their right names, without varnish or subterfuge. I am either to tell the simple and obvious truth, or I am not; I am to suppress, or I am not to suppress: this is the alternative upon which the present question calls us to decide. If suppression, concealment or falsehood can in any case be my duty, let it be known to be such; I shall at least have this advantage, I shall be aware that it can only be my duty in some extraordinary emergence. Secondly, whatever reason can be assigned for my not communicating the truth in the form in which it originally suggests itself to my mind must, if it be a good reason, ultimately resolve itself into a reason of utility. Sincerity itself is a duty only for reasons of utility; it seems absurd therefore, if, in any case, truth is not to be communicated in its most obvious form, to seek for the reason rather in the secondary principle of sincerity than in the paramount and original principle of general utility. Lastly, this distinction is of a nature that seems to deserve that we should regard it with a watchful and jealous eye, on account of its vague and indefinite application. If the question were respecting the mode of my communicating truth, there could not perhaps be a better maxim than that I should take care so to communicate it, that it might have the effects of truth, and not of falsehood. But it will be extremely dangerous if I accustom myself to make this the test whether I shall communicate it or no. It is a maxim that seems exactly fitted to fall in with that indolence and want of enterprise which, in some degree or other, are characteristic of all human minds. Add to which, it is a maxim which may be applied without the possibility of limitation. There is no instance in which truth can be communicated absolutely pure. We can only make approximations to such a proceeding, without ever being able fully to arrive at it. It will be liable to some misconstruction, to some want of clearness and precision, to the exciting some passions that ought to lie for ever dormant. This maxim therefore will either prove too much, or is one to which no recourse must be had, but after such an investigation of the capacities of the human mind in each individual instance as to make the idea of introducing a general maxim by way of compendium ridiculous.

Having cleared the subject of those ambiguities in which it has sometimes been involved, let us proceed to the investigation of the original question; and for this purpose it may be useful to take up the subject a little higher, and recur to the basis of moral obligation.

All just reasoning in subjects of morality has been found to depend upon this as its fundamental principle, that each man is bound to consider himself as a debtor in all his faculties, his opportunities, and his industry, to the general welfare. This is a debt which must be always paying, never discharged. Every moment of my life can be better employed, or it cannot; if it cannot, I am in that very instance, however seemingly inconsiderable, playing the part of a true patriot of human kind; if it can, I then inevitably incur some portion of delinquency. Considering the subject in this point of view, there are two articles, which will always stand among the leading principles of moral decision, the good to result from the action immediately proposed, and the advantage to the public of my preserving in existence and vigour the means of future usefulness. Every man, sufficiently impressed with a sense of his debt to the species, will feel himself obliged to scruple the laying out his entire strength, and forfeiting his life, upon any single instance of public exertion. There is a certain proceeding which, in itself considered, I ought this day to adopt; change the circumstances, and make it unquestionable that, if adopted, my life will be the forfeit, will that make no change in my duty? This is a question which has been previously anticipated.*

In the meantime, to render the decision in the subject before us still more satisfactory, let us suppose a case in which the uttering a falsehood shall be the only means by which I can escape from a menace of instant destruction. Let it be that of a virtuous man, proscribed and hunted by the unjust usurpers of the government of his country, and who has reason to know that, if discovered, he will fall an immediate victim to their sanguinary policy. Ought he, if questioned as to who he is, by their myrmidons, to render himself the instrument of their triumph in his death, rather than affirm an untruth? Ought the man to whom he may have entrusted his secret and his life to preserve his sincerity, at the expense of betraying his trust, and destroying his friend? Let us state the several arguments that offer themselves on both sides of this question.

The advantages affirmed of sincerity in general will be found equally to hold in this instance. All falsehood has a tendency to enervate the individual that practises it. With what sentiments of mind is he to utter the falsehood in question? Shall he endeavour to render it complete, and effectually to mislead the persons to whom it relates? This will require a systematical hypocrisy, and a vigilant attention lest his features and gestures should prove so many indications of what is passing in his mind. Add to this, that by such a conduct he is contributing his part to the cutting off the intercourse between men's tongues and their sentiments, infusing general distrust,

* Book II, Chap. VI, pp. 200–201; Book III, Chap. VI, p. 241.

and trifling with the most sacred pledge of human integrity. To assert, in a firm and resolute manner, the thing that is not, is an action from which the human mind unconquerably revolts. To avow the truth with a spirited defiance of consequences has something in it so liberal and magnanimous as to produce a responsive feeling in every human heart. Nor is it to be forgotten that the threatened consequences can scarcely, in any instance, be regarded as certain. The intrepidity of his behaviour, the sobriety and dignified moderation of his carriage, and the reasonableness of his expostulations may be such as to disarm the bitterest foe.

Let us consider the arguments on the other side of the question. And here it may be observed that there is nothing really humiliating in the discharge of our duty. If it can be shown that compliance, in the instance described, is that which it is incumbent to yield, then, without doubt, we ought to feel self-approbation, and not censure in the yielding it. There are many duties which the habits of the world make us feel it humiliating to discharge, as well as many vices in which we pride ourselves; but this is the result of prejudice, and ought to be corrected. Whatever it be that our duty requires of us, the man who is sufficiently enlightened will feel no repugnance to the performance. As to the influence of our conduct upon other men, no doubt, so far as relates to example, we ought to set an example of virtue, of real virtue, not of that which is merely specious. It will also frequently happen, in cases similar to that above described, that the memory of what we do will be entirely lost; our proceeding is addressed to prejudiced persons, who will admit no virtue in the man they hate or despise. Is it probable that the effect of my fortitude in this act of unvarying sincerity will be more extensively beneficial to society than all my future life, however industrious and however pure? Cases might easily have been put of private animosity, where my generous self-devotion would scarcely in any instance be heard of. No mistake can be more painful to an impartial observer than to see an individual of great utility irretrievably thrown away upon a trivial adventure. It may also be worth remarking that the most virtuous man that lives is probably guilty of some acts of insincerity in every day of his life. Though therefore he ought not lightly to add to the catalogue, yet surely there is something extremely contrary to reason in finding the same man deviating from a general rule of conduct for the most trifling and contemptible motives, and immediately after repelling an additional deviation at the expense of his life. As to the argument drawn from the uncertainty of the threatened consequences, it must be remembered that some degree of this uncertainty adheres to all human affairs; and that all calculation of consequences, or in other words all virtue, depends upon our adopting the greater probability, and rejecting the less.

No doubt considerable sacrifices (not only of the imbecility of our character, which ought in all instances to be sacrificed without mercy, but) of the real advantages of life, ought to be made, for the sake of preserving, with ourselves and others, a confidence in our veracity. He who, being sentenced by a court of judicature for some action that he esteems laudable, is offered the remission of his sentence, provided he will recant his virtue, ought probably, in every imaginable case, to resist the proposal. Much seems to depend upon the formality and notoriety of the action. It may probably be wrong to be minutely scrupulous with a drunken bigot in a corner, who should require of me an assent to his creed with a pistol at my breast; and right peremptorily to refuse all terms of qualification, when solemnly proposed by a court of judicature in the face of a nation.

If there be cases where I ought not to scruple to violate the truth, inasmuch as the alternative consists in my certain destruction, it is at least as much incumbent on me when the life of my neighbour is at stake. Indeed, the moment any exception is admitted to the general principle of unreserved sincerity, it becomes obviously impossible to fix the nature of all the exceptions. The rule respecting them must be that, wherever a great and manifest evil arises from disclosing the truth, and that evil appears to be greater than the evil to arise from violating, in this instance, the general barrier of human confidence and virtue, there the obligation of sincerity is suspended.

Nor is it a valid objection to say 'that, by such a rule, we are making every man a judge in his own case'. In the courts of morality it cannot be otherwise; a pure and just system of thinking admits not of the existence of any infallible judge to whom we can appeal. It might indeed be further objected 'that, by this rule, men will be called upon to judge in the moment of passion and partiality, instead of being referred to the past decisions of their cooler reason'. But this also is an inconvenience inseparable from human affairs. We must and ought to keep ourselves open, to the last moment, to the influence of such considerations as may appear worthy to influence us. To teach men that they must not trust their own understandings is not the best scheme for rendering them virtuous and consistent. On the contrary, to inure them to consult their understanding is the way to render it worthy of becoming their director and guide.

Nothing which has been alleged under this head of exception produces the smallest alteration in what was offered under the general discussion. All the advantages, the sublime and illustrious effects, which attend upon an ingenuous conduct, remain unimpeached. Sincerity, a generous and intrepid frankness, will still be found to occupy perhaps the first place in the catalogue of human virtues. This is the temper that ought to pervade the whole course of our reflections and actions. It should be acted upon every day, and confirmed in us every night. There is nothing which we ought to reject with more unalterable firmness than an action that, by its consequences, reduces us to the necessity of duplicity and concealment. No man can be eminently either respectable, or amiable, or useful, who is not distinguished for the frankness and candour of his manners. This is the grand fascination, by which we lay hold of the hearts of our neighbours, conciliate their attention, and render virtue an irresistible object of imitation. He that is not conspicuously sincere either very little partakes of the passion of doing good, or is pitiably ignorant of the means by which the purposes of true benevolence are to be effected.

Appendix II

OF THE MODE OF EXCLUDING VISITORS

Its impropriety argued. — Pretended necessity of this practice, 1. to preserve us from intrusion — 2. to free us from disagreeable acquaintance.

THIS principle respecting the observation of truth in the common intercourses of life cannot perhaps be better illustrated than from the familiar and trivial case, as it is commonly supposed, of a master directing his servant to say he is not at home. No question of morality can be foreign to the science of politics; nor will those few pages of the present work be found perhaps the least valuable which, here, and in other places,* are dedicated to the refutation of those errors in private individuals that, by their extensive sway, have perverted the foundation of moral and political justice. Not to mention that such speculations may afford an amusement and relief in the midst of discussions of a more comprehensive and abstracted character.

Let us then, according to the well known axiom of morality, put ourselves in the place of the man upon whom this ungracious task is imposed. Is there any of us that would be contented to perform it in person, and to say that our father or our brother was not at home, when they were really in the house? Should we not feel con-

---

* Vide Appendices to Book II, Chap. II.

taminated with the plebeian lie? Can we then be justified in requiring that from another which we should shrink from, as an act of dishonour, in ourselves?

Whatever sophistry we may employ to excuse our proceeding, certain it is that the servant understands the lesson we teach him, to be a lie. It is accompanied by all the retinue of falsehood. Before it can be skilfully practised, he must be no mean proficient in hypocrisy. By the easy impudence with which it is uttered, he best answers the purpose of his master, or in other words the purpose of deceit. By the same means, he stifles the upbraidings of his own mind, and conceals the shame imposed on him. Before this can be sufficiently done, he must have discarded all frankness of speech, and all ingenuousness of countenance. Some visitors are so ill-bred as not immediately to take this answer without further examination; and some, unknown to the servant, are upon such unceremonious terms with his master as to think themselves entitled to treat the denial with incredulous contempt. Upon either of these suppositions, the insolence and prevarication of the servant must be increased, or his confusion rendered more glaring and despicable. When he has learned this degenerate lesson upon one subject, who will undertake that it shall produce no unfavourable effects upon his general conduct?

But it is said, 'This lie is necessary, and the intercourse of human society cannot be carried on without it. My friend may visit me at a time when it would be exceedingly inconvenient to me to see him; and this practice affords a fortunate alternative between submitting to have my occupations at the mercy of any accidental visitor on the one hand, and offending him with a rude denial on the other.'

But let us ask, from what cause it is that truth, upon the simplest occasion, should be so offensive to our delicacy, and falsehood so requisite to soothe us? He must, in reality, be the weakest of mankind who should take umbrage at a plain answer in this case, when he was informed of the moral considerations that induced me to employ it. In fact, we are conscious of caprice in our mode of deciding respecting our visitors, and are willing to shelter our folly under this sort of irresponsibility. Would it be worthy of regret if we compelled ourselves to part with this refuge for our imbecility, and to do nothing which we were ashamed to be known to do?

A further argument which has been urged in favour of this disingenuous practice is that 'there is no other way by which we can free ourselves from disagreeable acquaintance'. Thus it is one of the perpetual effects of polished society to persuade us that we are incapable of doing the most trivial office for ourselves. It would be as reasonable to tell me 'that it is a matter of indispensable necessity to have a valet to put on my stockings'. If there be, in the list of our acquaintance, any person whom we particularly dislike, it usually happens that it is for some moral fault that we perceive or think we perceive in him. Why should he be kept in ignorance of our opinion respecting him, and prevented from the opportunity either of amendment or vindication? If he be too wise or too foolish, too virtuous or too vicious for us, why should he not be ingenuously told of his mistake in his intended kindness to us, rather than suffered to find it out by six months enquiry from our servant? If we practised no deceit, if we assumed no atom of cordiality and esteem we did not feel, we should be little pestered with these buzzing intruders. But one species of falsehood involves us in another; and he that pleads for these lying answers to our visitors in reality pleads the cause of a cowardice that dares not deny to vice the distinction and kindness that are due to virtue.

CHAPTER VII

OF FREE WILL AND NECESSITY

THUS we have engaged in the discussion of various
topics respecting the mode in which improvement may
most successfully be introduced into the institutions of
society. We have seen, under the heads of resistance,
revolution, associations and tyrannicide, that nothing is
more to be deprecated than violence and a headlong zeal,
that everything may be trusted to the tranquil and wholesome progress of knowledge, and that the office of the
enlightened friend of political justice, for the most part,
consists in this only, a vigilant and perpetual endeavour
to assist the progress. We have traced the effects which are
to be produced by the cultivation of truth and the practice of sincerity. It remains to turn our attention to the
other branch of the subject proposed to be investigated
in the present book; the mode in which, from the structure of the human mind, opinion is found to operate in
modifying the conduct of individuals.

Some progress was made in the examination of this

point in an earlier division of the present work.* An attentive enquirer will readily perceive that no investigation can be more material, to such as would engage in a careful development of the principles of political justice. It cannot therefore be unproductive of benefit that we should here trace into their remoter ramifications the principles which were then delivered; as well as turn our attention to certain other considerations connected with the same topic which we have not hitherto had occasion to discuss. Of the many controversies which have been excited relative to the operation of opinion, none are of more importance than the question respecting free will and necessity, and the question respecting self-love and benevolence. These will occupy a principal portion of the enquiry.†

We will first endeavour to establish the proposition that all the actions of men are necessary. It was impossible that this principle should not, in an indirect manner, be frequently anticipated in the preceding parts of this work. But it will be found strongly entitled to a separate consideration. The doctrine of moral necessity includes in it consequences of the highest moment, and leads to a more bold and comprehensive view of man in society than can possibly be entertained by him who has embraced the opposite opinion.

To the right understanding of any arguments that may be adduced under this head, it is requisite that we should have a clear idea of the meaning of the term necessity. He who affirms that all actions are necessary means that the man who is acquainted with all the circumstances under which a living or intelligent being is placed upon any given occasion is qualified to predict the conduct he will hold, with as much certainty as he can predict

---

* Book I, Chap. V.

† The reader who is indisposed to abstruse speculations will find the other members of the treatise sufficiently connected, without an express reference to this and the three following chapters of the present book.

any of the phenomena of inanimate nature. Upon this question the advocate of liberty in the philosophical sense must join issue. He must, if he mean anything, deny this certainty of conjunction between moral antecedents and consequents. Where all is constant and invariable, and the events that arise uniformly correspond to the circumstances in which they originate, there can be no liberty.

It is generally acknowledged that, in the events of the material universe, everything is subjected to this necessity. The tendency of investigation and enquiry, relatively to this topic of human science, has been more effectually to exclude the appearance of irregularity, as our improvements extended. Let us recollect what is the species of evidence that has satisfied philosophers upon this point. Their only solid ground of reasoning has been from experience. The argument which has induced mankind to conceive of the universe as governed by certain laws has been an observed similarity in the succession of events. If, when we had once remarked two events succeeding each other, we had never had occasion to see that individual succession repeated; if we saw innumerable events in perpetual progression, without any apparent order, so that all our observation would not enable us, when we beheld one, to pronounce that another, of such a particular class, might be expected to follow; we should never have formed the conception of necessity, or have had an idea corresponding to that of laws and system.

Hence it follows that all that, strictly speaking, we know of the material universe is this uniformity of events. When we see the sun constantly rise in the morning, and set at night, and have had occasion to observe this phenomenon invariably taking place through the whole period of our existence, we cannot avoid receiving this as a law of the universe, and a ground for future expectation. But we never see any principle or virtue by which one event is conjoined to, or made the antecedent of, another.

Let us take some familiar illustrations of this truth. Can it be imagined that any man, by the inspection and analysis of gunpowder, would have been enabled, previously to experience, to predict its explosion? Would he, previously to experience, have been enabled to predict that one piece of marble, having a flat and polished surface, might with facility be protruded along another in a horizontal, but would, with considerable pertinacity, resist separation in a perpendicular direction? The simplest phenomena, of the most hourly occurrence, were originally placed at an equal distance from human sagacity.

There is a certain degree of obscurity, incident to this subject, arising from the following circumstance. All human knowledge is the result of perception. We know nothing of any substance, a supposed material body, for example, but by experience. If it were unconjoined, and bore no relation, to the phenomena of any other substance, it would be no subject of human intelligence. We collect a number of these concurrences, and having, by their perceived uniformity, reduced them into classes, form a general idea annexed to that part of the subject which stands as the antecedent. It must be admitted that a definition of any substance, that is anything that deserves to be called knowledge respecting it, will enable us to predict some of its future probable consequences, and that for this plain reason that definition is prediction under another name. But, though, when we have gained the idea of impenetrability as a general phenomenon of matter, we can predict some of the variations to which it leads, there are others which we cannot predict: or, in other words, we know none of these variations but such as we have actually remarked, added to an expectation that similar events will arise under similar circumstances, proportioned to the constancy with which they have been observed to take place in our past experience. Finding, as we do by repeated experiments, that material substances have the property of resistance, and that one substance in a state of rest, when struck upon by another, passes into a state of motion, we are still in want of more particular observation to enable us to predict the specific varieties that will follow from this collision, in each of the bodies. Enquire of a man who knows nothing more of matter than its general property of impenetrability what will be the result of one ball of matter impinging upon another, and you will soon find how little this general property can inform him of the particular laws of motion. We suppose him to know that motion will follow in to the second ball. But what quantity of motion will be communicated? What result will follow upon the collision, in the impelling ball? Will it continue to move in the same direction? Will it recoil in the opposite direction? Will it fly off obliquely; or will it subside into a state of rest? All these events will be found equally probable by him whom a series of observations upon the past has not instructed as to what he is to expect from the future.

From these remarks we may sufficiently collect what is the species of knowledge we possess respecting the laws of the material universe. No experiments we are able to make, no reasonings we are able to deduce, can ever instruct us in the principle of causation, or show us for what reason it is that one event has, in every instance in which it has been known to occur, been the precursor of another event of a given description. Yet this observation does not, in the slightest degree, invalidate our inference from one event to another, or affect the operations of moral prudence and expectation. The nature of the human mind is such as to oblige us, after having seen two events perpetually conjoined, to pass, as soon as one of them occurs, to the recollection of the other: and, in cases where this transition never misleads us, but the ideal succession is always found to be an exact copy of the future event, it is impossible that this species of foresight should not be converted into a general foundation of inference and reasoning. We cannot take a single step upon this subject which does not partake of the species of operation we denominate abstraction. Till we have been led to consider the rising of the sun tomorrow as an incident of the same species as its rising today, we cannot deduce from it similar consequences. It is the business of science to carry this talk of generalization to its furthest extent, and to reduce the diversified events of the universe to a small number of original principles.

Let us proceed to apply these reasonings concerning matter to the illustration of the theory of mind. Is it possible in this latter theory, as in the former subject, to discover any general principles? Can intellect be made a topic of science? Are we able to reduce the multiplied phenomena of mind to any certain standard of reasoning? If the affirmative of these questions be conceded, the inevitable consequence appears to be that mind, as well as matter, exhibits a constant conjunction of events, and furnishes all the ground that any subject will afford for an opinion of necessity. It is of no importance that we cannot see the ground of that necessity, or imagine how sensations, pleasurable or painful, when presented to the mind of a percipient being, are able to generate volition and animal motion; for, if there be any truth in the above statement, we are equally incapable of perceiving a ground of connection between any two events in the material universe, the common and received opinion, that we do perceive such ground of connection, being, in reality, nothing more than a vulgar prejudice.

That mind is a topic of science may be argued from all those branches of literature and enquiry which have mind for their subject. What species of amusement or instruction would history afford, if there were no ground of inference from moral antecedents to their consequents, if certain temptations and inducements did not, in all ages and climates, introduce a certain series of actions, if we were unable to trace a method and unity of system in men's tempers, propensities and transactions? The amusement would be inferior to that which we derive from the perusal of a chronological table, where events have no order but that of time; since, however the chronologist may neglect to mark the regularity of conjunction between successive transactions, the mind of the reader is busied in supplying that regularity from memory or imagination: but the very idea of such regularity would never have suggested itself if we had never found the source of that idea in experience. The instruction arising from the perusal of history would be absolutely none; since instruction implies, in its very nature, the classing and generalizing of objects. But, upon the supposition on which we are arguing, all objects would be irregular and disjunct, without the possibility of affording any grounds of reasoning or principles of science.

The idea correspondent to the term character inevitably includes in it the assumption of necessity and system. The character of any man is the result of a long series of impressions, communicated to his mind and modifying it in a certain manner, so as to enable us, a number of these modifications and impressions being given, to predict his conduct. Hence arise his temper and habits, respecting which we reasonably conclude that they will not be abruptly superseded and reversed; and that, if ever they be reversed, it will not be accidentally, but in consequence of some strong reason persuading, or some extraordinary event modifying his mind. If there were not this original and essential conjunction between motives and actions, and, which forms one particular branch of this principle, between men's past and future actions, there could be no such thing as character, or as a ground of inference, enabling us to predict what men would be, from what they have been.

From the same idea of regularity and conjunction arise all the schemes of policy in consequence of which men propose to themselves, by a certain plan of conduct, to prevail upon others to become the tools and instruments of their purposes. All the arts of courtship and flattery, of playing upon men's hopes and fears, proceed upon the supposition, that mind is subject to certain laws, and that, provided we be skilful and assiduous enough in applying the motive, the action will envitably follow.

Lastly, the idea of moral discipline proceeds entirely upon this principle. If I carefully persuade, exhort, and exhibit motives to another, it is because I believe that motives have a tendency to influence his conduct. If I reward or punish him, either with a view to his own improvement, or as an example to others, it is because I have been led to believe that rewards and punishments are calculated to affect the dispositions and practices of mankind.

There is but one conceivable objection against the inference from these premises to the necessity of human actions. It may be alleged that 'though there is a real coherence between motives and actions, yet this coherence may not amount to a certainty, and of consequence, the mind still retains an inherent activity, by which it can at pleasure supersede and dissolve it. Thus for example, when I address argument and persuasion to my neighbour, to induce him to adopt a certain species of conduct, I do it not with a certain expectation of success, and am not utterly disappointed if my efforts fail of their object. I make a reserve for a certain faculty of liberty he is supposed to possess, which may at last counteract the best digested projects.'

But in this objection there is nothing peculiar to the case of mind. It is just so in matter. I see a part only of the premises, and therefore can pronounce only with uncertainty upon the conclusion. A philosophical experiment which has succeeded a hundred times may altogether fail in the next trial. But what does the philosopher conclude from this? Not that there is a liberty of choice in his retort and his materials; by which they baffle the best-formed expectations. Not that the established order of antecedents and consequents is imperfect, and that part of the consequent happens without an antecedent. But that there was some other antecedent concerned, to which at the time he failed to advert, but which a fresh investigation will probably lay open to him. When the science of the material universe was in its infancy, men were sufficiently prompt to refer events to accident and chance; but the further they have extended their enquiries and observation, the more reason they have found to conclude that everything takes place according to necessary and universal laws.

The case is exactly parallel with respect to mind. The politician and the philosopher, however they may speculatively entertain the opinion of free will, never think of introducing it into their scheme of accounting for events. If an incident turn out otherwise than they expected, they take it for granted that there was some unobserved bias, some habit of thinking, some prejudice of education, some singular association of ideas, that disappointed their prediction; and, if they be of an active and enterprising temper, they return, like the natural philosopher, to search out the secret spring of this unlooked-for event.

The reflections into which we have entered upon the laws of the universe not only afford a simple and impressive argument in favour of the doctrine of necessity, but suggest a very obvious reason why the doctrine opposite to this has been, in a certain degree, the general opinion of mankind. It has appeared that the idea of uniform conjunction between events of any sort is the lesson of experience, and the vulgar never arrive at the universal application of this principle even to the phenomena of the material universe. In the easiest and most familiar instances, such as the impinging of one ball of matter upon another and its consequences, they willingly admit the interference of chance and irregularity. In this instance however, as both the impulse and its consequences are subjects of observation to the senses, they readily imagine that they perceive the absolute principle which causes motion to be communicated from the first ball to the second. Now the very same prejudice and precipitate conclusion, which induce them to believe that they discover the principle of motion in objects of sense, act in an opposite direction with respect to such objects as cannot be subjected to the examination of sense. The power by which a sensation, pleasurable or painful, when presented to the mind of a percipient being, produces volition and animal motion, no one can imagine that he sees; and therefore they readily conclude that there is no uniformity of conjunction in these events.

But, if the vulgar will universally be found to be the advocates of free will, they are not less strongly, however inconsistently, impressed with the belief of the doctrine of necessity. It is a well known and a just observation that, were it not for the existence of general laws to which the events of the material universe always conform, man could never have been either a reasoning or a moral being. The most considerable actions of our lives are directed by foresight. It is because he foresees the regular succession of the seasons that the farmer sows his field, and, after the expiration of a certain term, expects a crop. There would be no kindness in my administering food to the hungry, and no injustice in my thrusting a drawn sword against the bosom of my friend, if it were not the established quality of food to nourish, and of a sword to wound.

But the regularity of events in the material universe will not of itself afford a sufficient foundation of morality and prudence. The voluntary conduct of our neighbours enters for a share into almost all those calculations upon which our plans and determinations are founded. If voluntary conduct, as well as material impulse, were not subjected to general laws, and a legitimate topic of prediction and foresight, the certainty of events in the material universe would be productive of little benefit. But, in reality, the mind passes from one of these topics of speculation to the other, without accurately distributing them into classes, or imagining that there is any difference in the certainty with which they are attended. Hence it appears that the most uninstructed peasant or artisan is practically a necessarian. The farmer calculates as securely upon the inclination of mankind to buy his corn when it is brought into the market, as upon the tendency of the seasons to ripen it. The labourer no more suspects that his employer will alter his mind, and not pay him his daily wages, than he suspects that his tools will refuse to perform those functions today in which they were yesterday employed with success.*

Another argument in favour of the doctrine of necessity, not less clear and irresistible than that from the uniformity of conjunction of antecedents and consequents, will arise from a reference to the nature of voluntary action. The motions of the animal system distribute themselves into two great classes, voluntary and involuntary. 'Voluntary action,' as we formerly observed,† 'is where the event is foreseen, previously to its occurrence, and the hope or fear of that event, forms the excitement, prompting our effort to forward or retard it.'

Here then the advocates of intellectual liberty have a clear dilemma proposed to their choice. They must ascribe this freedom, this imperfect conjunction of antecedents and consequents, either to our voluntary or our involuntary actions. They have already made their determination. They are aware that to ascribe freedom to that which is involuntary, even if the assumption could be maintained, would be altogether foreign to the great subjects of moral, theological or political enquiry. Man would not be in any degree more an agent or an accountable being, though it could be proved that all his involuntary motions sprung up in a fortuitous and capricious manner.

But, on the other hand, to ascribe freedom to our voluntary actions is an express contradiction in terms. No motion is voluntary any further than it is accompanied with intention and design, and has for its proper antecedent the apprehension of an end to be accomplished. So far as it flows, in any degree, from another source, it is involuntary. The new-born infant foresees nothing, there-

---

*The reader will find the substance of the above arguments in a more diffusive form in Hume's *Enquiry concerning Human Understanding*,[27] being the third part of his *Essays*.

† Book I, Chap. V, p. 119.

fore all his motions are involuntary. A person arrived at maturity, takes an extensive survey of the consequences of his actions, therefore he is eminently a voluntary and rational being. If any part of my conduct be destitute of all foresight of the events to result, who is there that ascribes to it depravity and vice? Xerxes acted just as soberly as such a reasoner when he caused his attendants to inflict a thousand lashes on the waves of the Hellespont.

The truth of the doctrine of necessity will be still more evident if we consider the absurdity of the opposite hypothesis. One of its principal ingredients is self-determination. Liberty, in an imperfect and popular sense, is ascribed to the motions of the animal system, when they result from the foresight and deliberation of the intellect, and not from external compulsion. It is in this sense that the word is commonly used in moral and political reasoning. Philosophical reasoners therefore who have desired to vindicate the property of freedom, not only to our external motions, but to the acts of the mind, have been obliged to repeat this process. Our external actions are then said to be free when they truly result from the determination of the mind. If our volitions, or internal acts, be also free, they must in like manner result from the determination of the mind, or in other words, 'the mind in adopting them' must be 'self-determined'. Now nothing can be more evident than that in which the mind exercises its freedom must be an act of the mind. Liberty therefore, according to this hypothesis, consists in this, that every choice we make has been chosen by us, and every act of the mind been preceded and produced by an act of the mind. This is so true that, in reality, the ultimate act is not styled free from any quality of its own, but because the mind, in adopting it, was self-determined, that is, because it was preceded by another act. The ultimate act resulted completely from the determination that was its precursor. It was itself necessary; and, if we would look for freedom, it must be to that preceding act. But, in that preceding act also, if the mind were free, it was self-determined, that is, this volition was chosen by a preceding volition, and, by the same reasoning, this also by another antecedent to itself. All the acts, except the first, were necessary, and followed each other as inevitably as the links of a chain do when the first link is drawn forward. But then neither was this first act free, unless the mind in adopting it were self-determined, that is, unless this act were chosen by a preceding act. Trace back the chain as far as you please, every act at which you arrive is necessary. That act, which gives the character of freedom to the whole, can never be discovered; and, if it could, in its own nature includes a contradiction.

Another idea which belongs to the hypothesis of free will is that the mind is not necessarily inclined this way or that, by the motives which are presented to it, by the clearness or obscurity with which they are apprehended, or by the temper and character which preceding habits may have generated; but that, by its inherent activity, it is equally capable of proceeding either way, and passes to its determination from a previous state of absolute indifference. Now what sort of activity is that which is equally inclined to all kinds of actions? Let us suppose a particle of matter endowed with an inherent propensity to motion. This propensity must either be to move in one particular direction, and then it must for ever move in that direction, unless counteracted by some external impression; or it must have an equal tendency to all directions, and then the result must be a state of perpetual rest.

The absurdity of this consequence is so evident that the advocates of intellectual liberty have endeavoured to destroy its force, by means of a distinction. 'Motive,' it has been said, 'is indeed the occasion, the *sine qua non* of volition, but it has no inherent power to compel volition. Its influence depends upon the free and unconstrained surrender of the mind. Between opposite motives and considerations, the mind can choose as it pleases, and, by its determination, can convert the motive which is weak and insufficient in the comparison into the strongest.' But this hypothesis will be found exceedingly inadequate to the purpose for which it is produced. Not to repeat what has been already alleged to prove, that inherent power of production in an antecedent, is, in all cases, a mere fiction of the mind, it may easily be shown, that motives must either have a fixed and certain relation to their consequents, or they can have none.

For first it must be remembered that the ground or reason of any event, of whatever nature it be, must be contained among the circumstances which precede that event. The mind is supposed to be in a state of previous indifference, and therefore cannot be, in itself considered, the source of the particular choice that is made. There is a motive on one side and a motive on the other: and between these lie the true ground and reason of preference. But, wherever there is tendency to preference, there may be degrees of tendency. If the degrees be equal, preference cannot follow: it is equivalent to the putting equal weights into the opposite scales of a balance. If one of them have a greater tendency to preference than the other, that which has the greatest tendency must ultimately prevail. When two things are balanced against each other, so much amount may be conceived to be struck off from each side as exists in the smaller sum, and the overplus that belongs to the greater is all that truly enters into the consideration.

Add to this, secondly, that, if motive have not a necessary influence, it is altogether superfluous. The mind cannot first choose to be influenced by a motive, and afterwards submit to its operation: for in that case the preference would belong wholly to this previous volition. The determination would in reality be complete in the first instance; and the motive, which came in afterwards, might be the pretext, but could not be the true source of the proceedings.*

* The argument from the impossibility of free will is treated with great force of reasoning in Jonathan Edwards's *Enquiry into the Freedom of the Will.*

Lastly, it may be observed upon the hypothesis of free will that the whole system is built upon a distinction where there is no difference, to wit, a distinction between the intellectual and active powers of the mind. A mysterious philosophy taught men to suppose that, when an object was already felt to be desirable, there was need of some distinct power to put the body in motion. But reason finds no ground for this supposition; nor is it possible to conceive (in the case of an intellectual faculty placed in an aptly organized body, where preference exists, together with a sentiment, the dictate of experience, of our power to obtain the object preferred) of anything beyond this that can contribute to render a certain motion of the animal frame the necessary result. We need only attend to the obvious meaning of the terms, in order to perceive that the will is merely, as it has been happily termed, 'the last act of the understanding,'* 'one of the different cases of the association of ideas'.† What indeed is preference but a feeling of something that really inheres, or is supposed to inhere, in the objects themselves? It is the comparison, true or erroneous, which the mind makes, respecting such things as are brought into competition with each other. This is indeed the same principle as was established upon a former occasion, when we undertook to prove that the voluntary actions of men originate in their opinions.‡ But, if this fact had been sufficiently attended to, the freedom of the will would never have been gravely maintained by philosophical writers; since no man ever imagined that we were free to feel or not to feel an impression made upon our organs, and to believe or not to believe a proposition demonstrated to our understanding.

It must be unnecessary to add any thing further on this head, unless it be a momentary recollection of the sort of benefit that freedom of the will would confer upon us, supposing it possible. Man being, as we have here found him to be, a creature whose actions flow from the simple principle, and who is governed by the apprehen-

* Clarke.   † Hartley.   ‡ Book I, Chap. V.

349

sions of his understanding, nothing further is requisite but the improvement of his reasoning faculty to make him virtuous and happy. But did he possess a faculty independent of the understanding, and capable of resisting from mere caprice the most powerful arguments, the best education and the most sedulous instruction might be of no use to him. This freedom we shall easily perceive to be his bane and his curse; and the only hope of lasting benefit to the species would be by drawing closer the connection between the external motions and the understanding, wholly to extirpate it. The virtuous man, in proportion to his improvement, will be under the constant influence of fixed and invariable principles; and such a being as we conceive God to be, can never in any one instance have exercised this liberty, that is, can never have acted in a foolish and tyrannical manner. Freedom of the will is absurdly represented as necessary to render the mind susceptible of moral principles; but in reality, so far as we act with liberty, so far as we are independent of motives, our conduct is as independent of morality as it is of reason, nor is it possible that we should deserve either praise or blame for a proceeding thus capricious and indisciplinable.

CHAPTER VIII

INFERENCES FROM THE DOCTRINE OF NECESSITY

Idea it suggests to us of the universe. – Influence on our moral ideas: action – virtue – exertion – persuasion – exhortation – ardour – complacence and aversion – punishment – repentance praise and blame – intellectual tranquillity. – Language of necessity recommended.

CONSIDERING then the doctrine of moral necessity as sufficiently established, let us proceed to the consequences that are to be deduced from it. This view of things presents us with an idea of the universe, as of a body of events in systematical arrangement, nothing in the boundless progress of things interrupting this system, or breaking in upon the experienced succession of antecedents and consequents. In the life of every human being there is a chain of events, generated in the lapse of ages which preceded his birth, and going on in regular procession through the whole period of his existence, in consequence of which it was impossible for him to act in any instance otherwise than he has acted.

The contrary of this having been the conception of the mass of mankind in all ages, and the ideas of contingency and accident having perpetually obtruded themselves, the established language of morality has been universally tinctured with this error. It will therefore be of no trivial importance to enquire how much of this language is founded in the truth of things, and how much of what is expressed by it is purely imaginary. Accuracy of language is the indispensable prerequisite of sound knowledge; and, without attention to that subject, we can never ascertain the extent and importance of the consequences of necessity.

First then it appears that, in the emphatical and refined sense in which the word has sometimes been used, there is no such thing as action. Man is in no case, strictly speaking, the beginner of any event or series of events that takes place in the universe, but only the vehicle through which certain antecedents operate, which antecedents, if he were supposed not to exist, would cease to have that operation. Action however, in its more simple and obvious sense, is sufficiently real, and exists equally both in mind and in matter. When a ball upon a billiard-board is struck by the mace, and afterwards impinges upon a second ball, the ball which was first in motion is said to act upon the second, though the results are in the strictest conformity to the impression received, and the motion it communicates is precisely determined by the circumstances of the case. Exactly similar to this, upon the reasonings already delivered, are the actions of the human mind. Mind is a real principle, an indispensable link in the great chain of the universe; but not, as has sometimes been supposed, a principle of that paramount description as to supersede all necessities, and be itself subject to no laws and methods of operation.

Is this view of things incompatible with the existence of virtue?

If by virtue we understand the operation of an intelligent being in the exercise of an optional power, so that, under the same precise circumstances, it might or might not have taken place, undoubtedly it will annihilate it.

But the doctrine of necessity does not overturn the nature of things. Happiness and misery, wisdom and error will still be distinct from each other, and there will still be a correspondence between them. Wherever there is that which may be the means of pleasure or pain to a sensitive being, there is ground for preference and desire, or on the contrary for neglect and aversion. Benevolence and wisdom will be objects worthy to be desired, selfishness and error worthy to be disliked. If therefore by virtue we mean that principle which asserts the preference of the former over the latter, its reality will remain undiminished by the doctrine of necessity.

Virtue, if we would reason accurately, should perhaps be considered by us, in the first instance, objectively, rather than as modifying any particular beings.* Virtuous conduct is conduct proposing to itself a certain end; by its tendency to answer that end, its value and purity are to be tried. Its purpose is the production of happiness, and the aptitude or inaptitude of particular beings in this respect will decide their importance in the scale of existence. This aptitude is usually termed capacity or power. Now power, in the sense of the hypothesis of liberty, is altogether chimerical. But power, in the sense in which it is sometimes affirmed of inanimate substances, is equally

* Book II, Chap. IV.

true of those which are animate. A candlestick has the power or capacity of retaining a candle in a perpendicular direction. A knife has a capacity of cutting. In the same manner a human being has a capacity of walking: though it may be no more true of him than of the inanimate substance that he has an option to exercise or not to exercise that capacity. Again, there are different degrees as well as different classes of capacity. One knife is better adapted for the purposes of cutting than another.

There are two considerations relative to any particular being that generate approbation, and this whether the being be possessed of consciousness or no. These considerations are capacity, and the application of capacity. We approve of a sharp knife rather than a blunt one, because its capacity is greater. We approve of its being employed in carving food, rather than in maiming men or other animals, because that application of its capacity is preferable. But all approbation or preference is relative to utility or general good. A knife is as capable as a man of being employed in purposes of utility; and the one is no more free than the other as to its employment. The mode in which a knife is made subservient to these purposes is by material impulse. The mode in which a man is made subservient is by inducement and persuasion. But both are equally the affair of necessity. The man differs from the knife, as the iron candlestick differs from the brass one; he has one more way of being acted upon. This additional way in man is motive; in the candlestick, is magnetism.

Virtue is a term which has been appropriated to describe the effects produced by men, under the influence of motives, in promoting the general good: it describes the application of sentient and human capacity, and not the application of capacity in inanimate substances. The word, thus explained, is to be considered as rather similar to grammatical distinction than to real and philosophical difference. Thus, in Latin, *bonus* is *good* as affirmed of a man, *bona* is *good* as affirmed of a woman. In the same manner we can as easily conceive of the capacity of an inanimate, as of an animate, substance being applied to the general good; and as accurately describe the best possible application of the one, as of the other. The end, that upon which the application depends for its value, is the same in both instances. But we call the latter virtue and duty, and not the former. These words may, in a popular sense, be considered as either masculine or feminine, but never neuter. The existence of virtue therefore, if by this term we mean the real and essential difference between virtue and vice, the importance of a virtuous character, and the approbation that is due to it, is not annihilated by the doctrine of necessity, but rather illustrated and confirmed.

But, if the doctrine of necessity do not annihilate virtue, it tends to introduce a great change into our ideas respecting it. According to this doctrine it will be absurd for a man to say, 'I will exert myself', 'I will take care to remember', or even 'I will do this'. All these expressions imply as if man were, or could be, something else than what motives make him. Man is in reality a passive, and not an active being. In another sense however he is sufficiently capable of exertion. The operations of his mind may be laborious, like those of the wheel of a heavy machine in ascending a hill, may even tend to wear out the substance of the shell in which it acts, without in the smallest degree impeaching its passive character. If we were constantly aware of this, our minds would not glow less ardently with the love of truth, justice, happiness and mankind. We should have a firmness and simplicity in our conduct, not wasting itself in fruitless struggles and regrets, not hurried along with infantine impatience, but seeing actions with their consequences, and calmly and unreservedly given up to the influence of those comprehensive views which this doctrine inspires.

As to our conduct towards others, in instances where we were concerned to improve and meliorate their minds, we should address our representations and remonstrances to them with double confidence. The believer in free will can expostulate with, or correct, his pupil, with faint and uncertain hopes, conscious that the clearest exhibition of truth is impotent, when brought into contest with the unhearing and indisciplinable faculty of will; or in reality, if he were consistent, secure that it could produce no effect. The necessarian on the contrary employs real antecedents, and has a right to expect real effects.

But, though he would represent, he would not exhort, for this is a term without a meaning. He would suggest motives to the mind, but he would not call upon it to comply, as if it had a power to comply, or not to comply. His office would consist of two parts, the exhibition of motives to the pursuit of a certain end, and the delineation of the easiest and most effectual way of attaining that end.

There is no better scheme for enabling us to perceive how far any idea that has been connected with the hypothesis of liberty has a real foundation than to translate the usual mode of expressing it into the language of necessity. Suppose the idea of exhortation, so translated, to stand thus: 'To enable any arguments I may suggest to you to make a suitable impression, it is necessary that they should be fairly considered. I proceed therefore to evince to you the importance of attention, knowing that, if I can make this importance sufficiently manifest, attention will inevitably follow.' I should surely be far better employed in enforcing directly the truth I am desirous to impress, than in having recourse to this circuitous mode of treating attention as if it were a separate faculty. Attention will, in reality, always be proportionate to our apprehension of the importance of the subject proposed.

At first sight it may appear as if, the moment I was satisfied that exertion on my part was no better than a fiction, and that I was the passive instrument of causes exterior to myself, I should become indifferent to the objects which had hitherto interested me the most deeply, and lose all that inflexible perseverance which seems inseparable from great undertakings. But this cannot be the true state of the case. The more I resign myself to the influence of truth, the clearer will be my perception of it. The less I am interrupted by questions of liberty and caprice, of attention and indolence, the more uniform will be my constancy. Nothing could be more unreasonable than that the sentiment of necessity should produce in me a spirit of neutrality and indifference. The more certain is the conjunction between antecedents and consequents, the more cheerfulness should I feel in yielding to painful and laborious employments.

It is common for men impressed with the opinion of free will, to entertain resentment, indignation, and anger against those who fall into the commission of vice. How much of these feelings is just, and how much erroneous? The difference between virtue and vice will equally remain upon the opposite hypothesis. Vice therefore must be an object of rejection, and virtue of preference; the one must be approved, and the other disapproved. But our disapprobation of vice will be of the same nature as our disapprobation of an infectious distemper.

One of the reasons why we are accustomed to regard the murderer with more accute feelings of displeasure than the knife he employs is that we find a more dangerous property, and greater cause for apprehension, in the one than in the other. The knife is only accidentally an object of terror, but against the murderer we can never be enough upon our guard. In the same manner we regard the middle of a busy street with less complacency, as a place for walking, than the side; and the ridge of a house with more aversion than either. Independently therefore of the idea of freedom, mankind in general will find in the enormously vicious a sufficient motive of apprehension and displeasure. With the addition of that idea, it is no wonder that they should be prompted to sentiments of the most intemperate abhorrence.

These sentiments, obviously lead to the examination of the prevailing conceptions on the subject of punishment. The doctrine of necessity would teach us to class punishment in the list of the means we possess of influencing the human mind, and may induce us to enquire into its utility as an instrument for reforming error. The more the human mind can be shown to be under the influence of motive, the more certain it is that punishment will produce a great and unequivocal effect. But the doctrine of necessity will teach us to look upon punishment with no complacence, and at all times to prefer the most direct means of encountering error, the development of truth. Whenever punishment is employed under this system, it will be employed, not for any intrinsic recommendation it possesses, but only as it shall appear to conduce to general utility.

On the contrary it is usually imagined that, independently of the supposed utility of punishment, there is proper desert in the criminal, a certain fitness in the nature of things that renders pain the suitable concomitant of vice. It is therefore frequently said that it is not enough that a murderer should be transported to a desert island, where there should be no danger that his malignant propensities should ever again have opportunity to act; but that it is also right the indignation of mankind against him should express itself in the infliction of some actual ignominy and pain. On the contrary, under the system of necessity, the terms, guilt, crime, desert and accountableness, in the abstract and general sense in which they have sometimes been applied, have no place.

Correlative to the feelings of resentment, indignation and anger against the offences of others are those of repentance, contrition and sorrow for our own. As long as we admit of an essential difference between virtue and vice, no doubt all erroneous conduct, whether of ourselves or others, will be regarded with disapprobation. But it will in both cases be considered, under the system of necessity, as a link in the great chain of events, which could not have been otherwise than it is. We shall therefore no more be disposed to repent of our own faults than of the faults of others. It will be proper to view them both as actions injurious to the public good, and the repetition of which is to be deprecated. Amidst our present imperfections, it will perhaps be useful to recollect what is the error by which we are most easily seduced. But, in proportion as our views extend, we shall find motives sufficient to the practice of virtue, without a partial retrospect to ourselves, or a recollection of our own propensities and habits.

In the ideas annexed to the words resentment and repentance, there is some mixture of true judgement and a sound conception of the nature of things. There is perhaps still more justice in the notions conveyed by praise and blame, though these also have been vitiated and distorted by the hypothesis of liberty. When I speak of a beautiful landscape or an agreeable sensation, I employ the language of panegyric. I employ it still more emphatically when I speak of a good action; because I am conscious that the panegyric to which it is entitled has a tendency to procure a repetition of such actions. So far as praise implies nothing more than this, it perfectly accords with the severest philosophy. So far as it implies that the man could have abstained from the virtuous action I applaud, it belongs only to the delusive system of liberty.

A further consequence of the doctrine of necessity is its tendency to make us survey all events with a tranquil and placid temper, and approve and disapprove without impeachment to our self-possession. It is true that events may be contingent, as to any knowledge we possess respecting them, however certain they are in themselves. Thus the advocate of liberty knows that his relation was either lost or saved in the great storm that happened two months ago; he regards this event as past and certain, and yet he does not fail to be anxious about it. But it is not less true that anxiety and perturbation for the most part include in them an imperfect sense of contingency, and a feeling as if our efforts could make some alteration in the event. When the person recollects with clearness that the event is over, his mind grows composed; but presently he feels as if it were in the power of God or man to alter it, and his agitation is renewed. To this may be further added the impatience of curiosity; but philosophy and reason have an evident tendency to prevent useless curiosity from disturbing our peace. He therefore who regards all things past, present, and to come as links of an indissoluble chain will, as often as he recollects this comprehensive view, find himself assisted to surmount the tumult of passion; and be enabled to reflect upon the moral concerns of mankind with the same clearness of perception, the same firmness of judgement, and the same constancy of temper, as we are accustomed to do upon the truths of geometry.

This however must be expected to be no more than a temporary exertion. A sound philosophy may afford us intervals of entire tranquillity. It will communicate a portion of this tranquillity to the whole of our character. But the essence of the human mind will still remain. Man is the creature of habit; and it is impossible for him to lose those things which afforded him a series of pleasurable sensations without finding his thoughts in some degree unhinged, and being obliged, under the pressure of considerable disadvantages, to seek, in paths untried, and in new associations, a substitute for the benefits of which he has been deprived.

It would be of infinite importance to the cause of science and virtue to express ourselves upon all occasions in the language of necessity. The contrary language is perpetually intruding, and it is difficult to speak two sentences, upon any topic connected with human action, without it. The expressions of both hypotheses are mixed in inextricable confusion, just as the belief of both hypotheses, however incompatible, will be found to exist in all uninstructed minds. The reformation of which I speak will probably be found exceedingly practicable in itself; though, such is the subtlety of error, that we should, at first, find several revisals and much laborious study necessary, before it could be perfectly weeded out. This must be the author's apology for not having attempted in the present work what he recommends to others.

CHAPTER IX

OF THE MECHANISM OF THE HUMAN MIND

Nature of Mechanism. – Its classes, material and intellectual. – Material system, or of vibrations. – The intellectual system most probable – from the consideration that thought would otherwise be a superfluity – from the established principles of reasoning from effects to causes. – Objections refuted. – Thoughts which produce animal motion may be – 1. involuntary – 2. unattended with consciousness. – The mind cannot have more than one thought at any one time. – Objection to this assertion from the case of complex ideas – from various mental operations – as comparison – apprehension. – Rapidity of the succession of ideas. – Application. – Duration measured by consciousness. – 3. a distinct thought to each motion may be unnecessary – apparent from the complexity of sensible impressions. – The mind always thinks. – Conclusion. – The theory applied to the phenomenon of walking – to the circulation of the blood. – Of motion in general. – Of dreams.

THE doctrine of necessity being admitted, it follows that the theory of the human mind is properly, like the theory of every other series of events with which we are acquainted, a system of mechanism; understanding by mechanism nothing more than a regular succession of phenomena, without any uncertainty of event, so that every consequent requires a specific antecedent, and could be no otherwise in any respect than as the antecedent determined it to be.

But there are two sorts of mechanism capable of being applied to the solution of this case, one which has for its medium only matter and motion, the other which has for its medium thought. Which of these is to be regarded as most probable?

According to the first, we may conceive the human body to be so constituted as to be susceptible of vibrations, in the same manner as the strings of a musical instrument. These vibrations, having begun upon the surface of the body, are conveyed to the brain; and, in a manner that is equally the result of construction, produce a second set of vibrations beginning in the brain, and conveyed to the different organs or members of the body. Thus it may be supposed that a piece of iron considerably heated is applied to the body of an infant, and that the report of this irritation and separation of parts being conveyed to the brain vents itself again in a shrill and piercing cry. It is in this manner that certain convulsive and spasmodic affections appear to take place in the body. The case, as here described, is similar to that of the bag of a pair of bagpipes, which, being pressed in a certain manner, utters a groan, without anything more being necessary to account for this phenomenon than the known laws of matter and motion. Let us add to these vibrations a system of associations to be carried on by traces to be made upon the medullary substance of the brain, by means of which past and present impressions are connected according to certain laws, as the traces happen to approach or run into each other; and we have then a complete scheme of a certain sort, of the phenomena of human action. It is to be observed that, according to this system, mind, or perception, is altogether unnecessary to explain the appearances. It might for other reasons be desirable or wise, in the author of the universe for example, to introduce a thinking substance, or a power of perception, as a spectator of the process. But this percipient power is altogether neutral, having apparently no concern, either as a medium or otherwise, in the events to be produced.*

The second system, which represents thought as the medium of operation, is not less a system of mechanism according to the doctrine of necessity, but it is a mechanism of a totally different kind.

There are various reasons calculated to persuade us that this last hypothesis is the most profitable. No inconsiderable argument may be derived from the singular and important nature of that property of human beings which we term thought; which it is surely somewhat violent to strike out of our system, as a mere superfluity.

A second reason still more decisive than the former arises from the constancy with which thought, in innumerable instances, accompanies the functions of this mechanism. Now this constancy of conjunction has been shown to be the only ground we have, in any imaginable subject, for proceeding from antecedent to consequent, and expecting, when we see one given event, that another event of a given sort will succeed it.† We cannot therefore reject the principle which supposes thought to be a real medium in the mechanism of man, but upon grounds that would vitiate our reasonings in every topic of human enquiry.

It may be objected 'that, though this regularity of event

---

*The above will be found to be a tolerably accurate description of the hypothesis of the celebrated Hartley. It was unnecessary to quote his words, as it would be foreign to the purpose of the present work to enter into a refutation of any individual writer. The sagacity of Hartley, in having arranged and analysed the phenomena of mind, and shown the practicability of reducing its different operations to a simple principle, cannot be too highly applauded. The reasonings of the present chapter, if just, may be considered as giving farther stability to his principal doctrine, by freeing it from the scheme of material automatism with which it was unnecessarily clogged.

† Chap. VII.

is the only rational principle of inference, yet thought may be found not to possess the character of a medium, motion being in all instances the antecedent, and thought never anything more than a consequent'. But this is contrary to everything we know of the system of the universe, in which each event appears to be alternately both the one and the other, nothing terminating in itself, but everything leading on to an endless chain of consequences.

It would be equally vain to object 'that we are unable to conceive how thought can have any tendency to produce motion in the animal system'; since it has just appeared that this ignorance is by no means peculiar to the subject before us. We are universally unable to perceive a foundation of necessary connection.*

It being then sufficiently clear that there are cogent reasons to persuade us that thought is the medium through which the motions of the animal system are generally carried on, let us proceed to consider what is the nature of those thoughts by which the limbs and organs of our body are set in motion. It will then probably be found that the difficulties which have clogged the intellectual hypothesis are principally founded in erroneous notions derived from the system of liberty; as if there were any essential difference between those thoughts which are the medium of generating motion, and thoughts in general.

First, thought may be the source of animal motion, without partaking, in any degree, of volition, or design. It is certain that there is a great variety of motions in the animal system which are, in every view of the subject, involuntary.† Such, for example, are the cries of an infant, when it is first impressed with the sensation of pain. In the first motions of the animal system, nothing of any sort could possibly be foreseen, and therefore nothing of any sort could be intended. Yet these motions have sensa-

* Chap. VII.
† Book I, Chap. V.

tion or thought for their constant concomitant; and therefore all the arguments which have been already alleged remain in full force, to prove that thought is the medium of their production.

Nor will this appear extraordinary, if we consider the nature of volition itself. In volition, if the doctrine of necessity be true, the mind is altogether passive. Two ideas present themselves in some way connected with each other; and a perception of preferableness necessarily follows. An object having certain desirable qualities is perceived to be within my reach; and my hand is necessarily stretched out with an intention to obtain it. If a perception of preference, or desirableness, irresistibly lead to animal motion, why may not the mere perception of pain? All that the adversary of automatism is concerned to maintain is that thought is an essential link in the chain; and that, the moment it is taken away, the links that were before no longer afford the slightest ground to expect motion in the links that were after. – It is possible that, as a numerous class of motions have their constant origin in thought, so there may be no thoughts altogether unattended with motion.

Secondly, thought may be the source of animal motion, and at the same time be unattended with consciousness. This is undoubtedly a distinction of considerable refinement, depending upon the precise meaning of words; and, if any person should choose to express himself differently on the subject, it would be useless obstinately to dispute that difference with him. By the consciousness which accompanies any thought, there seems to be something implied distinct from the thought itself. Consciousness is a sort of supplementary reflection, by which the mind not only has the thought, but adverts to its own situation, and observes that it has it. Consciousness therefore, however nice the distinction, seems to be a second thought.

In order to ascertain whether every thought be attended with consciousness, it may be proper to consider whether the mind can ever have more than one thought

at any one time. Now this seems altogether contrary to
the very nature of mind. My present thought is that to
which my present attention is yielded; but I cannot attend to several things at once. This assertion appears to
be of the nature of an intuitive axiom; and experience is
perpetually reminding us of its truth. In comparing two
objects, we frequently endeavour, as it were, to draw
them together in the mind, but we seem obliged to pass
successively from the one to the other.

But, though it be intuitively true that we can attend to
but one thing, or, in other words, have but one thought,
at one time, and though intuitive and self-evident propositions do not, properly speaking, admit of being supported by argument, yet there is a collateral consideration,
something in the nature of an argument, that may be
adduced in support of this proposition. It is at present
generally admitted, by all accurate reasoners upon the
nature of the human mind, that its whole internal history
may be traced to one single principle, association. There
are but two ways in which a thought can be excited in the
mind, first, by external impression, secondly, by the property which one thought existing in the mind is found
to have, of introducing a second thought through the
means of some link of connection between them. This
being premised, let us suppose a given mind to have two
ideas at the same time. There can be no reason why
either of these ideas should prove ungenerative, or why
the two ideas they are best fitted to bring after them
should not coexist as well as their predecessors. Let the
same process be repeated indefinitely. We have then two
trains of thinking exactly contemporary in the same
mind. Very curious questions will here arise. Have they
any communication? Do they flow separately, or occasionally cross and interrupt each other? Can any reason
be given, why one of them should not relate to the doctrine of fluxions, and the other to the drama? in other
words, why the same man should not, at the same time,
be both Newton and Shakespeare? Why may not one of

these coexisting trains be of a joyful, and the other of a sorrowful tenour? There is no absurdity that may not be supported upon the assumption of this principle. In fact we have no other conception of fidelity, as it relates to the human mind, than that of a single idea, supersedable by external impression, or regularly leading on, by means of various connections, to an indefinite train of ideas in uninterrupted succession.

But this principle, though apparently supported both by reason and intuition, is not unattended with difficulties. The first is that which arises from the case of complex ideas. This will best be apprehended if we examine it, as it relates to visible objects. 'Let us suppose that I am at present employed in the act of reading. I appear to take in whole words, and indeed clusters of words, by a single act of the mind. But let it be granted for a moment that I see each letter successively. Yet each letter is made up of parts: the letter D, for example, of a right line and a curve, and each of these lines of the successive addition or fluxion of points. If I consider the line as a whole, yet its extension is one thing, and its terminations another. I could not see the letter, if the black line that describes it, and the white surface that bounds it, were not each of them in the view of my organ. There must therefore, as it should seem, upon the hypothesis above stated, to be an infinite succession of ideas in the mind, before it could apprehend the simplest objects with which we are conversant. But we have no feeling of any such thing, but rather of the precise contrary. Thousands of human beings go out of the world, without ever apprehending that lines are composed of the addition or fluxion of points. An hypothesis that is in direct opposition to so many apparent facts must have a very uncommon portion of evidence to sustain it, if indeed it can be sustained.'

The true answer to this objection seems to be as follows. The mind can apprehend only a single idea at once, but that idea need not be a simple idea. The mind can apprehend two or more objects at a single effort, but it cannot apprehend them as two. There seems no sufficient reason to deny that all those objects which are painted at once upon the retina of the eye produce a joint and simultaneous impression upon the mind. But they are not immediately conceived by the mind as many, but as one: the recollection may occur that they are made up of parts, but these parts cannot be considered by us otherwise than successively. The resolution of objects into their simple elements is an operation of science and improvement; but it is altogether foreign to our first and original conceptions. In all cases, the operations of our understanding are rather analytical than synthetical, rather those of resolution than composition. We do not begin with the successive perception of elementary parts till we have obtained an idea of a whole; but beginning with a whole, are capable of reducing it into its elements.

A second difficulty is of a much subtler nature. It consists in the seeming 'impossibility of performing any mental operation, such as comparison for example, which has relation to two or more ideas, if we have not both ideas before us at once, if one of them be completely vanished and gone, before the other begins to exit'. The source of this difficulty seems to lie in the mistake of supposing that there is a real interval between the two ideas. It will perhaps be found upon an accurate examination that, though we cannot have two ideas at once, yet it is not just to say that the first has perished, before the second begins to exist. The instant that connects them is of no real magnitude, and produces no real division. The mind is always full. It is this instant therefore that is the true point of comparison.

It may be objected 'that comparison is rather a matter of retrospect, deciding between two ideas that have been completely apprehended, than a perception which occurs in the middle, before the second has been observed'. To this objection experience will perhaps be found to furnish the true answer. We find in fact that we cannot compare two objects till we have passed and repassed them in the mind.

'Supposing this account of the operation of the mind in comparison to be admitted, yet what shall we say to a complex sentence, containing twenty ideas, the sense of which I fully apprehend at a single hearing, nay, even, in some cases, by the time one half of it has been uttered?'

The mere talk of understanding what is affirmed to us is of a very different nature from that of comparison, or of any other species of judgement that is to be formed concerning this affirmation. When a number of ideas are presented in a train, though in one sense there be variety, yet in another there is unity. First, there is the unity of uninterrupted succession, the perennial flow as of a stream, where the drop indeed that succeeds is numerically distinct from that which went before, but there is no cessation. Secondly, there is the unity of method. The mind apprehends, as the discourse proceeds, a strict association, from similarity or some other source, between each idea as it follows in the process, and that which went before it.

The faculty of understanding the different parts of a discourse in their connection with each other, simple as it appears, is in reality of gradual and slow acquisition. We are, by various causes, excluded from a minute observation of the progress of the infant mind, and therefore do not readily conceive by how imperceptible advances it arrives at a quickness of apprehension, relative to the simplest sentences. But we more easily remark its subsequent improvement, and perceive how long it is, before it can apprehend a discourse of considerable length, or a sentence of great abstraction.

Nothing is more certain than the possibility of my perceiving the sort of relation that exists between the different parts of a methodical discourse, for example, Mr Burke's Speech upon Oeconomical Reform,[28] though it be impossible for me, after the severest attention, to consider the several parts otherwise than successively. I have a latent feeling of this relation as the discourse proceeds, but I cannot give a firm judgement respecting it, otherwise than by retrospect. It may however be suspected, even in the case of simple apprehension, that an accurate attention to the operations of the mind would show that we scarcely in any instance hear a single sentence without returning again and again upon the steps of the speaker and drawing more closely in our minds the preceding members of his period, before he arrives at its conclusion; though even this exertion of mind, subtle as it is, be not of itself thought sufficient to authorize us to give a judgement of the whole.

But, if the principle here stated be true, how infinitely rapid must be the succession of ideas? While I am speaking, no two ideas are in my mind at the same time, and yet with what facility do I pass from one to another? If my discourse be argumentative, how often do I pass in review the topics of which it consists, before I utter them; and, even while I am speaking, continue the review at intervals, without producing any pause in my discourse? How many other sensations are experienced by me during this period, without so much as interrupting, that is, without materially diverting the train of my ideas? My eye successively remarks a thousand objects that present themselves. My mind wanders to the different parts of my body, and receives a sensation from the chair upon which I sit, or the table upon which I lean; from the pinching of a shoe, from a singing in my ear, a pain in my head, or an irritation of the breast. When these most perceptibly occur, my mind passes from one to another without feeling the minutest obstacle, or being in any degree distracted by their multiplicity. From this cursory view of the subject, it appears that we have a multitude of different successive perceptions in every moment of our existence.* – To return.

*An attempt has been made to calculate these, but there is no reason to believe that the calculation deserves to be considered as a standard of truth. Sensations leave their images behind them, some

Consciousness, as it has been above defined, appears to be one of the departments of memory. Now the nature of memory, so far as it relates to the subject of which we are treating, is obvious. An infinite number of thoughts passed through my mind in the last five minutes of my existence. How many of them am I now able to recollect? How many of them shall I recollect tomorrow? One impression after another is perpetually effacing from this intellectual register. Some of them may with great attention and effort be revived; others obtrude themselves uncalled for; and a third sort are perhaps out of the reach of any power of thought to reproduce, as having never left their traces behind them for a moment. If the memory be capable of so many variations and degrees of intensity, may there not be some cases with which it never connects itself? If the succession of thought be so inexpressibly rapid, may they not pass over some topics with so delicate a touch as to elude the supplement of consciousness?

It seems to be consciousness, rather than the succession of ideas, that measures time to the mind. The succession of ideas is, in all cases, exceedingly rapid, and it is by no means clear that it can be accelerated. We find it impracticable in the experiment to retain any idea in our mind unvaried for any perceptible duration. Continual flux appears to take place in every part of the universe. Of thought, may be said, in a practical sense, what has been affirmed of matter, that it is infinitely divisible. Yet time seems, to our apprehension, to flow now with a precipitated, and now with a tardy course. The indolent man reclines for hours in the shade; and, though his mind be perpetually at work, the silent progress of time is unobserved. But, when acute pain, or uneasy expectation, obliges consciousness to recur with unusual force, the time appears insupportably long. Indeed it is a contra-

---

for a longer and some for a shorter time; so that, in two different instances, the calculation is in one case eight, and in another three hundred and twenty to a second. See Watson on Time, Ch. II.

diction in terms to suppose that the succession of thoughts, where there is nothing that perceptibly links them together, where they totally elude the memory and instantly vanish, can be a measure of time to the mind. That there is such a state of mind, in some cases assuming a permanent form, has been so much the general opinion of mankind that it has obtained a name, and is called reverie. It is probable from what has been said that thoughts of reverie, understanding by that appellation thoughts untransmitted to the memory, perpetually take their turn with our more express and digested thoughts, even in the most active scenes of our life.

Lastly, thought may be the source of animal motion, and yet there may be no need of a distinct thought producing each individual motion. This is a very essential point in the subject before us. In uttering a cry for example, the number of muscles and articulations of the body concerned in this operation is very great; shall we say that the infant has a distinct thought for each of these articulations?

The answer to this question will be considerably facilitated if we recollect the manner in which the impressions are blended which we receive from external objects. The sense of feeling is diffused over every part of my body, I feel the different substances that support me, the pen I guide, various affections and petty irregularities in different parts of my frame, nay, the very air that environs me. But all these impressions are absolutely simultaneous, and I can have only one perception at once. Out of these various impressions, the most powerful, or that which has the greatest advantage to solicit my attention, overcomes and drives out the rest; or, which not less frequently happens, some idea of association, suggested by the last preceding idea, wholly withdraws my attention from every external object. It is probable however that this perception is imperceptibly modified by the miniature impressions which accompany it, just as we actually find that the very same ideas presented to a sick man take a peculiar tinge which renders them exeedingly different from what they are in the mind of a man in health. It has been already shown that, though there is nothing less frequent than the apprehending of a simple idea, yet every idea, however complex, offers itself to the mind under the conception of unity. The blending of numerous impressions into one perception is a law of our nature; and the customary train of our perceptions is entirely of this denomination. After this manner, not only every perception is complicated by a variety of simultaneous impressions, but every idea that now offers itself to the mind is modified by all the ideas that ever existed in it. It is this circumstance that constitutes the insensible empire of prejudice; and causes every object which is exhibited to a number of individuals to assume as many forms in their mind as there are individuals who view it.

These remarks furnish us with an answer to the long disputed question, whether the mind always thinks? It appears that innumerable impressions are perpetually made upon our body; and the only way in which the slightest of these is prevented from conveying a distinct report to the mind is in consequence of its being overpowered by some more considerable impression. It cannot therefore be alleged 'that, as one impression is found to be overpowered by another while we wake, the strongest only of the simultaneous impressions furnishing an idea to the mind; so the whole set of simultaneous impressions during sleep may be overpowered by some indisposition of the sensorium, and entirely fail of its effect'. For, first, the cases are altogether different. From the explication above given, it appeared that not one of the impressions was really lost, but tended, though in a very limited degree, to modify the predominant impression. Secondly, nothing can be more absurd than this supposition. Sleep ought, according to this scheme, to cease of itself after the expiration of a certain term, but to be incapable of interruption from any experiment I might make upon the sleeper. To what purpose call or shake him? This act evinces my knowledge, and its success the truth of my knowledge, that he is in a state susceptible of impression. But, if susceptible of impression, then impressed, by bedclothes, etc. Shall we say, 'that it requires an impression of a certain magnitude to excite the sensorium'? But a clock shall strike in the room and not wake him, when a voice of a much lower key produces that effect. What is the precise degree of magnitude necessary? We actually find the ineffectual calls that are addressed to us, as well as various other sounds, occasionally mixing with our dreams, without our being aware from whence these new perceptions arose. Thus it appears that every, the most minute, impression that is made upon our bodies in a state of sleep or deliquium is conveyed to the mind, however faint may be its effect, or however it may be overpowered and swallowed up by other sensations or circumstances.

Let it however be observed that the question whether the mind always thinks is altogether different from the question, which has sometimes been confounded with it, whether a sleeping man always dreams. The arguments here adduced seem conclusive as to the first question, but there is some reason to believe that there have been men who never once dreamed in the whole course of their lives.

To apply these observations. If a number of impressions acting upon the mind may come to us so blended as to make up one thought or perception, why may not one thought, in cases where the mind acts as a principle, produce a variety of motions? It has already been shown that there is no essential difference between the two cases. The mind is completely passive in both. Is there any sufficient reason to show that, though it be possible for one substance, considered as the recipient of effects, to be the subject of a variety of simultaneous impressions, yet it is impossible for one substance, considered as a cause, to produce a variety of simultaneous motions? If it be granted that there is not, if the mere modification of a thought designing a motion in chief (a cry, for example, or a motion of the limbs), may produce a secondary motion, then it must perhaps further be confessed possible for that modification which my first thought produced in my second to carry on the motion, even though the second thought be upon a subject altogether different.

The consequences which seem deducible from this theory of mind are sufficiently memorable. By showing the extreme subtlety and simplicity of thought, it removes many of the difficulties that might otherwise rest upon its finer and more evanescent operations. If thought, in order to be the source of animal motion, need not have either the nature of volition, or the concomitant of consciousness, and if a single thought may become a complex source, and produce a variety of motions, it will then become exceedingly difficult to trace its operations, or to discover any circumstances in a particular instance of animal motion which can sufficiently indicate that thought was not the principle of its production, and by that means supersede the force of the general arguments adduced in the beginning of this chapter. Hence therefore it appears that all those motions which are observed to exist in substances having perception, and which are not to be discovered in substances of any other species, may reasonably be suspected to have thought, the distinguishing peculiarity of such substances, for their source.

There are various classes of motion which will fall under this definition, beside those already enumerated. An example of one of these classes suggests itself in the phenomenon of walking. An attentive observer will perceive various symptoms calculated to persuade him that every step he takes, during the longest journey, is the production of thought. Walking is, in all cases, originally a voluntary motion. In a child, when he learns to walk, in a rope-dancer, when he begins to practise that particular exercise, the distinct determination of mind, preceding each step, is sufficiently perceptible. It may be absurd to say that a long series of motions can be the result of so many express volitions, when these supposed volitions leave no trace in the memory. But it is not unreasonable to believe that a species of motion which began in express design may, though it ceases to be the subject of conscious attention, owe its continuance to a continued series of thoughts flowing in that direction, and that, if life were taken away, material impulse would not carry on the exercise for a moment. We actually find that, when our thoughts in a train are more than commonly earnest, our pace slackens, and sometimes our going forward is wholly suspended, particularly in any less common species of walking, such as that of descending a flight of stairs. In ascending the case is still more difficult, and accordingly we are accustomed wholly to suspend the regular progress of reflection during that operation.

Another class of motions of a still subtler nature are the regular motions of the animal economy, such as the circulation of the blood, and the pulsation of the heart. Are thought and perception the medium of these motions? We have the same argument here as in the former instances, conjunction of event. When thought begins, these motions also begin; and, when it ceases, they are at an end. They are therefore either the cause or effect of percipiency, or mind; but we shall be inclined to embrace the latter side of this dilemma when we recollect that we are probably acquainted with many instances in which thought is the immediate cause of motions, which scarcely yield in subtlety to these; but that, as to the origin of the faculty of thought, we are wholly uninformed. Add to this that there are probably no motions of the animal economy which we do not find it in the power of volition, and still more of our involuntary sensations, to hasten or retard.

It is far from certain that the phenomenon of motion can anywhere exist where there is not thought. Motion may be distributed into four classes; the simpler motions, which result from what are called the essential properties of matter, and the laws of impulse; the more complex ones, which cannot be accounted for by the assumption of these laws; such as gravitation, elasticity, electricity and magnetism, the motions of the vegetable, and of the animal systems. Each of these seems further than that which preceded it, from being accounted for by anything we understand of the nature of matter.

Some light may be derived from what has been here advanced, upon the phenomenon of dreams. 'In sleep we sometimes imagine,' for example, 'that we read long passages from books, or hear a long oration from a speaker. In all cases, scenes and incidents pass before us that, in various ways, excite our passions, and interest our feelings. Is it possible that these should be the unconscious production of our own minds?'

It has already appeared that volition is the accidental, and by no means the necessary concomitant, even of those thoughts which are most active and efficient in the producing of motion. It is therefore no more to be wondered at that the mind should be busied in the composition of books, which it appears to read, than that a train of thoughts of any other kind should pass through it, without a consciousness of its being the author. In fact we perpetually annex erroneous ideas to this phrase, that we are the authors. Though mind be a real and proper antecedent, it is in no case a first cause, a thing indeed of which we have in no case any experimental knowledge. Thought is the medium through which operations are produced. Ideas succeed each other in our sensorium according to certain necessary laws. The most powerful impression, either from without or within, constantly gets the better of its competitors, and forcibly drives out the preceding thought, till it is in the same irresistible manner driven out by its successor.

CHAPTER X

OF SELF-LOVE AND BENEVOLENCE

*Question stated. – Nature of voluntary action.
– Origin of benevolence. – Operation of habit
– of opinion. – Reflex operation of enjoyment.
– Complexity of motives. – Of malevolence. –
Scheme of self-love incompatible with virtue. –
Conclusion.*

THE subject of the mechanism of the human mind is the
obvious counterpart of that which we are now to examine.
Under the former of these topics we have entered, with
considerable minuteness, into the nature of our involuntary actions; the decision of the latter will, in a great
degree, depend upon an accurate conception of such as
are voluntary. The question of self-love and benevolence
is a question relative to the feelings and ideas by which
we ought to be governed, in our intercourse with our
fellow men, or, in other words, in our moral conduct. But
it is universally admitted that there can be no moral conduct, that we can be neither virtuous nor vicious, except
in instances where our actions flow from intention, and
are directed by foresight, or where they might have been
so directed; and this is the definition of voluntary actions.* The question therefore of self-love and benevolence is a question of voluntary action.

The enquiry here proposed is the same in effect as the
question whether we are capable of being influenced by
disinterested considerations. Once admit that we are, and
it will not be disputed that it is by such considerations
we ought to be influenced, in cases where our neighbour
or the public is to be eminently benefited.

This question has been long and eagerly contested, and
the majority of persons who are accustomed to give some
attention to speculations of this sort have ranged themselves on the side of self-love. Among the French, not a

* Book I, Chap. V, p. 119.

single writer upon the nature of the human mind is to be found who does not, with more or less explicitness, declare for this hypothesis. Among ourselves, several authors of eminence have undertaken to support the practicability of disinterested action.*

One of the writers who first contributed to render this enquiry a subject of general attention was the duke de la Rochefoucault.[31] He asserted the system of self-love in its grossest form; and his exposition of it amounts to little less than 'that, in every action of our lives, we are directed by a calculation of personal interest'. This notion has been gradually softened down by his successors; and the hypothesis of self-love is now frequently explained to mean only 'that, as every state of a percipient being has in it a mixture of pleasure or pain, the immediate sensation in either of these kinds is to be regarded as the sole, proper and necessary cause of the subsequent action'. This fluctuation among the adherents of self-love has had the effect of making some of the arguments with which their principle has been attacked apparently inapplicable to the newest state of the question. Let us see whether the point may not be put upon a simpler issue than has usually been attempted.

An unanswerable argument for the system of disinterestedness is contained in a proposition so obvious as for its very plainness to be exposed to the risque of contempt, *viz.* that the motive of every voluntary action consists in the view present to the mind of the agent at the time of his determination. This is an inference which immediately results from the nature of volition. Volition is an affair of foresight.† 'No motion is voluntary any further than it is accompanied with intention and design, and has for its proper antecedent the apprehension of an

---

* Particularly Shaftesbury, Butler,[29] Hutcheson[30] and Hume. The active and ardent spirit of the founders of religion has perhaps always carried them into the liberal system. See Matt. ch. xxii, ver. 37–41.

* Book I, Chap. V, p. 119.

end to be accomplished. So far as it flows in any degree from another source, it is involuntary.'* But, if this be a just description of voluntary action, then the converse of this assertion must also be true; that whatever is proposed by the mind as an end to be accomplished, whether it be life or death, pleasure or pain, and relate to myself or my neighbour, has in it the true essence of a motive. – To illustrate this in relation to the subject in hand.

Voluntary action cannot exist but as the result of experience. Neither desire nor aversion can have place till we have had a consciousness of agreeable and disagreeable sensations. Voluntary action implies desire, and the idea of certain means to be employed for the attainment of the thing desired.

The things first desired by every thinking being will be agreeable sensation, and the means of agreeable sensation. If he foresee anything that is not apprehended to be pleasure or pain, or the means of pleasure or pain, this will excite no desire, and lead to no voluntary action.

A disposition to promote the benefit of another, my child, my friend, my relation, or my fellow being, is one of the passions; understanding by the term passion a permanent and habitual tendency towards a certain course of action. It is of the same general nature as avarice, or the love of fame. The good of my neighbour could not, in the first instance, have been chosen but as the means of agreeable sensation. His cries, or the spectacle of his distress importune me, and I am irresistibly impelled to adopt means to remove this importunity. The child perceives, in his own case, that menaces or soothing tend to stop his cries, and he is induced to employ, in a similar instance, that mode of the two which seems most within his reach. He thinks little of the sufferings endured, and is only uneasy at the impression made upon his organs. To this motive, he speedily adds the idea of esteem and gratitude, which are to be purchased by his beneficence. Thus the good of our neighbour, like the

* Chap. VII, p. 345.

possession of money, is originally pursued for the sake of its advantage to ourselves.

But it is the nature of the passions speedily to convert what at first were means into ends. The avaricious man forgets the utility of money which first incited him to pursue it, fixes his passion upon the money itself and counts his gold, without having in his mind any idea but that of seeing and handling it. Something of this sort happens very early in the history of every passion. The moment we become attached to a particular source of pleasure, beyond any idea we have of the rank it holds in the catalogue of sources, it must be admitted that it is loved for its own sake. The man who pursues wealth or fame with any degree of ardour, soon comes to concentre his attention in the wealth or the fame, without carrying his mind beyond, or thinking of anything that is to result from them.

This is merely one case of the phenomena of habit.* All indulgence of the senses is originally chosen for the sake of the pleasure that accrues. But the quantity of accruing pleasure or pain is continually changing. This however is seldom adverted to; and when it is, the power of habit is frequently too strong to be thus subdued. The propensity to do again what we have been accustomed to do recurs when the motive that should restrain us has escaped from our thoughts. Thus the drunkard and the lecher continue to pursue the same course of action long after the pains have outweighed the pleasures, and even after they confess and know this to be the real state of the case. It is in this manner that men will often, for the sake of that which has become the object of a favourite passion, consent to sacrifice what they generally know to contain in it a greater sum of agreeable sensations. It is a trite and incontrovertible axiom 'that they will rather die, than part with it'.

If this be the case in the passion of avarice or the love of fame, it must also be true in the instance of beneficence

* Book I, Chap. V, p. 124.

that, after having habituated ourselves to promote the happiness of our child, our family, our country or our species, we are at length brought to approve and desire their happiness without retrospect to ourselves. It happens in this instance, as in the former, that we are occasionally actuated by the most perfect disinterestedness, and willingly submit to tortures and death, rather than see injury committed upon the object of our affections.

Thus far there is a parallel nature in avarice and benevolence. But ultimately there is a wide difference between them. When once we have entered into so auspicious a path as that of disinterestedness, reflection confirms our choice, in a sense in which it never can confirm any of the factitious passions we have named. We find by observation that we are surrounded by beings of the same nature with ourselves. They have the same senses, are susceptible of the same pleasures and pains, capable of being raised to the same excellence and employed in the same usefulness.* We are able in imagination to go out of ourselves, and become impartial spectators of the system of which we are a part. We can then make an estimate of our intrinsic and absolute value; and detect the imposition of that self-regard which would represent our own interest as of as much value as that of all the world beside. The delusion being thus sapped, we can, from time to time at least, fall back in idea into our proper post, and cultivate those views and affections which must be most familiar to the most perfect intelligence.

It is admitted on all hands that it is possible for a man to sacrifice his own existence to that of twenty others. Here then is an action possessing various recommendations: the advantage to arise to twenty men; their tranquillity and happiness through a long period of remaining existence; the benefits they will not fail to confer on thousands of their contemporaries, and through them on millions of posterity; and lastly his own escape from uneasiness, and momentary exultation in an act of virtue.

* Book II, Chap. III, p. 183.

The advocates of the system of self-love are compelled to assert that the last consideration only is of any value with him; and that he perceives the real state of the case without feeling himself in the smallest degree directly and properly affected by it. He engages in an act of generosity without one atom of true sympathy, and wholly and exclusively influenced by considerations of the most selfish description.

It is not easily to conceive an hypothesis more singular than this. It is in direct opposition to experience, and what every man seems to know of himself. It undertakes to maintain that we are under a delusion of the most extraordinary sort; and which would appear to a person not trained in a philosophical system of all others the most improbable. It affirms that we are wholly incapable of being influenced by motives which seem to have an absolute power; that the philanthropist has no love for mankind, nor the patriot for his country; that no child ever had an affection for his parent, or parent for his child; in a word that, when we imagine we are most generously concerned for another, we have no concern for him, but are anxious only for ourselves. Undoubtedly a thesis of this sort is in need of very cogent arguments to support it.

It must be admitted indeed as characteristic of every determination of the mind that, when made, we feel uneasiness in the apprehension of any obstacle, and pleasure in indulging the desire, and seeing events turn out conformably to the desire. But it would be absurd to say: 'that the motive of our proceeding, in this case, is impatience and uneasiness, and that we are impelled to the sacrifices which are frequently made, by the mere wish to free ourselves from intolerable pain'. Impatience and uneasiness are only generated by obstacles to the attainment of our desires; and we often fulfil our purposes with a swiftness and impetuosity that leave no leisure for the recurrence of pain. The uneasiness of unfulfilled desire implies the desire itself as the antecedent and parent of the uneasiness. It is because I wish my neighbour's advantage that I am uneasy at his misfortune. I should no more be uneasy about this than about the number of syllables contained in the present paragraph, if I had not previously loved it for its own sake.

This pleasure and pain however, though not the authors of my determination, undoubtedly tend to perpetuate and strengthen it. Such is conspicuously the case in the present instance. The man who vigilantly conforms his affections to the standard of justice, who loses the view of personal regards in the greater objects that engross his attention, who, from motives of benevolence, sits loose to life and all its pleasures, and is ready without a sigh, to sacrifice them to the public good, has an uncommonly exquisite source of happiness. When he looks back, he applauds the state of his own affections; and, when he looks out of himself, his sensations are refined, in proportion to the comprehensiveness of his sentiments. He is filled with harmony within; and the state of his thoughts is uncommonly favourable to what we may venture to style the sublime emotions of tranquillity. It is not to be supposed that an experience of the pleasures of benevolence should not tend to confirm in us a benevolent propensity.

The hypothesis of disinterestedness would never have had so many adversaries if the complexity of human motives had been sufficiently considered. To illustrate this, let it be recollected that every voluntary action has in it a mixture of involuntary.* In the sense in which we have used the word motive in an early part of this work,† it is equally descriptive of the cause of action in both cases. Motive may therefore be distinguished, according to its different relations, into direct and indirect; understanding by the direct, that which is present to the mind of the agent at the time of his determination, and which belongs to every voluntary action, and to so much of every action as is voluntary; and by the indirect, that

* Book I, Chap. V, p. 127.
† p. 119.

which operates without being adverted to by the mind, whether in the case of actions originally involuntary, or that have become so, in whole, or in part, by the force of habit. Thus explained, it is incontrovertibly evident that the direct motive to many of our actions is purely disinterested. We are capable of self-oblivion, as well as of sacrifice. All that is strictly voluntary, in the beneficence of a man habitually generous and kind, commences from this point: if other considerations intervene in the sequel, they are indebted for their intervention to the disinterested motive. But, at the same time that this truth is clearly established, it is not less true, first, that the indirect and original motive, that which laid the foundation of all our habits, is the love of agreeable sensation. Secondly, it is also to be admitted that there is probably something personal directly and perceptibly mixing itself with such of our beneficent actions as are of a sensible duration. We are so accustomed to fix our attention upon agreeable sensation that we can scarcely fail to recollect, at every interval the gratitude we shall excite, or the approbation we shall secure, the pleasure that will result to ourselves from our neighbour's well-being, the joys of self-applause, or the uneasiness that attends upon ungratified desire. Yet, after every deduction that can be made, the disinterested and direct motive, the profit and advantage of our neighbour, seems to occupy the principal place. This is at least the first, often the only, thing in the view of the mind, at the time the action is chosen. It is this from which, by way of eminence, it derives the character of voluntary action.

There is an observation arising in this place which it seems of some importance to mention. Pure malevolence is the counterpart of disinterested virtue; and almost all the considerations that prove the existence of the one are of equal avail to prove the existence of the other. It is not enough to say, I choose the pleasure or pain of my neighbour for the sake of the gratification I have in contemplating it. This only removes the difficulty a single step, and will not account for the phenomenon of habit in either case. Both the one and the other are originally chosen with a view to agreeable sensation; but in both cases the original view is soon forgotten. It is as certain that there are human beings who take pleasure in shrieks and agony, without a prospect to anything further or different; as that the miser comes at last to regard his guineas with delight, independently of a recollection of the benefits they may purchase.

There is one further remark which, though by no means so conclusive as many that have been adduced, ought not to be omitted. If self-love be the only principle of action, there can be no such thing as virtue. Benevolent intention is essential to virtue.* Virtue, where it exists in any eminence, is a species of conduct modelled upon a true estimate of the different reasons inviting us to preference. He that makes a false estimate, and prefers a trivial and partial good to an important and comprehensive one, is vicious. Virtue requires a certain disposition and view of the mind, and does not belong to the good which may accidentally and unintentionally result from our proceeding. The creditor that, from pure hardness of disposition, should cast a man into prison who, unknown to him, was upon the point of committing some atrocious and sanguinary action, would be not virtuous but vicious. The mischief to result from the project of his debtor was no part of his motive; he thought only of gratifying his inordinate passion. Just so, in the case stated a little before, the public benefactor, upon the system of self-love, prefers a single individual to twenty, or to twenty millions. So far as relates to the real merits of the case, his own advantage or pleasure is a very insignificant consideration, and the benefit to be produced, suppose to a world, is inestimable. Yet he falsely and unjustly prefers the first, and regards the latter, separately taken, as nothing. If there be such a thing as justice, if I have a real and absolute value upon which truth can de-

* Book II, Chap. IV.

cide, and which can be compared with what is greater or less, then, according to this system, the best action that ever was performed may, for anything we know, have been the action, in the whole world, of the most exquisite and deliberate injustice. Nay, it could not have been otherwise, since it produced the greatest good, and therefore was the individual instance in which the greatest good was most directly postponed to personal gratification. Such is the spirit of the doctrine we have endeavoured to refute.

On the other hand, the just result of the arguments above adduced is that men are capable of understanding the beauty of virtue, and the claims of other men upon their benevolence; and, understanding them, that these views, as well as every other perception which has relation to sensitive existence, are of the nature of motives, sometimes overpowered by other considerations, and sometimes overpowering them, but always in their own nature capable of exciting to action, when not counteracted by pleas of a different sort. Men are capable, no doubt, of preferring an inferior interest of their own to a superior interest of others; but this preference arises from a combination of circumstances and is not the necessary and invariable law of our nature.*

There is no doctrine in which the generous and elevated mind rests with more satisfaction than in that of which we are treating. If it be false, it is no doubt incumbent upon us to make the best of the small remnant of good that remains. But it is a discouraging prospect for the moralist, who, when he has done all, has no hope

---

* Some persons, friendly to the doctrine of this chapter, have objected to the remark that 'upon the system of self-love, there can be no such thing as virtue', as too broad, or too incautiously expressed. Undoubtedly it was not intended in this place to assert that the different tendencies of actions would not remain upon both systems, or that habits conducive to the general welfare would not deserve to be sedulously cultivated, in ourselves and others, however mean and ignoble might be the motives from which they sprung.

to persuade mankind to one atom of real affection towards any one individual of their species. We may be made indeed the instruments of good, but in a way less honourable than that in which a frame of wood, or a sheet of paper, may be made the instrument of good. The wood, or the paper, is at least neutral. But we are drawn into the service with affections of a diametrically opposite direction. When we perform the most benevolent action, it is with a view only to our own advantage, and with the most sovereign and unreserved neglect of that of others. We are instruments of good, in the same manner as bad men are said to be the instruments of providence, even when their inclinations are most refractory to its decrees. In this sense, we may admire the system of the universe, where public utility results from each man's contempt of that utility, and where the most beneficial actions, of those whom we have been accustomed to term the best men, are only instances in which justice and the real merits of the case are most flagrantly violated. But we can think with little complacence of the individuals of whom this universe is composed. It is no wonder that philosophers whose system has taught them to look upon their fellow men as thus perverse and unjust have been frequently cold in their temper, or narrow in their designs. It is no wonder that Rousseau, the most benevolent of them, and who most escaped the general contagion, has been driven to place the perfection of virtue in doing no injury.* Neither philosophy, nor morality, nor politics will ever show like itself till man shall be acknowledged for what he really is, a being capable of rectitude, virtue and benevolence, and who needs not always be led to actions of general utility, by foreign and frivolous considerations.

The system of disinterested benevolence proves to us that it is possible to be virtuous, and not merely to talk of virtue; that all which has been said by philosophers

---

* 'La plus sublime vertu est négative; elle nows instruit de ne jamais faire du mal à personne.' *Emile*, Liv. II.

and moralists respecting impartial justice is not an unmeaning rant; and that, when we call upon mankind to divest themselves of selfish and personal considerations, we call upon them for something they are able to practise. An idea like this reconciles us to our species; teaches us to regard, with enlightened admiration, the men who have appeared to lose the feeling of their personal existence, in the pursuit of general advantage; and gives us reason to expect that, as men collectively advance in science and useful institution, they will proceed more and more to consolidate their private judgement, and their individual will, with abstract justice, and the unmixed approbation of general happiness.

What are the inferences that ought to be made from this doctrine with respect to political institution? Certainly not that the interest of the individual ought to be made incompatible with the part he is expected to take in the interest of the whole. This is neither desirable, nor even possible. But that social institution needs not despair of seeing men influenced by other and better motives. The true politician is bound to recollect that the perfection of mind consists in disinterestedness. He should regard it as the ultimate object of his exertions to induce men to estimate themselves at their just value, and neither to grant to themselves, nor claim from others, a higher consideration than they deserve. Above all, he should be careful not to add vigour to the selfish passions. He should gradually wean men from contemplating their own benefit in all that they do, and induce them to view with complacence the advantage that is to result to others. Great mischief, in this respect, has probably been done by those moralists who think only of stimulating men to good deeds by considerations of frigid prudence and mercenary self-interest, and never apply themselves to excite one generous and magnanimous sentiment of our natures. This has been too much the case with the teachers of religion, even those of them who are most eager in their hostility to religious enthusiasm.

The last perfection of the sentiment here vindicated consists in that state of mind which bids us rejoice as fully in the good that is done by others, as if it were done by ourselves. The man who shall have attained to this improvement will be actuated neither by interest nor ambition, the love of honour, nor the love of fame. He has a duty indeed obliging him to seek the good of the whole; but that good is his only object. If that good be effected by another hand, he feels no disappointment. All men are his fellow labourers, but he is the rival of no man. Like Pedaretus in ancient story, he is ready to exclaim: 'I also have endeavoured to deserve; but there are three hundred citizens in Sparta better than myself, and I rejoice.'

CHAPTER XI

OF GOOD AND EVIL

Definitions. – Principle of the Stoics examined. Pleasure delineated. – Scale of happiness – the peasant and artisan – the man of wealth – the man of taste – the man of benevolence. – Inference. – System of optimism. – Errors of this system. – Mixture of truth. – Limitations. – Condition of the universe displayed. – Ill effects of optimism. – It is destructive of any consistent theory of virtue – blunts the delicacy of moral discrimination – reconciles us to the spectacle of perverseness in others. – Of persecution.

THERE is no disquisition more essential either in morality or politics than that which shall tend to give us clear and distinct ideas of good and evil, what it is we should desire, and what we should deprecate. We will therefore close the present volume with a few considerations upon this head.

The nature of good and evil, which is one of the plainest subjects upon which the human mind can be engaged, has been obscured by two sets of men: those who, from an eagerness to refine and exalt beyond measure the nature of virtue, have elevated it into something impossible and unmeaning: and those who, spurning the narrow limits of science and human understanding, have turned system-builders, and fabricated a universe after their own peculiar fancy. We shall see, as we proceed, what has been the operation of these two errors. In the meantime it may be most safe to examine the subject in its genuine simplicity, uninfluenced by the preconceptions of party.

Good is a general name, including pleasure, and the means by which pleasure is procured. Evil is a general name, including pain, and the means by which pain is produced. Of the two things included in these general names, the first is cardinal and substantive, the second has no intrinsic recommendations, but depends for its value on the other. Pleasure therefore is to be termed an absolute good; the means of pleasure are only relatively good. The same observation may be stated of pain.*

We inhabit a world where sensations do not come detached, but where everything is linked and connected together. Of consequence, among things absolutely good there may be two classes. There are some things that are good and only good, pleasures that do not draw after them mischief, anguish and remorse. There may be other pleasures that are attended in the sequel with an overbalance of pain, and which, though absolutely good, are relatively evil. There may also be pains which, taken together with their consequences, are salutary. But this does not alter the original proposition: where there is a mixture of evil, all is not good; just as, where there is a mixture of pain, all is not pleasure.

Let us see how this statement affects the theory and practice of virtue.

* Book III, Chap. III, p. 221.

First, we are hereby enabled to detect their mistake who denied that 'pleasure was the supreme good'. The error of the Epicurean philosophers seems to have been, not in affirming that 'pleasure was the supreme good', for this cannot be refuted; but in confining that pleasure which is the proper scope of human actions to the pleasure of the individual who acts, and not admitting that the pleasure of others was an object which, for its own sake, could, and ought to be pursued.*

That 'pleasure is the supreme good' cannot be denied by him who is sufficiently attentive to the meaning of words. That which will give pleasure neither to ourselves nor others, and from which the fruits of joy can be reaped, in no stage, and at no period, is necessarily good for nothing.

The opposers of the Epicurean maxim were terrified by a consequence which they hastily concluded might be built upon it. If pleasure were the only thing that is worthy to be desired, they thought that every man might reasonably be justified in 'walking in the sight of his own eyes', and there would be no longer any rule of human conduct. Each man might say, 'Pleasure is the proper object of my pursuit; I best know what pleases me; and therefore, however opposite is the plan of my conduct to your conceptions, it is unreasonable and unjust for you to interfere with me.'

An inference the opposite of this might, with more propriety, have been drawn from the maxim upon which we are descanting. Is 'pleasure the only good'? Then have we the most cogent reason for studying pleasure, and reducing it to a science, and not for leaving every man to pursue his own particular taste, which is nothing more than the result of his education, and of the circumstances in which he happens to have been placed, and which by other lessons and circumstances may be corrected.

No man is entitled to complain of my sober and dis-passionate expostulations respecting the species of plea-

* Chap. X.

sure he thinks proper to pursue, because no man stands alone, and can pursue his private conceptions of pleasure, without affecting, beneficially or injuriously, the persons immediately connected with him, and, through them, the rest of the world. Even if he have persuaded himself that it is his business to pursue his own pleasure, and that he is not bound to attend ultimately to the pleasure of others, yet it may easily be shown that it is, generally speaking, the interest of each individual that all should form their plan of personal pleasure with a spirit of deference and accommodation to the pleasure of each other.

But putting the circumstance of the action and re-action of men in society out of the question, still there will be a science of pleasure, and it will be idle and erroneous to consider each man separately, and leave each to find his source of pleasure suitable to his particular humour. We have a common nature, and that common nature ought to be consulted. There is one thing, or series of things, that constitutes the true perfection of man.*

In the discussions that took place a few years ago, in the English parliament and nation, respecting the slave-trade, the sentiment we are here combating was used as a topic of argument by some of those persons who, from certain deplorable prejudices, were able to prevail upon themselves to appear as advocates for this trade. 'The slaves in the West Indies,' they said, 'are contented with their situation, they are not conscious of the evils against which you exclaim; why then should you endeavour to alter their condition?'

The true answer to this question, even granting them their fact, would be: 'It is not very material to a man of a liberal and enlarged mind whether they are contented or no. Are they contented? I am not contented for them. I see in them beings of certain capacities, equal to certain pursuits and enjoyments. It is of no consequence in the question that they do not see this, that they do not know their own interests and happiness. They do not

* Book II, Chap. III, p. 183; Book III, Chap. VII, p. 249.

repine? Neither does a stone repine. That which you mention as an alleviation finishes in my conception the portrait of their calamity. Abridged as they are of independence and enjoyment, they have neither the apprehension nor spirit of men. I cannot bear to see human nature thus degraded. It is my duty, if I can, to make them a thousand times happier than they are, or have any conception of being.'

It is not difficult to form a scale of happiness. Suppose it to be something like the following.

The first class shall be such as we may perhaps sometimes find among the labouring inhabitants of the civilized states of Europe. We will conceive a man working with his hands every day to obtain his subsistence. He rises early to his labour, and leaves off every night weary and exhausted. He takes a tranquil or a boisterous refreshment, and spends the hours of darkness in uninterrupted slumber. He does not quarrel with his wife oftener than persons of his class regularly do; and his cares are few, as he has scarcely known the pressure of absolute want. He never repines but when he witnesses luxuries he cannot partake, and that sensation is transient; and he knows no diseases but those which rise from perpetual labour. The range of his ideas is scanty; and the general train of his sensations comes as near as the nature of human existence will admit to the region of indifference. This man is in a certain sense happy. He is happier than a stone.

Our next instance shall be taken from among the men of rank, fortune and dissipation. We will suppose the individual in question to have an advantageous person and a sound constitution. He enjoys all the luxuries of the palate, the choicest viands, and the best-flavoured wines. He takes his pleasures discreetly, so as not, in the pursuit of pleasure, to lose the power of feeling it. He shoots, he hunts. He frequents all public places. He sits up late in scenes of gay resort. He rises late. He has just time to ride and dress before he goes into company again. With a happy flow of spirits and a perpetual variety of amusements, he is almost a stranger to *ennui*. But he is a model of ignorance. He never reads, and knows nothing beyond the topic of the day. He can scarcely conceive the meaning of the sublime or pathetic; and he rarely thinks of anything beyond himself. This man is happier than the peasant. He is happier, by all the pleasures of the palate, and all the gratifications of neatness, elegance and splendour, in himself, and the objects around him. Every day he is alive, inventing some new amusement, or enjoying it. He tastes the pleasures of liberty; he is familiar with the gratifications of pride: while the peasant slides through life, with something of the contemptible insensibility of an oyster.

The man of taste and liberal accomplishments is more advantageously circumstanced than he whom we have last described. We will suppose him to possess as many of the gratifications of expense as he desires. But, in addition to these, like the mere man of fortune in comparison with the peasant, he acquires new senses, and a new range of enjoyment. The beauties of nature are all his own. He admires the overhanging cliff, the wide-extended prospect, the vast expanse of the ocean, the foliage of the woods, the sloping lawn and the waving grass. He knows the pleasures of solitude, when man holds commerce alone with the tranquil solemnity of nature. He has traced the structure of the universe; the substances which compose the globe we inhabit, and are the materials of human industry; and the laws which hold the planets in their course amidst the trackless fields of space. He studies; and has experienced the pleasures which result from conscious perspicacity and discovered truth. He enters, with a true relish, into the sublime and pathetic. He partakes in all the grandeur and enthusiasm of poetry. He is perhaps himself a poet. He is conscious that he has not lived in vain, and that he shall be recollected with pleasure, and extolled with ardour, by generations yet unborn. In this person, compared with the two preceding classes, we

acknowledge something of the features of man. They
were only a better sort of brutes; but he has sensations
and transports of which they have no conception.

But there is a rank of man more fitted to excite our
emulation than this, the man of benevolence. Study is
cold, if it be not enlivened with the idea of the happiness
to arise to mankind from the cultivation and improvement of sciences.* The sublime and pathetic are barren,
unless it be the sublime of true virtue, and the pathos of
true sympathy. The pleasures of the mere man of taste
and refinement, 'play round the head, but come not to
the heart'. There is no true joy but in the spectacle and
contemplation of happiness. There is no delightful melancholy but in pitying distress. The man who has once performed an act of exalted generosity knows that there is
no sensation of corporeal or intellectual taste to be compared with this. The man who has sought to benefit
nations rises above the mechanical ideas of barter and exchange. He asks no gratitude. To see that they are benefited, or to believe that they will be so, is its own reward.
He ascends to the highest of human pleasures, the pleasures of disinterestedness. He enjoys all the good that
mankind possess, and all the good that he perceives to be
in reserve for them. No man so truly promotes his own
interest as he that forgets it. No man reaps so copious a
harvest of pleasure as he who thinks only of the pleasures
of other men.

The inference from this survey of human life is that he
who is fully persuaded that pleasure is the only good
ought by no means to leave every man to enjoy his
peculiar pleasure according to his own peculiar humour.
Seeing the great disparity there is between different conditions of human life, he ought constantly to endeavour
to raise each class, and every individual of each class, to
a class above it. This is the true equalization of mankind. Not to pull down those who are exalted, and
reduce all to a naked and savage equality. But to raise

* Chap. V, p. 300.

those who are abased; to communicate to every man all genuine pleasures, to elevate every man to all true wisdom and to make all men participators of a liberal and comprehensive benevolence. This is the path in which the reformers of mankind ought to travel. This is the prize they should pursue. Do you tell me, 'that human society can never arrive at this improvement'? I do not stay to dispute that point with you. We can come nearer it than we are. We can come nearer and nearer yet. This will not be the first time that persons engaged in the indefatigable pursuit of some accomplishment have arrived at an excellence that surpassed their most sanguine expectations.

The result of this part of the subject is that those persons have been grossly mistaken who taught that virtue was to be pursued for its own sake, and represented pleasure and pain as trivial matters and unworthy consideration. Virtue is upon no other account valuable than as it is the instrument of the most exquisite pleasure. – Be it observed that it is one thing to say that pain is not an evil, which is absurd, and another thing to say that temporary pains and pleasures are to be despised, when the enduring of the one is necessary, and the declining the other unavoidable in the pursuit of excellent and permanent pleasure, which is a most fundamental precept of wisdom and morality.

Let us proceed to a second point announced by us in the outset, the consideration of how the subject of good and evil has been darkened by certain fabulists and system-builders. The system alluded to under this head is that of the optimists,[32] who teach 'that everything in the universe, is for the best; and that, if anything had happened otherwise than it has happened, the result would have been, a diminution of the degree of happiness and good'.

That we may escape the error into which these persons have been led, by the daringness of their genius, and their mode of estimating things in the gross, and not in detail, we must be contented to follow experience, and not to outrun it.

It has already appeared that there is in the universe absolute evil: and, if pain be evil (and it has been proved to be the only absolute evil), it cannot be denied that, in the part of the universe with which we are acquainted, it exists in considerable profusion. It has also appeared that there is a portion of absolute evil which is relatively good, and which therefore the preceding circumstances being assumed, was desirable. Such, for example, is the amputation of a gangrened limb.

Whether or no those preceding circumstances were, universally, and in a comprehensive sense, good, which rendered the introduction of the absolute evil in question necessary, is, to say the least, a very doubtful point. But, if there be some presumption in the negative even in the smallest instance, this presumption against universal good is incalculably increased, when we recollect all the vice, disorder and misery that exist in the world.

Let us consider what portion there is of truth that has been mixed with the doctrine of optimism. This is the same thing as to enquire by means of what plausibilities it gained footing in the world. The answer to the sequestions lies in two circumstances.

First, there is a degree of improvement real and visible in the world. This is particularly manifest in the history of the civilized part of mankind, during the three last centuries. The taking of Constantinople by the Turks (1453) dispersed among European nations the small fragment of learning which was, at that time, shut up within the walls of this metropolis. The discovery of printing was nearly contemporary with that event. These two circumstances greatly favoured the reformation of religion, which gave an irrecoverable shock to the empire of superstition and implicit obedience. From that time, the most superficial observation can trace the improvements of art and science, which may, without glaring impropriety, be styled incessant. Not to mention essential improvements which were wholly unknown to the ancients, the most important characteristics of modern literature are the extent of surface over which it is diffused, and the number of persons that participate in it. It has struck its roots deep, and there is no probability that it will ever be subverted. It was once the practice of moralists to extol past times, and declaim without bound on the degeneracy of mankind. But this fashion is nearly exploded. The true state of the fact is too gross to be mistaken. And, as improvements have long continued to be incessant, so there is no chance but they will go on. The most penetrating philosophy cannot prescribe limits to them, nor the most ardent imagination adequately fill up the prospect.

Secondly, the doctrine of necessity teaches us that all things in the universe are connected together. Nothing could have happened otherwise than it has happened. Do we congratulate ourselves upon the rising genius of freedom? Do we view with pride the improvements of mankind, and contrast, with wonder, man in the state in which he once was, naked, ignorant and brutal, with man as we now sometimes behold him, enriched with boundless stores of science, and penetrated with sentiments of the purest philanthropy? These things could not have existed in their present form without having been prepared by all the preceding events. Everything the most seemingly insignificant, the most loathsome, or the most retrograde, was indissolubly bound to all that we most admire in the prospect before us. We may perhaps go a step further than this. The human mind is a principle of the simplest nature, a mere faculty of sensation or perception. It must have begun from absolute ignorance; it must obtain its improvement by slow degrees; it must pass through various stages of folly and mistake. Such is, and could not but be, the history of mankind.

There are three considerations which limit that idea of optimism, which some men have been inclined to deduce from the above circumstances.

First, it applies only to that part of the universe with which we are acquainted. That deduction, whatever it is, which is authorized by the above circumstances depends upon their junction. The general tendency to improvement would be an insufficient apology for untoward events if everything were not connected; and the connection of all events would have no just tendency to reconcile us to the scene were it not for the visible improvement. But has improvement been the constant characteristic of the universe? The human species seems to be but, as it were, of yesterday. Will it continue forever? The globe we inhabit bears strong marks of convulsion, such as the teachers of religion, and the professors of natural philosophy, agree to predict will one day destroy the inhabitants of the earth. Vicissitude therefore, rather than unbounded progress, appears to be the characteristic of nature.

Secondly, the quantity of good deducible from these circumstances, instead of meriting the name of optimism, is, in one respect, directly contrasted with it. Nothing is positively best. So far from it that the considerations here alleged are calculated to prove that everything is valuable, for this reason among others, that it leads to something better than itself.

Lastly, the points here affirmed are by no means calculated to bear out the conclusion that, if something else had happened, in the place of what did actually happen in any given instance, it might not have been a fortunate event. We are taught, by the doctrine of necessity, that nothing else could possibly happen under the circumstances; not that, if something else had been possible, it would not have been attended with more desirable consequences. Caesar enslaved his country; the event was unavoidable; and the general progress of human improvement upon the whole went on, notwithstanding this disastrous occurrence. But, if it had been possible that Caesar should have been diverted from this detestable enterprise, if the republic could have been restored by the battle of Mutina, or made victorious in the plains of Philippi, it might have been a most fortunate event for the whole race of mankind. There is a difficulty in conceiving that things should have been, in any respect, otherwise than they are. It may be conjectured, with much plausibility, that this is in all cases impossible. But the consideration of this affords no ground of rejoicing in untoward events. More auspicious harbingers would have led to more extended improvements. As to what was stated of the simplicity of the human mind, it may be observed that the history of the species exhibits the united effects of this internal principle, and the structure of the human body, as well as of the material universe. Brutes appear to have the same internal principle of perception that we have, but they have never made our progress. There may be other conscious beings in existence who possess the most essential advantages over us.

It may be worthy of remark that the support the system of optimism derives from the doctrine of necessity is of a very equivocal nature. The doctrine of necessity teaches that each event is the only thing, under the circumstances, that could happen; it would, of consequence, be as proper, upon this system, to say that everything that happens is the worst, as that it is the best, that could possibly happen.

It was observed in the commencement of this discussion upon the subject of optimism that, though there is some pain, or absolute evil, which, relatively taken, must be admitted to be attended with an overbalance of good, yet it is a matter of great delicacy and difficulty, in most instances, to decide in favour of pain, which, whatever be its relative value, is certainly a negative quantity to be deducted in the sum total of happiness. There is perhaps some impropriety in the phrase, thus applied, of relative good. Pain, under the most favourable circumstances, must be admitted to be absolutely, though not relatively, an evil. In every instance of this kind we are reduced to a choice of evils: consequently, whichever way we determine our election, it is still evil that we choose.

Taking these considerations along with us, the rash-ness of the optimist will appear particularly glaring, while we recollect the vast portion of pain and calamity that is to be found in the world. Let us not amuse ourselves with a pompous and delusive survey of the whole, but let us examine parts serverally and individually. All nature swarms with life. This may, in one view, afford an idea of an extensive theatre of pleasure. But unfortunately every animal preys upon his fellow. Every animal, how-ever minute, has a curious and subtle structure, render-ing him susceptible, as it should seem, of piercing anguish. We cannot move our foot without becoming the means of destruction. The wounds inflicted are of a hundred kinds. These petty animals are capable of palpitating for days in the agonies of death. It may be said, with little licence of phraseology, that all nature suffers. There is no day nor hour in which, in some regions of the many-peopled globe, thousands of men, and millions of animals, are not tortured, to the utmost extent that organized life will afford. Let us turn our attention to our own species. Let us survey the poor; oppressed, hungry, naked, denied all the gratifications of life, and all that nourishes the mind. They are either tormented with the injustice, or chilled into lethargy. Let us view man, writhing under the pangs of disease, or the fiercer tortures that are stored up for him by his brethren. Who is there that will look on, and say, 'All this is well; there is no evil in the world?' Let us recollect the pains of the mind; the loss of friends, the rankling tooth of ingratitude, the unre-lenting rage of tyranny, the slow progress of justice, the brave and honest consigned to the fate of guilt. Let us plunge into the depth of dungeons. Let us observe youth languishing in hopeless despair, and talents and virtue shrouded in eternal oblivion. The evil does not consist merely in the pain endured. It is the injustice that inflicts it that gives it its sharpest sting. Malignity, an unfeeling disposition, vengeance and cruelty, are inmates of every climate. As these are felt by the sufferer with peculiar acuteness, so they propagate themselves. Severity begets severity, and hatred engenders hate.* The whole history of the human species, taken in one point of view, appears a vast abortion. Man seems adapted for wisdom and fortitude and benevolence. But he has always, through a vast majority of countries, been the victim of ignorance and superstition. Contemplate the physiognomy of the species. Observe the traces of stupidity, of low cunning, of rooted insolence, of withered hope, and narrow selfishness, where the characters of wisdom, independence and disinterestedness might have been inscribed. Recollect the horrors of war, that last invention of deliberate profligacy for the misery of man. Think of the variety of wounds, the multiplication of anguish, the desolation of countries, towns destroyed, harvests flaming, inhabitants perishing by thousands of hunger and cold.

A sound philosophy will teach us to contemplate this scene without madness. Instructed in its lessons, we shall remember that, though there is much of evil, there is also much of good in the world, much pleasure, as well as much pain. We shall not even pronounce that some small portion of this evil is not relatively not an evil. Above all, we shall be cheered with the thought of brighter prospects and happier times. But the optimist must be particularly rash who takes upon him to affirm of all this mass of evil without exception that it is relatively not evil, and that nothing could have happened otherwise than it has happened, without the total being worse than it is.

There is reason to think that the creed of optimism, or an opinion bearing some relation to that creed, has done much harm in the world.

It is calculated to overturn all distinction between virtue and vice. The essential part of these ideas, as has been already observed, consists in the tendency of the actions so denominated with respect to the general good.† But,

* Chap. II, p. 272.
† Book II, Chap. IV.

according to the doctrine of optimism, if I do a virtuous action, I contribute to the general good; and, if I do a vicious action, it is still the same. Every man, according to this system, is privileged, as the elect are privileged according to the system of certain religionists: 'he may live as he list, for he cannot commit sin'. Whether I murder my benefactor, or preserve him from being murdered by another, I still do the very best thing that could have been done or thought of.

It will be admitted on all hands that the conduct of a man may be such as to produce evil and pain to himself, to involve him in perpetual obloquy and remorse. It may be such as to inflict intolerable pain, and the most horrible mischief, upon another, or upon many others. A man therefore, upon this scheme, may reasonably study his own interest; he may study the benefit and advantage of his friends or his neighbours. But, if he affect to study the good of the whole, he is only deceiving himself. It is impossible for him to have the slightest notion what acts of an individual, under any given circumstances, will or will not contribute to the general good. Nero, when he pronounced sentence upon Lucan or Seneca, when he castrated Sporus, set fire to the city of Rome, or, enclosing the Christians in cloth of pitch, burned them by night after the manner of torches, adopted the conduct, though perhaps he was not aware of it, most aptly conducing to the happiness of the whole. It is not indeed, absolutely speaking, indifferent what I shall do; but, practically speaking, it is, since I am wholly unable to conjecture what will be beneficial or what injurious. We saw, upon the system of self-love, public utility resulting from each man's determining to postpone that utility to his private advantage: * but it is much more absurd and repulsive to suppose universal happiness to be essentially promoted by the profligacy, malevolence and misery of innumerable multitudes.

But, though optimism, pursued into its consequences,

* Chap. X, p. 386.

is destructive of the distinction between virtue and vice, or rather teaches that there neither is nor can be such a thing as vice, yet it is the fate of this, like many other errors, that the truths which lie undeveloped in the mind, and cannot be deracinated, serve to check its influence and counteract its evil tendency.

It may however be suspected that, while its pernicious effects are thus counteracted, they are not destroyed. It is unavoidable that men should, in some respects, imitate what they persuade themselves is right. Thus in religion, those persons who believe that a large portion of mankind are objects of God's wrath, and reserved for eternal perdition, can never be prevailed on to regard, with a true and genuine sympathy, those whom God has cursed. In the same manner it will probably happen in the present case: those who believe that all the unfortunate events and sufferings that exist in the world will be found, in some mysterious way, to have been the fittest instruments of universal good are in danger of being less scrupulous than they ought to be, in the means they shall themselves select for the accomplishment of their purposes. If pain, horrors and devastation be frequently found means of kindness in the system of the universe, it is impossible to assign a good reason why they should not be such under the direction of man.

There is another crude notion diffused in the world, which the principle of optimism is calculated to encourage, and which the views here explained have a tendency to correct. It is not uncommon to congratulate ourselves upon the perverseness and misconduct of those whose views we oppose, under the imagination that such misconduct conduces to the more speedy subversion of error and establishment of justice. But the maxim is safer and better founded than this, which should instruct us that we 'rejoice not in evil, but rejoice in the truth'. It has already appeared that it is a matter of great delicacy and difficulty to decide in favour of pain and calamity, as the probable means of a preponderance of good. It was sufficiently seen, when we treated of resistance and revolutions, that the angry passions are not the most promising instruments of human happiness. A perverse conduct tends to the production of confusion and violence. A government that employed every species of persecution against those who should desire its reform, and that involved the country over which it presided in war, for the purpose of checking or exterminating sentiments of reason and equality, would do harm, and not good. It might indeed defeat its own purposes; but it would produce resentment and contention. It might excite a revulsion in the public mind against its designs; but this revulsion would be the offspring of irritation, and not of the understanding. Diminish the irritation, and the progress of real knowledge would be more substantial and salutary. Real knowledge is benevolent, not cruel and retaliating. The change that grows up among any people from a calm conviction of the absurdity of their former errors is of the most admirable sort; but the change that grows from distress, distemper and crisis, is an explosion pregnant with fate to thousands. From all these considerations it appears that every departure from enormous vice should be accounted as so much gained to the cause of general happiness.

Let any person who entertains the contrary opinion ask himself whether, if he had a part in the government we have supposed, he would think himself obliged to act in the manner in which he professes to desire the government should act? If, as he imagines, that action be most conducive to the public good, most undoubtedly, were it his own case, he ought to adopt it. Again, would he advise or incite the government, in any way, to this perverse conduct? There cannot be a clearer principle in morals, than 'that the action it would be vice in us to adopt, it is vice in us to desire to see adopted by another'.

A further consequence that flows from these speculations is relative to the persecution and sufferings to be endured by the advocates of justice. The same reasoning that has persuaded men to rejoice in beholding acts of oppression has led them to court oppression and martyrdom. A sound philosophy, it should seem, would never instigate us to provoke the passions of others, or to regard injustice as the suitable means of public happiness. It is reason, and not anger, that will benefit mankind. Dispassionate enquiry, not bitterness and resentment, is the parent of reform. The wise man will avoid persecution, because a protracted life, and an unfettered liberty, are likely to enable him to produce a greater sum of good. He will avoid persecution, because he will be unwilling to add fuel to the flames of contention. He will regret it when it arrives, because he believes it to be both wicked and mischievous. But he will not avoid it by the sacrifice of a virtuous, but tempered, activity. He will not regret it with a mean and pusillanimous spirit, but will meet it, when it can no longer be prevented, with that dignity of soul and tranquillity of temper that are characteristic of true wisdom. He will not imagine that the cause of truth will perish, though he should be destroyed. He will make the best of the situation to which he is reduced, and endeavour that his death, like his life, may be of use to mankind.

BOOK V

OF LEGISLATIVE AND EXECUTIVE POWER

CHAPTER I

INTRODUCTION

Retrospect of principles already established. – Distribution of the remaining subjects. – Subject of the present book. – Forms of government. – Method of examinations to be adopted.

IN the preceding divisions of this work the ground has been sufficiently cleared to enable us to proceed, with considerable explicitness and satisfaction, to the practical detail: in other words, to attempt the tracing out that application of the laws of general justice which may best conduce to the gradual improvement of mankind.

It has appeared that an enquiry concerning the principles and conduct of social intercourse is the most important topic upon which the mind of man can be exercised;* that, upon these principles, well or ill conceived, and the manner in which they are administered, the vices and virtues of individuals depend;* that political institution, to be good, must have constant relation to the rules of immutable justice;† and that those rules, uniform in their nature, are equally applicable to the whole human race.‡

The different topics of political institution cannot perhaps be more perspicuously distributed than under the

* Book I.
† Book II, Chap. II.
‡ Book I, Chap. VI, VII. Book III, Chap. VII. Book II.

four following heads: provisions for general administration; provisions for the intellectual and moral improvement of individuals; provisions for the administration of criminal justice; and provisions for the regulation of property. Under each of these heads it will be our business, in proportion as we adhere to the great and comprehensive principles already established, rather to clear away abuses than to recommend further and more precise regulations, rather to simplify than to complicate. Above all we should not forget that government is, abstractedly taken, an evil, an usurpation upon the private judgement and individual conscience of mankind; and that, however we may be obliged to admit it as a necessary evil for the present, it behoves us, as the friends of reason and the human species, to admit as little of it as possible, and carefully to observe, whether, in consequence of the gradual illumination of the human mind, that little may not hereafter be diminished.

And first we are to consider the different provisions that may be made for general administration; including, under the phrase general administration, all that shall be found necessary, of what has usually been denominated, legislative and executive power. Legislation has already appeared to be a term not applicable to human society.* Men cannot do more than declare and interpret law; nor can there be an authority so paramount as to have the prerogative of making that to be law which abstract and immutable justice had not made to be law previously to that interposition. But it might, notwithstanding this, be found necessary that there should be an authority empowered to declare those general principles, by which the equity of the community will be regulated, in particular cases upon which it may be compelled to decide. The question concerning the reality and extent of this necessity, it is proper to reserve for after consideration.† Executive power consists of two very distinct parts:

* Book III, Chap. V.
† Book VII, Chap. VIII.

general deliberations relative to particular emergencies, which, so far as practicability is concerned, may be exercised either by one individual or a body of individuals, such as peace and war, taxation,* and the selection of proper periods for convoking deliberative assemblies: and particular functions, such as those of financial detail, or minute superintendence, which cannot be exercised unless by one or a small number of persons.

In reviewing these several branches of authority, and considering the persons to whom they may be most properly confided, we cannot perhaps do better than adopt the ordinary distribution of forms of government into monarchy, aristocracy and democracy. Under each of these heads we may enquire into the merits of their respective principles, first absolutely, and upon the hypothesis of their standing singly for the whole administration; and secondly, in a limited view, upon the supposition of their constituting one branch only of the system of government. It is usually alike incident to them all, to confide the minuter branches of executive detail to inferior agents.

One thing more it is necessary to premise. The merits of each of the three heads I have enumerated are to be considered negatively. The corporate duties of mankind are the result of their irregularities and follies in their individual capacity. If they had no imperfection, or if men were so constituted, as to be sufficiently, and sufficiently early, corrected by persuasion alone, society would cease from its functions. Of consequence, of the three forms of government, and their compositions, that is the best which shall least impede the activity and application of our intellectual powers. It was in the recollection of this truth that I have preferred the term political institution to that of government, the former appearing

---

* I state the article of taxation as a branch of executive government, since it is not, like law or the declaration of law, a promulgating of some general principle, but is a temporary regulation for some particular emergence.

to be sufficiently expressive of that relative form, whatever it be, into which individuals would fall, when there was no need of force to direct them into their proper channel, and were no refractory members to correct.

CHAPTER II

OF EDUCATION, THE EDUCATION OF A PRINCE

> *Nature of monarchy delineated. – School of adversity. – Tendency of superfluity to inspire effeminacy – to deprive us of the benefit of experience – illustrated in the case of princes. – Manner in which they are addressed. – Inefficacy of the instruction bestowed upon them.*

FIRST then of monarchy; and we will first suppose the succession to the monarchy to be hereditary. In this case we have the additional advantage of considering this distinguished mortal who is thus set over the heads of the rest of his species from the period of his birth.

The abstract idea of a king is of an extremely momentous and extraordinary nature; and, though the idea has, by the accident of education, been rendered familiar to us from our infancy, yet perhaps the majority of readers can recollect the period when it struck them with astonishment, and confounded their powers of apprehension. It being sufficiently evident that some species of government was necessary, and that individuals must concede a part of that sacred and important privilege by which each man is constituted judge of his own words and actions, for the sake of general good, it was next requisite to consider what expedients might be substituted in the room of this original claim. One of these expedients has been monarchy. It was the interest of each individual that his individuality should be invaded as rarely as possible; that no invasion should be permitted to flow from wanton caprice, from sinister and disingenuous views, or from the instigation of anger, partiality and passion; and that this bank, severely levied upon the peculium of each member of the society, should be administered with frugality and discretion. It was therefore, without doubt, a very bold adventure to commit this precious deposit to the custody of a single man. If we contemplate the human powers, whether of body or mind, we shall find them much better suited to the superintendence of our private concerns, and to the administering occasional assistance to others, than to the accepting the formal trust, of superintending the affairs, and watching for the happiness of millions. If we recollect the physical and moral equality of mankind, it will appear a very violent usurpation upon this principle to place one individual at so vast an interval from the rest of his species. Let us then consider how such persons are usually educated, or may be expected to be educated, and how well they are prepared for this illustrious office.

It is a common opinion 'That adversity is the school in which all extraordinary virtue must be formed. Henry the fourth of France, and Elizabeth of England, experienced a long series of calamities before they were elevated to a throne. Alfred, of whom the obscure chronicles of a barbarous age record such superior virtues, passed through the vicissitudes of a vagabond and a fugitive. Even the mixed, and, upon the whole, the vicious, yet accomplished, characters of Frederic and Alexander were not formed without the interference of injustice and persecution.'

This hypothesis however seems to have been pushed too far. It is no more reasonable to suppose that virtue cannot be matured without injustice than to believe, which has been another prevailing opinion, that human happiness cannot be secured without imposture and deceit.*
Both these errors have a common source, a distrust of the omnipotence of truth. If their advocates had reflected

* Chap. XV.

more deeply upon the nature of the human mind, they would have perceived that all our voluntary actions are judgements of the understanding, and that actions of the most judicious and useful nature must infallibly flow from a real and genuine conviction of truth.

But, though the exaggerated opinion here stated, of the usefulness of adversity, be erroneous, it is, like many other of our errors, allied to important truth. If adversity be not necessary, it must be allowed that prosperity is pernicious. Not a genuine and philosophical prosperity, which requires no more than sound health with a sound intellect, the capacity of procuring for ourselves, by a moderate and well regulated industry, the means of subsistence, virtue and wisdom: but prosperity as it is usually understood, that is, a competence provided for us by the caprice of human institution, inviting our bodies to indolence, and our minds to lethargy; and still more prosperity, as it is understood in the case of noblemen and princes, that is, a superfluity of wealth, which deprives us of all intercourse with our fellow men upon equal terms, and makes us prisoners of state, gratified indeed with baubles and splendour, but shut out from the real benefits of society, and the perception of truth. If truth be so intrinsically powerful as to make adversity unnecessary to excite our attention to it, it is nevertheless certain that luxury and wealth have the most fatal effects in distorting it. If it require no foreign aid to assist its energies, we ought however to be upon our guard against principles and situations the tendency of which may be perpetually to counteract it.

Nor is this all. One of the most essential ingredients of virtue is fortitude. It was the plan of many of the Grecian philosophers, and most of all of Diogenes, to show to mankind how very limited is the supply that our necessities require, and how little dependent our real welfare and prosperity are upon the caprice of others. Among innumerable incidents upon record that illustrate this principle, a single one may suffice to suggest to our minds its general spirit. Diogenes had a slave whose name was Menas, and Menas thought proper upon some occasion to elope. 'Ha!' said the philosopher, 'can Menas live without Diogenes, and cannot Diogenes live without Menas?' There can be no lesson more important than that which is here conveyed. The man that does not know himself not to be at the mercy of other men, that does not feel that he is invulnerable to all the vicissitudes of fortune, is incapable of a constant and inflexible virtue. He to whom the rest of his species can reasonably look up with confidence must be firm, because his mind is filled with the excellence of the object he pursues; and cheerful, because he knows that it is out of the power of events to injure him. If anyone should choose to imagine that this idea of virtue is strained too high, yet all must allow that no man can be entitled to our confidence who trembles at every wind, who can endure no adversity, and whose very existence is linked to the artificial character he sustains. Nothing can more reasonably excite our contempt than a man who, if he were once reduced to the genuine and simple condition of man, would be driven to despair, and find himself incapable of consulting and providing for his own subsistence. Fortitude is a habit of mind that grows out of a sense of our independence. If there be a man who dares not even trust his own imagination with the fancied change of his circumstances, he must necessarily be effeminate; irresolute and temporizing. He that loves sensuality or ostentation better than virtue may be entitled to our pity, but a madman only would entrust to his disposal anything that was dear to him.

Again, the only means by which truth can be communicated to the human mind is through the inlet of the senses. It is perhaps impossible that a man shut up in a cabinet can ever be wise. If we would acquire knowledge, we must open our eyes, and contemplate the universe. Till we are acquainted with the meaning of terms, and the nature of the objects around us, we cannot understand the propositions that may be formed concerning them. Till we are acquainted with the nature of the objects around us, we cannot compare them with the principles we have formed, and understand the modes of employing them. There are other ways of attaining wisdom and ability beside the school of adversity, but there is no way of attaining them but through the medium of experience. That is, experience brings in the materials with which intellect works; for it must be granted that a man of limited experience will often be more capable than he who has gone through the greatest variety of scenes; or rather perhaps, that one man may collect more experience in a sphere of a few miles square than another who has sailed round the world.

To conceive truly the value of experience, we must recollect the numerous improvements the human mind has received, and how far an enlightened European differs from a solitary savage. However multifarious are these improvements, there are but two ways in which they can be appropriated by any individual; either at second hand by books and conversation, or at first hand by our own observations of men and things. The improvement we receive in the first of these modes is unlimited; but it will not do alone. We cannot understand books till we have seen the subjects of which they treat.

He that knows the mind of man must have observed it for himself; he that knows it most intimately must have observed it in its greatest variety of situations. He must have seen it without disguise, when no exterior situation puts a curb upon its passions, and induces the individual to exhibit a studied, not a spontaneous character. He must have seen men in their unguarded moments, when the eagerness of temporary resentment tips their tongue with fire, when they are animated and dilated by hope, when they are tortured and wrung with despair, when the soul pours out its inmost self into the bosom of an equal and a friend. Lastly, he must himself have been an actor in the scene, have had his own passions brought into play, have known the anxiety of expectation and the transport of success, or he will feel and understand about as much of what he sees as mankind in general would of the transactions of the vitrified inhabitants of the planet Mercury, or the salamanders that live in the sun. – Such is the education of the true philosopher, the genuine politician, the friend and benefactor of human kind.

What is the education of a prince? Its first quality is extreme tenderness. The winds of heaven are not permitted to blow upon him. He is dressed and undressed by his lacqueys and valets. His wants are carefully anticipated; his desires, without any effort of his, profusely supplied. His health is of too much importance to the community to permit him to exert any considerable effort either of body or mind. He must not hear the voice of reprimand or blame. In all things it is first of all to be remembered that he is a prince, that is, some rare and precious creature, but not of human kind.

As he is the heir to a throne, it is never forgotten by those about him that considerable importance is to be annexed to his favour or his displeasure. Accordingly, they never express themselves in his presence frankly and naturally, either respecting him or themselves. They are supporting a part. They play under a mask. Their own fortune and emolument is always uppermost in their minds, at the same time that they are anxious to appear generous, disinterested and sincere. All his caprices are to be complied with. All his gratifications are to be studied, They find him a depraved and sordid mortal; they judge of his appetites and capacities by their own; and the gratifications they recommend serve to sink him deeper in folly and vice.

What is the result of such an education? Having never experienced contradiction, the young prince is arrogant and presumptuous. Having always been accustomed to the slaves of necessity or the slaves of choice, he does not understand even the meaning of the word freedom. His temper is insolent, and impatient of parley and expostulation. Knowing nothing, he believes himself sovereignly informed, and runs headlong into danger, not from firmness and courage, but from the most egregious wilfulness and vanity. Like Pyrrho among the ancient philosophers, if his attendants were at a distance, and he trusted himself alone in the open air, he would perhaps be run over by the next coach, or fall down the first precipice. His violence and presumption are strikingly contrasted with the extreme timidity of his disposition. The first opposition terrifies him, the first difficulty, seen and understood, appears insuperable. He trembles at a shadow, and at the very semblance of adversity is dissolved into tears. It has accordingly been observed that princes are commonly superstitious beyond the rate of ordinary mortals.

Above all, simple, unqualified truth is a stranger to his ear. It either never approaches; or, if so unexpected a guest should once appear, it meets with so cold a reception as to afford little encouragement to a second visit. The longer he has been accustomed to falsehood and flattery, the more grating will it sound. The longer he has been accustomed to falsehood and flattery, the more terrible will the talk appear to him to change his tastes, and discard his favourites. He will either place a blind confidence in all men, or, having detected the insincerity of those who were most agreeable to him, will conclude that all men are knavish and designing. As a consequence of this last opinion, he will become indifferent to mankind, and callous to their sufferings, and will believe that even the virtuous are knaves under a craftier mask. Such is the education of an individual who is destined to superintend the affairs, and watch for the happiness, of millions.

In this picture are contained the features which most obviously constitute the education of a prince, into the conduct of which no person of energy and virtue has by accident been introduced. In real life it will be variously modified, but the majority of the features, unless in rare instances, will remain the same. In no case can the education of a friend and benefactor of human kind, as sketched in a preceding page, by any speculative contrivance be communicated.

Nor is there any difficulty in accounting for the universal miscarriage. The wisest preceptor, thus circumstanced, must labour under insuperable disadvantages. No situation can be so artificial as that of a prince, so difficult to be understood by him who occupies it, so irresistibly propelling the mind to mistake. The first ideas it suggests are of a tranquillizing and soporific nature. It fills him with the opinion of his secretly possessing some inherent advantage over the rest of his species, by which he is formed to command, and they to obey. If you assure him of the contrary, you can expect only an imperfect and temporary credit; for facts, when, as in this case, they are continually deposing against you, speak a language more emphatic and intelligible than words. If it were not as he supposes, why should everyone that approaches be eager to serve him? The sordid and selfish motives by which they are really actuated, he is very late in detecting. It may even be doubted whether the individual who was never led to put the professions of others to the test by his real wants, has, in any instance, been completely aware of the little credit that is usually due to them. A prince finds himself courted and adored long before he can have acquired a merit entitling him to such distinctions. By what arguments can you persuade him laboriously to pursue what appears so completely superfluous? How can you induce him to be dissatisfied with his present acquisitions, while every other person assures him that his accomplishments are admirable, and his mind a mirror of sagacity? How will you persuade him who finds all his wishes anticipated to engage in any arduous undertaking, or propose any distant object for his ambition?

But, even should you succeed in this, his pursuits may be expected to be either mischievous or useless. His understanding is distorted; and the basis of all morality, the recollection that other men are beings of the same order with himself, is extirpated. It would be unreasonable to expect from him anything generous and humane. Unfortunate as he is, his situation is continually propelling him to vice, and destroying the germs of integrity and virtue, before they are unfolded. If sensibility begin to discover itself, it is immediately poisoned by the blighting winds of flattery. Amusement and sensuality call with an imperious voice, and will not allow him time to feel. Artificial as is the character he fills, even should he aspire to fame, it will be by the artificial methods of false refinement, or the barbarous inventions of usurpation and conquest, not by the plain and unornamented road of benevolence.

Some idea of the methods usually pursued, and the effects produced in the education of a prince, may be collected from a late publication of madame de Genlis, in which she gives an account of her own proceedings in relation to the children of the duke of Orleans. She thus describes the features of their disposition and habits, at the time they were committed to her care. 'The duke de Valois (the eldest) is frequently coarse in his manners, and ignoble in his expressions. He finds great humour in calling mean and common objects by their most vulgar appellations; all this seasoned with the proverbial propensity of Sancho, and set off with a loud forced laugh. His prate is eternal, nor does he suspect but that it must be an exquisite gratification to anyone to be entertained with it; and he frequently heightens the jest by a falsehood uttered in the gravest manner imaginable. Neither he nor his brother has the least regard for anybody but themselves; they are selfish and grasping, considering everything that is done for them as their due, and imagining that they are in no respect obliged to consult the happiness of others. The slightest reproof is beyond measure shocking to them, and the indignation they conceive at it immediately vents itself in sullenness or tears. They are in an uncommon degree effeminate, afraid of the wind or the cold, unable to run or to leap, or even so much as to walk at a round pace, or for more than half an hour at a time. The duke de Valois has an extreme terror of dogs, to such a degree as to turn pale and shriek at the sight of one.' 'When the children of the duke of Orleans were committed to my care, they had been accustomed, in winter, to wear under-waistcoats, two pair of stockings, gloves, muffs, etc. The eldest, who was eight years of age, never came downstairs without being supported by the arm of one or two persons; the domestics were obliged to render them the meanest services, and, for a cold or any slight indisposition, sat up with them for nights together.'*

* 'M. de Valois a encore des manières bien désagréables, des expressions ignobles, et de tems en tems le plus mauvais ton. A présent qu'il est à son aise avec moi, il me débite avec confiance toutes les gentillesses qu'on lui a apprises. Tout cela assaisonné de tous les proverbes de Sancho, et d'un gros rire forcé, qui n'est pas le moindre de ses désagréments. En outre, il est très bavard, grand conteur, et il ment souvent pour se divertir; avec cela la plus grande indifférence pour M. et Mde de Chartres, n'y pensant jamais, les voyant froidement, ne désirant point les voir. – Ils étoient l'un et l'autre de la plus grande impolitesse, *oui* et *non* tout court, ou un signe de tête, peu reconnoissant, parce qu'ils croient qu'il n'est point de soins, d'attentions, ni d'égards qu'on ne les doive. Il n'étoit pas possible de les reprendre sans les mettre au désespoir; dans ce cas, toujours des pleurs ou de l'humeur. Ils étoient très douillets, craignant le vent, le froid, ne pouvant, non seulement ni courir ni sauter, mais même ni marcher d'un bon pas, et plus d'une demi-heure. Et M. le duc de Valois ayant une peur affreuse des chiens au point de pâlir et de crier quand il en voyoit un.'

'Quand on m'a remis ceux que j'ai élevés, ils avoient l'habitude de porter en hiver des gillets, des doubles paires de bas, des grands manchons, etc. L'aîné, qui avoit huit ans, ne descendoit jamais un escalier sans s'appuyer sur le bras d'une ou deux personnes. On obligeoit des domestiques de ces enfans à leur rendre les services les plus vils: pour un rhume, pour une légère incommodité, ces domestiques passoient sans cesse les nuits, etc.' *Leçons d'une Gouvernante a ses Elèves.* par Mde de Sillery Brulart (ci-devant comtesse de Genlis), Tome II.

Madame de Genlis, a woman of uncommon talents, though herself infected with a considerable number of errors, corrected these defects in the young princes. But few princes have the good fortune to be educated by a person of so much independence and firmness as madame de Genlis, and we may safely take our standard for the average calculation rather from her predecessors than herself. Even were it otherwise, we have already seen what it is that a preceptor can do in the education of a prince. Nor should it be forgotten that the children under her care were not of the class of princes who seemed destined to a throne.

CHAPTER III

PRIVATE LIFE OF A PRINCE

Principles by which he is influenced – irresponsibility – impatience of control – habits of dissipation – ignorance – dislike of truth – dislike of justice. – Pitiable situation of princes.

Such is the culture; the fruit that it produces may easily be conjectured. The fashion which is given to the mind in youth, it ordinarily retains in age; and it is with ordinary cases only that the present argument is concerned. If there have been kings, as there have been other men, in the forming of whom particular have outweighed general causes, the recollection of such exceptions has little to do with the question whether monarchy be, generally speaking, a benefit or an evil. Nature has no particular mould in which she forms the intellects of princes; monarchy is certainly not *jure divino*; and of consequence, whatever system we may adopt upon the subject of natural talents, the ordinary rate of kings will possess, at best, but the ordinary rate of human understanding. In what has been said, and in what remains to say, we are not to fix our minds upon prodigies, but to think of the species as it is usually found.

But, though education for the most part determines the character of the future man, it may not be useless to follow the disquisition a little further. Education, in one sense, is the affair of youth; but, in a stricter and more accurate sense, the education of an intellectual being can terminate only with his life. Every incident that befalls us, is the parent of a sentiment, and either confirms or counteracts the preconceptions of the mind.

Now the causes that acted upon kings in their minority continue to act upon them in their maturer years. Everything is carefully kept out of sight that may remind them they are men. Every means is employed which may persuade them that they are of a different species of beings, and subject to different laws of existence. 'A king,' such at least is the maxim of absolute monarchies, 'though obliged by a rigid system of duties, is accountable for his discharge of those duties only to God.' That is, exposed to a hundredfold more seductions than ordinary men, he has not, like them, the checks of a visible constitution of things, perpetually, through the medium of the senses, making their way to the mind. He is taught to believe himself superior to the restraints that bind ordinary men, and subject to a rule peculiarly his own. Everything is trusted to the motives of an invisible world; which, whatever may be the estimate to which they are entitled in the view of philosophy, mankind are not now to learn, are weakly felt by those who are immersed in splendour or affairs, and have little chance of success, in contending with the impressions of sense, and the allurements of visible objects.

It is a maxim generally received in the world, 'that every king is a despot in his heart', and the maxim can seldom fail to be verified in the experiment. A limited monarch, and an absolute monarch, though in many respects different, approach in more points than they separate. A monarch strictly without limitation is perhaps a phenomenon that never yet existed. All countries have possessed some check upon despotism, which, to their deluded imaginations, appeared a sufficient security for their independence. All kings have possessed such a portion of luxury and ease, have been so far surrounded with servility and falsehood, and to such a degree exempt from personal responsibility, as to destroy the natural and wholesome complexion of the human mind. Being placed so high, they find but one step between them and the summit of social authority, and they cannot but eagerly desire to pass that step. Having so frequent occasions of seeing their commands implicitly obeyed, being trained in so long a scene of adulation and servility, it is impossible they should not feel some indignation at the honest firmness that sets limits to their omnipotence. But to say, 'that every king is a despot in his heart' will presently be shown to be the same thing as to say, that every king is, by unavoidable necessity, the enemy of the human race.

The principal source of virtuous conduct is to recollect the absent. He that takes into his estimate present things alone will be the perpetual slave of sensuality and selfishness. He will have no principle by which to restrain appetite, or to employ himself in just and benevolent pursuits. The cause of virtue and innocence, however urgent, will no sooner cease to be heard than it will be forgotten. Accordingly, nothing is found more favourable to the attainment of moral excellence than meditation: nothing more hostile than an uninterrupted succession of amusements. It would be absurd to expect from kings the recollection of virtue in exile or disgrace. It has generally been observed that, even for the loss of a flatterer or a favourite, they speedily console themselves. Image after image so speedily succeed in their sensorium that no one leaves a durable impression. A circumstance which contributes to this moral insensibility is the effeminacy and cowardice which grow out of perpetual indulgence. Their minds irresistibly shrink from painful ideas, from motives

that would awaken them to effort, and reflections that
demand severity of disquisition.

What situation can be more unfortunate than that of a
stranger who cannot speak our language,[33] knows nothing
of our manners and customs, and enters into the busy
scene of our affairs, without one friend to advise with or
assist him? If anything is to be got by such a man, we may
depend upon seeing him instantly surrounded with a
group of thieves, sharpers and extortioners. They will
impose upon him the most incredible stories, will overreach him in every article of his necessities or his commerce, and he will leave the country at last as unfriended,
and in as absolute ignorance, as he entered it. Such a
stranger is a king; but with this difference, that the
foreigner, if he be a man of sagacity and penetration, may
make his way through this crowd of intruders, and discover a set of persons worthy of his confidence, which
can scarcely in any case happen to a king. He is placed in
a sphere peculiarly his own. He is surrounded with an
atmosphere through which it is impossible for him to discover the true colours and figure of things. The persons
that are near him are in a cabal and conspiracy of their
own; and there is nothing about which they are more
anxious than to keep truth from approaching him. The
man who is not accessible to every comer, who delivers up
his person into the custody of another, and may, for anything that he can tell, be precluded from that very intercourse and knowledge it is most important for him to
possess, whatever name he may bear, is, in reality, a
prisoner.

Whatever the arbitrary institutions of men may pretend, the more powerful institutions of our nature forbid
one man to transact the affairs and provide for the welfare
of millions. A king soon finds the necessity of entrusting
his functions to the administration of his servants. He
acquires the habit of seeing with their eyes, and acting
with their hands. He finds the necessity of confiding implicitly in their fidelity. Like a man long shut up in a

dungeon, his organs are not strong enough to bear the irradiation of truth. Accustomed to receive information of the feelings and sentiments of mankind, through the medium of another, he cannot bear directly to converse with business and affairs. Whoever would detach his confidence from his present favourites, and induce him to pass over again, in scrutiny, the principles and data which he has already adopted, requires of him too painful a task. He hastens from his adviser, to communicate the accusation to his favourite; and the tongue that has been accustomed to gain credit easily varnishes over this new discovery. He flies from uncertainty, anxiety and doubt, to his routine of amusements; or amusement presents itself, is importunate to be received, and presently obliterates the tale that overspread his mind with melancholy and suspicion. Much has been said of intrigue and duplicity. They have been alleged to intrude themselves into the walks of commerce, to haunt the intercourse of men of letters, and to rend the petty concerns of a village with faction. But, wherever else they may be strangers, in courts they undoubtedly find a congenial climate. The intrusive tale-bearer, who carries knowledge to the ear of kings, is, within that circle, an object of general abhorrence. The favourite marks him for his victim; and the inactive and unimpassioned temper of the monarch soon resigns him to the vindictive importunity of his adversary. It is in the contemplation of these circumstances that Fénelon has remarked that 'kings are the most unfortunate and the most misled of all human beings'.*

But, in reality, were they in possession of purer sources of information, it would be to little purpose. Royalty inevitably allies itself to vice. Virtue, in proportion as it has taken possession of any character, is just, consistent and

* 'Les plus malheureux & les plus aveugles de tous les hommes.' *Télémaque*, Liv. XIII. More forcible and impressive description is scarcely anywhere to be found than that of the evils inseparable from monarchical government contained in this and the following book of Fénelon's work.

sincere. But kings, debauched from their birth, and ruined by their situation, cannot endure an intercourse with these attributes. Sincerity, that would tell them of their errors, and remind them of their cowardice; justice, that, uninfluenced by the trappings of majesty, would estimate the man at his true desert; consistency, that no temptation would induce to part with its integrity; are odious and intolerable in their eyes. From such intruders, they hasten to men of a pliant character, who will flatter their mistakes, put a varnish on their actions, and be visited by no scruples in assisting the indulgence of their appetites. There is scarcely in human nature an inflexibility that can resist perpetual flattery and compliance. The virtues that grow up among us are cultured in the open foil of equality, not in the artificial climate of greatness. We need the winds to harden as much as the heat to cherish us. Many a mind that promised well in its outset has been found incapable to stand the test of perpetual indulgence and ease, without one shock to waken, and one calamity to stop it in its smooth career.

Monarchy is, in reality, so unnatural an institution that mankind have, at all times, strongly suspected it was unfriendly to their happiness. The power of truth, upon important topics, is such that it may rather be said to be obscured than obliterated; and falsehood has scarcely ever been so successful as not to have had a restless and powerful antagonist in the heart of its votaries. The man who with difficulty earns his scanty subsistence cannot behold the ostentatious splendour of a king without being visited by some sense of injustice. He inevitably questions, in his mind, the utility of an officer whose services are hired at so enormous a price. If he consider the subject with any degree of accuracy, he is led to perceive, and that with sufficient surprise, that a king is nothing more than a common mortal, exceeded by many, and equalled by more, in every requisite of strength, capacity and virtue. He feels therefore that nothing can be more groundless and unjust than the supposing that one such man as this is the fittest and most competent instrument for regulating the affairs of nations.

These reflections are so unavoidable that kings themselves have often been aware of the danger to their imaginary happiness with which they are pregnant. They have sometimes been alarmed with the progress of thinking, and oftener regarded the ease and prosperity of their subjects as a source of terror and apprehension. They justly consider their functions as a sort of public exhibition, the success of which depends upon the credulity of the spectators, and which good sense and courage would speedily bring to contempt. Hence the well known maxims of monarchical government, that ease is the parent of rebellion; and that it is necessary to keep the people in a state of poverty and endurance, in order to render them submissive. Hence it has been the perpetual complaint of despotism that 'the restive knaves are overrun with ease, and plenty ever is the nurse of faction'.* Hence it has been the lesson perpetually read to monarchs: 'Render your subjects prosperous, and they will speedily refuse to labour; they will become stubborn, proud, unsubmissive to the yoke, and ripe for revolt. It is impotence and penury alone that will render them supple, and prevent them from rebelling against the dictates of authority.'†

It is a common and vulgar observation that the state of a king is greatly to be pitied. 'All his actions are hemmed in with anxiety and doubt. He cannot, like other men, indulge the gay and careless hilarity of his mind; but is obliged, if he be of an honest and conscientious disposition, to consider how necessary the time which he is thoughtlessly giving to amusement may be to the relief of a worthy and oppressed individual; how many benefits

---

* *Jane Shore*, Act III.

† 'Si vous mettez les peuples dans l'abondance, ils ne travailleront plus, ils deviendront fiers, indociles, et seront toujours prêt à se revolter: il n'y a que la foiblesse et la misère qui les rendent souples, et qui les empêchent de résister à l'autorité.' *Télémaque*, Liv. XIII.

might, in a thousand instances, result from his interference; how many a guileless and undesigning heart
might be cheered by his justice. The conduct of kings is
a subject for the severest criticism which the nature of
their situation disables them to encounter. A thousand
things are done in their name in which they have no participation; a thousand stories are so disguised to their
ear as to render the truth undiscoverable; and the king
is the general scape-goat, loaded with the offences of all
his dependents.'

No picture can be more just, judicious and humane
than that which is thus exhibited. Why then should the
advocates of antimonarchical principles be considered as
the enemies of kings? They would relieve them from 'a
load would sink a navy, too much honour'.* They would
exalt them to the happy and enviable condition of private
individuals. In reality, nothing can be more iniquitous
and cruel than to impose upon a man the unnatural
office of a king. It is not less inequitable towards him that
exercises it than towards them who are subjected to it.
Kings, if they understood their own interests, would be
the first to espouse these principles, the most eager to
listen to them, the most fervent in expressing their esteem
of the men who undertake to impress upon their species
this important truth.

* Shakespeare: *Henry the Eighth*, Act III.

CHAPTER IV

OF A VIRTUOUS DESPOTISM

Supposed excellence of this form of government controverted — from the narrowness of human powers. — Case of a vicious administration — of a virtuous administration intended to be formed. — Monarchy not adapted to the government of large states.

THERE is a principle, frequently maintained upon this subject,* which is entitled to impartial consideration. It is granted, by those who espouse it, 'that absolute monarchy, from the imperfection of those by whom it is administered, is, for the most part, productive of evil'; but they assert, 'that it is the best and most desirable of all forms under a good and virtuous prince. It is exposed,' say they, 'to the fate of all excellent natures, and, from the best thing, frequently, if corrupted, becomes the worst.' This remark is certainly not very decisive of the general question, so long as any weight shall be attributed to the arguments which have been adduced to evince what sort of character and disposition may be ordinarily expected in princes. It may however be allowed, if true, to create in the mind of a sort of partial retrospect to this happy and perfect despotism; and, if it can be shown to be false, it will render the argument for the abolition of monarchy, so far as it is concerned, more entire and complete.

Now, whatever dispositions any man may possess in favour of the welfare of others, two things are necessary to give them validity; discernment and power. I can promote the welfare of a few persons, because I can be sufficiently informed of their circumstances. I can promote the welfare of many in certain general articles, because, for this purpose, it is only necessary that I should be informed of the nature of the human mind as such, not of

* See *Tom Jones*, Book XII, Chap. XII.

the personal situation of the individuals concerned. But for one man to undertake to administer the affairs of millions, to supply, not general principles and perspicuous reasoning, but particular application, and measures adapted to the necessities of the moment, is of all undertakings the most extravagant and absurd.

The most simple and obvious system of practical administration is for each man to be the arbiter of his own concerns. If the imperfection, the narrow views, and the mistakes of human beings, render this, in certain cases, inexpedient and impracticable, the next resource is to call in the opinion of his peers, persons who, from their vicinity, may be presumed to have some general knowledge of the case, and who have leisure and means minutely to investigate the merits of the question. It cannot reasonably be doubted that the same expedient which is resorted to in our civil and criminal concerns would, by plain and uninstructed mortals, be adopted in the assessment of taxes, in the deliberations of commerce, and in every other article in which their common interests were involved, only generalizing the deliberative assembly, or panel, in proportion to the generality of the question to be decided.

Monarchy, instead of referring every question to the persons concerned or their neighbours, refers it to a single individual, placed at the greatest distance possible from the ordinary members of the society. Instead of distributing the causes to be judged into as many parcels as convenience would admit, for the sake of providing leisure and opportunities of examination, it draws them to a single centre, and renders enquiry and examination impossible. A despot, however virtuously disposed, is obliged to act in the dark, to derive his knowledge from other men's information, and to execute his decisions by other men's instrumentality. Monarchy seems to be a species of government proscribed by the nature of man; and those persons who furnished their despot with integrity and virtue forgot to add omniscience and omnipotence, qualities not less necessary to fit him for the office they had provided.

Let us suppose this honest and incorruptible despot to be served by ministers, avaricious, hypocritical and interested. What will the people gain by the good intentions of their monarch? He will mean them the greatest benefits, but he will be altogether unacquainted with their situation, their character and their wants. The information he receives will frequently be the very reverse of the truth. He will be taught that one individual is highly meritorious, and a proper subject of reward, whose only merit is the profligate servility with which he has fulfilled the purposes of his administration. He will be taught that another is the pest of the community, who is indebted for this report to the steady virtue with which he has traversed and defeated the wickedness of government. He will mean the greatest benefits to his people; but, when he prescribes something calculated for their advantage; his servants, under pretence of complying, shall, in reality, perpetrate diametrically the reverse. Nothing will be more dangerous than to endeavour to remove the obscurity with which his ministers surround him. The man who attempts so hardy a task will become the incessant object of their hatred. However incorruptible may be the justice of the sovereign, the time will come when his observation will be laid asleep, while malice and revenge are ever vigilant. Could he unfold the secrets of his prison-houses of state, he would find men committed in his name whose crimes he never knew, whose names he never heard of, perhaps men whom he honoured and esteemed. Such is the history of the benevolent and philanthropic despots whom memory has recorded; and the conclusion from the whole is that, wherever despotism exists, there it will always be attended with the evils of despotism, capricious measures and arbitrary infliction.

'But will not a wise king provide himself with good and virtuous servants?' Undoubtedly he will effect a part of this, but he cannot supersede the nature of things. He that executes an office as a deputy will never discharge it in the same spirit, as if he were the principal. Either the minister must be the author of the plans which he carries into effect, and then it is of little consequence, except so far as relates to his integrity in the choice of his servants, what sort of mortal the sovereign shall be found or he must play a subordinate part, and then it is impossible to transfuse into his mind the perspicacity and energy of his master. Wherever despotism exists, it can remain in a single hand, but must be transmitted whole and entire through the progressive links of authority. To render despotism auspicious and benign, it is necessary, not only that the sovereign should possess every human excellence, but that all his officers should be men of penetrating genius and unspotted virtue. If they fall short of this, they will, like the ministers of Elizabeth, be sometimes specious profligates,* and sometimes men who, however admirably adapted for the technical emergencies of business, consult, on many occasions exclusively, their private advantage, worship the rising sun, enter into vindictive cabals, and cuff down new-fledged merit.† Wherever the continuity is broken, the flood of vice will bear down all before it. One weak or disingenuous man will be the source of unbounded mischief.

Another position, not less generally asserted than the desirableness of a virtuous despotism, is 'that republicanism is a species of government practicable only in a small state, while monarchy is best fitted to embrace the concerns of a vast and flourishing empire'‡ The reverse of this, so far at least as relates to monarchy, appears at first sight to be the truth. The competence of any government cannot be measured by a purer standard than the extent and accuracy of its information. In this respect monarchy appears in all cases to be wretchedly deficient;

---

* Dudley earl of Leicester.

† Cecil earl of Salisbury, lord treasurer; Howard earl of Nottingham, lord admiral, etc.

‡ Paine's *Letter to the Republican.*

but, if it can ever be admitted, it must surely be in those narrow and limited instances where an individual can, with least absurdity, be supposed to be acquainted with the affairs and interests of the whole.

CHAPTER V

OF COURTS AND MINISTERS

Systematical monopoly of confidence. – Charac-
ter of ministers and their dependents. –
Dupliciy of courts. – Venality and corruption.
– Universality of this principle.

WE shall be better enabled to judge of the dispositions with which information is communicated, and measures are executed, in monarchical countries, if we reflect upon another of the ill consequences attendant upon this species of government, the existence and corruption of courts.

The character of this, as well as of every other human institution, arises out of the circumstances with which it is surrounded. Ministers and favourites are a sort of people who have a state prisoner in their custody, the whole management of whose understanding and actions they can easily engross. This they completely effect with a weak and credulous master, nor can the most cautious and penetrating entirely elude their machinations. They unavoidably desire to continue in the administration of his functions, whether it be emolument, or the love of homage, or any more generous motive, by which they are attached to it. But, the more they are confided in by the sovereign, the greater will be the permanence of their situation; and, the more exclusive is their possession of his ear, the more implicit will be his confidence. The wisest of mortals are liable to error; the most-judicious projects are open to specious and superficial objections; and it can rarely happen but a minister will find his ease and security in excluding, as much as possible, other and opposite advisers, whose acuteness and ingenuity are perhaps additionally whetted by a desire to succeed to his office.

Ministers become a sort of miniature kings in their turn. Though they have the greatest opportunity of observing the impotence and unmeaningness of the character, they envy it. It is their trade perpetually to extol the dignity and importance of the master they serve; and men cannot long anxiously endeavour to convince others of the truth of any proposition without becoming half convinced of it themselves. They feel themselves dependent for all that they most ardently desire, upon this man's arbitrary will; but a sense of inferiority is perhaps the never failing parent of emulation or envy. They assimilate themselves therefore, of choice, to a man to whose circumstances their own are considerably similar.

In reality the requisites without which monarchical government cannot be preserved in existence are by no means sufficiently supplied by the mere intervention of ministers. There must be the ministers of ministers, and a long beadroll of subordination, descending by tedious and complicated steps. Each of these lives on the smile of the minister, as he lives on the smile of the sovereign. Each of these has his petty interests to manage, and his empire to employ under the guise of servility. Each imitates the vices of his superior, and exacts from others the adulation he is obliged to pay.

It has already appeared that a king is necessarily, and almost unavoidably, a despot in his heart.* He has been used to hear those things only which were adapted to give him pleasure; and it is with a grating and uneasy sensation that he listens to communications of a different sort. He has been used to unhesitating compliance; and it is with difficulty he can digest expostulation and opposition. Of consequence the honest and virtuous character, whose principles are clear and unshaken, is least qualified

* p. 22.

for his service; he must either explain away the severity of his principles, or he must give place to a more crafty and temporizing politician. The temporizing politician expects the same pliability in others that he exhibits in himself; and the fault which he can least forgive is an ill timed an inauspicious scrupulosity.

Expecting this compliance from all the coadjutors and instruments of his designs, he soon comes to set it up as a standard by which to judge of the merit of other men. He is deaf to every recommendation but that of a fitness for the secret service of government, or a tendency to promote his interest, and extend the sphere of his influence. The worst man, with this argument in his favour, will seem worthy of encouragement; the best man, who has no advocate but virtue to plead for him, will be treated with superciliousness and neglect. The genuine criterion of human desert can scarcely indeed be superseded and reversed. But it will appear to be reversed, and appearance will produce many of the effects of reality. To obtain honour, it will be thought necessary to pay a servile court to administration, to bear, with unaltered patience, their contumely and scorn, to flatter their vices, and render ourselves useful to their private gratification. To obtain honour, it will be thought necessary, by assiduity and intrigue, to make ourselves a party, to procure the recommendation of lords, and the good word of women of pleasure, and clerks in office. To obtain honour, it will be thought necessary to merit disgrace. The whole scene conflicts in hollowness, duplicity and falsehood. The minister speaks fair to the man he despises, and the slave pretends a generous attachment, while he thinks of nothing but his personal interest. That these principles are interspersed, under the worst governments, with occasional deviations into better, it would be folly to deny; that they do not form the great prevailing features, wherever a court and a monarch are to be found, it would be madness to assert.

There is one feature above all others which has never

escaped the most superficial delineator of the manners of a court; I mean the profound dissimulation which is there cultivated. The minister has, in the first place, to deceive the sovereign, continually to pretend to feel whatever his master feels, to ingratiate himself by an uniform insincerity, and to make a show of the most unreserved affection and attachment. His next duty, is to cheat his dependents and the candidates for office; to keep them in a perpetual fever of desire and expectation. Recollect the scene of a ministerial levee. To judge by the external appearance, we should suppose this to be the chosen seat of disinterested kindness. All that is erect and decisive in man is shamelessly surrendered. No professions of submission can be so base, no forms of adulation so extravagant, but that they are eagerly practised by these voluntary prostitutes. Yet it is notorious that, in this scene above all others, hatred has fixed its dwelling; jealousy rankles in every breast; and the most of its personages would rejoice in the opportunity of ruining each other for ever. Here it is that promises, protestations and oaths are so wantonly multiplied as almost to have lost their meaning. There is scarcely a man so weak as, when he has received a court promise, not to tremble, lest it should be found as false and unsubstantial by him, as it has proved to so many others.

At length, by the constant practice of dissimulation, the true courtier comes to be unable to distinguish, among his own sentiments, the pretended from the real. He arrives at such proficiency in his art as to have neither passions nor attachments. Personal kindness, and all consideration for the merit of others, are swallowed up in a narrow and sordid ambition; not that generous ambition for the esteem of mankind, which reflects a sort of splendour upon vice itself, but an ambition of selfish gratification and illiberal intrigue. Such a man has bid a long farewell to every moral restraint, and thinks his purposes cheaply promoted by the sacrifice of honour, sincerity and justice. His chief study and greatest boast are to be impenetrable; that no man shall be able to discover what he designs; that, though you discourse with him for ever, he shall constantly elude your detection. Consummate in his art, he will often practise it without excuse or necessity. Thus history records her instances of the profuse kindness and endearment with which monarchs have treated those they had already resolved to destroy. A gratuitous pride seems to have been placed in exhibiting the last refinement of profligacy and deceit. Ministers of this character are the mortal enemies of virtue in others. A cabal of such courtiers is in the utmost degree deadly. They destroy by secret ways that give no warning, and leave no trace. If they have to do with a blunt, just man who knows no disguise, or a generous spirit that scorns to practise dissimulation and artifice, they mark him their certain victim. No good or liberal character can escape their machinations; and the immorality of the court, which throws into shade all other wickedness, spreads its contagion through the land, and emasculates the sentiments of the most populous nation.

A fundamental disadvantage in monarchical government is that it renders things of the most essential importance, subject, through successive gradations, to the caprice of individuals. The suffrage of a body of electors will always bear a resemblance, more or less remote, to the public sentiment. The suffrage of an individual will depend upon caprice, personal convenience or pecuniary corruption. If the king be himself inaccessible to injustice, if the minister disdain a bribe, yet the fundamental evil remains, that kings and ministers, fallible themselves, must, upon a thousand occasions, depend upon the recommendation of others. Who will answer for these, through all their classes, officers of state, and deputies of office, humble friends, and officious valets, wives and daughters, concubines and confessors?

It is supposed by many that the existence of permanent hereditary distinction is necessary to the maintenance of order, among beings so imperfect as the human species.

But it is allowed by all that permanent hereditary distinction is a fiction of policy, not an ordinance of immutable truth. Wherever it exists, the human mind, so far as relates to political society, is prevented from settling upon its true foundation. There is a constant struggle between the genuine sentiments of the understanding, which tell us that all this is an imposition, and the imperious voice of government, which bids us, Reverence and obey. In this unequal contest, alarm and apprehension will perpetually haunt the minds of those who exercise usurped power. In this artificial state of man, powerful engines must be employed to prevent him from rising to his true level. It is the business of the governors to persuade the governed that it is their interest to be slaves. They have no other means by which to create this fictitious interest but those which they derive from the perverted understandings, and burdened property, of the public, to be returned in titles, ribands and bribes. Hence that system of universal corruption without which monarchy could not exist.

It has sometimes been supposed that corruption is particularly incident to a mixed government. 'In such a government the people possess a portion of freedom; privilege finds its place as well as prerogative; a certain sturdiness of manner, and consciousness of independence, are the natives of these countries. The country-gentleman will not abjure the dictates of his judgement without a valuable consideration. There is here more than one road to success; popular favour is as sure a means of advancement as courtly patronage. In despotic countries the people may be driven like sheep: however unfortunate is their condition, they know no other, and they submit to it as an inevitable calamity. Their characteristic feature is a torpid dullness, in which all the energies of man are forgotten. But, in a country calling itself free, the minds of the inhabitants are in a perturbed and restless state, and extraordinary means must be employed to calm their vehemence.' It has sometimes happened to men whose hearts have been pervaded with the love of virtue, of which pecuniary prostitution is the most odious corruption, to prefer, while they have contemplated this picture, an acknowledged despotism to a state of specious and imperfect liberty.

But the picture is not accurate. As much of it as relates to a mixed government must be acknowledged to be true. But the features of despotism are too favourably touched. Whether privilege be conceded by the forms of the constitution or no, a whole nation cannot be kept ignorant of its force. No people were ever yet so sunk in stupidity as to imagine one man, because he bore the appellation of a king, literally equal to a million. In a whole nation, as monarchical nations at least must be expected to be constituted, there will be nobility and yeomanry, rich and poor. There will be persons who, by their situation, their wealth, or their talents, form a middle rank between the monarch and the vulgar, and who, by their confederacies and their intrigues, can hold the throne in awe. These men must be bought or defied. There is no disposition that clings so close to despotism as incessant terror and alarm. What else gave birth to the armies of spies, and the numerous state prisons, under the old government of France? The eye of the tyrant is never closed. How numerous are the precautions and jealousies that these terrors dictate? No man can go out or come into the country, but he is watched. The press must issue no productions that have not the imprimatur of government. All coffee houses, and places of public resort, are objects of attention. Twenty people cannot be collected together, unless for the purposes of superstition, but it is immediately suspected that they may be conferring about their rights. Is it to be supposed that, where the means of jealousy are employed, the means of corruption will be forgotten? Were it so indeed, the case would not be much improved. No picture can be more disgustful, no state of mankind more depressing, that that in which a whole nation is held in obedience by the mere operation of fear, in which all that is most eminent among them, and that should give example to the rest, is prevented, under the severest penalties, from expressing its real sentiments, and, by necessary consequence, from forming any sentiments that are worthy to be expressed. But, in reality, fear was never the only instrument employed for these purposes. No tyrant was ever so unsocial as to have no confederates in his guilt. This monstrous edifice will always be found supported by all the various instruments for perverting the human character, severity, menaces, blandishments, professions and bribes. To this it is, in a great degree, owing that monarchy is so costly an establishment. It is the business of the despot to distribute his lottery of seduction into as many prizes as possible. Among the consequences of a pecuniary polity these are to be reckoned the foremost that every man is supposed to have his price, and that, the corruption being managed in an underhand manner, many a man who appears a patriot may be really a hireling; by which means virtue itself is brought into discredit, is either regarded as mere folly and romance, or observed with doubt and suspicion, as the cloak of vices, which are only the more humiliating the more they are concealed.

CHAPTER VI

OF SUBJECTS

Monarchy founded in imposture. – Kings not entitled to superiority – inadequate to the functions they possess. – Means by which the imposture is maintained – 1. splendour – 2. exaggeration. – This imposture generates – 1. indifference to merit – 2. indifference to truth – 3. artificial desires – 4. pusillanimity. – Moral incredulity of monarchical countries. – Injustice of luxury – of the inordinate admiration of wealth.

LET us proceed to consider the moral effects which the institution of monarchical government is calculated to produce upon the inhabitants of the countries in which it flourishes. And here it must be laid down as a first principle that monarchy is founded in imposture. It is false that kings are entitled to the eminence they obtain. They possess no intrinsic superiority over their subjects. The line of distinction that is drawn is the offspring of pretence, an indirect means employed for effecting certain purposes, and not the language of truth. It tramples upon the genuine nature of things, and depends for its support upon this argument, 'that, were it not for impositions of a similar nature, mankind would be miserable'.

Secondly, it is false that kings can discharge the functions of royalty. They pretend to superintend the affairs of millions, and they are necessarily unacquainted with these affairs. The senses of kings are constructed like those of other men: they can neither see nor hear what is transacted in their absence. They pretend to administer the affairs of millions, and they possess no such supernatural powers, as should enable them to act at a distance. They are nothing of what they would persuade us to believe them. The king is often ignorant of that of which half the inhabitants of his dominions are informed.

His prerogatives are administered by others, and the lowest clerk in office is frequently, to this and that individual, more effectually the sovereign than the king himself. He is wholly unacquainted with what is solemnly transacted in his name.

To conduct this imposture with success, it is necessary to bring over to its party our eyes and our ears. Accordingly kings are always exhibited with all the splendour of ornament, attendance and equipage. They live amidst a sumptuousness of expense; and this, not merely to gratify their appetites but as a necessary instrument of policy. The most fatal opinion that could lay hold upon the minds of their subjects is that kings are but men. Accordingly, they are carefully withdrawn from the profaneness of vulgar inspection; and, when they are shown to the public, it is with every artifice that may dazzle our sense, and mislead our judgement.

The imposture does not stop with our eyes, but address itself to our ears. Hence the inflated style of regal formality. The name of the king everywhere obtrudes itself upon us. It would seem as if everything in the country, the lands, the houses, the furniture, and the inhabitants, were his property. Our estates are the king's dominions. Our bodies and minds are his subjects. Our representatives are his parliament. Our courts of law are his deputies. All magistrates, throughout the realm, are the king's officers. His name occupies the foremost place in all statutes and decrees. He is the prosecutor of every criminal. He is 'Our Sovereign Lord the King'. Were it possible that he should die, 'the fountain of our blood, the means by which we live', would be gone: every political function would be suspended. It is therefore one of the fundamental principles of monarchical government that 'the king cannot die'. Our moral principles accommodate themselves to our veracity: and, accordingly, the sum of our political duties (the most important of all duties) is loyalty; to be true and faithful to the king; to honour a man whom, it may be, we ought to despise; and to obey; that is, to convert our shame into our pride, and to be ostentatious of the surrender of our own understandings. The morality of adults in this situation is copied from the basest part of the morality sometimes taught to children; and the perfection of virtue is placed in blind compliance and unconditional submission.

What must be the effects of this machine upon the moral principles of mankind? Undoubtedly we cannot trifle with the principles of morality and truth with impunity. However gravely the imposture may be carried on, it is impossible but that the real state of the case should be strongly suspected. Man in a state of society, if undebauched by falsehoods like these, which confound the nature of right and wrong, is not ignorant of what it is in which merits consists. He knows that one man is not superior to another, except so far as he is wiser or better. Accordingly these are the distinctions to which he aspires for himself. These are the qualities he honours and applauds in another, and which therefore the feelings of each man instigate his neighbours to acquire. But what a revolution is introduced among these original and undebauched sentiments by the arbitrary distinctions which monarchy engenders? We still retain in our minds the standard of merit: but it daily grows more feeble and powerless; we are persuaded to think that it is of no real use in the transactions of the world, and presently lay it aside as Utopian and visionary.

Nor is this the whole of the injurious consequences produced by the hyperbolical pretensions of monarchy. There is a simplicity in truth'that refuses alliance with this impudent mysticism. No man is entirely ignorant of the nature of man. He will not indeed be incredulous to a degree of energy and rectitude that may exceed the standard of his preconceived ideas. But for one man to pretend to think and act for a nation of his fellows is so preposterous as to set credibility at defiance. Is he persuaded that the imposition is salutary? He willingly assumes the right of introducing similar falsehoods into his private affairs. He becomes convinced that veneration for truth is to be classed among our errors and prejudices, and that, so far from being, as it pretends to be, in all cases salutary, it would lead, if ingenuously practised, to the destruction of mankind.

Again, if kings were exhibited simply as they are in themselves to the inspection of mankind, the 'salutary prejudice', as it has been called,* which teaches us to venerate them would speedily be extinct: it has therefore been found necessary to surround them with luxury and expense. Thus luxury and expense are made the standard of honour, and of consequence the topics of anxiety and envy. However fatal this sentiment may be to the morality and happiness of mankind, it is one of those illusions which monarchical government is eager to cherish. In reality, the first principle of virtuous feeling, as has been elsewhere said,† is the love of independence. He that would be just must, before all things, estimate the objects about him at their true value. But the principle in regal states has been to think your father the wisest of men, because he is your father,‡ and your king the foremost of his species because he is a king. The standard of intellectual merit is no longer the man, but his title. To be drawn in a coach of state by eight milk-white horses is the highest of all human claims to our veneration. The same principle inevitably runs through every order of the state, and men desire wealth under a monarchical government

* Burke's Reflection. † p. 413.

‡ 'The persons whom you ought to love infinitely more than me are those to whom you are indebted for your existence.' 'Their conduct ought to regulate yours and be the standard of your sentiments.' 'The respect we owe to our father and mother is a sort of *worship*, as the phrase *filial piety* implies.' 'Ce que vous devez aimer avant moi sans aucune comparaison, ce sont ceux à qui vous devez la vie.' 'Leur conduite doit régler la vôtre et fixer votre opinion.' 'Le respect que nous devons à notre père et a notre mère est un *culte*, comme l'exprime le mot *piété filiale*.' *Leçons d'une Gouvernante*, Tome I.

for the same reason that, under other circumstances, they would have desired virtue.

Let us suppose an individual who by severe labour earns a scanty subsistence, to become, by accident or curiosity, a spectator of the pomp of a royal progress. Is it possible that he should not mentally apostrophize this elevated mortal, and ask, 'What has made thee to differ from me?' If no such sentiment pass through his mind, it is a proof that the corrupt institutions of society have already divested him of all sense of justice. The more simple and direct is his character, the more certainly will these sentiments occur. What answer shall we return to his enquiry? That the well being of society requires men to be treated otherwise than according to their intrinsic merit? Whether he be satisfied with this answer or no, will he not aspire to possess that (which in this instance is wealth) to which the policy of mankind has annexed such high distinction? Is it not indispensable that, before he believes in the rectitude of this institution, his original feelings of right and wrong should be wholly reversed? If it be indispensable, then let the advocate of the monarchical system ingenuously declare that, according to that system, the interest of society, in the first instance, requires the subversion of all principles of moral truth and justice.

With this view let us again recollect the maxim adopted in monarchical countries, 'that the king never dies'. Thus, with true oriental extravagance, we salute this imbecile mortal, 'O king, live for ever!' Why do we this? Because upon his existence the existence of the state depends. In his name the courts of law are opened. If his political capacity be suspended for a moment, the centre to which all public business is linked is destroyed. In such countries everything is uniform: the ceremony is all, and the substance nothing. In the riots in the year 1780, the mace of the house of lords was proposed to be sent into the passages, by the terror of its appearance to quiet the confusion but it was observed that, if the mace should be

rudely detained by the rioters, the whole would be
thrown into anarchy. Business would be at a stand; their
insignia, and, with their insignia, their legislative and
deliberative functions would be gone. Who can expect
firmness and energy in a country where everything is
made to depend, not upon justice, public interest and
reason, but upon a piece of gilded wood? What conscious
dignity and virtue can there be among a people who, if
deprived of the imaginary guidance of one vulgar mortal,
are taught to believe that their faculties are benumbed,
and all their joints unstrung?

Lastly, one of the most essential ingredients in a virtuous character is undaunted firmness; and nothing can
more powerfully tend to destroy this principle than the
spirit of a monarchical government. The first lesson of
virtue is, Fear no man; the first lesson of such a constitution is, Fear the king. The true interest of man requires
the annihilation of factitious and imaginary distinctions;
it is inseparable from monarchy to support and render
them more palpable than ever. He that cannot speak to
the proudest despot with a consciousness that he is a man
speaking to a man, and a determination to yield him no
superiority to which his inherent qualifications do not
entitle him, is wholly incapable of an illustrious virtue.
How many such men are bred within the pale of
monarchy? How long would monarchy maintain its
ground in a nation of such men? Surely it would be wisdom in society, instead of conjuring up a thousand
phantoms to seduce us into error, instead of surrounding
us with a thousand fears to deprive us of energy, to remove every obstacle to our progress, and smooth the
path of improvement.

Virtue was never yet held in much honour and esteem
in a monarchical country. It is the inclination and the
interest of courtiers and kings to bring it into disrepute;
and they are but too successful in the attempt. Virtue is,
in their conception, arrogant, intrusive, unmanageable
and stubborn. It is an assumed outside, by which those

who pretend to it, intend to gratify their rude tempers, or their secret views. Within the circle of monarchy, virtue is always regarded with dishonourable incredulity. The philosophical system, which affirms self-love to be the first mover of all our actions, and the falsity of human virtues, is the growth of these countries.* Why is it that the language of integrity and public spirit is constantly regarded among us as hypocrisy? It was not always thus. It was not till the usurpation of Caesar, that books were written, by the tyrant and his partisans, to prove that Cato was no better than a snarling pretender.†

There is a further consideration which has seldom been adverted to upon this subject, but which seems to be of no inconsiderable importance. In our definition of justice, it appeared that our debt to our fellow men extended to all the efforts we could make for their welfare, and all the relief we could supply to their necessities. Not a talent do we possess, not a moment of time, not a shilling of property, for which we are not responsible at the tribunal of the public, which we are not obliged to pay into the general bank of common advantage. Of every one of these things there is an employment which is best, and that best justice obliges us to select. But how extensive is the consequence of this principle with respect to the luxuries and ostentation of human life? How many of these luxuries are there that would stand the test, and approve themselves, upon examination, to be the best objects upon which our property could be employed? Will it often come out to be true that hundreds of individuals ought to be subjected to the severest and most incessant labour, that one man may spend in idleness what would afford to the general mass ease, leisure and consequently wisdom?

Whoever frequents the habitations of the luxurious

* *Maximes*, par M. le Duc de la Rochefoucault: *De la Fausseté des Vertus Humaines*, par M. Esprit.

† See Plutarch's Lives; Lives of Caesar and Cicero: *Ciceronis Epistolæ ad Atticum*, Lib. XII, Epist. xl, xli.

will speedily be infected with the vices of luxury. The ministers and attendants of a sovereign, accustomed to the trappings of magnificence, will turn with disdain from the merit that is obscured with the clouds of adversity. In vain may virtue plead, in vain may talents solicit distinction, if poverty seem, to the fastidious sense of the man in place, to envelop them, as it were, with its noisome effluvia. The very lacquey knows how to repel unfortunate merit from the great man's door.

Here then we are presented with the lesson which is, loudly and perpetually, read through all the haunts of monarchy. Money is the great requisite, for the want of which nothing can atone. Distinction, the homage and esteem of mankind, are to be bought, not earned. The rich man need not trouble himself to invite them, they come unbidden to his surly door. Rarely indeed does it happen that there is any crime that gold cannot expiate, any baseness and meanness of character that wealth cannot shroud in oblivion. Money therefore is the only object worthy of your pursuit, and it is of little importance by what sinister and unmanly means, so it be but obtained.

It is true that virtue and talents do not stand in need of the great man's assistance, and might, if they did but know their worth, repay his scorn with a just and enlightened pity. But, unfortunately, they are often ignorant of their strength, and adopt the errors they see universally espoused. Were it otherwise, they would indeed be happier, but the general manners would perhaps remain the same. The general manners are fashioned by the form and spirit of the national government; and if, in extraordinary cases, they cease to yield to the mould, they speedily change the form to which they fail to submit.

The evils indeed that arise out of avarice, an inordinate admiration of wealth and an intemperate pursuit of it are so obvious that they have constituted a perpetual topic of lamentation and complaint. The object in this place is to consider how far they are extended and aggravated by a monarchical government, that is, by a constitution the very essence of which is to accumulate enormous wealth upon a single head, and to render the ostentation of splendour the established instrument for securing honour and veneration. The object is to consider in what degree the luxury of courts, the effeminate softness of favourites, the system, never to be separated from the monarchical form, of putting men's approbation and good word at a price, of individuals buying the favour of government, and government buying the favour of individuals, is injurious to the moral improvement of mankind. As long as the unvarying practice of courts is cabal, and as long as the unvarying tendency of cabal is to bear down talents, and discourage virtue, to recommend cunning in the room of sincerity, a servile and supple disposition in preference to firmness and inflexibility, a pliant and selfish morality as better than an ingenuous one, and the study of the red book of promotion rather than the study of the general welfare, so long will monarchy be the bitterest and most potent of all the adversaries of the true interests of mankind.

CHAPTER VII

OF ELECTIVE MONARCHY

Disorders attendant on such an election. – Election is intended either to provide a man of great or of moderate talents. – Consequences of the first – of the second. – Can elective and hereditary monarchy be combined?

HAVING considered the nature of monarchy in general, it is incumbent on us to examine how far its mischiefs may be qualified by rendering the monarchy elective.

One of the most obvious objections to this remedy is the difficulty that attends upon the conduct of such an election. There are machines that are too mighty for the human hand to conduct; there are proceedings that are too gigantic and unwieldy for human institutions to regulate. The distance between the mass of mankind and a sovereign is so immense, the trust to be confided so incalculably great, the temptations of the object to be decided on so alluring, as to set every passion that can vex the mind in tumultuous conflict. Election will therefore either dwindle into an empty form, a *congé d'élire* with the successful candidate's name at full length in the conclusion, an election perpetually continued in the same family, perhaps in the same lineal order of descent; or will become the signal of a thousand calamities, foreign cabal, and domestic war. These evils have been so generally understood that elective monarchy, in the strict sense of that appellation, has had very few advocates.

Rousseau, who, in his advice to the Polish nation, appears to be one of those few, that is, one of those who, without loving monarchy, conceive an elective sovereignty to be greatly preferable to an hereditary one, endeavours to provide against the disorders of an election by introducing into it a species of sortition.* In another part of the present enquiry, it will be our business to examine how far chance, and the decision by lot, are compatible with the principles, either of sound morality, or sober reason. For the present, it will be sufficient to say that the project of Rousseau will probably fall under one part of the following dilemma, and of consequence will be refuted by the same arguments that bear upon the mode of election in its most obvious idea.

The design with which election can be introduced into the constitution of a monarchy must either be that of raising to the kingly office a man of superlative talents and uncommon genius, or of providing a moderate portion of wisdom and good intention for these functions,

* *Considérations sur le Gouvernement de Pologne*, Chap. VIII.

and preventing them from falling into the hands of persons of notorious imbecility. To the first of these designs it will be objected by many 'that genius is frequently nothing more in the hands of its possessor than an instrument for accomplishing the most pernicious intentions'. And, though in this assertion there is much partial and mistaken exaggeration, it cannot however be denied that genius, such as we find it amidst the present imperfections of mankind, is compatible with very serious and essential errors. If then genius can, by temptations of various sorts, be led into practical mistake, may we not reasonably entertain a fear respecting the effect of that situation which is so singularly pregnant with temptation? If considerations of inferior note be apt to mislead the mind, what shall we think of this most intoxicating draught, of a condition superior to restraint, stripped of all those accidents and vicissitudes from which the morality of human beings has flowed, with no salutary check, with no intellectual warfare, where mind meets mind on equal terms, but perpetually surrounded with sycophants, servants and dependents? To suppose a mind in which genius and virtue are united and permanent is also undoubtedly to suppose something which no calculation will teach us to expect should offer upon every vacancy. And, if the man could be found, we must imagine to ourselves electors almost as virtuous as the elected, or else error and prejudice, faction and intrigue, will render his election at least precarious, perhaps improbable. Add to this that it is sufficiently evident, from the unalterable evils of monarchy already enumerated, and which we shall presently have occasion to recapitulate, that the first act of sovereignty in a virtuous monarch whose discernment was equal to his virtue would be to annihilate the constitution which had raised him to a throne.

But we will suppose the purpose of instituting an elective monarchy, not to be that of constantly filling the throne with a man of sublime genius, but merely to prevent the office from falling into the hands of a person of notorious imbecility. Such is the strange and pernicious nature of monarchy that it may be doubted whether this be a benefit. Wherever monarchy exists, courts and administrations must, as long as men can see only with their eyes, and act only with their hands, be its constant attendants. But these have already appeared to be institutions so mischievous that perhaps one of the greatest injuries that can be done to mankind is to persuade them of their innocence. Under the most virtuous despot, favour and intrigue, the unjust exaltation of one man, and depression of another, will not fail to exist. Under the most virtuous despot, the true spring there is in mind, the desire to possess merit, and the consciousness that merit will not fail to make itself perceived by those around it, and through their esteem to rise to its proper sphere, will be cut off; and mean and factitious motives be substituted in its room. Of what consequence is it that my merit is perceived by mortals who have no power to advance it? The monarch, shut up in his sanctuary, and surrounded with formalities, will never hear of it. How should he? Can he know what is passing in the remote corners of his kingdom? Can he trace the first tender blossoms of genius and virtue? The people themselves will lose their discernment of these things, because they will perceive their discernment to be powerless in effects. The birth of mind is daily sacrificed by hecatombs to the genius of monarchy. The seeds of reason and truth become barren and unproductive in this unwholesome climate. And the example perpetually exhibited, of the preference of wealth and craft over integrity and talents, produces the most powerful effects upon that mass of mankind, who at first sight may appear least concerned in the objects of generous ambition. This mischief, to whatever it amounts, becomes more strongly fastened upon us under a good monarch than under a bad one. In the latter case, it only restrains our efforts by violence; in the former, it seduces our understandings. To palliate the defects and skin over the deformity of what is fundamentally wrong is certainly very perilous, perhaps very fatal to the best interests of mankind.

Meanwhile the ideas here suggested should be listened to with diffidence and caution. Great doubts may well be entertained respecting that benefit which is to be produced by vice and calamity. If I lived under an elective monarchy, I certainly should not venture to give my vote to a fickle, intemperate or stupid candidate, in preference to a sober and moderate one. Yet may it not happen that a succession, such as that of Trajan, Adrian and the Antonines, familiarizing men to despotism, and preparing them to submit to the tyranny of their successors, may be fraught with more mischief than benefit? It should seem that a mild and insidious way of reconciling mankind to a calamity, before they are made to feel it, is a real and a heavy misfortune.

A question has been started whether it be possible to blend elective and hereditary monarchy, and the constitution of England has been cited as an example of this possibility. What was it that the parliament effected at the revolution, and when they settled the succession upon the house of Hanover? They elected not an individual, but a new race of men to fill the throne of these kingdoms. They gave a practical instance of their power, upon extraordinary emergencies to change the succession. At the same time however that they effected this in action, they denied it in words. They employed the strongest expressions that language could furnish to bind themselves, their heirs and posterity, for ever, to adhere to this settlement. They considered the present as an emergence which, taking into the account the precautions and restrictions they had provided, could never occur again.

In reality what sort of sovereignty is that which is partly hereditary and partly elective? That the accession of a family, or race of men, should originally be a matter of election has nothing particular in it. All government is founded in opinion; and undoubtedly some sort of election, made by a body of electors more or less extensive, originated every new establishment. To whom, in this amphibious government, does the sovereignty belong, upon the death of the first possessor? To his heirs and descendants. What sort of choice shall that be considered which is made of a man half a century before he begins to exist? By what designation does he succeed? Undoubtedly by that of hereditary descent. A king of England therefore holds his crown independently, or, as it has been energetically expressed, 'in contempt', of the choice of the people.*

CHAPTER VIII

OF LIMITED MONARCHY

Liable to most of the preceding objections – to further objections peculiar to itself. – Responsibility considered. – Maxim, that the king can do no wrong. – Functions of a limited monarch. – Impossibility of maintaining the neutrality required. – Of the dismission of ministers. – Responsibility of ministers. – Appointment of ministers, its importance – its difficulties. – Recapitulation. – Strength and weakness of the human species.

I PROCEED to consider monarchy, not as it exists in countries where it is unlimited and despotic, but, as in certain instances it has appeared, a branch merely of the general constitution.

Here it is only necessary to recollect the objections which applied to it in its unqualified state in order to

---

* This argument is stated, with great copiousness, and irresistible force of reasoning, by Mr Burke, towards the beginning of his *Reflections on the Revolution in France.*

perceive that they bear upon it, with the same explicitness, if not with equal force, under every possible modification. Still the government is founded in falsehood, affirming that a certain individual is eminently qualified for an important situation, whose qualifications are perhaps scarcely superior to those of the meanest member of the community. Still the government is founded in injustice, because it raises one man, for a permanent duration, over the heads of the rest of the community, not for any moral recommendation he possesses, but arbitrarily and by accident. Still it reads a constant and powerful lesson of immorality to the people at large, exhibiting pomp and splendour and magnificence, instead of virtue, as the index to general veneration and esteem. The individual is, not less than in the most absolute monarchy, unfitted by his education to become either respectable or useful. He is unjustly and cruelly placed in a situation that engenders ignorance, weakness and presumption, after having been stripped, in his infancy, of all the energies that should defend him against their inroads. Finally, his existence implies that of a train of courtiers, and a series of intrigue, of servility, secret influence, capricious partialities and pecuniary corruption. So true is the observation of Montesquieu, that 'we must not expect, under a monarchy, to find the people virtuous'.*

But, if we consider the question more narrowly, we shall perhaps find that limited monarchy has other absurdities and vices which are peculiarly its own. In an absolute sovereignty, the king may, if he please, be his own minister; but, in a limited one, a ministry and a cabinet are essential parts of the constitution. In an absolute sovereignty, princes are acknowledged to be responsible only to God; but, in a limited one, there is a responsibility of a very different nature. In a limited

---

* 'Il n'est pas rare qu'il y ait des princes vertueux, mais il est très difficile dans une monarchie que le peuple le soit.' *Esprit des Lois,* Liv. III, Chap. V.

monarchy, there are checks, one branch of the government counteracting the excesses of another, and a check without responsibility is the most flagrant contradiction.

There is no subject that deserves to be more maturely considered than this of responsibility. To be responsible is to be liable to be called into an open judicature, where the accuser and the defendant produce their allegations and evidence on equal terms. Everything short of this is mockery. Everything that would give, to either party, any other influence, than that of truth and virtue is subversive of the great ends of justice. He that is arraigned of any crime must descend, a private individual, to the level plain of justice. If he can bias the sentiments of his judges by his possession of power, or by any compromise previous to his resignation, or by the mere sympathy excited in his successors, who will not be severe in their censures, lest they should be treated with severity in return, he cannot truly be said to be responsible. From the honest insolence of despotism we may perhaps promise ourselves better effects than from the hypocritical disclaimers of a limited government. Nothing can be more pernicous than falsehood, and no falsehood can be more palpable than that which pretends to put a weapon into the hands of the general interest, which constantly proves blunt and powerless in the very act to strike.

It was a confused feeling of these truths that introduced into limited monarchies the principle 'that the king can do no wrong'. Observe the peculiar consistency of this proceeding. Consider what a specimen it affords of plain dealing, frankness and ingenuous sincerity. An individual is first appointed, and endowed with the most momentous prerogatives; and then it is pretended that, not he, but other men, are answerable for the abuse of these prerogatives. This pretence may appear tolerable to men bred among the fictions of law, but justice, truth and virtue revolt from it with indignation.

Having first invented this fiction, it becomes the business of such constitutions, as nearly as possible, to realize it. A ministry must be regularly formed; they must concert together; and the measures they execute must originate in their own discretion. The king must be reduced, as nearly as possible, to a cypher. So far as he fails to be completely so, the constitution must be imperfect.

What sort of figure is it that this miserable wretch exhibits in the face of the world? Everything is, with great parade, transacted in his name. He assumes all the inflated and oriental style which has been already described,* and which indeed was, upon that occasion, transcribed from the practice of a limited monarchy. We find him like Pharaoh's frogs, 'in our houses, and upon our beds, in our ovens, and our kneading troughs'.

Now observe the man himself to whom all this importance is annexed. To be idle is the abstract of his duties. He is paid an immense revenue only to hunt and to eat, to wear a scarlet robe and a crown. He may not choose any one of his measures. He must listen, with docility, to the consultations of his ministers, and sanction, with a ready assent, whatever they determine. He must not hear any other advisers; for they are his known and constitutional counsellors. He must not express to any man his opinion; for that would be a sinister and unconstitutional interference. To be absolutely perfect, he must have no opinion, but be the vacant and colourless mirror by which theirs is reflected. He speaks; for they have taught him what he should say: he affixes his signature; for they inform him that it is necessary and proper.

A limited monarchy, in the articles we have described, might be executed with great facility and applause if a king were, what such a constitution endeavours to render him, a mere puppet regulated by pulleys and wires. But it is among the most egregious and palpable of all political mistakes to imagine that we can reduce a human being to this neutrality and torpor. He will not exert any useful and true activity, but he will be far from

* See above, Chap. VI, p. 441.

passive. The more he is excluded from that energy that characterizes wisdom and virtue, the more depraved and unreasonable will he be in his caprices. Is any promotion vacant, and do we expect that he will never think of bestowing it on a favourite, or of proving, by an occasional election of his own, that he really exists? This promotion may happen to be of the utmost importance to the public welfare; or, if not – every promotion unmeritedly given is pernicious to national virtue, and an upright minister will refuse to assent to it. A king does not fail to hear his power and prerogatives extolled, and he will, no doubt, at some time, wish to essay their reality in an unprovoked war against a foreign nation, or against his own citizens.

To suppose that a king and his ministers should, through a period of years, agree in their genuine sentiments, upon every public topic, is what human nature, in no degree, authorizes. This is to attribute to the king talents equal to those of the most enlightened statesmen of his age, or at least to imagine him capable of understanding all their projects, and comprehending all their views. It is to suppose him unspoiled by education, undebauched by rank, and with a mind disposed to receive the impartial lessons of truth.

'But if they disagree, the king can choose other ministers.' We shall presently have occasion to consider this prerogative in a general view; let us for the present examine it, in its application to the differences that may occur between the sovereign and his servants. It is an engine for ever suspended over the heads of the latter, to persuade them to depart from the singleness of their integrity. The compliance that the king demands from them is perhaps, at first, but small; and the minister, strongly pressed, thinks it better to sacrifice his opinion, in this inferior point, than to sacrifice his office. One compliance of this sort leads on to another, and he that began, perhaps only with the preference of an unworthy candidate for distinction, ends with the most atrocious political guilt. The more we consider this point, the greater will its magnitude appear. It will rarely happen but that the minister will be more dependent for his existence on the king than the king upon his minister. When it is otherwise, there will be a mutual compromise, and both in turn will part with everything that is firm, generous, independent and honourable in man.

And, in the meantime, what becomes of responsibility? The measures are mixed and confounded as to their source, beyond the power of human ingenuity to unravel. Responsibility is, in reality, impossible. 'Far otherwise,' cries the advocate of monarchical government: 'it is true that the measures are partly those of the king, and partly those of the minister, but the minister is responsible for all.' Where is the justice of that? It were better to leave guilt wholly without censure than to condemn a man for crimes of which he is innocent. In this case the grand criminal escapes with impunity, and the severity of the law falls wholly upon his coadjutors. The coadjutors receive that treatment which constitutes the essence of all bad policy: punishment is profusely menaced against them, and antidote is wholly forgotten. They are propelled to vice by irresistible temptations, the love of power, and the desire to retain it; and then censured with a rigour altogether disproportioned to their fault. The vital principle of the society is tainted with injustice; and the same neglect of equity, and partial respect of persons, will extend itself over the whole.

I proceed to consider that prerogative in limited monarchy which, whatever others may be given or denied, is inseparable from its substance, the prerogative of the king to nominate to public offices. If anything be of importance, surely this must be of importance, that such a nomination be made with wisdom and integrity, that the fittest persons be appointed to the highest trusts the state has to confer, that an honest and generous ambition be cherished, and that men who shall most ardently qualify themselves for the care of the public welfare be secure of having the largest share in its superintendence.

This nomination is a most arduous task, and requires the wariest circumspection. It falls, more accurately than any other affair of political society, within the line of a pure, undefinable discretion. In other cases the path of rectitude seems visible and distinct. Justice in the contests of individuals, justice in questions of peace and war, justice in the establishment of maxims and judicature, will not perhaps obstinately withdraw itself from the research of an impartial and judicious enquirer. But to observe the various portions of capacity scattered through a nation, and minutely to weigh the qualifications of multiplied candidates, must, after all our accuracy, be committed to some degree of uncertainty.

The first difficulty that occurs is to discover those whom genius and ability have made, in the best sense, candidates for the office. Ability is not always intrusive; talents are often to be found in the remoteness of a village, or the obscurity of a garret. And, though self-consciousness and self-possession are, to a certain degree, the attributes of genius, yet there are many things beside false modesty that may teach its possessor to shun the air of a court.

Of all men a king is least qualified to penetrate these recesses, and discover merit in its hiding place. Encumbered with forms, he cannot mix at large in the society of his species. He is too much engrossed with the semblance of business, or a succession of amusements, to have leisure for such observations as should afford a just estimate of men's characters. In reality, the task is too mighty for any individual, and the benefit can only be secured through the mode of election.

Other disadvantages, attendant on this prerogative of choosing his own ministers, it is needless to enumerate. If enough have not been already said to explain the character of a monarch as growing out of the functions with which he is invested, a laboured repetition in this place would be both tedious and useless. If there be any dependence to be placed upon the operation of moral causes, a king will, in almost every instance, be found among the most undiscriminating, the most deceived, the least informed, and the least heroically disinterested of mankind.

Such then is the genuine and uncontrovertible scene of a mixed monarchy. An individual placed at the summit of the edifice, the centre and the fountain of honour, and who is neutral, or must seem neutral, in the current transactions of his government. This is the first lesson of honour, virtue and truth which mixed monarchy reads to its subjects. Next to the king come his administration, and the trible of courtiers; men driven by a fatal necessity to be corrupt, intriguing and venal; selected for their trust by the most ignorant and ill formed inhabitant of the realm; made solely accountable for measures of which they cannot solely be the authors; threatened, if dishonest, with the vengeance of an injured people; and, if honest, with the surer vengeance of their sovereign's displeasure. The rest of the nation, the subjects at large –

Was ever name so fraught with degradation and meanness as this of subjects? I am, it seems, by the very place of my birth, become a subject. A subject I know I ought to be to the laws of justice; a subject I know I am to the circumstances and emergencies under which I am placed. But to be the subject of an individual, of a being with the same form, and the same imperfections as myself; how much must the human mind be degraded, how much must his grandeur and independence be emasculated, before I can learn to think of this with patience, with indifference, nay, as some men do, with pride and exultation? Such is the idol that monarchy worships, in lieu of the divinity of truth, and the sacred obligation of public good. It is of little consequence whether we vow fidelity to the king and the nation, or to the nation and the king, so long as the king intrudes himself to tarnish and undermine the true simplicity, the altar of virtue.

Are mere names beneath our notice, and will they produce no sinister influence upon the mind? May we bend the knee before the shrine of vanity and folly without injury? Far otherwise. Mind had its beginning in sensation, and it depends upon words and symbols for the progress of its associations. The truly good man must not only have a heart resolved, but a front erect. We cannot practise abjection, hypocrisy and meanness, without becoming degraded in other men's eyes and in our own. We cannot 'bow the head in the temple of Rimmon', without in some degree apostatizing from the divinity of truth. He that calls a king a man will perpetually hear from his own mouth the lesson that he is unfit for the trust reposed in him: he that calls him by any sublimer appellation is hastening fast into the grossest and most dangerous errors.

But perhaps 'mankind are so weak and imbecile that it is in vain to expect, from the change of their institutions, the improvement of their character'. Who made them weak and imbecile? Previously to human institutions and human society, they had certainly none of this defect. Man, considered in himself, is merely a being capable of impression, a recipient of perceptions. What is there in this abstract character that precludes him from advancement? We have a faint discovery in individuals at present of what our nature is capable: why should individuals be fit for so much, and the species for nothing? Is there anything in the structure of the globe that forbids us to be virtuous? If no, if nearly all our impressions of right and wrong flow from our intercourse with each other, why may not that intercourse be susceptible of modification and amendment? It is the most cowardly of all systems that would represent the discovery of truth as useless, and teach us that, when discovered, it is our wisdom to leave the mass of our species in error.

There is, in reality, little room for scepticism respecting the omnipotence of truth. Truth is the pebble in the lake; and, however slowly, in the present case, the circles succeed each other, they will infallibly go on, till they overspread the surface. No order of mankind will for ever remain ignorant of the principles of justice, equality and public good. No sooner will they understand them than they will perceive the coincidence of virtue and public good with private interest: nor will any erroneous establishment be able effectually to support itself against general opinion. In this contest sophistry will vanish, and mischievous institutions sink quietly into neglect. Truth will bring down all her forces, mankind will be her army, and oppression, injustice, monarchy and vice, will tumble into a common ruin.

CHAPTER IX

OF A PRESIDENT WITH REGAL POWERS

Enumeration of powers – that of appointing to inferior offices – of pardoning offences – of convoking deliberative assemblies – of affixing a veto to their decrees. – Conclusion. – The title of king estimated. – Monarchical and aristocratical systems, similarity of their effects.

STILL monarchy it seems has one refuge left. 'We will not,' say some men, 'have an hereditary monarchy, we acknowledge that to be an enormous injustice. We are not contented with an elective monarchy, we are not contented with a limited one. We admit the office however reduced, if the tenure be for life, to be an intolerable grievance. But why not have kings, as we have magistrates and legislative assemblies, renewable by frequent elections? We may then change the holder of the office as often as we please.'

Let us not be seduced by a mere plausibility of phrase, nor employ words without having reflected on their meaning. What are we to understand by the appellation a king? If the office have any meaning, it seems reasonable that the man who holds it should possess the privilege, either of appointing to certain employments at his own discretion, or of remitting the decrees of criminal justice, or of convoking and dismissing popular assemblies, or of affixing and refusing his sanction to the decrees of those assemblies. Most of these privileges may claim a respectable authority in the powers delegated to their president by the United States of America.

Let us however bring these ideas to the touchstone of reason. Nothing can appear more adventurous than the reposing, unless in cases of absolute necessity, the decision of any affair of importance to the public in the breast of one man. But this necessity will scarcely be alleged in any of the articles just enumerated. What advantage does one man possess over a society or council of men in any of these respects? The disadvantages under which he labours are obvious. He is more easily corrupted, and more easily misled. He cannot possess so many advantages for obtaining accurate information. He is abundantly more liable to the attacks of passion and caprice, of unfounded antipathy to one man and partiality to another, of uncharitable censure or blind idolatry. He cannot be always upon his guard; there will be moments in which the most exemplary vigilance is liable to surprise. Meanwhile, we are placing the subject in much too favourable a light. We are supposing his intentions to be upright and just; but the contrary of this will be more frequently the truth. Where powers beyond the capacity of human nature are entrusted, vices, the disgrace of human nature, will be engendered. Add to this that the same reasons which prove that government, wherever it exists, should be directed by the sense of the people at large, equally prove that, wherever public officers are necessary, the sense of the whole, or of a body of men most nearly approaching in spirit to the whole, ought to decide on their pretensions.

These objections are applicable to the most innocent of the privileges above enumerated, that of appointing to the exercise of certain employments. The case will be still worse if we consider the other privileges. We shall have occasion hereafter to examine the propriety of pardoning offences, considered independently of the persons in whom that power is vested: but, in the meantime, can anything be more intolerable than for an individual to be authorized, without assigning a reason, or assigning a reason upon which no one is allowed to pronounce, to supersede the grave decisions of a court of justice, founded upon a careful and public examination of evidence? Can anything be more unjust than for an individual to assume the function of informing a nation, when they are to deliberate, and when they are to cease from deliberation?

The remaining privilege is of too iniquitous a nature to be an object of much terror. It is not in the compass of credibility to conceive that any people would remain quiet spectators while the sense of one man was, openly and undisguisedly, set against the sense of the national representative in frequent assembly, and suffered to overpower it. Two or three direct instances of the exercise of this negative could not fail to annihilate it. Accordingly, wherever it is supposed to exist, we find it softened and nourished by the genial dew of pecuniary corruption; either rendered unnecessary beforehand, by a sinister application to the frailty of individual members, or disarmed and made palatable in the sequel, by a copious effusion of venal emollients. If it can in any case be endured, it must be in countries where the degenerate representative no longer possesses the sympathy of the public, and the haughty president is made sacred by the blood of an exalted ancestry which flows through his veins, or the holy oil which the representatives of the Most High have poured on his head. A common mortal, periodically selected by his fellow-citizens to watch over their interests, can never be supposed to possess this stupendous virtue.

If there be any truth in these reasonings, it inevitably

follows that there are no important functions of general superintendence which can justly be delegated to a single individual. If the office of a president be necessary, either in a deliberative assembly, or an administrative council, supposing such a council to exist, his employment will have relation to the order of their proceedings, and by no means consist in the arbitrary preferring and carrying into effect his private decision. A king, if unvarying usage can give meaning to a word, describes a man upon whose single discretion some part of the public interest is made to depend. What use can there be for such a man in an unperverted and well ordered state? With respect to its internal affairs, certainly none. How far the office can be of advantage, in our transactions with foreign governments, we shall hereafter have occasion to decide.

Let us beware, by an unjustifiable perversion of terms, of confounding the common understanding of mankind. A king is the well known and standing appellation for an office, which, if there be any truth in the arguments of the preceding chapters, has been the bane and the grave of human virtue. Why endeavour to purify and exorcize what is entitled only to execration? Why not suffer the term to be as well understood, and as cordially detested, as the once honourable appellation of tyrant afterwards was among the Greeks? Why not suffer it to rest a perpetual monument of the folly, the cowardice and misery of our species?

*

In proceeding from the examination of monarchical to that of aristocratical government, it is impossible not to remark that there are several disadvantages common to both. One of these is the creation of a separate interest. The benefit of the governed is made to lie on one side, and the benefit of the governors on the other. It is to no purpose to say that individual interest, accurately understood, will always be found to coincide with general, if it appear in practice that the opinions and errors of mankind are perpetually separating them, and placing them in opposition to each other. The more the governors are fixed in a sphere distinct and distant from the governed, the more will this error be cherished. Theory, in order to produce an adequate effect upon the mind, should be favoured, not counteracted, by practice. What principle in human nature is more universally confessed than self-love, that is, than a propensity to think individually of a private interest, to discriminate and divide objects which the laws of the universe have indissolubly united? None, unless it be the *esprit de corps*, the tendency of bodies of men to aggrandize themselves, a spirit, which, though less ardent than self love, is still more vigilant, and not exposed to the accidents of sleep, indisposition and mortality. Thus it appears that, of all impulses to a narrow, self-interested conduct, those afforded by monarchy and aristocracy are the greatest.

Nor must we be too hasty and undistinguishing in applying the principle that individual interest, accurately understood, will always be found to coincide with general. Relatively to individuals considered as men, it is, for the most part, certainly true; relatively to individuals considered as lords and kings, it is false. The man will perhaps be served by the sacrifice of all his little peculium to the public interest, but the king will be annihilated. The first sacrifice that justice demands, at the hand of monarchy and aristocracy, is that of their immunities and prerogatives. Public interest dictates the unlimited dissemination of truth, and the impartial administration of justice. Kings and lords subsist only under favour of error and oppression. They will therefore resist the progress of knowledge and illumination; the moment the deceit is dispelled, their occupation is gone.

In thus concluding however, we are taking for granted that aristocracy will be found an arbitrary and pernicious institution, as monarchy has already appeared to be. It is time that we should enquire in what degree this is actually the case.

CHAPTER X

OF HEREDITARY DISTINCTION

Birth considered as a physical cause – as a moral cause. – Education of the great. – Recapitulation.

A PRINCIPLE deeply interwoven with both monarchy and aristocracy in their most flourishing state, but most deeply with the latter, is that of hereditary pre-eminence. No principle can present a deeper insult upon reason and justice. Examine the new-born son of a peer, and of a mechanic. Has nature designated in different lineaments their future fortune? Is one of them born with callous hands and an ungainly form? Can you trace in the other the early promise of genius and understanding, of virtue and honour? We have been told indeed 'that nature will break out',* and that

> The eaglet of a valiant nest will quickly tower
> Up to the region of his fire;*

and the tale was once believed. But mankind will not soon again be persuaded that the birthright of one lineage of human creatures is beauty and virtue, and of another, dullness, grossness and deformity.

It is difficult accurately to decide how much of the characters of men is produced by causes that operated upon them in the period preceding their birth, and how much is the moral effect of education, in its extensive sense. Children certainly bring into the world with them a part of the character of their parents; nay, it is probable that the human race is meliorated, somewhat in the same way as the races of brutes, and that every generation, in a civilized state, is further removed, in its physical structure, from the savage and uncultivated man.

But these causes operate too uncertainly to afford any just basis of hereditary distinction. If a child resembles his

* *Tragedy of Douglas*, Act iii.

father in many particulars, there are particulars, perhaps more numerous and important, in which he differs from him. The son of a poet is not a poet, the son of an orator an orator, nor the son of a good man a saint; and yet, in this case, a whole volume of moral causes is often brought to co-operate with the physical. This has been aptly illustrated, by a proposition, humorously suggested,* for rendering the office of poet laureat hereditary. But, if the qualities and dispositions of the father were found descendible in the son, in a much greater degree than we have any reason to suppose, the character must be expected to wear out in a few generations, either by the mixture of breeds, or by, what there is great reason to suppose is still more pernicious, the want of mixture. The title made hereditary will then remain a brand upon the degenerate successor. It is not satire, but a simple statement of fact, when we observe that it is not easy to find a set of men in society sunk more below the ordinary standard of man in his constituent characteristics than the body of the English, or any other, peerage.

Let us proceed to enquire into the efficacy of high birth and nobility, considered as a moral cause.

The persuasion of its excellence in this respect is an opinion probably as old as the institution of nobility itself. The etymology of the word expressing this particular form of government may perhaps be considered as having a reference to this idea. It is called aristocracy, or the government of the best [αριςοι]. In the writings of Cicero, and the speeches of the Roman senate, this order of men is styled the '*optimates*', the 'virtuous', the 'liberal', and the 'honest'. It is asserted, and with some degree of justice, 'that the multitude is an unruly beast, with no fixed sentiments of honour or principle, guided by sordid venality, or not less sordid appetite, envious, tyrannical, inconstant and unjust'. Hence they deduced as a consequence 'the necessity of maintaining an order of men of liberal education and elevated sentiments, who should either engross the government of the humbler and

* Paine's *Rights of Man*.

more numerous class incapable of governing themselves, or at least should be placed as a rigid guard upon their excesses, with powers adequate to their correction and restraint'. The greater part of these reasonings will fall under our examination when we consider the disadvantages of democracy.* So much as relates to the excellence of aristocracy it is necessary at present to discuss.

The whole proceeds upon a supposition that 'if nobility should not, as its hereditary constitution might seem to imply, be found originally superior to the ordinary rate of mortals, it is at least rendered eminently so by the power of education. Men who grow up in unpolished ignorance and barbarism, and are chilled with the icy touch of poverty, must necessarily be exposed to a thousand sources of corruption, and cannot have that delicate sense of rectitude and honour which literature and manly refinement are found to bestow. It is under the auspices of indulgence and ease that civilzation is engendered. A nation must have surmounted the disadvantages of a first establishment, and have arrived at some degree of leisure and prosperity, before the love of letters can take root among them. It is in individuals, as in large bodies of men. A few exceptions will occur; but, excluding these, it can scarcely be expected that men who are compelled in every day by laborious manual efforts to provide for the necessities of the day should arrive at great expansion of mind and comprehensiveness of thinking.'

In certain parts of this argument there is considerable truth. The sound moralist will be the last man to deny the power and importance of education. It is therefore necessary, either that a system should be discovered for securing leisure and prosperity to every member of the community; or that a certain influence and authority should be given to the liberal and the wise, over the illiterate and ignorant. Now, supposing, for the present, that the former of these measures is impossible, it may yet be reasonable to enquire whether aristocracy be the most judicious scheme for obtaining the latter. Some light may

* Chap. XIV.

be collected on this subject from what has already appeared respecting education under the head of monarchy.

Education is much, but opulent education is of all its modes the least efficacious. The education of words is not to be despised, but the education of things is on no account to be dispensed with. The former is of admirable use in enforcing and developing the latter; but, when taken alone, it is pedantry and not learning, a body without a soul. Whatever may be the abstract perfection of which mind is capable, we seem at present frequently to need being excited, in the case of any uncommon effort, by motives that address themselves to the individual. But, so far as relates to these motives, the lower classes of mankind, had they sufficient leisure, have greatly the advantage. The plebeian must be the maker of his own fortune; the lord finds his already made. The plebeian must expect to find himself neglected and despised in proportion as he is remiss in cultivating the objects of esteem; the lord will always be surrounded with sycophants and slaves. The lord therefore has no motive to industry and exertion; no stimulus to rouse him from the lethargic, 'oblivious pool', out of which every human intellect originally rose. It must indeed be confessed that truth does not need the alliance of circumstances, and that a man may arrive at the temple of fame by other paths than those of misery and distress. But the lord does not content himself with discarding the stimulus of adversity: he goes further than this, and provides fruitful sources of effeminacy and error. Man cannot offend with impunity against the great principle of universal good. He that monopolizes to himself luxuries and titles and wealth to the injury of the whole becomes degraded from the rank of man; and, however he may be admired by the multitude, will be pitied by the wise, and not seldom be wearisome to himself. Hence it appears that to elect men to the rank of nobility is to elect them to a post of moral danger and a means of depravity; but that to constitute them hereditarily noble is to preclude them, exclusively of a few extraordinary accidents, from all the causes that generate ability and virtue.

The reasonings here repeated upon the subject of hereditary distinction are so obvious that nothing can be a stronger instance of the power of prejudice instilled in early youth than the fact of their having been, at any time, disputed or forgotten. From birth as a physical cause, it sufficiently appears that little fundamental or regular can be expected: and, so far as relates to education, it is practicable, in a certain degree, nor is it easy to set limits to that degree, to infuse emulation into a youthful mind; but wealth is the fatal blast that destroys the hopes of a future harvest. There was once indeed a gallant kind of virtue that, by irresistibly seizing the senses, seemed to communicate extensively, to young men of birth, the mixed and equivocal accomplishments of chivalry; but, since the subjects of moral emulation have been turned from personal prowess to the energies of intellect, and especially since the field of that emulation has been more widely opened to the species, the lists have been almost uniformly occupied by those whose narrow circumstances have goaded them to ambition, or whose undebauched habits and situation in life have rescued them from the poison of flattery and effeminate indulgence.

CHAPTER XI

MORAL EFFECTS OF ARISTOCRACY

Nature of aristocracy. – Importance of practical justice. – Species of injustice which aristocracy creates. – Estimate of the injury produced. – Examples.

THE features of aristocratical institution are principally two: privilege, and an aggravated monopoly of wealth.

The first of these is the essence of aristocracy; the second, that without which aristocracy can rarely be supported. They are both of them in direct opposition to all sound morality, and all generous independence of character.

Inequality of wealth is perhaps the necessary result of the institution of property, in any state of progress at which the human mind has yet arrived; and cannot, till the character of the human species is essentially altered, be superseded but by a despotic and positive interference, more injurious to the common welfare, than the inequality it attempted to remove. Inequality of wealth involves with it inequality of inheritance.

But the mischief of aristocracy is that it inexpressibly aggravates and embitters an evil which, in its mildest form, is deeply to be deplored. The first sentiment of an uncorrupted mind, when it enters upon the theatre of human life, is, Remove from me and my fellows all arbitrary hindrances; let us start fair; render all the advantages and honours of social institution accessible to every man, in proportion to his talents and exertions.

Is it true, as has often been pretended, that generous and exalted qualities are hereditary in particular lines of descent? They do not want the alliance of positive institution to secure to them their proper ascendancy, and enable them to command the respect of mankind. Is it false? Let it share the fate of exposure and detection with other impostures. If I conceived of a young person that he was destined, from his earliest infancy, to be a sublime poet, or a profound philosopher, should I conceive that the readiest road to the encouraging and fostering his talents was, from the moment of his birth, to put a star upon his breast, to salute him with titles of honour, and to bestow upon him, independently of all exertion, those advantages which exertion usually proposes to itself as its ultimate object of pursuit? No; I should send him to the school of man, and oblige him to converse with his fellows upon terms of equality.

Privilege is a regulation rendering a few men, and those

only, by the accident of their birth, eligible to certain situations. It kills all liberal ambition in the rest of mankind, by opposing to it an apparently insurmountable bar. It diminishes it in the favoured class itself, by showing them the principal qualification as indefeasibly theirs. Privilege entitles a favoured few to engross to themselves gratifications which the system of the universe left at large to all her sons; it puts into the hands of these few the means of oppression against the rest of their species; it fills them with vain-glory, and affords them every incitement to insolence and a lofty disregard to the feelings and interests of others.

Privilege, as we have already said, is the essence of aristocracy; and, in a rare condition of human society, such as that of the ancient Romans, privilege has been able to maintain itself without the accession of wealth, and to flourish in illustrious poverty. But this can be the case only under a very singular coincidence of circumstances. In general, an aggravated monopoly of wealth has been one of the objects about which the abettors of aristocracy have been most incessantly solicitous. Hence the origin of entails, rendering property, in its own nature too averse to a generous circulation, a thousand times more stagnant and putrescent than before, of primogeniture, which disinherits every other member of a family, to heap unwholesome abundance upon one; and of various limitations, filling the courts of civilized Europe with endless litigation, and making it in many cases impossible to decide who it is that has the right of conveying a property, and what shall amount to a legal transfer.

There is one thing, more than all the rest, of importance to the well being of mankind, justice. A neglect of justice is not only to be deplored for the direct evil it produces; it is perhaps still more injurious by its effects in perverting the understanding, overturning our calculations of the future, and thus striking at the root of moral discernment, and genuine power and decision of character.

Of all the principles of justice, there is none so material to the moral rectitude of mankind as that no man can be distinguished but by his personal merit. When a man has proved himself a benefactor to the public, when he has already, by laudable perseverance, cultivated in himself talents which need only encouragement and public favour to bring them to maturity, let that man be honoured. In a state of society where fictitious distinctions are unknown, it is impossible he should not be honoured. But that a man should be looked up to with servility and awe because the king has bestowed on him a spurious name, or decorated him with a ribband; that another should revel in luxury because his ancestor three centuries ago bled in the quarrel of Lancaster or York; do we imagine that these iniquities can be practised without injury?

Let those who entertain this opinion converse a little with the lower orders of mankind. They will perceive that the unfortunate wretch who, with unremitted labour, finds himself incapable adequately to feed and clothe his family has a sense of injustice rankling at his heart.

But let us suppose that their sense of injustice were less acute than is here supposed, what favourable inference can be deduced from that? Is not the injustice real? If the minds of men are so withered and stupified by the constancy with which it is practised that they do not feel the rigour that grinds them into nothing, how does that improve the picture?

Let us fairly consider, for a moment, what is the amount of injustice included in the institution of aristocracy. I am born, suppose, a Polish prince with an income of £300,000 per annum. You are born a manerial serf, or a Creolian Negro, attached to the soil, and transferable, by barter or otherwise, to twenty successive lords. In vain shall be your most generous efforts, and your unwearied industry, to free yourself from the intolerable yoke. Doomed, by the law of your birth, to wait at the gates of the palace you must never enter; to sleep under a ruined, weather-beaten roof, while your master sleeps under canopies of state; to feed on putrefied offals, while the world is ransacked for delicacies for his table; to labour, without moderation or limit, under a parching sun, while he basks in perpetual sloth; and to be rewarded at last with contempt, reprimand, stripes and mutilation. In fact the case is worse than this. I could endure all that injustice or caprice could inflict provided I possessed, in the resource of a firm mind, the power of looking down with pity on my tyrant, and of knowing that I had that within that sacred character of truth, virtue and fortitude which all his injustice could not reach. But a slave and a serf are condemned to stupidity and vice, as well as to calamity.

Is all this nothing? Is all this necessary for the maintenance of civil order? Let it be recollected that, for this distinction, there is not the smallest foundation in the nature of things, that, as we have already said, there is no particular mould for the construction of lords, and that they are born neither better nor worse than the poorest of their dependents. It is this structure of aristocracy, in all its sanctuaries and fragments, against which reason and morality have declared war. It is alike unjust, whether we consider it in the calls of India; the villainage of the feudal system; or the despotism of ancient Rome, where the debtors were dragged into personal servitude, to expiate, by stripes and slavery, the usurious loans they could not repay. Mankind will never be, in an eminent degree, virtuous and happy, till each man shall possess that portion of distinction and no more, to which he is entitled by his personal merits. The dissolution of aristocracy is equally the interest of the oppressor and the oppressed. The one will be delivered from the listlessness of tyranny, and the other from the brutalizing operation of servitude. How long shall we be told in vain 'that mediocrity of fortune is the true rampart of personal happiness'?

CHAPTER XII

OF TITLES

Their origin and history. – Their miserable absurdity. – Truth the only adequate reward of merit.

THE case of mere titles is so absurd that it would deserve to be treated only with ridicule were it not for the serious mischiefs they impose on mankind. The feudal system was a ferocious monster, devouring, wherever it came, all that the friend of humanity regards with attachment and love. The system of titles appears under a different form. The monster is at length destroyed, and they who followed in his train, and fattened upon the carcases of those he slew, have stuffed his skin, and, by exhibiting it, hope still to terrify mankind into patience and pusillanimity. The system of the Northern invaders, however odious, escaped the ridicule of the system of titles. When the feudal chieftains assumed a geographical appellation, it was from some place really subject to their authority; and there was no more absurdity in the style they assumed than in our calling a man, at present, the governor of Tangiers or the governor of Gibraltar. The commander in chief, or the sovereign, did not then give an empty name; he conferred an earldom or a barony, a substantial tract of land, with houses and men, and producing a real revenue. He now grants nothing but a privilege, equivalent to that of calling yourself Tom, who were beforetime called Will; and, to add to the absurdity, your new appellation is borrowed from some place perhaps you never saw, or some country you never visited. The style however is the same; we are still earls and barons, governors of provinces and commanders of forts, and that with the same evident propriety as the elector of Hanover, and arch treasurer of the empire, styles himself king of France.

Can there be anything more ludicrous than that the

man who was yesterday Mr St John, the most eloquent speaker of the British house of commons, the most penetrating thinker, the umpire of maddening parties, the restorer of peace to bleeding and exhausted Europe, should be today lord Bolingbroke?[34] In what is he become greater and more venerable than he was? In the pretended favour of a stupid and besotted woman, who always hated him, as she uniformly hated talents and virtue, though, for her own interest, she was obliged to endure him.

The friends of a man upon whom a title has recently been conferred must either be wholly blinded by the partiality of friendship, not to feel the ridicule of his situation; or completely debased by the parasitical spirit of dependence, not to betray their feelings. Every time they essay to speak, they are in danger of blundering upon the inglorious appellations of Mr and Sir.* Every time their tongue falters with unconfirmed practice, the question rushes upon them with irresistible force. 'What change has my old friend undergone; in what is he wiser or better, happier or more honourable?' The first week of a new title is a perpetual war of the feelings in every spectator; the genuine dictates of common sense, against the arbitrary institutions of society. To make the farce more perfect, these titles are subject to perpetual fluctuations, and the man who is today earl of Kensington will tomorrow resign, with unblushing effrontery, all appearance of character and honour, to be called marquis of Kew. History labours under the Gothic and unintelligible burden; no mortal patience can connect the different stories, of him who is today lord Kimbolton, and tomorrow earl of Manchester; today earl of Mulgrave, and tomorrow marquis of Normanby and duke of Buckinghamshire.

The absurdity of these titles strikes us the more, because they are usually the reward of intrigue and cor-

* In reality these appellations are little less absurd than those by which they are superseded.

ruption. But, were it otherwise, still they would be unworthy of the adherents of reason and justice. When we speak of Mr St John, as of the man who by his eloquence swayed contending parties, who withdrew the conquering sword from suffering France, and gave thirty years of peace and calm pursuit of the arts of life and wisdom to mankind, we speak of something eminently great. Can any title express these merits? Is not truth the consecrated and single vehicle of justice? Is not the plain and simple truth worth all the cunning substitutions in the world? Could an oaken garland, or a gilded coronet, have added one atom to his real greatness? Garlands and coronets may be bestowed on the unworthy, and prostituted to the intriguing. Till mankind be satisfied with the naked statement of what they really perceive, till they confess virtue to be then most illustrious, when she most disdains the aid of ornament, they will never arrive at that manly justice of sentiment at which they seem destined one day to arrive. By this scheme of naked truth, virtue will be every day a gainer; every succeeding observer will more fully do her justice, while vice, deprived of that varnish with which she delighted to gloss her actions, of that gaudy exhibition which may be made alike by every pretender, will speedily sink into unheeded contempt.

CHAPTER XIII

OF THE ARISTOCRATICAL CHARACTER

Intolerance of aristocracy – dependent for its success upon the ignorance of the multitude. – Precautions necessary for its support. – Different kinds of aristocracy. – Aristocracy of the Romans: its virtues – its vices. Aristocratical distribution of property – regulations by which it is maintained – avarice it engenders. – Argument against innovation from the present happy establishment of affairs considered. – Conclusion.

ARISTOCRACY, in its proper signification, is neither less nor more than a scheme for rendering more permanent and visible, by the interference of political institution, the inequality of mankind. Aristocracy, like monarchy, is founded in falsehood, the offspring of art foreign to the real nature of things, and must therefore, like monarchy, be supported by artifice and false pretences. Its empire however is founded in principles more gloomy and unsocial than those of monarchy. The monarch often thinks it advisable to employ blandishments and courtship with his barons and officers; but the lord deems it sufficient to rule with a rod of iron.

Both depend for their perpetuity upon ignorance. Could they, like Omar, destroy the productions of profane reasoning, and persuade mankind that the Alcoran contained everything which it became them to study, they might then renew their lease of empire. But here again aristocracy displays its superior harshness. Monarchy admits of a certain degree of monkish learning among its followers. But aristocracy holds a stricter hand. Should the lower ranks of society once come to be generally able to write and read, its power would be at an end. To make men serfs and villains, it is indispensibly necessary to make them brutes. This is a question which has long

479

been canvassed with eagerness and avidity. The resolute advocates of the old system have, with no contemptible foresight, opposed the communication of knowledge as a most alarming innovation. In their well known observation 'that a servant who has been taught to write and read ceases to be any longer the passive machine they require', is contained the embryo from which it would be easy to explain the whole philosophy of European society.

And who is there that can ponder with unruffled thoughts the injurious contrivances of these self-centred usurpers, contrivances the purpose of which is to retain the human species in a state of endless degradation? It is in the subjects we are here examining that the celebrated maxim of 'many made for one' is brought to the test. Those reasoners were, no doubt, 'wise in their generation', who two centuries ago conceived alarm at the blasphemous doctrine 'that government was instituted for the benefit of the governed, and, if it proposed to itself any other object, was no better than an usurpation'. It will perpetually be found that the men who, in every age, have been the earliest to give the alarm of innovation, and have been ridiculed on that account as bigoted and timid, were, in reality, persons of more than common discernment, who saw, though but imperfectly, in the rude principle, the inferences to which it inevitably led. It is time that men of reflection should choose between the two sides of the alternative: either to go back, fairly and without reserve, to the primitive principles of tyranny; or, adopting any one of the maxims opposite to these, however neutral it may at first appear, not feebly and ignorantly to shut their eyes upon the system of consequences it draws along with it.

It is not necessary to enter into a methodical disquisition of the different kinds of aristocracy, since, if the above reasonings have any force, they are equally cogent against them all. Aristocracy may vest its prerogatives principally in the individual, as in Poland; or restrict them to the nobles in their corporate capacity, as in

Venice. The former will be more tumultuous and disorderly; the latter more jealous, intolerant and severe. The magistrates may either recruit their body by election among themselves, as in Holland; or by the choice of the people, as in ancient Rome.

The aristocracy of ancient Rome was incomparably the most venerable and illustrious that ever existed. It may not therefore be improper to contemplate in them the degree of excellence to which aristocracy may be raised. They included in their institution some of the benefits of democracy, as, generally speaking, no man became a member of the senate but in consequence of his being elected by the people to the superior magistracies. It was reasonable therefore to expect that the majority of the members would possess some degree of capacity. They were not like modern aristocratical assemblies, in which, as primogeniture, and not selection, decides upon their prerogatives, we shall commonly seek in vain for capacity, except in a few of the lords of recent creation. As the plebeians were long restrained from looking for candidates, except among the patricians, that is, the posterity of senators, it was reasonable to suppose that the most eminent talents would be confined to that order. A circumstance which contributed to this was the monopoly of liberal education and the cultivation of the mind, a monopoly which the invention of printing has at length fully destroyed. Accordingly, all the great literary ornaments of Rome were either patricians, or of the equestrian order, or their immediate dependents. The plebeians, though, in their corporate capacity, they possessed, for some centuries, the virtues of sincerity, intrepidity, love of justice and of the public, could scarcely boast of any of those individual characters in their party that reflect lustre on mankind, except the two Gracchi: while the patricians told of Brutus, Valerius, Coriolanus, Cincinnatus, Camillus, Fabricius, Regulus, the Fabii, the Decii, the Scipios, Lucullus, Marcellus, Cato, Cicero and innumerable others. With this retrospect continually suggested to their minds, it was almost venial for the stern heroes of Rome, and the last illustrious martyrs of the republic, to entertain aristocratical sentiments.

Let us however consider impartially this aristocracy, so superior to any other of ancient or modern times. Upon the first institution of the republic, the people possessed scarcely any authority, except in the election of magistrates, and even here their intrinsic importance was eluded by the mode of arranging the assembly, so that the whole decision vested in the richer classes of the community. No magistrates of any description were elected but from among the patricians. All causes were judged by the patricians, and from their judgement there was no appeal. The patricians intermarried among themselves, and thus formed a republic of narrow extent, in the midst of the nominal one, which was held by them in a state of abject servitude. The idea which purified these usurpations in the minds of the usurpers was 'that the vulgar are essentially coarse, grovelling and ignorant, and that there can be no security for the empire of justice and consistency, but in the decided ascendancy of the liberal'. Thus, even while they opposed the essential interests of mankind, they were animated with public spirit and an unbounded enthusiasm of virtue. But it is not less true that they did oppose the essential interests of mankind. What can be more memorable in this respect than the declamations of Appius Claudius, whether we consider the moral greatness of mind by which they were dictated, or the cruel intolerance they were intended to enforce? It is inexpressibly painful to see so much virtue, through successive ages, employed in counteracting the justest requisitions. The result was that the patricians, notwithstanding their immeasurable superiority in abilities, were obliged to resign, one by one, the exclusions to which they clung. In the interval they were led to have recourse to the most odious methods of opposition; and every man among them contended who should be loudest in applause of the nefarious murder of the Gracchi. If the

Romans were distinguished for so many virtues, constituted as they were, what might they not have been but for the iniquity of aristocratical usurpation? The indelible blemish of their history, the love of conquest, originated in the same cause. Their wars, through every period of the republic, were nothing more than the contrivance of the patricians, to divert their countrymen from attending to the sentiments of political truth, by leading them to scenes of conquest and carnage. They understood the art, common to all governments, of confounding the understandings of the multitude, and persuading them that the most unprovoked hostilities were merely the dictates of necessary defence.

Aristocracy, as we have already seen, is intimately connected with an extreme inequality of possessions. No man can be a useful member of society except so far as his talents are employed in a manner conducive to the general advantage. In every society, the produce, the means of contributing to the necessities and conveniences of its members, is of a certain amount. In every society, the bulk at least of its members contribute by their personal exertions to the creation of this produce. What can be more desirable and just than that the produce itself should, with some degree of equality, be shared among them? What more injurious than the accumulating upon a few every means of superfluity and luxury, to the total destruction of the ease, and plain, but plentiful subsistence of the many? It may be calculated that the king, even of a limited monarchy, receives as the salary of his office, an income equivalent to the labour of fifty thousand men.* Let us set out in our estimate from this point, and figure to ourselves the shares of his counsellors, his nobles, the wealthy commoners by whom the nobility will be emulated, their kindred and dependents. Is it any wonder that, in such countries, the lower orders of the community are exhausted by the hardships of penury and immoderate fatigue? When we see the wealth of a pro-

* Taking the average price of labour at one shilling per diem.

vince spread upon the great man's table, can we be surprised that his neighbours have not bread to satiate the cravings of hunger?

Is this a state of human beings that must be considered as the last improvement of political wisdom? In such a state it is impossible that eminent virtue should not be exceedingly rare. The higher and the lower classes will be alike corrupted by their unnatural situation. But to pass over the higher class for the present, what can be more evident than the tendency of want to contract the intellectual powers? The situation which the wise man would desire, for himself, and for those in whose welfare he was interested, would be a situation of alternate labour and relaxation, labour that should not exhaust the frame, and relaxation that was in no danger of degenerating into indolence. Thus industry and activity would be cherished, the frame preserved in a healthful tone, and the mind accustomed to meditation and improvement. But this would be the situation of the whole human species if the supply of our wants were fairly distributed. Can any system be more worthy of disapprobation than that which converts nineteen-twentieths of them into beasts of burden, annihilates so much thought, renders impossible so much virtue, and extirpates so much happiness?

But it may be alleged 'that this argument is foreign to the subject of aristocracy; the inequality of conditions being the inevitable consequence of the institution of property'. It is true that many disadvantages have hitherto flowed out of this institution, in the simplest form in which it has yet existed; but these disadvantages, to whatever they may amount, are greatly aggravated by the operations of aristocracy. Aristocracy turns the stream of property out of its natural course, in following which it would not fail to fructify and gladden, in turn at least, every division of the community; and forwards, with assiduous care, its accumulation in the hands of a very few persons.

At the same time that it has endeavoured to render the acquisition of permanent property difficult, aristocracy has greatly increased the excitements to that acquisition. All men are accustomed to conceive a thirst after distinction and pre-eminence, but they do not all fix upon wealth as the object of this passion, but variously upon skill in any particular art, grace, learning, talents, wisdom and virtue. Nor does it appear that these latter objects are pursued by their votaries with less assiduity than wealth is pursued by those who are anxious to acquire it. Wealth would be still less capable of being mistaken for the universal passion, were it not rendered by political institution, more than by its natural influence, the road to honour and respect.

There is no mistake more thoroughly to be deplored on this subject than that of persons sitting at their ease and surrounded with all the conveniences of life who are apt to exclaim, 'We find things very well as they are'; and to inveigh bitterly against all projects of reform, as 'the romances of visionary men, and the declamations of those who are never to be satisfied'. Is it well that so large a part of the community should be kept in abject penury, rendered stupid with ignorance, and disgustful with vice, perpetuated in nakedness and hunger, goaded to the commission of crimes, and made victims to the merciless laws which the rich have instituted to oppress them? Is it sedition to enquire whether this state of things may not be exchanged for a better? Or can there be anything more disgraceful to ourselves than to exclaim that 'All is well', merely because we are at our ease, regardless of the misery, degradation and vice that may be occasioned in others?

It is undoubtedly a pernicious mistake which has insinuated itself among certain reformers that leads them to the perpetual indulgence of acrimony and resentment, and renders them too easily reconciled to projects of commotion and violence. But, if we ought to be aware that mildness and an unbounded philanthropy are the most effectual instruments of public welfare, it does not follow that we are to shut our eyes upon the calamities that exist, or to cease from the most ardent aspirations for their removal.

There is one argument to which the advocates of monarchy and aristocracy always have recourse, when driven from every other pretence; the mischievous nature of democracy. 'However imperfect the two former of these institutions may be in themselves, they are found necessary,' we are told, 'as accommodations to the imperfection of human nature.' It is for the reader who has considered the arguments of the preceding chapters to decide how far it is probable that circumstances can occur which should make it our duty to submit to these complicated evils. Meanwhile let us proceed to examine that democracy of which so alarming a picture has usually been exhibited.

CHAPTER XIV

GENERAL FEATURES OF DEMOCRACY

Definition. – Supposec evils of this form of government – ascendancy of the ignorant – of the crafty – inconstancy – rash confidence – groundless suspicion. – Merits and defects of democracy compared. – Its moral tendency. – Tendency of truth. – Representation.

DEMOCRACY is a system of government according to which every member of society is considered as a man, and nothing more. So far as positive regulation is concerned, if indeed that can, with any propriety, be termed regulation, which is the mere recognition of the simplest of all moral principles, every man is regarded as equal. Talents and wealth, wherever they exist, will not fail to obtain a certain degree of influence, without requiring positive institution to second their operation.

But there are certain disadvantages that may seem the necessary result of democratical equality. In political society, it is reasonable to suppose that the wise will be outnumbered by the unwise; and it will be inferred 'that the welfare of the whole will therefore be at the mercy of ignorance and folly'. It is true that the ignorant will generally be sufficiently willing to listen to the judicious, 'but their very ignorance will incapacitate them from discerning the merit of their guides. The turbulent and crafty demagogue will often possess greater advantages for inveigling their judgement than the man who, with purer intentions, may possess a less brilliant talent. Add to this that the demagogue has a never failing resource, in the ruling imperfection of human nature, that of preferring the specious present to the substantial future. This is what is usually termed playing upon the passions of mankind. Politics have hitherto presented an enigma that all the wit of man has been insufficient to solve. Is it to be supposed that the uninstructed multitude should always be able to resist the artful sophistry, and captivating eloquence, that may be employed to perplex the subject with still further obscurity? Will it not often happen that the schemes proposed by the ambitious disturber will possess a meretricious attraction which the severe and sober project of the discerning statesman shall be unable to compensate?

'One of the most fruitful sources of human happiness is to be found in the steady and uniform operation of certain fixed principles. But it is the characteristic of a democracy to be wavering and inconstant. The speculator only, who has deeply meditated his principles, is inflexible in his adherence to them. The mass of mankind, as they have never arranged their reflections into system, are at the mercy of every momentary impulse, and liable to change with every wind. But this inconstancy is directly the reverse of political justice.

'Nor is this all. Democracy is a monstrous and unwieldy vessel, launched upon the sea of human passions, without ballast. Liberty, in this unlimited form, is in danger to be lost almost as soon as it is obtained. The ambitious man finds nothing, in this scheme of human affairs, to set bounds to his desires. He has only to dazzle and deceive the multitude, in order to rise to absolute power.

'A further ill consequence flows out of this circumstance. The multitude, conscious of their weakness in this respect, will, in proportion to their love of liberty and equality, be perpetually suspicious and uneasy. Has any man displayed uncommon virtues, or rendered eminent services to his country? He will presently be charged with secretly aiming at the tyranny. Various circumstances will come in aid of this accusation; the general love of novelty, envy of superior merit, and the incapacity of the multitude to understand the motives and character of those who excel them. Like the Athenian, they will be tired of hearing Aristides constantly called the Just. Thus will merit be too frequently the victim of ignorance and envy. Thus will all that is liberal and refined, whatever the human mind in its highest state of improvement is able to conceive, be often overpowered by the turbulence of unbridled passion, and the rude dictates of savage folly.'

If this picture must be inevitably realized wherever democratical principles are established, the state of human nature would be peculiarly unfortunate. No form of government can be devised which does not partake of monarchy, aristocracy or democracy. We have taken a copious survey of the two former, and it would seem impossible that greater or more inveterate mischiefs can be inflicted on mankind than those which are inflicted by them. No portrait of injustice, degradation and vice can be exhibited that can surpass the fair and inevitable inferences from the principle upon which they are built. If then democracy can, by any arguments, be brought down to a level with such monstrous institutions as these, in which there is neither integrity nor reason, our prospects of the future happiness of mankind will indeed be deplorable.

But this is impossible. Supposing that we should even be obliged to take democracy with all the disadvantages that were ever annexed to it, and that no remedy could be discovered for any of its defects, it would still be preferable to the exclusive system of other forms. Let us take Athens, with all its turbulence and instability; with the popular and temperate usurpations of Pisistratus and Pericles; with its monstrous ostracism, by which, with undisguised injustice, they were accustomed periodically to banish some eminent citizen, without the imputation of a crime; with the imprisonment of Miltiades, the exile of Aristides, and the murder of Phocion: – with all these errors on its head, it is incontrovertible that Athens exhibited a more illustrious and enviable spectacle than all the monarchies and aristocracies that ever existed. Who would reject their gallant love of virtue and independence because it was accompanied with irregularities? Who would pass an unreserved condemnation upon their penetrating mind, their quick discernment, and their ardent feeling because they were subject occasionally to be intemperate and impetuous? Shall we compare a people of such incredible achievements, such exquisite refinement, gay without insensibility, and splendid without intemperance, in the midst of whom grew up the greatest poets, the noblest artists, the most finished orators, and the most disinterested philosophers, the world ever saw – shall we compare this chosen seat of patriotism, independence and generous virtue with the torpid and selfish realms of monarchy and aristocracy? All is not happiness that looks tranquillity. Better were a portion of turbulence and fluctuation than that unwholesome calm in which all the best faculties of the human mind are turned to putrescence and poison.

In the estimate that is usually made of democracy, one of the sources of our erroneous judgement lies in our taking mankind such as monarchy and aristocracy have made them, and thence judging how fit they are to manage for themselves. Monarchy and aristocracy would be no evils if their tendency were not to undermine the virtues and the understandings of their subjects. The thing most necessary is to remove all those restraints which prevent the human mind from attaining its genuine strength. Implicit faith, blind submission to authority, timid fear, a distrust of our powers, an inattention to our own importance and the good purposes we are able to effect, these are the chief obstacles to human improvement. Democracy restores to man a consciousness of his value, teaches him, by the removal of authority and oppression, to listen only to the suggestions of reason, gives him confidence to treat all other men with frankness and simplicity, and induces him to regard them no longer as enemies against whom to be upon his guard, but as brethren whom it becomes him to assist. The citizen of a democratical state, when he looks upon the oppression and injustice that prevail in the countries around him, cannot but entertain an inexpressible esteem for the advantages he enjoys, and the most unalterable determination to preserve them. The influence of democracy upon the sentiments of its members is altogether of the negative sort, but its consequences are inestimable. Nothing can be more unreasonable than to argue from men as we now find them to men as they may hereafter be made. Strict and accurate reasoning, instead of suffering us to be surprised that Athens did so much, would at first induce us to wonder that she retained so many imperfections.

The road to the improvement of mankind is in the utmost degree simple, to speak and act the truth. If the Athenians had had more of this, it is impossible they should have been so flagrantly erroneous. To express ourselves to all men with honesty and unreserve, and to administer justice without partiality, are principles which, when once thoroughly adopted, are in the highest degree prolific. They enlighten the understanding, give decision to the judgement, and strip misrepresentation of its speciousness. In Athens, men suffered themselves to be dazzled by splendour and show. If the error in their constitution which led to this defect can be discovered, if a form of political society can be devised in which men shall be accustomed to judge simply and soberly, and be habitually exercised to the manliness of truth, democracy will, in that society, cease from the turbulence, instability, fickleness and violence that have too often characterized it. Nothing can be more worthy to be depended on than the omnipotence of truth, or, in other words, than the connection between the judgement and the outward behaviour.* The contest between truth and falsehood is of itself too unequal for the former to stand in need of support from any political ally. The more it is discovered, especially that part of it which relates to man in society, the more simple and self-evident will it appear; and it will be found impossible any otherwise to account for its having been so long concealed than from the pernicious influence of positive institution.

There is another obvious consideration that has frequently been alleged to account for the imperfection of ancient democracies, which is worthy of our attention, though it be not so important as the argument which has just been stated. The ancients were unaccustomed to the idea of deputed or representative assemblies; and it is reasonable to suppose that affairs might often be transacted with the utmost order, in such assemblies, which might be productive of much tumult and confusion if submitted to the personal discussion of the citizens at large.† By this happy expedient, we secure many of the pretended benefits of aristocracy, as well as the real benefits of democracy. The discussion of national affairs is brought before persons of superior education and wisdom: we

---

* Book I, Chap. V.

† The general grounds of this institution have been stated, Book III, Chap. IV. The exceptions which limit its value will be seen in the twenty-third chapter of the present book.

may conceive them, not only the appointed medium of the sentiments of their constituents, but authorized, upon certain occasions, to act on their part, in the same manner as an unlearned parent delegates his authority over his child to a preceptor of greater accomplishments than himself. This idea, within proper limits, might probably be entitled to approbation, provided the elector had the wisdom not to recede from the exercise of his own understanding in political concerns, exerted his censorial power over his representative, and were accustomed, if the representative were unable, after the fullest explanation, to bring him over to his opinion, to transfer his deputation to another.

The true value of the system of representation seems to be as follows. Large promiscuous assemblies, such as the assemblies of the people in Athens and Rome, must perhaps always be somewhat tumultuous, and liable to many of the vices of democracy enumerated in the commencement of this chapter. A representative assembly, deputed on the part of the multitude, will escape many of their defects. But representative government is necessarily imperfect. It is, as was formerly observed,* a point to be regretted, in the abstract notion of civil society, that a majority should overbear a minority, and that the minority, after having opposed and remonstrated, should be obliged practically to submit to that which was the subject of their remonstrance. But this evil, inseparable from political government, is aggravated by representation, which removes the power of making regulations one step further from the people whose lot it is to obey them. Representation therefore, though a remedy, or rather a palliative, for certain evils, is not a remedy so excellent or complete as should authorize us to rest in it as the highest improvement of which the social order is capable.†

Such are the general features of democratical government: but this is a subject of too much importance to be

* Book III, Chap. II.
† See this subject pursued in Chap. XXIII, XXIV.

dismissed without the fullest examination of everything that may enable us to decide upon its merits. We will proceed to consider the further objections that have been alleged against it.

CHAPTER XV

OF POLITICAL IMPOSTURE

Importance of this topic. – Example in the doctrine of eternal punishment. – Its inutility argued – from history – from the nature of mind. – Second example: the religious sanction of a legislative system. – This idea is, 1. in strict construction impracticable – 2. injurious. – Third example: principle of political order. – Vice has no essential advantage over virtue. – Motives of political imposture. – Effects that attend it. – Situation of the advocates of this system. – Absurdity of their reasonings.

ALL the arguments that have been employed to prove the insufficiency of democracy grow out of this one root, the supposed necessity of deception and prejudice for restraining the turbulence of human passions. Without the assumption of this principle the argument could not be sustained for a moment. The direct and decisive answer would be, 'Are kings and lords intrinsically wiser and better than their humbler neighbours? Can there be any solid ground of distinction except what is founded in personal merit? Are not men, really and strictly considered, equal, except so far as what is personal and inalienable, establishes a difference?' To these questions there can be but one reply, 'Such is the order of reason and absolute truth, but artificial distinctions are necessary for the happiness of mankind. Without deception and prejudice the turbulence of human passions cannot be

493

restrained.' Let us then examine the merits of this theory; and these will be best illustrated by an instance.

It has been held, by some divines and some politicians, 'that the doctrine which teaches that men will be eternally tormented in another world, for their errors and misconduct in this, is in its own nature unreasonable and absurd, but that it is necessary, to keep mankind in awe. Do we not see', say they, 'that, notwithstanding this terrible denunciation, the world is overrun with vice? What then would be the case if the irregular passions of mankind were set free from their present restraint, and they had not the fear of this retribution before their eyes?'

This argument seems to be founded in a singular inattention to the dictates of history and experience, as well as to those of reason. The ancient Greeks and Romans had nothing of this dreadful apparatus of fire and brimstone, and a torment 'the smoke of which ascends for ever and ever'. Their religion was less personal than political. They confided in the Gods as protectors of the state, and this inspired them with invincible courage. In periods of public calamity, they found a ready consolation in expiatory sacrifices to appease the anger of the Gods. The attention of these beings was conceived to be principally directed to the ceremonial of religion, and very little to the moral excellencies and defects of their votaries, which were supposed to be sufficiently provided for by the inevitable tendency of moral excellence or defect to increase or diminish individual happiness. If their systems included the doctrine of a future existence, little attention was paid by them to the connecting the moral deserts of individuals in this life with their comparative situation in another. In Homer, the Elysian fields are a seat of perpetual weariness and languor: Elysium and Tartarus are enclosed in the same circuit; and the difference between them, as most, amounts to no more than the difference between sadness and misery. The same omission, of future retribution as the basis of moral obligation, runs through the systems of the

Persians, the Egyptians, the Celts, the Phenicians, the Jews, and indeed every system which has not been, in some manner or other, the offspring of the Christian. If we were to form our judgement of these nations by the above argument, we should expect to find every individual among them cutting his neighbour's throat, and inured to the commission of every enormity. But they were, in reality, as susceptible of the regulations of government, and the order of society, as those whose imaginations have been most artfully terrified by the threats of future retribution; and some of them were much more generous, determined and attached to the public weal.

Nothing can be more contrary to a just observation of the nature of the human mind than to suppose that these speculative tenets have much influence in making mankind more virtuous than they would otherwise be found. Human beings are placed in the midst of a system of things, all the parts of which are strictly connected with each other, and exhibit a sympathy and unison, by means of which the whole is rendered familiar, and, as it were, inmate to the mind. The respect I shall obtain, and the happiness I shall enjoy, for the remainder of my life are topics of which I feel the entire comprehension. I understand the value of ease, liberty and knowledge, to myself, and my fellow men. I perceive that these things, and a certain conduct intending them, are connected, in the visible system of the world, and not by any supernatural and unusual interposition. But all that can be told me of a future world, a world of spirits, or of glorified bodies, where the employments are spiritual, and the first cause is to be rendered a subject of immediate perception, or of a scene of retribution, where the mind, doomed to everlasting inactivity, shall be wholly a prey to the upbraidings of remorse, and the sarcasms of devils, is so foreign to everything with which I am acquainted, that my mind in vain endeavours to believe or to understand it. If doctrines like these occupy the habitual reflections of any, it is not of the lawless, the violent and ungovernable, but of the sober and conscientious, overwhelming them with gratuitous anxiety, or persuading them passively to submit to despotism and injustice, that they may receive the recompense of their patience hereafter. This objection is equally applicable to every species of deception. Fables may amuse the imagination; but can never stand in the place of reason and judgement as the principles of human conduct. – Let us proceed to a second instance.

It is affirmed by Rousseau, in his treatise of the Social Contract, 'that no legislator could ever establish a grand political system without having recourse to religious imposture. To render a people who are yet to receive the impressions of political wisdom susceptible of the evidence of that wisdom would be to convert the effect of civilization into the cause. The legislator being deprived of assistance from the two grand operative causes among men, reasoning and force, is obliged to have recourse to an authority of a different sort, which may draw without compulsion, and persuade without elucidation.'*

* 'Pour qu'un peuple naissant pût goûter les saines maximes de la politique et suivre les règles fondamentales de la raison de l'état, il faudroit que l'effet pût devenir la cause, que l'esprit social, qui doit être l'ouvrage de l'institution, présidât à l'institution même, et que les hommes fussent avant les lois ce qu'ils doivent devenir par elles. Ainsi donc le législateur ne pouvant employer ni la force ni le raisonnement; c'est une necessité qu'il recour a une autorité d'un autre ordre, qui puisse entraîner sans violence, et persuader sans convaincre.' *Du Contrat Social*, Liv. II, Chap. vii.

Having frequently quoted Rousseau in the course of this work, it may be allowable to say one word of his general merits, as a moral and political writer. He has been subjected to continual ridicule for the extravagance of the proposition with which he began his literary career; that the savage state was the genuine and proper condition of man. It was however by a very slight mistake that he missed the opposite opinion which it is the business of the present enquiry to establish. He only substituted, as the topic of his eulogium, the period that preceded government and laws, instead of the period that may possibly follow upon

These are the dreams of a fertile conception, busy in the erection of imaginary systems. To a wary and sceptical mind, that project would seem to promise little substantial benefit, which set out from so erroneous a principle. To terrify or seduce men into the reception of a system the reasonableness of which they were unable to perceive is surely a very questionable method for rendering them sober, judicious, reasonable and happy.

In reality, no grand political system ever was introduced in the manner Rousseau describes. Lycurgus, as he observes, obtained the sanction of the oracle at Delphi to the constitution he had established. But was it by an appeal to Apollo that he persuaded the Spartans to renounce the use of money, to consent to an equal division of land, and to adopt various other regulations, the most contrary to their preconceived habits and ideas? No: it was by an appeal to their understandings, in the

---

their abolition. It is sufficiently observable that, where he describes the enthusiastic influx of truth that first made him a moral and political writer (in his second letter to Malesherbes), he does not so much as mention his fundamental error, but only the just principles which led him into it. He was the first to teach that the imperfections of government were the only perennial source of the vices of mankind; and this principle was adopted from him by Helvetius and others. But he saw further than this, that government, however formed, was little capable of affording solid benefit to mankind, which they did not. This principle has since (probably without being suggested by the writings of Rousseau) been expressed with great perspicuity and energy, but not developed, by Thomas Paine, in the first page of his *Common Sense*.

Rousseau, notwithstanding his great genius, was full of weakness and prejudice. His *Emile* deserves perhaps, upon the whole, to be regarded as one of the principal reservoirs of philosophical truth as yet existing in the world; though with a perpetual mixture of absurdity and mistake. In his writings expressly political, *Du Contrat Social* and *Considérations sur la Pologne*, the superiority of his genius seems to desert him. To his merits as an investigator, we should not forget to add that the term eloquence is perhaps more precisely descriptive of his mode of composition than of that of any other writer that ever existed.

midst of long debate and perpetual counteraction, and through the inflexibility of his courage and resolution, that he at last attained his purpose. Lycurgus thought proper, after the whole was concluded, to obtain the sanction of the oracle, conceiving that it became him to neglect no method of substantiating the benefit he had conferred on his countrymen. It is indeed scarcely possible to persuade a society of men to adopt any system without convincing them that it is their wisdom to adopt it. It is difficult to conceive a company of such miserable dupes, as to receive a code, without any imagination that it is salutary or wise or just, but upon this single recommendation that it is delivered to them from the Gods. The only reasonable, and infinitely the most efficacious method of changing the established customs of any people is by creating in them a general opinion of their erroneousness and insufficiency.

But, if it be indeed impracticable to persuade men into the adoption of any system without employing as our principal argument the intrinsic rectitude of that system, what is the argument which he would desire to use who had most at heart the welfare and improvement of the persons concerned? Would he begin by teaching them to reason well, or to reason ill? by unnerving their mind with prejudice, or new stringing it with truth?

How many arts, and how noxious to those towards whom we employ them, are necessary, if we would successfully deceive? We must not only leave their reason in indolence at first, but endeavour to supersede its exertion in any future instance. If men be, for the present, kept right by prejudice, what will become of them hereafter, if, by any future penetration, or any accidental discovery, this prejudice shall be annihilated? Detection is not always the fruit of systematical improvement, but may be effected by some solitary exertion of the faculty, or some luminous and irresistible argument, while everything else remains as it was. If we would first deceive, and then maintain our deception unimpaired, we shall need penal statutes, and licensers of the press, and hired ministers of falsehood and imposture. Admirable modes these for the propagation of wisdom and virtue!

There is another case, similar to that stated by Rousseau, upon which much stress has been laid by political writers. 'Obedience,' say they, 'must either be courted or compelled. We must either make a judicious use of the prejudices and the ignorance of mankind, or be contented to have no hold upon them but their fears, and to maintain social order entirely by the severity of punishment. To dispense us from this painful necessity, authority ought carefully to be invested with a sort of magic persuasion. Citizens should serve their country, not with a frigid submission that scrupulously weighs its duties, but with an enthusiasm that places its honour in its loyalty. For this reason, our governors and superiors must not be spoken of with levity. They must be considered, independently of their individual character, as deriving a sacredness from their office. They must be accompanied with splendour and veneration. Advantage must be taken of the imperfection of mankind. We ought to gain over their judgements through the medium of their senses, and not leave the conclusions to be drawn to the uncertain process of immature reason.*

This is still the same argument under another form. It takes for granted that a true observation of things is inadequate to teach us our duty; and of consequence recommends an equivocal engine, which may with equal ease be employed in the service of justice and injustice, but would surely appear somewhat more in its place in the service of the latter. It is injustice that stands most in need of superstition and mystery, and will most frequently be a gainer by the imposition. This hypothesis proceeds upon an assumption which young men sometimes impute to their parents and preceptors. It says,

* This argument is the great common place of Mr Burke's *Reflections on the Revolution in France*, and of a multitude of other works, ancient and modern, upon the subject of government.

'Mankind must be kept in ignorance: if they know vice, they will love it too well; if they perceive the charms of error, they will never return to the simplicity of truth.' And, strange as it may appear, this bare-faced and unplausible argument has been the foundation of a very popular and generally received hypothesis. It has taught politicians to believe that a people, once sunk into decrepitude, as it has been termed, could never afterwards be endured with purity and vigour.*

There are two modes according to which the minds of human beings may be influenced by him who is desirous to conduct them. The first of these is a strong and commanding picture, taking hold of the imagination, and surprising the judgement; the second, a distinct and unanswerable statement of reasons, which, the oftener they are reflected upon, and the more they are sifted, will be found by so much the more cogent.

One of the tritest and most general, as well as most self-evident, maxims in the science of the human mind is that the former of these is only adapted to a temporary purpose, while the latter alone is adequate to a purpose that is durable. How comes it then that, in the business of politics and government, the purposes of which are evidently not temporary, the fallacious mode of proceeding should have been so generally and so eagerly resorted to?

This may be accounted for from two considerations: first the diffidence, and secondly, the vanity and self-applause, of legislators and statesmen. It is an arduous task always to assign reasons to those whose conduct we would direct; it is by no means easy to answer objections and remove difficulties. It requires patience; it demands profound science and severe meditation. This is the reason why, in the instance already alluded to, parents and preceptors find a refuge for their indolence, while by false pretences they cheat the young into compliance, in preference to showing them, as far as they may be capable of understanding it, the true face of things.

* Book I, Chap. VII.

Statesmen secretly distrust their own powers, and therefore substitute quackery in the room of principle.

But, beside the recommendations that quackery derives from indolence and ignorance, it is also calculated to gratify the vanity of him that employs it. He that would reason with another, and honestly explain to him the motives of the action he recommends, descends to a footing of equality. But he who undertakes to delude us, and fashion us to his purpose by a specious appearance, has a feeling that he is our master. Though his task is neither so difficult nor so honourable as that of the ingenuous dealer, he regards it as more flattering. At every turn he admires his own dexterity; he triumphs in the success of his artifices, and delights to remark how completely mankind are his dupes.

There are disadvantages of no ordinary magnitude that attend upon the practice of political imposture.

It is utterly incompatible with the wholesome tone of the human understanding. Man, we have seen some reason to believe, is a being of progressive nature, and capable of unlimited improvement. But his progress must be upon the plain line of reason and truth. As long as he keeps the open road, his journey is prosperous and promising; but, if he turn aside into by-paths, he will soon come to a point where there is no longer either avenue or track. He that is accustomed to a deceitful medium will be ignorant of the true colours of things. He that is often imposed on will be no judge of the fair and the genuine. Human understanding cannot be tampered with, with impunity; if we admit prejudice, deception and implicit faith in one subject, the inquisitive energies of the mind will be more or less weakened in all. This is a fact so well known that the persons who recommend the governing mankind by deception are, to a man, advocates of the opinion that the human species is essentially stationary.

A further disadvantage of political imposture is that the bubble is hourly in danger of bursting, and the delusion of coming to an end. The playing upon our passions and our imagination, as we have already said, can never fully answer any but a temporary purpose. In delusion there is always inconsistency. It will look plausibly, when placed in a certain light; but it will not bear handling, and examining on all sides. It suits us in a certain animated tone of mind; but, in a calm and tranquil season, it is destitute of power. Politics and government are affairs of a durable concern; they should therefore rest upon a basis that will abide the test.

The system of political imposture divides men into two classes, one of which is to think and reason for the whole, and the other to take the conclusions of their superiors on trust. This distinction is not founded in the nature of things; there is no such inherent difference between man and man as it thinks proper to suppose. Nor is it less injurious than it is unfounded. The two classes which it creates must be more and less than man. It is too much to expect of the former, while we consign to them an unnatural monopoly, that they should rigidly consult for the good of the whole. It is an iniquitous requisition upon the latter that they should never employ their understandings, or penetrate into the essences of things, but always rest in a deceitful appearance. It is iniquitous to deprive them of that chance for additional wisdom which would result from a greater number of minds being employed in the enquiry, and from the distinterested and impartial spirit that might be expected to accompany it.

How strangely incongruous is that state of mind which the system we are here examining is adapted to recommend. Shall those persons who govern the springs, and carry on the deception, be themselves in the secret of the imposition or not? This is a fundamental question. It has often been started in relation to the authors or abettors of a new fabric of superstition. On the one hand, we should be apt to imagine that, for a machine to be guided well, it is desirable that those who guide it should be acquainted with its principle. We should suppose that, otherwise, the governors we speak of would not always know the extent and the particulars as to which the deception was salutary and that, where 'the blind led the blind', the public welfare would not be in a much better condition than the greatest advocates of imposture could suppose it to be under the auspices of truth. But then again, on the other hand, no man can be powerful in persuasion in a point where he has not first persuaded himself. Beside that the secret must, first or last, be confided to so many hands that it will be continually in danger of being discovered by the public at large. So that for these reasons it would seem best that he who first invented the art of leading mankind at pleasure, and set the wheels of political craft in motion, should suffer his secret to die with him.

And what sort of character must exist in a state thus modified? Those at the head of affairs, if they be acquainted with the principle of the political machine, must be perpetually anxious lest mankind should unexpectedly recover the use of their faculties. Falsehood must be their discipline and incessant study. We will suppose that they adopt this system of imposture, in the first instance, from the most benevolent motives. But will the continual practice of concealment, hypocrisy and artifice make no breaches in their character? Will they, in despite of habit, retain all that ingenuousness of heart which is the first principle of virtue?

With respect to the multitude, in this system, they are placed in the middle between two fearful calamities, suspicion on one side, and infatuation on the other. Even children, when their parents explain to them that there is one system of morality for youth and another for mature age, and endeavour to cheat them into submission, are generally found to suspect the trick. It cannot reasonably be thought that the mass of the governed in any country should be less clear sighted than children. Thus they are kept in perpetual vibration, between rebellious discontent, and infatuated credulity. Sometimes they suppose their governors to be the messengers and favourites of heaven, a supernatural order of beings; and sometimes they suspect them to be a combination of usurpers to rob and oppress them. For they dare not indulge themselves in solving the dilemma, because they are held in awe by oppression and the gallows.

Is this the genuine state of man? Is this a condition so desirable that we should be anxious to entail it upon posterity for ever? Is it high treason to enquire whether it may be meliorated? Are we sure that every change from such a situation of things is severely to be deprecated? Is it not worth while to suffer that experiment which shall consist in a gradual, and almost insensible, abolition of such mischievous institutions?

It may not be uninstructive to consider what sort of discourse must be held, or book written, by him who should make himself the champion of political imposture. He cannot avoid secretly wishing that the occasion had never existed. What he undertakes is to lengthen the reign of 'salutary prejudices'. For this end, he must propose to himself the two opposite purposes, of prolonging the deception, and proving that it is necessary to deceive. By whom is it that he intends his book should be read? Chiefly by the governed; the governors need little inducement to continue the system. But, at the same time that he tells us, we should cherish the mistake as mistake, and the prejudice as prejudice, he is himself lifting the veil, and destroying his own system. While the affair of our superiors and the enlightened is simply to impose upon us, the task is plain and intelligible. But, the moment they begin to write books, to persuade us that we ought to be willing to be deceived, it may well be suspected that their system is upon the decline. It is not to be wondered at if the greatest genius, and the sincerest and most benevolent champion, should fail in producing a perspicuous or very persuasive treatise, when he undertakes so hopeless a task.

The argument of such a system must, when attentively examined, be the most untenable that can be imagined. It undertakes to prove that we must not be governed by reason. To prove! How prove? Necessarily, from the resources of reason. What can be more contradictory? If I must not trust the conclusions of reason relative to the intrinsic value of things, why trust to your reasons in favour of the benefit of being deceived? You cut up your own argument by the roots. If I must reject the dictates of reason in one point, there can be no possible cause why I should adopt them in another. Moral reasons and inducements, as we have repeatedly shown, consist singly in this, an estimate of consequences. What can supersede this estimate? Not an opposite estimate; for, by the nature of morality, the purpose, in the first instance, is to take into account all the consequences. Not something else, for a consideration of consequences is the only thing with which morality and practical wisdom are directly concerned. The moment I dismiss the information of my own eyes and my own understanding, there is, in all justice, an end to persuasion, expostulation or conviction. There is no pretence by which I can disallow the authority of inference and deduction in one instance that will not justify a similar proceeding in every other. He that, in any case, designedly surrenders the use of his own understanding is condemned to remain for ever at the beck of contingence and caprice, and is even bound in consistency no more to frame his course by the results of demonstration than by the wildest dreams of delirium and insanity.

CHAPTER XVI

OF THE CAUSES OF WAR

Offensive war contrary to the nature of democracy. – Defensive war exceedingly rare. – Erroneousness of the ideas usually annexed to the phrase, our country. – Nature of war delineated. – Insufficient causes of war – the acquiring a healthful and vigorous tone to the public mind – the putting a termination upon private insults – the menaces or preparations of our neighbours – the dangerous consequences of concession – the vindication of national honour. – Two legitimate causes of war.

EXCLUSIVELY of those objections which have been urged against the democratical system, as it relates to the internal management of affairs, there are others, upon which considerable stress has been laid, in relation to the transactions of a state with foreign powers, to war and peace, and to treaties of alliance and commerce.

There is indeed an eminent difference, with respect to these, between the democratical system and all others. It is perhaps impossible to show that a single war ever did or could have taken place, in the history of mankind, that did not in some way originate with those two great political monopolies, monarchy and aristocracy. This might have formed an additional article, in the catalogue of the evils to which they have given birth, little inferior to any of those we have enumerated. But nothing could be more idle than to overcharge a subject the evidence of which is irresistible.

What could be the source of misunderstanding between states, where no man, or body of men, found encouragement to the accumulation of privileges to himself, at the expense of the rest? Why should they pursue additional wealth or territory? These would lose their value the moment they became the property of all. No man can cultivate more than a certain portion of land. Money is respresentative, and not real wealth. If every man in the society possessed a double portion of money, bread, and every other commodity, would sell at double their present price, and the relative situation of each individual would be just what it had been before. War and conquest cannot be beneficial to the community. Their tendency is to elevate a few at the expense of the rest; and consequently they will never be undertaken but where the many are the instruments of the few. But this cannot happen in a democracy till the democracy shall become such only in name. If expedients can be devised for maintaining this species of government in its purity, or if there be anything, in the nature of wisdom and intellectual improvement, which has a tendency daily to make truth more prevalent over falsehood, the principle of offensive war will be extirpated. But this principle enters into the very essence of monarchy and aristocracy.

It is not meant here to be insinuated that democracy has not repeatedly been a source of war. It was eminently so among the ancient Romans; the aristocracy found in it an obvious expedient for diverting the attention and encroachments of the people. It may be expected to be so wherever the form of government is complicated, and the nation at large is enabled to become formidable to a band of usurpers. But war will be foreign to the character of any people in proportion as their democracy becomes simple and unalloyed.

Meanwhile, though the principle of offensive war be incompatible with the genius of democracy, a democratical state may be placed in the neighbourhood of states whose government is less equal, and therefore it will be proper to enquire into the supposed disadvantages which the democratical state may sustain in the contest. The only species of war in which it can consistently be engaged will be that the object of which is to repel wanton invasion. Such invasions will be little likely frequently to occur. For what purpose should a corrupt state attack a country that has no feature in common with itself upon which to build a misunderstanding and that presents, in the very nature of its government, a pledge of its inoffensiveness and neutrality? Add to which, it will presently appear that this state which yields the fewest incitements to provoke an attack will prove a very undesirable adversary to those by whom an attack shall be commenced.

One of the most essential principles of political justice is diametrically the reverse of that which impostors, as well as patriots, have too frequently agreed to recommend. Their perpetual exhortation has been, 'Love your country. Sink the personal existence of individuals in the existence of the community. Make little account of the particular men of whom the society consists, but aim at the general wealth, prosperity and glory. Purify your mind from the gross ideas of sense, and elevate it to the single contemplation of that abstract individual, of which particular men are so many detached members, valuable only for the place they fill.'*

The lessons of reason on this head are different from these. 'Society is an ideal existence, and not, on its own account, entitled to the smallest regard. The wealth, prosperity and glory of the whole are unintelligible chimeras. Set no value on anything but in proportion as you are convinced of its tendency to make individual men happy and virtuous. Benefit, by every practicable mode, man wherever he exists; but be not deceived by the specious idea of affording services to a body of men, for which no individual man is the better. Society was instituted, not for the sake of glory, not to furnish splendid materials for the page of history, but for the benefit of its members. The love of our country, as the term has usually been understood, has too often been found to be one of those specious illusions which are employed by impostors for the purpose of rendering the multitude the blind instruments of their crooked designs.'

* *Du Contrat Social*, etc. etc. etc.

In the meantime, the maxims which are here controverted have had by so much the more success in the world as they bear some resemblance to the purest sentiments of virtue. Virtue is nothing else but kind and sympathetic feelings reduced into principle. Undisciplined feeling would induce me, now to interest myself exclusively for one man, and now for another, to be eagerly solicitous for those who are present to me, and to forget the absent. Feeling ripened into virtue embraces the interests of the whole human race, and constantly proposes to itself the production of the greatest quantity of happiness. But, while it anxiously adjusts the balance of interests, and yields to no case, however urgent, to the prejudice of the whole, it keeps aloof from the unmeaning rant of romance, and uniformly recollects that happiness, in order to be real, must necessarily be individual.

The love of our country has often been found to be a deceitful principle, as its direct tendency is to set the interests of one division of mankind in opposition to another, and to establish a preference built upon accidental relations, and not upon reason. Much of what has been understood by the appellation is excellent, but perhaps nothing that can be brought within the strict interpretation of the phrase. A wise and well informed man will not fail to be the votary of liberty and justice. He will be ready to exert himself in their defence, wherever they exist. It cannot be a matter of indifference to him, when his own liberty and that of other men with whose merits and capacities he has the best opportunity of being acquainted are involved in the event of the struggle to be made. But his attachment will be to the cause, as the cause of man, and not to the country. Wherever there are individuals who understand the value of political justice, and are prepared to assert it, that is his country. Whereever he can most contribute to the diffusion of these principles and the real happiness of mankind, that is his country. Nor does he desire, for any country, any other benefit than justice.

To apply these principles to the subject of war. – And, before that application can be adequately made, it is necessary to recollect, for a moment, the force of the term.

Because individuals were liable to error, and suffered their apprehensions of justice to be perverted by a bias in favour of themselves, government was instituted. Because nations were susceptible of a similar weakness, and could find no sufficient umpire to whom to appeal, war was introduced. Men were induced deliberately to seek each other's lives, and to adjudge the controversies between them, not according to the dictates of reason and justice, but as either should prove most successful in devastation and murder. This was no doubt in the first instance the extremity of exasperation and rage. But it has since been converted into a trade. One part of the nation pays another part, to murder and be murdered in their stead; and the most trivial causes, a supposed insult, or a sally of youthful ambition, have sufficed to deluge provinces with blood.

We can have no adequate idea of this evil unless we visit, at least in imagination, a field of battle. Here men deliberately destroy each other by thousands, without resentment against, or even knowledge of, each other. The plain is strewed with death in all its forms. Anguish and wounds display the diversified modes in which they can torment the human frame. Towns are burned; ships are blown up in the air, while the mangled limbs descend on every side; the fields are laid desolate; the wives of the inhabitants exposed to brutal insult; and their children driven forth to hunger and nakedness. It is an inferior circumstance, though by no means unattended with the widest and most deplorable effects, when we add, to these scenes of horror, and the subversion of all ideas of moral justice they must occasion in the auditors and spectators, the immense treasures which are wrung, in the form of taxes, from those inhabitants whose residence is removed from the seat of war.

After this enumeration, we may venture to enquire what are the justifiable causes and rules of war.

It is not a justifiable reason 'that we imagine our own people would be rendered more cordial and orderly, if we could find a neighbour with whom to quarrel, and who might serve as a touchstone to try the characters and dispositions of individuals among ourselves'.* We are not at liberty to have recourse to the most complicated and atrocious of all mischiefs, in the way of an experiment.

It is not a justifiable reason, 'that we have been exposed to certain insults, and that tyrants, perhaps, have delighted in treating with contempt, the citizens of our happy state who have visited their dominions'. Government ought to protect the tranquillity of those who reside within the sphere of its functions; but, if individuals think proper to visit other countries, they must be delivered over to the protection of general reason. Some proportion must be observed between the evil of which we complain and the evil which the nature of the proposed remedy inevitably includes.

It is not a justifiable reason 'that our neighbour is preparing, or menacing, hostilities'. If we be obliged to prepare in our turn, the inconvenience is only equal; and it is not to be believed that a despotic country is

* The reader will easily perceive that the pretences by which the people of France were instigated to a declaration of war, in April 1792, were in the author's mind in this and the two following articles. Nor will a few lines be misspent in this note in stating the feelings of a dispassionate observer, upon the wantonness with which they have appeared ready, upon different occasions, to proceed to extremities. If policy were in question, it might be doubted whether the confederacy of kings would ever have been brought into action against them, had it not been for their precipitation; and it might be asked, what impression they must expect to find produced upon the minds of other states; by their intemperate commission of hostility? But that equal humanity, which prescribes to us never, by a hasty interference, to determine the doubtful balance in favour of murder, is a superior consideration, in comparison with which policy is scarcely worthy to be named.

capable of more exertion than a free one, when the task incumbent on the latter is indispensable precaution.

It has sometimes been held to be sound reasoning upon this subject 'that we ought not to yield little things, which may not, in themselves, be sufficiently valuable to authorize this tremendous appeal, because a disposition to yield only invites further experiments'. Much otherwise; at least when the character of such a nation is sufficiently understood. A people that will not contend for nominal and trivial objects, that adheres to the precise line of unalterable justice, and that does not fail to be moved at the moment that it ought to be moved, is not the people that its neighbours will delight to urge to extremities.

'The vindication of national honour' is a very insufficient reason for hostilities. True honour is to be found only in integrity and justice. It has been doubted how far a view to reputation ought, in matters of inferior moment, to be permitted to influence the conduct of individuals; but, let the case of individuals be decided as it may, reputation, considered as a separate motive in the instance of nations, can perhaps never be justifiable. In individuals, it seems as if I might, consistently with the utmost real integrity, be so misconstrued and misrepresented by others as to render my efforts at usefulness almost necessarily abortive. But this reason does not apply to the case of nations. Their real story cannot easily be suppressed. Usefulness and public spirit, in relation to them, chiefly belong to the transactions of their members among themselves; and their influence in the transactions of neighbouring nations is a consideration evidently subordinate – The question which respects the justifiable causes of war would be liable to few difficulties, if we were accustomed, along with the word, strongly to call up to our minds the thing which that word is intended to represent.

Accurately considered, there can probably be but two causes of war that can maintain any plausible claim to justice; and one of them is among those which the logic of sovereigns, and the law of nations, as it has been termed, have been thought to proscribe: these are the defence of our own liberty, and of the liberty of others. The well known objection to the latter of these cases is 'that one nation ought not to interfere in the internal transactions of another'. But certainly every people is fit for the possession of any immunity, as soon as they understand the nature of that immunity, and desire to possess it and it is probable that this condition may be sufficiently realized in cases where, from the subtlety of intrigue, and the tyrannical jealousy of neighbouring kingdoms, they may be rendered incapable of effectually asserting their rights. This principle is capable of being abused by men of ambition and intrigue; but, accurately considered, the very same argument that should induce me to exert myself for the liberties of my own country is equally cogent, so far as my opportunities and ability extend, with respect to the liberties of any other country. But what is my duty in this case is the duty of all; and the exertion must be collective, where collective exertion only can be effectual.

CHAPTER XVII

OF THE OBJECT OF WAR

The repelling an invader. – Not reformation – not restraint – not indemnification. – Nothing can be a sufficient object of war that is not a sufficient cause for beginning it. – Reflections on the balance of power.

LET us pass, from the causes to the objects of war. As defence is the only legitimate cause, the object pursued, reasoning from this principle, will be circumscribed within very narrow limits. It can extend no further than the repelling the enemy from our borders. It is perhaps desirable that, in addition to this, he should afford some proof that he does not propose immediately to renew his invasion; but this, though desirable, affords no sufficient apology for the continuance of hostilities. Declarations of war, and treaties of peace, were the inventions of a barbarous age, and would probably never have grown into established usages if war had customarily gone no further than to the limits of defence.

The criminal justice, as it has been termed, of nations within themselves has only three objects that it can be imagined to have in view, the reformation of the criminal, the restraining him from future excesses, and example. But none of these objects, whatever may be thought of them while confined to their original province, can sufficiently apply to the case of war between independent states. War, as we have already seen, perhaps never originates, on the offending side, in the sentiments of a nation, but of a comparatively small number of individuals: and, were it otherwise, there is something so monstrous in the idea of changing the principles of a whole country by the mode of military execution that every man not lost to sobriety and common sense may be expected to shrink from it with horror.

Restraint appears to be sometimes necessary, with respect to the offenders that exist in the midst of a community, because it is customary for such offenders to assail us with unexpected violence; but nations cannot move with such secrecy as to make an unforeseen attack an object of considerable apprehension. The only effectual means of restraint, in this case, is by disabling, impoverishing and depopulating the country of our adversaries; and, if we recollected that they are men as well as ourselves, and the great mass of them innocent of the quarrel against us, we should be little likely to consider these expedients with complacency. – The idea of making an example of an offending nation is reserved for that God whom the church, as by law established, instructs us to adore.

Indemnification is another object of war which the

same mode of reasoning will not fail to condemn. The true culprits can never be discovered, and the attempt would only serve to confound the innocent and the guilty: not to mention that, nations having no common umpire, the reverting, in the conclusion of every war, to the justice of the original quarrel, and the indemnification to which the parties were entitled, would be a means of rendering the controversy endless. The question respecting the justifiable objects of war would be liable to few difficulties if we laid it down as a maxim that, as often as the principle or object of a war already in existence was changed, it was to be considered as equivalent to the commencement of a new war. This maxim, impartially applied, would not fail to condemn objects of prevention, indemnification and restraint.

The celebrated topic of the balance of power is a mixed consideration, having sometimes been proposed as the cause for beginning a war, and sometimes as an object to be pursued in a war already begun. A war undertaken to maintain the balance of power may be either of defence, as to protect a people who are oppressed, or of prevention, to counteract new acquisitions, or to reduce the magnitude of old possessions. We shall be in little danger of error however if we pronounce wars undertaken to maintain the balance of power to be universally unjust. If any people be oppressed, it is our duty, as has been already said, as far as a favourable opportunity may invite us, to fly to their succour. But it would be well if, in such cases, we called our interference by the name which justice prescribes, and fought against the oppression, and not the power. All hostilities against a neighbouring people, because they are powerful, or because we impute to them evil designs which they have not begun to carry in execution, are incompatible with every principle of morality. If one nation choose to be governed by the monarch, or an individual allied to the monarch, of another, as seems to have been the case in Spain, upon the extinction of the elder branch of the house of Austria, we may endeavour, as individuals, to enlighten them on the subject of government, and imbue them with principles of liberty; but it is an execrable piece of tyranny to tell them, 'You shall exchange the despot you love for the despot you hate, on account of certain remote consequences we apprehend from the accession of the former.' The pretence of the balance of power has, in a multitude of instances, served as a veil to the intrigue of courts; but it would be easy to show that the present independence of the different states of Europe has, in no instance, been materially assisted by the wars undertaken for that purpose. The fascination of a people desiring to become the appendage of a splendid despotism will rarely occur; and, when it does, can justly be counteracted only by peaceable means. The succouring a people in their struggle against oppression must always be just, with this limitation, that to attempt it without an urgent need on their part may uselessly extend the calamities of war, and has a tendency to diminish those energies among themselves the exertion of which might contribute to their virtue and happiness. Add to this, that the object itself, the independence of the different states of Europe, is of an equivocal nature. The despotism which at present prevails in the majority of them is certainly not so excellent as to make us very anxious for its preservation. The press is an engine of so admirable a nature for the destruction of despotism as to elude the sagacity perhaps of the most vigilant police; and the internal checks upon freedom in a mighty empire and distant provinces can scarcely be expected to be equally active with those of a petty tyrant. The reasoning will surely be good with respect to war, which has already been employed upon the subject of government, that an instrument, evil in its own nature, ought never to be selected as the means of promoting our purpose, in any case in which selection can be practised.

CHAPTER XVIII

OF THE CONDUCT OF WAR

*Offensive operations. – Fortifications. – General
action. – Stratagem. – Military contributions. –
Capture of mercantile vessels. – Naval war. –
Humanity. – Military obedience. – Foreign
possessions.*

ANOTHER topic respecting war, which it is of importance
to consider in this place, relates to the mode of conducting it. Upon this article, our judgement will be greatly
facilitated by a recollection of the principles already
established, first, that no war is justifiable but a war
purely defensive; and secondly, that a war already begun
is liable to change its character in this respect, the
moment the object pursued in it becomes in any degree
varied. From these principles it follows as a direct corollary that it is never allowable to make an expedition into
the provinces of the enemy, unless for the purpose of
assisting its oppressed inhabitants. It is scarcely necessary
to add that all false casuistry respecting the application of
this exception would be particularly odious; and that it is
better undisguisedly to avow the corrupt principles of
policy by which we conduct ourselves than hypocritically
to claim the praise of better principles, which we fail not
to wrest to the justification of whatever we desire. The
case of relieving the inhabitants of our enemy's territory,
and their desire of obtaining relief, ought to be unequivocal; we shall be in great danger of misapprehension
on the subject when the question comes under the form
of immediate benefit to ourselves; and, above all, we
must recollect that human blood is not to be shed upon
a precarious experiment.

The occasional advantages of war that might be gained
by offensive operations might be abundantly compensated
by the character of magnanimous forbearance that a rigid
adherence to defence would exhibit, and the effects that

character would produce, both upon foreign nations, and upon our own people. Great unanimity at home can scarcely fail to be the effect of a direct and clear conformity to political justice. The enemy who penetrates into our country, wherever he meets a man will meet a foe. Every obstacle will oppose itself to his progress, while everything will be friendly and assisting to our own forces. He will scarcely be able to procure the slightest intelligence, or understand in any case his relative situation. The principles of defensive war are so simple as to procure an almost infallible success. Fortifications are a very equivocal species of protection, and will perhaps oftener be of advantage to the enemy, by being first taken, and then converted into magazines for his armies. A moving force on the contrary, if it only hovered about his march, and avoided general action, would always preserve the real supriority. The great engine of military success or miscarriage is the article of provisions; and the further the enemy advanced into our country, the more easy would it be to cut off his supply; at the same time that, so long as we avoided general action, any decisive success on his part would be impossible. These principles, if rigidly practised, would soon be so well understood that the entering in a hostile manner the country of a neighbouring nation would come to be regarded as the infallible destruction of the invading army. Perhaps no people were ever conquered at their own doors, unless they were first betrayed, either by divisions among themselves, or by the abject degeneracy of their character. The more we come to understand of the nature of justice, the more it will show itself to be stronger than a host of foes. Men whose bosoms are truly pervaded with this principle cannot perhaps be other than invincible. Among the various examples of excellence, in almost every department, that ancient Greece has bequeathed us, the most conspicuous is her resistance with a handful of men against three millions of invaders.*

* These chapters were written during the month of September

One branch of the art of war, as well as of every other human art, has hitherto consisted in deceit. If the principles of this work be built upon a sufficiently solid basis, the practice of deceit ought, in almost all instances, to be condemned, whether it proceed from false tenderness to our friends, or from a desire to hasten the downfall of injustice. Vice is neither the most allowable nor effectual weapon with which to contend against vice. Deceit is certainly not less deceit, whether the falsehood be formed into words, or be conveyed through the medium of fictitious appearances. A virtuous and upright nation would be scarcely more willing to mislead the enemy, by false intelligence, or treacherous ambuscade, than by the breach of their engagements, or by feigned demonstrations of friendship. There seems to be no essential difference between throwing open our arms to embrace them and advancing towards them with neutral colours, or covering ourselves with a defile or a wood. By the practice of surprise and deceit, we shall oftenest cut off their straggling parties, and shed most blood. By an open display of our force, we shall prevent detachments from being made, and intercept the possibility of supply, without unnecessary bloodshed; and there seems no reason to believe that our ultimate success will be less secure. Why should war be made the science of disingenuousness and mystery, when the plain dictates of good sense would answer all its legitimate purposes? The first principle of defence is firmness and vigilance. The second perhaps, which is not less immediately connected with the end to be attained, is frankness, and the open disclosure of our purpose, even to our enemies. What astonishment, admiration and terror might this conduct excite in those with whom we had to contend? What confidence and magnanimity would accompany it in our own bosoms? Why should not war, as a step towards its complete

1792, before the intelligence of Dumouriez's success, and while the heart of every lover of liberty ached for the event of the campaign.

abolition, be brought to such perfection as that the purposes of the enemy might be baffled without firing a musket, or drawing a sword?

Another corollary, not less inevitable, from the principles which have been delivered is that the operations of war should be limited, as accurately as possible, to the generating no further evils than defence inevitably requires. Ferocity ought carefully to be banished from it. Calamity should, as entirely as possible, be prevented, to every individual who is not actually in arms, and whose fate has no immediate reference to the event of the war. This principle condemns the levying military contributions, and the capture of mercantile vessels. Each of these atrocities would be in another way precluded, by the doctrine of simple defence. We should scarcely think of levying such contributions if we never attempted to pass the limits of our own territory; and every species of naval war would probably be proscribed.

The utmost benevolence ought to be practised towards our enemies. We should refrain from the unnecessary destruction of a single life, and afford every humane accommodation to the unfortunate. The bulk of those against whom we have to contend are, comparatively speaking, innocent of the projected injustice. Those by whom it has been most assiduously fostered are entitled to our kindness as men, and to our compassion as mistaken. It has already appeared that all the ends of punishment are foreign to the transactions of war. It has appeared that the genuine melioration of war, in consequence of which it may be expected absolutely to cease, is by gradually disarming it of its ferocity. The horrors of war have sometimes been attempted to be vindicated by a supposition that the more intolerable it was made, the more quickly would it cease to infest the world. But the direct contrary of this is the truth. Severities beget severities. It is a most mistaken way of teaching men to feel that they are brothers, by imbuing their minds with unrelenting hatred. The truly just man cannot feel animosity, and is therefore little likely to act as if he did.

Having examined the conduct of war as it respects our enemies, let us next consider it in relation to the various descriptions of persons by whom it is to be supported. We have seen how little a just and upright war stands in need of secrecy. The plans for conducting a campaign, instead of being, as artifice and ambition have hitherto made them, inextricably complicated, will probably be reduced to two or three variations, suited to the different circumstances, that can possibly occur in a war of simple defence. The better these plans are known to the enemy, the more advantageous will it be to the resisting party. Hence it follows that the principles of implicit faith and military obedience, as they are now understood, will be no longer necessary. Soldiers will cease to be machines. The circumstance that constitutes men machines, in this sense of the word, is not the uniformity of their motions, when they see the reasonableness of that uniformity: it is their performing any motion, or engaging in any action, the object and utility of which they do not clearly understand. It is true that, in every state of human society, there will be men of an intellectual capacity much superior to their neighbours. But defensive war, and every other species of operation, in which it will be necessary that many individuals should act in concert, will perhaps be found so simple in their operations as not to exceed the apprehension of the most common capacities. It is ardently to be desired that the time should arrive when no man should lend his assistance to any operation without, in some degree, exercising his judgement, respecting the honesty, and the expected event, of that operation.

The principles here delivered on the conduct of war lead the mind to a very interesting subject, that of foreign and distant territories. Whatever may be the value of these principles considered in themselves, they become altogether nugatory the moment the idea of foreign dependencies is admitted. But, in reality, what argument possessing the smallest degree of plausibility can be alleged in favour of that idea? The mode in which dependencies are acquired must be either conquest, cession or colonization. The first of these no true moralist or politician will attempt to defend. The second is to be considered as the same thing in substance as the first, but with less openness and ingenuity. Colonization, which is by much the most specious pretence, is however no more than a pretence. Are these provinces held in a state of dependence for our sake or for theirs? If for ours, we must recollect that this is still a usurpation, and that justice requires we should yield to others what we demand for ourselves, the privilege of being governed by the dictates of their own reason. If for theirs, they must be told that it is the business of associations of men to defend themselves, or, if that be impracticable, to look for support to a confederation with their neighbours. They must be told that defence against foreign enemies is a very inferior consideration, and that no people were ever either wise or happy who were not left to the fair development of their inherent powers. Can anything be more absurd than for the West India islands, for example, to be defended by fleets and armies to be transported across the Atlantic? The support of a mother country extended to her colonies is much oftener a means of involving them in danger than of contributing to their security. The connection is maintained by vanity on one side and prejudice on the other. If they must sink into a degrading state of dependence, how will they be the worse in belonging to one state rather than another? Perhaps the first step towards putting a stop to this fruitful source of war would be to annihilate that monopoly of trade which enlightened reasoners at present agree to condemn, and to throw open the ports of our colonies to all the world. The principle which will not fail to lead us right upon this subject of foreign dependencies, as well as upon a thousand others, is the principle delivered in entering upon the topic of war, that that attribute, however splendid, is not really beneficial to a nation that is not beneficial to the great mass of individuals of which the nation consists.

CHAPTER XIX

OF MILITARY ESTABLISHMENTS AND TREATIES

A country may look for its defence either to a standing army, or an universal militia. – The former condemned. – The latter objected to, as of pernicious tendency – as unnecessary – either in respect to courage – or discipline. – Of a commander. – Of treaties. – Conclusion.

THE last topic which it may be necessary to examine, as to the subject of war, is the conduct it becomes us to observe respecting it, in a time of peace. This article may be distributed into two heads, military establishments, and treaties of alliance.

If military establishments in time of peace be judged proper, their purpose may be effected either by consigning the practice of military discipline to a certain part of the community, or by making every man, whose age is suitable for that purpose, a soldier.

The preferableness of the latter of these methods to the former is obvious. The man that is merely a soldier must always be uncommonly depraved. War, in his case, inevitably degenerates from the necessary precautions of a personal defence into a trade, by which a man sells his skill in murder, and the safety of his existence, for a pecuniary recompense. The man that is merely a soldier ceases to be, in the same sense as his neighbours, a citizen. He is cut off from the rest of the community, and has sentiments and a rule of judgement peculiar to himself. He considers his countrymen as indebted to him for their security; and, by an unavoidable transition of reasoning, believes that, in a double sense, they are at his mercy. On the other hand, that every citizen should exercise in his turn the functions of a soldier seems peculiarly favourable to that confidence in himself, and in the resources of his country, which it is so desirable he should entertain. It is congenial to that equality which must operate to a considerable extent before mankind in general can be either virtuous or wise. And it seems to multiply the powers of defence in a country, so as to render the idea of its falling under the yoke of an enemy in the utmost degree improbable.

There are reasons however that will oblige us to doubt respecting the propriety of cultivating, under any form, the system of military discipline in time of peace. It is, in this respect, with nations as it is with individuals. The man that, with a pistol-bullet, is sure of his mark, or that excels his contemporaries in the exercise of the sword, can scarcely escape those obliquities of understanding which accomplishments of this sort are adapted to nourish. It is not to be expected that he should entertain all that confidence in justice, and distaste of violence, which reason prescribes. It is beyond all controversy that war, though the practice of it, under the present state of the human species, should be found, in some instances, unavoidable, is a proceeding pregnant with calamity and vice. It cannot be a matter of indifference for the human mind to be systematically familiarized to thoughts of murder and desolation. The pupil of nature would not fail, at the sight of a musket or a sword, to be impressed with sentiments of abhorrence. Why expel these sentiments? Why connect the discipline of death with ideas of festivity and splendour; which will inevitably happen if the citizens, without oppression, are accustomed to be drawn out to encampments and reviews? Is it possible that he who has not learned to murder his neighbour with a grace is imperfect in the trade of man?

If it be replied 'that the generating of error is not inseparable from military discipline, and that men may at some time be sufficiently guarded against the abuse, even while they are taught the use of arms'; it will be found upon reflection that this argument is of little weight. If error be not unalterably connected with the science of arms, it will for a long time remain so. When men are sufficiently improved to be able to handle, familiarly, and with application of mind, the instruments of death, without injury to their dispositions, they will also be sufficiently improved to be able to master any study with much greater facility than at present, and consequently the cultivation of the art military in time of peace will have still fewer inducements to recommend it to our choice – To apply these considerations to the present situation of mankind.

We have already seen that the system of a standing army is altogether indefensible, and that a universal militia is a more formidable defence, as well as more agreeable to the principles of justice and political happiness. It remains to be seen what would be the real situation of a nation, surrounded by other nations, in the midst of which standing armies were maintained, that should nevertheless, upon principle, wholly neglect the art military in seasons of peace. In such a nation it will probably be admitted that, so far as relates to mere numbers, an army may be raised upon the spur of occasion nearly as soon as in a nation the citizens of which had been taught to be soldiers. But this army, though numerous, would be in want of many of those principles of combination and activity which are of material importance in a day of battle. There is indeed included in the supposition that the internal state of this people is more equal and free than that of the people by whom they are invaded. This will infallibly be the case in a comparison between a people with a standing army and a people without one; between a people who can be brought blindly and wickedly to the invasion of their peaceful neighbours, and a people who will not be induced to fight but in their own defence. The latter therefore will be obliged to compare the state of society and government, in their own country, and among their neighbours, and will not fail to be impressed with great ardour in defence of the inestimable superiority they possess. Ardour, even in the day of battle, might prove sufficient. A body of men, however undisciplined, whom nothing could induce to quit the field would infallibly be victorious over their veteran adversaries who, under the circumstances of the case, could have no accurate conception of the object for which they were fighting, and therefore could not entertain an inextinguishable love for it. It is not certain that activity and discipline, opposed to ardour, have even a tendency to turn the balance of slaughter against the party that wants them. Their great advantage consists in their power over the imagination to astonish, to terrify and confound. An intrepid courage in the party thus assailed would soon convert them from sources of despair into objects of contempt.

But it would be extremely unwise in us to have no other resource but in the chance of this intrepidity. A resource much surer, and more agreeable to justice, is in recollecting that the war of which we treat is a war of defence. Battle is not the object of such a war. An army which, like that of Fabius, by keeping on the hills, or by whatever other means, rendered it impracticable for the enemy to force them to an engagement might look with indifference upon his impotent efforts to enslave the country. One advantage included in such a system of war is that, as its very essence is protraction, the defending army might, in a short time, be rendered as skilful as the assailants. Discipline, like every other art, has been represented, by vain and interested men, as surrounded with imaginary difficulties, but is, in reality exceedingly simple; and would be learned much more effectually in the scene of a real war than in the puppet-show exhibitions of a period of peace.

It is desirable indeed that we should have a commander of considerable skill, or rather of considerable wisdom, to reduce this patient and indefatigable system into practice. This is of greater importance than the mere discipline of the ranks. But the nature of military wisdom has been greatly misrepresented. Experience in this, as well as in other arts, has been unreasonably magnified, and the general power of a cultivated mind been thrown into shade. It will probably be no long time before this quackery of professional men will be thoroughly exploded. How often do we meet with those whom experience finds incorrigible; while it is recorded of one of the greatest generals of antiquity that he set out for his appointment wholly unacquainted with his art, and was indebted for that skill, which broke out immediately upon his arrival, to the assiduity of his enquiries, and a careful examination of those writers by whom the art had most successfully been illustrated?* In all events it will be admitted that the maintenance of a standing army, or the perpetual discipline of a nation, is a very dear price to pay for the purchase of a general, as well as that the purchase would be extremely precarious if we were even persuaded to consent to the condition. It may perhaps be true, though this is not altogether clear, that a nation by whom military discipline was wholly neglected would be exposed to some disadvantage. In that case, it becomes us to weigh the neglect and cultivation together, and to cast the balance on the side to which, upon mature examination, it shall appear to belong.

A second article which belongs to the military system in a season of peace is that of treaties of alliance. This subject may easily be dispatched. Treaties of alliance, if we examine and weigh the history of mankind, will perhaps be found to have been, in all cases, nugatory, or worse. Governments, and public men, will not, and ought not, to hold themselves bound to the injury of the concerns they conduct, because a parchment, to which they or their predecessors were a party, requires it. If the concert demanded in time of need approve itself to their

* *Ciceronis Lucullus, five Academicorum Liber Secundus, init.*

judgement, and correspond with their inclination, it will be yielded, though they are under no previous engagement for that purpose. Treaties of alliance serve to no other end than to exhibit, by their violation, an appearance of profligacy and vice, which unfortunately becomes too often a powerful encouragement to the inconsistency of individuals. Add to this, that if alliances were engines as powerful as they are really important, they could seldom be of use to a nation uniformly adhering to the principles of justice. They would be useless, because they are, in reality, ill calculated for any other purposes than those of ambition. They might be pernicious, because it would be beneficial for nations, as it is for individuals, to look for resources at home, instead of depending upon the precarious compassion of their neighbours.

It would be unjust to dismiss the consideration of this most dreadful, yet perhaps, in the present state of things, sometimes unavoidable, calamity of war, without again reminding the reader of its true character. It is that state of things where a man stands prepared to deal slaughter and death to his fellow men. Let us image to ourselves a human being, surveying, as soon as his appetite for carnage is satiated, the scene of devastation he has produced. Let us view him surrounded with the dying and the dead, his arms bathed to the very elbow in their blood. Let us investigate along with him the features of the field, attempt to divide the wounded from the slain, observe their distorted countenances, their mutilated limbs, their convulsed and palpitating flesh. Let us observe the long-drawn march of the hospital-waggons, every motion attended with pangs unutterable, and shrieks that rend the air. Let us enter the hospital itself, and note the desperate and dreadful cases that now call for the skill of the surgeon, even omitting those to which neither skill nor care is ever extended. Whence came all this misery? What manner of creature shall we now adjudge the warrior to be? What had these men done to him? Alas! he knew them not; they had never offended; he smote them to the death, unprovoked by momentary anger, coldly deliberating on faults of which they were guiltless, and executing plans of wilful and meditated destruction. Is not this man a murderer? Yet such is the man who goes to battle, whatever be the cause that induces him. Who that reflects on these things does not feel himself prompted to say, 'Let who will engage in the business of war; never will I, on any pretence, lift up a word against my brother'?

We have entered, in these chapters, somewhat more at large into the subject of war than the question of democracy, might seem to require. So far as this is a digression, the importance of the topic may perhaps plead our excuse.

CHAPTER XX

OF DEMOCRACY AS CONNECTED WITH THE TRANSACTIONS OF WAR

External affairs are of subordinate consideration. – Application. – Further objections to democracy – 1. it is unfavourable to secrecy – this proved to be an excellence – 2. its movements are too slow – 3. too precipitate.

HAVING thus endeavoured to reduce the question of war to its true principles, it is time that we should recur to the maxim delivered at our entrance upon this subject, that individuals are everything, and society, abstracted from the individuals of which it is composed, nothing. An immediate consequence of this maxim is that the internal affairs of the society are entitled to our principal attention, and the external are matters of inferior and subordinate consideration. The internal affairs are subjects of perpetual and hourly concern, the external are periodical and precarious only. That every man should be impressed with the consciousness of his independence, and rescued from the influence of extreme want and artificial desires, are purposes the most interesting that can suggest themselves to the human mind; but the life of man might pass in a state uncorrupted by ideal passions without its tranquillity being so much as once disturbed by foreign invasions. The influence that a certain number of millions, born under the same climate with ourselves, and known by the common appellation of English or French, shall possess over the administrative councils of their neighbour millions, is a circumstance of much too airy and distant consideration to deserve to be made a principal object in the institutions of any people. The best influence we can exert is that of a sage and upright example.

If therefore it should appear that of these two articles, internal and external affairs, one must, in some degree, be sacrificed to the other, and that a democracy will, in certain respects, be less fitted for the affairs of war than some other species of government, good sense will not hesitate in the alternative. We shall have sufficient reason to be satisfied if, together with the benefits of justice and virtue at home, we have no reason to despair of our safety from abroad. A confidence in this article will seldom deceive us if our countrymen, however little trained to formal rules, and the uniformity of mechanism, have studied the profession of man, understand his attributes and his nature, and have their necks unbroken to the yoke of blind credulity and abject submission. Such men, inured, as we are now supposing them, to a rational state of society, will be full of calm confidence and penetrating activity, and these qualities will stand them in stead of a thousand lessons in the school of military mechanism. If democracy can be proved adequate to wars of defence, and other governments be better fitted for wars of a different sort, this would be an argument, not of its imperfection, but its merit.

It has been one of the objections to the ability of a democracy in war 'that it cannot keep secrets. The legislative assembly, whether it possess the initiative, or a power of control only, in executive affairs, will be perpetually calling for papers, plans and information, cross-examining ministers, and sifting the policy and justice of public undertakings. How shall we be able to cope with an enemy, if he know precisely the points we mean to attack, the state of our fortifications, and the strength and weakness of our armies? How shall we manage our treaties with skill and address, if he be precisely informed of ur sentiments, and have access to the instructions of our ambassadors?'

It happens in this instance that that which the objection attacks as the vice of democracy is one of its most essential excellencies. The trick of a mysterious carriage is the prolific parent of every vice; and it is an eminent advantage incident to democracy that, though the proclivity of the human mind has hitherto reconciled this species of administration, in some degree, to the keeping of secrets, its inherent tendency is to annihilate them. Why should disingenuity and concealment be thought virtuous or beneficial on the part of nations in cases where they would inevitably be discarded with contempt by an upright individual? Where is there an igenuous and enlightened man who is not aware of the superior advantage that belongs to a proceeding, frank, explicit and direct? Who is there that sees not that this inextricable labyrinth of reasons of state was artfully invented, lest the people should understand their own affairs, and, understanding, become inclined to conduct them? With respect to treaties, it is to be suspected that they are, in all instances, superfluous. But, if public engagements ought to be entered into, what essential difference is there between the governments of two countries endeavouring to overreach each other, and the buyer and seller in any private transaction adopting a similar proceeding?

This whole system proceeds upon the idea of national grandeur and glory, as if, in reality, these words had any specific meaning. These contemptible objects, these airy names, have, from the earliest page of history, been made a colour for the most pernicious undertakings. Let us take a specimen of their value from the most innocent and laudable pursuits. If I aspire to be a great poet or a great historian, so far as I am influenced by the dictates of reason, it is that I may be useful to mankind, and not that I may do honour to my country. Is Newton the better because he was an Englishman; or Galileo the worse because he was an Italian? Who can endure to put this high-sounding nonsense in the balance against the best interests of mankind, which will always suffer a mortal wound when dexterity, artifice and concealment are made the topics of admiration and applause? The understanding and the virtues of mankind will always keep pace with the manly simplicity of their designs, and the undisguised integrity of their hearts.

It has further been objected to a democratical state, in its transactions with foreign powers, 'that it is incapable of those rapid and decisive proceedings which, in some situations, have so eminent a tendency to ensure success'. If by this objection it be understood that a democratical state is ill fitted for dexterity and surprise, the rapidity of an assassin, it has already received a sufficient answer. If it be meant that the regularity of its proceedings may ill accord with the impatience of a neighbouring despot, and, like the Jews of old, we desire a king 'that we may be like the other nations', this is a very unreasonable requisition. A just and impartial enquirer will be little desirous to see his country placed high in the diplomatical roll, deeply involved in the intrigues of nations, and assiduously courted by foreign princes, as the instrument of their purposes. A more groundless and absurd passion cannot seize upon any people than that of glory, the preferring their influence in the affairs of the globe to their internal happiness and virtue; for these objects will perpetually counteract and clash with each other.

But democracy is by no means necessarily of a phlegmatic character, or obliged to take every proposition that is made to it, *ad referendum*, for the consideration of certain primary assemblies, like the states of Holland. The first principle in the institution of government itself is the necessity, under the present imperfections of mankind, of having some man, or body of men, to act on the part of the whole. Wherever government subsists, the authority of the individual must be, in some degree, superseded. It does not therefore seem unreasonable for a representative national assembly to exercise, in certain cases, a discretionary power. Those privileges which are vested in individuals selected out of the mass by the voice of their fellows, and who will speedily return to a private station, are by no means liable to the same objections as the executive and unsympathetic privileges of an aristocracy. Representation, together with many disadvantages, has this benefit, that it is able, impartially, and with discernment, to call upon the most enlightened part of the nation to deliberate for the whole, and may thus generate a degree of wisdom, and a refined penetration of sentiment, which it would have been unreasonable to expect as the result of primary assemblies.

A third objection more frequently offered against democratical government is 'that it is incapable of that mature and deliberate proceeding, which is alone suitable to the decision of such important concerns. Multitudes of men have appeared subject to fits of occasional insanity: they act from the influence of rage, suspicion and despair: they are liable to be hurried into the most unjustifiable extremes, by the artful practices of an impostor.' One of the most obvious answers to this objection is that for all men to share the privileges of all is the law of our nature, and the dictate of justice. The case, in this instance, is parallel to that of an individual in his private concerns. It is true that, while each man is master of his own affairs, he is liable to the starts of passion. He is attacked by the allurements of temptation and the tempest of rage, and may be guilty of fatal error, before reflection and judgement come forward to his aid. But this is no sufficient reason for depriving men of the direction of their own concerns. We should endeavour to make them wise, not to make them slaves. The depriving men of their self-government is, in the first place, unjust, while, in the second, this self-government, imperfect as it is, will be found more salutary than anything that can be substituted in its place. – Another answer to this objection will occur in the concluding chapters of the present book.

CHAPTER XXI

OF THE COMPOSITION OF GOVERNMENT

Houses of assembly. – This institution unjust.
– Deliberate proceeding the proper antidote.
– Separation of legislative and executive power
considered. – Superior importance of the latter.
– Functions of ministers.

ONE of the articles which has been most eagerly insisted on, by the advocates of complexity in political institutions, is that of 'checks, by which a rash proceeding may be prevented, and the provisions under which mankind have hitherto lived with tranquillity, may not be reversed without mature deliberation'. We will suppose that the evils of monarchy and aristocracy are, by this time, too notorious to incline the speculative enquirer to seek for a remedy in either of these. 'Yet it is possible, without the institution of privileged orders, to find means that may answer a similar purpose in this respect. The representatives of the people may be distributed, for example, into two assemblies; they may be chosen with this particular view, to constitute an upper and a lower house, and may be distinguished from each other either by various qualifications of age or fortune, or by being chosen by a greater or smaller number of electors, or for a shorter or longer term.'

To every inconvenience that experience can produce,

or imagination suggest, there is probably an appropriate remedy. This remedy may either be sought in a more strict prosecution of the principles of reason and justice, or in artificial combinations encroaching upon those principles. Which are we to prefer? No doubt, the institution of two houses of assembly is contrary to the primary dictates of reason and justice. How shall a nation be governed? Agreeably to the opinions of its inhabitants, or in opposition to them? Agreeably to them undoubtedly. Not, as we cannot too often repeat, because their opinion is a standard of truth, but because, however erroneous that opinion may be, we can do no better. There is no effectual way of improving the institutions of any people, but by enlightening their understandings. He that endeavours to maintain the authority of any sentiment, not by argument, but by force, may intend a benefit, but really inflicts an extreme injury. To suppose that truth can be instilled through any medium but that of its intrinsic evidence is a flagrant and pernicious error. He that believes the most fundamental proposition through the influence of authority does not believe a truth, but a falsehood. The proposition itself he does not understand, for thoroughly to understand it is to perceive the degree of evidence with which it is accompanied; is to know the full meaning of its terms, and, by necessary consequence, to perceive in what respects they agree or disagree with each other. All that he believes is that it is very proper he should submit to usurpation and injustice.

It was imputed to the late government of France that, when they called an assembly of notables in 1787, they contrived, by dividing the assembly into seven distinct corps, and not allowing them to vote otherwise than in these corps, that the vote of fifty persons should be capable of operating, as if they were a majority, in an assembly of one hundred and forty-four. It would have been still worse if it had been ordained that no measure should be considered as the measure of the assembly, unless it were adopted by the unanimous voice of all the corps: eleven persons might then, in voting a negative, have operated as a majority of one hundred and forty four. This may serve as a specimen of the effects of distributing a representative national assembly into two or more houses. Nor should we suffer ourselves to be deceived under the pretence of the innocence of a negative in comparison with an affirmative. In a country in which universal justice was already established, there would be little need of a representative assembly. In a country into whose institutions error has insinuated itself, a negative upon the repeal of those errors is the real affirmative.

The institution of two houses of assembly is the direct method to divide a nation against itself. One of these houses will, in a greater or less degree, be the asylum of usurpation, monopoly and privilege. Parties would expire, as soon as they were born, in a country where opposition of sentiments, and a struggle of interests, were not allowed to assume the formalities of distinct institution.

Meanwhile, a species of check perfectly simple, and which appears sufficiently adequate to the purpose, suggests itself in the idea of a slow and deliberate proceeding, which the representative assembly should prescribe to itself. Perhaps no proceeding of this assembly should have the force of a general regulation, till it had undergone five or six successive discussions in the assembly, or till the expiration of one month from the period of its being proposed. Something like this is the order of the English house of commons, nor does it appear to be, by any means, among the worst features of our constitution. A system like this would be sufficiently analogous to the proceedings of a wise individual, who certainly would not wish to determine upon the most important concerns of his life without a severe examination; and still less would omit this examination if his decision were destined to be a rule for the conduct, and a criterion to determine upon the rectitude, of other men.

Perhaps, as we have said, this slow and gradual proceeding ought, in no instance, to be dispensed with, by the national representative assembly. This seems to be the true line of separation between the functions of the assembly as such and the executive power, whether we suppose the executive separate, or simply place it in a committee of the representative body. A plan of this sort would produce a character of gravity and good sense, eminently calculated to fix the confidence of the citizens. The mere votes of the assembly, as distinguished from its acts and decrees, might serve as an encouragement to the public functionaries, and as affording a basis of expectation, respecting the speedy cure of those evils of which the public might complain; but they should never be allowed to be pleaded as the complete justification of any action. A precaution like this would not only tend to prevent the fatal consequences of any precipitate judgement of the assembly within itself, but of tumult and disorder from without. An artful demagogue would find it more easy to work up the people into a fit of momentary insanity than to retain them in it for a month, in opposition to the efforts of their real friends to undeceive them. Meanwhile, the consent of the assembly to take their demand into consideration might reasonably be expected to moderate their impatience.

Scarcely any plausible argument can be adduced in favour of what has been denominated by political writers a division of powers. Nothing can seem less reasonable than to prescribe any positive limits to the topics of deliberation in an assembly adequately representing the people; or peremptorily to forbid them the exercise of functions the depositaries of which are placed under their inspection and censure. Perhaps, upon any emergence, totally unforeseen at the time of their election, and uncommonly important, they would prove their wisdom by calling upon the people to elect a new assembly, with a direct view to that emergence. But the emergence, as we shall have occasion more fully to observe in the sequel, cannot with any propriety be prejudged, and a rule laid down for their conduct, by a body prior to, or distinct from, themselves. The distinction of legislative and executive powers, however intelligible in theory, will by no means authorize their separation in practice.

Legislation, that is, the authoritative enunciation of abstract or general propositions, is a function of equivocal nature, and will never be exercised in a pure state of society, or a state approaching to purity, but with great caution and unwillingness. It is the most absolute of the functions of government, and government itself is a remedy that inevitably brings its own evils along with it. Administration, on the other hand, is a principle of perpetual application. So long as men shall see reason to act in a corporate capacity, they will always have occasions of temporary emergency for which to provide. In proportion as they advance in social improvement, executive power will, comparatively speaking, become everything, and legislative nothing. Even at present, can there be any articles of greater importance than those of peace and war, taxation and the selection of proper periods for the meeting of deliberative assemblies, which, as was observed in the commencement of the present book, are articles of temporary regulation?* Is it decent, can it be just, that these prerogatives should be exercised by any power less than the supreme, or be decided by any authority but that which most adequately represents the voice of the nation? This principle ought, beyond question, to be extended universally. There can be no just reason for excluding the national representative from the exercise of any function, the exercise of which, on the part of the society, is, in any case, necessary.

The functions therefore of ministers and magistrates, commonly so called, do not relate to any particular topic respecting which they have a right exclusive of the representative assembly. They do not relate to any supposed necessity for secrecy; for secrecy, in political affairs, as we have had occasion to perceive,† is rarely salutary or wise;

* Chap. 1, p. 409.
† Chap. XVIII, p. 519; Chap. XX, p. 531.

and secrets of state will commonly be found to consist of that species of information relative to the interests of a society, respecting which the chief anxiety of its depositaries is that it should be concealed from the members of that society. It is the duty of the assembly to desire information without reserve, for themselves and the public, upon every subject of general importance; and it is the duty of ministers and others to communicate such information, though it should not be expressly desired. The utility therefore of ministerial functions being, in a majority of instances, less than nothing in these respects, there are only two classes of utility that remain to them; particular functions, such as those of financial detail or minute superintendence, which cannot be exercised unless by one or a small number of persons;* and measures proportioned to the demand of those necessities which will not admit of delay, and subject to the revision and censure of the deliberative assembly. The latter of these classes will perpetually diminish as men advance in improvement; nor can anything politically be of greater importance than the reduction of that discretionary power in an individual which may greatly affect the interests, or fetter the deliberations of the many.

* Chap. I, p. 409.

CHAPTER XXII

OF THE FUTURE HISTORY OF POLITICAL
SOCIETIES

Quantity of administration necessary to be maintained. — Objects of administration: national glory — rivalship of nations. — Inferences: 1. complication of government unnecessary — 2. extensive territory superfluous — 3. constraint, its limitations. — Project of government: police — defence.

THUS we have endeavoured to unfold and establish certain general principles upon the subject of legislative and executive power. But there is one interesting topic that remains to be discussed. How much of either of these powers does the public benefit require us to maintain?

We have already seen* that the only legitimate object of political institution is the advantage of individuals. All that cannot be brought home to them, national wealth, prosperity and glory, can be advantageous only to those self-interested impostors who, from the earliest accounts of time, have confounded the understandings of mankind, the more securely to sink them in debasement and misery.

The desire to gain a more extensive territory, to conquer or to hold in awe our neighbouring states, to surpass them in arts or arms, is a desire sounded in prejudice and error. Usurped authority is a spurious and unsubstantial medium of happiness. Security and peace are more to be desired than a national splendour that should terrify the world. Mankind are brethren. We associate in a particular district or under a particular climate, because association is necessary to our internal tranquillity, or to defend us against the wanton attacks of a common enemy. But the rivalship of nations is a creature

* Chap. XVI, p. 508; Chap. XX, p. 531.

of the imagination. If riches be our object, riches can only be created by commerce; and the greater is our neighbour's capacity to buy, the greater will be our opportunity to sell. The prosperity of all is the interest of all.

The more accurately we understand our own advantage, the less shall we be disposed to disturb the peace of our neighbour. The same principle is applicable to him in return. It becomes us therefore to desire that he may be wise. But wisdom is the growth of equality and independence, not of injury and oppression. If oppression had been the school of wisdom, the improvement of mankind would have been inestimable, for they have been in that school for many thousand years. We ought therefore to desire that our neighbour should be independent. We ought to desire that he should be free; for wars do not originate in the unbiased propensities of nations, but in the cabals of government and the propensities that governments inspire into the people at large.* If our neighbour invade our territory, all we should desire is to repel him from it†, and, for that purpose, it is not necessary we should surpass him in prowess, since upon our own ground his match is unequal.‡ Not to say that to conceive a nation attacked by another, so long as its own conduct is sober, equitable and moderate, is an exceedingly improbable supposition.§

Where nations are not brought into avowed hostility, all jealousy between them is an unintelligible chimera. I reside upon a certain spot because that residence is most conducive to my happiness or usefulness. I am interested in the political justice and virtue of my species because they are men, that is, creatures eminently capable of justice and virtue ;and I have perhaps additional reason to interest myself for those who live under the same government as myself because I am better qualified to understand their claims, and more capable of exerting myself in their behalf. But I can certainly have no in-

* Chap. XVI.　　　　　† Chap. XVII.
‡ Chap. XVIII.　　　　§ Chap. XVI.

terest in the infliction of pain upon others, unless so far as they are expressly engaged in acts of injustice. The object of sound policy and morality is to draw men nearer to each other, not to separate them; to unite their interests, not to oppose them.

Individuals ought, no doubt, to cultivate a more frequent and confidential intercourse with each other than at present subsists; but political societies of men, as such, have no interests to explain and adjust, except so far as error and violence may render explanation necessary. This consideration annihilates, at once, the principal objects of that mysterious and crooked policy which has hitherto occupied the attention of governments. Before this principle, officers of the army and the navy, ambassadors and negotiators, all the train of artifices that has been invented to hold other nations at bay, to penetrate their secrets, to traverse their machinations, to form alliances and counter-alliances, sink into nothing. The expense of government is annihilated, and, together with its expense, the means of subduing and undermining the virtues of its subjects.*

Another of the great opprobriums of political science is, at the same time, completely removed, that extent of territory, subject to one head, respecting which philosophers and moralists have alternately disputed whether it be most unfit for a monarchy, or for a democratical government. The appearance which mankind, in a future state of improvement, may be expected to assume is a policy that, in different countries, will wear a similar form, because we have all the same faculties and the same wants but a policy the independent branches of which will extend their authority over a small territory, because neighbours are best informed of each others concerns, and are perfectly equal to their adjustment. No recommendation can be imagined of an extensive rather than a limited territory, except that of external security.

Whatever evils are included in the abstract idea of

* Hume's *Essays*, Part I, Essay V.

government, they are all of them extremely aggravated by the extensiveness of its jurisdiction, and softened under circumstances of an opposite nature. Ambition, which may be no less formidable than a pestilence in the former, has no room to unfold itself in the latter. Popular commotion is like the waters of the earth, capable where the surface is large, of producing the most tragical effects, but mild and innocuous when confined within the circuit of a humble lake. Sobriety and equity are the obvious characteristics of a limited circle.

It may indeed be objected 'that great talents are the offspring of great passions, and that, in the quiet mediocrity of a petty republic, the powers of intellect may be expected to subside into inactivity'. This objection, if true, would be entitled to the most serious consideration. But it is to be considered that, upon the hypothesis here advanced, the whole human species would constitute, in some sense, one great republic, and the prospects of him who desired to act beneficially upon a great surface of mind would become more animating than ever. During the period in which this state was growing, but not yet complete, the comparison of the blessings we enjoyed with the iniquities practising among our neighbours would afford an additional stimulus to exertion.*

Ambition and tumult are evils that arise out of government, in an indirect manner, in consequence of the habits, which government introduces, of concert and combination extending themselves over multitudes of men. There are other evils inseparable from its existence. The object of government is the suppression of such violence, as well external as internal, as might destroy, or bring into jeopardy, the well being of the community or its members; and the means it employs are constraint and violence of a more regulated kind. For this purpose the concentration of individual forces becomes necessary, and the method in which this concentration is usually ob-

---

* This objection will be fully discussed in the eighth book of the present work.

tained is also constraint. The evils of constraint have been considered on a former occasion.* Constraint employed against delinquents, or persons to whom delinquency is imputed, is by no means without its mischiefs. Constraint employed by the majority of a society against the minority, who may differ from them upon some question of public good, is calculated, at first sight at least, to excite a still greater disapprobation.

Both these exertions may indeed appear to rest upon the same principle. Vice is unquestionably no more, in the first instance, than error of judgement, and nothing can justify an attempt to correct it by force, but the extreme necessity of the case.† The minority, if erroneous, fall under precisely the same general description, though their error may not be of equal magnitude. But the necessity of the case can seldom be equally impressive. If the idea of secession, for example, were somewhat more familiarized to the conceptions of mankind, it could seldom happen that the secession of the minority from difference of opinion could in any degree compare, in mischievous tendency, with the hostility of a criminal offending against the most obvious principles of social justice. The cases are parallel to those of offensive and defensive war. In putting constraint upon a minority, we yield to a suspicious temper that tells us the opposing party may hereafter, in some way, injure us, and we will anticipate his injury. In putting constraint upon a criminal, we seem to repel an enemy who has entered our territory, and refuses to quit it.

Government can have no more than two legitimate purposes, the suppression of injustice against individuals within the community, and the common defence against external invasion. The first of these purposes, which alone can have an uninterrupted claim upon us, is sufficiently answered by an association, of such an extent, as to afford room for the institution of a jury to decide upon the

* Book II, Chap. VI.
† Book II, Chap. VI: Book IV, Chap. VIII.

offences of individuals within the community, and upon the questions and controversies respecting property which may chance to arise. It might be easy indeed for an offender to escape from the limits of so petty a jurisdiction; and it might seem necessary, at first, that the neighbouring parishes,* or jurisdictions, should be governed in a similar maner, or at least should be willing, whatever was their form of government, to co-operate with us in the removal or reformation of an offender whose present habits were alike injurious to us and to them. But there will be no need of any express compact, and still less of any common centre of authority, for this purpose. General justice, and mutual interest, are found more capable of binding men than signatures and seals. In the meantime, all necessity for causing the punishment of the crime, to pursue the criminal would soon, at least, cease, if it ever existed. The motives to offence would become rare: its aggravations few: and rigour superfluous. The principal object of punishment is restraint upon a dangerous member of the community; and the end of this restraint would be answered by the general inspection that is exercised by the members of a limited circle over the conduct of each other, and by the gravity and good sense that would characterize the censures of men, from whom all mystery and empiricism were banished. No individual would be hardy enough in the cause of vice to defy the general consent of sober judgement that would surround him. It would carry despair to his mind, or, which is better, it would carry conviction. He would be obliged, by a force not less irresistible than whips and chains, to reform his conduct.

In this sketch is contained the rude outline of political government. Controversies between parish and parish would be, in an eminent degree, unreasonable, since, if

* The word parish is here used without regard to its origin, and merely in consideration of its being a word descriptive of a certain small portion of territory, whether in population or extent, which custom has rendered familiar to us.

any question arose, about limits, for example, the obvious principles of convenience could scarcely fail to teach us to what district any portion of land should belong. No association of men, so long as they adhered to the principles of reason, could possibly have an interest in extending their territory. If we would produce attachment in our associates, we can adopt no surer method than that of practising the dictates of equity and moderation; and, if this failed in any instance, it could only fail with him who, to whatever society he belonged, would prove an unworthy member. The duty of any society to punish offenders is not dependent upon the hypothetical consent of the offender to be punished, but upon the duty of necessary defence.

But however irrational might be the controversy of parish with parish in such a state of society, it would not be the less possible. For such extraordinary emergencies therefore, provision ought to be made. These emergencies are similar in their nature to those of foreign invasion. They can only be provided against by the concert of several district declaring and, if needful, enforcing the dictates of justice.

One of the most obvious remarks that suggests itself, upon these two cases, of hostility between district and district, and of foreign invasion which the interest of all calls upon them jointly to repel, is that it is their nature to be only of occasional recurrence, and that therefore the provisions to be made respecting them need not be, in the strictest sense, of perpetual operation. In other words, the permanence of a national assembly, as it has hitherto been practised in France, cannot be necessary in a period of tranquillity, and may perhaps be pernicious. That we may form a more accurate judgement of this, let us recollect some of the principal features that enter into the constitution of a national assembly.

CHAPTER XXIII

OF NATIONAL ASSEMBLIES

*They produce a fictitious unanimity – an un-
natural uniformity of opinion. – Causes of this
uniformity. – Consequences of the mode of
decision by vote – 1. perversion of reason – 2.
contentious disputes – 3. the triumph of ignorance and vice. – Society incapable of acting
from itself – of being well conducted by others.
– Conclusion. – Modification of democracy that
results from these considerations.*

IN the first place, the existence of a national assembly
introduces the evils of a fictitious unanimity. The public,
guided by such an assembly, must act with concert, or the
assembly is a nugatory excrescence. But it is impossible
that this unanimity can really exist. The individuals who
constitute a nation cannot take into consideration a
variety of important questions without forming different
sentiments respecting them. In reality, all questions that
are brought before such an assembly are decided by a
majority of votes, and the minority, after having exposed,
with all the power of eloquence, and force of reasoning,
of which they are capable, the injustice and folly of the
measures adopted, are obliged, in a certain sense, to
assist in carrying them into execution. Nothing can
more directly contribute to the depravation of the human
understanding and character. It inevitably renders mankind timid, dissembling and corrupt. He that is not accustomed exclusively to act upon the dictates of his own
understanding must fall inexpressibly short of that energy
and simplicity of which our nature is capable. He that
contributes his personal exertions, or his property, to the
support of a cause which he believes to be unjust will
quickly lose that accurate discrimination, and nice sensibility of moral rectitude, which are the principal ornaments of reason.

Secondly, the existence of national councils produces a certain species of real unanimity, unnatural in its character, and pernicious in its effects. The genuine and wholesome state of mind is to be unloosed from shackles, and to expand every fibre of its frame, according to the independent and individual impressions of truth upon that mind. How great would be the progress of intellectual improvement if men were unfettered by the prejudices of education, unseduced by the influence of a corrupt state of society, and accustomed to yield without fear, to the guidance of truth, however unexplored might be the regions, and unexpected the conclusions to which she conducted us? We cannot advance in the voyage of happiness unless we be wholly at large upon the stream that carry us thither: the anchor that we at first looked upon as the instrument of our safety will, at last, be found to be the means of detaining our progress. Unanimity of a certain sort is the result to which perfect freedom of enquiry is calculated to conduct us; and this unanimity would, in a state of perfect freedom, become hourly more conspicuous. But the unanimity that results from men's having a visible standard by which to adjust their sentiments is deceitful and pernicious.

In numerous assemblies, a thousand motives influence our judgements, independently of reason and evidence. Every man looks forward to the effects which the opinions he avows will produce on his success. Every man connects himself with some sect or party. The activity of his thought is shackled, at every turn, by the fear that his associates may disclaim him. This effect is strikingly visible in the present state of the British parliament, where men, whose faculties are comprehensive almost beyond all former example, may probably be found influenced by these motives sincerely to espouse the grossest and most contemptible errors.

Thirdly, the debates of a national assembly are distorted from their reasonable tenour by the necessity of their being uniformly terminated by a vote. Debate and discussion are, in their own nature, highly conducive to intellectual improvement; but they lose this salutary character, the moment they are subjected to this unfortunate condition. What can be more unreasonable than to demand that argument, the usual quality of which is gradually and imperceptibly to enlighten the mind, should declare its effect in the close of a single conversation? No sooner does this circumstance occur than the whole scene changes its character. The orator no longer enquires after permanent conviction, but transitory effect. He seeks rather to take advantage of our prejudices than to enlighten our judgement. That which might otherwise have been a scene of patient and beneficent enquiry is changed into wrangling, tumult and precipitation.

Another circumstance that arises out of the decision by vote is the necessity of constructing a form of words that shall best meet the sentiments, and be adapted to the preconceived ideas, of a multitude of men. What can be conceived at once more ludicrous and disgraceful than the spectacle of a set of rational beings employed for hours together in weighing particles, and adjusting commas? Such is the scene that is incessantly witnessed in clubs and private societies. In parliaments, this sort of business is usually adjusted before the measure becomes a subject of public inspection. But it does not the less exist; and sometimes it occurs in the other mode, so that, when numerous amendments have been made to suit the corrupt interest of imperious pretenders, the Herculean task remains at last to reduce the chaos into a grammatical and intelligible form.

The whole is then wound up, with that flagrant insult upon all reason and justice, the deciding upon truth by the casting up of numbers. Thus everything that we have been accustomed to esteem most sacred is determined, at best, by the weakest heads in the assembly, but, as it not less frequently happens, through the influence of the most corrupt and dishonourable intentions.

In the last place, national assemblies will by no means

be thought to deserve our direct approbation if we recollect, for a moment, the absurdity of that fiction by which society is considered, as it has been termed, as a moral individual. It is in vain that we endeavour to counteract the laws of nature and necessity. A multitude of men, after all our ingenuity, will still remain a multitude of men. Nothing can intellectually unite them, short of equal capacity and identical perception. So long as the varieties of mind shall remain, the force of society can no otherwise be concentrated than by one man, for a shorter or a longer term, taking the lead of the rest, and employing their force, whether material, or dependent on the weight of their character, in a mechanical manner, just as he would employ the force of a tool or a machine. All government corresponds, in a certain degree, to what the Greeks denominated a tyranny. The difference is that, in despotic countries, mind is depressed by an uniform usurpation; while, in republics, it preserves a greater portion of its activity, and the usurpation more easily conforms itself to the fluctuations of opinion.

The pretence of collective wisdom is among the most palpable of all impostures. The acts of the society can never rise above the suggestions of this or that individual, who is a member of it. Let us enquire whether society, considered as an agent, can really become the equal of certain individuals, of whom it is composed. And here, without staying to examine what ground we have to expect that the wisest member of the society will actually take the lead in it, we find two obvious reasons to persuade us that, whatever be the degree of wisdom inherent in him that really superintends, the acts which he performs in the name of the society will be both less virtuous and less able than the acts he might be expected to perform in a simpler and more unencumbered situation. In the first place, there are few men who, with the consciousness of being able to cover their responsibility under the name of a society, will not venture upon measures less direct in their motives, or less justifiable in the experiment, than they would have chosen to adopt in their own persons. Secondly, men who act under the name of a society are deprived of that activity and energy which may belong to them in their individual character. They have a multitude of followers to draw after them, whose humours they must consult, and to whose slowness of apprehension they must accommodate themselves. It is for this reason that we frequently see men of the most elevated genius dwindle into vulgar leaders when they become involved in the busy scenes of public life.

From these reasonings we seem sufficiently authorized to conclude that national assemblies, or, in other words, assemblies instituted for the joint purpose of adjusting the differences between district and district, and of consulting respecting the best mode of repelling foreign invasion, however necessary to be had recourse to upon certain occasions, ought to be employed as sparingly as the nature of the case will admit. They should either never be elected but upon extraordinary emergencies, like the dictator of the ancient Romans, or else sit periodically, one day for example in a year, with a power of continuing their sessions within a certain limit, to hear the complaints and representations of their constituents. The former of these modes is greatly to be preferred. Several of the reasons already adduced are calculated to show that election itself is of a nature not to be employed but when the occasion demands it. There would probably be little difficulty in suggesting expedients, relative to the regular originating of national assemblies. It would be most suitable to past habits and experience that a general election should take place whenever a certain number of districts demanded it. It would be most agreeable to rigid simplicity and equity that an assembly of two or two hundred districts should take place, in exact proportion to the number of districts by whom that measure was desired.

It will scarcely be denied that the objections which have been most loudly reiterated against democracy become null in an application to the form of government which has now been delineated. Here we shall with difficulty find an opening for tumult, for the tyranny of a multitude drunk with unlimited power, for political ambition on the part of the few, or restless jealousy and precaution on the part of the many. Here the demagogue would discover no suitable occasion for rendering the multitude the blind instrument of his purposes. Men, in such a state of society, might be expected to understand their happiness, and to cherish it. The true reason why the mass of mankind has so often been made the dupe of knaves has been the mysterious and complicated nature of the social system. Once annihilate the quackery of government, and the most homebred understanding might be strong enough to detect the artifices of the state juggler that would mislead him.

CHAPTER XXIV

OF THE DISSOLUTION OF GOVERNMENT

*Political authority of a national assembly –
of juries. – Consequence from the whole.*

IT remains for us to consider what is the degree of authority necessary to be vested in such a modified species of national assembly as we have admitted into our system. Are they to issue their commands to the different members of the confederacy? Or is it sufficient that they should invite them to co-operate for the common advantage, and, by arguments and addresses, convince them of the reasonableness of the measures they propose? The former of these might at first be necessary. The latter would afterwards become sufficient.* The

* Such is the idea of the author of *Gulliver's Travels* (Part IV), a man who appears to have had a more profound insight into the true principles of political justice than any preceding or contem-

Amphictyonic council of Greece possessed no authority but that which flowed from its personal character. In proportion as the spirit of party was extirpated, as the restlessness of public commotion subsided, and as the political machine became simple, the voice of reason would be secure to be heard. An appeal, by the assembly, to the several districts would not fail to unite the approbation of reasonable men unless it contained in it something so evidently questionable as to make it perhaps desirable that it should prove abortive.

This remark leads us one step further. Why should not the same distinction between commands and invitations, which we have just made in the case of national assemblies, be applied to the particular assemblies or juries of the several districts? At first, we will suppose that some degree of authority and violence would be necessary. But this necessity does not appear to arise out of the nature of man, but out of the institutions by which he has been corrupted. Man is not originally vicious. He would not refuse to listen to, or to be convinced by, the expostulations that are addressed to him, had he not been accustomed to regard them as hypocritical, and to conceive that, while his neighbour, his parent, and his political governor pretended to be actuated by a pure regard to his interest or pleasure, they were, in reality, at the expense of his, promoting their own. Such are the fatal effects of mysteriousness and complexity. Simplify the social system in the manner which every motive but those of usurpation and ambition powerfully recommends; render the plain dictates of justice level to every capacity; remove the necessity of implicit faith; and we may expect the whole species to become reasonable and virtuous. It might then be sufficient for juries to recommend a certain mode of

porary author. It was unfortunate that a work of such inestimable wisdom failed at the period of its publication from the mere playfulness of its form, in communicating adequate instruction to mankind. Posterity only will be able to estimate it as it deserves.

adjusting controversies, without assuming the prerogative of dictating that adjustment. It might then be sufficient for them to invite offenders to forsake their errors. If their expostulations proved, in a few instances, ineffectual, the evils arising out of this circumstance would be of less importance than those which proceed from the perpetual violation of the exercise of private judgement. But, in reality, no evils would arise: for, where the empire of reason was so universally acknowledged, the offender would either readily yield to the expostulations of authority; or, if he resisted, though suffering no personal molestation, he would feel so uneasy, under the unequivocal disapprobation, and observant eye, of public judgement, as willingly to remove to a society more congenial to his errors.

The reader has probably anticipated the ultimate conclusion from these remarks. If juries might at length cease to decide, and be contented to invite, if force might gradually be withdrawn and reason trusted alone, shall we not one day find that juries themselves and every other species of public institution may be laid aside as unnecessary? Will not the reasonings of one wise man be as effectual as those of twelve? Will not the competence of one individual to instruct his neighbours be a matter of sufficient notoriety, without the formality of an election? Will there be many vices to correct, and much obstinacy to conquer? This is one of the most memorable stages of human improvement. With what delight must every well informed friend of mankind look forward to the auspicious period, the dissolution of political government, of that brute engine which has been the only perennial cause of the vices of mankind, and which, as has abundantly appeared in the progress of the present work, has mischiefs of various sorts incorporated with its substance, and no otherwise removable than by its utter annihilation!

BOOK VI

OF OPINION CONSIDERED AS A SUBJECT OF POLITICAL INSTITUTION

CHAPTER 1

GENERAL EFFECTS OF THE POLITICAL SUPERINTENDENCE OF OPINION

Arguments in favour of this superintendence. – Answer. – The exertions of society in its corporate capacity are, 1. unwise – 2. incapable of proper effect. – Of sumptuary laws, agrarian laws and rewards. – Of spies. – Political degeneracy not incurable. – 3. superfluous – in commerce – in speculative enquiry – in morality – 4. pernicious – as undermining the best qualities of the mind – as hostile to its future improvement. – Conclusion.

A PRINCIPLE which has entered deeply into the systems of the writers on political law is that of the duty of governments to watch over the manners of the people. 'Government,' say they, 'plays the part of an unnatural step mother, not of an affectionate parent, when she is contented by rigorous punishments to avenge the commission of a crime, while she is wholly inattentive beforehand to imbue the mind with those virtuous principles which might have rendered punishment unnecessary. It is the business of a sage and patriotic magistracy to have its attention ever alive to the sentiments of the people, to encourage such as are favourable to virtue, and to check, in the bud, such as may lead to disorder and corruption.

How long shall government be employed to display its terrors without ever having recourse to the gentleness of invitation? How long shall she deal in retrospect and censure to the utter neglect of prevention and remedy?' These reasonings have, in some respects, gained additional strength by means of the latest improvements, and clearest views, upon the subject of political truth. It is now more evident than it was in any former period that government, instead of being an object of secondary consideration, has been the principal vehicle of extensive and permanent evil to mankind. It was unavoidable therefore to say 'since government can produce so much positive mischief, surely it can do some positive good'.

But these views, however specious and agreeable they may in the first instance appear, are liable to very serious question. If we would not be seduced by visionary good, we ought here, more than ever, to recollect the fundamental principles laid down and illustrated in this work, 'that government is, in all cases, an evil', and 'that it ought to be introduced as sparingly as possible'. Man is a species of being whose excellence depends upon his individuality; and who can be neither great nor wise but in proportion as he is independent.

But, if we would shut up government within the narrowest practicable limits, we must beware how we let it loose in the field of opinion. Opinion is the castle, or rather the temple, of human nature; and, if it be polluted, there is no longer anything sacred or venerable in sublunary existence.

In treating of the subject of political obedience,* we settled, perhaps with some degree of clearness, the line of demarcation between the contending claims of the individual and of the community. We found that the species of obedience which sufficiently discharged the claims of the community was that which is paid to force, and not which is built upon a sentiment of deference; and that this species of obedience was, beyond all others, least a source

* Book III, Chap. VI.

of degeneracy in him that paid it. But, upon this hypothesis, whatever exterior compliance is yielded, opinion remains inviolate.

Here then we perceive in what manner the purposes of government may be answered, and the independence of the individual suffer the smallest degree of injury. We are shown how government, which is, in all cases, an evil, may most effectually be limited as to the noxiousness of its influence.

But, if this line be overstepped, if opinion be rendered a topic of political superintendence, we are immediately involved in a slavery to which no imagination of man can set a termination. The hopes of our improvement are arrested; for government fixes the mercurialness of man to an assigned station. We can no longer enquire or think; for enquiry and thought are uncertain in their direction, and unshackled in their termination. We sink into motionless inactivity and the basest cowardice; for our thoughts and words are beset on every side with penalty and menace.

It is not the business of government, as will more fully appear in the sequel, to become the preceptor of its subjects. Its office is not to inspire our virtues, that would be a hopeless task; it is merely to check those excesses which threaten the general security.

But, though this argument ought perhaps to be admitted as sufficiently decisive of the subject under consideration, and cannot be set aside but upon grounds that would invalidate all the reasonings of this work, yet the prejudice in favour of the political superintendence of opinion has, with some persons, been so great, and the principle, in some of its applications, has been stated with such seeming plausibility, as to make it necessary that we should follow it in these applications, and endeavour in each instance to expose its sophistry.

In the meantime it may not be improper to state some further reasons in confirmation of the general unfitness of government as a superintendent of opinion.

One of these may be drawn from the view we have recently taken of society considered as an agent.* A multitude of men may be feigned to be an individual, but they cannot become a real individual. The acts which go under the name of the society are really the acts now of one single person and now of another. The men who by turns usurp the name of the whole perpetually act under the pressure of incumbrances that deprive them of their true energy. They are fettered by the prejudices, the humours, the weakness and the vice of those with whom they act; and, after a thousand sacrifices to these contemptible interests, their project comes out at last, distorted in every joint, abortive and monstrous. Society therefore, in its corporate capacity, can by no means be busy and intrusive with impunity, since its acts must be expected to be deficient in wisdom.

Secondly, they will not be less deficient in efficacy than they are in wisdom. The object at which we are supposing them to aim is to improve the opinions, and through them the manners, of mankind; for manners are nothing but opinions carried out into action: such as is the fountain, such will be the streams that are supplied from it. But what is it upon which opinion must be founded? Surely upon evidence, upon the perceptions of the understanding. Has society then any particular advantage, in its corporate capacity, for illuminating the understanding? Can it convey, into its addresses and expostulations, a compound or sublimate of the wisdom of all its members, superior in quality to the individual wisdom of any? If so, why have not societies of men written treatises of morality, of the philosophy of nature, or the philosophy of mind? Why have all the great steps of human improvement been the work of individuals?

If then society, considered as an agent, have no particular advantage for enlightening the understanding, the real difference between the *dicta* of society and the *dicta* of individuals must be looked for in the article of auth-

* Book V, Chap. XXIII, p. 550.

ority. But authority is, by the very nature of the case, inadequate to the task it assumes to perform. Man is the creature of habit and judgement; and the empire of the former of these, though not perhaps more absolute, is at least more conspicuous. The most efficacious instrument I can possess for changing a man's habits is to change his judgements. Even this instrument will seldom produce a sudden, though, when brought into full operation, it is perhaps sure of producing a gradual revolution. But this mere authority can never do. Where it does most in changing the characters of men, it only changes them into base and despicable slaves. Contending against the habits of an entire society, it can do nothing. It excites only contempt of its frivolous endeavours. If laws were a sufficient means for the reformation of error and vice, it is not to be believed but that the world, long ere this, would have become the seat of every virtue. Nothing can be more easy than to command men to be just and good to love their neighbours, to practise universal sincerity, to be content with a little, and to resist the enticements of avarice and ambition. But, when we have done, will the actions of men be altered by our precepts? These commands have been issued for thousands of years; and, if it had been decreed that every man should be hanged that violated them, it is vehemently to be suspected that this would not have secured their influence.

But it will be answered 'that laws need not deal thus in generals, but may descend to particular provisions calculated to secure their success. We may institute sumptuary laws, limiting the expense of our citizens in dress and food. We may institute agrarian laws, forbidding any man to possess more than a certain annual revenue. We may proclaim prizes as the reward of acts of justice, benevolence and public virtue'. And, when we have done this, how far are we really advanced in our career? If the people are previously inclined to moderation in expense, the laws are a superfluous parade. If they are not inclined, who shall execute them, or prevent their evasion? It is the misfortune in these cases that regulations cannot be executed but by the individuals of that very people they are meant to restrain. If the nation at large be infested with vice, who shall secure us a succession of magistrates that are free from the contagion? Even if we could surmount this difficulty, still it would be vain. Vice is ever more ingenious in evasion than authority in detection. It is absurd to imagine that any law can be executed that directly contradicts the propensities and spirit of the nation. If vigilance were able fully to countermine the subterfuges of art, the magistrates who thus pertinaciously adhered to the practice of their duty could scarcely fail to become the miserable victims of depravity exasperated into madness.

What can be more contrary to all liberal principles of human intercourse than the inquisitorial spirit which such regulations imply? Who shall enter into my house, scrutinize my expenditure, and count the dishes upon my table? Who shall detect the stratagems I employ, to cover my real possession of an enormous income, while I seem to receive but a small one? Not that there is really anything unjust and unbecoming, as has been too often supposed, in my neighbour's animadverting with the utmost freedom upon my personal conduct.* But that all watchfulness that proposes for its object the calling in of force as the corrective of error is invidious. Observe my conduct; you do well. Report it as widely as possible, provided you report it fairly; you are entitled to commendation. But the heart of man unavoidably revolts against the attempt to correct my error by the infliction of violence. We disapprove of the superior, however well informed he may be, who undertakes, by chastisement, to induce me to alter in my opinion, or vary in my choice; but we disapprove still more, and we do well, of the man who officiates as the Argus of my tyrant; who reports my conduct, not for the purpose of increasing my wisdom and prudence, not for the purpose of instructing others, but

* Book II, Chap. V, p. 194.

that he may bring down upon me the brute, the slavish and exasperating arm of power.

Such must be the case in extensive governments: in governments of smaller dimensions opinion would be all-sufficient; the inspection of every man over the conduct of his neighbours, when unstained with caprice, would constitute a censorship of the most irresistible nature. But the force of this censorship would depend upon its freedom, not following the positive dictates of law, but the spontaneous decisions of the understanding.

Again, in the distribution of rewards who shall secure us against error, partiality and intrigue, converting that which was meant for the support of virtue into a new engine for her ruin? Not to add that prizes are a very feeble instrument for the generation of excellence, always inadequate to its reward where it exists, always in danger of being bestowed on its semblance, continually misleading the understanding by foreign and degenerate motives of avarice and vanity.

The force of this argument, respecting the inefficacy of regulations, has often been felt, and the conclusions that are deduced from it have been in a high degree, discouraging. 'The character of nations,' it has been said, 'is unalterable, or at least, when once debauched, can never be recovered to purity. Laws are an empty name when the manners of the people are become corrupt. In vain shall the wisest legislator attempt the reformation of his country when the torrent of profligacy and vice has once broken down the bounds of moderation. There is no longer any instrument left for the restoration of simplicity and frugality. It is useless to declaim against the evils that arise from inequality of riches and rank, where this inequality has already gained an establishment. A generous spirit will admire the exertions of a Cato and a Brutus; but a calculating spirit will condemn them, as inflicting useless torture upon a patient whose disease was irremediable. It was from a view of this truth that the poets derived their fictions respecting the early history of mankind; well aware that, when luxury was introduced, and the springs of intellect unbent, it would be a vain expectation that should hope to recall men from passion to reason, and from effeminacy to energy.'* But this conclusion from the inefficacy of regulations is so far from being valid that in reality,

A third objection to the positive interference of society in its corporate capacity for the propagation of truth and virtue is that such interference is altogether unnecessary. Truth and virtue are competent to fight their own battles. They do not need to be nursed and patronized by the hand of power.

The mistake which has been made in this case is similar to the mistake which is now universally exploded upon the subject of commerce. It was long supposed that, if any nation desired to extend its trade, the thing most immediately necessary was for government to interfere, and institute protecting duties, bounties and monopolies. It is now generally admitted by speculative enquirers that commerce never flourishes so much as when it is delivered from the guardianship of legislators and ministers, and is conducted upon the principle, not of forcing other people to buy our commodities dear, when they might purchase them elsewhere cheaper or better, but of ourselves feeling the necessity of recommending them by their intrinsic advantages. Nothing can be at once so unreasonable and hopeless as to attempt, by positive regulations, to supersede the dictates of common sense, and the essential principles of human understanding.

The same truth which has gained such extensive footing under the article of commerce has made some progress in its application to speculative enquiry. Formerly it was thought that the true religion was to be defended by acts of uniformity, and that one of the first duties of the magistrate was to watch the progress of heresy. It was truly judged that the connection between error and vice is of the most intimate nature; and it was concluded that no

* Book I, Chap. VII.

means could be more effectual to prevent men from deviating into error than to check their wanderings by the scourge of authority. Thus writers whose political views in other respects have been uncommonly enlarged have been found to maintain 'that men ought indeed to be permitted to think as they please, but not to propagate their pernicious opinions; as they may be permitted to keep poisons in their closet, but not to offer them to sale under the denomination of cordials'.* Or, if humanity have forbidden them to recommend the extirpation of a sect which has already got footing in a country, they have however earnestly advised the magistrate to give no quarter to any new extravagance that might be attempted to be introduced.† – The reign of these two errors, respecting commerce, and theoretical speculation, is nearly at an end; and it is reasonable to believe that the idea of teaching virtue through the instrumentality of regulation and government will not long survive them.

All that we should require on the part of government, in behalf of morality and virtue, seems to be a clear stage upon which for them to exert their own energies, and perhaps some restraint, for the present, upon the violent disturbers of the peace of society, that the operations of these principles may be permitted to go on uninterrupted to their genuine conclusion. Who ever saw an instance in which error, unallied to power, was victorious over truth? Who is there that can bring himself to believe that, with equal arms, truth can be ultimately defeated? Hitherto it seems as if every instrument of menace or influence had been employed to counteract her. Has she made no progress? Has the mind of man the capacity to choose falsehood, and reject truth, when evidence is fairly presented? When it has been once thus presented, and has gained a few converts, does she ever fail to go on increasing the number of her votaries? Exclusively of the

* *Gulliver's Travels*, Part II, Chap. VI.

† Mably, *de la Législation*, Liv. IV, Chap. III: *des Etats Unis d'Amérique*, Lettre III.

fatal interference of government, and the violent irruptions of barbarism threatening to sweep her from the face
of the earth, has not this been, in all instances, the history
of science?

Nor are these observations less true in their application
to the manners and morals of mankind. Do not men always
act in the manner which they esteem best upon the whole,
or most conducive to their interest? Is it possible then that
evidence of what is best, or what is most beneficial,
can be stated to no purpose? The real history of the
changes of character they experience in this respect seems
to be this. Truth, for a long time, spreads itself unobserved. Those who are the first to embrace it are little
aware of the extraordinary events with which it is pregnant. But it goes on to be studied and illustrated. It increases in clearness and amplitude of evidence. The number of those by whom it is embraced is gradually enlarged.
If it have relation to their practical interests, if it show
them that they may be a thousand times more happy and
more free than at present, it is impossible that, in its perpetual increase of evidence and energy, it should not, at
last, break the bounds of speculation, and become an operative principle of action. What can be less plausible than
the opinion which has so long prevailed 'that justice, and
an equal distribution of the means of happiness, may
appear, with the utmost clearness, to be the only reasonable basis of social institution, wihout ever having a
chance of being reduced into practice? that oppression
and misery are draughts of so intoxicating a nature that,
when once tasted, we can never afterwards refuse to partake of them? that vice has so many advantages over virtue as to make the reasonableness and wisdom of the latter,
however powerfully exhibited, incapable of obtaining a
firm hold upon our affections?'

While therefore we demonstrate the inefficacy of naked
and unassisted regulations, we are far from producing any
discouragement in the prospect of social improvement.
The true tendency of this view of the subject is to suggest

indeed a different, but a more consistent and promising, method by which this improvement is to be produced. The legitimate instrument of effecting political reformation is knowledge. Let truth be incessantly studied, illustrated and propagated, and the effect is inevitable. Let us not vainly endeavour, by laws and regulations, to anticipate the future dictates of the general mind, but calmly wait till the harvest of opinion is ripe. Let no new practice in politics be introduced, and no old one anxiously superseded, till the alteration is called for by the public voice. The task which, for the present, should occupy the first rank in the thoughts of the friend of man is enquiry, communication, discussion. The time may come when his task shall appear to be of another sort. Error indeed, if, with unaltered constancy to sink into unnoticed oblivion, without almost one partisan adventurous enough to intercept her fall. Such would probably be the event were it not for the restless and misjudging impetuosity of mankind. But the event may be otherwise. Political change, advancing too rapidly to its crisis, may be attended with commotion and hazard; and it may then be incumbent on the generous and disinterested man, suspending, to a certain degree, general speculations, and the labours of science, to assist in unfolding the momentous catastrophe, and to investigate and recommend the measures which the pressure of temporary difficulties shall appear successively to require. If this should at any time be the case, if a concert of action can become preferable to a concert of disquisition, the duty of the philanthropist will then change its face. Instead of its present sober, cheerful and peaceable character, it will be full of arduousness, solicitude and uncertainty, evils which nothing but an assured simplicity and independence of conduct can ever purify or relieve. – To return.

In the fourth place, the interference of an organized society, for the purpose of influencing opinions and manners, is not only useless, but pernicious. We have already found that such interference is in one view of the subject ineffectual. But here a distinction is to be made. Considered with a view to the introduction of any favourable changes in the state of Society, it is altogether impotent. But, though it be inadequate to change it, it is powerful to prolong. This property is political regulation is so far from being doubtful that to it alone we are to ascribe all the calamities that government has inflicted on mankind. When regulation coincides with the habits and propensities of mankind at the time it is introduced, it will be found capable of maintaining those habits and propensities, in the greater part, unaltered for centuries. In this view it is doubly entitled to jealousy and distrust.

To understand this more accurately, let us apply it to the case of rewards, which has always been a favourite topic with the advocates of an improved legislation. How often have we been told 'that talents and virtues would spring up spontaneously in a country, one of the objects of whose constitution should be to secure to them an adequate reward'? Now, to judge of the propriety of this aphorism, we should begin with recollecting that the discerning of merit is an individual, not a social capacity. What can be more reasonable than that each man, for himself, should estimate the merits of his neighbour? To endeavour to institute a general judgement in the name of the whole, and to melt down the different opinions of mankind into one common opinion, appears, at first sight, so monstrous an attempt that it is impossible to augur well of its consequences. Will this judgement be wise, reasonable or just? Wherever each man is accustomed to decide for himself, and the appeal of merit is immediately to the opinion of its contemporaries, there, were it not for the false bias of some positive institution, we might expect a genuine ardour in him who aspired to excellence, creating and receiving impressions in the preference of an impartial audience. We might expect the judgement of the auditors to ripen by perpetual exercise, and mind, ever curious and awake, continually to approach nearer to its genuine standard. What do we gain in compensation for this, by setting up authority as the oracle, from which the active mind is to inform itself what sort of excellence it should seek to acquire, and the public at large what judgement they should pronounce upon the efforts of their contemporaries? What should we think of an act of parliament appointing some individual president of the court of criticism, and judge in the last resort of the literary merit of dramatic compositions? Is there any solid reason why we should expect better things from authority usurping the examination of moral or political excellence?

Nothing can be more unreasonable than the attempt to retain men in one common opinion by the dictate of authority. The opinion thus obtruded upon the minds of the public is not their real opinion; it is only a project by which they are rendered incapable of forming an opinion. Whenever government assumes to deliver us from the trouble of thinking for ourselves, the only consequences it produces are torpor and imbecility. This point was perhaps sufficiently elucidated when we had occasion directly to investigate the principle of the right of private judgement.*

We shall be still more completely aware of the pernicious tendency of positive institutions if we proceed explicitly to contrast the nature of mind, and the nature of government. One of the most unquestionable characteristics of the human mind has appeared to be its progressive nature. Now, on the other hand, it is the express tendency of positive institution to retain that with which it is conversant for ever in the same state. Is then the perfectibility of understanding an attribute of trivial importance? Can we recollect, with coldness and indifference, the advantages with which this quality seems pregnant to the latest posterity? And how are these advantages to be secured? By incessant industry, by a curiosity never to be disheartened or fatigued, by a spirit of enquiry to which a philanthropic mind will allow no pause. The circumstance most indispensably necessary is that we should never stand

* Book II, Chap. VI.

still, that everything most interesting to the general welfare, wholly delivered from restraint, should be in a state of change, moderate and as it were imperceptible, but continual. Is there anything that can look with a more malignant aspect upon the general welfare than an institution tending to give permanence to certain systems and opinions? Such institutions are two ways pernicious; first, which is most material, because they render the future advances of mind inexpressibly tedious and operose; secondly because, by violently confining the stream of reflection and holding it for a time in an unnatural state, they compel it at last to rush forward with impetuosity, and thus occasion calamities which, were it free from restraint, would be found extremely foreign to its nature. If the interference of positive institution had been out of the question, would the progress of intellect, in past ages, have been so slow as to have struck the majority of ingenuous observers with despair? The science of Greece and Rome upon the subject of politics was, in many respects, extremely imperfect: yet could we have been so long in appropriating their discoveries, had not the allurements of reward, and the menace of persecution, united to induce us not to trust to the direct and fair verdict of our own understandings?

The just conclusion from the above reasonings is nothing more than a confirmation, with some difference in the mode of application, of the fundamental principle that government is little capable of affording benefit of the first importance to mankind. It is calculated to induce us to lament, not the apathy and indifference, but the inauspicious activity of government. It incites us to look for the moral improvement of the species, not in the multiplying of regulations, but in their repeal. It teaches us that truth and virtue, like commerce, will then flourish most when least subjected to the mistaken guardianship of authority and laws. This maxim will rise upon us in its importance in proportion as we connect it with the numerous departments of political justice to which it will be found to have relation. As fast as it shall be adopted into the practice of mankind, it may be expected to deliver us from a weight, intolerable to mind, and, in the highest degree, hostile to the progress of truth.

CHAPTER II

OR RELIGIOUS ESTABLISHMENTS

Their general tendency. – Effects on the clergy: they introduce, 1. implicit faith – 2. hypocrisy: topics by which an adherence to them is vindicated. – Effects on the laity. – Application.

ONE of the most striking instances of the injurious effects of the political patronage of opinion, as it at present exists in the world, is to be found in the system of religious conformity. Let us take our example from the church of England, by the constitution of which subscription is required from its clergy to thirty-nine articles of precise and dogmatical assertion, upon almost every subject of moral and metaphysical enquiry. Here then we have to consider the whole honours and revenues of the church, from the archbishop, who takes precedence next after the princes of the blood royal, to the meanest curate in the nation, as employed in support of a system of blind submission and abject hypocrisy. Is there one man, through this numerous hierarchy, that is at liberty to think for himself? Is there one man among them that can lay his hand upon his heart, and declare, upon his honour and conscience, that the emoluments of his profession have no effect in influencing his judgement? The supposition is absurd. The most that an honest and discerning man, under such circumstances, can say, is, 'I hope not; I endeavour to be impartial.'

First, the system of religious conformity is a system of blind submission. In every country possessing a religious establishment, the state, from a benevolent care, it may be, for the manners and opinions of its subjects, publicly excites a numerous class of men to the study of morality and virtue. What institution, we might obviously be led to enquire, can be more favourable to public happiness? Morality and virtue are the most interesting topics of human speculation; and the best effects might be expected to result from the circumstance, of many persons perpetually receiving the most liberal education, and setting themselves apart from the express cultivation of these topics. But, unfortunately, these very men are fettered in the outset by having a code of propositions put into their hands, in a conformity to which all their enquiries must terminate. The direct tendency of science is to increase from age to age, and to proceed, from the slenderest beginnings, to the most admirable conclusions. But care is taken, in the present case, to anticipate these conclusions, and to bind men, by promises and penalties, not to improve upon the science of their ancestors. The plan is designed indeed to guard against degeneracy and decline; but it makes no provision for advance. It is founded in the most sovereign ignorance of the nature of mind, which never fails to do either the one or the other.

Secondly, the tendency of a code of religious conformity is to make men hypocrites. To understand this, it may be sufficient to recollect the various subterfuges that have been invented by ingenious men to apologize for the subscription of the English clergy. It is observable, by the way, that the articles of our church are founded upon the creed of the Calvinists, though, for one hundred and fifty years past, it has been accounted disreputable among the clergy to be of any other than the opposite, or Arminian tenets. Volumes have been written to prove that, while these articles express Calvinistic sentiments, they are capable of a different construction, and that the subscriber has a right to take advantage of that construction. Divines of another class have rested their arguments upon the known good character and benevolent intentions of the first reformers, and have concluded that they could never intend to tyrannize over the consciences of men, or to preclude the advantage of further information. Lastly, there are many who have treated the articles as articles of peace; and inferred that, though you did not believe, you might allow yourself the disingenuity of subscribing them, provided you added the further guilt of constantly refraining to oppose what you considered as an adulteration of divine truth.

It would perhaps be regarded as incredible, if it rested upon the evidence of history alone, that a whole body of men, set apart as the instructors of mankind, weaned, as they are expected to be, from temporal ambition, and maintained upon the supposition that the existence of human virtue and divine truth depends on their exertions, should, with one consent, employ themselves in a casuistry the object of which is to prove the propriety of a man's declaring his assent to what he does not believe. These men either credit their own subterfuges, or they do not. If they do not, what can be expected from men so unprincipled and profligate? With what front can they exhort other men to virtue, with the brand of infamy upon their own foreheads? If they do yield this credit, what must be their portion of moral sensibility and discernment? Can we believe that men shall enter upon their profession with so notorious a perversion of reason and truth, and that no consequences will flow from it, to infect their general character? Rather, can we fail to compare their unnatural and unfortunate state with the wisdom and virtue which the same industry and exertion might unquestionably have produced, if they had been left to their genuine operation? They are like the victims of Circe, to whom human understanding was preserved entire, that they might more exquisitely feel their degraded condition. They are incited, like Tantalus, to contemplate and desire an object, the fruition of which is constantly withheld from their unsuccessful attempts. They are held up to their contemporaries as the votaries of truth, while political institution tyrannically commands them, in all their varieties of understanding, and through a succession of ages, to model themselves by one invariable standard.

Such are the effects that a code of religious conformity produces upon the clergy; let us consider the effects that are produced upon their countrymen. They are bid to look for instruction and morality to a denomination of men, formal, embarrassed and hypocritical, in whom the main spring of intellect is unbent and incapable of action. If the people be not blinded with religious zeal, they will discover and despise the imperfections of their spiritual guides. If they be so blinded, they will not the less transplant into their own characters the imbecile and unworthy spirit they are not able to detect. Is virtue so deficient in attractions, as to be incapable of gaining adherents to her standard? Far otherwise. Nothing can bring the wisdom of a just and pure conduct into question but the circumstance of its being recommended to us from an equivocal quarter. The most malicious enemy of mankind could not have invented a scheme more destructive of their true happiness than that of hiring, at the expense of the state, a body of men whose business it should seem to be to dupe their contemporaries into the practice of virtue.

One of the lessons that powerful facts are perpetually reading to the inhabitants of such countries is that of duplicity and prevarication in an order of men, which, if it exists at all, ought to exist only for reverence. Can it be thought that this prevarication is not a subject of general notoriety? Can it be supposed that the first idea that rises to the understanding of the multitude at sight of a clergyman is not that of a man, inculcates certain propositions not so properly because he thinks them true, or thinks them interesting, as because he is hired to the employment? Whatever instruction a code of religious uniformity may fail to convey, there is one that it always communicates, the wisdom of sacrificing our understandings, and maintaining a perpetual discord between our professions and our sentiments. Such are the effects that are produced by political institution, in a case in which it most zealously intends, with parental care, to guard its subjects from seduction and depravity.

These arguments do not apply to any particular articles and creeds, but to the notion of ecclesiastical establishments in general. Wherever the state sets apart a certain revenue for the support of religion, it will infallibly be given to the adherents of some particular opinions, and will operate, in the manner of prizes, to induce men to embrace and profess those opinions. Undoubtedly, if I think it right to have a spiritual instructor, to guide me in my researches, and, at stated intervals, publicly to remind me of my duty, I ought to be at liberty to take the proper steps to supply myself in this respect. A priest, who thus derives his mission from the unbiassed judgement of his parishioners, will stand a chance to possess, beforehand, and independently of corrupt influence, the requisites they demand. But why should I be compelled to contribute to the support of an institution, whether I approve of it or no? If public worship be conformable to reason, reason without doubt will prove adequate to its vindication and support. If it be from God, it is profanation to imagine that it stands in need of the alliance of the state. It must be, in an eminent degree, artificial and exotic, if it be incapable of preserving itself in existence otherwise than by the inauspicious interference of political institution.

CHAPTER III

OF THE SUPPRESSION OF ERRONEOUS OPINIONS IN RELIGION AND GOVERNMENT

Of heresy. – Arguments by which the suppression of heresy has been recommended. – Answer. – Ignorance not necessary to make men virtuous. – Reason, and not force, the proper corrective of sophistry. – Incongruity of the attempt to restrain thought – to restrain the freedom of speech. – Consequences that would result. – Fallibility of the men by whom authority is exercised. – Of erroneous opinions in government. – Iniquity of the attempt to restrain them. – Difficulty of suppressing opinions by force. – Severities that would be necessary. – Without persecution and oppression, opinions do not lead to violence.

THE same views which have prevailed for the introduction of religious establishments have inevitably led to the idea of provisions against the rise and progress of heresy. No arguments can be adduced in favour of the political patronage of truth that will not be equally cogent in behalf of the political discouragement of error. Nay, they will, of the two, perhaps be most cogent in the latter case; as to prevent men from going wrong is a milder and more temperate assumption of power than to compel them to go right. It has however happened that this argument, though more tenable, has had fewer adherents. Men are more easily reconciled to abuse in the distribution of rewards, than in the infliction of penalties. It seems therefore the less necessary laboriously to insist upon the refutation of this principle; its discussion is principally requisite for the sake of method.

Various arguments have been alleged in defence of this restraint. 'The importance of opinion, as a general proposition, is notorious and unquestionable. Ought not political institution to take under its inspection that root from which all our voluntary actions are ultimately derived? The opinions of men must be expected to be as various as their education and their temper: ought not government to exert its foresight, to prevent this discord from breaking out into anarchy and violence? There is no proposition so absurd, or so hostile to morality and public good, as not to have found its votaries: will there be no danger in suffering these eccentricities to proceed unmolested, and every perverter of truth and justice to make as many converts as he is able? It may be found indeed to be a hopeless task to endeavour to extirpate by the hand of power errors already established; but is it not the duty of government to prevent their ascendancy, to check the growth of their adherents, and the introduction of heresies hitherto unknown? Can those persons to whom the care of the general welfare is confided, or who are fitted, by their situation, or their talents, to suggest proper regulations to the adoption of the community, be justified in conniving at the spread of such extravagant and pernicious opinions as strike at the root of order and morality? Simplicity of mind, and an understanding undebauched with sophistry, have ever been the characteristics of a people among whom virtue has flourished: ought not government to exert itself, to exclude the inroad of qualities opposite to these? It is thus that the friends of moral justice have ever contemplated with horror the progress of infidelity and latitudinarian principles. It was thus that the elder Cato viewed with grief the importation into his own country of that plausible and loquacious philosophy by which Greece had already been corrupted.'*

There are several trains of reflection which these reasoning suggest. None of them can be more important than that which may assist us in detecting the error of the elder Cato, and of other persons who have been the zealous, but

---

* The reader will consider this as the language of the objectors. The most eminent of the Greek philosophers were, in reality, distinguished from all the other teachers by the fortitude with which they conformed to the precepts they taught.

mistaken, advocates of virtue. Ignorance is not necessary to render men virtuous. If it were, we might reasonably conclude that virtue was an imposture, and that it was our duty to free ourselves from its shackles. The cultivation of the understanding has no tendency to corrupt the heart. A man who should possess all the science of Newton, and all the genius of Shakespeare, would not, on that account, be a bad man. Want of great and comprehensive views had as considerable a share as benevolence in the grief of Cato. The progress of science and intellectual cultivation, in some degree, resembles the taking to pieces a disordered machine, with a purpose, by reconstructing it, of enhancing its value. An uninformed and timid spectator might be alarmed at the temerity of the artist, at the confused heap of pins and wheels that are laid aside at random, and might take it for granted that nothing but destruction could be the consequence. But he would be disappointed. It is thus that the extravagant sallies of mind are the prelude of the highest wisdom, and that the dreams of Ptolemy were destined to precede the discoveries of Newton.

The event cannot be other than favourable. Mind would else cease to be mind. It would be more plausible to say that the incessant cultivation of the understanding will terminate in madness than that it will terminate in vice. As long as enquiry is suffered to proceed, and science to improve, our knowledge is perpetually increased. Shall we know everything else, and nothing of ourselves? Shall we become clear-sighted and penetrating in all other subjects, without increasing our penetration upon the subject of man? Is vice most truly allied to wisdom, or to folly? Can mankind perpetually increase in wisdom, without increasing in the knowledge of what it is wise for them to do? Can a man have a clear discernment, unclouded with any remains of former mistake, that this is the action he ought to perform, most conducive to his own interest, and to the general good, most delightful at the instant, and satisfactory in the review, most agreeable to reason, justice and the nature of things, and refrain from performing it? Every system which has been constructed relative to the nature of superior beings and Gods, amidst its other errors, has reasoned truly upon these topics, and taught that the accession of wisdom and knowledge led, not to malignity and tyranny, but to benevolence and justice.

Secondly, the injustice of punishing men for their opinions and arguments will be still more visible if we reflect on the nature of punishment. Punishment is one of the classes of coercion, and, as such, may perhaps be allowed to have an occasional propriety, where the force introduced is the direct correlative of corporal violence previously exerted. But the case of false opinions and perverse arguments is of a very different nature. Does any man assert falsehood? Nothing further can appear requisite than that it should be confronted with truth. Does he bewilder us with sophistry? Introduce the light of reason, and his deceptions will vanish. Where argument, erroneous statements, and misrepresentation alone are employed, argument alone should be called forth to encounter them.

To enable us to estimate properly the value of laws for the punishment of heresy, let us suppose a country to be sufficiently provided with such laws, and observe the result. The object is to prevent men from entertaining certain opinions, or, in other words, from thinking in a certain way. What can be more absurd than to undertake to put fetters upon the subtlety of thought? How frequently does the individual who desires to restrain it in himself fail in the attempt? Add to this that prohibition and menace, in this respect, will frequently give new restlessness to the curiosity of the mind. I must not so much as think of the propositions that there is no God; that the stupendous miracles of Moses and Christ were never really performed; that the dogmas of the Athanasian creed are erroneous. I must shut my eyes, and run blindly into all the opinions, religious and political, that my ancestors regarded as sacred. Will this, in all instances, be possible?

There is another consideration, trite indeed, but the triteness of which is an additional argument of its truth. Swift says 'Men ought to be permitted to think as they please, but not to propagate their pernicious opinions.'* The obvious answer to this is, 'We are much obliged to him: how would he be able to punish our heresy, even if he desired it, so long as it was concealed?' The attempt to punish opinion is absurd: we may be silent respecting our conclusions, if we please; the train of thinking by which those conclusions are generated cannot fail to be silent.

'But, if men be not punished for their thoughts, they may be punished for uttering those thoughts.' No. This is not less impossible than the other. By what arguments will you persuade every man in the nation to exercise the trade of an informer? By what arguments will you persuade my bosom-friend, with whom I repose all the feelings of my heart, to repair immediately from my company to a magistrate, in order to procure my commitment, for so doing, to the prisons of the inquisition? In countries where this is attempted, there will be a frequent struggle, the government endeavouring to pry into our most secret transactions, and the people excited to countermine, to outwit and to execrate their superintendents.

But the most valuable consideration which this part of the subject suggests is, Supposing all this were done, what judgement must we form of the people among whom it is done? Though all this cannot, yet much may be performed; though the embryo cannot be annihilated, it may be prevented from expanding itself into the dimensions of a man. The arguments by which we were supposing a system for the restraint of opinion to be recommended were arguments derived from a benevolent anxiety for the virtue of mankind, and to prevent their degeneracy. Will this end be accomplished? Let us contrast a nation of men daring to think, to speak, and to act what they believe to be right, and fettered with no spurious motives

* See above, Chap. I, p. 563.

to dissuade them from right, with a nation that fears to speak, and fears to think, upon the most interesting subjects of human enquiry. Can any spectacle be more degrading than this timidity? Can men in whom mind is thus annihilated be capable of any good or valuable purpose? Can this most abject of all slaveries be the genuine state, the true perfection of the human species?*

Another argument, though it has often been stated to the world, deserves to be mentioned in this place. Governments no more than individual men are infallible. The cabinets of princes and the parliaments of kingdoms, if there by any truth in considerations already stated,† are often less likely to be right in their conclusions than the theorist in his closet. But, dismissing the estimate of greater and less, it was to be presumed from the principles of human nature, and is found true in fact, that cabinets and parliaments are liable to vary from each other in opinion. What system of religion or government has not, in its turn, been patronized by national authority? The consequence therefore of admitting this authority is not merely attributing to government a right to impose some, but any, or all, opinions upon the governed. Are Paganism and Christianity, the religions of Mahomet, Zoroaster and Confucius, are monarchy and aristocracy, in all their forms, equally worthy to be perpetuated among mankind? Is it certain that the greatest of human calamities is change? Must we never hope for advance and improvement? Have no revolution in government, and no reformation in religion, been productive of more benefit than disadvantage? There is no species of reasoning, in defence of the suppression of heresy, which may not be brought back to this monstrous principle, that the knowledge of truth, and the introduction of right principles of policy, are circumstances altogether indifferent to the welfare of mankind.

The same reasonings that are here employed against

* Book II, Chap. VI.
† Book V, Chap. XXIII, p. 550.

the forcible suppression of religious heresy will be found equally valid with respect to political. The first circumstance that will not fail to suggest itself to every reflecting mind is, What sort of constitution must that be which must never be examined? whose excellencies must be the constant topic of eulogium, but respecting which we must never permit ourselves to enquire in what they consist? Can it be the interest of society to proscribe all investigation respecting the wisdom of its regulations? Or must our debates be occupied with provisions of temporary convenience; and are we forbid to ask whether there may not be something fundamentally wrong in the principles of the structure? Reason and good sense will not fail to augur ill of that system of things which is too sacred to be looked into; and to suspect that there must be something essentially weak in what thus shrinks from the eye of curiosity. Add to which that, however we may doubt of the importance of religious disputes, nothing can less reasonably be exposed to question than that the happiness of mankind is essentially connected with the improvement of political science.

That indeed, in the present situation of human affairs, is sufficiently evident, which was formerly endeavoured to be controverted, that the opinions of men are calculated essentially to affect their social condition. We can no longer, with any plausibility, lay claim to toleration, upon pretence of the innocence of error. It would not, at this time, be mere indifference, it would be infatuation, in our rulers, to say, We will leave the busily idle votaries of speculation to manage their controversies for themselves, secure that their disputes are, in no degree, of concern to the welfare of mankind.

Opinion is the most potent engine that can be brought within the sphere of political society. False opinion, superstition and prejudice, have hitherto been the true supporters of usurpation and despotism. Enquiry, and the improvement of the human mind, are now shaking to the centre those bulwarks that have so long held mankind in thraldom. This is the genuine state of the case: how ought our governors, and the friends of public tranquillity, to conduct themselves in this momentous crisis?

We no longer claim toleration, as was formerly occasionally done, from the unimportance of opinion; we claim it because a contrary system will be found pregnant with the most fatal disasters, because toleration only can give a mild and auspicious character to the changes that are impending.

It has lately become a topic of discussion with political enquirers whether it be practicable forcibly to effect the suppression of novel opinions. Instances have been cited in which this seems to have been performed. A cool and deliberate calculation has been made, as to the number of legal or illegal murders that must be committed, the quantity of misery that must be inflicted, the extent and duration of the wars that must be carried on, according to the circumstances of the case, to accomplish this purpose.

In answer to this sort of reasoning, it may be observed, first, that, if there are instances where a spreading opinion seems to have been extirpated by violence, the instances are much more numerous where this expedient has been employed in vain. It should appear that an opinion must be in a particular degree of reception, and not have exceeded it, in order to give to this engine a chance of effecting its purpose. Above all, it is necessary that the violence by which a set of opinions is to be suppressed should be unintermitted and invariable. If it should happen, as often has happened in similar cases, that the partisans of the new opinion should alternately gain the ascendancy over their oppressors, we shall then have only an alternate succession of irritation and persecution. If there be the least intermission of the violence, it is to be expected that the persecuted party will recover their courage, and the whole business will be to be begun over again. However seriously anyone may be bent upon the suppression of opinions, it would be absurd for him to build upon the supposition that the powers of government will never be transferred to other hands, and that the measures now adopted will be equably pursued to a distant termination.

Secondly, we must surely be induced on strong grounds to form a terrible idea of the consequences to result from the ascendancy of new opinions, before we can bring ourselves to assent to such severe methods for their suppression. Inexpressible must be the enormities committed by us, before we can expect to succeed in such an undertaking. To persecute men for their opinions is, of all the denominations of violence, that to which an ingenuous mind can with the greatest difficulty be reconciled. The persons, in this case, most obnoxious to our hostility are the upright and conscientious. They are of all men the most true to their opinions, and the least reluctant to encounter the evils in which those opinions may involve them. It may be they are averse to every species of disorder, pacific, benevolent, and peculiarly under the guidance of public spirit and public affections. A gallant spirit would teach us to encounter opinion with opinion, and argument with argument. It is a painful species of cowardice to which we have recourse, whatever be our motive, when we determine to overbear an opponent by violence, whom we cannot convince. The tendency of persecution is to generate the most odious vices: in one part of the community, those malevolent passions which teach us to regard our brethren as prodigies and monsters, and that treacherous and vindictive spirit which is ever lying in wait to destroy: in the other part of the community, terror, hatred, hypocrisy and falsehood. Supposing us ultimately to succeed in our object, what sort of a people will be the survivors of this infernal purification?

Thirdly, opinion, though formidable in its tendencies, is perhaps never calamitous in its operation but so far as it is encountered with injustice and violence. In countries where religious toleration has been established, opposite sectaries have been found to pursue their disputes in tranquillity. It is only where measures of severity are adopted that animosity is engendered. The mere prospect of melioration may inspire a sedate and consistent ardour; but oppression and suffering are necessary to render men bitter, impatient and sanguinary. If we persecute the advocates of improvement, and fail of our object, we may fear a terrible retribution; but, if we leave the contest to its genuine course, and only apply ourselves to prevent mutual exasperation, the issue perhaps, whichever way it is determined, will be beneficent and auspicious.

CHAPTER IV

OF TESTS

Their supposed advantages are attended with injustice – are nugatory. – Illustration. – Their disadvantages. – They ensnare. – Example. – Second example. – Influence of tests on the latitudinarian – on the purist. – Conclusion.

THE majority of the arguments above employed, on the subject of penal laws in matters of opinion, are equally applicable to tests, religious and political. The distinction between prizes and penalties, between greater and less, has little tendency to change the state of the question, if we have already proved that any discouragement extended to the curiosity of intellect, and any authoritative countenance afforded to one set of opinions in preference to another, is in its own nature unjust, and evidently hostile to the general welfare,

Leaving out of the consideration religious tests, as being fully comprehended in the preceding discussion,* let us attend for a moment to an article which has had its advocates among men of considerable liberality, the supposed propriety of political tests. 'Shall we have no federal oaths,

* Chap. II.

no oaths of fidelity to the nation, the law and the republic? How in that case shall we distinguish between the enemies and the friends of freedom?'

Certainly there cannot be a method devised for this purpose at once more iniquitous and ineffectual than a federal oath. What is the language that, in strictness of interpretation, belongs to the act of the legislature imposing this oath? To one party it says, 'We know that you are our friends; the oath, as it relates to you, we acknowledge to be superfluous; nevertheless you must take it, as a cover to our indirect purposes, in imposing it upon persons whose views are less unequivocal than yours.' To the other party it says, 'It is vehemently suspected that you are hostile to the cause in which we are engaged: this suspicion is either true or false; if false, we ought not to suspect you, and much less ought we to put you to this corrupting and nugatory purgation; if true, you will either candidly confess your difference, or dishonestly prevaricate: be candid, and we will indignantly banish you; be dishonest, and we will receive you as bosom-friends.'

Those who say this, however, promise too much. Duty and common sense oblige us to watch the man we suspect, even though he should swear he is innocent. Would not the same precautions, which we are still obliged to employ, to secure us against his duplicity have sufficiently answered our purpose, without putting him to this purgation? Are there no methods by which we can find whether a man be the proper subject in whom to repose an important trust, without putting the question to himself? Will not he who is so dangerous an enemy that we cannot suffer him at large, discover his enmity by his conduct, without reducing us to the painful necessity of tempting him to an act of prevarication? If he be so subtle a hypocrite that all our vigilance cannot dectect him, will he scruple to add to his other crimes the guilt of perjury?

Whether the test we impose be merely intended to operate as an exclusion from office, or to any more considerable disadvantage, the disability it introduces is still in the nature of a punishment. It treats the individual in question as an unsound member of society, as distinguished, in an unfavourable sense, from the majority of his countrymen, and possessing certain attributes detrimental to the general interest. In the eye of reason, human nature is capable of no other guilt than this.* Society is authorized to animadvert upon a certain individual, in the case of murder, for example, not because he has done an action that he might have avoided, not because he was sufficiently informed of the better, and obstinately chose the worse; for this is impossible, every man necessarily does that which he at the time apprehends to be best: but because his habits and character render him dangerous to society, in the same sense as a wolf or a blight would be dangerous.* It must, no doubt, be an emergency of no common magnitude that can justify a people in putting a mark of displeasure upon a man for the opinions he entertains, be they what they may. But, taking for granted, for the present, the propriety of such a measure, it would certainly be just as equitable to administer, to the man accused for murder, an oath of purgation, as to the man accused of disaffection to the established order of society. The proof of this injustice is to be found in the nature of punishment. It would be well, in ordinary cases at least, that a man were allowed to propose to his neighbour what questions he pleased, and, in general, his duty would prompt him to give an explicit answer. But, when you punish a man, you suspend the treatment that is due to him as a rational being, and consequently your own claim to a reciprocation of that treatment. You demand from him an impartial confession at the same time that you employ a most powerful motive to prevarication, and menace him with a serious injury in return for his ingenuousness.

These reasonings being particularly applicable to a people in a state of revolution, like the French, it may perhaps be allowable to take, from their revolution, an

* Book IV, Chap. VIII.

example of the injurious and ensnaring effects with which tests, and oaths of fidelity, are usually attended. It was required of all men, in the year 1791, to swear, 'that they would be faithful to the nation, the law and the king'. In what sense can they be said to have adhered to their oath who, twelve months after their constitution had been established on its new basis, have taken a second oath declaratory of their everlasting abjuration of monarchy? What sort of effect, favourable or unfavourable, must this precarious mutability in their solemn appeals to heaven have upon the minds of those by whom they are made?

And this leads us, from the consideration of the supposed advantages of tests, religious and political, to their disadvantages. The first of these disadvantages consists in the impossibility of constructing a test in such a manner as to suit the various opinions of those upon whom it is imposed, and not to be liable to reasonable objection. When the law was repealed imposing upon the dissenting clergy of England a subscription, with certain reservations, to the articles of the established church, an attempt was made to invent an unexceptionable test that might be substituted in its room. This test simply affirmed 'that the books of the Old and New Testament, in the opinion of the person who took it, contained a revelation from God'; and it was supposed that no Christian could scruple such a declaration. But is it impossible that I should be a Christian, and yet doubt of the canonical authority of the amatory eclogues of Solomon, or of certain other books, contained in a selection that was originally made in a very arbitrary manner? 'Still however I may take the test, with a persuasion that the books of the Old and New Testament contain a revelation from God, and something more.' In the same sense I might take it, and if the Koran, the Talmud, and the sacred books of the Hindoos, were added to the list. What sort of influence will be produced upon the mind that is accustomed to this looseness of construction in its most solemn engagements?

Let us examine, with the same view, the federal oath of the French, proclaiming the determination of the swearer, 'to be faithful to the nation, the law and the king'. Fidelity to three several interests, which may, in various cases, be placed in opposition to each other, will appear at first sight to be no very reasonable engagement. The propriety of vowing fidelity to the king has already been brought to the trial, and received its condemnation.* Fidelity to the law is an engagement of so complicated a nature as to strike terror into every mind of serious reflection. It is impossible that a system of law, the composition of men, should ever be presented to such a mind, that shall appear faultless. But, with respect to laws that appear to me to be unjust, I am bound to every kind of hostility short of open violence; I am bound to exert myself incessantly, in proportion to the magnitude of the injustice, for their abolition. Fidelity to the nation is an engagement scarcely less equivocal. I have a paramount engagement to the cause of justice, and the benefit of the human race. If the nation undertake what is unjust, fidelity in that undertaking is a crime. If it undertake what is just, it is my duty to promote its success, not because I was born one of its citizens, but because such is the command of justice.

It may be alleged with respect to the French federal oath, as well as with respect to the religious test before cited, that it may be taken with a certain laxity of interpretation. When I swear fidelity to the law, I may mean only that there are certain parts of it that I approve. When I swear fidelity to the nation, the law and the king, I may mean, so far only as these three authorities shall agree with each other, and all of them agree with the general welfare of mankind. In a word, the final result of this laxity of interpretation explains the oath to mean, 'I swear that I believe it is my duty to do everything that appears to me to be just'. Who can look without indignation and regret at this prostitution of language? Who

* Book V, Chap. II–VIII.

can think, without horror, of the consequences of the public and perpetual lesson of duplicity which is thus read to mankind?

But, supposing there should be certain members of the community, simple and uninstructed enough to conceive that an oath contained some real obligation, and did not leave the duty of the person to whom it was administered precisely where it found it, what is the lesson that would be read to such members? They would listen, with horror, to the man who endeavoured to persuade them that they owed no fidelity to the nation, the law and the king, as to one who was instigating them to sacrilege. They would tell him that it was too late, and that they must not allow themselves to hear his arguments. They would perhaps have heard enough, before their alarm commenced, to make them look with envy on the happy state of this man. who was free to listen to the communications of others without terror, who could give a loose to his thoughts, and intrepidly follow the course of his enquiries wherever they led him. For themselves they had promised to think no more for the rest of their lives. Compliance indeed in this case is impossible; but will a vow of inviolable adherence to a certain constitution have no effect in checking the vigour of their contemplations, and the elasticity of their minds?

We put a miserable deception upon ourselves when we promise ourselves the most favourable effects from the abolition of monarchy and aristocracy, and retain this wretched system of tests, overturning, in the apprehensions of mankind at large the fundamental distinctions of justice and injustice. Sincerity is not less essential than equality to the well-being of mankind. A government that is perpetually furnishing motives to jesuitism and hypocrisy is not less in hostility with reason than a government of orders and hereditary distinction. It is not easy to imagine how soon men would become frank, explicit in their declarations, and unreserved in their manners, were there no positive institutions inculcating upon them the necessity of falsehood and disguise. Nor is it possible for any language to describe the inexhaustible benefits that would arise from the universal practice of sincerity.

CHAPTER V

OF OATHS

Oaths of office and duty. – Their absurdity. – Their immoral consequences. – Oaths of evidence – less atrocious. – Opinion of the liberal and resolved respecting them. – Their essential features: contempt of veracity – false morality. – Their particular structure. – Abstract principles assumed by them to be true. – Their inconsistency wih these principles.

THE same arguments that prove the injustice of tests may be applied universally to all oaths of duty and office. If I entered upon the office without an oath, what would be my duty? Can the oath that is imposed upon me make any alteration in my duty? If not, does not the very act of imposing it by implication assert a falsehood? Will this falsehood have no injurious effect upon a majority of the persons concerned? What is the true criterion that I shall faithfully discharge the office that conferred upon me? Surely my past life, not any protestations I may be compelled to make. If my life have been unimpeachable, this compulsion is an unmerited insult; if it have been otherwise, it is something worse.

It is with no common disapprobation that a man of undebauched understanding will reflect upon the prostitution of oaths, which marks the history of modern European countries, and particularly of our own. This is one of the means that government employs to discharge itself of its proper functions, by making each man security for himself. It is one of the means that legislators have provided to cover the inefficiency and absurdity of their regulations, by making individuals promise the execution of that which the police is not able to execute. It holds out, in one hand, the temptation to do wrong, and, in the other, the obligation imposed not to be influenced by that temptation. It compels a man to engage, not only for his own conduct, but for that of all his dependents. It obliges certain officers (church-wardens in particular) to promise an inspection beyond the limits of human faculties, and to engage for a proceeding, on the part of those under their jurisdiction, which they neither intend, nor are empowered to enforce. Will it be believed in after ages that every considerable trader in exciseable articles in this country is induced, by the constitution of its government, to reconcile his mind to the guilt of perjury, as to the condition upon which he is allowed to exercise his profession?

There remains only one species of oaths to be considered, which have found their advocates among persons sufficiently speculative to reject every other species of oath, I mean, oaths administered to a witness in a court of justice. 'These are certainly free from many of the objections that apply to oaths of fidelity, duty or office. They do not call upon a man to declare his assent to a certain proposition which the legislator has prepared for his acceptance; they only require him solemnly to pledge himself to the truth of assertions, dictated by his own apprehension of things, and expressed in his own words. They do not require him to engage for something future, and, of consequence, to shut up his mind against further information, as to what his conduct in that future ought to be; but merely to pledge his veracity to the apprehended order of things past.'

These considerations palliate the evil, but do not convert it into good. Wherever, in any quarter of the globe, men of peculiar energy and dignity of mind have existed, they have felt the degradation of binding their assertions with an oath. The English constitution recognizes, in a

partial and imperfect manner, the force of this principle,
and therefore provides, that, while the common herd of
mankind shall be obliged to confirm their declarations
with an oath, nothing more shall be required from the
order of nobles, in the very function which, in all other
cases, has emphatically received the appellation of juror,
than a declaration upon honour. Will reason justify this
distinction?

Can there be a practice more pregnant with false morality than that of administering oaths in a court of justice?
The language it expressly holds is, 'You are not to be
believed upon your mere word'; and there are few men
firm enough resolutely to preserve themselves from con-
tamination, when they are accustomed, upon the most
solemn occasions, to be treated with contempt. To the
unthinking it comes like a plenary indulgence to the occasional tampering with veracity in affairs of daily occurrence, that they are not upon their oath; and we may
affirm, without risk of error, that there is no cause of
insincerity, prevarication and falsehood more powerful
than that we are here considering. It treats veracity, in
the scenes of ordinary life, as a thing not to be looked
for. It takes for granted that no man, at least of plebeian
rank, is to be credited upon his bare affirmation; and what
it thus takes for granted, it has an irresistible tendency to
produce.

Add to this, a feature that runs through all the abuses
of political institution, it saps the very foundations of
moral principle. Why is it that I am bound to be more
especially careful of what I affirm in a court of justice?
Because the subsistence, the honest reputation, or the
life, of a fellow man, is there peculiarly at issue. All these
genuine motives are, by the contrivance of human institution, thrown into shade, and we are expected to speak
the truth only because government demands it of us upon
oath, and at the times in which government has thought
proper, or recollected, to administer this oath. All attempts to strengthen the obligations of morality by fic-

titious and spurious motives will, in the sequel, be found to have no tendency but to relax them.

Men will never act with that liberal justice, and conscious integrity, which are their highest ornament till they come to understand what men are. He that contaminates his lips with an oath must have been thoroughly fortified with previous moral instruction, if he be able afterwards to understand the beauty of an unconstrained and simple integrity. If our political institutors had been but half as judicious in perceiving the manner in which excellence and worth were to be generated, as they have been ingenious and indefatigable in the means of depraving mankind, the world, instead of a slaughterhouse, would have been a paradise.

Let us leave, for a moment, the general consideration of the principle of oaths, to reflect upon their particular structure, and the precise meaning of the term. They take for granted, in the first place, the existence of an invisible governor of the world, and the propriety of our addressing petitions to him, both which a man may deny, and yet continue a good member of society. What is the situation in which the institution of which we treat places this man? But we must not suffer ourselves to be stopped by trivial considerations. – Oaths are also so constructed, as to take for granted the religious system of the country whatever it may happen to be.

Now what are the words with which we are taught, in this instance, to address the creator whose existence we have thus recognized? 'So help me God, and the contents of his holy word.' It is the language of imprecation. I pray him to pour down his everlasting wrath and curse upon me if I utter a lie. – It were to be wished that the name of that man had been recorded who first invented this mode of binding men to veracity. He had surely himself very slight and contemptuous notions of the Supreme Being, who could thus tempt men to insult him, by braving his displeasure. If it be thought to be our duty to invoke his blessing, yet surely it must be a most

hardened profaneness that can thus be content to put all
the calamity with which he is able to overwhelm us to
the test of one moment's rectitude or frailty.

CHAPTER VI

OF LIBELS

*Public libels. – Injustice of an attempt to pre-
scribe the method in which public questions
shall be discussed. – Its pusillanimity. – Invitations to tumult. – Private libels. – Reasons in
favour of their being subjected to restraint. –
Answer. – 1. It is necessary the truth should be
told. – Salutary effects of the unrestrained
investigation of character. – Objection: freedom
of speech would be productive of calumny, not
of justice. – Answer. – Future history of libel.
– 2. It is necessary men should be taught to be
sincere. – Extent of the evil which arises from
a command to be insincere. – The mind spontaneously shrinks from the prosecution of a
libel. – Conclusion.*

IN the examination already bestowed upon the article
of heresy, political and religious,* we have anticipated
one of the heads of the law of libel; and, if the arguments
there adduced be admitted for valid, it will follow that no
punishment can justly be awarded against any writing or
words derogatory to religion or political government.

It is impossible to establish any solid ground of distinction upon this subject, or to lay down rules in conformity
to which controversies, political or religious, must be
treated. It is impossible to tell me, when I am penetrated
with the magnitude of the subject, and I must be logical,
and not eloquent: or, when I feel the absurdity of the
theory I am combating, that I must not express it in terms

* Chap. III.

that shall produce feelings of ridicule in my readers. It were better to forbid me the discussion of the subject altogether than forbid me to describe it in the manner I conceive to be most suitable to its merits. It would be a most tyrannical species of candour to tell me, 'You may write against the system we patronize, provided you will write in an imbecile and ineffectual manner; you may enquire and investigate as much as you please, provided, when you undertake to communicate the result, you carefully check your ardour, and be upon your guard that you do not convey any of your own feelings to your readers.' In subjects connected with the happiness of mankind, the feeling is the essence. If I do not describe the miserable effects of fanaticism and abuse, if I do not excite in the mind a sentiment of aversion and ardour, I had better leave the subject altogether, for I am betraying the cause of which I profess to be the advocate. Add to this, that rules of distinction, as they are absurd in relation to the dissidents, will prove a continual instrument of usurpation and injustice to the ruling party. No reasonings will appear fair to them but such as are futile. If I speak with energy, they will deem me inflammatory; and if I describe censurable proceedings in plain and homely but pointed language, they will cry out upon me as a buffoon.

It must be truly a deplorable case if truth, savoured by the many, and patronized by the great, should prove too weak to enter the lists with falsehood. It is in a manner self-evident that that which will stand the test of examination cannot need the support of penal statutes. After our adversaries have exhausted their eloquence, and exerted themselves to mislead us, truth has a clear, nervous and simple story to tell, which, if force be excluded on all sides, will not fail to put down their arts. Misrepresentation will speedily vanish if the friends of truth be but half as alert as the advocates of falsehood. Surely then it is a most ungracious plea to offer, 'We are too idle to reason with you, and are therefore determined to silence you by force.' So long as the adversaries of justice confine themselves to expostulation, there can be no ground for serious alarm. As soon as they begin to act with violence and riot, it will be time enough to encounter them with force.

There is however one class of libel that seems to demand a separate consideration. A libel may either not confine itself to any species of illustration of religion or government, or it may leave illustration entirely out of its view. Its object may be to invite a multitude of persons to assemble, as the first step towards acts of violence. A public libel is any species of writing in which the wisdom of some established system is controverted; and it cannot be denied that a dispassionate and severe demonstration of its injustice tends, not less than the most alarming tumult, to the destruction of such institutions. But writing and speech are the proper and becoming methods of operating changes in human society, and tumult is an improper and equivocal method. In the case then of the specific preparations of riot, it should seem that the regular force of the society may lawfully interfere. But this interference may be of two kinds. It may consist of precautions to counteract all tumultuous concourse, or it may arraign the individual for the offences he has committed against the peace of the community. The first of these seems sufficiently commendable and wise, and would perhaps, if vigilantly exerted, be, in almost all cases, adequate to the purpose. A firm and explicit language as to the preceding steps, a careful attention to avoid unecessary irritation and violence, and a temperate display of strength in case of extremity, might be expected always to extricate the government in safety in these delicate exigencies. It must be a very uncommon occasion in which the mass of the sober and effective part of the community will not be found inimical to disorderly and tumultuous proceedings. The second idea, that of bringing the individual to account for a proceeding of this sort, is of a more doubtful nature. A libel the avowed intention of which is to lead to immediate violence is altogether different from a publication in which the general merits of any institution are treated with the utmost freedom, and may well be supposed to fall under different rules. The difficulty here arises from the consideration of the general nature of punishment, which is abhorrent to the true principles of mind, and ought to be restrained within as narrow limits as possible, if not immediately abolished.* A distinction to which observation and experience, in cases of judicial proceeding, have uniformly led is that between crimes that exist only in intention, and over acts. So far as prevention only is concerned, the former would seem, in many cases, not less entitled to the animadversion of society than the latter; but the evidence of intention usually rests upon circumstances equivocal and minute, and the friend of justice will tremble to erect any grave proceedings upon so uncertain a basis.† These reasonings on exhortations to tumult will also be found applicable, with slight variation, to incendiary letters addressed to private persons.

But the law of libel, as we have already said, distributes itself into two heads, libels against public establishments and measures, and libels against private character. Those who have been willing to admit that the first ought to pass unpunished have generally asserted the propriety of counteracting the latter by censures and penalties. It shall be the business of the remainder of this chapter to show that they were erroneous in their decision.

The arguments upon which their decision is built must be allowed to be both popular and impressive. 'There is no external possession more solid, or more valuable than an honest fame. My property, in goods or estate, is appropriated only by convention. Its value is, for the most part, the creature of a debauched imagination; and, if I were sufficiently wise and philosophical, he that deprived me of it would do me very little injury. He that inflicts a stab upon my character is a much more formidable enemy. It is a very serious inconvenience that my countrymen

* See the following Book.
† Book VII, Chap. VII.

should regard me as destitute of principle and honesty. If the mischief were entirely to myself, it is not possible to be regarded with levity. I must be void of all sense of justice, if I am callous to the contempt and detestation of the world. I must cease to be a man, if I am unaffected by the calumny that deprives me of the friend I love, and leaves me perhaps without one bosom in which to repose my sympathies. But this is not all. The same stroke that annihilates my character extremely abridges, if it do not annihilate, my usefulness. It is in vain that I would exert my good intentions and my talents for the assistance of others, if my motives be perpetually misinterpreted. Men will not listen to the arguments of him they despise; he will be spurned during life, and execrated as long as his memory endures. What then are we to conclude but that to an injury greater than robbery, greater perhaps than murder, we ought to award an exemplary punishment?'

The answer to this statement may be given in the form of an illustration of two propositions: first, that it is necessary the truth should be told; secondly, that it is necessary men should be taught to be sincere.

First, it is necessary the truth should be told. How can this ever be done if I be forbidden to speak upon more than one side of a question? The case is here exactly similar to the case of religion and political establishment. If we must always hear the praise of things as they are, and allow no man to urge an objection, we may be lulled into torpid tranquillity, but we can never be wise.

If a veil of partial favour is to be drawn over the indiscretions and faults of mankind, it is easy to perceive whether virtue or vice will be the gainer. There is no terror that comes home to the heart of vice like the terror of being exhibited to the public eye. On the contrary, there is no reward worthy to be bestowed upon eminent virtue but this one, the plain, unvarnished proclamation of its excellence in the face of the world.

If the unrestrained discussion of abstract enquiry be of the highest importance to mankind, the unrestrained investigation of character is scarcely less to be cultivated. If truth were universally told of men's dispositions and actions, gibbets and wheels might be dismissed from the face of the earth. The knave unmasked would be obliged to turn honest in his own defence. Nay, no man would have time to grow a knave. Truth would follow him in his first irresolute essays, and public disapprobation arrest him in the commencement of his career.

There are many men at present who pass for virtuous that tremble at the boldness of a project like this. They would be detected in their effeminacy and imbecility. Their imbecility is the growth of that inauspicious secrecy which national manners, and political institutions, at present draw over the actions of individuals. If truth were spoken without reserve, there would be no such men in existence. Men would act with clearness and decision if they had no hopes in concealment, if they saw, at every turn, that the eye of the world was upon them. How great would be the magnanimity of the man who was always sure to be observed, sure to be judged with discernment, and to be treated with justice? Feebleness of character would hourly lose its influence in the breast of those over whom it now domineers. They would feel themselves perpetually urged, with an auspicious violence, to assume manners more worthy of the form they bear.

To these reasonings it may perhaps be rejoined, 'This indeed is an interesting picture. If truth could be universally told, the effects would no doubt be of the most excellent nature; but the expectation is to be regarded as visionary.'

Not so: the discovery of individual and personal truth is to be effected in the same manner as the discovery of general truth, by discussion. From the collision of disagreeing accounts, justice and reason will be produced. Mankind seldom think much of any particular subject without coming to think right at last.

'Is it then to be supposed that mankind will have the discernment and the justice, of their own accord, to reject the libel?' Yes; libels do not at present deceive mankind from their intrinsic power, but from the restraint under which they labour. The man who, from his dungeon, is brought to the light of day cannot accurately distinguish colours; but he that has suffered no confinement feels no difficulty in the operation. Such is the state of mankind at present: they are not exercised to employ their judgement, and therefore they are deficient in judgement. The most improbable tale now makes a deep impression; but then men would be accustomed to speculate upon the possibilities of human action.

At first, it may be, if all restraint upon the freedom of writing and speech were removed, and men were encouraged to declare what they thought, as publicly as possible, every press would be burdened with an inundation of scandal. But the stories, by their very multiplicity, would defeat themselves. No one man, if the lie were successful, would become the object of universal persecution. In a short time, the reader, accustomed to the dissection of character, would acquire discrimination. He would either detect the imposition by its internal absurdity, or at least would attribute to the story no further weight than that to which its evidence entitled it.

Libel, like every other human concern, would soon find its level, if it were delivered from the injurious interference of political institution. The libeller, that is, he who utters an unfounded calumny, either invents the story he tells, or delivers it with a degree of assurance to which the evidence that has offered itself to him is by no means entitled. In each case he would meet with his proper punishment in the judgement of the world. The consequences of his error would fall back upon himself. He would either pass for a malignant accuser, or for a rash and headlong censurer. Anonymous scandal would be almost impossible in a state where nothing was concealed. But, if it were attempted, it would be wholly pointless, since, where there could be no honest and rational excuse for concealment, the desire to be concealed would prove the baseness of the motive.

Secondly, force ought not to intervene for the suppression of private libels, because men ought to learn to be sincere. There is no branch of virtue more essential than that which consists in giving language to our thoughts. He that is accustomed to utter what he knows to be false, or to suppress what he knows to be true, is in a state of perpetual degradation. If I have had particular opportunity to observe any man's vices, justice will not fail to suggest to me that I ought to admonish him of his errors, and to warn those whom his errors might injure. There may be very sufficient ground for my representing him as a vicious man, though I may be totally unable to demonstrate his vices, so as to make him a proper subject of judicial punishment. Nay, it cannot be otherwise; for I ought to describe his character exactly as it appears to be, whether it be virtuous or vicious, or of an ambiguous nature. Ambiguity would presently cease if every man avowed his sentiments. It is here as in the intercourses of friendship: a timely explanation seldom fails to heal a broil; misunderstandings would not grow considerable were we not in the habit of brooding over imaginary wrongs.

Laws for the suppression of private libels are, properly speaking, laws to restrain men from the practice of sincerity. They create a warfare between the genuine dictates of unbiassed private judgement and the apparent sense of the community; throwing obscurity upon the principles of virtue, and inspiring an indifference to the practice. This is one of those consequences of political institution that presents itself at every moment: morality is rendered the victim of uncertainty and doubt. Contradictory systems of conduct contend with each other for the preference, and I become indifferent to them all. How is it possible that I should imbibe the divine enthusiasm of benevolence and justice, when I am prevented from discerning what it is in which they consist? Other laws assume for the topic of their animadversion actions of unfrequent occurrence. But the law of libels usurps the office of directing me in my daily duties, and, by perpetually menacing me with the scourge of punishment, undertakes to render me habitually a coward, continually governed by the basest and most unprincipled motives.

Courage consists more in this circumstance than in any other, the daring to speak everything the uttering of which may conduce to good. Actions the performance of which requires an inflexible resolution call upon us but seldom; but the virtuous economy of speech is our perpetual affair. Every moralist can tell us that morality eminently consists in 'the government of the tongue'. But this branch of morality has long been inverted. Instead of studying what we shall tell, we are taught to consider what we shall conceal. Instead of an active virtue, 'going about doing good', we are instructed to believe that the chief end of man is to do no mischief. Instead of fortitude, we are carefully imbued with maxims of artifice and cunning, misnamed prudence.

Let us contrast the character of those men with whom we are accustomed to converse, with the character of men such as they ought to be, and will be. On the one side, we perceive a perpetual caution that shrinks from the observing eye, that conceals, with a thousand folds, the genuine emotions of the heart, and that renders us unwilling to approach the men that we suppose accustomed to read it, and to tell what they read. Such characters as ours are the mere shadows of men, with a specious outside perhaps, but destitute of substance and soul. When shall we arrive at the land of realities, where men shall be known for what they are, by energy of thought, and intrepidity of action! It is fortitude that must render a man superior alike to caresses and threats, enable him to derive his happiness from within, and accustom him to be, upon all occasions, prompt to assist and to inform. Everything therefore favourable to fortitude must be of inestimable value: everything that inculcates dissimulation, worthy of our fullest disapprobation.

There is one thing more that is of importance to be observed upon this subject of libel, which is the good effects that would spring from every man's being accustomed to encounter falsehood with its only proper antidote, truth. After all the arguments that have been industriously accumulated to justify prosecution for libel, every man that will retire into himself feels himself convinced of their insufficiency. The modes in which an innocent and a guilty man would repel an accusation against them might be expected to be opposite; but the law of libel confounds them. He that was conscious of his rectitude, and undebauched by ill systems of government, would say to his adversary, 'Publish what you please against me, I have truth on my side, and will confound your misrepresentations.' His sense of fitness and justice would not permit him to say, 'I will have recourse to the only means that are congenial to guilt, I will compel you to be silent.' A man urged by indignation and impatience may commence a prosecution against his accuser; but he may be assured, the world, that is a disinterested spectator, feels no cordiality for his proceedings. The language of their sentiments upon such occasions is, 'What! he dares not even let us hear what can be said against him.'

The arguments in favour of justice, however different may be the views under which it is considered, perpetually run parallel to each other. The recommendations under this head are precisely the same as those under the preceding, the generation of activity and fortitude. The tendency of all false systems of political institution is to render the mind lethargic and torpid. Were we accustomed not to recur either to public or individual force, but upon occasions that unequivocally justified their employment, we should then come to have some respect for reason, for we should know its power. How great must be the difference between him who answers me with a writ of summons or a challenge, and him who employs the sword and the shield of truth alone? He knows that force only is to be encountered with force, and allegation with allegation; and he scorns to change places with the offender by being the first to break the peace. He does that which, were it not for the degenerate habits of society, would scarcely deserve the name of courage, dares to meet, upon equal ground, with the sacred armour of truth, an adversary who possesses only the perishable weapons of falsehood. He calls up his understanding; and does not despair of baffling the shallow pretences of calumny. He calls up his firmness; and knows that a plain story, every word of which is marked with the emphasis of sincerity, will carry conviction to every hearer. It were absurd to expect that truth should be cultivated, so long as we are accustomed to believe that it is an impotent incumbrance. It would be impossible to neglect it, if we knew that it was as impenetrable as adamant, and as lasting as the world.

CHAPTER VII

OF CONSTITUTIONS

Distinction of regulations constituent and legislative. – Supposed character of permanence that ought to be given to the former – inconsistent with the nature of man. – Source of the error. – Remark. – Absurdity of the system of permanence. – Its futility. – Mode to be pursued in framing a constitution. – Constituent laws not more important than others. – In what manner the consent of the districts is to be declared. – Tendency of the principle which requires this consent. – It would reduce the number of constitutional articles – parcel out the legislative power – and produce the gradual extinction of law. – Objection. – Answer.

A QUESTION intimately connected with the political superintendence of opinion is presented to us relative to a doctrine which has lately been taught upon the subject of constitutions. It has been said 'that the laws of every regular state naturally distribute themselves under two heads, fundamental and temporary; laws the object of which is the distribution of political power, and directing the permanent forms according to which public business is to be conducted; and laws the result of the deliberations of powers already constituted.' This distinction being established in the first instance, it has been inferred 'that these laws are of very unequal importance, and that, of consequence, those of the first class ought to be originated with much greater solemnity, and to be declared much less susceptible of variation, than those of the second'. The French national assembly of 1789 pushed this principle to the greatest extremity, and seemed desirous of providing every imaginable security for rendering the work they had formed immortal. It was not to be touched, upon any account, under the term of ten years; every alteration it was to receive must be recognized as necessary by two successive national assemblies of the ordinary kind; after these formalities an assembly of revision was to be elected, and they to be forbidden to amend the constitution in any other points than those which had been previously marked out for their consideration.

It is easy to perceive that these precautions are in direct hostility with the principles established in this work. 'Man and for ever!' was the motto of the labours of this assembly. Just broken loose from the thick darkness of an absolute monarchy, they assumed to prescribe lessons of wisdom to all future ages. They seem not so much as to have dreamed of that purification of intellect, that climax of improvement, which may very probably be the destiny of posterity. The true state of man, as has been already said, is, not to have his opinions bound down in the fetters of an eternal quietism, but, flexible and unrestrained, to yield with facility to the impressions of accumulating observation and experience. That form of society will, of consequence, appear most eligible which is least founded in a principle of permanence. But, if this view of the subject be just, the idea, of giving permanence to what is called the constitution of any government, and rendering one class of laws, under the appellation of fundamental, less susceptible of change than another, must be founded in misapprehension and error.

The error probably originally sprung out of the forms of political monopoly which we see established over the whole civilized world. Government could not justly flow, in the first instance, but from the choice of the people; or, perhaps more accurately speaking, ought to be adjusted in its provisions to the prevailing apprehensions of equity and truth. We see government as present administered, either in whole or in part, by a king and a body of noblesse; and we reasonably say that the laws made by these authorities are one thing, and the laws from which they derived their existence another. Now this, and indeed every species of exclusive institution, presents us with a dilemma, memorable in its nature, and hard of solution. If the prejudices of a nation are decisively favourable to a king or a body of noblesse, it seems impossible to say that a king, or a body of noblesse, should not form part of their government. But then, on the other hand, the moment you admit this species of exclusive institution, you counteract the purpose for which it was admitted, and deprive the sentiments of the people of their genuine operation.

If we had never seen arbitrary and capricious forms of government, we should probably never have thought of cutting off certain laws from the code, under the name of constitutional. When we behold certain individuals, or bodies of men, exercising an exclusive superintendence over the affairs of a nation, we inevitably ask how they came by their authority, and the answer is, By the constitution. But, if we saw no power existing in the state but that of the people, having a body of representatives, and a certain number of official secretaries and clerks acting in their behalf, subject to their revival, and renewable at their pleasure, the question how the people came by this authority would never have suggested itself.

A celebrated objection that has been urged against the

governments of modern Europe is 'that they have no constitutions'.* If, by this objection, it be understood that they have no written code bearing this appellation, and that their constitutions have been less an instantaneous than a gradual production, the criticism seems to be rather verbal than of essential moment. In any other sense, it is to be suspected that the remark would amount to an eulogium, but an eulogium to which they are certainly by no means entitled.

But to return to the question of permanence. Whether we admit or reject the distinction between constitutional and ordinary legislation, it is not less true than the power of a nation to change its constitution, morally considered, must be briefly and universally coeval with the existence of a constitution. The languages of permanence, in this case, is the grossest absurdity. It is to say to a nation, 'Are you convinced that something is right, perhaps immediately necessary, to be done? It shall be done ten years hence.'

The folly of this system may be further elucidated, if further elucidation be necessary, from the following dilemma. Either a people must be governed according to their own apprehensions of justice and truth, or they must not. The last of these assertions cannot be avowed, but upon the unequivocal principles of tyranny. But, if the first be true, then it is just as absurd to say to a nation, 'This government, which you chose nine years ago, is the legitimate government, and the government which your present sentiments approve, the illegitimate'; as to insist upon their being governed by the *dicta* of their remotest ancestors, even of the most insolent usurper.

It is extremely probable that a national assembly, chosen in the ordinary forms, is just as well entitled to change the fundamental laws as to change any of the least important branches of legislation. This function would never perhaps be dangerous but in a country that still preserved a portion of monarchy or aristocracy; and, in such a country,

* Paine's *Rights of Man*.

a principle of permanence would be found a very feeble antidote against the danger. The true principle upon the subject is that no assembly, though chosen with the most unexampled solemnity, is competent to impose any regulations contrary to the public apprehension of right; and a very ordinary authority, fairly originated, will be sufficient to facilitate the harmonious adoption of a change that is dictated by national opinion. The distinction of constitutional and ordinary topics will always appear in practice unintelligible and vexatious. The assemblies of more frequent recurrence will find themselves arrested in the intention of confering eminent benefit on their own country, by the apprehension that they shall invade the constitution. In a country where the people are habituated to sentiments of equality, and where no political monopoly is tolerated, there is little danger that any national assembly should be disposed to enforce a pernicious change, and there is still less that the people should submit to the injury, or not possess the means easily and with small interruption of public tranquillity, to avert it. The language of reason on this subject is, 'Give us equality and justice, but no constitution. Suffer us to follow, without restraint, the dictates of our own judgement, and to change our forms of social order, as fast as we improve in understanding and knowledge.'

The opinion upon this head, most popular in France at the time (1792) that the national convention entered upon its functions, was that the business of a convention extended only to the presenting the draft of a constitution, to be submitted in the sequel to the approbation of the districts, and, subsequently only to that approbation, to be considered as law. This opinion is deserving of a serious examination.

The first idea that suggests itself respecting it is that, if constitutional laws ought to be subjected to the revision of the districts, then all laws ought to undergo the same process, understanding by laws all declarations of a general principle to be applied to particular cases as they may happen to occur, and even including all provisions for individual emergencies that will admit of the delay incident to the revision in question. It is a mistake to imagine that the importance of these articles is in a descending ratio, from fundamental to ordinary, and from ordinary to particular. It is possible for the most odious injustice to be perpetrated by the best constituted legislature that ever was framed. A law rendering it capital to oppose the doctrine of transubstantiation would be more injurious to the public welfare than a law changing the duration of the national representative from two years, to one year, or to three. Taxation has been shown to be an article rather of executive than legislative administration*; and yet a very oppressive and unequal tax would be scarcely less ruinous than any single measure that could possibly be devised.

It may further be remarked that an approbation demanded from the districts to certain constitutional articles, whether more or less numerous, will be either real or delusive, according to the mode adopted for that purpose. If the districts be required to decide upon these articles by a simple affirmative or negative, it will then be delusive. It is impossible for any man or body of men, in the due exercise of their understanding, to decide upon any complicated system in that manner. It can scarcely happen but that there will be some things that they would approve, and some that they would disapprove. On the other hand, if the articles be unlimitedly proposed for discussion in the districts, a transaction will be begun to which it is not easy to foresee termination. Some districts will object to certain articles; and, if these articles be modelled to obtain their approbation, it is possible that the very alteration, introduced to please one part of the community, may render the code less acceptable to another. How are we to be assured that the dissidents will not set up a separate government for themselves? The reasons that might be offered to persuade a minority of districts to yield to the sense of a majority are by no means so perspicuous and

* Book V, Chap. I.

forcible as those which sometimes persuade the minority of members in a given assembly to that species of concession.

It is desirable, in all cases of the practical adoption of any given principle, that we should fully understand the meaning of the principle, and perceive the conclusions to which it inevitably leads. This principle of a consent of districts has an immediate tendency, by a salutary gradation perhaps, to lead to the dissolution of all government. What then can be more absurd than to see it embraced by those very men who are, at the same time, advocates for the complete legislative unity of a great empire? It is founded upon the same basis as the principle of private judgement, which, in proportion as it impresses itself on the minds of men, may be expected perhaps to supersede the possibility of the action of society in a collective capacity. It is desirable that the most important acts of the national representatives should be subject to the approbation or rejection of the districts, whose representatives they are, for exactly the same reason that it is desirable that the acts of the districts themselves should, as speedily as practibility will admit, be in force only so far as relates to the individuals by whom those acts are approved.

The first consequence that would result, not from the delusive, but the real establishment of this principle would be the reduction of the constitution to a very small number of articles. The impracticability of obtaining the deliberate approbation of a great number of districts to a very complicated code would speedily manifest itself. In reality, the constitution of a state, governed either in whole or in part by a political monopoly, must necessarily be complicated. But what need of complexity in a country where the people are destined to govern themselves? The whole constitution of such a country ought scarcely to exceed two articles; first, a scheme for the division of the whole into parts equal in their population, and, secondly, the fixing of stated periods for the election of a national assembly:

not to say that the latter of these articles may very probably be dispensed with.

A second consequence that results from the principle of which we are treating is as follows. It has already appeared that the reason is no less cogent for submitting important legislative articles to the revisal of the districts than for submitting the constitutional articles themselves. But, after a few experiments of this sort, it cannot fail to suggest itself that the mode of sending laws to the districts for their revision, unless in cases essential to the general safety, is a proceeding unecessarily circuitous, and that it would be better, in as many instances as possible, to suffer the districts to make laws for themselves, without the intervention of the national assembly. The justness of this consequence is implicitly assumed in the preceding paragraph, while we stated the very narrow bounds within which the constitution of an empire, such as that of France for example, might be circumscribed. In reality, provided the country were divided into convenient districts with a power of sending representatives to the general assembly, it does not appear that any ill consequences would ensue to the common cause from these districts being permitted to regulate their internal affairs, in conformity to their own apprehensions of justice. Thus, that which was, at first, a great empire with legislative unity would speedily be transformed into a confederacy of lesser republics, with a general congress or Amphictyonic council, answering the purpose of a point of co-operation upon extraordinary occasions. The ideas of a great empire, and legislative unity, are plainly the barbarous remains of the days of military heroism. In proportion as political power is brought home to the citizens, and simplified into something of the nature of parish regulation, the danger of misunderstanding and rivalship will be nearly annihilated. In proportion as the science of government is divested of its present mysterious appearances, social truth will become obvious, and the districts pliant and flexible to the dictates of reason.

A third consequence, sufficiently memorable, from the same principle, is the gradual extinction of law. A great assembly, collected from the different provinces of an extensive territory, and constituted the sole legislator of those by whom the territory is inhabited, immediately conjures up to itself an idea of the vast multitude of laws that are necessary for regulating the concerns of those whom it represents. A large city, impelled by the principles of commercial jealousy, is not slow to digest the volume of its by-laws and exclusive privileges. But the inhabitants of a small parish, living with some degree of that simplicity which best corresponds to the real nature and wants of a human being, would soon be led to suspect that general laws were unnecessary, and would adjudge the causes that came before them, not according to certain axioms previously written, but according to the circumstances and demand of each particular cause. – It was proper that this consequence should be mentioned in this place. The benefits that will arise from the abolition of law will come to be considered in detail in the following book.*

The principal objection that is usually made to the idea of confederacy, considered as the substitute of legislative unity, is 'the possibility that arises of the members of the confederacy detaching themselves from the support of the public cause'. To give this objection every advantage, let us suppose 'that the seat of the confederacy, like France, is placed in the midst of surrounding nations, and that the governments of these nations are anxious, by every means of artifice and violence, to suppress the insolent spirit of liberty that has started up among this neighbour people'. It is to be believed that, even under these circumstances, the danger is more imaginary than real. The national assembly, being precluded by the supposition, from the use of force against the malcontent districts, is obliged to confine itself to expostulation; and it is sufficiently observable that our powers of expostulation are tenfold increased, the moment our hopes are confined to expostulation alone. They have to display, with the utmost perspicuity and simplicity, the benefits of in-

* Book VII, Chap. VIII.

dependence; to convince the public at large that all they intend is to enable every district, and, as far as possible, every individual, to pursue unmolested its own ideas of propriety; and that, under their auspices, there shall be no tyranny, no arbitrary punishments, such as proceed from the jealousy of councils and courts, no exactions, almost no taxation. Some ideas respecting this last subject will speedily occur.* It is not possible but that, in a country rescued from the inveterate evils of despotism, the love of liberty should be considerably diffused. The adherents therefore of the public cause will be many: the malcontents few. If a small number of districts were so far blinded as to be willing to surrender themselves to oppression and slavery, it is probable they would soon repent. Their desertion would inspire the more enlightened and courageous with additional energy. It would be a fascinating spectacle, to see the champions of the general welfare eagerly declaring that they desired none but willing supporters. It is not possible that so magnanimous a principle should not contribute more to the advantage than the injury of their cause.

CHAPTER VIII

OF NATIONAL EDUCATION

> *Arguments in its favour. – Answer. – 1. It produces permanence of opinion. – Nature of prejudice and judgement described. – 2. It requires uniformity of operation. – 3. It is the mirror and tool of national government. – The right of punishing, not founded in the previous function of instructing.*

A MODE in which government has been accustomed to interfere, for the purpose of influencing opinion, is by

* pp. 625, 626.

the superintendence it has in a greater or less degree, exerted in the article of education. It is worthy of observation that the idea of this superintendence has obtained the countenance of several of the zealous advocates of political reform. The question relative to its propriety or impropriety is entitled, on that account, to the more deliberate examination.

The argument in its favour have been already anticipated. 'Can it be justifiable in those persons who are appointed to the functions of magistracy, and whose duty it is to consult for the public welfare, to neglect the cultivation of the infant mind, and to suffer its future excellence or depravity to be at the disposal of fortune? Is it possible for patriotism and the love of the public to be made the characteristic of a whole people in any other way so successfully as by rendering the early communication of these virtues a national concern? If the education of our youth be entirely confided to the prudence of their parents, or the accidental benevolence of private individuals, will it not be a necessary consequence that some will be educated to virtue, others to vice, and others again entirely neglected?' To these considerations it has been added, 'That the maxim which has prevailed in the majority of civilized countries, that ignorance of the law is no apology for the breach of it, is in the highest degree iniquitous; and that government cannot justly punish us for our crimes when committed unless it have forewarned us against their commission, which cannot be adequately done without something of the nature of public education.'

The propriety or impropriety of any project for this purpose must be determined by the general consideration of its beneficial or injurious tendency. If the exertions of the magistrate in behalf of any system of instruction will stand the test, as conducive to the public service, undoubtedly he cannot be justified in neglecting them. If, on the contrary, they conduce to injury, it is wrong and unjustifiable that they should be made.

The injuries that result from a system of national education are, in the first place, that all public establishments include in them the idea of permanence. They endeavour, it may be, to secure and to diffuse whatever of advantageous to society is already known, but they forget that more remains to be known. If they realized the most substantial benefits at the time of their introduction, they must inevitably become less and less useful as they increased in duration. But to describe them as useless is a very feeble expression of their demerits. They actively restrain the flights of mind, and fix it in the belief of exploded errors. It has frequently been observed of universities, and extensive establishments for the purpose of education, that the knowledge taught there is a century behind the knowledge which exists among the unshackled and unprejudiced members of the same political community. The moment any scheme of proceeding gains a permanent establishment, it becomes impressed, as one of its characteristic features, with an aversion to change. Some violent concussion may oblige its conductors to change an old system of philosophy for a system less obsolete; and they are then as pertinaciously attached to this second doctrine as they were to the first. Real intellectual improvement demands that mind should, as speedily as possible, be advanced to the height of knowledge already existing among the enlightened members of the community, and start from thence in the pursuit of further acquisitions. But public education has always expended its energies in the support of prejudice; it teaches its pupils, not the fortitude that shall bring every proposition to the test of examination, but the art of vindicating such tenets as may chance to be established. We study Aristotle, or Thomas Aquinas, or Bellarmine, or chief justice Coke, not that we may detect their errors, but that our minds may be fully impregnated with their absurdities. This feature runs through every species of public establishment; and, even in the petty institution of Sunday schools, the chief lessons that are taught are a superstitious veneration for the church of England, and to bow to every man in a handsome coat. All this is directly contrary to the true interests of mankind. All this must be unlearned before we can begin to be wise.

It is the characteristic of mind to be capable of improvement. An individual surrenders the best attribute of man, the moment he resolves to adhere to certain fixed principles, for reasons not now present to his mind, but which formerly were.* The instant in which he shuts upon himself the career of enquiry is the instant of his intellectual decease. He is no longer a man; he is the ghost of departed man. There can be no scheme more egregiously stamped with folly than that of separating a tenet from the evidence upon which its validity depends. If I cease from the habit of being able to recall this evidence, my belief is no longer a perception, but a prejudice: it may influence me like a prejudice; but cannot animate me like a real apprehension of truth. The difference between the man thus guided and the man that keeps his mind perpetually alive is the difference between cowardice and fortitude. The man who is, in the best sense, an intellectual being delights to recollect the reasons that have convinced him, to repeat them to others, that they may produce conviction in them, and stand more distinct and explicit in his own mind; and he adds to this a willingness to examine objections, because he takes no pride in consistent error. The man who is not capable of this salutary exercise, to what valuable purpose can he be employed? Hence it appears that no vice can be more destructive than that which teaches us to regard any judgement as final, and not open to review. The same principle that applies to individuals applies to communities. There is no proposition at present apprehended to be true so valuable as to justify the introduction of an establishment for the purpose of inculcating it on mankind. Refer them to reading, to conversation, to meditation; but teach them neither creeds nor catechisms, either moral or political.

* Book I, Chap. V, p. 127.

Secondly, the idea of national education is founded in an inattention to the nature of mind. Whatever each man does for himself is done well; whatever his neighbours or his country undertake to do for him is done ill. It is our wisdom to incite men to act for themselves, not to retain them in a state of perpetual pupillage. He that learns because he desires to learn will listen to the instructions he receives, and apprehend their meaning. He that teaches because he desires to teach will discharge his occupation with enthusiasm and energy. But the moment political institution undertakes to assign to every man his place, the functions of all will be discharged with supineness and indifference. Universities and expensive establishments have long been remarked for formal dullness. Civil policy has given me the power to appropriate my estate to certain theoretical purposes; but it is an idle presumption to think I can entail my views, as I can entail my fortune. Remove those obstacles which prevent men from seeing, and which restrain them from pursuing their real advantage; but do not absurdly undertake to relieve them from the activity which this pursuit requires. What I earn, what I acquire only because I desire to acquire it, I estimate at its true value; but what is thrust upon me may make me indolent, but cannot make respectable. It is an extreme folly to endeavour to secure to others, independently of exertion on their part, the means of being happy. – This whole proposition of national education is founded upon a supposition which has been repeatedly refuted in this work, but which has recurred upon us in a thousand forms, that unpatronized truth is inadequate to the purpose of enlightening mankind.

Thirdly, the project of a national education ought uniformly to be discouraged on account of its obvious alliance with national government. This is an alliance of a more formidable nature than the old and much contested alliance of church and state. Before we put so powerful a machine under the direction of so ambiguous an agent, it behoves us to consider well what it is that we do. Government will not fail to employ it, to strengthen its hands, and perpetuate its institutions. If we could even suppose the agents of government not to propose to themselves an object which will be apt to appear in their eyes, not merely innocent, but meritorious; the evil would not the less happen. Their views as institutors of a system of education will not fail to be analogous to their views in their political capacity: the data upon which their conduct as statesmen is vindicated will be the data upon which their instructions are founded. It is not true that our youth ought to be instructed to venerate the constitution, however excellent; they should be led to venerate truth; and the constitution only so far as it corresponds with their uninfluenced deductions of truth. Had the scheme of a national education been adopted when despotism was most triumphant, it is not to be believed that it could have for ever stifled the voice of truth. But it would have been the most formidable and profound contrivance for that purpose that imagination can suggest. Still, in the countries where liberty chiefly prevails, it is reasonably to be assumed that there are important errors, and a national education has the most direct tendency to perpetuate those errors, and to form all minds upon one model.

It is not easy to say whether the remark 'that government cannot justly punish offenders, unless it have previously informed them what is virtue and what is offence' be entitled to a separate answer. It is to be hoped that mankind will never have to learn so important a lesson through so incompetent a channel. Government may reasonably and equitably presume that men who live in society know that enormous crimes are injurious to the public weal, without its being necessary to announce them as such, by laws, to be proclaimed by heralds, or expounded by curates. It has been alleged that 'mere reason may teach me not to strike my neighbour; but will never forbid my sending a sack of wool from England, or printing the French constitution in Spain'. This objection leads to the true distinction upon the subject. All real crimes that that can be supposed to be the fit objects of judicial animadversion are capable of being discerned without the teaching of law. All supposed crimes not capable of being so discerned are truly and unalterably placed beyond the cognisance of a sound criminal justice. It is true that my own understanding would never have told me that the exportation of wool was a crime: neither do I believe it is a crime, now that law has been made affirming it to be such. It is a feeble and contemptible palliation of iniquitous punishments to signify to mankind beforehand that you intend to inflict them. Men of a lofty and generous spirit would almost be tempted to exclaim: Destroy us if you please; but do not endeavour, by a national education, to destroy in our understandings the discernment of justice and injustice. The idea of such an education, or even perhaps of the necessity of a written law, would never have occurred if government and jurisprudence had never attempted the arbitrary conversion of innocence into guilt.

CHAPTER IX

OF PENSIONS AND SALARIES

Reasons by which they are vindicated. – Labour in its usual acceptation and labour for the public compared. – Immoral effects of the institution of salaries. – Source from which they are derived. – Unnecessary for the subsistence of the public functionary – for dignity. – Salaries of inferior officers – may also be superseded. – Taxation. – Qualifications.

AN article which deserves the maturest consideration, and by means of which political institution does not fail to produce the most important influence upon opinion, is that of the mode of rewarding public services. The mode which has obtained in all European countries is that of pecuniary reward. He who is employed to act in behalf of the public is recompensed with a salary. He who retires from that employment is recompensed with a pension. The arguments in support of this system are well known. It has been remarked 'that indeed it may be creditable to individuals to be willing to serve their country without a reward; but that it is a becoming pride on the part of the public to refuse to receive as an alms that for which they are well able to pay. If one man, animated by the most disinterested motives, be permitted to serve the public upon these terms, another will assume the exterior of disinterestedness, as a step towards the gratification of a sinister ambition. If men be not openly and directly paid for the services they perform, we may rest assured that they will pay themselves, by ways a thousand times more injurious. He who devotes himself to the public ought to devote himself entire: he will therefore be injured in his personal fortune, and ought to be replaced. Add to this that the servants of the public ought, by their appearance and mode of living, to command respect both from their countrymen, and from foreigners; and that this circumstance will require an expense, for which it is the office of their country to provide.'*

Before this argument can be sufficiently estimated, it will be necessary for us to consider the analogy between labour in its most usual acceptation, and labour for the public service, what are the points in which they resemble, and in which they differ. If I cultivate a field the produce of which is necessary for my subsistence, this is an innocent and laudable action; the first object it proposes is my own emolument; and it cannot be unreasonable that that object should be much in my comtemplation, while the labour is performing. If I cultivate a field the produce of which is not necessary to my subsistence, but which I

* The substance of these arguments may be found in Burke's Speech on Oeconomical Reform.

propose to give in barter for a garment, the case becomes different. The action here does not, properly speaking, begin in myself. Its immediate object is to provide food for another; and it seems to be, in some degree, a perversion of intellect that causes me to place in an inferior point of view the inherent quality of the action, and to do that which is, in the first instance, beneficent, from a partial retrospect to my own advantage. Still the perversion here, at least to our habits of reflecting and judging, does not appear violent. The action differs only in form from that which is direct. I employ that labour in cultivating a field which must otherwise be employed in manufacturing a garment. The garment I propose to myself as the end of my labour. We are not apt to conceive of this species of barter and trade as greatly injurious to our moral discernment.

But then this is an action, in the slightest degree, indirect. It does not follow, because we are induced to do some actions immediately beneficial to others from a selfish motive, that we can admit of this, in all instances, with impunity. It does not follow, because we are sometimes inclined to be selfish, that we must never be generous. The love of our neighbour is the great ornament of a moral nature: the perception of truth is the most solid improvement of an intellectual nature. He that sees nothing in the universe deserving of regard but himself, is a consummate stranger to the dictates of general and impartial reason. He that is not influenced in his conduct by the real and inherent nature of things is rational to no purpose. Admitting that it is venial to do some actions, immediately beneficial to my neighbour, from a partial retrospect to myself, surely there must be other actions in which I ought to forget, or endeavour to forget myself. This duty is most obligatory in actions most extensive in their consequences. If a thousand men are to be benefited, I ought to recollect that I am only an atom in the comparison, and to reason accordingly.

These considerations may enable us to decide upon

the article of pensions and salaries. Surely it ought not to be the end of a good political institution to increase our selfishness, instead of suffering it to dwindle and decay. If we pay an ample salary to him who is employed in the public service how are we sure that he will not have more regard to the salary than to the public? If we pay a small salary, yet the very existence of such a payment will oblige men to compare the work performed, and the reward bestowed; and all the consequence that will result will be to drive the best men from the service of their country, a service first degraded by being paid, and then paid with an ill-timed parsimony. Whether the salary be large or small, if a salary exist, many will desire the office for the sake of its appendage. Functions the most extensive in their consequences, will be converted into a trade. How humiliating will it be to the functionary himself, amidst the complication and subtlety of motives, to doubt whether the salary were not one of his inducements to the accepting the office? If he stand acquitted to himself, it is however still to be regretted that grounds should be afforded to his countrymen which tempt them to misrepresent his views.

Another consideration of great weight in this instance is that of the source from which salaries are derived: from public revenue, from taxes imposed upon the community. The nature of taxation has perhaps seldom been sufficiently considered. By some persons it has been supposed that the superfluities of the community might be collected, and placed under the disposition of the representative or executive power. But this is a gross mistake. The superfluities of the rich are, for the most part, inaccessible to taxation; the burthen falls, almost exclusively, upon the laborious and the poor. All wealth, in a state of civilized society, is the produce of human industry.* To be rich is merely to possess a patent, entitling one man to dispose of the produce of another man's industry. Taxation therefore can no otherwise fall upon the rich but so far as it

* Book VIII, Chap. II.

operates to diminish their luxuries. But this it does in a very few instances, and in a very small degree. Its genuine operation is to impose a new portion of labour upon those whom labour has already plunged deep in ignorance, degradation, and misery. The higher and governing part of the community are like the lion who hunted in concert with the weaker beasts. The landed proprietor first takes a very disproportionate share of the produce to himself; the capitalist follows, and shows himself equally voracious. Both these classes, in the form in which they now appear, might, under a different mode of society, be dispensed with. Taxation comes in next, and lays a new burthen upon those who are bowed down to the earth already. Who is there, allowed the choice of an alternative, and possessing the spirit of a man, that would choose to be thus fed, with the hard-earned morsel that, through the medium of taxation, is wrested from the gripe of the peasant?

Too much stress however is not to be laid upon this argument. There is no profession, there is perhaps no mode of life compatible with liberal and intellectual pursuits, that does not include in it a portion of inquiry. It is one of the evils of a corrupt state of society that it forces the most enlightened and the most virtuous unwillingly to participate in its injustice. It would be weakness, and not magnanimity, that should teach us to view these things with a microscopical scrupulosity; and to refuse to be useful because no usefulness is pure. The most important objection to emoluments flowing from a public revenue is built upon their tendency to corrupt the mind of the receiver, and the views of the spectators.

Let us proceed to consider the extent of the difficulty that would result from the abolition of salaries. The majority of persons nominated to eminent employments, under any state of mankind approaching to the present, will possess a personal fortune adequate to their support. Those selected from a different class will probably be selected for extraordinary talents, which will naturally lead to extraordinary resources. It has been deemed dishonourable to subsist upon private liberality; but this dishonour is produced only by the difficulty of reconciling this mode of subsistence and intellectual independence. It is true that the fortunes of individuals, like public salaries, are merely a patent, empowering them to engross the produce of other men's labour. But large private fortunes cannot cease to exist till a spirit of sobriety and reflection, hitherto unknown, has been infused into the great mass of mankind. In the meantime the possessors of them are bound to consider of the best mode of disposing of their incomes for the public interest: and it would perhaps be difficult to point out a better than that here alluded to. By this method no new addition would be made to the burthens of the laborious; and the distribution would perhaps produce a better effect, than if it were made in douceurs and prizes to the more ordinary classes of mankind. As to the receiver, he, by the supposition, receives no more than his due; and therefore prejudice alone can represent him as degraded, or imbue him with servility. This source of emolument is free from many of the objections that have been urged against a public stipend. I ought to receive your superfluity as my due, while I am employed in affairs more important than that of earning a subsistence; but at the same time to receive it with a total indifference to personal advantage, taking only what I deem necessary for the supply of my wants. He that listens to the dictates of justice, and turns a deaf ear to the suggestions of pride, will probably wish that the customs of his country should cast him for support on the virtue of individuals, rather than on the public revenue. That virtue may be expected, in this, as in all other instances, to increase, the more it is called into action.

'But what if he have a wife and children?' Let many aid him, if the aid of one be insufficient. Let him do in his lifetime what Eudamidas did at his decease, bequeath his daughter to be subsisted by one friend, and his mother by another. This is the only true taxation, which he, in whom civil policy has vested the means, assesses on himself, not which he endeavours to discharge upon the shoulders of the poor. It is a striking example of the power of venal governments in generating prejudice that this scheme of serving the public functions without salaries, so common among the ancient republicans, should, by liberal-minded men of the present day, be deemed impracticable. Nor let us imagine that the safety of the community will depend upon the services of an individual. In the country in which individuals fit for the public service are rare, the post of honour will probably be his, not that fills an official situation, but that, from his closet, endeavours to waken the sleeping virtues of mankind. In the country where they are frequent, it will not be difficult, by the short duration of the employment, to compensate for the slenderness of the means of him that fills it.

It is not easy to describe the advantages that must result from this proceeding. The public functionary would, in every article of his charge, recollect the motives of public spirit and benevolence. He would hourly improve in the vigour and disinterestedness of his character. The habits created by a frugal fare and a cheerful poverty, not hid as now in obscure retreats, but held forth to public view, and honoured with public esteem, would speedily pervade the community, and auspiciously prepare them for still further improvements.

The objection 'that it is necessary for him who acts on the part of the public to make a certain figure, and to live in a style calculated to excite respect, is scarcely to be considered as deserving a separate answer. The whole spirit of this enquiry is in direct hostility to such an objection. If therefore it have not been answered already, it would be vain to attempt an answer in this place. It is recorded of the burghers of the Netherlands who conspired to throw off the Austrian yoke, that they came to the place of consultation, each man with his knapsack of provisions: who is there that feels inclined to despise this simplicity and honourable poverty? Who would not exclaim with the imperial minister when he viewed the spectacle, Men thus resolute and austere, are neither to be despised nor subdued? – The abolition of salaries would doubtless render necessary the simplification and abridgement of public business. This would be a benefit, and not a disadvantage.

It will further be objected that there are certain functionaries, in the lower departments of government, such as clerks and tax-gatherers, whose employment is perpetual, and whose subsistence ought, for that reason, to be made the result of their employment. If this objection were admitted, its consequences would be of subordinate importance. The office of a clerk or a tax-gatherer is considerably similar to those of mere barter and trade; and therefore to degrade it altogther to their level would have little resemblance to the fixing such a degradation upon offices that demand the most elevated character. The annexation of a stipend to such employments, if considered only as a matter of temporary accommodation, might perhaps be endured.

But the exception, if admitted, ought to be admitted with great caution. He that is employed in an affair of direct public necessity ought to be conscious, while he discharges it, of its true character. We should never allow ourselves to undertake an office of a public nature without feeling ourselves animated with a public zeal. We shall otherwise discharge our trust with comparative coldness and neglect. Nor is this all. The abolition of salaries would lead to the abolition of those offices to which salaries are thought necessary. If we had neither foreign wars nor domestic stipends, taxation would be almost unknown; and, if we had no taxes to collect, we should want no clerks to keep an account of them. In the simple scheme of political institution which reason dictates, we could scarely have any burthensome offices to discharge; and, if we had any that were so in their abstract nature, they might be rendered light by the perpetual rotation of their holders.

If we have salaries, for a still further reason we ought to

have no pecuniary qualifications, or, in other words, no regulation requiring the possession of a certain property as a condition to the right of electing, or the capacity of being elected. It is an uncommon strain of tyranny to call upon men to appoint for themselves a delegate, and at the same time forbid them to appoint exactly the man whom they may judge fittest of the office. Qualification in both kinds is a most flagrant injustice. It asserts the man to be of less value than his property. It furnishes to the candidate a new stimulus to the accumulation of wealth; and this passion, when once set in motion, is not easily allayed. It tells him, 'Your intellectual and moral qualifications may be of the highest order; but you have not enough of the means of luxuries and vice.' To the non-elector it holds the most detestable language. It says, 'You are poor; you are unfortunate; the institutions of society oblige you to be the perpetual witness of other men's superfluity: because you are sunk this low, we will trample you yet lower; you shall not even be reckoned for a man, you shall be passed by, as one of whom society makes no account, and whose welfare and moral existence she disdains to recollect.'

CHAPTER X

OF THE MODES OF DECIDING A QUESTION ON THE PART OF THE COMMUNITY

Decision by lot, its origin – founded in moral imbecility – or cowardice. – Decision by ballot – inculcates timidity – and hypocrisy. – Decision by vote, its recommendations.

WHAT has been here said upon the subject of qualifications naturally leads to a few observations upon the three principal modes of determining public questions and elections, by sortition, ballot and vote.

The idea of sortition was first introduced by the dictates of superstition. It was supposed that, when human reason piously acknowledged its insufficiency, the Gods, pleased with so unfeigned a homage, interfered to guide the decision. This imagination is now exploded. Every man who pretends to philosophy will confess that, whereever sortition is introduced, the decision is exclusively guided by the laws of impulse and gravitation. – Strictly speaking, we know of no such thing as contingence. But, so far as relates to the exercise of apprehension and judgement on the particular question to be determined, all decision by lot is the decision of contingence. The operations of impulse and gravitation either proceed from a blind and unconscious principle; or, if they be the offspring of a superintending mind, it is mind executing general laws, not temporizing with every variation of human caprice.

All reference of public questions and elections to lot includes in it one of two evils, moral imbecility or cowardice. There is no situation in which we can be placed that has not its corresponding duties. There is no alternative that can be offered to our choice that does not include in it a better and a worse. The idea of sortition therefore springs either from an effeminacy that will not enquire, or a timidity that dares not pronounce its desision.

The path of virtue is simple and direct. The first attributes of a virtuous character are a mind awake, and a quick and observant eye. A man of right dispositions will enquire out the lessons of duty. The man, on the contrary, who is spoiled by stupidity or superstition will wait till these lessons are brought to him in a way that he cannot resist. A superficial survey will perhaps lead him to class a multitude of human transactions among the things that are indifferent. But, if we be indefatigably benevolent, we shall, for the most part, find, even among things ordinarily so denominated, a reason for preference. He may well be concluded to have but a small share of moral principle who easily dispenses himself from seeking the occasion to exercise it. Add to which, they are not trifles, but matters of serious import that it has been customary to commit to the decision of lot.

But, supposing us to have a sentiment of preference, or a consciousness that to attain such a perception is our duty, if we afterwards desert it this is the most contemptible cowardice. Nothing can be more unworthy than a propensity to take refuge in indolence and neutrality, simply because we have not the courage to encounter the consequences of ingenuousness and sincerity.

Ballot is a mode of decision still more censurable than sortition. It is scarcely possible to conceive a political institution that includes a more direct and explicit patronage of vice. It has been said 'that ballot may in certain cases be necessary to enable a man of a feeble character to act with ease and independence, and to prevent bribery, corrupt influence and faction'. Hypocrisy is an ill remedy to apply to the cure of weakness. A feeble and irresolute character might before be accidental; ballot is a contrivance to render it permanent, and to scatter its seeds over a wider surface. The true remedy for a want of constancy and public spirit is to inspire firmness, not to inspire timidity. Sound and just conceptions, if communicated to the mind with perspicuity, may be expected to be a sufficient basis for virtue. To tell men that it is necessary they should form their decision by ballot is to tell them that it is necessary they should be ashamed of their integrity.

If sortition taught us to desert our duty, ballot teaches us to draw a veil of concealment over our performance of it. It points out to us a method of acting unobserved. It incites us to make a mystery of our sentiments. If it did this in the most trivial article, it would not be easy to bring the mischief it would produce, within the limits of calculation. But it dictates this conduct in our most important concerns. It calls upon us to discharge our duty to the public with the most virtuous constancy; but at the same time directs us to hide our discharge of it. One of the most beneficial principles in the structure of the material universe will perhaps be found to be its tendency to prevent our withdrawing ourselves from the consequences of our own actions. A political institution that should attempt to counteract this principle would be the only true impiety. How can a man have the love of the public in his heart, without the dictates of that love flowing to his lips? When we direct men to act with secrecy, we direct them to act with frigidity. Virtue will always be an unusual spectacle among men, till they shall have learned to be at all times ready to avow their actions, and assign the reasons upon which they are founded.

If then sortition and ballot be institutions pregnant with vice, it follows that all social decisions should be made by open vote; that, wherever we have a function to discharge, we should reflect on the purpose for which it ought to be exercised; and that, whatever conduct we are persuaded to adopt, especially in matters of routine and established practice, be adopted in the face of the world.

BOOK VII

OF CRIMES AND PUNISHMENTS.

CHAPTER I

LIMITATIONS OF THE DOCTRINE OF PUNISHMENT WHICH RESULT FROM THE PRINCIPLES OF MORALITY

Definition of punishment. – Nature of crime. – Retributive justice not independent and absolute – not to be vindicated from the system of nature. – Force of the term, desert. – Conclusion.

THE subject of punishment is perhaps the most fundamental in the science of politics. Men associated for the sake of mutual protection and benefit. It has already appeared that the internal affairs of such associations are of an inexpressibly higher importance than their external.* It has appeared that the action of society, in conferring rewards, and superintending opinion, is of pernicious effect.† Hence it follows that government, or the action of society in its corporate capacity, can scarcely be of any utility except so far as it is requisite for the suppression of force by force; for the prevention of the hostile attack of one member of the society, upon the person or property of another, which prevention is usually called by the name of criminal justice, or punishment.

Before we can properly judge of the necessity or urgency of this action of government, it will be of some importance

* Book V, Chap. XX.
† Book V, Chap. XII; Book VI, throughout.

to consider the precise import of the word punishment. I may employ force to counteract the hostility that is actually committing on me. I may employ force to compel any member of the society to occupy the post that I conceive most conducive to the general advantage, either in the mode of impressing soldiers and sailors, or by obliging a military officer, or a minister of state, to accept, or retain his appointment. I may put a valuable man to death for the common good, either because he is infected with a pestilential disease, or because some oracle has declared it essential to the public safety. None of these, though they consist in exertion of force for some moral purpose, comes within the import of the word punishment. Punishment is also often used to signify the voluntary infliction of evil upon a vicious being, not merely because the public advantage demands it, but because there is apprehended to be a certain fitness and propriety in the nature of things that render suffering, abstractedly from the benefit to result, the suitable concomitant of vice.

The justice of punishment however, in this import of the word, can only be a deduction from the hypothesis of free will, if indeed that hypothesis will sufficiently support it; and must be false, if human actions are necessary. Mind, as was sufficiently apparent when we treated of that subject,* is an agent in no other sense than matter is an agent. It operates and is operated upon, and the nature, the force and line of direction of the first, is exactly in proportion to the nature, force and line of direction of the second. Morality, in a rational and designing mind, is not essentially different from morality in an inanimate substance. A man of certain intellectual habits is fitted to be an assassin; a dagger of a certain form is fitted to be his instrument. The one or the other excites a greater degree of disapprobation, in proportion as its fitness for mischievous purposes appears to be more inherent and direct. I view a dagger, on this account, with more disapprobation than a knife, which is perhaps equally adapted for the

* Book IV, Chap. VIII.

purposes of the assassin; because the dagger has few or no beneficial uses to weigh against those that are hurtful, and because it has a tendency by means of association to the exciting of evil thoughts. I view the assassin with more disapprobation than the dagger because he is more to be feared, and it is more difficult to change his vicious structure, or to take from him his capacity to injure. The man is propelled to act by necessary causes and irresistible motives, which, having once occurred, are likely to occur again. The dagger has no quality adapted to the contraction of habits, and, though it have committed a thousand murders, is not more likely (unless so far as those murders, being known, may operate as a slight associated motive with the possessor) to commit murder again. Except in the articles he specified, the two cases are exactly parallel. The assassin cannot help the murder he commits, any more than the dagger.

These arguments are merely calculated to set in a more perspicuous light a principle which is admitted by many by whom the doctrine of necessity has never been examined; that the only measure of equity is utility, and whatever is not attended with any beneficial purpose is not just. This is so evident that few reasonable and reflecting minds will be found inclined to deny it. Why do I inflict suffering on another? If neither for his own benefit nor the benefit of others, can I be right? Will resentment, the mere indignation and horror I have conceived against vice, justify me in putting a being to useless torture? 'But suppose I only put an end to his existence.' What, with no prospect of benefit either to himself or others? The reason in mind more easily reconciles itself to this supposition is that we conceive existence to be less a blessing than a curse to a being incorrigibly vicious. But, in that case, the supposition does not fall within the terms of the question: I am in reality conferring a benefit. It has been asked, 'If we conceive to ourselves two beings, each of them solitary, but the first virtuous, and the second vicious, the first inclined to be the highest acts of benevolence, if his situation were changed for the social, the second to malignity, tyranny and injustice, do we not feel that the first is entitled to felicity in preference to the second?' If there be any difference in the question, it is wholly caused by the extravagance of the supposition. No being can be either virtuous, or vicious, who has no opportunity of influencing the happiness of others. He may indeed, though now solitary, recollect or imagine a social state; but this sentiment, and the propensities it generates, can scarcely be vigorous, unless he have hopes of being, at some future time, restored to that state. The true solitaire cannot be considered as a moral being, unless the morality we contemplate be that which has relation to his own permanent advantage. But, if that be our meaning, punishment, unless for reform, is peculiarly absurd. His conduct is vicious, because it has a tendency to render him miserable: shall we inflict calamity upon him, for this reason only, because he has already inflicted calamity upon himself? It is difficult for us to imagine to ourselves a solitary intellectual being, whom no future accident shall ever render social. It is difficult for us to separate, even an idea, virtue and vice from happiness and misery; and, of consequence, not to imagine that, when we bestow a benefit upon virtue, we bestow it where it will turn to account; and when we bestow a benefit upon vice, we bestow it where it will be unproductive. For these reasons, the question of desert, as it relates to a solitary being, will always have a tendency to mislead and perplex.

It has sometimes been alleged that the course of nature has annexed suffering to vice, and has thus led us to the idea of punishment here referred to. Arguments of this sort should be listened to with great caution. It was by reasonings of a similar nature that our ancestors justified the practice of religious persecution: 'Heretics and unbelievers are the objects of God's indignation; it must therefore be meritorious in us to maltreat those whom God has cursed.' We know too little of the system of the universe, are too liable to error respecting it, and see too small a portion, to entitle us to form our moral principles upon an imitation of what we conceive to be the course of nature.

Thus it appears, whether we enter philosophically into the principle of human actions, or merely analyse the ideas of rectitude and justice which have the universal consent of mankind, that, in the refined and absolute sense in which that term has frequently been employed, there is no such thing as desert; in other words, that it cannot be just that we should inflict suffering on any man, except so far as it tends to good. Hence it follows also that punishment, in the last of the senses enumerated towards the beginning of this chapter, by no means accords with any sound principles of reasoning. It is right that I should inflict suffering, in every case where it can be clearly shown that such infliction will produce an overbalance of good. But this infliction bears no reference to the mere innocence or guilt of the person upon whom it is made. An innocent man is the proper subject of it, if it tend to good. A guilty man is the proper subject of it under no other point of view. To punish him, upon any hypothesis, for what is past and irrecoverable, and for the consideration of that only, must be ranked among the most pernicious exhibitions of an untutored barbarism. Every man upon whom discipline is employed is to be considered as to the purpose of this discipline as innocent. The only sense of the word punishment that can be supposed to be compatible with the principles of the present work is that of pain inflicted on a person convicted of past injurious action, for the purpose of preventing future mischief.

It is of the utmost importance that we should bear these ideas constantly in mind, during our examination of the theory of punishment. This theory would, in the past transactions of mankind, have been totally different if they had divested themselves of the emotions of anger and resentment; if they had considered the man who torments another for what he has done as upon a par with the child who beats the table; if they had conjured up to their imagination, and properly estimated, the man who should shut up in prison and periodically torture some atrocious criminal, from the mere consideration of the abstract congruity of crime and punishment, without a possible benefit to others or to himself; if they had regarded punishment as that which was to be regulated solely, by a dispassionate calculation of the future, without suffering the past, on its own account, for a moment to enter into the proceeding.

CHAPTER II

GENERAL DISADVANTAGES OF PUNISHMENT

Conscience in matters of religion considered – in the conduct of life. – Best practicable criterion of duty – not the decision of other men, but of our own understanding. – Tendency of coercion. – Its various classes considered.

HAVING thus endeavoured to show what denominations of punishment justice, and a sound idea of the nature of man, would invariably proscribe, it belongs to us, in the further prosecution of the subject, to consider merely that coercion, which it has been supposed right to employ, against persons convicted of past injurious action, for the purpose of preventing future mischief. And here we will, first, recollect what is the quantity of evil which accrues from all such coercion; and secondly, examine the cogency of the various reasons by which it is recommended. It will not be possible to avoid the repetition of some of the reasons which occurred in the preliminary discussion of the exercise of private judgement.* But those reasonings will now be extended, and will perhaps derive additional advantage from a fuller arrangement.

It is commonly said 'that no man ought to be compelled,

* Book II, Chap. VI.

in matters of religion, to act contrary to the dictates of his conscience. Religion is a principle which the practice of all ages has deeply impressed upon the human mind. He that discharges what his apprehensions prescribe to him on the subject stands approved to the tribunal of his own mind, and, conscious of rectitude in his intercourse with the author of nature, cannot fail to obtain the greatest of those advantages, whatever may be their amount, which religion has to bestow. It is in vain that I endeavour, by persecuting statutes, to compel him to resign a false religion for a true. Arguments may convince, but persecution cannot. The new religion, which I oblige him to profess contrary to his own conviction, however pure and holy it may be in its own nature, has no benefits in store for him. The sublimest worship becomes transformed into a source of depravity when it is not consecrated by the testimony of a pure conscience. Truth is the second object in this respect, integrity of heart is the first: or rather, a proposition that, in its abstract nature, is truth itself converts into rank falsehood and mortal poison, if it be professed with the lips only, and abjured by the understanding. It is then the foul garb of hypocrisy. Instead of elevating the mind above sordid temptations, it perpetually reminds the worshipper of the degrading subjection to which he has yielded. Instead of filling him with sacred confidence, it overwhelms him with confusion and remorse.'

The inference that has been made from these reasonings is 'that criminal law is eminently misapplied in affairs of religion, and that its true province is civil misdemeanours'. But this distinction is by no means so satisfactory and well founded as at first sight it may appear.* Is it not strange that men should have affirmed religion to be the sacred province of conscience, while moral duty is to be left undefined to the decision of the magistrate? Is it of no consequence whether I be the benefactor of my species, or their bitterest enemy? whether I be an informer, or

* Book II, Chap. VI.

a robber, or a murderer? whether I be employed, as a soldier, to extirpate my fellow beings, or, as a citizen, contribute my property to their extirpation? whether I declare the truth, with that firmness and unreserve which an ardent philanthropy will not fail to inspire, or suppress science, lest I be convicted of blasphemy, and fact, lest I be convicted of a libel? whether I contribute my efforts for the furtherance of political improvement, or quietly submit to the exile of a prince of whose claims I am an advocate, or to the subversion of liberty, the most valuable of all human possessions? Nothing can be more clear than that the value of religion, or of any other species of opinion, lies in its moral tendency. If I am to hold as of no account the civil power, for the sake of that which is the means, how much more when it rises in contradiction to the end?

Of all human concerns morality is the most interesting. It is the constant associate of all our transactions: there is no situation in which we can be placed, no alternative that can be presented to our choice, respecting which duty is silent. 'What is the standard of morality and duty?' Justice. Not the arbitrary decrees that are in force in a particular climate; but those laws of reason that are equally obligatory wherever man is to be found. There is an obvious distinction between those particulars in each instance which constitute the permanent nature of the case before us, and those interpositions of a peremptory authority to which it may be prudent to submit, but which cannot alter our ideas of the conduct to which independent man ought to adhere. What then are the consequences that will result from the obedience of compulsion, and not of the uderstanding?

No principle of moral science can be more obvious and fundamental than that the motive by which we are induced to an action constitutes an essential part of its character. This idea has perhaps sometimes been carried too far. A good motive is of little value when it is not joined to a salutary exertion. But, without a good motive, the most extensively useful action that ever was performed can contribute little to the improvement or honour of him that performs it. We owe him no respect if he has been induced to perform it by ideas of personal advantage, or the influence of a bribe. It is, in some respects, worse, if the motive that governed him were the sentiment of fear. If we hold in any estimation the attributes of man, if we desire the improvement of our species, we ought particularly to desire that they should be led in the path of usefulness by generous and liberal considerations, that their obedience should be the obedience of the heart, and not that of a slave.

Nothing can be of higher importance to the improvement of the human mind than that, whatever be the conduct we may be compelled to pursue, we should have distinct and accurate notions of the merits of every moral question in which we may be concerned. In all doubtful questions, there are but two criterions possible, the decisions of other men's wisdom, and the decisions of our own understanding. Which of these is conformable to the nature of man? Can we surrender our own understanding? However we may strain after implicit faith, will not conscience in spite of ourselves whisper us, 'The decree is equitable, and this is founded in mistake?' Will there not be in the minds of the votaries of superstition a perpetual dissatisfaction, a desire to believe what is dictated to them, accompanied with a want of that in which belief consists, evidence and conviction? If we could surrender our understanding, what sort of beings should we become?

The direct tendency of coercion is to set our understanding and our fears, our duty and our weakness, at variance with each other. Coercion first annihilates the understanding of the subject upon whom it is exercised, and then of him who employs it. Dressed in the supine prerogatives of a master, he is excused from cultivating the faculties of a man. What would not man have been, long before this, if the proudest of us had no hopes but in argument, if he knew of no resort beyond, if he were obliged to sharpen his faculties, and collect his powers, as the only means of effecting his purposes?

Let us reflect a little upon the species of influence that coercion employs. It avers to its victim that he must necessarily be in the wrong, because I am more vigorous or more cunning than he. Will vigour and cunning be always on the side of truth? It appeals to force, and represents superior strength as the standard of justice. Every such exertion implies in its nature a species of contest. The contest is often decided before it is brought to open trial, by the despair of one of the parties. The ardour and paroxysm of passion being over, the offender surrenders himself into the hands of his superiors, and calmly awaits the declaration of their pleasure. But it is not always so. The depredator that by main force surmounts the strength of his pursuers, or by stratagem and ingenuity escapes their toils, so far as this argument is valid, proves the justice of his cause. Who can refrain from indignation when he sees justice thus miserably prostituted? Who does not feel, the moment the contest begins, the full extent of the absurdity that the appeal includes? The magistracy, the represenative of the social system, that declares war against one of its members, in behalf of justice, or in behalf of oppression, appears almost equally, in both cases, entitled to our censure. In the first case, we see truth throwing aside her native arms and her intrinsic advantage, and putting herself upon a level with falsehood. In the second, we see falsehood confident in the casual advantage she possesses, artfully extinguishing the new born light that would shame her in the midst of her usurped authority. The exhibition in both is that of an infant crushed in the merciless grasp of a giant.

No sophistry can be more gross than that which pretends to bring the parties to an impartial hearing. Observe the consistency of this reasoning! We first vindicate political coercion, because the criminal has committed an offence against the community at large, and then pretend, while we bring him to the bar of the community, the offended party, that we bring him before an impartial umpire. Thus in England, the king by his attorney is the prosecutor, and the king by his representative is the judge. How long shall such inconsistencies impose on mankind? The pursuit commenced against the supposed offender is the *posse comitatus*, the armed force of the whole, drawn out in such portions as may be judged necessary; and, when seven millions of men have got one poor, unassisted individual in their power, they are then at leisure to torture or to kill him, and to make his agonies a spectacle to glut their ferocity.

The argument against political coercion is equally strong against the infliction of private penalties, between master and slave, and between parent and child. There was, in reality, not only more of gallantry, but more of reason in the Gothic system of trial by duel than in these. The trial of force is over in these, as we have alealy said, before the exertion of force is begun. All that remains is the leisurely infliction of torture, my power to inflict it being placed in my joints and my sinews. This whole argument seems liable to an irresistible dilemma. The right of the parent over his offspring lies either in his superior strength, or his superior reason. If in his strength, we have only to apply this right universally in order to drive all morality out of the world. If in his reason, in that reason let him confide. It is a poor argument of my superior reason that I am unable to make justice be apprehended and felt, in the most necessary cases, without the intervention of blows.

Let us consider the effect that coercion produces upon the mind of him against whom it is employed. It cannot begin with convincing; it is no argument. It begins with producing the sensation of pain, and the sentiment of distaste. It begins with violently alienating the mind from the truth with which we wish it to be impressed. It includes in it a tacit confession of imbecility. If he who employs coercion against me could mould me to his purposes by argument, no doubt he would. He pretends to punish me because his argument is strong; but he really punishes me because his argument is weak.

CHAPTER III

OF THE PURPOSES OF PUNISHMENT

Nature of defence considered. – Punishment for restraint – for reformation. – Supposed uses of adversity – defective – unnecessary. – Punishment for example – 1. nugatory. – 2. unjust. – Unfeeling character of this species of coercion.

LET us proceed to consider the three principal ends that punishment proposes to itself, restraint, reformation and example. Under each of these heads the arguments on the affirmative side must be allowed to be cogent, not irresistible. Under each of them considerations will occur that will oblige us to doubt universally of the propriety of punishment.

The first and most innocent of all the classes of coercion is that which is employed in repelling actual force. This has but little to do with any species of political institution, but may nevertheless deserve to be first considered. In this case I am employed (suppose, for example, a drawn sword is pointed at my own breast or that of another, with threats of instant destruction) in preventing a mischief that seems about inevitably to ensue. In this case there appears to be no time for experiments. And yet, even here, a strict research will suggest to us important doubts. The powers of reason and truth are yet unfathomed. That truth which one man cannot communicate in less than a year, another can communicate in a fortnight. The shortest term may have an understanding commensurate to it. When Marius said, with a stern look and a commanding countenance, to the soldier that was sent down into his dungeon to assassinate him, 'Wretch, have you the temerity to kill Marius!' and with these few words drove him to flight; it was that the grandeur of the idea conceived in his own mind made its way with irresistible force to the mind of his executioner. He had no arms for resistance; he had no vengeance to threaten; he was debilitated and deserted; it was by the force of sentiment only that he disarmed his destroyer. If there were falsehood and prejudice mixed with the idea communicated, in this case, can we believe that truth is not still more powerful? It would be well for the human species if they were all, in this respect, like Marius, all accustomed to place an intrepid confidence in the single energy of intellect. Who shall say what there is that would be impossible to men thus bold, and actuated only by the purest sentiments? Who shall say how far the whole species might be improved, did they cease to respect force in others, and did they refuse to employ it for themselves?

The difference however between this species of coercion, and the species which usually bears the denomination of punishment, is obvious. Punishment is employed against an individual whose violence is over. He is, at present, engaged in no hostility against the community, or any of its members. He is quietly pursuing, it may be, those occupations which are beneficial to himself, and injurious to none. Upon what pretence is this man to be the subject of violence?

For restraint. Restraint from what? 'From some future injury which is to be feared he will commit.' This is the very argument which has been employed to justify the most execrable tyrannies. By what reasonings have the inquisition, the employment of spies, and the various kinds of public censure directed against opinion been vindicated? By recollecting that there is an intimate connection between men's opinions and their conduct; that immoral sentiments lead, by a very probable consequence, to immoral actions. There is not more reason, in many cases at least, to apprehend that the man who has once committed robbery will commit it again than the man who has dissipated his property at the gaming-table or who is accustomed to profess that, upon any emergency, he will not scruple to have recourse to this expedient. Nothing can be more obvious than that, whatever precautions may be allowable with respect to the future, justice will reluctantly class among these precautions a violence to be committed on my neighbour. Nor it is oftener unjust than it is superfluous. Why not arm myself with vigilance and energy, instead of locking up every man whom my imagination may bid me fear, that I may spend my days in undisturbed inactivity? If communities, instead of aspiring, as they have hitherto done, to embrace a vast territory, and glut their vanity with ideas of empire, were contented with a small district, with a proviso of confederation in cases of necessity, every individual would then live under the public eye; and the disapprobation of his neighbours, a species of coercion not derived from the caprice of men, but from the system of the universe, would inevitably oblige him either to reform or to emigrate. – The sum of the arguments under this head is that all punishment for the sake of restraint is punishment upon suspicion, a species of punishment the most abhorrent to reason, and arbitrary in its application, that can be devised.

The second object which punishment may be imagined to propose to itself is reformation. We have already seen various objections that may be offered to it in this point of view. Coercion cannot convince, cannot conciliate, but on the contrary alienates the mind of him against whom it is employed. Coercion has nothing in common with reason, and therefore can have no proper tendency to the cultivation of virtue. It is true that reason is nothing more than a collation and comparison of various emotions and feelings; but they must be the feelings originally appropriate to the question, not those which an arbitrary will, stimulated by the possession of power, may annex to it. Reason is omnipotent: if my conduct be wrong, a very simple statement, flowing from a clear and comprehensive view, will make it appear to be such; nor is it probable that there is any perverseness that would persist in vice in the face of all the recommendations with which virtue might be invested, and all the beauty in which it might be displayed.

But to this it may be answered 'that this view of the subject may indeed be abstractedly true, but that it is not true relative to the present imperfection of human faculties. The grand requisite for the reformation and improvement of the human species seems to consist in the rousing of the mind. It is for this reason that the school of adversity has so often been considered as the school of virtue.* In an even course of easy and prosperous circumstances, the faculties sleep. But, when great and urgent occasion is presented, it should seem that the mind rises to the level of the occasion. Difficulties awaken vigour and engender strength; and it will frequently happen that the more you check and oppress me, the more will my faculties swell, till they burst all the obstacles of oppression.'

The opinion of the excellence of adversity is built upon a very obvious mistake. If we will divest ourselves of paradox and singularity, we shall perceive that adversity is a bad thing, but that there is something else that is worse. Mind can neither exist, nor be improved, without the reception of ideas. It will improve more in a calamitous than a torpid state. A man will sometimes be found wiser at the end of his career, who has been treated with severity than with neglect. But, because severity is one way of generating thought, it does not follow that it is the best.

It has already been shown that coercion, absolutely considered, is injustice. Can injustice be the best mode of disseminating principles of equity and reason? Oppression, exercised to a certain extent, is the most ruinous of all things. What is it but this that has habituated mankind to so much ignorance and vice for so many thousand years? Is it probable that that which has been thus terrible in

* Book V, Chap. II, p. 411.

its consequences should, under any variation of circumstances, be made a source of eminent good? All coercion sours the mind. He that suffers it is practically persuaded of the want of a philanthropy sufficiently enlarged, in those with whom he has intercourse. He feels that justice prevails only with great limitations, and that he cannot depend upon being treated with justice. The lesson which coercion reads to him is, 'Submit to force, and abjure reason. Be not directed by the convictions of your understanding, but by the basest part of your nature, the fear of personal pain, and a compulsory awe of the injustice of others.' It was thus Elizabeth of England and Frederic of Prussia were educated in the school of adversity. The way in which they profited by this discipline was by finding resources in their own minds, enabling them to regard, with an unconquered spirit, the violence employed against them. Can this be the best mode of forming men to virtue? If it be, perhaps it is further requisite that the coercion we use should be flagrantly unjust, since the improvement seems to lie, not in submission, but resistance.

But it is certain that truth is adequate to excite the mind, without the aid of adversity. By truth is here understood a just view of all the attractions of industry, knowledge and benevolence. If I apprehend the value of any pursuit, shall I not engage in it? If I apprehend it clearly, shall I not engage in it zealously? If you would awaken my mind in the most effectual manner, speak to the genuine and honourable feelings of my nature. For that purpose, thoroughly understand yourself that which you would recommend to me, impregnate your mind with its evidence, and speak from the clearness of your view, and with fullness of conviction. Were we accustomed to an education in which truth was never neglected from indolence, or told in a way treacherous to its excellence, in which the preceptor subjected himself to the perpetual discipline of finding the way to communicate it with brevity and force, but without prejudice and acrimony, it cannot be believed but that such an education would be more effectual for the improvement of the mind, than all the modes of angry or benevolent coercion that ever were devised.

The last object which punishment proposes is example. Had legislators confined their views to reformation and restraint, their exertions of power, though mistaken, would still have borne the stamp of humanity. But, the moment vengeance presented itself as a stimulus on the one side, or the exhibition of a terrible example on the other, no barbarity was thought too great. Ingenious cruelty was busied to find new means of torturing the victim, or of rendering the spectacle impressive and horrible.

It has long since been observed that this system of policy constantly fails of its purpose. Further refinements in barbarity produce a certain impression, so long as they are new; but this impression soon vanishes, and the whole scope of a gloomy invention is exhausted in vain.* The reason of this phenomenon is that, whatever may be the force with which novelty strikes the imagination, the inherent nature of the situation speedily recurs, and asserts its indestructible empire. We feel the emergencies to which we are exposed, and we feel, or think we feel, the dictates of reason inciting us to their relief. Whatever ideas we form in opposition to the mandates of law, we draw, with sincerity, though it may be with some mixture of mistake, from the essential conditions of our existence. We compare them with the despotism which society exercises in its corporate capacity; and, the more frequent is our comparison, the greater are our murmurs and indignation against the injustice to which we are exposed. But indignation is not a sentiment that conciliates; barbarity possesses none of the attributes of persuasion. It may terrify; but it cannot produce in us candour and docility. Thus ulcerated with injustice, our distresses, our temptations, and all the eloquence of feeling present themselves again and again. Is it any wonder they should prove victorious?

Punishment for example is liable to all the objections

* Beccaria, *Dei Delitti e delle Pene*.

which are urged against punishment for restraint or reformation, and to certain other objections peculiar to itself. It is employed against a person not now in the commission of offence, and of whom we can only suspect that he ever will offend. It supersedes argument, reason and conviction, and requires us to think such a species of conduct our duty, because such is the good pleasure of our superiors, and because, as we are taught by the example in question, they will make us rue our stubbornness if we think otherwise. In addition to this it is to be remembered that, when I am made to suffer as an example to others, I am myself treated with supercilious neglect, as if I were totally incapable of feeling and morality. If you inflict pain upon me, you are either just or unjust, If you be just, it should seem necessary that there should be something in me that makes me the fit subject of pain, either absolute desert, which is absurd, or mischief I may be expected to perpetrate, or lastly, a tendency in what you do to produce my reformation. If any of these be the reason why the suffering I undergo is just, then example is out of the question: it may be an incidental consequence of the procedure, but it forms no part of its principle. It must surely be a very inartificial and injudicious scheme for guiding the sentiments of mankind, to fix upon an individual as a subject of torture or death, respecting whom this treatment has no direct fitness, merely that we may bid others look on, and derive instruction from his misery. This argument will derive additional force from the reasonings of the following chapter.

CHAPTER IV

OF THE APPLICATION OF PUNISHMENT

Delinquency and punishment incommensurable. — External action no proper subject of criminal animadversion — how far capable of proof. — Iniquity of this standard in a moral — and in a political view. — Propriety of a retribution to be measured by the intention of the offender considered. — Such a project would overturn criminal law — would abolish punishment. — Inscrutability, 1. of motives. — Doubtfulness of history. — Declarations of sufferers. — 2. of the future conduct of the offender. — Uncertainty of evidence — either of the facts — or the intention. — Disadvantages of the defendant in a criminal suit.

A FURTHER consideration, calculated to show not only the absurdity of punishment for example, but the iniquity of punishment in general, is that delinquency and punishment are, in all cases, incommensurable. No standard of delinquency ever has been, or ever can be, discovered. No two crimes were ever alike; and therefore the reducing them, explicitly or implicitly, to general classes, which the very idea of example implies, is absurd. Nor is it less absurd to attempt to proportion the degree of suffering to the degree of delinquency, when the latter can never be discovered. Let us endeavour to clear the truth of these propositions.

Man, like every other machine the operations of which can be made the object of our senses, may, in a certain sense, be affirmed to consist of two parts, the external and the internal. The form which his actions assume is one thing; the principle from which they flow is another. With the former it is possible we should be acquainted; respecting the latter there is no species of evidence that can adequately inform us. Shall we proportion the degree of suffering to the former or the latter, to the injury sustained by the community, or to the quantity of ill intention conceived by the offender? Some philosophers, sensible of the inscrutability of intention, have declared in favour of our attending to nothing but the injury sustained. The humane and benevolent Beccaria[35] has treated this as a truth of the utmost importance, 'unfortunately neglected by the majority of political institutors, and preserved only in the dispassionate speculation of philosophers.'*

It is true that we may, in many instances, be tolerably informed respecting external actions, and that there will, at first sight, appear to be no great difficulty in reducing them to general rules. Murder, according to this system, suppose, will be the exertion of any species of action affecting my neighbour so as that the consequences terminate in death. The difficulties of the magistrate are much abridged upon this principle, though they are by no means annihilated. It is well known how many subtle disquisitions, ludicrous or tragical according to the temper with which we view them, have been introduced to determine, in each particular instance, whether the action were or were not the real occasion of the death. It never can be demonstratively ascertained.

But dismissing this difficulty, how complicated is the iniquity of treating all instances alike in which one man has occasioned the death of another? Shall we abolish the imperfect distinctions, which the most odious tyrannies have hitherto thought themselves compelled to admit, between chance-medley, manslaughter and malice prepense? Shall we inflict on the man who, in endeavouring to save the life of a drowning fellow creature, oversets a boat, and occasions the death of a second, the same suffering as on him who, from gloomy and vicious habits, is incited to the murder of his benefactor? In reality, the injury sustained by the community is, by no means, the same as these two

---

* Questa è una di quelle palpabili verità, che per una maravigliosa combinazione di circonstanze non sono con decisa sicurezza conosciute, che da alcuni pochi pensatori uomini d'ogni nazione, e d'ogni secolo.' *Dei Delitti e delle Pene.*

cases; the injury sustained by the community is to be measured by the antisocial dispositions of the offender, and, if that were the right view of the subject, by the encouragement afforded to similar dispositions from his impunity. But this leads us at once from the external action to the unlimited consideration of the intention of the actor. The iniquity of the written laws of society is of precisely the same nature, though not of so atrocious a degree, in the confusion they actually introduce between various intentions, as if this confusion were unlimited. One man shall commit murder to remove a troublesome observer of his depraved disposition, who will otherwise counteract and expose him to the world. A second, because he cannot hear the ingenuous sincerity with which he is told of his vices. A third, from his intolerable envy of superior merit. A fourth, because he knows that his adversary meditates an act pregnant with extensive mischief, and perceives no other mode by which its perpetration can be prevented. A fifth, in defence of his father's life or his daughter's chastity. Each of these men, except perhaps the last, may act either from momentary impulse, or from any of the infinite shades and degrees of deliberation. Would you award one individual punishment to all these varieties of action? Can a system that levels these inequalities, and confounds these differences, be productive of good? That we may render men beneficent towards each other, shall we subvert the very nature of right and wrong? Or is it not this system, from whatever pretences introduced, calculated in the most powerful manner to produce general injury? Can there be a more flagrant injury than to inscribe, as we do in effect, upon our courts of judgement, 'This is the Hall of Justice, in which the principles of right and wrong are daily and systematically slighted, and offences of a thousand different magnitudes are confounded together, by the insolent supineness of the legislator, and the unfeeling selfishness of those who have engrossed the produce of the general labour to their particular emolument!'

But suppose, secondly, that we were to take the inten-

tion of the offender, and the future injury to be apprehended, as the standard of infliction. This would no doubt
be a considerable improvement. This would be the true
mode of reconciling punishment and justice, if, for reasons
already assigned, they were not, in their own nature, incompatible. It is earnestly to be desired that this mode
of administering retribution should be seriously attempted. It is hoped that men will one day attempt to establish
an accurate criterion, and not go on for ever, as they have
hitherto done, with a sovereign contempt of equity and
reason. This attempt would lead, by a very obvious process, to the abolition of all punishment.

It would immediately lead to the abolition of all criminal law. An enlightened and reasonable judicature would
have recourse, in order to decide upon the cause before
them, to no code but the code of reason. They would feel
the absurdity of other men's teaching them what they
should think, and pretending to understand the case before it happened, better than they who had all the circumstances under their inspection. They would feel the
absurdity of bringing every offence to be compared with a
certain number of measures previously invented, and com-
pelling it to agree with one of them. But we shall shortly
have occasion to return to this topic.*

The great advantage that would result from men's
determining to govern themselves, in the suffering to be
inflicted, by the motives of the offender, and the future
injury to be apprehended, would consist in their being
taught how vain and presumptuous it is in them to attempt to wield the rod of retribution. Who is it that, in
his sober reason, will pretend to assign the motives that
influenced me in any article of my conduct, and upon
them to found a grave, perhaps a capital, penalty against
me? The attempt would be iniquitous and absurd, even
though the individual who was to judge me had made the
longest observation of my character, and been most intimately acquainted with the series of my actions. How often

* Chap. VIII.

does a man deceive himself in the motives of his conduct, and assign to one principle what, in reality, proceeded from another? Can we expect that a mere spectator should form a judgement sufficiently correct, when he who has all the sources of information in his hands is nevertheless mistaken? Is it not to be this hour a dispute among philosophers whether I be capable of doing good to my neighbour for his own sake? 'To ascertain the intention of a man, it is necessary to be precisely informed of the actual impression of the objects upon his senses, and of the previous disposition of his mind, both of which vary in different persons, and even in the same person at different times, with a rapidity commensurate to the succession of ideas, passions and circumstances.'* Meanwhile the individuals whose office it is to judge of this inscrutable mystery are possessed of no previous knowledge, utter strangers to the person accused, and collecting their only materials from the information of two or three ignorant and prejudiced witnesses.

What a vast train of actual and possible motives enter into the history of a man, who has been incited to destroy the life of another? Can you tell how much in these there was of apprehended justice, and how much of inordinate selfishness? How much of sudden passion, and how much of rooted depravity? How much of intolerable provocation, and how much of spontaneous wrong? How much of that sudden insanity which hurries the mind into a certain action by a sort of incontinence of nature, almost without any assignable motive, and how much of incurable habit? Consider the uncertainty of history. Do we not still dispute whether Cicero were more a vain or a virtuous man, whether the heroes of ancient Rome were impelled

* 'Questa [l'intenzione] dipende dalla impressione attuale degli oggetti, e dalla precedente disposizione della mente: esse variano in tutti gli uomini e in ciascun uomo colla velocissima successione delle idee, delle passioni, e delle circostanze.' He adds, 'Sarebbe dunque necessario formare non solo un codice particolare per ciascun cittadino, ma una nuova legge ad ogni delitto.'

Dei Delitti e delle Pene.

by vain glory or disinterested benevolence, whether Voltaire were the stain of his species, or their most generous and intrepid benefactor? Upon these subjects moderate men perpetually quote the impenetrableness of the human heart. Will moderate men pretend that we have not an hundred times more evidence upon which to found our judgement in these cases than in that of the man who was tried last week at the Old Bailey? This part of the subject will be put in a striking light if we recollect the narratives that have been published by condemned criminals. In how different a light do they place the transactions that proved fatal to them, from the construction that was put upon them by their judges? And yet these narratives were written under the most awful circumstances, and many of them without the least hope of mitigating their fate, and with marks of the deepest sincerity. Who will say that the judge, with his slender pittance of information, was more competent to decide upon the motives than the prisoner after the severest scrutiny of his own mind? How few are the trials which an humane and just man can read, terminating in a verdict of guilty, without feeling an uncontrollable repugnance against the verdict? If there be any sight more humiliating than all others, it is that of a miserable victim acknowledging the justice of a sentence against which every enlightened spectator exclaims with horror.

But this is not all. The motive, when ascertained, is a subordinate part of the question. The point upon which only society can equitably animadvert, if it had any jurisdiction in the case, is a point, if possible, still more inscrutable than that of which we have been treating. A legal inquisition into the minds of men, considered by itself, all rational enquirers have agreed to condemn. What we want to ascertain is not the intention of the offender, but the chance of his offending again. For this purpose we reasonably enquire first into his intention. But, when we have found this, our task is but begun. This is one of our materials, to enable us to calculate the probability of his repeating his offence, or being imitated by others. Was this an habitual state of his mind, or was it a crisis in his history likely to remain an unique? What effect has experience produced on him; or what likelihood is there that the uneasiness and suffering that attend the perpetration of eminent wrong may have worked a salutary change in his mind? Will he hereafter be placed in circumstances that shall impel him to the same enormity? Precaution is, in its own nature, a step in a high degree precarious. Precaution that consists in inflicting injury on another will at all times be odious to an equitable mind. Meanwhile, be it observed that all which has been said upon the uncertainty of crime tends to aggravate the injustice of punishment for the sake of example. Since the crime upon which I animadvert in one man can never be the same as the crime of another, it is as if I should award a grievous penalty against persons with one eye, to prevent any man in future from putting out his eyes by design.

One more argument, calculated to prove the absurdity of the attempt to proportion delinquency and suffering to each other, may be derived from the imperfection of evidence. The veracity of witnesses will, to an impartial spectator, be a subject of continual doubt. Their competence, so far as relates to just observation and accuracy of understanding, will be still more doubtful. Absolute impartiality it would be absurd to expect from them. How much will every word and every action come distorted by the medium through which it is transmitted? The guilt of a man, to speak in the phraseology of law, may be proved either by direct or circumstantial evidence. I am found near to the body of a man newly murdered. I come out of his apartment with a bloody knife in my hand, or with blood upon my clothes. If under these circumstances, and unexpectedly charged with murder, I falter in my speech, or betray perturbation in my countenance, this is an additional proof. Who does not know that there is not a man in England, however blameless a life he may lead, who is secure that he shall not end it at the gallows? This is one of the most obvious and universal blessings that civil government has to bestow. In what is called direct evidence, it is necessary to identify the person of the offender. How many instances are there upon recond of persons condemned upon this evidence who, after their death, have been proved entirely innocent? Sir Walter Raleigh,[36] when a prisoner in the Tower, heard some high words accompanied with blows under his window. He enquired of several eye-witnesses, who entered his apartment in succession, into the nature of the transaction. But the story they told varied in such material circumstances that he could form no just idea of what had been done. He applied this to prove the uncertainty of history. The parallel would have been more striking if he had applied it to criminal suits.

But, supposing the external action, the first part of the question to be ascertained, we have next to discover through the same garbled and confused medium the intention. How few men should I choose to entrust with the drawing up a narrative of some delicate and interesting transaction of my life? How few, though, corporally speaking, they were witnesses of what was done, would justly describe my motives, and properly report and interpret my words? Yet, in an affair that involves my life, my fame and future usefulness, I am obliged to trust to any vulgar and casual observer.

A man properly confident in the force of truth would consider a public libel upon his character as a trivial misfortune. But a criminal trial in a court of justice is inexpressibly different. Few men, thus circumstanced, can retain the necessary presence of mind, and freedom from embarrassment. But if they do, it is with a cold and unwilling ear that their tale is heard. If the crime charged against them be atrocious, they are half condemned in the passions of mankind before their cause is brought to a trial. All that is interesting to them is decided amidst the first burst of indignation; and it is well if their story be impartially estimated ten years after their body has mouldered in the grave. Why, if a considerable time elapse between the trial and the execution, do we find the severity of the public changed into compassion? For the same reason that a master, if he do not beat his slave in the moment of resentment, often feels a repugnance to the beating him at all. Not so much, perhaps, as is commonly supposed, from forgetfulness of the offence, as that the sentiments of reason have time to recur, and he feels, in a confused and indefinite manner, the injustice of punishment. Thus every consideration tends to show that a man tried for a crime is a poor deserted individual, with the whole force of the community conspiring his ruin. The culprit that escapes, however conscious of innocence, lifts up his hands with astonishment, and can scarcely believe his senses, having such mighty odds against him. It is easy for a man who desires to shake off an imputation under which he labours to talk of being put on his trial; but no man ever seriously wished for this ordeal who knew what a trial was.

CHAPTER V

OF PUNISHMENT CONSIDERED AS A TEMPORARY EXPEDIENT

Arguments in its favour. – Answer. – It cannot fit men for a better order of society. – The true remedy to private injustice described – is adapted to immediate practice. – Duty of the community in this respect. – Duty of individuals. – Illustration from the case of war – of individual defence. – Application. Disadvantages of anarchy – want of security – of progressive enquiry. – Correspondent disadvantages of despotism. – Anarchy awakens, despotism depresses the mind. – Final result of anarchy – how determined. – Supposed purposes of punishment in a temporary view – reformation – example – restraint. – Conclusion.

THUS much for the general merits of punishment, considered as an instrument to be applied in the government of men. It is time that we should enquire into the apology which may be offered in its behalf, as a temporary expedient. No introduction seemed more proper to this enquiry than such a review of the subject upon a comprehensive scale; that the reader might be inspired with a suitable repugnance against so pernicious a system, and prepared firmly to resist its admission, in all cases where its necessity cannot be clearly demonstrated.

The arguments in favour of punishment as a temporary expedient are obvious. It may be alleged that 'however suitable an entire immunity in this respect may be to the nature of mind absolutely considered, it is impracticable with regard to men as we now find them. The human species is at present infected with a thousand vices, the offspring of established injustice. They are full of factitious appetites and perverse habits: headstrong in evil, inveterate in selfishness, without sympathy and forbearance for the welfare of others. In time they may become accommodated to the lessons of reason; but at present they would be found deaf to her mandates, and eager to commit every species of injustice.'

One of the remarks that most irresistibly suggest themselves upon this statement is that punishment has no proper tendency to prepare men for a state in which punishment shall cease. It were idle to expect that force should begin to do that which it is the office of truth to finish, should fit men, by severity and violence, to enter with more favourable auspices into the schools of reason.

But, to omit this gross misrepresentation in behalf of the supposed utility of punishment, it is of importance, in the first place, to observe that there is a complete and unanswerable remedy to those evils, the cure of which has hitherto been sought in punishment, that is within the reach of every community, whenever they shall be persuaded to adopt it. There is a state of society, the outline of which has been already sketched,* that, by the mere simplicity of its structure, would lead to the extermination of offence: a state in which temptation would be almost unknown, truth brought down to the level of all apprehensions, and vice sufficiently checked, by the general discountenance, and sober condemnation of every spectator. Such are the consequences that might be expected to spring from an abolition of the craft and mystery of governing; while, on the other hand, the innumerable murders that are daily committed under the sanction of legal forms are solely to be ascribed to the pernicious notion of an extensive territory; to the dreams of glory, empire and national greatness, which have hitherto proved the bane of the human species, without producing entire benefit and happiness to a single individual.

Another observation which this consideration immediately suggests is that it is not, as the objection supposed, by any means necessary that mankind should pass through a state of purification, and be freed from the vicious propensities which ill constituted governments have im-

* Book V, Chap. XXII, p. 544.

planted, before they can be dismissed from the coercion to which they are at present subjected. Their state would indeed be hopeless if it were necessary that the cure should be effected before we were at liberty to discard those practices to which the disease owes its most alarming symptoms. But it is the characteristic of a well formed society, not only to maintain in its members those virtues with which they are already imbued, but to extirpate their errors, and render them benevolent and just to each other. It frees us from the influence of those phantoms which before misled us, shows us our true advantage as consisting in independence and integrity, and binds us, by the general consent of our fellow citizens, to the dictates of reason more strongly than with fetters of iron. It is not to the sound of intellectual health that the remedy so urgently addresses itself as to those who are infected with diseases of the mind. The ill propensities of mankind no otherwise tend to postpone the abolition of coercion than as they prevent them from perceiving the advantages of political simplicity. The moment in which they can be persuaded to adopt any rational plan for this abolition is the moment in which the abolition ought to be effected.

A further consequence that may be deduced from the principles that have been delivered is that a coercion to be employed upon its own members can, in no case, be the duty of the community. The community is always competent to change its institutions, and thus to extirpate offence in a way infinitely more rational and just than that of punishment. If, in this sense, punishment has been deemed necessary as a temporary expedient, the opinion admits of satisfactory refutation. Punishment can at no time, either permanently or provisionally, make part of any political system that is built upon the principles of reason.

But, though, in this sense, punishment cannot be admitted for so much as a temporary expedient, there is another sense in which it must be so admitted. Coercion, exercised in the name of the state upon its respective members, cannot be the duty of the community; but coercion may be the duty of individuals within the community. The duty of individuals, in their political capacity, is, in the first place, to endeavour to meliorate the state of society in which they exist, and to be indefatigable in detecting its imperfections. But, in the second place, it behoves them to recollect that their efforts cannot be expected to meet with instant success, that the progress of knowledge has, in all cases, been gradual, and that their obligation to promote the welfare of society during the intermediate period is certainly not less real than their obligation to promote its future and permanent advantage. Even the future advantage cannot be effectually procured if we be inattentive to the present security. But, as long as nations shall be so far mistaken as to endure a complex government, and an extensive territory, coercion will be indispensably necessary to general security. It is therefore the duty of individuals to take an active share upon occasion in so much coercion, and in such parts of the existing system, as shall be sufficient to counteract the growth of universal violence and tumult. It is unworthy of a rational enquirer to say, 'These things are necessary, but I am not obliged to take my share in them.' If they be necessary, they are necessary for the general welfare; of consequence, are virtuous, and what no just man will refuse to perform.

The duty of individuals is, in this respect, similar to the duty of independent communities upon the subject of war. It is well known what has been the prevailing policy of princes under this head. Princes, especially the most active and enterprising among them, are seized with an inextinguishable rage for augmenting their dominions. The most innocent and inoffensive conduct on the part of their neighbours will not, at all times, be a sufficient security against their ambition. They indeed seek to disguise their violence under plausible pretences; but it is well known that, where no such pretences occur, they are not, on that account, disposed to relinquish the pursuit.

Let us imagine then a land of freemen invaded by one of these despots. What conduct does it behove them to adopt? We are not yet wise enough to make the sword drop out of the hands of our oppressors, by the mere force of reason. Were we resolved, like quakers, neither to oppose nor, where it could be avoided, to submit to them, much bloodshed might perhaps be prevented: but a more lasting evil would result. They would fix garrisons in our country, and torment us with perpetual injustice. Supposing it were even granted that, if the invaded nation should demean itself with unalterable constancy, the invaders would become tired of their fruitless usurpation, it would prove but little. At present we have to do, not with nations of philosophers, but with nations of men whose virtues are alloyed with weakness, fluctuation and inconstancy. At present it is our duty to consult respecting the procedure which, to such nations, may be attended with the most favourable result. It is therefore proper that we should choose the least calamitous mode of obliging the enemy speedily to withdraw himself from our territories.

The case of individual defence is of the same nature. It does not appear that any advantage can result from my forbearance, adequate to the disadvantages of suffering my own life, or that of another, a peculiarly valuable member of the community, as it may happen, to become a prey to the first ruffian who inclines to destroy it. Forbearance, in this case, will be the conduct of a singular individual, and its effect may very probably be trifling. Hence it appears that I ought to arrest the villain in the execution of his designs, though at the expense of a certain degree of coercion.

The case of an offender who appears to be hardened in guilt, and to trade in the violation of social security, is clearly parallel to these. I ought to take up arms against the despot by whom my country is invaded, because my capacity does not enable me by arguments to prevail on him to desist, and because my countrymen will not preserve their intellectual independence in the midst of oppression. For the same reason I ought to take up arms against the domestic spoiler, because I am unable either to persuade him to desist, or the community to adopt a just political institution by means of which security might be maintained consistently with the abolition of punishment.

To understand the full extent of this duty, it is incumbent upon us to remark that anarchy as it is usually understood , and a well conceived form of society without government, are exceedingly different from each other. If the government of Great Britain were dissolved tomorrow, unless that dissolution were the result of consistent and digested views of political truth previously disseminated among the inhabitants, it would be very far from leading to the abolition of violence. Individuals, freed from the terrors by which they had been accustomed to be restrained, and not yet placed under the happier and more rational restraint of public inspection, or convinced of the wisdom of reciprocal forbearance, would break out into acts of injustice, while other individuals, who desired only that this irregularity should cease, would find themselves obliged to associate for its forcible suppression. We should have all the evils and compulsory restraint to a regular government, at the same time that we were deprived of that tranquillity and leisure which are its only advantages.

It may not be useless in this place to consider, more accurately than we have hitherto done, the evils of anarchy. Such a review may afford us a criterion by which to discern, as well the comparative value of different institutions, as the precise degree of coercion which is required for the exclusion of universal violence and tumult.

Anarchy, in its own nature, is an evil of short duration. The more horrible are the mischiefs it inflicts, the more does it hasten to a close. But it is nevertheless necessary that we should consider both what is the quantity of mischief it produces in a given period, and what is the scene in which it promises to close. The first victim that is sacrificed at its shrine is personal security. Every man who has a secret foe ought to dread the dagger of that foe. There is no doubt that, in the worst anarchy, multitudes of men will sleep in happy obscurity. But woe to him who, by whatever means, excites the envy, the jealousy or the suspicion of his neighbour! Unbridled ferocity instantly marks him for its prey. This is indeed the principal evil of such a state, that the wisest, the brightest, the most generous and bold will often be most exposed to an immature fate. In such a state we must bid farewell to the patient lucubrations of the philosopher, and the labour of the midnight oil. All is here, like the society in which it exists, impatient and headlong. Mind will frequently burst forth, but its appearance will be like the coruscations of the meteor, not like the mild and equable illumination of the sun. Men who start forth into sudden energy will resemble in temper the state that brought them to this unlooked for greatness. They will be rigorous, unfeeling and fierce; and their ungoverned passions will often not stop at equality, but incite them to grasp at power.

With all these evils, we must not hastily conclude that the mischiefs of anarchy are worse than those which government is qualified to produce. With respect to personal security, anarchy is perhaps a condition more deplorable than despotism; but then it is to be considered that despotism is as perennial as anarchy is transitory. Despotism, as it existed under the Roman emperors, marked out wealth for its victim, and the guilt of being rich never failed to convict the accused of every other crime. This despotism continued for centuries. Despotism, as it has existed in modern Europe, has been ever full of jealousy and intrigue, a tool to the rage of courtiers, and the resentment of women. He that dared utter a word against the tyrant, or endeavour to instruct his countrymen in their interests, was never secure that the next moment would not conduct him to a dungeon. Here despotism wreaked her vengeance at leisure; and forty years of misery and solitude were sometimes insufficient to satiate her fury. Nor was this all. An usurpation that defied all the rules of justice was obliged to purchase its own safety by assisting tyranny through all its subordinate ranks. Hence the rights of nobility, of feudal vassalage, of primogeniture, of fines and inheritance. When the philosophy of law shall be properly understood, the true key to its spirit and history will probably be found, not, as some men have fondly imagined, in a desire to secure the happiness of mankind, but in the venal compact by which superior tyrants have purchased the countenance and alliance of the inferior.

There is one point remaining in which anarchy and despotism are strongly contrasted with each other. Anarchy awakens thought, and diffuses energy and enterprise through the community, though it does not effect this in the best manner, as its fruits, forced into ripeness, must not be expected to have the vigorous stamina of true excellence. But, in despotism, mind is trampled into an equality of the most odious sort. Everything that promises greatness is destined to fall under the exterminating hand of suspicion and envy. In despotism, there is no encouragement to excellence. Mind delights to expatiate in a field where every species of distinction is within its reach. A scheme of policy under which all men are fixed in classes, or levelled with the dust, affords it no encouragement to pursue its career. The inhabitants of countries in which despotism is complete are frequently but a more vicious species of brutes. Oppression stimulates them to mischief and piracy and superior force of mind often displays itself only in deeper treachery, or more daring injustice.

One of the most interesting questions, in relation to anarchy, is that of the result in which it may be expected to terminate. The possibilities as to this termination are as wide as the various schemes of society which the human imagination can conceive. Anarchy may and has terminated in despotism; and, in that case, the introduction of anarchy will only serve to afflict us with variety of evils. It may lead to a modification of despotism, a milder and more equitable government than that which had gone before. It cannot immediately lead to the best form of society, since it necessarily leaves mankind in a state of ferment, which requires a strong hand to control, and a slow and wary process to tranquillize.

The scene in which anarchy shall terminate principally depends upon the state of mind by which it has been preceded. All mankind were in a state of anarchy, that is, without government, previously to their being in a state of policy. It would not be difficult to find, in the history of almost every country, a period of anarchy. The people of England were in a state of anarchy immediately before the Restoration. The Roman people were in a state of anarchy at the moment of their secession to the Sacred Mountain. Hence it follows that anarchy is neither so good nor so ill a thing in relation to its consequences as it has sometimes been represented.

Little good can be expected from any species of anarchy that should subsist, for instance, among American savages. In order to anarchy being rendered a seed-plot of future justice, reflection and enquiry must have gone before, the regions of philosophy must have been penetrated, and political truth have opened her school to mankind. It is for this reason that the revolutions of the present age (for revolution is a species of anarchy) promise a more auspicious ultimate result than the revolutions of any former period. For the same reason, the more anarchy can be held at bay, the more fortunate will it be for mankind. Falsehood may gain by precipitating the crisis; but a genuine and enlightened philanthropy will wait, with unaltered patience, for the harvest of instruction. The arrival of that harvest may be slow, but it is perhaps infallible. If vigilance and wisdom be successful in their present opposition to anarchy, every benefit may ultimately be expected, untarnished with violence, and unstained with blood.

Of Punishment Considered as a Temporary Expedient

These observations are calculated to lead us to an accurate estimate of the mischiefs of anarchy, and, of consequence, to show the importance we are bound to attach to the exclusion of it. Government is frequently a source of peculiar evils; but an enlarged view will teach us to endure those evils which experience seems to evince are inseparable from the final benefit of mankind. From the savage state to the highest degree of civilization, the passage is long and arduous; and, if we aspire to the final result, we must submit to that portion of misery and vice which necessarily fills the space between. If we would free ourselves from these inconveniences, unless our attempt be both skilful and cautious, we shall be in danger, by our impatience, of producing worse evils than those we would escape. Now it is the first principle of morality and justice that directs us, where one of two evils is inevitable, to choose the least. Of consequence, the wise and just man, being unable, as yet, to introduce the form of society which his understanding approves, will contribute to the support of so much coercion as is necessary to exclude what is worse, anarchy.

If then constraint as the antagonist of constraint must, in certain cases, and under temporary circumstances, be admitted, it is an interesting enquiry to ascertain which of the three ends of punishment, already enumerated, must be selected by the individuals by whom punishment is employed. And here it will be sufficient very briefly to recollect the reasonings that have been stated under each of these heads.

It cannot be reformation. Reformation is improvement; and nothing can take place in a man worthy the name of improvement otherwise than by an appeal to the unbiassed judgement of his mind, and the essential feelings of his nature. If I would improve a man's character, who is there that knows not that the only effectual mode is by removing all extrinsic influences and incitements, by inducing him to observe, to reason and enquire, by leading him to the forming a series of sentiments that are truly his own, and not slavishly modelled upon the sentiments of another?

To conceive that compulsion and punishment are the proper means of reformation is the sentiment of a barbarian; civilization and science are calculated to explode so ferocious an idea. It was once universally admitted and approved; it is now necessarily upon the decline.

Punishment must either ultimately succeed in imposing the sentiments it is employed to inculcate upon the mind of the sufferer; or it must forcibly alienate him against them.

The last of these can never be the intention of its employer, or have a tendency to justify its application. If it were so, punishment ought to follow upon deviations from vice, not deviations from virtue. Yet to alienate the mind of the sufferer from the individual that punishes, and from the sentiments he entertains, is perhaps the most common effect of punishment.

Let us suppose however that its effect is of an opposite nature; that it produces obedience, and even a change of opinion. What sort of a being does it leave the man thus reformed? His opinions are not changed upon evidence. His conversion is the result of fear. Servility has operated that within him which liberal enquiry and instruction were not able to do.

Punishment undoubtedly may change a man's behaviour. It may render his external conduct beneficial from injurious, though it is no very promising expedient for that purpose. But it cannot improve his sentiments, or lead him to the form of right proceeding but by the basest and most despicable motives. It leaves him a slave, devoted to an exclusive self-interest, and actuated by fear, the meanest of the selfish passions.

But it may be said, 'however strong may be the reasons I am able to communicate to a man in order to his reformation, he may be restless and impatient of expostulation, and of consequence render it necessary that I should retain him by force, till I can properly instil these reasons into his mind'. It must be remembered that the idea here is not that of precaution, to prevent the mischiefs he might perpetrate, for that belongs to another of the three ends of punishment, that of restraint. But, separately from this idea, the argument is peculiarly weak. If the reasons I have to communicate be of an energetic and impressive nature if they stand forward perspicuous and distinct in my own mind, it will be strange if they do not, at the outset, excite curiosity and attention in him to whom they are addressed. It is my duty to choose a proper reason to communicate them, and not to betray the cause of justice by an ill-timed impatience. This prudence I should infallibly exercise if my object were to obtain something interesting to myself; why should I be less quick-sighted when I purpose the benefit of another? It is a miserable way of preparing a man for conviction to compel him by violence to hear an expostulation which he is eager to avoid. – These arguments prove, not that we should lose sight of reformation, if punishment for any other reason appear to be necessary; but that reformation cannot reasonably be made the object of punishment.

Punishment for the sake of example is a theory that can never be justly maintained. The suffering proposed to be inflicted, considered absolutely, is either right or wrong. If it be right, it should be inflicted for its intrinsic recommendations. If it be wrong, what sort of example does it display? To do a thing for the sake of example is, in other words, to do a thing today in order to prove that I will do a similar thing tomorrow. This must always be a subordinate consideration. No argument has been so grossly abused as this of example. We found it, under the subject of war,* employed to prove the propriety of my doing a thing otherwise wrong, in order to convince the opposite party that I should, when occasion offered, do something else that was right. He will display the best example, who carefully studies the principles of justice, and assiduously practises them. A better effect will be

* Book V, Chap. XVI, p. 511.

produced in human society by my conscientious adherence to them than by my anxiety to create a specific expectation respecting my future conduct. This argument will be still further enforced if we recollect what has already been said respecting the inexhaustible differences of different cases, and the impossibility of reducing them to general rules.*

The third object of punishment according to the enumeration already made is restraint. If punishment be, in any case, to be admitted, this is the only object it can reasonably propose to itself. The serious objections to which, even in this point of view, it is liable have been stated in another stage of the enquiry†: the amount of the necessity tending to supersede these objections has also been considered. The subject of this chapter is of great importance in proportion to the length of time that may possibly elapse before any considerable part of mankind shall be persuaded to exchange the present complexity of political institution for a mode which promises to supersede the necessity of punishment. It is highly unworthy of the cause of truth, to suppose that, during this interval, I have no active duties to perform, that I am not obliged to co-operate for the present welfare of the community, as well as for its future regeneration. The temporary obligation that arises out of this circumstance exactly corresponds with what was formerly delivered on the subject of duty. Duty is the best possible application of a given power to the promotion of the general good.‡ But my power depends upon the disposition of the men by whom I am surrounded. If I were enlisted in an army of cowards, it might be my duty to retreat, though, absolutely considered, it should have been the duty of the army to come to blows. Under every possible circumstance, it is my duty to advance the general good, by the best means which the circumstances under which I am placed will admit.

* Chap. IV.　　　　　　　　　　† Chap. III.
‡ Book II, Chap. IV.

CHAPTER VI

SCALE OF PUNISHMENT

IT is time to proceed to the consideration of certain inferences that may be deduced from the theory of punishment which has now been delivered; nor can anything
be of greater importance than these inferences will be
found, to the virtue, the happiness and improvement of
mankind.

And, first, it evidently follows that punishment is an
act of painful necessity, inconsistent with the true character and genius of mind, the practice of which is tem-
porarily imposed upon us by the corruption and ignorance
that reign among mankind. Nothing can be more absurd
than to look to it as a source of improvement. It contributes to the generation of excellence, just as the keeper
of the course contributes to the fleetness of the race. Nothing can be more unjust than to have recourse to it, but
upon the most unquestionable emergency. Instead of
multiplying occasions of coercion, and applying it as the
remedy of every moral evil, the true politician will anxiously confine it within the narrowest limits, and per-

petually seek to diminish the occasions of its employment. There is but one reason which can, in any case, be
admitted as its apology, and that is where the allowing
the offender to be at large shall be notoriously hazardous
to public security.

Secondly, the consideration of restraint as the only
justifiable ground of punishment will furnish us with a
simple and satisfactory criterion by which to measure the
justice of the suffering inflicted.

The infliction of a lingering and tormenting death
cannot be vindicated upon this hypothesis; for such infliction can only be dictated by sentiments of resentment on
the one hand, or by the desire to exhibit a terrible example on the other.

To deprive an offender of his life in any manner will
appear to be unjust, as it seems always sufficiently practicable, without this, to prevent him from further offence.
Privation of life, though by no means the greatest injury
that can be inflicted, must always be considered as a very
serious injury; since it puts a perpetual close upon the
prospects of the sufferer as to all the enjoyments, the
virtues and the excellence of a human being.

In the story of those whom the merciless laws of Europe
doom to destruction, we sometimes meet with persons
who, subsequently to their offence, have succeeded to a
plentiful inheritance, or who for some other reason appear
to have had the fairest propects of tranquillity and happiness opened upon them. Their story, with a little accommodation, may be considered as the story of every offender. If there be any man whom it may be necessary, for
the safety of the whole, to put under restraint, this circumstance is a powerful plea to the humanity and justice
of those who conduct the affairs of the community, in his
behalf. This is the man who most stands in need of their
assistance. If they treated him with kindness, instead of
supercilious and unfeeling neglect, if they made him
understand with how much reluctance they had been induced to employ the force of the society against him, if they

represented the true state of the case with calmness, perspicuity and benevolence to his mind, if they employed those precautions which an humane disposition would not fail to suggest, to keep from him the motives of corruption and obstinacy, his reformation would be almost infallible. These are the prospects to which his wants and his misfortunes powerfully entitle him; and it is from these prospects that the hand of the executioner cuts him off for ever.

It is a mistake to suppose that this treatment of criminals tends to multiply crimes. On the contrary, few men would enter upon a course of violence with the certainty of being obliged, by a slow and patient process, to amputate their errors. It is the uncertainty of punishment under the existing forms that multiplies crimes. Remove this uncertainty, and it would be as reasonable to expect that a man would wilfully break his leg, for the sake of being cured by a skilful surgeon. Whatever gentleness the intellectual physician may display, it is not to be believed that men can part with rooted habits of injustice and vice without considerable pain.

The true reasons in consequence of which these forlorn and deserted members of the community are brought to an ignominious death are, first, the peculiar iniquity of the civil institutions of that community, and, secondly, the supineness and apathy of their superiors. In republican and simple forms of government, punishments are rare, and the punishment of death almost unknown. On the other hand, the more there is in any country of inequality and oppression, the more punishments are multiplied. The more the institutions of society contradict the genuine sentiments of the human mind, the more severely is it necessary to avenge their violation. At the same time the rich and titled members of the community, proud of their fancied eminence, behold, with total unconcern, the destruction of the destitute and the wretched, disdaining to recollect that, if there be any intrinsic difference between them, it is the offspring of their different circumstances, and that the man whom they now so much despise might have been found as accomplished and susceptible as they if he had only changed situations. When we behold a company of poor wretches brought out for execution, reflection will present to our affrighted fancy all the hopes and possibilities which are thus brutally extinguished, the genius, the daring invention, the unshrinking firmness, the tender charities and ardent benevolence, which have occasionally, under this system, been sacrificed, at the shrine of torpid luxury and unrelenting avarice.

The species of suffering commonly known by the apellation of corporal punishment is also proscribed by the system above established. Corporal punishment, unless so far as it is intended for example, appears, in one respect, in a very ludicrous point of view. It is an expeditious mode of proceeding which has been invented in order to compress the effect of much reasoning and long confinement, that might otherwise have been necessary, into a very short compass. In another view, it is difficult to express the abhorrence it ought to create. The genuine propensity of man is to venerate mind in his fellow man. With what delight do we contemplate the progress of intellect, its efforts for the discovery of truth, the harvest of virtue that springs up under the genial influence of instruction, the wisdom that is generated through the medium of unrestricted communication? How completely do violence and corporal infliction reverse the scene? From this moment, all the wholesome avenues of mind are closed, and, on every side, we see them guarded with a train of disgraceful passions, hatred, revenge, despotism, cruelty, hypocrisy, conspiracy and cowardice. Man becomes the enemy of man; and stronger are seized with the lust of unbridled domination, and the weaker shrink, with hopeless disgust, from the approach of a fellow. With what feelings must an enlightened observer contemplate the furrow of a lash imprinted upon the body of a man? What heart beats not in unison with the sublime law of antiquity, 'Thou shalt not inflict stripes upon the body of a Roman?' There is but one alternative in this case, on the part of the sufferer. Either his mind must be subdued by the arbitrary dictates of the superior (for to him all is arbitrary that does not stand approved to the judgement of his own understanding); he will be governed by something that is not reason, and ashamed of something that is not disgrace; or else every pang he endures will excite the honest indignation of his heart, and fix the clear disapprobation of his intellect, will produce contempt and alienation against his punisher.

The justice of punishment is built upon this simple principle: Every man is bound to employ such means as shall suggest themselves for preventing evils subversive of general security, it being first ascertained, either by experience or reasoning, that all milder methods are inadequate to the exigency of the case. The conclusion from this principle is that we are bound, under certain urgent circumstances, to deprive the offender of the liberty he has abused. Further than this perhaps no circumstance can authorize us. He whose person is imprisoned (if that be the right kind of seclusion) cannot interrupt the peace of his fellows; and the infliction of further evil, when his power to injure is removed, is the wild and unauthorized dictate of vengeance and rage, the wanton sport of unquestioned superiority.

When indeed the person of the offender has been first seized, there is a further duty incumbent on his punisher, the duty of endeavouring his reform. But this makes no part of the direct consideration. The duty of every man to contribute to the intellectual health of his neighbour is of general application. Beside which it is proper to recollect, what has been already proved, that coercion of no sort is among the legitimate means of reformation. Restrain the offender as long as the safety of the community prescribes it, for this is just. Restrain him not an instant from a simple view to his own improvement, for this is contrary to reason and morality.

Meanwhile, there is one circumstance by means of which

restraint and reformation are closely connected. The person of the offender is to be restrained as long as the public safety would be endangered by his liberation. But the public safety will cease to be endangered as soon as his propensities and dispositions have undergone a change. The connection which thus results from the nature of things renders it necessary that, in deciding upon the species of restraint to be imposed, these circumstances be considered jointly, how the personal liberty of the offender may be least entrenched upon, and how his reformation may be best promoted.

The most common method pursued in depriving the offender of the liberty he has abused is to erect a public jail, in which offenders of every description are thrust together, and left to form among themselves what species of society they can. Various circumstances contribute to imbue them with habits of indolence and vice, and to discourage industry; and no effort is made to remove or soften these circumstances. It cannot be necessary to expatiate upon the atrociousness of this system. Jails are, to a proverb, seminaries of vice; and he must be an uncommon proficient in the passion and the practice of injustice, or a man of sublime virtue, who does not come out of them a much worse man than he entered.

An active observer of mankind,* with the purest intentions, and who had paid a singular attention to this subject, was struck with the mischievous tendency of the reigning system, and called the attention of the public to a scheme of solitary imprisonment. But this, though free from the defects of the established mode, is liable to very weighty objections.

It must strike every reflecting mind as uncommonly tyrannical and severe. It cannot therefore be admitted into the system of mild coercion which forms the topic of our enquiry. Man is a social animal. How far he is necessarily so will appear if we consider the sum of advantages resulting from the social, and of which he would be de-

* Mr Howard.[37]

prived in the solitary state. But, independently of his original structure, he is eminently social by his habits. Will you deprive the man you imprison of paper and books, of tools and amusements? One of the arguments in favour of solitary imprisonment is that it is necessary the offender should be called off from wrong habits of thinking, and obliged to enter into himself. This the advocates of solitary imprisonment probably believe will be most effectually done the fewer be the avocations of the prisoner. But let us suppose that he is indulged in these particulars, and only deprived of society. How many men are there that can derive amusement from books? We are, in this respect, the creatures of habit, and it is scarcely to be expected from ordinary men that they should mould themselves to any species of employment to which in their youth they were strangers. But he that is most fond of study has his moments when study pleases no longer. The soul yearns, with inexplicable longings, for the society of its like. Because the public safety unwillingly commands the confinement of an offender, must he for that reason never light up his countenance with a smile? Who can tell the sufferings of him who is condemned to uninterrupted solitude? Who can tell that this is not, to the majority of mankind, the bitterest torment that human ingenuity can inflict? A mind sufficiently sublime might perhaps conquer this inconvenience: but the powers of such a mind do not enter into the present question.

From the examination of solitary imprisonment, in itself considered, we are naturally led to enquire into its real tendency as to the article of reformation. To be virtuous, it is requisite that we should consider men, and their relation to each other. As a preliminary to this study, is it necessary that we should be shut out from the society of men? Shall we be most effectually formed to justice, benevolence and prudence in our intercourse with each other, in a state of solitude? Will not our selfish and unsocial dispositions be perpetually increased? What temptation has he to think of benevolence or justice, who has no opportunity to exercise it? The true soil in which atrocious crimes are found to germinate is a gloomy and morose disposition. Will his heart become much either softened or expanded, who breathes the atmosphere of a dungeon? Surely it would be better in this respect to imitate the system of the universe, and, if we would teach justice and humanity, transplant those we would teach into a simple and reasonable state of society. Solitude, absolutely considered, may instigate us to serve ourselves, but not to serve our neighbours. Solitude, imposed under too few limitations, may be a nursery for madmen and idiots, but not for useful members of society.

Another idea which has suggested itself with regard to the removal of offenders from the community they have injured is that of reducing them to a state of slavery or hard labour. The true refutation of this system is anticipated in what has been already said. To the safety of the community it is unnecessary. As a means to the reformation of the offender, it is inexpressibly ill-conceived. Man is an intellectual being. There is no way to make him virtuous but in calling forth his intellectual powers. There is no way to make him virtuous but by making him independent. He must study the laws of nature, and the necessary consequence of actions, not the arbitrary caprice of his superior. Do you desire that I should work? Do not drive me to it with the whip; for, if, before, I thought it better to be idle, this will but increase my alienation. Persuade my understanding, and render it the subject of my choice. It can only be by the most deplorable perversion of reason that we can be induced to believe any species of slavery, from the slavery of the school-boy to that of the most unfortunate Negro in our West India plantations, favourable to virtue.*

* The institution of personal slavery has, within a few years, made a considerable progress in the island of Great Britain. The first step was that of sending criminals, whose guilt was of an inferior description, to raise ballast from the bed of the Thames. The second step, more serious in its nature, appears to have re-

A scheme greatly preferable to any of these, and which has been tried under various forms, is that of transportation or banishment. This scheme under the most judicious modifications, is liable to objection. It would be strange if any scheme of coercion or violence were not so. But it has been made appear still more exceptional than it will be found in its intrinsic nature by the crude and incoherent circumstances with which it has usually been executed.

Banishment in its simple form, that is, a mere prohibition of residence has, at least in certain aggravated cases, a strong appearance of injustice. The citizen whose presence we will not endure in our own country, we have a very questionable right to impose upon any other.

Banishment has sometimes been joined with slavery. Such was the practice of Great Britain previously to the defection of her American colonies. This cannot stand in need of a separate refutation.

A very usual species of banishment is removal to a country yet unsettled. Something may be alleged in favour of this mode of proceeding. The labour by which the undisciplined mind is best weaned from the vicious habits of a corrupt society is the labour, not which is prescribed by the mandate of a superior, but which is imposed by

---

sulted fom the well intended, but misguided, philanthropy of Mr Howard. This consisted in the erecting jails of solitary confinement in various parts of the country. The prisoners in these jails spend a large proportion of their time shut up in silent and dreary cells, like so many madmen. The rest of their time is employed in what is called hard labour, under the inspection of certain ignorant and insolent task-masters. It is asserted that, in one of these jails (Clerkenwell New Prison), its unfortunate tenants are engaged for five hours in each day in trundling a wheel-barrow round in a circle. The cruelty of this imposition is inexpressibly heightened by its impudent uselessness. From this instance we may perceive that the inventiveness of tyranny did not perish with the race of Dionysii. Cases of this sort it is our duty, as citizens, to notice, that the chance of their existing without the knowledge of those to whose province their superintendence belongs may be removed.

the necessity of subsistence. The first settlement of Rome, by Romulus and his vagabonds, is a happy image of this, whether we consider it as a real history, or as the ingenious fiction of a writer well acquainted with the principles of mind. Men who are freed from the injurious institutions of European government, and obliged to begin the world for themselves, are in the direct road to be virtuous.

Two circumstances have hitherto contributed to render this project abortive. First, that the mother-country pursues this species of colony with her hatred. The chief anxiety is, in reality, to render its residence odious and uncomfortable, with the vain idea of deterring offenders. The chief anxiety ought to be to smooth their difficulties, and contribute to their happiness. We should recollect that the colonists are men, for whom we ought to feel no sentiments but those of kindness and compassion. If we were reasonable, we should regret the cruel exigence that obliges us to treat them in a manner unsuitable to the nature of mind; and having complied with the demand of that exigence, we should next be anxious to confer upon them every benefit in our power. But we are unreasonable. We harbour a thousand savage feelings of resentment and vengeance. We thrust them out to the remotest corner of the world. We subject them to perish by multitudes with hardship and hunger. Perhaps, if our treatment of such unfortunate men were sufficiently humane, banishment to the Hebrides would prove as effectual as banishment to the Antipodes.

Secondly, it is absolutely necessary, upon the principles here explained, that these colonists, after having been sufficiently provided in the outset, should be left to themselves. We do worse than nothing if we pursue them into their obscure retreat with the inauspicious influence of our European institutions. Why trouble ourselves with sending magistrates and officers to govern and direct them? Do we suppose that, if left to themselves, they would universally destroy each other? On the contrary, new situations make new minds. The worst criminals, when turned adrift in a body, and reduced to feel the churlish fang of necessity, conduct themselves upon reasonable principles, and have been found to proceed with a sagacity and public spirit that might put the proudest monarchy to the blush.

Meanwhile let us not forget the inherent vices of punishment, which present themselves from whatever point the subject is viewed. Colonization may be thought the most eligible of those expedients which have been stated, but it is attended with considerable difficulties. The community judges of a certain individual that his residence cannot be tolerated among them consistently with the general safety. In denying him his choice among other communities do they not exceed their commission? What treatment shall be awarded him if he return from the banishment to which he was sentenced? – These difficulties (and many others might be subjoined to these) are calculated to bring back the mind to the absolute injustice of punishment, and to render us inexpressibly anxious for the period at which it shall be abolished.

To conclude. The observations of this chapter are relative to a theory which affirmed that it might be the duty of individuals, but never of communities, to exert a certain species of political coercion; and which founded this duty upon a consideration of the benefits of public security. Under these circumstances then, every individual is bound to judge for himself, and to yield his countenance to no other coercion than that which is indispensably necessary. He will, no doubt, endeavour to meliorate those institutions, with which he cannot prevail upon his countrymen to part. He will decline all concern in the execution of such, as abuse the plea of public security to atrocious purposes. Laws may easily be found in almost every code which, on account of the iniquity of their provisions, are suffered to fall into disuse by general consent. Every lover of justice will, in this way, contribute to the repeal of laws that wantonly usurp upon the independence of mankind, whether by the mutiplicity of their restrictions, or the severity of their sanctions.

CHAPTER VII

OF EVIDENCE

*Difficulties to which this subject is liable –
exemplified in the distinction between overt
actions and intentions. – Reasons against this
distinction. – Principle in which it is founded.*

HAVING sought to ascertain the decision in which questions of offence against the general safety ought to terminate, it only remains under this head of enquiry to consider the principles according to which the trial should be conducted. These principles may for the most part be referred to two points, the evidence that is to be required, and the method to be pursued by us in classing offences.

The difficulties to which the subject of evidence is liable have been stated in the earlier divisions of this work.* It may be worth while, in this place, to recollect the difficulties which attend upon one particular class of evidence, it being scarcely possible that the imagination of every reader should not suffice him to apply this text, and to perceive how easily the same kind of enumeration might be extended to any other class.

It has been asked, 'Why intentions are not subjected to the animadversion of criminal justice, in the same manner as direct acts of offence?'

The arguments in favour of their being thus subjected are obvious. 'The proper object of political superintendence is not the past, but the future. Society cannot justly employ punishment against any individual, however atrocious may have been his misdemeanours, from any other than a prospective consideration, that is, a consideration of the danger with which his habits may be pregnant to the general safety. Past conduct cannot properly fall under the animadversion of government, except so far as it is an indication of the future. But past conduct appears, at first sight, to afford a slighter presumption as to what the delinquent will do hereafter than declared in-

* Particularly Chap. IV.

tention. The man who professes his determination to commit murder seems to be scarcely a less dangerous member of society than he who, having already committed murder, has no apparent intention to repeat his offence.' Yet all governments have agreed either to pass over the menace in silence, or to subject the offender to a much less degree of punishment than they employ against him by whom the crime has been perpetrated. It may be right perhaps to yield them some attention when they thus agree in forbearance, though little is probably due to their agreement in inhumanity.

This distinction, so far as it is founded in reason, has relation prinicpally to the uncertainty of evidence. Before the intention of any man can be ascertained, in a court of justice, from the consideration of the words he has employed, a variety of circumstances must be taken into the account. The witness heard the words which were employed: does he repeat them accurately, or has not his want of memory caused him to substitute, in the room of some of them, words of his own? Before it is possible to decide, upon the confident expectation I may entertain, that these words will be followed with correspondent actions, it is necessary I should know the exact tone with which they were delivered, and gesture with which they were accompanied. It is necessary I should be acquainted with the context, and the occasion that produced them. Their construction will depend upon the quantity of momentary heat or rooted malice with which they were delivered; and words which appear at first sight of tremendous import will sometimes be found, upon accurate investigation, to have had a meaning purely ironical in the mind of the speaker. These considerations, together with the odious nature of punishment in general, and the extreme mischief that may attend our restraining the faculty of speech, in addition to the restraint we conceive ourselves obliged to put on men's actions, will probably be found to afford a sufficient reason why words ought seldom or never to be made a topic of political animadversion.

CHAPTER VIII

OF LAW

A FURTHER article of great importance in the trial of
offences is that of the method to be pursued by us in classing them, and the consequent apportioning the degree
of animadversion to the cases that may arise. This article
brings us to the direct consideration of law, which is, without doubt, one of the most important topics upon which
human intellect can be employed. It is law that has hitherto been regarded, in countries calling themselves civilized,
as the standard by which to measure all offences and
irregularities that fall under public animadversion. Let us
fairly investigate the merits of this choice.

The comparison which has presented itself, to those by
whom the topic has been investigated, has hitherto been
between law on one side, and the arbitrary will of a despot
on the other. But if we would estimate truly the merits of
law, we should first consider it as it is in itself, and then,
if necessary, search for the most eligible principle that
may be substituted in its place.

It has been recommended as 'affording information to
the different members of the community, respecting the

principles which will be adopted in deciding upon their actions'. It has been represented as the highest degree of iniquity 'to try men by an *ex post facto* law, or indeed in any other manner than by the letter of a law, formally made, and sufficiently promulgated'.

How far it will be safe altogether to annihilate this principle, we shall presently have occasion to enquire. It is obvious, at first sight, to remark that it is of most importance in a country where the system of jurisprudence is most capricious and absurd. If it be deemed criminal in any society to wear clothes of a particular texture, or buttons of a particular composition, it is unavoidable to exclaim that it is high time the jurisprudence of that society should inform its members what are the fantastic rules by which they mean to proceed. But, if a society be contented with the rules of justice, and do not assume to itself the right of distorting or adding to those rules, there law is evidently a less necessary institution. The rules of justice would be more clearly and effectually taught by an actual intercourse with human society, unrestrained by the fetters of prepossession, than they can be by catechisms and codes.*

One result of the institution of law is that the institution, once begun, can never be brought to a close. Edict is heaped upon edict, and volume upon volume. This will be most the case where the government is most popular, and its proceedings have most in them of the nature of deliberation. Surely this is no slight indication that the principle is wrong, and that, of consequence, the further we proceed in the path it marks out to us, the more we shall be bewildered. No talk can be less hopeful than that of effecting a coalition between a right principle and a wrong. He that seriously and sincerely attempts it will perhaps expose himself to more palpable ridicule than he who, instead of professing two opposite systems, should adhere to the worst.

There is no maxim more clear than this, 'Every case is

* Book VI, Chap. VIII.

a rule to itself.' No action of any man was ever the same as any other action had ever the same degree of utility or injury. It should seem to be the business of justice to distinguish the qualities of men, and not, which has hitherto been the practice, to confound them. But what has been the result of an attempt to do this in relation to law? As new cases occur, the law is perpetually found deficient. How should it be otherwise? Lawgivers have not the faculty of unlimited prescience, and cannot define that which is boundless. The alternative that remains is either to wrest the law to include a case which was never in the contemplation of its authors, or to make a new law to provide for this particular case. Much has been done in the first of these modes. The quibbles of lawyers, and the arts by which they refine and distort the sense of the law, are proverbial. But, though much is done, everything cannot be thus done. The abuse will sometimes be too palpable. Not to say that the very education that enables the lawyer, when he is employed for the prosecutor, to find out offences the lawgiver never meant, enables him, when he is employed for the defendant, to discover subterfuges that reduce the law to nullity. It is therefore perpetually necessary to make new laws. These laws, in order to escape evasion, are frequently tedious, minute and circumlocutory. The volume in which justice records her prescriptions is for ever increasing, and the world would not contain the books that might be written.

The consequence of the infinitude of law is its uncertainty. This strikes at the principle upon which law is founded. Laws were made to put an end to ambiguity, and that each man might know what he had to expect. How well have they answered this purpose? Let us instance in the article of property. Two men go to law for a certain estate. They would not go to law if they had not both of them an opinion of the success. But we may suppose them partial in their own case. They would not continue to go to law if they were not both promised success by their lawyers. Law was made that a plain man might know what he had to expect; and yet the most skilful practitioners differ about the event of my suit. It will sometimes happen that the most celebrated pleader in the kingdom, or the first counsel in the service of the crown, shall assure me of infallible success, five minutes before another law-officer, styled the keeper of the king's conscience, by some unexpected juggle decides it against me. Would the issue have been equally uncertain if I had had nothing to trust to but the plain unperverted sense of a jury of my neighbours, founded in the ideas they entertained of general justice? Lawyers have absurdly maintained that the expensiveness of law is necessary to prevent the unbounded multiplication of suits; but the true source of this multiplication is uncertainty. Men do not quarrel about that which is evident, but that which is obscure.

He that would study the laws of a country accustomed to legal security must begin with the volumes of the statutes. He must add a strict enquiry into the common or unwritten law; and he ought to digress into the civil, the ecclesiastical and canon law. To understand the intention of the authors of a law, he must be acquainted with their characters and views, and with the various circumstances to which it owed its rise, and by which it was modified while under deliberation. To understand the weight and interpretation that will be allowed to it in a court of justice, he must have studied the whole collection of records, decisions and precedents. Law was originally devised that ordinary men might know what they had to expect; and there is not, at this day, a lawyer existing in Great Britain vain-glorious enough to pretend that he has mastered the code. Nor must it be forgotten that time and industry, even were they infinite, would not suffice. It is a labyrinth without end; it is a mass of contradictions that cannot be disentangled. Study will enable the lawyer to find in it plausible, perhaps unanswerable, arguments for any side of almost any question; but it would argue the utmost folly to suppose that the study of law can lead to knowledge and certainty.

A further consideration that will demonstrate the absurdity of law in its most general acceptation is that it is of the nature of prophecy. Its task is to describe what will be the actions of mankind, and to dictate decisions respecting them. Its merits, in this respect, have already been decided under the head of promises.* The language of such a procedure is 'We are so wise that we can draw no additional knowledge from circumstances as they occur; and we pledge ourselves that, if it be otherwise, the additional knowledge we acquire shall produce no effect upon our conduct.' It is proper to observe that this subject of law may be considered, in some respects, as more properly belonging to the topic of the preceding book. Law tends, no less than creeds, catechisms and tests, to fix the human mind in a stagnant condition, and to substitute a principle of permanance in the room of that unceasing progress which is the only salubrious element of mind. All the arguments therefore which were employed upon that occasion may be applied to the subject now under consideration.

The fable of Procrustes presents us with a faint shadow of the perpetual effort of law. In defiance of the great principle of natural philosophy, that there are not so much as two atoms of matter of the same form through the whole universe, it endeavours to reduce the actions of men, which are composed of a thousand evanescent elements, to one standard. We have already seen the tendency of this endeavour in the article of murder.† It was in the contemplation of this system of jurisprudence that the strange maxim was invented that 'strict justice would often prove the highest injustice.'‡ There is no more real justice in endeavouring to reduce the actions of men into classes than there was in the scheme to which we have just alluded, of reducing all men to the same stature. If, on the contrary, justice be a result flowing from the contem-

* Book III, Chap. III.
† Chap. IV.
‡ Summum jus summa injuria.

plation of all the circumstances of each individual case, if only the criterion of justice be general utility, the inevitable consequence is that the more we have of justice, the more we shall have of truth, virtue and happiness.

From all these considerations we can scarcely hesitate to conclude universally that law is an institution of the most pernicious tendency.

The subject will receive some additional elucidation if we consider the perniciousness of law in its immediate relation to those who practise it. If there ought to be no such thing as law, the profession of lawyer is no doubt entitled to our disapprobation. A lawyer can scarcely fail to be a dishonest man. This is less a subject for censure than for regret. Men are, in an eminent degree, the creatures of the circumstances under which they are placed. He that is habitually goaded by the incentives of vice will not fail to be vicious. He that is perpetually conversant in quibbles, false colours and sophistry cannot equally cultivate the generous emotions of the soul, and the nice discernment of rectitude. If a single individual can be found who is but superficially tainted with the contagion, how many men on the other hand in whom there appeared a promise of the sublimest virtues have by this trade been rendered indifferent to consistency, or accessible to a bribe? Be it observed that these remarks apply principally to men eminent or successful in their profession. He that enters into an employment carelessly, and by way of amusement, is much less under its influence (though even he will not escape) than he that enters into it with ardour and devotion.

Let us however suppose, a circumstance which is perhaps altogether impossible, that a man shall be a perfectly honest lawyer. He is determined to plead no cause that he does not believe to be just, and to employ no argument that he does not apprehend to be solid. He designs, as far as his sphere extends, to strip law of its ambiguities, and to speak the manly language of reason. This man is, no doubt, highly respectable, so far as relates to himself; but it may be questioned whether he be not a more pernicious member of society than the dishonest lawyer. The hopes of mankind in relation to their future progress depend upon their observing the genuine effects of erroneous institutions. But this man is employed in softening and masking these effects. His conduct has a direct tendency to postpone the reign of sound policy, and to render mankind tranquil in the midst of imperfection and ignorance.

What is here stated however in favour of the dishonest lawyer, like that stated in favour of an imbecile monarch,* should be considered as advanced in the way of conjecture only. As there is some pain which is requisite as the means of an overbalance of pleasure, so there may, in a few extraordinary instances, be some vice (understanding by vice, evil intention or rooted depravity) which is productive of the effects of virtue. In questions of this kind however, it becomes us to be more than usually scrupulous and guarded. It is of the most pernicious consequence for us to confound the distinctions of virtue and vice. It can scarcely be considered as the part of a philanthropist to rejoice in the depravity of others. It is safer for us, in almost every imaginable instance, to regard 'every departure from enormous vice, as so much gained to the cause of general happiness'.†

The only principle which can be substituted in the room of law is that of reason exercising an uncontrolled jurisdiction upon the circumstances of the case. To this principle no objection can arise on the score of wisdom. It is not to be supposed that there are not men now existing whose intellectual accomplishments rise to the level of law. Law we sometimes call the wisdom of our ancestors. But this is a strange imposition. It was as frequently the dictate of their passion, of timidity, jealousy, a monopolizing spirit, and a lust of power that knew no bounds. Are we not obliged perpetually to revise and remodel this misnamed wisdom of our ancestors? to cor-

* Book V, Chap. VII.
† Book IV, Chap. XI.

rect it by a detection of their ignorance, and a censure of their intolerance? But if men can be found among us whose wisdom is equal to the wisdom of law, it will scarcely be maintained that the truths they have to communicate will be the worse for having no authority but that which they derive from the reasons that support them.

It may however be alleged that 'if there be little difficulty in securing a current portion of wisdom, there may nevertheless be something to be feared from the passions of men. Law may be supposed to have been constructed in the tranquil serenity of the soul, a suitable monitor, to check the inflamed mind, with which the recent memory of ills might induce us to proceed to the infliction of punishment.' This is the most considerable argument that can be adduced in favour of the prevailing system, and therefore deserves a mature examination.

The true answer to this objection is that nothing can be improved but in conformity to its nature. If we consult for the welfare of man, we must bear in mind the structure of man. It must be admitted that we are imperfect, ignorant, the slaves of appearance. These defects can be removed by no indirect method, but only by the introduction of knowledge. A specimen of the indirect method we have in the doctrine of spiritual infallibility. It was observed that men were liable to error, to dispute for ever without coming to a decision, and to mistake in their most important interests. What was wanting was supposed to be a criterion and a judge of controversies. What was attempted was to indue truth with a visible form, and then repair to the oracle we had erected.

The case respecting law is parallel to this. Men were aware of the deceitfulness of appearances, and they sought a talisman to guard them from imposition. Suppose I were to determine, at the commencement of every day, upon a certain code of principles to which I would conform the conduct of the day; and, at the commencement of every year, the conduct of the year. Suppose I were to determine that no circumstances should be allowed, by the light they afforded, to modify my conduct, lest I should become the dupe of appearances, and the slave of passion. This is a just and accurate image of every system of permanence. Such systems are formed upon the idea of stopping the perpetual motion of the machine, lest it should sometimes fall into disorder.

This consideration must sufficiently persuade an impartial mind that, whatever inconveniences may arise from the passions of men, the introduction of fixed laws cannot be the genuine remedy. Let us consider what would be the operation and progressive state of these passions, provided men were trusted to the guidance of their own discretion. Such is the discipline that a reasonable state of society employs with respect to man in his individual capacity: * why should it not be equally valid with respect to men acting in a collective capacity? Inexperience and zeal would prompt me to restrain my neighbour whenever he is acting wrong, and, by penalties and inconveniences designedly interposed, to cure him of his errors. But reason evinces the folly of this proceeding, and teaches me that, if he be not accustomed to depend upon the energies of intellect, he will never rise to the dignity of a rational being. As long as a man is held in the trammels of obedience, and habituated to look to some foreign guidance for the direction of his conduct, his understanding and the vigour of his mind will sleep. Do I desire to raise him to the energy of which he is capable? I must teach him to feel himself, to bow to no authority, to examine the principles he entertains, and render to his mind the reason of his conduct.

The habits which are thus salutary to the individual will be equally salutary in the transactions of communities. Men are weak at present, because they have always been told they are weak, and must not be trusted with themselves. Take them out of their shackles, bid them enquire, reason and judge, and you will soon find them

* Book V, Chap. XX, p. 533.

very different beings. Tell them that they have passions, are occasionally hasty, intemperate and injurious, but they must be trusted with themselves. Tell them that the mountains of parchment in which they have been hitherto entrenched are fit only to impose upon ages of superstition and ignorance; that henceforth we will have no dependence but upon their spontaneous justice; that, if their passions be gigantic, they must rise with gigantic energy to subdue them; that, if their decrees be iniquitous, the iniquity shall be all their own. The effect of this disposition of things will soon be visible; mind will rise to the level of its situation; juries and umpires will be penetrated with the magnitude of the trust reposed in them.

It may be no uninstructive spectacle to survey the progressive establishment of justice in the state of things which is here recommended. At first, it may be, a few decisions will be made uncommonly absurd or atrocious. But the authors of these decisions will be confounded, with the unpopularity and disgrace in which they have involved themselves. In reality, whatever were the original source of law, it soon became cherished as a cloak for oppression. Its obscurity was of use to mislead the inquisitive eye of the sufferer. Its antiquity served to divert a considerable part of the odium from the perpetrator of the injustice to the author of the law; and, still more, to disarm that odium by the influence of superstitious awe. It was well known that unvarnished, barefaced oppression could not fail to be the victim of its own operations.

To this statement it may indeed be objected 'that bodies of men have often been found callous to censure, and that the disgrace, being amicably divided, is intolerable to none'. In this observation there is considerable force, but it is inapplicable to the present argument. To this species of abuse one of two things is indispensably necessary, either numbers of secrecy. To this abuse therefore it will be a sufficient remedy that each jurisdiction be considerably limited, and all transactions conducted in an open and explicit manner. – To proceed.

The juridical decisions that were made immediately after the abolition of law would differ little from those during its empire. They would be the decisions of prejudice and habit. But habit, having lost the centre about which it revolved, would diminish in the regularity of its operations. Those to whom the arbitration of any question was entrusted would frequently recollect that the whole case was committed to their deliberation; and they could not fail occasionally to examine themselves respecting the reason of those principles which had hitherto passed uncontroverted. Their understandings would grow enlarged, in proportion as they felt the importance of their trust, and the unbounded freedom of their investigation. Here then would commence an auspicious order of things, of which no understanding of man at present in existence can foretell the result, the dethronement of implicit faith, and the inauguration of reason and justice.

Some of the conclusions of which this state of things would be the harbinger have been already seen, in the judgement that would be made of offences against the community.* Offences arguing a boundless variety in the depravity from which they sprung would no longer be confounded under some general name. Juries would grow as perspicacious in distinguishing, as they are now indiscriminate in confounding, the merit of actions and characters.

The effects of the abolition of law, as it respects the article of property, would not be less auspicious. Nothing can be more worthy of regret than the manner in which property is at present administered, so far as relates to courts of justice. The doubtfulness of titles, the different measures of legislation as they relate to different classes of property, the tediousness of suits, and the removal of causes by appeal from court to court, are a perpetual round of artifice and chicane to one part of the community, and of anguish and misery to another. Who can describe the baffled hopes, the fruitless years of expecta-

* Chap. IV, p. 651.

tion, which thus consume away the strength and the lives of numerous individuals? In vain is the intention of a testator, while the disputes between the legal and the testamentary heir, or a mere quibble upon the phraseology of the bequest, shall supply food for endless controversy. In vain shall be all the assurances I can heap together for the establishment of my right, since the obscurity of records, and the complexity of law, will, almost in all cases, enable an ingenious man, who is at the same time a rich one, to dispute my tenure. The imbecility of law is strikingly illustrated by the vulgar maxim of the importance of possession. Possession could not be thus advantageous were it not for the opportunity that law affords for procrastination and evasion. Property could not be thus disputable were the persons who are called upon to decide concerning it left to the direction of their own understanding. The contention of opposing claims arises more from the jargon in which these claims are recorded than from the complexity of the subject to which they relate. The intention of a testator is much more easily settled than the quibbles to which the expression of that intention may be subjected. Those who were appointed for the decision of suits would not indeed be such gainers, under the system here delineated, as at present; but every other description of persons that were interested in questions of property would, no doubt, find their advantage.

An observation which cannot have escaped the reader in the perusal of this chapter is that law is merely relative to the exercise of political force, and must perish when the necessity for that force ceases, if the influence of truth do not still sooner extirpate it from the practice of mankind.

CHAPTER IX

OF PARDONS

Their absurdity. – Their origin. – Their abuses. – Their arbitrary character. – Destructive of morality.

THERE is one other topic which belongs to the subject of the present book, but which may be dismissed in a very few words, because, though it has unhappily been, in almost all cases, neglected in practice, it is a point that seems to admit of uncommonly simple and irresistible evidence: I mean the topic of pardons.

The very word, to a reflecting mind, is fraught with absurdity. 'What is the rule that ought, in all cases, to direct my conduct?' Surely justice; understanding by justice the greatest utility of the whole mass of beings that may be influenced by my conduct. 'What then is clemency?' It can be nothing but the pitiable egotism of him who imagines he can do something better than justice. 'Is it right that I should suffer constraint for a certain offence?' The reasonableness of my suffering must be founded in its consonance with the general welfare. He therefore that pardons me iniquitously prefers the supposed interest of an individual, and utterly neglects what he owes to the whole. He bestows that which I ought not to receive, and which he has no right to give. 'Is it right, on the contrary, that I should not undergo the suffering in question? Will he, by rescuing me from suffering, confer a benefit on me, and inflict no injury on others?' He will then be a notorious delinquent, if he allows me to suffer. There is indeed a considerable defect in this last supposition. If, while he benefits me, he inflicts no injury upon others, he is infallibly performing a public service. If I suffered in the arbitrary manner which the supposition includes, the public would sustain an unquestionable injury in the injustice that was perpetrated. And yet the man who prevents this odious injustice has been accustomed to arrogate to himself the attribute of clement, and the apparently sublime, but, in reality, tyrannical, name of forgiveness. For, if he do more than has been here described, instead of glory, he ought to take shame to himself, as an enemy to human kind. If every action, and especially every action in which the happiness of a rational being is concerned, be susceptible of a certain rule, then caprice must be in all cases excluded: there can be no action which, if I neglect, I shall have discharged my duty, and, if I perform, I shall be entitled to applause.

The pernicious effect of the system of pardons is peculiarly glaring. It was first invented as the miserable supplement to a sanguinary code, the atrociousness of which was so conspicuous that its ministers either dreaded the resistance of the people, if it were indiscriminately executed, or themselves shrunk with unconquerable repugnance from the devastation it commanded. The system of pardons obviously associates with the system of law; for, though we may call every case, for instance, in which one man occasions the death of another, by the name of murder, yet the injustice would be too great to apply to all cases the same treatment. Define murder as accurately as we please, the same consequence, the same disparity of cases, will obtrude itself. It is necessary therefore to have a court of reason to which the decisions of a court of law shall be brought for revisal.

But how is this court, inexpressibly more important than the other, to be constituted? Here lies the essence of the matter; the rest is form. A jury is empanelled to tell you the generical name of the action; a judge presides, to read out of the volume of the law the prescription annexed to that name; last of all comes the court of enquiry, which is to decide whether the prescription of the dispensatory is suitable to the circumstances of this particular case. This authority we are accustomed to invest, in the first instance with the judge, and in the last resort with the king in council. Now, putting aside the propriety or impropriety of this particular selection, there is one grievous abuse which ought to strike the most superficial observer. These persons with whom the principal trust is reposed consider their functions in this respect as a matter purely incidental, exercise them with supineness, and, in many instances, with the most scanty materials to guide their judgement. This grows in a considerable degree out of the very name of pardon, by which we are accustomed to understand a work of supererogatory benevolence.

From the manner in which pardons are dispensed inevitably flows the uncertainty of punishment. It is too evident that punishment is inflicted by no certain rules, and therefore creates no uniformity of expectation. Uniformity of treatment, and constancy of expectation, form the sole basis of a genuine morality. In a just form of society, this would never go beyond the sober expression of those sentiments of approbation or disapprobation with which different modes of conduct inevitably impress us. But, if we at present exceed this line, it is surely an execrable refinement of injustice that should exhibit the perpetual menace of suffering, unaccompanied with any certain rule foretelling its application. Not more than one third of the offenders whom the law condemns to death in this metropolis are made to suffer the punishment that is awarded. Is it possible that each offender should not flatter himself that he shall be among the number that escapes? Such a system, to speak it truly, is a lottery of death, in which each man draws his ticket for reprieve or execution, as undefinable accidents shall decide.

It may be asked whether 'the abolition of law would not produce equal uncertainty?' By no means. The principles of king and council, in such cases, are very little understood, either by themselves or others. The principles of a jury of his neighbours, commissioned to pronounce upon the whole of the case, the criminal easily guesses. He has only to appeal to his own sentiments and experience. Reason is a thousand times more explicit and intelligible than law; and when we were accustomed to consult her, the certainty of her decisions would be such as men, practised in our present courts, are totally unable to conceive.

Another important consequence grows out of the system of pardons. A system of pardons is a system of unmitigated slavery. I am taught to expect a certain desirable event, from what? From the clemency, the uncontrolled, unmerited kindness of a fellow mortal. Can any lesson be more degrading? The pusillanimous servility of the man, who devotes himself with everlasting obsequiousness to another, because that other, having begun to be unjust, relents in his career; the ardour with which he confesses the equity of his sentence and the enormity of his deserts will constitute a tale that future ages will find it difficult to understand.

What are the sentiments in this respect that are alone worthy of a rational being? Give me that, and that only, which without injustice you cannot refuse. More than justice it would be disgraceful for me to ask, and for you to bestow. I stand upon the foundation of right. This is a title which brute force may refuse to acknowledge, but which all the force in the world cannot annihilate. By resisting this plea, you may prove yourself unjust; but, in yielding to it, you grant me but my due. If, all things considered, I be the fit subject of a benefit, the benefit is merited: merit, in any other sense, is contradictory and absurd. If you bestow upon me unmerited advantage, you are a recreant from the general good. I may be base enough to thank you; but, if I were virtuous, I should condemn you.

These sentiments alone are consistent with true independence of mind. He that is accustomed to regard virtue as an affair of favour and grace cannot be eminently virtuous. If he occasionally perform an action of apparent kindness, he will applaud the generosity of his sentiments; and, if he abstain, he will acquit himself with the question, 'May I not do what I will with my own?' In the same manner, when he is treated benevolently by another, he will, in the first place, be unwilling to examine strictly into the reasonableness of this treatment, because benevolence, as he imagines, is not subject to any inflexibility of rule; and, in the second place, he will not regard his benefactor with that erect and unembarrassed mien, that manly sense of equality, which is the only unequivocal basis of virtue and happiness.

BOOK VIII

OF PROPERTY

CHAPTER I

PRELIMINARY OBSERVATIONS

Importance of this topic. – Plan for its discussion. – Definition. – Subject of the present chapter – of the next. – Principle of decision stated. – Rights of man. – Superfluities appreciated – Love of distinction. – Direction which this passion is capable of receiving. – Of merit and reward. – System of popular morality on this subject. – Its defects.

THE subject of property is the key-stone that completes the fabric of political justice. According as our ideas respecting it are crude or correct, they will enlighten us as to the consequences of a *simple form of society without government*, and remove the prejudices that attach us to complexity. There is nothing that more powerfully tends to distort our *judgement* and *opinions* than erroneous notions concerning the goods of fortune. Finally, the period that must put an end to the system of *coercion* and *punishment* is intimately connected with the circumstance of property's being placed upon an equitable basis.

Various abuses of the most incontrovertible nature have insinuated themselves into the administration of property. Each of these abuses might usefully be made the subject of a separate investigation. We might enquire into the vexations of this sort that are produced by the dreams of national greatness, and the sumptuousness of public offices and magistrates. This would lead us to a just estimate of the different kinds of taxation, landed or mercantile, having the necessaries or the luxuries of life for their subject of operation. We might examine into the abuses which have adhered to the commercial system; monopolies, charters, patents, protecting duties, prohibitions and bounties. We might consider the claims of the church: first fruits and tithes. All these disquisitions would tend to show the incalculable importance of this subject. But, excluding them all from the present enquiry, it shall be the business of what remains of this work to examine the subject in its most general principles, and by that means endeavour to discover the source, not only of the abuses above enumerated, but of others of innumerable kinds, too multifarious and subtle to enter into so brief a catalogue.

The subject to which the doctrine of property relates is all those things which conduce, or may be conceived to conduce, to the benefit or pleasure of man, and which can no otherwise be applied to the use of one or more persons than by a permanent or temporary exclusion of the rest of the species. Such things in particular are food, clothing, habitation and furniture.

Upon this subject two questions unavoidably arise. Who is the person entitled to the use of any particular article of this kind? Who is the person in whose hands the preservation and distribution of any number of these articles will be most justly and beneficially vested?

The answer to the first of these questions is easy upon the principles of the present work. Justice has been proved to be a rule applicable to all the concerns of man. It pronounces upon every case that can arise, and leaves nothing to the disposal of a momentary caprice.* There is not an article of the kinds above specified which will not ultimately be the instrument of more benefit and happiness in one individual mode of application than in any

* Book II, Chap. II.

other than can be devised. This is the application it ought
to receive.

We are here led to the consideration of that species of
rights which was designedly postponed in an earlier division of this work.* Every man has a right to that, the
exclusive possession of which being awarded to him, a
greater sum of benefit or pleasure will result than could
have arisen from its being otherwise appropriated. This
is the same principle as that just delivered, with a slight
variation of form. If man have a right to anything, he
has a right to justice. These terms, as they have ordinarily
been used in moral enquiry, are, strictly and properly
speaking, convertible terms.

Let us see how this principle will operate in the inferences it authorizes us to make. Human beings are partakers of a common nature; what conduces to the benefit
or pleasure of one man will conduce to the benefit or
pleasure of another.† Hence it follows, upon the principles of equal and impartial justice, that the good things
of the world are a common stock, upon which one man
has as valid a title as another to draw for what he wants.
It appears in this respect, as formerly it appeared in the
case of our claim to the forbearance of each other,‡ that
each man has a sphere the limit and termination of which
is marked out by the equal sphere of his neighbour. I have
a right to the means of subsistence; he has an equal right.
I have a right to every pleasure I can participate without
injury to myself or others; his title in this respect is of
similar extent.

This view of the subject will appear the more striking
if we pass in review the good things of the world. They
may be divided into four classes; subsistence; the means
of intellectual and moral improvement; inexpensive
gratifications; and such gratifications as are by no means
essential to healthful and vigorous existence, and cannot

---

* Book II, Chap. V, p. 199.
† Book III, Chap. III, p. 183.
‡ Book II, Chap. V, p. 198.

be purchased but with considerable labour and industry. It is the last class principally that interposes an obstacle in the way of equal distribution. It will be matter of after-consideration how far and how many articles of this class would be admissible into the purest mode of social existence.* But, in the meantime, it is unavoidable to remark the inferiority of this class to the three preceding. Without it we may enjoy to a great extent activity, contentment and cheerfulness. And in what manner are these seeming superfluities usually procured? By abridging multitudes of men to a deplorable degree in points of essential moment, that one man may be accommodated, with sumptuous yet, strictly considered, insignificant luxuries. Supposing the alternative could fairly be brought home to a man, and it could depend upon his instant decision, by the sacrifice of these to give to five hundred of his fellow beings leisure, independence, conscious dignity, and whatever can refine and enlarge the human understanding, it is difficult to conceive him to hesitate. But, though this alternative cannot be produced in the case of an individual, it will perhaps be found to be the true alternative, when taken at once in reference to the species.

To the forming a just estimate of costly gratifications, it is necessary that we should abstract the direct pleasure, on the one hand, from the pleasure they afford us only as instruments for satisfying our love of distinction. It must be admitted in every system of morality not tainted with monastic prejudices, but adapted to the nature of intelligent beings, that, so far as relates to ourselves, and leaving our connection with the species out of the consideration, we ought not to refuse any pleasure, except as it tends to the exclusion of some greater pleasure.† But it has already been shown‡ that the difference in the pleasures of the palate, between a simple and wholesome

* Chap. VII.
† Book IV, Chap. XI, p. 391.
‡ Book I, Chap. V, pp. 129, 130.

diet on the one hand, and all the complexities of the most splendid table on the other, is so small that few men would even think it worth the tedium that attends upon a change of services, if the pleasure of the palate were the only thing in question, and they had no spectator to admire their magnificence. 'He who should form himself, with the greatest care, upon a system of solitary sensualism, would probably come at last to a decision not different from that which Epicurus is said to have adopted in favour of fresh herbs, and water from the spring.'* The same observation applies to the splendour of furniture, equipage and dress. So far as relates to the gratification of the eye, this pleasure may be reaped, with less trouble, and in greater refinement, from the beauties which nature exhibits to our observation. No man, if the direct pleasure were the only thing in consideration, would think the difference to himself worth purchasing by the oppression of multitudes.

But these things, though trivial in themselves, are highly prized, from that love of distinction which is characteristic of every human mind. The creditable artisan or tradesman exerts a certain species of industry to supply his immediate wants. But these are soon supplied. The rest is exerted that he may wear a better coat, that he may clothe his wife with gay attire, that he may have not merely a shelter, but a handsome habitation, not merely bread and flesh to eat, but that he may set it out with suitable decorum. How many of these things would engage his attention if he lived in a desert island, and had no spectator of his economy? If we survey the appendages of our persons, there is scarcely an article that is not in some respect an appeal to the good will of our neighbours, or a refuge against their contempt. It is for this that the merchant braves the perils of the ocean, and the mechanical inventor brings forth the treasures of his meditation. The soldier advances even to the cannon's mouth, and the statesman exposes himself to the rage of

* Book I, Chap. V, pp. 129, 130.

an indignant people, because he cannot bear to pass through life without distinction and esteem. Exclusively of certain higher motives which will hereafter be mentioned,* this is the purpose of all the great exertions of mankind. The man who has nothing to provide for but his animal wants scarcely ever shakes off the lethargy of his mind; but the love of honour hurries us on to the most incredible achievements.

It must be admitted indeed that the love of distinction appears, from experience and the past history of mankind, to have been their ruling passion. But the love of distinction is capable of different directions. At present, there is no more certain road to the general deference of mankind than the exhibition of wealth. The poet, the wit, the orator, the saviour of his country, and the ornament of his species may upon certain occasions be treated with neglect and biting contempt; but the man who possesses and disburses money in profusion can scarcely fail to procure the attendance of the obsequious man and the flatterer. But let us conceive this erroneous and pernicious estimate of things to be reversed. Let us suppose the avaricious man, who is desirous of monopolizing the means of happiness, and the luxurious man, who expends without limitation, in pampering his appetites, that which, in strict justice, is the right of another, to be contemplated with as much disapprobation as they are now beheld by a mistaken world with deference and respect. Let us imagine the direct and unambiguous road to public esteem to be the acquisition of talent, or the practice of virtue, the cultivation of some species of ingenuity, or the display of some generous and expansive sentiment; and that the persons who possess these talents were as conspicuously treated with affection and esteem as the wealthy are now treated with slavish attention. This is merely, in other words, to suppose good sense, and clear and correct perceptions, at some time to gain the ascendancy in the world. But it is plain that, under the reign

* Chap. VI.

of such sentiments, the allurements that now wait upon costly gratification, would be, for the most part, annihilated. If, through the spurious and incidental recommendations it derives from the love of distinction, it is now rendered, to many, a principal source of agreeable sensation, under a different state of opinion, it would not merely be reduced to its intrinsic value in point of sensation, but, in addition to this, would be connected with ideas of injustice, unpopularity and dislike. So small is the space which costly gratifications are calculated unalterably to fill in the catalogue of human happiness.

It has sometimes been alleged, as an argument against the equal rights of men in the point of which we are treating, 'that the merits of men are different, and ought to be differently rewarded'. But it may be questioned whether this proposition, though true, can with any show of plausibility be applied to the present subject. Reasons have been already suggested to prove that positive institutions do not afford the best means for rewarding virtue, and that human excellence will be more effectually forwarded by those encouragements which inevitably arise from the system of the universe.* But, exclusively of this consideration, let us recollect, upon the grounds of what has just been stated, what sort of reward is thus proposed to exertion. 'If you show yourself deserving, you shall have the essence of a hundred times more food than you can eat, and a hundred times more clothes than you can wear. You shall have a patent for taking away from others the means of a happy and respectable existence, and for consuming them in riotous and unmeaning extravagance.' Is this the reward that ought to be offered to virtue, or that virtue should stoop to take?

The doctrine of the injustice of accumulated property has been the foundation of all religious morality. Its most energetic teachers have been irresistibly led to assert the precise truth in this respect. They have taught the rich

* Book V, Chap. XII; Book VI, Chap. I.

that they hold their wealth only as a trust, that they are strictly accountable for every atom of their expenditure, that they are merely administrators, and by no means proprietors in chief.* But, while religion thus inculcated on mankind the pure principles of justice, the majority of its prossessors have been but too apt to treat the practice of justice, not as a debt, which it ought to be considered, but as an affair of spontaneous generosity and bounty.

The effect which is produced by this accommodating doctrine is to place the supply of our wants in the disposal of a few, enabling them to make a show of generosity with what is not truly their own, and to purchase the submission of the poor by the payment of a debt. Theirs is a system of clemency and charity, instead of a system of justice. It fills the rich with unreasonable pride, by the spurious denominations with which it decorates their acts; and the poor with servility, by leading them to regard the slender comforts they obtain, not as their incontrovertible due, but as the good pleasure and grace of their opulent neighbours.

* Mark, ch. x, ver. 21: Acts, ch. ii, ver. 44, 45. See also Swift's Sermon on Mutual Subjection.

CHAPTER II

PRINCIPLES OF PROPERTY

*Definitions. — Degrees of property — 1. in the
means of subsistence and happiness — 2. in the
fruits of our labour — 3. in the labour of others.
— Unfavourable features of this species of property. — Ground of obligation respecting it. —
Origin of property — of inheritance and testation. — Instances of gratuitous inequality. —
Legislation of titles. — Limitations on the
preceding reasoning. — Sacredness of property.
— Conclusion.*

HAVING considered at large the question of the person
entitled to the use of the means of benefit or pleasure, it is
time that we proceed to the second question, of the person
in whose hands the preservation and distribution of any
of these means will be most justly and beneficially vested.
An interval must inevitably occur between the production
of any commodity and its consumption. Those things
which are necessary for the accommodation of man in
society cannot be obtained without the labour of man.
When fit for his use, they do not admit of being left at
random, but require that some care and vigilance should
be exerted to preserve them, for the period of actual
consumption. They will not, in the first instance, fall
into the possession of each individual, in the precise
proportion necessary for his consumption. Who then is
to be the factor or warehouseman that is to watch over
their preservation, and preside at their distribution?

This is strictly speaking the question of property. We
do not call the person who accidentally takes his dinner
at my table the proprietor of what he eats, though it is
he, in the direct and obvious sense, who receives the benefit of it. Property implies some permanence of external
possession, and includes in it the idea of a possible com-
petitor.

Of property there are three degrees.

The first and simplest degree is that of my permanent right in those things the use of which being attributed to me, a greater sum of benefit or pleasure will result than could have arisen from their being otherwise appropriated. It is of no consequence, in this case, how I came into possession of them, the only necessary conditions being their superior usefulness to me, and that my title to them is such as is generally acquiesced in by the community in which I live. Every man is unjust who conducts himself in such a manner respecting these things as to infringe, in any degree, upon my power of using them, at the time when the using them will be of real importance to me.

It has already appeared* that one of the most essential of the rights of man is my right to the forbearance of others; not merely that they shall refrain from every thing that may, by direct consequence, affect my life, or the possession of my powers, but that they shall refrain from usurping upon my understanding, and shall leave me a certain equal sphere for the exercise of my private judgement. This is necessary because it is possible for them to be wrong, as well as for me to be so, because the exercise of the understanding is essential to the improvement of man, and because the pain and interruption I suffer are as real, when they infringe, in my conception only, upon what is of importance to me, as if the infringement had been, in the utmost degree, palpable. Hence it follows that no man may, in ordinary cases, make use of my apartment, furniture or garments, or of my food, in the way of barter or loan, without having first obtained my consent.

The second degree of property is the empire to which every man is entitled over the produce of his own industry, even that part of it the use of which ought not to be appropriated to himself. It has been repeatedly shown that all the rights of man which are of this description

* Book II, Chap. V, VI.

are passive.* He has no right of option in the disposal of anything which may fall into his hands. Every shilling of his property, and even every, the minutest, exertion of his powers have received their destination from the decrees of justice. He is only the steward. But still he is the steward. These things must be trusted to his award, checked only by the censorial power that is vested, in the general sense, and favourable or unfavourable opinion, of that portion of mankind among whom he resides. Man is changed from the capable subject of illimitable excellence, into the vilest and most despicable thing that imagination can conceive, when he is restrained from acting upon the dictates of his understanding. All men cannot individually be entitled to exercise compulsion on each other, for this would produce universal anarchy. All men cannot collectively be entitled to exercise unbounded compulsion, for this would produce universal slavery: the interference of government, however impartially vested, is, no doubt, only to be resorted to upon occasions of rare occurrence, and indispensable urgency.

It will readily be perceived that this second species of property is in a less rigorous sense fundamental than the first. It is, in one point of view, a sort of usurpation. It vests in me the preservation and dispensing of that which in point of complete and absolute right belongs to you.

The third degree of property is that which occupies the most vigilant attention in the civilized states of Europe. It is a system, in whatever manner established, by which one man enters into the faculty of disposing of the produce of another man's industry. There is scarcely any species of wealth, expenditure or splendour, existing in any civilized country, that is not, in some way, produced by the express manual labour, and corporeal industry, of the inhabitants of that country. The spontaneous productions of the earth are few, and contribute little to wealth, expenditure or splendour. Every man may calculate, in every glass of wine he drinks, and every

* Book II, Chap. V.

ornament he annexes to his person, how many individuals have been condemned to slavery and sweat, incessant drudgery, unwholesome food, continual hardships, deplorable ignorance, and brutal insensibility, that he may be supplied with these luxuries. It is a gross imposition that men are accustomed to put upon themselves when they talk of the property bequeathed to them by their ancestors. The property is produced by the daily labour of men who are now in existence. All that their ancestors bequeathed to them was a mouldy patent which they show as a title to extort from their neighbours what the labour of those neighbours has produced.

It is clear therefore that the third species of property is in direct contradiction to the second.

The most desirable state of human society would require that the quantity of manual labour and corporal industry to be exerted, and particularly that part of it which is not the uninfluenced choice of our own judgement, but is imposed upon each individual by the necessity of his affairs, should be reduced within as narrow limits as possible. For any man to enjoy the most trivial accommodation, while, at the same time, a similar accommodation is not accessible to every other member of the community, is, absolutely speaking, wrong. All refinements of luxury, all inventions that tend to give employment to a great number of labouring hands, are directly adverse to the propagation of happiness. Every additional tax that is laid on, every new channel that is opened for the expenditure of the public money, unless it be compensated (which is scarcely ever the case) by an equivalent deduction from the luxuries of the rich, is so much added to the general stock of ignorance, drudgery and hardship. The country-gentleman who, by levelling an eminence, or introducing a sheet of water into his park, finds work for hundreds of industrious poor is the enemy, and not, as has commonly been imagined, the friend, of his species. Let us suppose that, in any country, there is now ten times as much industry and manual labour as there was three centuries ago. Except so far as this is applied to maintain an increased population, it is expended in the more costly indulgences of the rich. Very little indeed is employed to increase the happiness or conveniences of the poor. They barely subsist at present, and they did as much at the remoter period of which we speak. Those who, by fraud or force, have usurped the power of buying and selling the labour of the great mass of the community are sufficiently disposed to take care that they should never do more than subsist. An object of industry added to or taken from the general stock produces a momentary difference, but things speedily fall back into their former state. If every labouring inhabitant of Great Britain were able and willing today to double the quantity of his industry, for a short time he would derive some advantage from the increased stock of commodities produced. But the rich would speedily discover the means of monopolizing this produce, as they had done the former. A small part of it only could consist in commodities essential to the subsistence of man, or be fairly distributed through the community. All that is luxury and superfluity would increase the accommodations of the rich, and perhaps, by reducing the price of luxuries, augment the number of those to whom such accommodations were accessible. But it would afford no alleviation to the great mass of the community. Its more favoured members would give their inferiors no greater wages for twenty hours' labour, suppose, than they now do for ten.

What reason is there then that this species of property should be respected? Because, ill as the system is, it will perhaps be found that it is better than any other, which, by any means, except those of reason, the love of distinction, or the love of justice, can be substituted in its place. It is not easy to say whether misery or absurdity would be most conspicious in a plan which should invite every man to seize upon everything he conceived himself to want. If, by positive institution, the property of every man were equalized today, without a contemporary change in men's dispositions and sentiments, it would become unequal tomorrow. The same evils would spring up with a rapid growth; and we should have gained nothing, by a project which, while it violated every man's habits, and many men's inclinations, would render thousands miserable. We have already shown,* and shall have occasion to show more at large,† how pernicious the consequences would be if government were to take the whole permanently into their hands, and dispense to every man his daily bread. It may even be suspected that agrarian laws, and others of a similar tendency which have been invented for the purpose of keeping down the spirit of accumulation, deserve to be regarded as remedies more pernicious than the disease they are intended to cure.‡

An interesting question suggests itself in this stage of the discussion. How far is the idea of property to be considered as the offspring of positive institution? The decision of this question may prove extremely essential to the point upon which we are engaged. The regulation of property by positive laws may be a very exceptionable means of reforming its present inequality, at the same time that an equal objection may by no means lie against a proceeding the object of which shall be merely to supersede positive laws, or such positive laws as are peculiarly exceptionable.

In pursuing this enquiry, it is necessary to institute a distinction between such positive laws, or established practices (which are often found little less efficacious than laws), as are peculiar to certain ages and countries, and such laws or practices as are common to all civilized communities, and may therefore be perhaps interwoven with the existence of society.

The idea of property, or permanent empire, in those things which ought to be applied to our personal use, and

---

* Book VI, Chap. VIII, p. 616.
† Chap. VIII.
‡ Book VI, Chap. I, p. 559.

still more in the produce of our industry, unavoidably suggests the idea of some species of law or practice by which it is guaranteed. Without this, property could not exist. Yet we have endeavoured to show that the maintenance of these two kinds of property is highly beneficial. Let us consider the consequences that grow out of this position.

Every man should be urged to the performance of his duty, as much as possible, by the instigations of reason alone.* Compulsion to be exercised by one human being over another, whether individually, or in the name of the community, if in any case to be resorted to, is at least to be resorted to only in cases of indispensable urgency. It is not therefore to be called in for the purpose of causing one individual to exert a little more, or another a little less, of productive industry. Neither is it to be called in for the purpose of causing the industrious individual to make the precise distribution of his produce which he ought to make. Hence it follows that, while the present erroneous opinions and prejudices respecting accumulation continue, actual accumulation will, in some degree, take place.

For, let it be observed that, not only no well informed community will interfere with the quantity of any man's industry, or the disposal of its produce, but the members of every such well informed community will exert themselves to turn aside the purpose of any man who shall be inclined, to dictate to, or restrain, his neighbour in this respect.

The most destructive of all excesses is that where one man shall dictate to another, or undertake to compel him to do, or refrain from doing, anything (except, as was before stated, in cases of the most indispensable urgency) otherwise than with his own consent. Hence it follows that the distribution of wealth in every community must be left to depend upon the sentiments of the individuals of that community. If, in any society,

* Book II, Chap. VI; Book VII, passim.

wealth be estimated at its true value, and accumulation and monopoly be regarded as the seals of mischief, injustice and dishonour, instead of being treated as titles to attention and deference, in that society the accommodations of human life will tend to their level, and the inequality of conditions will be destroyed.* A revolution of opinions is the only means of attaining to this inestimable benefit. Every attempt to effect this purpose by means of regulation will probably be found ill conceived and abortive. Be this as it will, every attempt to correct the distribution of wealth by individual violence is certainly to be regarded as hostile to the first principles of public security.

If one individual, by means of greater ingenuity or more indefatigable industry, obtain a great proportion of the necessaries or conveniences of life than his neighbour, and, having obtained them, determine to convert them into the means of permanent inequality, this proceeding is not of a sort that it would be just or wise to undertake to repress by means of coercion. If, inequality being thus introduced, the poorer member of the community shall be so depraved as to be willing, or so unfortunately circumstanced as to be driven, to make himself the hired servant or labourer of his richer neighbour, this probably is not an evil to be corrected by the interposition of government. But, when we have gained this step, it will be difficult to set bounds to the extent of accumulation in one man, or of poverty and wretchedness in another.

It has already appeared that reason requires that no man shall endeavour, by individual violence, to correct this inequality. Reason would probably, in a well ordered community, be sufficient to restrain men from the attempt so to correct it. Where society existed in the simplicity which has formerly been described,† accumulation itself would be restrained by the very means that restrained

* Chap. I, p. 706.
† Book V, Chap. XXIV.

depredation, the good sense of the community, and the inspection of all exercised upon all. Violence therefore would, on the one hand, have little to tempt it as, on the other, it would be incessantly and irresistibly repressed.

But, if reason prove insufficient for this fundamental purpose, other means must doubtless be employed.* It is better that one man should suffer than that the community should be destroyed. General security is one of those indispensable preliminaries without which nothing good or excellent can be accomplished. It is therefore right that property, with all its inequalities, such as it is sanctioned by the general sense of the members of any state, and so long as that sanction continues unvaried should be defended, if need be, by means of coercion.

We have already endeavoured to show that coercion would probably, in no case, be necessary but for the injudicious magnitude and complication of political societies.† In a general and absolute sense therefore it cannot be vindicated. But there are duties incumbent upon us of a temporary and local nature; and we may occasionally be required, by the pressure of circumstances, to suspend and contravene principles, the most sound in their general nature.‡ Till men shall be persuaded to part with the ideas of a complicated government and an extensive territory, coercion will be necessary, as an expedient to counteract the most imminent evils. There are however various reasons that would incline a just man to confine the province of coercion within the severest limits. It is never to be regarded but as a temporary expedient, the necessity of having recourse to which is deeply to be regretted. It is an expedient, protecting one injustice, the accumulation of property, for the sake of keeping out another evil, still more formidable and destructive. Lastly, it is to be considered that this injustice, the unequal distribution of property, the grasping and

* Book VII, Chap. V.
† Book VII, Chap. V.
‡ Vol. I, Book IV, Chap. VI, App. No. I.

selfish spirit of individuals, is to be regarded as one of the original sources of government, and, as it rises in its excesses, is continually demanding and necessitating new injustice, new penalties and new slavery.

Thus far then it should seem the system of coercion must be permitted to extend. We should set bounds to no man's accumulation. We should repress by wise and effectual, yet moderate and humane, penalties, all forcible invasion to be committed by one man upon the acquisitions of another. But it may be asked, are there not various laws or practices, established among civilized nations, which do not, like these we have described, stop at the toleration of unequal property, but which operate to its immediate encouragement, and to the rendering this inequality still wider and more oppressive?

What are we to conceive in this respect of the protection given to inheritance, and testamentary bequest? 'There is no merit in being born the son of a rich man, rather than of a poor one, that should justify us in raising this man to affluence, and condemning that to invincible depression. Surely,' we might be apt to exclaim, 'it is enough to maintain men in their usurpation [for let it never be forgotten that accumulated property is usurpation], during the term of their lives. It is the most extravagant fiction, which would enlarge the empire of the proprietor beyond his natural existence, and enable him to dispose of events, when he is himself no longer in the world.'

The arguments however that may be offered, in favour of the protection given to inheritance and testamentary bequest, are more forcible than might at first be imagined. We have attempted to show that men ought to be protected in the disposal of the property they have personally acquired; in expending it, in the necessaries they require, or the luxuries in which they think proper to indulge; in transferring it, in such portions, as justice shall dictate, or their erroneous judgement suggest. To attempt therefore to take the disposal out of their hands, at the period of their decease, would be an abortive and pernicious project. If we prevented them from bestowing it in the open and explicit mode of bequest, we could not prevent them from transferring it before the close of their lives, and we should open a door to vexatious and perpetual litigation. Most persons would be inclined to bestow their property, after the period of their lives, upon their children or nearest relatives. Where therefore they have failed to express their sentiments in this respect, it is reasonable to presume what they would have been; and this disposal of the property on the part of the community is the mildest, and therefore the most justifiable, interference. Where they have expressed a capricious partiality, this iniquity also is, in most cases, to be protected, because, for the reasons above assigned, it cannot be prevented without exposing us to still greater iniquities.

But, though it may possibly be true, that inheritance, and the privilege of testation, are necessary consequences of the system of property in a community the members of which are involved in prejudice and ignorance, it will not be difficult to find the instances, in every political country of Europe, in which civil institution, instead of granting, to the inequalities of accumulation, only what could not prudently be withheld, has exerted itself, for the express purpose of rendering these inequalities greater and more oppressive. Such instances are, the feudal system, and the system of ranks, seignorial duties, fines, conveyances, entails, the distinction, in landed property, of freehold, copyhold and manor, the establishment of vassalage, and the claim of primogeniture. We here distinctly recognize the policy of men who, having first gained a superiority, by means of the inevitable openings before cited, have made use of this superiority for the purpose of conspiring to monopolize whatever their rapacity could seize, in direct opposition to every dictate of the general interest. These articles fall under the distinction, brought forward in the outset,* of laws or practices not

* p. 714.

common to all civilized communities, but peculiar to certain ages and countries.

It should seem therefore that these are institutions the abolition of which is not to be entirely trusted to the silent hostility of opinion, but that they are to be abrogated by the express and positive decision of the community. For their abrogation, it is not necessary that any new law or regulation should be promulgated, an operation which, to say the least, should always be regarded with extreme jealousy. Property, under every form it can assume, is upheld by the direct interference of institution; and that species which we at present contemplate must inevitably perish the moment the protection of the state is withdrawn. Of the introduction of new regulations of whatever description it becomes the friend of man to be jealous; but we may allow ourselves to regard with a more friendly eye a proceeding which consists merely in their abolition.

The conclusion however in this instance must not be pushed further than the premises will justify. The articles enumerated will perhaps, all of them, be found to tally with the condition annexed; they depend for their existence upon the positive protection of the state. But there are particulars which have grown up under their countenance that are of a different sort. Such, for instance, are titles, armorial bearings and liveries. If the community refuse to countenance feudal and seignorial claims, and the other substantial privileges of an aristocracy, they must inevitably cease. But the case is different in the instances last cited. It is one thing to abolish a law, or refuse to persist in a practice that is made the engine of tyranny; and a thing of a totally different sort, by a positive law to prohibit actions, however irrational, by which no man's security is directly invaded. It should seem unjustifiable to endeavour, by penalties, to deter a man from calling himself by any name, or attiring himself or others, with their own consent, in any manner he thinks proper. Not that these things are, as they have sometimes been represented, in their own nature trivial. We have endeavoured to prove the reverse of this.* They ought to be assailed with every weapon of argument and ridicule. In an enlightened community, the man who assumes to himself a pompous appellation will be considered as a fool or a madman. But fulminations and penalties are not the proper instruments to repress an ecstasy of this sort.

There is another circumstance necessary to be stated, by way of qualification to the preceding conclusion. Evils often exist in a community, which, though mere excrescences at first, at length become so incorporated with the principle of social existence that they cannot suddenly be separated without the risk of involving the most dreadful calamities. Feudal rights, and the privileges of rank, are, in themselves considered, entitled to no quarter. The inequalities of property perhaps constituted a state through which it was at least necessary for us to pass, and which constituted the true original excitement to the unfolding the powers of the human mind.† But it would be difficult to show that feudality and aristocracy ever produced an overbalance of good. Yet, were they to be suddenly and instantly abolished, two evils would necessarily follow. First, the abrupt reduction of thousands to a condition the reverse of that to which they had hitherto been accustomed, a condition, perhaps the most auspicious to human talent and felicity, but for which habit had wholly unfitted them, and which would be to them a continual source of dejection and suffering. It may be doubted whether the genuine cause of reform ever demands that, in its name, we should sentence whole classes of men to wretchedness. Secondly, an attempt abruptly to abolish practices which had originally no apology to plead for their introduction would be attended with as dreadful convulsions, and as melancholy a series of public calamities, as an attack upon the first principles of society itself. All the reasonings therefore which were formerly adduced

* Book V, Chap. XII.
† Chap. VII.

under the head of revolutions* are applicable to the present case.

Having now accomplished what was last proposed,† and endeavoured to ascertain in what particulars the present system of property is to be considered as the capricious offspring of positive institution, let us return to the point which led us to that enquiry, the question concerning the degree of respect to which property in general is entitled. And here it is only necessary that we should recollect the principle in which the doctrine of property is founded, the sacred and indefeasible right of private judgement. There are but two objects for which government can rationally be conceived to have been originated: first, as a treasury of public wisdom, by which individuals might, in all cases, with advantage be directed, and which might actively lead us, with greater certainty, in the path of happiness: or, secondly, instead of being forward to act itself as an umpire, that the community might fill the humbler office of guardian of the rights of private judgement, and never interpose but when one man appeared, in this respect, alarmingly to encroach upon another. All the arguments of this work have tended to show that the latter, and not the former, is the true end of civil institution. The first idea of property then is a deduction from the right of private judgement; the first object of government is the preservation of this right. Without permitting to every man, to a considerable degree, the exercise of his own discretion, there can be no independence, no improvement, no virtue and no happiness. This is a privilege in the highest degree sacred; for its maintenance, no exertions and sacrifices can be too great. Thus deep is the foundation of the doctrine of property. It is, in the last resort, the palladium of all that ought to be dear to us, and must never be approached but with awe and veneration. He that seeks to loosen the hold of this principle upon our minds, and that would lead us

* Book IV, Chap. II.
† p. 714.

to sanction any exceptions to it without the most deliberate and impartial consideration, however right may be his intentions, is, in that instance, an enemy to the whole. A condition indispensably necessary to every species of excellence is security. Unless I can foresee, in a considerable degree, the treatment I shall receive from my species, and am able to predict, to a certain extent, what will be the limits of their irregularity and caprice, I can engage in no valuable undertaking. Civil society maintains a greater proportion of security among men than can be found in the savage state: this is one of the reasons why, under the shade of civil society, arts have been invented, sciences perfected and the nature of man, in his individual and relative capacity, gradually developed.

One observation it seems proper to add to the present chapter. We have maintained* the equal rights of men, that each man has a perfect claim upon everything the possession of which will be productive of more benefit to him than injury to another. 'Has he then,' it will be asked, 'a right to take it? If not, what sort of right is that which the person in whom it vests is not entitled to enforce?'

The difficulty here is in appearance, and not in reality. The feature specified in the present instance adheres to every department of right. It is right that my actions should be governed by the dictates of my own judgement; and every man is an intruder who endeavours to compel me to act by his judgement instead of my own. But it does not follow that I shall always do wisely or well in undertaking to repel his intrusion by force. Persuasion, and not force, is the legitimate instrument for influencing the human mind; and I shall never be justifiable in having recourse to the latter, while there is any rational hope of succeeding by the former. Add to which, the criterion of morals is utility. When it has once been determined that my being constituted the possessor of a certain article will be beneficial, it does not follow that my attempting,

* Chap. I.

or even succeeding, violently to put myself in possession of it will be attended with a beneficial result. If I were quietly installed, it may be unquestionable that that would be an absolute benefit; and yet it may be true that my endeavours to put myself in possession, whether effectual or ineffectual, will be attended with worse consequences than all the good that would follow from right being done as to the object itself. The doctrine of rights has no rational or legitimate connection with the practice of tumult.

But, though I may not, consistently with rectitude, attempt to put myself in possession of many things which it is right I should have, yet this sort of right is by no means futile and nugatory. It may prove to be a great truth, resting upon irresistible evidence, and may, in that case, be expected to make hourly progress in the convictions of mankind. If it be true, it is an interesting truth, and may therefore be expected to germinate in the mind, and produce corresponding effects upon the conduct. It may appear to be a truth of that nature which is accustomed to sink deep in the human understanding, insensibly to mix itself with all our reasonings, and ultimately to produce, without shadow of violence, the most complete revolution in the maxims of civil society.

CHAPTER III

BENEFITS ATTENDANT ON A SYSTEM OF EQUALITY

Contrasted with the mischiefs of the present system – 1. a sense of dependence. 2. the perpetual spectacle of injustice, leading men astray in their desires – and perverting the integrity of their judgements. – The rich are the true pensioners. – 3. the discouragement of intellectual attainments. – 4. the multiplication of vice – generating the crimes of the poor – the passions of the rich – and the misfortunes of war. – 5. depopulation.

HAVING seen the justice of an equal distribution of the good things of life, let us next proceed to consider, in detail, the benefits with which it would be attended. And here with grief it must be confessed that, however great and extensive are the evils that are produced by monarchies and courts,* by the imposture of priests† and the iniquity of criminal laws,‡ all these are imbecile and impotent compared with the evils that arise out of the established administration of property.

Its first effect is that we have already mentioned,§ a sense of dependence. It is true that courts are mean-spirited, intriguing and servile, and that this disposition is transferred by contagion from them to all ranks of society. But accumulation brings home a servile and truckling spirit, by no circuitous method, to every house in the nation. Observe the pauper fawning with abject vileness upon his rich benefactor, speechless with sensations of gratitude, for having received that which he ought to have claimed, not indeed with arrogance, or a dictatorial and overbearing temper, but with the spirit of a man discussing with a man, and resting his cause only

* Book V.   † Book VI.
‡ Book VII.   § Chap. I, p. 708.

on the justice of his claim. Observe the servants that follow in a rich man's train, watchful of his looks, anticipating his commands, not daring to reply to his insolence, all their time and their efforts under the direction of his caprice. Observe the tradesman, how he studies the passions of his customers, not to correct, but to pamper them, the vileness of his flattery and the systematical constancy with which he exaggerates the merit of his commodities. Observe the practices of a popular election, where the great mass are purchased by obsequiousness, by intemperance and bribery, or driven by unmanly threats of poverty and persecution. Indeed 'the age of chivalry is' not 'gone'!* The feudal spirit still survives that reduced the great mass of mankind to the rank of slaves and cattle for the service of a few.

We have heard much of visionary and theoretical improvements. It would indeed be visionary to expect integrity from mankind while they are thus subjected to hourly corruption, and bred, from father to son, to sell their independence and their conscience for the vile rewards that oppression has to bestow. No man can be either useful to others, or happy in himself, who is a stranger to the grace of firmness, or who is not habituated to prefer the dictates of his own understanding to the tyranny of command, and the allurements of temptation. Here again, as upon a former occasion,† religion comes in to illustrate our thesis. Religion was the generous ebullition of men who let their imagination loose on the grandest subjects, and wandered without restraint in the unbounded field of enquiry. It is not to be wondered at therefore if they brought home imperfect ideas of the sublimest views that intellect can furnish. In this instance, religion teaches that the pure perfection of man is to arm himself against the power of sublunary enticements and sublunary terrors; that he must suffer no artificial wants, sensuality, or fear, to come in competition with the dic-

---

* Burke's *Reflections*.
† Chap. I, p. 708.

tates of rectitude and reflection. But to expect a constancy
of this sort from the human species, under the present
system, is an extravagant speculation. The enquirer after
truth, and the benefactor of mankind, will be desirous of
removing from them those external impressions by which
their evil propensities are cherished. The true object that
should be kept in view is to extirpate all ideas of con-
descension and superiority, to oblige every man to feel that
the kindness he exerts is what he is bound to perform,
and to examine whether the assistance he asks be what he
has a right to claim.

A second evil that arises out of the established administration of property is the continual spectacle of injustice
it exhibits. The effect of this consists partly in the creation
of wrong propensities, and partly in a hostility to right
ones. There is nothing more pernicious to the human
mind than the love of opulence. Essentially active when
the original cravings of appetite have been satisfied, we
necessarily fix on some object of pursuit, benevolent or
personal, and, in the latter case, on the attainment of
some excellence, or something which shall command the
esteem and deference of others. Few propensities, absolutely considered, can be more valuable than this. But
the established administration of property directs it into
the channel of the acquisition of wealth. The ostentation
of the rich perpetually goads the spectator to the desire of
opulence. Wealth, by the sentiments of servility and dependence it produces, makes the rich man stand forward
as the principal object of general esteem and deference.
In vain are sobriety, integrity and industry, in vain the
sublimest powers of mind, and the most ardent benevolence, if their possessor be narrow in his circumstances.
To acquire wealth and to display it is therefore the universal passion. The whole structure of human society is
made a system of the narrowest selfishness. If the state
of society were such that self-love and benevolence were
apparently reconciled as to their object, a man might
then set out with the desire of eminence, and yet become

every day more generous and philanthropical in his views. But the passion we are here describing is accustomed to be gratified at every step by inhumanly trampling upon the interest of others. Wealth is acquired by overreaching our neighbour, and is spent in insulting him.

The spectacle of injustice which the established administration of property exhibits operates also in the way of hostility to right propensities. If you would cherish in any man the love of rectitude, you must see that its principles be impressed on him, not only by words, but actions. It happens perhaps, during the period of education, that maxims of integrity and consistency are repeatedly enforced, and the preceptor gives no quarter to the base suggestions of selfishness and cunning. But how is the lesson that has been read to the pupil confounded and reversed when he enters upon the scene of the world? If he ask, 'Why is this man honoured?' the ready answer is, 'Because he is rich.' If he enquire further, 'Why is he rich?' the answer, in most cases, is, 'From the accident of birth, or from a minute and sordid attention to the cares of gain.' Humanity weeps over the distresses of the peasantry in all civilized nations; and, when she turns from this spectacle, to behold the luxury of their lords, gross, imperious and prodigal, her sensations certainly are not less acute. This spectacle is the school in which mankind have been educated. They have been accustomed to the sight of injustice, oppression and iniquity, till their feelings are made callous, and their understandings incapable of apprehending the principles of virtue.

In beginning to point out the evils of accumulated property, we compared the extent of those evils with the correspondent evils of monarchies and courts.* No circumstances, under the latter, have excited a more pointed disapprobation than pensions and pecuniary corruption, by means of which hundreds of individuals are rewarded, not for serving, but betraying the public, and the hard earnings of industry are employed to fatten the servile

* p. 725.

adherents of despotism. But the rent-roll of the lands of England is a much more formidable pension-list than that which is supposed to be employed in the purchase of ministerial majorities. All riches, and especially hereditary riches, are to be considered as the salary of a sinecure office, where the labourer and the manufacturer perform the duties, and the principal spends the income in luxury and idleness.* Hereditary wealth is in reality a premium paid to idleness, an immense annuity expended to retain mankind in brutality and ignorance. The poor are kept in ignorance by the want of leisure. The rich are furnished indeed with the means of cultivation and literature,

---

* This idea is to be found in an *Essay on the Right of Property in Land*, published about twelve years ago by an ingenious inhabitant of North Britain,[38] Part I, Sect. iii, par. 38, 39. The reasonings of this author have sometimes considerable merit, though he has, by no means, gone to the source of the evil.

It might be amusing to some readers to recollect the authorities, if the citation of authorities were a proper mode of reasoning, by which the system of accumulated property is openly attacked. The best known is Plato in his treatise of a *Republic*. His steps have been followed by Sir Thomas More[39] in his *Utopia*. Specimens of very powerful reasoning on the same side may be found in *Gulliver's Travels*, particularly Part IV, Chap. VI Mably,[40] in his book *De la Législation*, has displayed at large the advantages of equality, and then quits the subject in despair, from an opinion of the incorrigibleness of human depravity. Wallace,[41] the contemporary and antagonist of Hume, in a treatise entitled, *Various Prospects of Mankind, Nature and Providence*, is copious in his eulogium in the same system, and deserts it only from fear of the earth becoming too populous: see below, Chap. IX. The great practical authorities are Crete, Sparta, Peru and Paraguay. We should swell the lift to an inconvenient size if we added examples where an approach only to these principles was attempted, and authors who have incidentally confirmed a doctrine so interesting and clear as never to have been wholly eradicated from any human understanding.

It would be trifling to object that the systems of Plato and others are full of imperfections. This rather strengthens their authority; since the evidence of the truth they maintained was so great as still to preserve its hold on their understandings, though they knew not how to remove the difficulties that attended it.

but they are paid for being dissipated and indolent. The most powerful means that malignity could have invented are employed to prevent them from improving their talents, and becoming useful to the public.

This leads us to observe, thirdly, that the established administration of property is the true levelling system with respect to the human species, by as much as the cultivation of intellect is more valuable, and more characteristic of man, than the gratifications of vanity or appetite. Accumulated property treads the powers of thought in the dust, extinguishes the sparks of genius, and reduces the great mass of mankind to be immersed in sordid cares; beside depriving the rich, as we have already said, of the most salubrious and effectual motives to activity. If superfluity were banished, the necessity for the greater part of the manual industry of mankind would be superseded; and the rest, being amicably shared among the active and vigorous members of the community, would be burthensome to none. Every man would have a frugal, yet wholesome diet; every man would go forth to that moderate exercise of his corporal functions that would give hilarity to the spirits; none would be made torpid with fatigue, but all would have leisure to cultivate the kindly and philanthropical affections, and to let loose his faculties in the search of intellectual improvement. What a contrast does this scene present to the present state of society, where the peasant and the labourer work till their understandings are benumbed with toil, their sinews contracted and made callous by being for ever on the stretch, and their bodies invaded with infirmities, and surrendered to an untimely grave? What is the fruit they obtain from this disproportioned and unceasing toil? In the evening they return to a family, famished with hunger, exposed half naked to the inclemencies of the sky, hardly sheltered, and denied the slenderest instruction, unless in a few instances, where it is dispensed by the hands of ostentatious charity, and the first lesson communicated is unprincipled servility. All this while their rich neighbour – but we visited him before.*

How rapid would be the advances of intellect if all men were admitted into the field of knowledge? At present ninety-nine persons in a hundred are no more excited to any regular exertions of general and curious thought than the brutes themselves. What would be the state of public mind in a nation where all were wise, all had laid aside the shackles of prejudice and implicit faith, all adopted, with fearless confidence, the suggestions of reason, and the lethargy of the soul was dismissed for ever? It is to be presumed that the inequality of mind would, in a certain degree, be permanent; but it is reasonable to believe that the geniuses of such an age would greatly surpass the utmost exertions of intellect hitherto known. Genius would not be depressed with false wants and niggardly patronage. It would not exert itself with a sense of neglect and oppression rankling in its bosom. It would be delivered from those apprehensions that perpetually recall us to the thought of personal emolument; and, of consequence, would expatiate freely among sentiments of generosity and public good.

From ideas of intellectual, let us turn to moral, improvement. And here it is obvious that the great occasions of crime would be cut off for ever.†

The fruitful source of crimes consists in this circumstance, one man's possessing in abundance that of which another man is destitute. We must change the nature of mind before we can prevent it from being powerfully influenced by this circumstance, when brought strongly home to its perceptions by the nature of its situation. Man must cease to have senses, the pleasures of appetite and vanity must cease to gratify, before he can look on tamely at the monopoly of these pleasures. He must cease to have a sense of justice, before he can clearly and fully approve this mixed scene of superfluity and want. It is

*p. 728.
† Book I, Chap. III.

true that the proper method of curing this inequality is by reason and not by violence. But the immediate tendency of the established administration is to persuade men that reason is impotent. The injustice of which they complain is upheld by force; and they are too easily induced by force to attempt its correction. All they endeavour is the partial correction of an injustice which education tells them is necessary, but more powerful reason affirms to be tyrannical.

Force grew out of monopoly. It might accidentally have occurred among savages, whose appetites exceeded their supply, or whose passions were inflamed by the presence of the object of their desire; but it would gradually have died away, as reason and civilization advanced. Accumulated property has fixed its empire; and henceforth all is an open contention of the strength and cunning of one party against the strength and cunning of the other. In this case, the violent and premature struggles of the necessitous are undoubtedly an evil. They tend to defeat the very cause in the success of which they are most deeply interested; they tend to procrastinate the triumph of justice. But the true crime, in every instance, is in the selfish and partial propensities of men, thinking only of themselves, and despising the emolument of others; and, of these, the rich have their share.

The spirit of oppression, the spirit of servility, and the spirit of fraud, these are the immediate growth of the established administration of property. They are alike hostile to intellectual and moral improvement. The other vices of envy, malice and revenge are their inseparable companions. In a state of society where men lived in the midst of plenty, and where all shared alike the bounties of nature, these sentiments would inevitably expire. The narrow principle of selfishness would vanish. No man being obliged to guard his little store, or provide, with anxiety and pain, for his restless wants, each would lose his individual existence, in the thought of the general good. No man would be an enemy to his neighbour, for they would have no subject of contention; and of consequence, philanthropy would resume the empire which reason assigns her. Mind would be delivered from her perpetual anxiety about corporal support, and free to expatiate in the field of thought which is congenial to her. Each would assist the enquiries of all.

Let us fix our attention, for a moment, upon the alteration of principles and habits that immediately grows out of an unequal distribution of property. Till it was thus distributed, men felt what their wants required, and sought the supply of those wants. All that was more than this was regarded as indifferent. But no sooner is accumulation introduced than they begin to study a variety of methods, for disposing of their superfluity with least emolument to their neighbour, or, in other words, by which it shall appear to be most their own. They do not long continue to buy commodities before they begin to buy men. He that possesses, or is the spectator of, superfluity, soon discovers the hold which it affords him on the minds of others. Hence the passions of vanity and ostentation. Hence the despotic manners of such, as recollect with complacence the rank they occupy; and the restless ambition of those, whose attention is engrossed by the possible future.

Ambition is, of all the passions of the human mind, the most extensive in its ravages. It adds district to district, and kingdom to kingdom. It spreads bloodshed and calamity and conquest over the face of the earth. But the passion itself, as well as the means of gratifying it, is the produce of the prevailing administration of property.* It is only by means of accumulation that one man obtains an unresisted sway over multitudes of others. It is by means of a certain distribution of income that the present governments of the world are retained in existence. Nothing more easy than to plunge nations, so organized, into war. But, if Europe were at present covered with inhabitants all of them possessing competence, and none of

* Book V, Chap. XVI.

them superfluity, what could induce its different countries to engage in hostility? If you would lead men to war, you must exhibit certain allurements. If you be not enabled, by a system already prevailing, and which derives force from prescription, to hire them to your purposes, you must bring over each individual by dint of persuasion. How hopeless a task by such means to excite mankind to murder each other? It is clear then that war, in all its aggravations, is the growth of unequal property. As long as this source of jealousy and corruption shall remain, it is visionary to talk of universal peace. As soon as the source shall be dried up, it will be impossible to exclude the consequence. It is accumulation that forms men into one common mass, and makes them fit to be played upon like a brute machine. Were this stumbling-block removed, each man would be united to his neighbour, in love and mutual kindness, a thousand times more than now: but each man would think and judge for himself. Let then the advocates for the prevailing administration at least consider what it is for which they plead, and be well assured that they have arguments in its favour which will weigh against these disadvantages.

There is one other circumstance which, though inferior to those above enumerated, deserves to be mentioned. This is population. It has been calculated that the average cultivation of Europe might be so improved as to maintain five times her present number of inhabitants.* There is a principle in human society by which population is perpetually kept down to the level of the means of subsistence. Thus, among the wandering tribes of America and Asia, we never find, through the lapse of ages, that population has so increased as to render necessary the cultivation of the earth. Thus, among the civilized nations of Europe, by means of territorial monopoly, the sources of subsistence are kept within a certain limit, and, if the population became overstocked, the lower ranks of the inhabitants would be still more incapable of procur-

* *Essay on Property*, Part I, Sect. iii, par. 35.

ing for themselves the necessaries of life. There are, no doubt extraordinary concurrences of circumstances by means of which changes are occasionally introduced in this respect; but, in ordinary cases, the standard of population is held, in a manner, stationary for centuries. Thus the established administration of property may be considered as strangling a considerable portion of our children in their cradle. Whatever may be the value of the life of man, or rather whatever would be his capability of happiness in a free and equal state of society, the system we are here opposing may be considered as arresting, upon the threshold of existence, four fifths of that value and that happiness.

CHAPTER IV

OBJECTION TO THIS SYSTEM FROM THE FRAILTY OF THE HUMAN MIND

Recapitulation. – Objection stated. – General answer to his objection. – Particular answer. – Influence of public opinion upon the conduct of individuals.

HAVING proceeded thus far in our investigation, it may be proper to recapitulate the principles already established. The discussion, under each of its branches, as it relates to the equality of men,* and the inequalities of property,† may be considered as a discussion either of right or duty; and, in that respect, runs parallel to the two great heads of which we treated in our original development of the principles of society.‡ I have a right to the assistance of my neighbour; he has a right that it should not be extorted from him by force. It is his duty

* Chap. I, III.
† Chap. II.
‡ Book II, Chap. IV, V.

to afford me the supply of which I stand in need; it is my duty not to violate his province in determining, first, whether he is to supply me, and, secondly, in what degree.

Equality of conditions, or, in other words, an equal admission to the means of improvement and pleasure, is a law rigorously enjoined upon mankind by the voice of justice. All other changes in society are good, only as they are fragments of this, or steps to its attainment. All other existing abuses are to be deprecated, only as they serve to increase and perpetuate the inequality of conditions.

We have however arrived at another truth not less evident than this. Equality of conditions cannot be produced by individual compulsion, and ought not to be produced by compulsion in the name of the whole. There remains therefore but one mode of arriving at this great end of justice and most essential improvement of society, and that consists in rendering the cession by him that has to him that wants an unrestrained and voluntary action. There remain but two instruments for producing this volition, the illumination of the understanding and the love of distinction.

These instruments have commonly been supposed wholly inadequate to their object. It has usually been treated as 'the most visionary of all systems, to expect the rich to "sell all that they have, and give to the poor".* It is one thing to convince men that a given conduct, on their part, would be most conducive to the general interest, and another to persuade them actively to postpone, to considerations of general interest, every idea of personal ambition or pleasure. The sober calculator will often doubt whether it be reasonable, in consistence with the nature of a human being, to expect from him such a sacrifice: and the man of a lively and impetuous temper, even when satisfied that it is his duty, will be in hourly danger of deserting it, at the invitation of some allurement, too powerful for mortal frailty to resist.'

* Mark, ch. x, ver. 21.

There is certainly considerable force in this statement; and there is good reason to believe, though the human mind be unquestionably accessible to disinterested motives,* that virtue would be in most instances an impracticable refinement; were it not that self-love and social, however different in themselves, are found upon strict examination to prescribe the same system of conduct.

But this observation by no means removes the difficulty intended to be suggested in the objection. 'Though frugality, moderation and plainness may be the joint dictate of these two authorities, yet it is the property of the human mind to be swayed by things present more than by things absent. In affairs of religion, we often find men indulging themselves in offences of small gratification, in spite of all the threats that can be held out to them of eternal damnation. It is in vain that, for the most part, you would preach the pleasures of abstinence amidst the profusion of a feast; or the unsubstantialness of fame and power to him who is tortured with the goadings of ambition. The case is similar to that of the exacerbations of grief, the attempt to cure which by the consolations of philosophy has been a source of inexhaustible ridicule.'

The answer to these remarks has been anticipated.† The ridicule lies in supposing the endeavour to cure a man of his weakness to consist in one phlegmatic and solitary expostulation, instead of conceiving it to be accompanied with the vigour of conscious truth, and the progressive regularity of a course of instruction.

Let us take up the subject in a view, in some degree varying from that in which it was formerly considered. We have endeavoured to establish, in the commencement of the present book, the principles of justice, relative to the distribution of the goods of fortune. Let us enquire whether the principles there delivered can be made productive of conviction to the rich; whether they can be

* Book IV, Chap. X.
† Book I Chap, V. § 3.

made productive of conviction, in cases not immediately connected with personal interest; and whether they can be made productive of conviction to the poor?

Is it possible for a rich man to see that the costly gratifications in which he indulges are comparatively of little value, and that he may arrive at everything that is most essential in happiness or pleasure, by means of the three other sources formerly enumerated,* subsistence, unexpensive gratifications, and the means of intellectual and moral improvement? Is it possible for him to understand the calculation, 'in every glass that he drinks, and every ornament that he annexes to his person', of 'how many individuals have been condemned to slavery and sweat, incessant drudgery, unwholesome food, continual hardships, deplorable ignorance and brutal insensibility, that he may be supplied with these luxuries'?† Is it possible for a man to have these ideas so repeatedly suggested to his mind, so strongly impressed, and so perpetually haunting him, as finally to induce a rich man to desire, with respect to personal gratifications, to live as if he were a poor one? It is not conceivable but that every one of these questions must be answered in the affirmative.

Be it observed by the way that the motives for a rich man to live as if he were a poor one are very inferior now to what they would be when a general sympathy upon this subject had taken place, and a general illumination had diffused itself.

If then it be possible for a rich man, from the mere apprehensions of justice, voluntarily to desire to live as if he were a poor one, we shall have still less hesitation in affirming that a sentiment of justice in this matter may be made productive of conviction, in cases not immediately connected with personal interest, and of conviction to the poor.

Undoubtedly an apprehension of the demands of justice in this respect has some tendency to the instigation

* Chap. I, p. 704.
† Chap. II. pp. 711, 712.

of violence and tumult, were we not to suppose the gradual development of this impression to be accompanied with a proportionable improvement of the mind in other respects, and a slow, but incessant, melioration of the institutions and practices of society. With this supposition, it could not however fail to happen that, in proportion as the prejudices and ignorance of the great mass of society declined, the credit of wealth, and the reverent admiration with which it is now contemplated, must also decline. But, in proportion as it lost credit with the great mass of society, it would relax its hold upon the minds of those who possess it, or have the means of acquiring it. We have already seen* that the great incitement to the acquisition of wealth is the love of distinction. Suppose then that, instead of the false glare which wealth, through the present puerility of the human mind, reflects on its possessor, his conduct in amassing and monopolizing it were seen in its true light. We should not then demand his punishment, but we should look on him as a man uninitiated in the plainest sentiments of reason. He would not be pointed at with the finger, or hooted as he passed along through the resorts of men, but he would be conscious that he was looked upon as the meanest of mankind. He would be incited to the same assiduity in hiding his acquisitions then as he employs in displaying them now. He would be regarded with no terror, for his conduct would appear too absurd to excite imitation. Add to which, his acquisitions would be small, as the independent spirit and sound discretion of mankind would allow but little chance of his being able to retain them in his service, as now, by generously rewarding them with a part of the fruit of their own labours. Thus it appears, with irresistible probability, when the subject of wealth shall be understood, and correct ideas respecting it familiarized to the human mind, that the present disparity of conditions will subside, by a gradual and incessant progress, into its true level.

* Chap. I, p. 705.

CHAPTER V

OBJECTION TO THIS SYSTEM FROM THE QUESTION OF PERMANENCE

Grounds of the objection. – Its serious import. –
Nature of the equality under consideration –
as produced by a stricter sense of justice – and
a purer theory of happiness.

THE change we are here contemplating consists in the
disposition of every member of the community voluntarily
to resign that which would be productive of a much
higher degree of benefit and pleasure when possessed by
his neighbour than when occupied by himself. Undoubtedly, this state of society is remote from the modes of
thinking and acting which at present prevail. A long
period of time must probably elapse before it can be
brought entirely into practice. All we have been attempting to establish is that such a state of society is agreeable
to reason, and prescribed by justice; and that, of consequence, the progress of science and political truth among
mankind is closely connected with its introduction. The
inherent tendency of intellect is to improvement. If therefore this inherent tendency be suffered to operate, and
no concussion of nature or inundation of barbarism arrest
its course, the state of society we have been describing
must, at some time, arrive.

But it has frequently been said 'that if an equality of
conditions could be introduced today, it would be destroyed tomorrow. It is impossible to reduce the varieties
of the human mind to such a uniformity as this system
demands. One man will be more industrious than another; one man will be provident and avaricious, and
another dissipated and thoughtless. Misery and confusion
would be the result of an attempt to equalize, in the
first instance, and the old vices and monopolies would
succeed, in the second. All that the rich could purchase
by the most generous sacrifice would be a period of bar-

barism, from which the ideas and regulations of civil society must recommence, as from a new infancy.'

Upon this statement, it is first to be remarked that, if true, it presents to us a picture in the highest degree melancholy and discouraging. It discovers a disease to which it is probable there is no remedy. Human knowledge must proceed. What we see and admire we shall at some time or other seek to attain: Such is the inevitable law of our nature. It is impossible not to see the beauty of equality, and not to be charmed with the benefits it appears to promise. It is impossible not to regret the unbounded mischiefs and distress that grow out of the opposite system. The consequence is sure. Man, according to these reasoners, is prompted, for some time, to advance with success: but after that, in the very act of pursuing further improvement, he necessarily plunges beyond the compass of his powers, and has his petty career to begin afresh: always pursuing what is beautiful, always frustrated in his object, always involved in calamities by the very means he employs to escape them.

Secondly, it is to be observed that there is a wide difference between the equality here spoken of, and the equality which has frequently constituted a subject of discussion among mankind. This is not an equality introduced by force, or maintained by the laws and regulations of a positive institution. It is not the result of accident, of the authority of a chief magistrate, or the over-earnest persuasion of a few enlightened thinkers; but is produced, by the serious and deliberate conviction of the public at large. It is one thing for men to be held to a certain system by the force of laws, and the vigilance of those who administer them; and a thing entirely different to be held by the firm and habitual persuasion of their own minds. We can readily conceive their finding means to elude the former; but it is not so easy to comprehend a disobedience to the latter. If the force of truth shall be strong enough gradually to wean men from the most rooted habits, and to introduce a mode of society so remote from that which at present exists, it will also probably be strong enough to hold them in the course they have commenced, and to prevent the return of vices which have once been extirpated. This probability will be increased if we recollect the two principles which must have led men into such a system of action; a stricter sense of justice, and a purer theory of happiness.

Equality of conditions cannot begin to assume a fixed appearance in human society till the sentiment becomes deeply impressed, as well as widely diffused, that the genuine wants of any man constitute his only just claim to the ultimate appropriation, and the consumption, of any species of commodity. It must previously be seen that the claims of one man are originally of the same extent as the claims of another; and that the only difference which can arise must relate to extraordinary infirmity, or the particular object of utility which any individual is engaged in promoting. It must be felt that the most fundamental and noxious of all kinds of injustice is for one man actively to withhold from his neighbours the most indispensable benefits, for the sake of some trivial accommodation to himself. Men who are habituated to these views can scarcely be tempted to monopolize; and the sense of the community respecting him who yields to the temptation will be so decisive in its tenor, and unequivocal in its manifestation, as to afford small encouragement to perseverance or imitation.

A spontaneous equality of conditions also implies a purer theory of happiness than has hitherto obtained. Men will cease to regard with complacence the happiness that consists in spendour and ostentation, of which the true object, however disguised, is to insult our neighbours, and to feed our own vanity, with the recollection of the goods that we possess, and from which, though endowed with an equal claim, they are debarred. They will cease to derive pleasure from the empire to be possessed over others, or the base servility and terror with which they may address us. They will be contented, for the most part, with the means of healthful existence, and of unexpensive pleasure. They will find the highest gratification in promoting and contemplating the general happiness. They will regard superfluities, absolutely considered, with no impatience of desire; and will abhor the idea of obtaining them through the medium of oppression and injustice. This conduct they would be induced to observe, even were their own gratification only in view; and, instead of repining at the want of exorbitant indulgencies, they will stand astonished that men could ever have found gratification in that which was visibly stamped and contaminated with the badge of extortion.

CHAPTER VI

OBJECTION TO THIS SYSTEM FROM THE ALLUREMENTS OF SLOTH

Objection proposed. – Such a state of society preceded by great intellectual improvement. – The manual labour required will be small. – Universality of the love of distinction. – Operation of this motive under the system in question – finally superseded by a better motive.

ANOTHER objection which has been urged against the system which counteracts the accumulation of property is 'that it would put an end to industry. We behold, in commercial countries, the miracles that are operated by the love of gain Their inhabitants cover the sea with their fleets, astonish mankind by the refinements of their ingenuity, hold vast continents in subjection, in distant parts of the world, by their arms, are able to defy the most powerful confederacies, and, oppressed with taxes and debts, seem to acquire fresh prosperity under their accumulated burthens. Shall we lightly part with a motive which appears so great and stupendous in its in-

fluence? Once establish it as a principle in society that
no man is to apply to his personal use more than his
necessities require; and every man will become indifferent to the exertions which now call forth the energy of
his faculties. Once establish it as a principle that each
man, without being compelled to exert his own powers,
is entitled to partake of the superfluity of his neighbour;
and indolence will speedily become universal. Such a
society must either starve, or be obliged, in its own defence, to return to that system of monopoly and sordid
interest which theoretical reasoners will for ever arraign
to no purpose.'

In reply to this objection, the reader must again be re-
minded that the equality for which we are pleading is an
equality which would succeed to a state of great intellectual improvement. So bold a revolution cannot take
place in human affairs till the general mind has been
highly cultivated. Hasty and undigested tumults may be
produced by a superficial idea of equalization; but it is
only a clear and calm conviction of justice, of justice
mutually to be rendered and received, of happiness to
be produced by the desertion of our most rooted habits,
that can introduce an invariable system of this sort. Attempts, without this prepartion, will be productive only
of confusion. Their effect will be momentary, and a new
and more barbarous inequality will succeed. Each man,
with unaltered appetite, will watch the opportunity, to
gratify his love of power or of distinction, by usurping
on his inattentive neighbours.

Is it to be believed then that a state of so great intellectual improvement can be the forerunner of universal
ignorance and brutality? Savages, it is true, are subject
to the weakness of indolence. But civilized and refined
states are the theatre of a peculiar activity. It is thought,
acuteness of disquisition, and ardour of pursuit that set
the corporeal faculties at work. Thought begets thought.
Nothing perhaps can put a stop to the advances of mind
but oppression. But here, so far from being oppressed,

every man is equal, every man independent and at his ease. It has been observed that the introduction of a republican government is attended with public enthusiasm and irresistible enterprise. Is it to be believed that equality, the true republicanism, will be less effectual? It is true that in republics this spirit, sooner or later, is found to languish. Republicanism is not a remedy that strikes at the root of the evil. Injustice, oppression and misery can find an abode in those seeming happy seats. But what shall stop the progress of ardour and improvement where the monopoly of property is unknown?

This argument will be strengthened if we reflect on the amount of labour that a state of equality will require. What is this quantity of exertion from which the objection supposes many individuals to shrink? It is so light as rather to assume the guise of agreeable relaxation and gentle exercise than of labour. In such a community, scarcely anyone can be expected, in consequence of his situation or avocations, to consider himself as exempted from the obligation to manual industry. There will be no rich man to recline in indolence, and fatten upon the labour of his fellows. The mathematician, the poet and the philosopher will derive a new stock of cheerfulness and energy from the recurring labour that makes them feel they are men. There will be no persons devoted to the manufacture of trinkets and luxuries; and none whose office it should be to keep in motion the complicated machine of government, tax-gatherers, beadles, excisemen, tide-waiters, clerks and secretaries. There will be neither fleets nor armies, neither courtiers nor lacqueys. It is the unnecessary employments that, at present, occupy the great mass of every civilized nation, while the peasant labours incessantly to maintain them in a state more pernicious than idleness.

It may be computed that not more than one twentieth of the inhabitants of England is substantially employed in the labours of agriculture. Add to this that the nature of agriculture is such as to give full occupation in some parts of the year, and to leave other parts comparatively vacant. We may consider the latter as equivalent to a labour which, under the direction of sufficient skill, might suffice, in a simple state of society, for the fabrication of tools, for weaving, and the occupation of tailors, bakers and butchers. The object, in the present state of society, is to multiply labour; in another state, it will be to simplify it. A vast disproportion of the wealth of the community has been thrown into the hands of a few; and ingenuity has been continually upon the stretch to find ways in which it may be expended. In the feudal times, the great lord invited the poor to come and eat of the produce of his estate, upon condition of wearing his livery, and forming themselves in rank and file to do honour to his well born guests. Now that exchanges are more facilitated, he has quitted this inartificial mode, and obliges the men who are maintained from his income to exert their ingenuity and industry in return. Thus, in the instance just mentioned, he pays the tailor to cut his clothes to pieces that he may sew them together again, and to decorate them with stitching and various ornaments, without which they would be, in no respect, less convenient and useful. We are imagining, in the present case, a state of the most rigid simplicity.

From the sketch which has been given, it seems by no means impossible that the labour of every twentieth man in the community would be sufficient to supply to the rest all the absolute necessaries of life. If then this labour, instead of being performed by so small a number, were amicably divided among the whole, it would occupy the twentieth part of every man's time. Let us compute that the industry of a labouring man engrosses ten hours in every day, which, when we have deducted his hours of rest, recreation and meals, seems an ample allowance. It follows that half an hour a day employed in manual labour by every member of the community would sufficiently supply the whole with necessaries. Who is there that would shrink from this degree of industry? Who is there that sees the incessant industry exerted in this city and island, and would believe that, with half an hour's industry *per diem*, the sum of happiness to the community at large might be much greater than at present? Is it possible to contemplate this fair and generous picture of independence and virtue, where every man would have ample leisure for the noblest energies of mind, without feeling our very souls refreshed with admiration and hope?

When we talk of men's sinking into idleness, if they be not excited by the stimulus of gain, we seem to have little considered the motives that, at present, govern the human mind. We are deceived by the apparent mercenariness of mankind, and imagine that the accumulation of wealth is their great object. But it has sufficiently appeared that the present ruling passion of man is the love of distinction.* There is, no doubt, a class in society that is perpetually urged by hunger and need, and has no leisure for motives less gross and material. But is the class next above them less industrious than they? Will any man affirm that the mind of the peasant is as far removed from inaction and sloth as the mind of the general or statesman, of the natural philosopher who macerates himself with perpetual study, or the poet, the bard of Mantua for example, who can never believe that he has sufficiently revised, reconsidered and polished his compositions?

In reality, those by whom this reasoning has been urged have mistaken the nature of their own objection. They did not suppose that men could be roused into action only by the love of gain; but they conceived that, in a state of equality, men would have nothing to occupy their attention. What degree of truth there is in this idea we shall presently have occasion to estimate.†

Meanwhile, it is sufficiently obvious that the motives which arise from the love of distinction are by no means cut off by a state of society incompatible with the ac-

* Chap. I, p. 705.
† Chap. VII, VIII.

cumulation of property. Men, no longer able to acquire
the esteem, or avoid the contempt, of their neighbours,
by circumstances of dress and furniture, will divert the
passion for distinction into another channel. They will
avoid the reproach of indolence as carefully as they now
avoid the reproach of poverty. The only persons who,
at present, neglect the effect which their appearance and
manners may produce are those whose faces are ground
with famine and distress. But, in a state of equal society,
no man will be oppressed, and, of consequence, the more
delicate affections will have time to expand themselves.
The general mind having, as we have already shown,
arrived at a high degree of improvement, the impulse
that carries it into action will be stronger. The fervour
of public spirit will be great. Leisure will be multiplied;
and the leisure of a cultivated understanding is the precise period in which great designs, designs the tendency
of which is to secure applause and esteem, are conceived.
In tranquil leisure, it is impossible for any but the sublimest mind to exist without the passion for distinction.
This passion, no longer permitted to lose itself in indirect
channels and useless wanderings, will seek the noblest
course, and perpetually fructify the seeds of public good.
Mind, though it will perhaps at no time arrive at the
termination of its possible discoveries and improvements,
will nevertheless advance with a rapidity and firmness of
progression of which we are, at present, unable to conceive the idea.

The love of fame is no doubt a delusion. This, like
every other delusion, will take its turn to be detected and
abjured. It is an airy phantom, which will indeed afford
us an imperfect pleasure so long as we worship it, but will
always, in a considerable degree, disappoint us, and will
not stand the test of examination. We ought to love
nothing but a substantial happiness, that happiness which
will bear the test of recollection, and which no clearness
of perception, and improvement of understanding, will
tend to undermine. If there be any principle more sub-

stantial than the rest, it is justice, a principle that rests upon this single postulatum, that man and man are beings of the same nature, and susceptible, under certain limitations, of the same advantages. Whether the benefit which is added to the common flock proceed from you or me is a pitiful distinction. Fame therefore is an unsubstantial and delusive pursuit. If it signify an opinion entertained of me greater than I deserve, to desire it is vicious. If it be the precise mirror of my character, it is valuable only as a means, in as much as I shall be able most essentially to benefit those who best know the extent of my capacity, and the rectitude of my intentions.

The love of fame, when it perishes in minds formed under the present system, often gives place to a principle still more reprehensible. Selfishness is the habit that grows out of monopoly. When therefore selfishness ceases to seek its gratification in public exertion, it too often narrows into some frigid conception of personal pleasure, perhaps sensual, perhaps intellectual. But this cannot be the process where monopoly is banished. Selfishness has there no kindly circumstances to foster it. Truth, the overpowering truth of general good, then seizes us irresistibly. It is impossible we should want motives, so long as we see clearly how multitudes and ages may be benefited by our exertions, how causes and effects are connected in an endless chain, so that no honest effort can be lost, but will operate to good, centuries after its author is consigned to the grave.* This will be the general passion, and all will be animated by the example of all.

* Book IV, Chap. X.

CHAPTER VII

OBJECTION TO THIS SYSTEM FROM THE BENEFITS OF LUXURY

Nature of the objection. – Extent of its influence. – Luxury a stage to be passed through. – Meanings of the term luxury distinguished. – Application.

THE objections we have hitherto examined attack the practicability of a system of equality. But there are not wanting reasoners the tendency of whose arguments is to show that, omitting the practicability, it is not even desirable. One of the objections they advance is as follows.

They lay it down as a maxim, in the first instance, and the truth of this maxim we shall not contend with them, 'that refinement is better than ignorance. It is better to be a man than a brute. Those attributes therefore which separate the man from the brute are most worthy of our affection and cultivation. Elegance of taste, refinement of sentiment, depth of penetration, and largeness of science, are among the noblest ornaments of man. But all these,' say they, 'are connected with inequality; they are the growth of luxury. It is luxury by which palaces are built, and cities peopled. It is for the purpose of obtaining a share of the luxury which he witnesses in his richer neighbours that the artificer exerts the refinements of his skill. To this cause we are indebted for the arts of architecture, painting, music and poetry. Art would never have been cultivated if a state of inequality had not enabled some men to purchase, and excited others to acquire the talent which was necessary to sell. In a state of equality, we must always have remained, and, with equality restored, we must again become, barbarians. Thus we see (as in the system of optimism*) disorder, selfishness, monopoly and distress, all of them seeming discords, contributing to the admirable harmony and magnificence of the

* Book IV, Chap. XI.

whole. The intellectual improvement and enlargement we witness and hope for was worth purchasing at the expense of partial injustice and distress.'*

This view of the subject, under various forms, has been very extensive in its effects. It probably contributed to make Rousseau an advocate of the savage state. Undoubtedly, we must not permit ourselves to think slightly of the mischiefs that accrue from a state of inequality. If it be necessary that the great mass of mankind should be condemned to slavery, and, stranger still, to ignorance, that a few may be enlightened, certainly those moralists are not to be blamed who doubted whether perpetual rudeness were not preferable to such a gift. Fortunately this is by no means the real alternative.

Perhaps a state of luxury, such as is here described, and a state of inequality, might be a stage through which it was necessary to pass in order to arrive at the goal of civilization. The only security we can ultimately have for an equality of conditions is a general persuasion of the iniquity of accumulation, and the usefulness of wealth, in the purchase of happiness. But this persuasion could not be established in a savage state; nor indeed can it be maintained, if we should fall back into barbarism. It was the spectacle of inequality that first excited the grossness of barbarians to persevering exertion, as a means of ac-

---

* The great champion of this doctrine is Mandeville.[42] It is not however easy to determine whether he is seriously, or only ironically, the defender of the present system of society. His principle work (*Fable of the Bees*) is highly worthy the attention of every man who would learn profoundly to philosophize upon human affairs. No author has displayed, in stronger terms, the deformity of existing abuses, or proved more satisfactorily how inseparably these abuses are connected together. Hume (*Essays*; Part II, Essay II.) has endeavoured to communicate to the Mandevilian system his own lustre and brilliancy of colouring. But it has unfortunately happened that what he adds in beauty he has subtracted from profoundness. The profoundness of Hume, which has never been surpassed, and which ranks him with the most illustrious and venerable of men, is for the most part the profoundness of logical distinction, rather than of moral analysis.

quiring. It was persevering exertion that first gave the reality, and the sense, of that leisure which has served the purposes of literature and art.

But, though inequality were necessary as the prelude to civilization, it is not necessary to its support. We may throw down the scaffolding, when the edifice is complete. We have at large endeavoured to show* that the love of our fellow men, the love of distinction, and whatever motive is most allied to the energies of the human mind, will remain when the enchantments of wealth are dissolved. He who has tasted the pleasures of refinement and knowledge will not relapse into ignorance.

The better to understand the futility of the present objection, it may be proper to enter into a more accurate consideration of the sense of the term luxury. It depends upon the meaning in which it is understood to determine whether it is to be regarded as a virtue or a vice. If we understand by a luxury something which is to be enjoyed exclusively by some, at the expense of undue privations, and a partial burthen upon others; to indulge ourselves in luxury is then a vice. But, if we understand by luxury, which is frequently the case, every accommodation which is not absolutely necessary to maintain us in sound and healthful existence, the procuring and communicating luxuries may then be virtuous. The end of virtue is to add to the sum of pleasurable sensation. The beacon and regulator of virtue is impartiality, that we shall not give that exertion to procure the pleasure of an individual which might have been employed in procuring the pleasure of many individuals. Within these limits every man is laudably employed who procures to himself or his neighbour a real accession of pleasure; and he is censurable who neglects any occasion of being so employed. We ought not to study that we may live, but to live that we may replenish existence with the greatest number of unallayed, exquisite and substantial enjoyments.

Let us apply these reflections to the state of equality we

* Chap. I, IV, VI.

have endeavoured to delineate. It appeared in that delineation* that the labour of half an hour *per diem* on the part of every individual in the community would probably be sufficient to procure for all the necessaries of life. This quantity of industry therefore, though prescribed by no law, and enforced by no direct penalty, would be most powerfully imposed upon the strong in intellect, by a sense of justice, and upon the weak, by a sense of shame. After this, how would men spend the remainder of their time? Not probably in idleness, not all men, and the whole of their time, in the pursuit of intellectual attainments. There are many things, the fruit of human industry, which, though not to be classed among the necessaries of life, are highly conducive to our well being. The criterion of these things will appear when we have ascertained what those accommodations are which will give us real pleasure, after the insinuations of vanity and ostentation shall have been dismissed. A considerable portion of time would probably be dedicated, in an enlightened community, to the production of such accommodations. A labour of this sort is perhaps not inconsistent with the most desirable state of human existence. Laborious employment is a calamity now, because it is imperiously prescribed upon men as the condition of their existence, and because it shuts them out from a fair participation in the means of knowledge and improvement. When it shall be rendered in the strictest sense voluntary, when it shall cease to interfere with our improvement, and rather become a part of it, or at worst be converted into a source of amusement and variety, it may then be no longer a calamity, but a benefit. Thus it appears that a state of equality need not be a state of Stoical simplicity, but is compatible with considerable accommodation, and even, in some sense, with splendour; at least, if by splendour we understand copiousness of accommodation, and variety of invention for the purposes of accommodation. Those persons therefore may be con-

* Chap. VI, p. 746.

cluded to have small appearance of reason who confound such a state with the state of the savage; or who suppose that the acquisition of the former is to be considered as having a tendency to lead to the latter.

CHAPTER VIII

OBJECTION TO THIS SYSTEM FROM THE INFLEXIBILITY OF ITS RESTRICTIONS

Objection stated. – Natural and moral independence distinguished. – Tendency of restriction properly so called. – The system of equality not a system of restriction.

AN objection that has often been urged against a system of equality is 'that it is inconsistent with personal independence. Every man, according to this scheme, is a passive instrument in the hands of the community. He must eat and drink, and play and sleep, at the bidding of others. He has no habitation, no period at which he can retreat into himself, and not ask another's leave. He has nothing that he can call his own, not even his time or his person. Under the appearance of a perfect freedom from oppression and tyranny, he is in reality subjected to the most unlimited slavery'.

To understand the force of this objection it is necessary that we should distinguish two sorts of independence, one of which may be denominated natural, and the other moral. Natural independence, a freedom from all constraint, except that of reasons and inducements presented to the understanding, is of the utmost importance to the welfare and improvement of mind. Moral independence, on the contrary, is always injurious. The dependence, which is essential, in this respect, to the wholesome temperament of society, includes in it articles that are, no doubt, unpalatable to a multitude of the present race of mankind, but that owe their unpopularity only to weakness and vice. It includes a censure to be exercised by every individual over the actions of another, a promptness to enquire into and to judge them. Why should we shrink from this? What could be more beneficial than for each man to derive assistance for correcting and moulding his conduct from the perspicacity of his neighbours? The reason that this species of censure is at present exercised with illiberality is because it is exercised clandestinely, and because we submit to its operation with impatience and aversion. Moral independence is always injurious: for, as has abundantly appeared in the course of the present enquiry, there is no situation in which I can be placed where it is not incumbent upon me to adopt a certain conduct in preference to all others, and, of consequence, where I shall not prove an ill member of society if I act in any other than a particular manner. The attachment that is felt by the present race of mankind to independence in this respect, and the desire to act as they please, without being accountable to the principles of reason, are highly detrimental to the general welfare.

But, if we ought never to act independently of the principles of reason, and, in no instance, to shrink from the candid examination of another, it is nevertheless essential that we should, at all times, be free to cultivate the individuality, and follow the dictates, of our own judgement. If there be anything in the idea of equality that infringes this principle, the objection ought probably to be conclusive. If the scheme be, as it has often been represented, a scheme of government, constraint and regulation, it is, no doubt, in direct hostility with the principles of this work.

But the truth is that a system of equality requires no restrictions or superintendence. There is no need of common labour, meals or magazines. These are feeble and mistaken instruments for restraining the conduct without making conquest of the judgement. If you cannot bring over the hearts of the community to your party, expect no success from brute regulations. If you can, regulation is unnecessary. Such a system was well enough adapted to the military constitution of Sparta; but it is wholly unworthy of men enlisted in no cause but that of reason and justice. Beware of reducing men to the state of machines. Govern them through no medium but that of inclination and conviction.

Can there be a good reason for men's eating together, except where they are prompted to it by the impulse of their own minds? Ought I to come at a certain hour, from the museum where I am working, the retreat in which I meditate, or the observatory where I remark the phenomena of nature, to a certain hall appropriated to the office of eating; instead of eating, as reason bids me, at the time and place most suited to my avocations? Why have common magazines? For the purpose of carrying our provisions to a certain distance, that we may afterwards bring them back again? Or is this precaution really necessary, after all that has been said, to guard us against the knavery and covetousness of our associates?

Appendix

OF CO-OPERATION, COHABITATION AND MARRIAGE

Advantages of social refinement – of individuality. – Evils of co-operation. – Ideas of the state of co-operation. – Is limits. – Its legitimate province. – Evils of cohabitation – of the received system of marriage. – Consequences of their abolition. – A promiscuous commerce of the sexes estimated. – Inconstancy estimated. – Education need not be a subject of positive institution. – Of the division of labour.

IT is a curious subject to enquire into the due medium between individuality and concert. On the one hand, it is to be observed that human beings are formed for society. Without society, we shall probably be deprived of the most eminent enjoyments of which our nature is susceptible. In society, no man possessing the genuine marks of a man can stand alone. Our opinions, our tempers and our habits are modified by those of each other. This is by no means the mere operation of arguments and persuasives; it occurs in that insensible and gradual way which no resolution can enable us wholly to counteract. He that would attempt to counteract it by insulating himself will fall into a worse error than that which he seeks to avoid. He will divest himself of the character of a man, and be incapable of judging his fellow men, or of reasoning upon human affairs.

On the other hand, individuality is of the very essence of intellectual excellence. He that resigns himself wholly to sympathy and imitation can possess little of mental strength or accuracy. The system of his life is a species of sensual dereliction. He is like a captive in the garden of Armida; he may revel in the midst of a thousand delights; but he is incapable of the enterprise of a hero, or the severity of a philosopher. He lives forgetting and forgot. He has deserted his station in human society. Mankind cannot be benefited by him. He neither animates them to exertion, nor leads them forward to unexpected improvement. When his country or his species call for him, he is not found in his rank. They can owe him no obligations; and, if one spark of a generous spirit remain within him, he will view his proceedings with no complacency. The truly venerable, and the truly happy, must have the fortitude to maintain his individuality. If he indulge in the gratifications, and cultivate the feelings of man, he must at the same time be strenuous in following the train of his disquisitions, and exercising the powers of his understanding.

The objectors of a former chapter* were partly in the right when they spoke of the endless variety of mind. It would be absurd to say that we are not capable of truth,

* Chap. V.

of evidence and agreement. In these respects, so far as mind is in a state of progressive improvement, we are perpetually coming nearer to each other. But there are subjects about which we shall continually differ, and ought to differ. The ideas, associations and circumstances of each man are properly his own; and it is a pernicious system that would lead us to require all men, however different their circumstances, to act by a precise general rule. Add to this that, by the doctrine of progressive improvement, we shall always be erroneous, though we shall every day become less erroneous. The proper method for hastening the decline of error, and producing uniformity of judgement, is not by brute force, by laws, or by imitation; but, on the contrary, by exciting every man to think for himself.

From these principles it appears that everything that is usually understood by the term co-operation is, in some degree, an evil. A man in solitude is obliged to sacrifice or postpone the execution of his best thoughts, in compliance with his necessities, or his frailties. How many admirable designs have perished in the conception, by means of this circumstance? It is still worse when a man is also obliged to consult the convenience of others. If I be expected to eat or to work in conjunction with my neighbour, it must either be at a time most convenient to me, or to him, or to neither of us. We cannot be reduced to a clockwork uniformity.

Hence it follows that all supererogatory co-operation is carefully to be avoided, common labour and common meals. 'But what shall we say to a co-operation that seems dictated by the nature of the work to be performed?' It ought to be diminished. There is probably considerably more of injury in the concert of industry than of sympathies. At present, it is unreasonable to doubt that the consideration of the evil of co-operation is, in certain urgent cases, to be postponed to that urgency. Whether, by the nature of things, co-operation of some sort will always be necessary is a question we are scarcely competent to decide. At present, to pull down a tree, to cut a canal, to navigate a vessel, require the labour of many. Will they always require the labour of many? When we recollect the complicated machines of human contrivance, various sorts of mills, of weaving engines, steam engines, are we not astonished at the compendium of labour they produce? Who shall say where this species of improvement must stop? At present, such inventions alarm the labouring part of the community; and they may be productive of temporary distress, though they conduce, in the sequel, to the most important interests of the multitude. But, in a state of equal labour, their utility will be liable to no dispute. Hereafter it is by no means clear that the most extensive operations will not be within the reach of one man; or, to make use of a familiar instance, that a plough may not be turned into a field, and perform its office without the need of superintendence. It was in this sense that the celebrated Franklin conjectured that 'mind would one day become omnipotent over matter'.*

The conclusion of the progress which has here been sketched is something like a final close to the necessity of manual labour. It may be instructive in such cases to observe how the sublime geniuses of former times anticipated what seems likely to be the future improvement of mankind. It was one of the laws of Lycurgus that no Spartan should be employed in manual labour. For this purpose, under his system, it was necessary that they should be plentifully supplied with slaves devoted to drudgery. Matter, or, to speak more accurately, the certain and unintermitting laws of the universe, will be the Helots of the period we are contemplating. We shall end in this respect, oh immortal legislator! at the point from which you began.

To return to the subject of co-operation. It may be a

---

* I have no authority to quote for this expression but the conversation of Doctor Price.[43] I am happy to find upon enquiry, that Mr William Morgan, the nephew of Dr Price, and editor of his works, distinctly recollects to have heard it from his uncle.

curious speculation to attend to the progressive steps by which this feature of human society may be expected to decline. For example: shall we have concerts of music? The miserable state of mechanism of the majority of the performers is so conspicuous as to be, even at this day, a topic of mortification and ridicule. Will it not be practicable hereafter for one man to perform the whole? Shall we have theatrical exhibitions? This seems to include an absurd and vicious co-operation. It may be doubted whether men will hereafter come forward in any mode formally to repeat words and ideas that are not their own? It may be doubted whether any musical performer will habitually execute the compositions of others? We yield supinely to the superior merit of our predecessors, because we are accustomed to indulge the inactivity of our faculties. All formal repetition of other men's ideas seems to be a scheme for imprisoning, for so long a time, the operations of our own mind. It borders perhaps, in this respect, upon a breach of sincerity, which requires that we should give immediate utterance to every useful and valuable idea that occurs.

Having ventured to state these hints and conjectures, let us endeavour to mark the limits of individuality. Every man that receives an impression from any external object has the current of his own thoughts modified by force; and yet, without external impressions, we should be nothing. Every man that reads the composition of another suffers the succession of his ideas to be, in a considerable degree, under the direction of his author. But it does not seem as if this would ever form a sufficient objection against reading. One man will always have stored up reflections and facts that another wants; and mature and digested discourse will perhaps always, in equal circumstances, be superior to that which is extempore. Conversation is a species of co-operation, one or the other party always yielding to have his ideas guided by the other; yet conversation, and the intercourse of mind with mind, seem to be the most fertile sources of improvement. It is here as it is with punishment. He that, in the gentlest manner, undertakes to reason another out of his vices will probably occasion pain; but this species of punishment ought, upon no account, to be superseded.

Let not these views of the future individuality of man be misapprehended, or overstrained. We ought to be able to do without one another. He is the most perfect man to whom society is not a necessary of life, but a luxury, innocent and enviable, in which he joyfully indulges. Such a man will not fly to society, as to something requisite for the consuming of his time, or the refuge of his weakness. In society he will find pleasure; the temper of his mind will prepare him for friendship and for love. But he will resort with a scarcely inferior eagerness to solitude; and will find in it the highest complacence and the purest delight.

Another article which belongs to the subject of co-operation is cohabitation. The evils attendant on this practice are obvious. In order to the human understanding's being successfully cultivated, it is necessary that the intellectual operations of men should be independent of each other.* We should avoid such practices as are calculated to melt our opinions into a common mould. Cohabitation is also hostile to that fortitude which should accustom a man, in his actions, as well as in his opinions, to judge for himself, and feel competent to the discharge of his own duties. Add to this, that it is absurd to expect the inclinations and wishes of two human beings to coincide, through any long period of time. To oblige them to act and to live together is to subject them to some inevitable portion of thwarting, bickering and unhappiness. This cannot be otherwise, so long as men shall continue to vary in their habits, their preferences and their views. No man is always cheerful and kind; and it is better that his fits of irritation should subside of themselves, since the mischief in that case is more limited,

* Book IV, Chap. III, p. 284.

and since the jarring of opposite tempers, and the suggestions of a wounded pride, tend inexpressibly to increase the irritation. When I seek to correct the defects of a stranger, it is with urbanity and good humour. I have no idea of convincing him through the medium of surliness and invective. But something of this kind inevitably obtains where the intercourse is too unremitted.

The subject of cohabitation is particularly interesting as it includes in it the subject of marriage. It will therefore be proper to pursue the enquiry in greater detail. The evil of marriage, as it is practised in European countries, extends further than we have yet described. The method is for a thoughtless and romantic youth of each sex to come together, to see each other, for a few times and under circumstances full of delusion, and then to vow eternal attachment. What is the consequence of this? In almost every instance they find themselves deceived. They are reduced to make the best of an irretrievable mistake. They are led to conceive it their wisest policy to shut their eyes upon realities, happy, if, by any perversion of intellect, they can persuade themselves that they were right in their first crude opinion of each other. Thus the institution of marriage is made a system of fraud; and men who carefully mislead their judgements in the daily affair of their life must be expected to have a crippled judgement in every other concern.

Add to this that marriage, as now understood, is a monopoly, and the worst of monopolies. So long as two human beings are forbidden, by positive institution, to follow the dictates of their own mind, prejudice will be alive and vigorous. So long as I seek, by despotic and artificial means, to maintain my possession of a woman, I am guilty of the most odious selfishness. Over this imaginary prize, men watch with perpetual jealousy; and one man finds his desire, and his capacity to circumvent, as much excited as the other is excited to traverse his projects, and frustrate his hopes. As long as this state of society continues, philanthropy will be crossed and checked in a thousand ways, and the still augmenting stream of abuse will continue to flow.

The abolition of the present system of marriage appears to involve no evils. We are apt to represent that abolition to ourselves as the harbinger of brutal lust and depravity. But it really happens, in this, as in other cases, that the positive laws which are made to restrain our vices irritate and multiply them. Not to say that the same sentiments of justice and happiness which, in a state of equality, would destroy our relish for expensive gratifications might be expected to decrease our inordinate appetites of every kind, and to lead us universally to prefer the pleasures of intellect to the pleasures of sense.

It is a question of some moment whether the intercourse of the sexes, in a reasonable state of society, would be promiscuous, or whether each man would select for himself a partner to whom he will adhere as long as that adherence shall continue to be the choice of both parties. Probability seems to be greatly in favour of the latter. Perhaps this side of the alternative is most favourable to population. Perhaps it would suggest itself in preference to the man who would wish to maintain the several propensities of his frame, in the order due to their relative importance, and to prevent a merely sensual appetite from engrossing excessive attention. It is scarcely to be imagined that this commerce, in any state of society, will be stripped of its adjuncts, and that men will as willingly hold it with a woman whose personal and mental qualities they disapprove as with one of a different description. But it is the nature of the human mind to persist, for a certain length of time, in its opinion or choice. The parties therefore, having acted upon selection, are not likely to forget this selection when the interview is over. Friendship, if by friendship we understand that affection for an individual which is measured singly by what we know of his worth, is one of the most exquisite gratifications, perhaps one of the most improving exercises, of a rational mind. Friendship therefore may be expected to come in aid of the sexual intercourse, to refine its grossness, and increase its delight. All these arguments are calculated to determine our judgement in favour of marriage as a salutary and respectable institution, but not of that species of marriage in which there is no room for repentance and to which liberty and hope are equally strangers.

Admitting these principles therefore as the basis of the sexual commerce, what opinion ought we to form respecting infidelity to this attachment? Certainly no ties ought to be imposed upon either party, preventing them from quitting the attachment, whenever their judgement directs them to quit it. With respect to such infidelities as are compatible with an intention to adhere to it, the point of principal importance is a determination to have recourse to no species of disguise. In ordinary cases, and where the periods of absence are of no long duration, it would seem that any inconstancy would reflect some portion of discredit on the person that practised it. It would argue that the person's propensities were not under that kind of subordination which virtue and self-government appear to prescribe. But inconstancy, like any other temporary dereliction, would not be found incompatible with a character of uncommon excellence. What, at present, renders it, in many instances, peculiarly loathsome is its being practised in a clandestine manner. It leads to a train of falsehood and a concerted hypocrisy, than which there is scarcely anything that more eminently depraves and degrades the human mind.

The mutual kindness of persons of an opposite sex will, in such a state, fall under the same system as any other species of friendship. Exclusively of groundless and obstinate attachments, it will be impossible for me to live in the world without finding in one man a worth superior to that of another. To this man I shall feel kindness in exact proportion to my apprehension of his worth. The case will be the same with respect to the other sex. I shall assiduously cultivate the intercourse of that woman whose moral and intellectual accomplishments strike me in the most powerful manner. But 'it may happen that other men will feel for her the same preference that I do'. This will create no difficulty. We may all enjoy her conversation; and, her choice being declared, we shall all be wise enough to consider the sexual commerce as unessential to our regard. It is a mark of the extreme depravity of our present habits that we are inclined to suppose the sexual commerce necessary to the advantages arising from the purest friendship. It is by no means indispensable that the female to whom each man attaches himself in that matter should appear to each the most deserving and excellent of her sex.

Let us consider the way in which this state of society will modify education. It may be imagined that the abolition of the present system of marriage would make education, in a certain sense, the affair of the public; though, if there be any truth in the reasonings of this work, to provide for it by the positive institutions of a community would be extremely inconsistent with the true principles of an intellectual nature.* Education may be regarded as consisting of various branches. First, the personal cares which the helpless state of an infant requires. These will probably devolve upon the mother; unless, by frequent parturition, or by the nature of these cares, that be found to render her share of the burthen unequal; and then it will be amicably and willingly participated by others. Secondly, food and other necessary supplies. These will easily find their true level, and spontaneously flow, from the quarter in which they abound, to the quarter that is deficient. Lastly, the term education may be used to signify instruction. The task of instruction, under such a form of society, will be greatly simplified and altered from what it is at present. It will then scarcely be thought more necessary to make boys slaves than to make men so. The business will not then be to bring forward so many adepts in the egg-shell, that the vanity of parents may be flattered by hearing their praises. No man will

* Book VI, Chap. VIII.

think of vexing with premature learning the feeble and inexperienced, lest, when they came to years of discretion, they should refuse to be learned. The mind will be suffered to expand itself in proportion as occasion and impression shall excite it, and not tortured and enervated by being cast in a particular mould. No creature in human form will be expected to learn anything but because he desires it, and has some conception of its value; and every man, in proportion to his capacity, will be ready to furnish such general hints and comprehensive views as will suffice for the guidance and encouragement of him who studies from the impulse of desire.

These observations lead us to the consideration of one additional difficulty, which relates to the division of labour. Shall each man manufacture his tools, furniture and accommodations? This would perhaps be a tedious operation. Every man performs the task to which he is accustomed, more skilfully, and in a shorter time than another. It is reasonable that you should make for me that which perhaps I should be three or four times as long in making, and should make imperfectly at last. Shall we then introduce barter and exchange? By no means. The moment I require any further reason for supplying you than the cogency of your claim, the moment, in addition to the dictates of benevolence, I demand a prospect of reciprocal advantage to myself, there is an end of that political justice and pure society of which we treat.

The division of labour, as it has been developed by commercial writers, is the offspring of avarice. It has been found that ten persons can make two hundred and forty times as many pins in a day as one person.* This refinement is the growth of monopoly. The object is to see into how vast a surface the industry of the lower classes may be beaten, the more completely to gild over the indolent and the proud. The ingenuity of the merchant is whetted by new improvements of this sort to transport more of the wealth of the powerful into his coffers. The practic-

* Smith's *Wealth of Nations*, Book I, Chap. I.

ability of effecting a compendium of labour by this means will be greatly diminished when men shall learn to deny themselves partial superfluities. The utility of such a saving of labour, where labour shall be changed from a burthen into an amusement, will scarcely balance the evils of so extensive a co-operation. From what has been said it appears that there will be a division of labour if we compare the society in question with the state of the solitaire and the savage. But it will produce an extensive simplification of labour if we compare it with that to which we are at present accustomed in civilized Europe.

CHAPTER IX

OBJECTION TO THIS SYSTEM FROM THE PRINCIPLE OF POPULATION

Objection stated. – Opinions that have been entertained on this subject. – Population adapted to find its own level. – Precautions that have been exerted to check it. – Conclusion.

AN author who has speculated widely upon subjects of government* has recommended equality (or, which was rather his idea, a community of goods to be maintained by the vigilance of the state), as a complete remedy for the usurpation and distress which are, at present, the most powerful enemies of human kind; for the vices which infect education in some instances, and the neglect it encounters in more; for all the turbulence of passion, and all the injustice of selfishness. But, after having exhibited this brilliant picture, he finds an argument that demolishes the whole, and restores him to indifference or despair, in 'the excessive population that would ensue'.

* Wallace: *Various Prospects of Mankind, Nature and Providence*, 1761.

The question of population, as it relates to the science of politics and society, is considerably curious. Several writers upon these topics have treated it in a way calculated to produce a very gloomy impression, and have placed precautions to counteract the multiplication of the human species among the most important objects of civil prudence. These precautions appear to have occupied much attention in several ancient nations, among whom there prevailed a great solicitude that the number of citizens in the state should suffer no augmentation. In modern times a contrary opinion has frequently obtained, and the populousness of a country has been said to constitute its true wealth and prosperity.

Perhaps however express precautions in either kind are superfluous and nugatory. There is a principle in the nature of human society by means of which everything seems to tend to its level, and to proceed in the most auspicious way, when least interfered with by the mode of regulation. In a certain stage of the social progress, population seems rapidly to increase; this appears to be the case in the United States of America. In a subsequent stage, it undergoes little change, either in the way of increase or diminution; this is the case in the more civilized countries of Europe. The number of inhabitants in a country will perhaps never be found, in the ordinary course of affairs, greatly to increase beyond the facility of subsistence.

Nothing is more easy than to account for this circumstance. So long as there is a facility of subsistence, men will be encouraged to early marriages, and to a careful rearing of their children. In America, it is said, men congratulate themselves upon the increase of their families as upon a new accession of wealth. The labour of their children, even in an early stage, soon redeems, and even repays with interest, the expense and effort of rearing them. In such countries the wages of the labourer are high, for the number of labourers bears no proportion to the demand, and to the general spirit of enterprise. In many European countries, on the other hand, a large family has become a proverbial expression for an uncommon degree of poverty and wretchedness. The price of labour in any state, so long as the spirit of accumulation shall prevail, is an infallible barometer of the state of its population. It is impossible where the price of labour is greatly reduced, and an added population threatens a still further reduction, that men should not be considerably under the influence of fear, respecting an early marriage, and a numerous family.

There are various methods by the practice of which population may be checked; by the exposing of children, as among the ancients, and, at this day, in China; by the art of procuring abortion, as it is said to subsist in the island of Ceylon; by a promiscuous intercourse of the sexes, which is found extremely hostile to the multiplication of the species; or, lastly, by a systematical abstinence, such as must be supposed, in some degree, to prevail in monasteries of either sex. But, without any express institution of this kind, the encouragement or discouragement that arises from the general state of a community will probably be found to be all-powerful in its operation.

Supposing however that population were not thus adapted to find its own level, it is obvious to remark upon the objection of this chapter that to reason thus is to foresee difficulties at a great distance. Three fourths of the habitable globe are now uncultivated. The improvements to be made in cultivation, and the augmentations the earth is capable of receiving in the article of productiveness, cannot, as yet be reduced to any limits of calculation. Myriads of centuries of still increasing population may pass away, and the earth be yet found sufficient for the support of its inabitants. It were idle therefore to conceive discouragement from so distant a contingency. The rational anticipations of human improvement are unlimited, not eternal. The very globe that we inhabit, and the solar system, may, for anything that we know, be subject to decay. Physical casualties of different denominations may interfere with the progressive nature of intellect. But, putting these out of the question, it is certainly most reasonable to commit so remote a danger to the chance of such remedies (remedies of which perhaps we may, at this time, not have the smallest idea) as shall suggest themselves at a period sufficiently early for their practical application.

Appendix

OF HEALTH, AND THE PROLONGATION OF HUMAN LIFE

Omnipotence of mind. – Application of this principle to the animal frame. – Causes of decrepitude. – Theory of voluntary and involuntary action. – Present utility of these reasonings. – Recapitulation. – Application to the future state of society.

THE question respecting population is, in some degree, connected with the subject of health and longevity. It may therefore be allowed us to make use of this occasion for indulging in certain speculations upon this article. What follows must be considered as eminently a deviation into the land of conjecture. If it be false, it leaves the system to which it is apppended, in all sound reason, as impregnable as ever.

Let us then, in this place, return to the sublime conjecture of Franklin, a man habitually conversant with the system of the external universe, and by no means propense to extravagant speculations, that 'mind will one day become omnipotent over matter'.* The sense which

* Chap. VIII, Appendiix, p. 759. The authors who have published their conjectures respecting the possibility of extending the term of human life are many. The most illustrious of these is probably lord Bacon; the most recent is Condorcet,[44] in his *Out-*

he annexed to this expression seems to have related to the improvements of human invention, in relation to machines and the compendium of labour. But, if the power of intellect can be established over all other matter, are we not inevitably led to ask why not over the matter of our own bodies? If over matter at however great a distance, why not over matter which, ignorant as we may be of the tie that connects it with the thinking principle, we seem always to carry about with us, and which is our medium of comunication with the external universe?

The different cases in which thought modifies the structure and members of the human body are obvious to all. First, they are modified by our voluntary thoughts or design. We desire to stretch out our hand, and it is stretched out. We perform a thousand operations of the same species every day, and their familiarity annihilates the wonder. They are not in themselves less wonderful than any of those modifications we are least accustomed to conceive. Secondly, mind modifies body involuntarily. To omit, for the present, what has been offered upon this subject by way of hypothesis and inference,* there are many instances in which this fact presents itself in the most unequivocal manner. Has not a sudden piece of good news been frequently found to dissipate a corporal indisposition? Is it not still more usual for mental impressions to produce indisposition, and even what is called a broken heart? And shall we believe that that which is so powerful in mischief can be altogether impotent for happiness? How common is the remark that those accidents which are to the indolent a source of disease are forgotten and extirpated in the busy and active? I walk twenty miles in

_____

lines of a *History of the Progress of the Human Mind*, published since the first appearance of this work. These authors however have inclined to rest their hopes rather upon the growing perfection of art than, as is here done, upon the immediate and unavoidable operation of an improved intellect.

* Book IV, Chap. IX.

an indolent and half determined temper, and am extremely fatigued. I walk twenty miles full of ardour, and with a motive that engrosses my soul, and I arrive as fresh and alert as when I began my journey. Emotion, excited by some unexpected word, by a letter that is delivered to us, occasions the most extraordinary revolutions in our frame, accelerates the circulation, causes the heart to palpitate, the tongue to refuse its office, and has been known to occasion death by extreme anguish or extreme joy. There is nothing of which the physician is more frequently aware than of the power of the mind in assisting or retarding convalescence.

Why is it that a mature man loses that elasticity of limb which characterizes the heedless gaiety of youth? The origin of this appears to be that he desists from youthful habits. He assumes an air of dignity, incompatible with the lightness of childish sallies. He is visited and vexed with the cares that rise out of our mistaken institutions, and his heart is no longer satisfied and gay. His limbs become stiff, unwieldy and awkward. This is the forerunner of old age and of death.

A habit peculiarly favourable to corporeal vigour is cheerfulness. Every time that our mind becomes morbid, vacant and melancholy, our external frame falls into disorder. Listlessness of thought is the brother of death. But cheerfulness gives new elasticity to our limbs, and circulation to our juices. Nothing can long be stagnant in the frame of him whose heart is tranquil, and his imagination active.

A further requisite in the case of which we treat is clear and distinct apprehension. Disease seems perhaps in all instances to be the concomitant of confusion. When reason resigns the helm, and our ideas fluctuate without order or direction, we sleep. Delirium and insanity are of the same nature. Fainting appears principally to consist in a relaxation of intellect, so that the ideas seem to mix in painful disorder, and nothing is distinguished. He that continues to act, or is led to a renewal of action with perspicuity and decision, is almost inevitably a man in health.

The surest source of cheerfulness is benevolence. To a youthful mind, while everything strikes with its novelty, the individual situation must be peculiarly unfortunate, if gaiety of thought be not produced, or, when interrupted, do not speedily return with its healing virtue. But novelty is a fading charm, and perpetually decreases. Hence the approach of inanity and listlessness. After we have made a certain round, life delights no more. A deathlike apathy invades us. Thus the aged are generally cold and indifferent; nothing interests their attention, or rouses their sluggishness. How should it be otherwise? The objects of human pursuit are commonly frigid and contemptible, and the mistake comes at last to be detected. But virtue is a charm that never fades. The mind that overflows with kindness and sympathy will always be cheerful. The man who is perpetually busied in contemplations of public good can scarcely be inactive. Add to this, that a benevolent temper is peculiarly irreconcileable with those sentiments of anxiety, discontent, rage, revenge and despair which so powerfully corrode the frame, and hourly consign their miserable victims to an untimely grave.

Thus far we have discoursed of a negative power which, if sufficiently exercised, would, it is to be presumed, eminently tend to the prolongation of human life. But there is a power of another description, which seems entitled to our attention in this respect. We have frequently had occasion to point out the distinction between our voluntary and involuntary motions.* We have seen that they are continually running into each other; our involuntary motions gradually becoming subject to the power of volition, and our voluntary motions degenerating into involuntary. We concluded in an early part of this work,† and that, as it should seem, with sufficient

* Book I, Chap. V: Book IV, Chap. VII, X.
† Book I, Chap. V, § 2.

reason, that the true perfection of man was to attain, as nearly as possible, to the perfectly voluntary state; that we ought to be, upon all occasions, prepared to render a reason of our actions; and should remove ourselves to the furthest distance from the state of mere inanimate machines, acted upon by causes of which they have no understanding.

Our involuntary motions are frequently found gradually to become subject to the power of volition. It seems impossible to set limits to this species of metamorphosis. Its reality cannot be questioned, when we consider that every motion of the human frame was originally involuntary.* Is it not then highly probable, in the process of human improvement, that we may finally obtain an empire over every articulation of our frame? The circulation of the blood is a motion, in our present state, eminently involuntary. Yet nothing is more obvious than that certain thoughts, and states of the thinking faculty, are calculated to affect this process. Reasons have been adduced which seem to lead to an opinion that thought and animal motion are, in all cases, to be considered as antecedent and consequent.† We can now perhaps by an effort of the mind correct certain commencing irregularities of the system, and forbid, in circumstances where those phenomena would otherwise appear, the heart to palpitate, and the limbs to tremble. The voluntary power of some men over their animal frame is found to extend to various articles in which other men are impotent.

A further probability will be reflected upon these conjectures if we recollect the picture which was formerly exhibited,‡ of the rapidity of the succession of ideas. If we can have a series of three hundred and twenty ideas in a second of time, why should it be supposed that we may not hereafter arrive at the skill of carrying on a great number of contemporaneous processes without disorder?

* Book IV, Chap. IX, p. 364.
† Book IV, Chap. IX.
‡ Book IV, Chap. IX, p. 369.

Nothing can be more irreconcilable to analogy than to conclude, because a certain species of power is beyond the train of our present observations, that it is beyond the limits of the human mind.* We talk familiarly indeed of the extent of our faculties; and our vanity prompts us to suppose that we have reached the goal of human capacity. But there is little plausibility in so arrogant an assumption. If it could have been told to the savage inhabitants of Europe in the times of Theseus and Achilles that man was capable of predicting eclipses and weighing the air, of reducing to settled rules the phenomena of nature so that no prodigies should remain, and of measuring the distance and size of the heavenly bodies, this would not have appeared to them less incredible than if we had told them of the possibility of maintaining the human body in perpetual youth and vigour. But we have not only this analogy, showing that the discovery in question forms, as it were, a regular branch of the acquisitions that belong to an intellectual nature; but, in addition to this, we seem to have a glimpse of the manner in which the acquisition will be secured.

One remark may be proper in this place. If the remedies here proposed tend to a total extirpation of the infirmities of our nature, then, though we should not be able to promise them an early or complete success, we may probably find them of some utility. They may contribute to prolong our vigour, if not to immortalize it, and, which is of more consequence, to make us live while we live. Every time the mind is invaded with anguish and gloom, the frame becomes disordered. Every time languor and indifference creep upon us, our functions fall into decay. In proportion as we cultivate fortitude and equanimity, our circulations will be cheerful. In proportion as we cultivate a kind and benevolent propensity, we may be secure of finding something to interest and engage us.

Medicine may reasonably be stated to consist of two branches, animal and intellectual. The latter of these

* Book I, Chap. VIII.

has been infinitely too much neglected. It cannot be employed to the purposes of a profession; or, where it has been incidentally so employed, it has been artificially and indirectly, not in an open and avowed manner. 'Herein the patient must minister to himself.'* It would no doubt be of extreme moment to us to be thoroughly acquainted with the power of motives, perseverance, and what is called resolution, in this respect.

The sum of the arguments which have been here offered amounts to a species of presumption that the term of human life may be prolonged, and that by the immediate operation of intellect, beyond any limits which we are able to assign. It would be idle to talk of the absolute immortality of man. Eternity and immortality are phrases to which it is impossible for us to annex any distinct ideas, and the more we attempt to explain them, the more we shall find ourselves involved in contradiction.

To apply these remarks to the subject of population. One tendency of a cultivated and virtuous mind is to diminish our eagerness for the gratifications of the senses. They please at present by their novelty, that is, because we know not how to estimate them. They decay in the decline of life, indirectly because the system refuses them, but directly and principally because they no longer excite the ardour of the mind. The gratifications of sense please at present by their imposture. We soon learn to despise the mere animal function, which, apart from the delusions of intellect, would be nearly the same in all cases; and to value it only as it happens to be relieved by personal charms or mental excellence.

The men therefore whom we are supposing to exist, when the earth shall refuse itself to a more extended population, will probably cease to propagate. The whole will be a people of men, and not of children. Generation will not succeed generation, nor truth have, in a certain degree, to recommence her career every thirty years. Other improvements may be expected to keep pace with

* Shakespeare: *Macbeth*, Act V.

those of health and longevity. There will be no war, no crimes, no administration of justice, as it is called, and no government. Beside this, there will be neither disease, anguish, melancholy, nor resentment. Every man will seek, with ineffable ardour, the good of all. Mind will be active and eager, yet never disappointed. Men will see the progressive advancement of virtue and good, and feel that, if things occasionally happen contrary to their hopes, the miscarriage itself was a necessary part of that progress. They will know that they are members of the chain, that each has his several utility, and they will not feel indifferent to that utility. They will be eager to enquire into the good that already exists, the means by which it was produced, and the greater good that is yet in store. They will never want motives for exertion; for that benefit which a man thoroughly understands and earnestly loves he cannot refrain from endeavouring to promote.

Before we dismiss this subject it is proper once again to remind the reader that the substance of this appendix is given only as matter of probable conjecture, and that the leading argument of this division of the work is altogether independent of its truth or falsehood.

CHAPTER X

REFLECTIONS

WE have now taken a general survey of the system of equality, and there remains only to state a few incidental remarks with which it may be proper to wind up the subject.

No idea has excited greater horror in the minds of a multitude of persons than that of the mischiefs that will ensue from the dissemination of what they call levelling principles. They believe 'that these principles will inevitably ferment in the minds of the vulgar, and that the attempt to carry them into execution will be attended with every species of calamity'. They represent to themselves 'the uninformed and uncivilized part of mankind, as let loose from restraint, and hurried into every kind of excess. Knowledge and taste, the improvements of intellect, the discoveries of sages, the beauties of poetry and art, are trampled under foot and extinguished by barbarians. It is another inundation of Goths and Vandals, with this bitter aggravation, that the viper that stings us to death was fostered in our own bosom'. They conceive the scene as beginning in massacre. They suppose 'all that is great, preeminent and illustrious as ranking among the first victims. Such as are distinguished by peculiar refinement of manners, or energy of understanding and virtue, will be the inevitable objects of envy and jealousy. Such as intrepidly exert themselves to succour the persecuted, or to declare to the public what they are least inclined, but is most necessary for them, to hear, will be marked out for assassination.'

Whatever may be the abstract recommendations of the system of equality, we must not allow ourselves any such partiality upon a subject in which the welfare of the species is involved as should induce us to shrink from a due attention to the ideas here exhibited. Massacre is the too possible attendant upon revolution, and massacre is perhaps the most hateful scene, allowing for its momentary duration, that any imagination can suggest. The fearful, hopeless expectation of the defeated, and the blood-hound fury of their conquerors, is a complication of mischief that all which has been told of infernal regions can scarcely surpass. The cold-blooded massacres that are perpetrated under the name of criminal justice fall short of these in some of their most frightful aggravations. The ministers and instruments of law have by custom reconciled their minds to the dreadful task they perform, and often bear their parts in the most shocking enormities without being sensible to the passions allied to these enormities. They do not always accompany their murders with the rudeness of an insulting triumph; and, as they conduct themselves, in a certain sort, by known principles of injustice, the evil we have reason to apprehend has its limits. But the instruments of massacre are discharged from every restraint. Whatever their caprice dictates, their hands are instantly employed to perpetrate. Their eyes emit flashes of cruelty and rage. They pursue their victims from street to street and from house to house. They tear them from the arms of their fathers and their wives. They glut themselves with barbarity, and utter shouts of horrid joy at the spectacle of tortures.

In answer to this representation it has sometimes been alleged by the friends of reform 'that the advantages possessed by a system of liberty are so great, as to be worth purchasing at any price; that the evils of the most sanguinary revolution are temporary; that the vices of despotism, which few pens indeed have ventured to record in all their demerits, are scarcely less atrocious in the hour of their commission, and infinitely more terrible by their extent and duration; and finally, that the crimes perpetrated in a revolutionary movement can in no just estimate be imputed to the innovators; that they were engendered by the preceding oppression, and ought to be regarded as the last struggles of expiring tyranny'.

But, not to repeat arguments that have already been fully exhibited,* it must be recollected that 'the benefits which innovation may seem to promise are not to be regarded as certain. After all, it may not be utterly impossible that the nature of man will always remain, for the most part, unaltered, and that he will be found incapable of that degree of knowledge and constancy which seems essential to a liberal democracy or a pure equality. However cogent may be the arguments for the practicability of human improvement, is it then justifiable, upon the mere credit of predictions, to expose mankind to the greatest calamities? Who that has a just conception of the nature of human understanding will vindicate such a proceeding? A careful enquirer is always detecting his past errors; each year of his life produces a severe comment upon the opinions of the last; he suspects all his judgements, and is certain of none. We wander in the midst of appearances; and plausible appearances are to be found on all sides. The wisest men perhaps have generally proved the most confirmed sceptics. Speculations therefore upon the new modes in which human affairs may be combined, different from any that occur in the

* Book IV, Chap. I, II.

history of past ages, may seem fitter to amuse men of acuteness and leisure than to be depended on in deciding the dearest interests of mankind. Proceedings the effects of which have been verified by experience furnish a surer ground of dependence than the most laboured reason can afford us in regard to schemes as yet untried.'

Undoubtedly in the views here detailed there is considerable force; and it would be well if persons who are eager to effect abrupt changes in human society would give them an attentive consideration. They do not however sufficiently apply to the question proposed to be examined. Our enquiry was not respecting revolution, but disquisition. We are not concerned to vindicate any species of violence; we do not assume that levelling principles are to be acted upon through the medium of force; we have simply affirmed that he who is persuaded of their truth ought to endeavour to render them a subject of attention. To be convinced of this we have only to consider the enormous and unquestionable political evils that are daily before our eyes, and the probability there is that, by temperate investigation, these evils may be undermined, with little or no tumultuary concussion.* In every affair of human life we are obliged to act upon a simple probability; and therefore, while it is highly worthy of a conscientious philanthropist to recollect the universal uncertainty of opinion, he is bound not to abstain from acting, with caution and sobriety, upon the judgements of his understanding, from a fear left, at the time that he intends to produce benefit, he should unintentionally be the occasion of evil.

But there is another consideration worthy of serious attention in this place. Granting, for a moment, the utmost weight to the objections of those who remind us of the mischief of political experiments, it is proper to ask, Can we suppress discussion? Can we arrest the progress of the enquiring mind? If we can, it must be by the most unmitigated despotism. Intellect has a perpetual

* Book IV, Chap. II.

tendency to proceed. It cannot be held back, but by a power that counteracts its genuine tendency, through every moment of its existence. Tyrannical and sanguinary must be the measures employed for this purpose. Miserable and disgustful must be the scene they produce. Their result will be barbarism, ignorance, superstition, servility, hypocrisy. This is the alternative, so far as there is any alternative in their choice, to which those who are impowered to consult for the general welfare must inevitably resort, if the suppression of enquiry be the genuine dictate of public interest.

Such has been, for the most part, the policy of governments through every age of the world. Have we slaves? We assiduously retain them in ignorance. Have we colonies and dependencies? The great effort of our care is to keep them from being populous and prosperous. Have we subjects? It is 'by impotence and misery that we endeavour to render them supple: plenty is fit only to make them unmanageable, disobedient and mutinous'.* If this were the true philosophy of social institutions, well might we shrink from it with horror. How tremendous an abortion would the human species be if all that tended to invigorate their understandings tended to make them unprincipled and profligate!

In the meantime it ought not to be forgotten that to say that a knowledge of political truth can be injurious to the true interests of mankind is to affirm an express contradiction. Political truth is that science which teaches us to weigh in the balance of an accurate judgement, the different proceedings that may be adopted, for the purpose of giving welfare and prosperity to communities of men. The only way in which discussion can be a reasonable object of terror is by its power of giving to falsehood, under certain circumstances, the speciousness of truth, or by that partial propagation the tendency of which is to intoxicate and mislead those understandings that, by

* Book V, Chap. III, p. 426.

an adequate instruction, would have been sobered and enlightened.

These considerations will scarcely permit us to doubt that it is the duty of governments to maintain the most inflexible neutrality, and of individuals to publish the truths with which they appear to be acquainted. The more truth is discovered, the more it is known in its true dimensions, and not in parts, the less is it possible that it should coalesce with, or leave room for the effects of, error. The true philanthropist, instead of suppressing discussion, will be eager to take a share in the scene, to exert the full strength of his faculties in investigation, and to contribute by his exertions to render the operation of enquiry at once perspicuous and profound.

The condition of the human species at the present hour is critical and alarming. We are not without grounds of reasonable hope that the issue will be uncommonly beneficial. There is however much to apprehend from the narrow views, and angry passions, of the contending parties. Every interval that can be gained, provided it is not an interval of torpor and indifference, is perhaps to be considered in the light of an advantage.

Meanwhile, in proportion as the just apprehensions of explosion shall increase, there are high duties incumbent upon every branch of the community.

First, upon those who are fitted to be precursor to their fellows in the discovery of truth.

They are bound to be active, indefatigable and disinterested. It is incumbent upon them to abstain from inflammatory language, and expressions of acrimony and resentment. It is absurd in any government to erect itself into a court of criticism in this respect, and to establish a criterion of liberality and decorum*; but, for that very reason, it is doubly incumbent on those who communicate their thoughts to the public to exercise a rigid censure over themselves. The lessons of liberty and equality are lessons of good will to all orders of men. They free the

* Book VI, Chap. VI.

peasant from the iniquity that depresses his mind, and the privileged from the luxury and despotism by which he is corrupted. It is disgraceful to those who teach these lessons, if they stain their benignity by showing that that benignity has not become the inmate of their hearts.

Nor is it less necessary that they should express themselves with explicitness and sincerity. No maxim can be more suspicious than that which teaches us to consult the temper of the times, and tell only as much as we imagine our contemporaries will be able to bear.* This practice is at present almost universal, and it will perhaps not be difficult to observe its pernicious effects. We retail and mangle truth. We impart it to our fellows, not with the liberal measure with which we have received it, but with such parsimony as our own miserable prudence may chance to prescribe. That we may deceive others with a tranquil conscience, we begin with deceiving ourselves. We put shackles upon our minds, and dare not trust ourselves at large in the pursuit of truth. This practice seems to have been greatly promoted by the machinations of party, and the desire of one wise and adventurous leader to lead a troop of weak, timid and selfish adherents in his train. There can scarcely be a sufficient reason why I should not declare in any assembly upon the face of the earth 'that I am a republican'. There is no more reason to apprehend that, being a republican under a monarchical government, I shall enter into a desperate faction to invade the public tranquillity, than if I were monarchical under a republic. Every community of men, as well as every individual, must govern itself according to its ideas of justice.† What I should desire is, not by violence to change its institutions, but by discussion to change its ideas. I have no concern, if I would study merely the public good, with factions or intrigue; but simply to promulgate the truth, and to wait the tranquil progress of conviction. If there be any assembly that cannot bear

* Book III, Chap. VII, p. 251.
† Book III, Chap. VIII; Book IV, Chap. I.

this, of such an assembly I ought to be no member. It probably happens, much oftener than we are willing to imagine, that 'the post of honour', or, which is better, the post of utility, 'is a private station'.*

The dissimulation here censured, beside its ill effects upon him who practises it, and, by degrading and un-nerving his character, upon society at large, has a particular ill consequence with respect to the point we are considering. It lays a mine, and prepares an explosion. This is the tendency of all unnatural restraint. The unfettered progress of investigation is perhaps always salutary. Its advances are gradual, and each step prepares the general mind for that which is to follow. They are sudden and unprepared, and therefore necessarily partial, emanations of truth that have the greatest tendency to deprive men of their sobriety and self-command. Reserve in this respect is calculated, at once, to give a rugged and angry tone to the multitude, whenever they shall happen to dis-cover what is thus concealed, and to mislead the deposi-taries of political power. It soothes them into false security, and prompts them to maintain an inauspicious obstin-acy.

Having considered what it is that belongs in such a crisis to the enlightened and wise, let us next turn our attention to a very different class of society, the rich and great. And here, in the first place, it be remarked that it is a false calculation that leads us universally to despair of having these for the advocates of political jus-tice. Mankind are not so miserably selfish as satirists and courtiers have supposed. We perhaps never engage in any action of moment without having enquired what is the decision of justice respecting it. We are at all times anxious to satisfy ourselves that what our inclinations lead us to do is innocent and right to be done.† Since therefore justice occupies so large a share in the con-templations of the human mind, it cannot reasonably be

* Addison's *Cato*, Act IV.
† Book I, Chap. V, p. 122.

doubted that a strong and commanding view of justice would prove a powerful motive to influence the choice of that description of men we are now considering. But that virtue which, for whatever reason, we have chosen soon becomes recommended to us by a thousand other reasons. We find in it reputation, honour and self-complacence, in addition to the recommendations it derives from impartial justice.

The rich and great are far from callous to views of general felicity, when such views are brought before them with that evidence and attraction of which they are susceptible. From one dreadful disadvantage their minds are free. They have not been soured with unrelenting tyranny, or narrowed by the perpetual pressure of distress. They are peculiarly qualified to judge of the emptiness of that pomp and those gratification which are always most admired when they are seen from a distance. They will frequently be found considerably indifferent to these things, unless confirmed by habit and rendered inveterate by age. If you show them the attractions of gallantry and magnanimity in resigning them, they will often be resigned without reluctance. Wherever accident of any sort has introduced an active mind, there enterprise is a necessary consequence; and there are few persons so inactive as to sit down for ever in the supine enjoyment of the indulgences to which they were born. The same spirit that has led forth the young nobility of successive ages to encounter the hardships of a camp might render them the champions of the cause of equality: nor is it to be believed that the consideration of superior virtue in this latter exertion will be without its effect.

But let us suppose a considerable party of the rich and great to be actuated by no view but to their emolument and ease. It is not difficult to show them that their interest in this sense will admit of no more than a temperate and yielding resistance. To such we may say: 'It is in vain for you to fight against truth. It is like endeavouring with the human hand to stop the inroad of the ocean.

Be wise betimes. Seek your safety in concession. If you will not come over to the standard of political justice, temporize at least with an enemy whom you cannot overcome. Much, inexpressibly much depends upon you. If your proceedings be moderate and judicious, it is not probable that you will suffer the privation even of that injurious indulgence and accommodation to which you are so strongly attached. The genuine progress of political improvement is kind and attentive to the sentiments of all. It changes the opinions of men by insensible degrees; produces nothing by shock and abruptness; and is far from requiring the calamity of any. Confiscation, and the proscription of bodies of men, form no branch of its story. These evils, which by wise and sober men will always be regretted, will in all probability never occur, unless brought on by your indiscretion and obstinacy. Even in the very tempest and fury of explosion, if such an event shall arise, it may perhaps still be in your power to make advantageous conditions, and to be little or nothing sufferers by the change.

'Above all, do not be lulled into a rash and headlong security. Do not imagine that innovation is not at hand; or that the spirit of innovation can be defeated. We have already seen* how much the hypocrisy and instability of the wise and enlightened of the present day, those who confess much, and have a confused view of still more, but dare not examine the whole with a steady and unshrinking eye, are calculated to increase this security. But there is a danger still more palpable. Do not be misled by the unthinking and seemingly general cry of those who have no fixed principles. Addresses have been found in every age a very uncertain criterion of the future conduct of a people. Do not count upon the numerous train of your adherents, retainers and servants. They afford a feeble dependence. They are men, and cannot be unconcerned as to the interests and claims of mankind. Some of them will adhere to you as long as a sordid interest

*pp. 783, 784.

seems to draw them in that direction. But the moment yours shall appear to be the losing cause, the same interest will carry them over to the enemy's standard. They will disappear like the morning's mist.

'Can it be supposed that you are incapable of receiving impression from another argument? Will you feel no compunction at the thought of resisting the greatest of all benefits? Are you content to be regarded by your impartial contemporaries, and to be recollected, as long as your memory shall endure, as the obstinate adversaries of phil-anthropy and justice? Can you reconcile it to your own minds that, for a sordid interest, for the cause of general corruption and abuse, you should be found active in stifling truth, and strangling the new-born happiness of mankind?' Would it were possible to make this argument felt by the enlightened and accomplished advocates of aristocracy! that they could be persuaded to consult neither passion, nor prejudice, nor the reveries of imagination, in deciding so momentous a question! 'We know,' I would say, 'that truth will be triumphant, even though you refuse to be her ally. We do not fear your enmity. But our hearts bleed to see such gallantry, talents and virtue employed in perpetuating the calamities of mankind. We recollect with grief that, when the lustre of your merits shall fill distant generations with astonishment, they will not be less astonished that you could be made the dupes of prejudice, and deliberately surrender the larger portion of the good you might have achieved, and the unqualified affection that might have pursued your memory.'*

* While this sheet is in the press for the third impression, I receive the intelligence of the death of Burke, who was principally in the author's mind while he penned the preceding sentences. In all that is most exalted in talents, I regard him as the inferior of no man that ever adorned the face of earth; and, in the long record of human genius, I can find for him very few equals. In subtlety of discrimination, in magnitude of conception, in sagacity and profoundness of judgement, he was never surpassed. But his characteristic excellencies were vividness and justness of painting,

To the general mass of the adherents of equality, it may be proper to address a few words. 'If there be any force in the arguments of this work, we seem authorized to deduce thus much from them, that truth is irresistible. Let then this axiom be the rudder of our undertakings. Let us not precipitately endeavour to accomplish that today which the dissemination of truth will make unavoidable tomorrow. Let us not over-anxiously watch for occasions and events: of particular events the ascendancy of truth is independent. Let us anxiously refrain from violence: force is not conviction, and is extremely unworthy of the cause of justice. Let us admit into our bosoms neither contempt, animosity, resentment nor revenge. The cause of justice is the cause of humanity. Its advocates should be penetrated with universal good-will.

---

and that boundless wealth of imagination that adorned the most ungrateful subjects, and heightened the most interesting. Of this wealth he was too lavish; and, though it is impossible for the man of taste not to derive gratification from almost every one of his images and metaphors while it passes before him, yet their exuberance subtracts, in no considerable degree, from that irresistibleness and rapidity of general effect which is the highest excellence of composition. No impartial man can recall Burke to his mind without confessing the grandeur and integrity of his feelings of morality, and being convinced that he was eminently both the patriot and the philanthropist. His excellencies however were somewhat tinctured with a vein of dark and saturnine temper; so that the same man strangely united a degree of the rude character of his native island with an urbanity and a susceptibility of the kinder affections that have rarely been paralleled. But his principal defect consisted in this; that the false estimate as to the things entitled to our deference and admiration, which could alone render the aristocracy with whom he lived unjust to his worth, in some degree infected his own mind. He therefore sought wealth and plunged in expense, instead of cultivating the simplicity of independence; and he entangled himself with a petty combination of political men, instead of reserving his illustrious talents unwarped, for the advancement of intellect, and the service of mankind. He has unfortunately left us a memorable example of the power of a corrupt system of government to undermine and divert from their genuine purposes the noblest faculties that have yet been exhibited to the observation of the world.

We should love this cause; for it conduces to the general happiness of mankind. We should love it; for there is not a man that lives who, in the natural and tranquil progress of things, will not be made happier by its approach. The most powerful circumstance by which it has been retarded is the mistake of its adherents, the air of ruggedness, brutishness and inflexibility which they have given to that which, in itself, is all benignity. Nothing less than this could have prevented the great mass of enquirers from bestowing upon it a patient examination. Be it the care of the now increasing advocates of equality to remove this obstacle to the success of their cause. We have but two plain duties, which, if we set out right, it is not easy to mistake. The first is an unwearied attention to the great instrument of justice, reason. We should communicate our sentiments with the utmost frankness. We should endeavour to press them upon the attention of others. In this we should give way to no discouragement. We should sharpen our intellectual weapons; add to the stock of our knowledge; be pervaded with a sense of the magnitude of our cause; and perpetually add to that calm presence of mind and self-possession which must enable us to do justice to our principles. Our second duty is tranquillity.'

It will not be right to pass over a question that will inevitably suggest itself to the mind of the reader. 'If an equalization of conditions be to take place, not by law, regulation or public institution, but only through the private conviction of individuals, in what manner shall it begin?' In answering this question it is not necessary to prove so simple a proposition as that all republicanism, all reduction of ranks and immunities, strongly tends towards an equalization of conditions. If men go on to improve in discernment, and this they certainly will with peculiar rapidity, when the ill-constructed governments which now retard their progress are removed, the same arguments which showed them the injustice of ranks will show them the injustice of one man's wanting that which, while it is in the possession of another, conduces in no respect to his well being.

It is a common error to imagine 'that this injustice will be felt only by the lower orders who suffer from it'; and from thence to conclude 'that it can only be corrected by violence'. But in answer to this it may, in the first place, be observed that all suffer from it, the rich who engross, as well as the poor who want. Secondly, it has been endeavoured to be shown in the course of the present work* that men are not so entirely governed by self-interest as has frequently been supposed. It appears, if possible, still more clearly that the selfish are not governed solely by sensual gratification or the love of gain, but that the desire of eminence and distinction is, in different forms, an universal passion.† Thirdly and principally, the progress of truth is the most powerful of all causes. Nothing can be more improbable than to imagine that theory, in the best sense of the word, is not essentially connected with practice. That which we can be persuaded clearly and distinctly to approve will inevitably modify our conduct. When men shall habitually perceive the folly of individual splendour, and when their neighbours are impressed with a similar disdain, it will be impossible they should pursue the means of it with the same avidity as before.

It will not be difficult to trace, in the progress of modern Europe from barbarism to refinement, a tendency towards the equalization of conditions. In the feudal times, as now in India and other parts of the world, men were born to a certain station, and it was nearly impossible for a peasant to rise to the rank of a noble. Except the nobles, there were no men that were rich; for commerce, either external or internal, had scarcely an existence. Commerce was one engine for throwing down this seemingly impregnable barrier, and shocking the prejudices of nobles, who were sufficiently willing to believe

* Book IV, Chap. X.
† Chap. I, p. 705.

that their retainers were a different species of beings from themselves. Learning was another, and more powerful engine. In all ages of the church we see men of the basest origin rising to the highest eminence. Commerce proved that others could rise to wealth beside those who were cased in mail; but learning proved that the low-born were capable of surpassing their lords. The progressive effect of these ideas may easily be traced. Long after learning began to unfold its powers, its votaries still submitted to those obsequious manners and servile dedications which no man reviews at the present day without astonishment. It is but lately that men have known that intellectual excellence can accomplish its purposes without a patron. At present, among the civilized and well informed, a man of slender income, but of great intellectual powers and a firm and virtuous mind, is constantly received with attention and deference; and his purse-proud neighbour who should attempt to treat him superciliously is sure to encounter a general disapprobation. The inhabitants of distant villages, where long established prejudices are slowly destroyed, would be astonished to see how comparatively small a share wealth has in determining the degree of attention with which men are treated in enlightened circles.

These no doubt are but slight indications. It is with morality in this respect as it is with politics. The progress is at first so slow as, for the most part, to elude the observation of mankind; nor can it be adequately perceived but by the contemplation and comparison of events during a considerable portion of time. After a certain interval, the scene is more fully unfolded, and the advances appear more rapid and decisive. While wealth was everything, it was to be expected that men would acquire it, though at the expense of conscience and integrity. The abstract ideas of justice had not yet been so concentred as to be able to overpower what dazzles the eye, or promises a momentary gratification. In proportion as the monopolies of rank and corporation are abolished, the value of superfluities will decline. In proportion as republicanism gains ground, men will be estimated for what they are, and not for their accidental appendages.

Let us reflect on the gradual consequences of this revolution of opinion. Liberality of dealing will be among its earliest results; and, of consequence, accumulation will become less frequent and enormous. Men will not be disposed, as now, to take advantage of each other's distresses. They will not consider how much they can extort, but how much it is reasonable to require. The master-tradesman who employs labourers under him will be disposed to give a more ample reward to their industry; which he is at present enabled to tax, chiefly by the accidental advantage of possessing a capital. Liberality on the part of his employer will complete in the mind of the artisan what ideas of political justice will probably have begun. He will no longer spend the surplus of his earnings in that dissipation, which is one of the principal of those causes that at present subject him to the arbitrary pleasure of a superior. He will escape from the irresolution of slavery and the fetters of despair, and perceive that independence and ease are scarcely less within his reach than that of any other member of the community. This is an obvious step towards the still further progression, in which the labourer will receive entire whatever the consumer may be required to pay, without having a capitalist, an idle and useless monopolizer, as he will then be found, to fatten upon his spoils.

The same sentiments that lead to liberality of dealing will also lead to liberality of distribution. The trader, who is unwilling to grow rich by extorting from his customers or his workmen, will also refuse to become rich by the not inferior injustice of withholding from his indigent neighbour the gratuitous supply of which he stands in need. The habit which was created in the former case of being contented with moderate gains is closely connected with the habit of being contented with slender accumulation. He that is not anxious to add to his heap will not be reluctant by a benevolent distribution to prevent its increase. Wealth was at one period almost the single object of pursuit that presented itself to the gross and uncultivated mind. Various objects will hereafter divide men's attention, the love of liberty, the love of equality, the pursuits of art and the desire of knowledge. These objects will not, as now, be confined to a few, but will gradually be laid open to all. The love of liberty obviously leads to a sentiment of union, and a disposition to sympathize in the concerns of others. The general diffusion of truth will be productive of general improvement; and men will daily approximate towards those views according to which every object will be appreciated at its true value. Add to which, that the improvement of which we speak is public, and not individual. The progress is the progress of all. Each man will find his sentiments of justice and rectitude echoed by the sentiments of his neighbours. Apostasy will be made eminently improbable, because the apostate will incur, not only his own censure, but the censure of every beholder.

One objection may perhaps be inferred from these considerations. 'If the inevitable progress of improvement insensibly lead towards equality, what need was there of proposing it as a specific object to men's consideration?' The answer to this objection is easy. The improvement in question consists in a knowledge of truth. But our knowledge will be very imperfect, so long as this great branch of universal justice fails to constitute a part of it. All truth is useful; can this truth, which is perhaps the most fundamental of all moral principles, be without its benefit? Whatever be the object towards which mind irresistibly advances, it is of no mean importance to us to have a distinct view of that object. Our advances will thus become accelerated. It is a well known principle of morality 'that he who proposes perfection to himself, though he will inevitably fall short of what he pursues, will make a more rapid progress than he who is contented to aim only at what is imperfect'. The benefits to be derived in the interval from a view of equality as one of the great objects to which we are tending are exceedingly conspicuous. Such a view will strongly conduce to make us disinterested now. It will teach us to look with contempt upon mercantile speculations, commercial prosperity, and the cares of gain. It will impress us with a just apprehension of what it is of which man is capable, and in which his perfection consists; and will fix our ambition and activity upon the worthiest objects. Intellect cannot arrive at any great and illustrious attainment, however much the nature of intellect may carry us towards it, without feeling some presages of its approach; and it is reasonable to believe that, the earlier these presages are introduced, and the more distinct they are made, the more auspicious will be the event.

Editor's Notes

1. 'these volumes': The *Enquiry* was originally published in two volumes. See the Note on the Text.

2. 'Sydney': Algernon Sydney (1622–83), republican writer and activist; author of *Discourses Concerning Government*, executed in 1683 by Charles II.

3. 'Locke': John Locke (1632–1704), philosopher and political theorist; author in 1680 of *The Second Treatise of Civil Government*.

4. 'The author of the *Rights of Man*': Thomas Paine (1737–1809), republican, revolutionary; author of *Common Sense* and *Rights of Man*.

5. 'Rousseau': Jean-Jacques Rousseau (1712–78), famous theorist of democracy; author of numerous works, including *Social Contract* (1762).

6. 'Helvétius': Claude-Adrien Helvétius (1715–71), French writer on politics and education; author of *Of the Spirit* (1758) and *Of Man* (1772).

7. 'salutary prejudices and useful delusions': References to themes found in Edmund Burke's *Reflections on the Revolution in France* (1791), defending ancient ideas and institutions.

8. 'author of the *Characteristics*': Anthony Ashley Cooper, Third Earl of Shaftesbury (1671–1713), philosopher and moralist; author in 1711 of *Characteristics of Men, Manners, Opinions, and Times*.

9. 'Hartley': David Hartley (1705–57), philosopher and founder of psychological theory of associationism; author in 1749 of *Observations on Man*.

10. 'Clarke': Samuel Clarke (1695–1729), religious writer, critic of Trinitarian doctrine; auhor in 1712 of *Scripture Doctrine of The Trinity*.

11. 'Whiston': William Whiston (1667–1752), religious writer, critic of Trinitarian doctrine; author in 1711 of *Primitive Christianity Revived*.

12. 'Collins': Anthony Collins (1676–1729), leading deist in

early eighteenth-century England; author in 1709 of *Priest-craft in Perfection*.

13. 'Woolston': Thomas Woolston (1670–1733), free-thinker and critic of notion of miracles; author in 1727 of *Discourse on The Miracles of Our Savior*.

14. 'Influence of Climate': This chapter deals directly with the ideas of Charles de Secondat, Baron de Montesquieu (1689–1755); French writer on politics who stressed the important role of climate as a political determinant in his *Spirit of the Laws* (1748).

15. 'Fénelon': François de Salignac de la Motte (1651–1715), Archbishop of Cambray; author of *Telemachus* (1699), a bitter satire of Louis XIV's rule.

16. 'Jonathan Edwards' (1703–58); Leading colonial American writer on religion, whose important book on free will in 1754 had a lasting influence on Godwin.

17. 'Lycurgus' ?–*c.* 783 B.C.): Celebrated law giver of Ancient Sparta; Model for subsequent ages of the great founding statesman.

18. 'Everard Digby' (1581–1606): Conspirator along with Guy Fawkes in the gunpowder plot (1605) in which papist sympathizers plotted to blow up the Houses of Parliament.

19. 'Jacobites': Followers of the deposed Stuart monarchy, who as backers of the Pretender James to the Hanoverian throne rose in unsuccessful rebellion in 1715 and 1745.

20. 'Tertullian': Quintus Septimus Florens (*c.* 194–216?), The first Latin writer of the primitive Christian Church who wrote against heathens and heretics.

21. 'Voltaire': Marie-François Arouet de Voltaire (1694–1779); great French writer and philosopher. He was particularly important for publicizing English thought in France.

22. 'Cranmer': Thomas Cranmer (1489–1556), first protestant archbishop of Canterbury; presided over Henry VIII's divorces and the dissolution of the monasteries.

23. 'Milton's devil': Godwin refers here to the protagonist, Lucifer, in John Milton's (1608–74) epic poem *Paradise Lost* (1667).

24. 'Epictetus': An illustrious philosopher of the Stoic School who flourished in the first century of the Christian era.

25. 'Cato': Marius Portius (232–147 B.C.), great Roman censor and Tribune. Famous for his exploits in war as well as for his common touch, his return to his fields after battle.

26. 'Johnson': Samuel Johnson (1709–84), giant of English letters in the eighteenth century; author in 1781 of *Lives of the Poets*.

27. 'Hume's *Enquiry* . . .': Godwin is here citing the essay by David Hume (1711–76), Scottish philosopher, in which the theory of causality is most clearly developed.

28. 'Mr Burke's speech upon Oeconomical Reform': A reference to a famous speech in Commons delivered by Burke in 1780 in which Burke attacked the expenditures and corrupt influence of George III and demanded reforms in the royal household.

29. 'Butler': Joseph Butler (1692–1752), Bishop of Durham and writer on moral subjects.

30. 'Hutcheson': Francis Hutcheson (1694–1747), distinguished moral philosopher who argued in *A System of Moral Philosophy* (pub. 1755) that there is a distinct class of benevolent feelings in human nature.

31. 'duke de la Rochefoucault': François Doudeauville, Duc de La Rochefoucauld (1613–80); author of a famous book of *Maxims*, the principal theme of which is the importance of self-love.

32. 'the optimists': Godwin refers here to various theorists of theodicy like Leibnitz (1646–1716), who argued that all events are part of God's inscrutable design for the ultimate happiness of his created universe.

33. 'a stranger who cannot speak our language': A reference to George I, who it is alleged could barely speak English when in 1714 he came from Hanover to become English King.

34. 'Lord Bolingbroke': Henry St John (1678–1751); author of the Treaty of Utrecht in 1713 ending the great war between England and the France of Louis XIV.

35. 'Beccaria': Cesare Bonesana, Marchese de Beccaria (1735–1793); author in 1764 of the celebrated book on penal reform *On Crimes and Punishment*.

36. 'Sir Walter Raleigh' (1552–1618): Eminent Elizabethan statesman, courtier, and writer; accused, tried and executed for high treason by James I.

37. 'Mr Howard': John Howard (1726–90), philanthropist and prison reformer; author of numerous works based on first-hand study of English and European prisons and hospitals.

38. 'ingenious inhabitant of North Britain': Godwin is referring here to Thomas Spence (1750–1814), economic reformer and early advocate of land nationalization, author in 1775 of *The Real Rights of Man*.

39. 'Sir Thomas More' (1480–1535): Lord Chancellor, writer, religious martyr in the reign of Henry VIII; author in 1518 of the classic utopian vision, *Utopia*.

40. 'Mably': Gabriel Bonnot, Abbé de (1709–85), churchman, statesman and writer; early advocate of communal property holdings.

41. 'Wallace': Robert Wallace (1697–1771), writer on population; author in 1761 of *Various Prospects of Mankind, Nature, and Providence*, believed to have stimulated Malthus to some of his notions.

42. 'Mandeville': Bernard de Mandeville (1670–1733), medical doctor, writer on political and ethical themes; controversial author of *Fable of the Bees*, proclaiming the public good served by rigorous egoism.

43. 'Doctor Price': Richard Price (1723–91), distinguished dissenting minister, political writer, and mathematician; his sermon 'On the Love of our Country' in 1789 provoked the wrath of Burke as expressed in the latter's answering *Reflections on the Revolution in France*.

44. 'Condorcet': Marie Jean Antoine Nicholas Caritat, Marquis de (1743–1794), eminent French philosopher and mathematician; author of lyrical praise to progress and man's potential for perfection in his *Historical Sketch of the Progress of the Human Mind* (1793).

Suggestions for Further Reading

A. *Godwin's writings:*

Caleb Williams (London, 1794).
The Enquirer: Reflections on Education, Manners and Literature (London, 1797).
Fleetwood (London, 1805).
Of Population (London, 1820).
Thoughts on Man (London, 1830).
William Godwin: His Friends and Contemporaries (ed. L. Kegan Paul) (London, 1876).

B. *On Godwin and his milieu*

H. N. Brailsford, *Shelley, Godwin, and Their Circle* (O.U.P., London, 1951).
F. K. Brown, *The Life of William Godwin* (London, 1926).
C. B. Cone, *The English Jacobins* (Scribner, New York, 1968).
D. Fleisher, *William Godwin: A Study in Liberalism* (Allen & Unwin, London, 1951).
R. G. Grylls, *William Godwin and His World* (Odhams Press, London, 1953).
E. Halévy, *The Growth of Philosophical Radicalism* (Faber, London, 1928).
I. Kramnick, 'On Anarchism and the Real World: William Godwin and Radical England,' *American Political Science Review*, Vol. LXVI, No. 1, March 1972.
A. H. Lincoln, *Some Political and Social Ideas of English Dissent 1763–1800* (Cambridge University Press, 1938).
D. H. Monro, *Godwin's Moral Philosophy* (O.U.P., London, 1953).
B. R. Pollin, *Education and Enlightenment in the Works of William Godwin* (Las Americas, New York, 1962).
F. E. L. Priestley, *Critical Introduction and Notes to Enquiry Concerning Political Justice* (Toronto, 1946).
E. P. Thompson, *The Making of the English Working Class* (Penguin Books, Harmondsworth, 1968).
G. Woodcock, *William Godwin, A Biographical Study* (Porcupine Press, London, 1946).

Index

Abstraction, inseparable from the existence of mind, 198. Necessary to the formation of language, and assisted by language in return, 160

Abuses, political, conviction of the understanding an adequate means of abolishing them, 275

Achilles, 775

Action, voluntary and involuntary distinguished, 118–19, 345, 378, 773–4. Voluntary actions originate in opinions, 120, 275, 349. Virtuous action defined, 185. Injurious actions often proceed from conscientious motives, 187–8. Actions of men regulated by the nature of things, 201. By positive institution, 201. Action considered in relation to the doctrine of necessity, 351. External action no proper subject of criminal animadversion, 649–50

Addison, 81, 785

Addresses, an equivocal mode of collecting the sense of a nation, 217. An uncertain criterion of the future conduct of a people, 787

Administration, quantity of,

necessary for social benefit, 540

Admonition, right of giving it, considered, 194

Adversity, school of, 411. Its supposed uses, 645. Defective, 645. Unnecessary, 646

Agincourt, *see* Cressy

Alexander, 84, 193

Alfred, 411

Alliance, *see* Treaties

Alphabetical writing, difficulty of its invention, 161. Probable manner in which an alphabet was produced, 162

Ambition, attainments to which it leads, 305

Ambition of princes, its destructive nature, 733

Amphictyonic council, 553

Anarchy, its evils, 663–4. Its disadvantages compared with the disadvantages of despotism, 664. Its final result, 665–6

Anaxarchus, 135

Aquinas, Thomas, 614

Ardour, considered in relation to the doctrine of necessity, 355–6

Aristides, 489

Aristocracy, source of the system of, 296. Principles in

MORE ABOUT PENGUINS
AND PELICANS

Penguinews, which appears every month, contains details of all the new books issued by Penguins as they are published. From time to time it is supplemented by *Penguins in Print*, which is our complete list of titles available. (There are some five thousand of these.)

A specimen copy of *Penguinews* will be sent to you free on request. Please write to Dept EP, Penguin Books Ltd, Harmondsworth, Middlesex, for your copy.

In the U.S.A.: For a complete list of books available from Penguin in the United States write to Dept CS, Penguin Books Inc., 7110 Ambassador Road, Baltimore, Maryland 21207.

In Canada: For a complete list of books available from Penguin in Canada write to Penguin Books Canada Ltd, 41 Steelcase Road West, Markham, Ontario.

BOOKS ON WORLD AFFAIRS AND CURRENT EVENTS
PUBLISHED BY PENGUIN BOOKS

BOOKS ON WORLD AFFAIRS AND CURRENT EVENTS
PUBLISHED BY PENGUIN BOOKS

THE PELICAN CLASSICS

'A boon to students young and perennial . . . the admirable introductions by reputable scholars are required reading' – *The Times Literary Supplement*